GREAT AMERICAN
BOMBERS
OF WWII

B-17 FLYING FORTRESS

William N. Hess

MBI Publishing Company

First published in 1998 by MBI Publishing Company,
729 Prospect Avenue, PO Box 1, Osceola, WI 54020-0001 USA

MBI Publishing Company books are also available at discounts in bulk quantity for industrial or sales-promotional use. For details write to Special Sales Manager at Motorbooks International Wholesalers & Distributors, 729 Prospect Avenue, Osceola, WI 54020-0001 USA.

Library of Congress Cataloging-in-Publication Data Available
ISBN 0-7603-0650-8

Printed in Hong Kong

On the front cover: A Boeing B-29 Superfortress from the 9th Bomber Group, 313th Wing on Tinian en route to deliver a payload of bombs to the Japanese mainland below. *Claude Logan collection*

On the back cover: Top: This is a spectacular view from the nose of a 39th Bomb Group B-29 captures incendiary bombs dropping from proceeding planes on the city of Hiratsuka, Japan, July 16, 1945. One hundred thirty two B-29s of the 314th Bomb Wing based at Guam dropped 1,163 tons of incendiary bombs from altitudes of 10-15,000 feet. Only three planes of the entire strike force failed to drop their bombs on the primary target, the urban area of the city. Emergency landings were made by 11 planes at Iwo Jima on the return flight to their home base. *Air Force photo* Bottom left: A formation of Superforts from the 73rd Wing out of Saipan dropping incendiary bombs on Yokahama, Japan. Bottom right: A formation of B-29s from the 500th Group, 73rd Wing off of Saipan, passing near Mount Fujiama on way to drop bombs on a target in Tokyo. *Claude Logan collection*

Photo on page 143: *Roundtrip Jack* flew with the 385th Bomb Group.

Photo on page 147: *Joy Rider* was a Pacific Privateer. *L. M. Myers Collection*

Photo on page 289: This picture shows some of the women who made up a large part of Boeing's work force, inserting wiring in the bomb bays and in the pressurized tunnel passageway from one compartment to another, above the bomb bays. *Boeing Archives*

Contents

B-17 Flying Fortress

B-24 Liberator

B-29 Superfortress

Acknowledgments

There are a number of people I would like to thank for material, photos, and favors that greatly aided me in writing this book. In particular, I owe a debt to my fellow historian Russell Strong, of the 306th Bombardment Group, for permission to quote from his history, *First over Germany,* and for many of the excellent photos that he provided. Mike Chambers loaned me his father's invaluable diary and photo albums from his B-17 days in the Pacific. John Mitchell, author of *On Wings We Conquer,* gave me permission to quote, and also provided rare photographs. The Rev. James Good Brown gave me permission to quote from his history of the 381st Bombardment Group, and C. B. Rollins, Jr., loaned me a copy of his 385th Bombardment Group book and valuable photographs. I would also like to thank the Boeing Corporation, John Bardwell, Jeffrey Ethell, Robert Gill, Tom Ivie, J. Griffin Murphey III, and Warren Thompson for their generous assistance with photographs for the book.

Introduction

When my editor, Greg Field, asked me if I would like to do a book on the Boeing B-17 it was almost like being asked to go home again. I fully realize that after so many years have passed you can't *really* go home again, but your memory can.

I grew up in an oil patch about forty-five miles from Barksdale Field, Louisiana (now Barksdale Air Force Base), and was privileged to see practically all of the different aircraft of the US Army Air Corps from 1932 onward. Their fighters and attack planes used to use some of the oil derricks for pylons, and they had a ball enjoying their own aerial circus of the 1930s. Barksdale was not a bomber base in those days, so I didn't get to see many of the multiengine aircraft, but it was always a great thrill to see the early Boeing B-17s fly over my home. I think that one of the most memorable sights I ever witnessed was watching the Boeing B-15 with a Boeing B-17 on each wing passing over one Sunday afternoon at about 1,000ft.

When I was assigned to a B-17 crew in 1944, it was once more a thrill and led to experiences that I would not want to live through again, but that I wouldn't take a million dollars for. To all of us who flew combat in its interior, the Fortress was a queen of the sky. The B-17 graced the sky with its beauty, and its formations made unforgettable sights that I can still see if I close my eyes. No truer legion ever charged than did the airborne attackers who unwaveringly entered the black fields of flak to carry out their mission. While many Fortresses fell, hundreds more brought their shattered airframes and wounded crews home where others might have failed.

I trust that in these pages I have painted just a little of the overall picture of the Fortress in combat. Writing this book brought back a lot of memories, and I hope that those readers who have experienced this story will find it accurate and informative. For those who seek to further their knowledge of the queen of the sky, I hope I have provided you with a valuable addition.

Chapter 1

The Flying Fortress

In May of 1934 the US Army Air Corps requested bids on Project X, which would comprise a bomber capable of carrying a bomb load of 2,000lb and possess a range of 5,000 miles. Boeing Airplane Company and the Glenn L. Martin Company submitted bids that resulted in Boeing Model 294 being ordered in 1935. The four-engine aircraft would be considered gigantic by 1935 standards, with a wingspan of 149ft and a length of 87ft 7in. The original request was that a 1,000hp engine be utilized, but the only thing available at the time was a Pratt and Whitney 850hp Twin Wasp. The original Air Corps designation of the aircraft XBLR-1 was changed to XB-15 before its completion.

The Air Corps issued another request in April of 1934 for a multiengine aircraft that would carry a 2,000lb bomb load for not less than 1,020 miles and if possible, 2,200 miles at a speed of 200 mph and possibly as high as 250mph. A flyable prototype was to be available not later than August 1935.

In August 1934, Boeing set out to build the prototype of design Model 299. Their board of directors approved a sum of $275,000 to build the aircraft. The aircraft had all-metal construction, with a conservative semi-monocoque fuselage with a forward gun turret in the extreme nose. The pilot and copilot were seated side by side in conventional commercial airline configuration. The bomb bay had

a capacity for 4,800lb of bombs. The radio room was a separate compartment aft of the bomb bay. Aerial gunners were provided with blisters on each side of the rear fuselage and another blister in the belly aft of the radio room. Full arma-

A Y1B-17 flies over cloud cover with Mount Rainier in the background. Boeing

ment consisted of five machine guns. The Model 299 was powered by four Pratt & Whitney R-1690 radial engines each developing 750hp.

The name "Flying Fortress" was coined by Dick Williams, a reporter for the *Seattle Times* who gave this name to Model 299 when it was rolled out displaying its colorful five machine-gun installations. Boeing quickly recognized the value of the title and had it copyrighted.

The first flight test was carried out on July 28, 1935, with Boeing chief test pilot Les Tower at the controls. The flight test program lasted only three weeks and consisted of seven flights totaling 14 hours and 5 minutes.

Following the company test program the Model 299 took off for Wright Field, Ohio, on August 20, 1935. The aircraft flew the 2,100 mile trip in only 9 hours and 3 minutes—an amazing ground speed of 233mph. The performance of the aircraft completely stole the show from Douglas' new B-18, which was essentially a bomber version of the DC-2 transport and Martin's worked-over, obsolete B-10.

On October 30, 1935, with Army Air Corps chief test pilot Ployer Hill at the controls and Les Tower flying as an observer, the aircraft took off on a second evaluation flight. Unfortunately, Hill forgot to take off the control locks. The aircraft took off and started to climb, then nosed over and plunged to the earth. Hill was killed in the crash and Tower succumbed to injuries a few days later.

The aircraft was not a complete loss, but the crash did dash the hopes that Boeing had for a sizeable contract. The bulk of orders for a new Army Air Corps bomber went to Douglas for the B-18.

Boeing was finally granted a contract on January 17, 1936, for thirteen aircraft to be designated YB-17. A number of changes were made on the aircraft from the original Model 299. The most significant was the change of engines. The new aircraft was fitted with Wright R-1820-39 Cyclone engines which developed 850hp. The first flight of the revised aircraft was made on December 2,

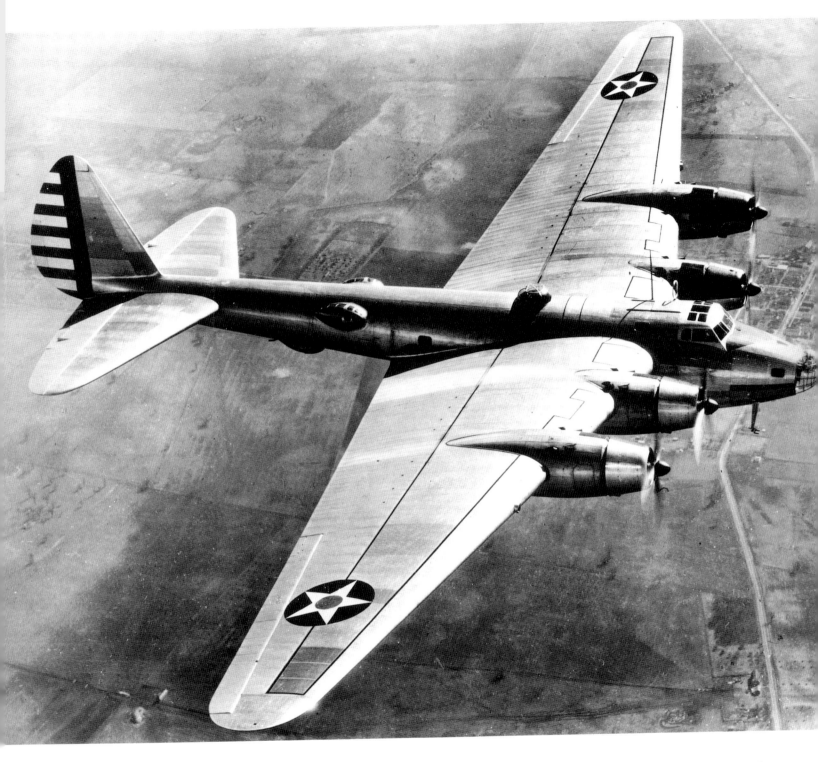

The gigantic Boeing B-15 was not a predecessor to the B-17. Its development was parallel, and it did not fly until 1937. Only one B-15 was built. It had a 149ft wing span and was 87ft, 7in in length. Its Pratt & Whitney 850hp engines were just not powerful enough for its size. Boeing

The nose turret was deleted on the Boeing B-17B. Superchargers were installed for the Wright Cyclone R-1820 engines. Boeing

Next page
The gun blisters were eliminated on the Boe-
ing B-17C. In place of the ventral blister was
a new bathtub ventral gun position. Boeing

A B-17B in all its shiny glory at rest as a heavy overcast moves in. Boeing

A B-17B of the 2nd Bomb Group. This aircraft was named Flagship *and was undoubtedly a lead aircraft for this famous 1930s unit. Boeing*

1936, with an Air Corps crew at the controls. The bombers were delivered to the 2nd Bomb Group at Langley Field, Virginia, where they served well and made many historic flights in the aircraft while compiling a record 9,293 accident-free hours.

While the 2nd Bomb Group was making record good-will flights to South America and attracting all kinds of attention to the B-17, there were those in Congress who were opposed to putting so much money into very large aircraft. Douglas continued to get contracts for B-18s, while the only thing new that Boeing came up with was the Y1B-17A, which was utilized to develop turbo-superchargers on the aircraft. Although not fully realized at the time, the work being done on superchargers would have great effect on later B-17 models.

In August 1937, Boeing got the first installment of contracts for the B-17B. Eventually, thirty-nine aircraft of this designation would be built. The primary change in this model was the elimination of the rotating nose turret, which was replaced with a bombardier's flat-glass aiming window, a larger rudder, and improved engines.

Even up until the outbreak of World War II in Europe, there was constant opposition from the Air Corps regarding the price of the B-17 and the desirability of the aircraft. At one time it appeared that no further contracts would be granted to Boeing. It was not until September 20, 1939, while Poland was being overrun by Germany, that the Army Air Corps contracted for thirty-eight B-17Cs. This new model eliminated the glass blisters on the aircraft and put the waist gunners behind a flat, tear-shaped opening. The belly gun position had a bathtub-type installation whereby the gunner could kneel and fire downward. In addition, the first self-sealing fuel tanks were fitted into the wings. Twenty B-17Cs went to England where they saw combat with the Royal Air Force (RAF).

The first B-17Ds were contracted in April 1940. These aircraft were originally to have been equipped with Sperry upper and lower gun turrets, but these turrets were still in the testing stage and were not installed in the aircraft. Instead, the aircraft got cowl flaps and dual gun installations in the radio room and in the belly. Most of the B-17Ds would see action in the Pacific, from the Pearl Harbor attack up until the time that most of them were lost in combat or associated operations.

As desperate as the Army Air Corps was for additional B-17s, when the contract came up for the sorely needed B-17E, which incorporated crucial improvements, it was held up in the US War Department for overpricing until August 30, 1940. The primary changes to the E model were in armament. The B-17E had a Sperry power turret just aft of the flight deck, a remote twin gun turret in the belly, and most significantly, a repositioned tail gun in the completely redesigned tail structure. The new tail, rudder, and dorsal fin drastically changed the look of the aircraft. A total of 512 B-17Es were contracted. A major change was implemented starting with the 113th B-17E when the Sperry ball turret was substituted for the remote turret, which had proved to be unsatisfactory.

The B-17E saw action in the Pacific, England, and North Africa, and was the real combat pioneer Flying Fortress. With the aircraft in great demand it was only natural that large quantities would be ordered. In fact, the orders were so large that when the B-17F began production, some orders were farmed out. The B-17F was basically the B-17E with over 400 small modifications. Boeing built 2,300 examples of the model in Seattle while another 500 were built in Burbank, California, by Lockheed/Vega. Douglas built 604 B-17Fs at Long Beach, California.

The biggest visible difference between the E and F model was the new one-piece, molded, clear plastic nose cone on the B-17F. As with the E model, there were four sockets for .30 caliber guns. With the Fortresses taking scores of vicious nose-on attacks over Europe, it was only natural that numerous field modifications would be made. The primary goal was to get more than one .50 caliber gun in the nose. Some units installed small window-type gun positions while others came up with the cheek type that would be standard equipment on the B-17G.

The B-17F also had new fuel tanks installed in outer wing panels which became known as "Tokyo tanks," and added another 1,100 gallons to the fuel capacity. Larger paddle-type propeller blades were fitted to give the engines more "bite" at high altitude.

The final and largest model of the Fortress was the B-17G. Like the F model, they were built at three factories. The totals were 4,035 in Seattle, 2,250 at Burbank, and 2,395 at Long Beach. The most welcome addition on the G model was the twin .50 caliber guns mounted in the chin turret beneath the bombardier's station. Many of the G models received a Cheyenne tail gun position which was installed at the United Air Lines modification center in Cheyenne, Wyoming. This gave the tail gunner a more comfortable bicycle seat and an optic head gun sight rather than the old ring and post. Waist windows were staggered and covered with plexiglass, eliminating the "butt bumping" by the waist gunners and the frigid air blast from the open windows.

There were other modifications of the Fortress that saw little or limited use. One major design variant was made when Lockheed/Vega built one model fitted with Allison V-1710-89 engines. The model was designated XB-38 and made its initial flight on May 19, 1943.

In an effort to assist the Fortress formations in their fight against the Luftwaffe before fighter escorts came along, twenty or more B-17Fs were converted to YB-40 escort gun ships. These Fortresses had chin turrets, a twin .50 caliber gun turret in the radio room, and twin gun installations in the waist positions. If cheek guns were installed, the aircraft carried at least fourteen .50 caliber guns. These modified ships were used on some Eighth Air Force missions, but it was found that the YB-40s could not keep up with the regular B-17s in formation, particularly after the B-17s had dropped their bombs. The idea was abandoned after nine missions.

B-17C assigned to the test section at Wright Field, Ohio. Ethell

Another B-17C in shiny splendor while assigned to Wright Field, Ohio. Ethell

B-17E in war colors. Its new olive-drab paint job shows up well against the clouds. Ethell

A Boeing B-17B that belonged to the 2nd Bomb Group at Langley Field, Virginia. This unit pioneered the virtues of the aircraft. US-AAF

This shiny new B-17D featured self-sealing fuel tanks, a new electrical system, and more armor. The B-17D was the first Flying Fortress model to see combat when it was used against the Japanese in 1942. Boeing

Brand-new B-17Cs on the hardstands outside the Boeing factory. Note how the lack of gun blisters gives the C-model sleeker lines.
Boeing

The B-17E was a completely new aircraft. The tail was redesigned and a tail gunner's position was added. It featured a Sperry top turret behind the flight deck and a remotely operated turret in the belly. Boeing

A Boeing B-17F in full war paint. With the Sperry ball turret and new plexiglass one-piece nose, the Flying Fortress was finally ready for war. This aircraft is from the 390th Bomb Group, Eighth Air Force. USAAF

This B-17G from the 91st Bomb Group, Eighth Air Force, features the chin turret in the nose and the improved tail gunner's station with an optical gun sight. Havelaar

The most heavily armed Fortress was the YB-40 which carried fourteen .50 caliber guns. The YB-40 was much more heavily armed than the standard B-17F from which it was modified. The YB-40 was given a chin turret, a power turret in the radio room and twin .50s in the waist windows. Boeing

Chapter 2

Royal Air Force Fortresses

In early 1941, the British Purchasing Commission accepted twenty Boeing B-17Cs for duty with the RAF. It was thought that with the aircraft's ability to operate at high altitude and with its speed and armament, it might be able to operate over Europe in daylight. The aircraft was not fitted with the secret Norden bombsight, and the RAF had to settle for one made by Sperry.

The first Forts began to arrive in England in May of 1941 and were assigned to No. 90 Squadron, which went in training on the aircraft at once. The aviators seemed quite pleased with the Fortress I, as it was called, and were eager to put it in action. The only real problems they encountered during their training was with the oxygen system and the cold weather. They were forced to change the oxygen system, and also came up with a serviceable electrically heated suit.

On July 8, 1941, three Fortress I aircraft took off on their first operation mission which was to bomb the docks at Wilhelmshaven, Germany. One aircraft was forced to salvo its bombs because of mechanical troubles, and a second aircraft had its bombs hang up over the target. The third Fortress dropped its bombs over the target with unknown results. Two of the aircraft sighted Messerschmitt Bf 109s climbing, but got up to 32,000ft and the enemy was not able to climb up to them. It was well that

they did not, for all the Fortress guns were frozen solid.

All through the summer of 1941, No. 90 Squadron mounted very high altitude missions against various targets. Most resulted in little or no damage to the enemy. It turned out that the bombsight

Fortress I airborne in service with No. 90 Squadron, RAF. Boeing

they were using was not accurate for such high-altitude bombing, and the aircraft was experiencing various other

A Fortress I on a test flight before leaving for England. Note that the rudder and vertical stabilizer have received camouflage paint while the balance of the aircraft is shiny silver. Boeing

problems resulting from the extreme cold at high altitudes.

For all practical purposes, operations ended for No. 90 Squadron, and the Fortress I aircraft in late September 1941. A number of the surviving aircraft were sent to North Africa where they flew some bombing missions against enemy shipping in the Mediterranean. The Fortress I had not been successful for

A Boeing Fortress I in full camouflage paint.
The one operationsl squadron with the RAF,
No. 90 Squadron, had all sorts of troubles
with the aircraft, primarily due to freezing
temperatures in their attempt at high altitude
bombing. Boeing

the RAF, but a great deal of knowledge was learned about the aircraft, and this knowledge was put to good use by the US Army Air Forces when it went to war with the Fortress.

The RAF received Boeing B-17Es and Gs later on in the war, and they served in Coastal Command where they did yeoman duty escorting ships and going after German U-boats. The Fortresses of Coastal Command were credited with the destruction of twelve U-boats before the end of the war.

Another in-flight photo of AM528. The Fortress I was undergunned, without self-sealing fuel tanks and the US Army Air Corps would not permit the secret Norden bomb sight to accompany the aircraft. Boeing

Chapter 3

The Pacific

The war did not come to the B-17 in the Pacific. Rather, the B-17 flew into it headlong. As part of the buildup in the Philippine Islands, an additional sixteen Fortresses were to stage through Hawaii in late November 1941. These aircraft came from the 38th Reconnaissance Squadron at Albuquerque, New Mexico, and the 88th Reconnaissance Squadron at Fort Douglas, Utah. Their departure was delayed by modifications and weather that held them in California. Army Chief of Staff Gen. George Marshall became alarmed at the delay and had Gen. H. H. Arnold, Army Air Corps chief of staff, get them going.

When the commander of the B-17 flight, Maj. Truman H. Landon, asked General Arnold why they weren't carrying ammunition if their departure was so urgent, Arnold told him they didn't need the extra weight. The second leg of the trip would be the dangerous one, and they could pick up ammunition for their guns in Hawaii.

As the flight prepared to leave Hamilton Field, California, two of the B-17s experienced engine trouble and were held over. Another Fortress had problems and did not take off, and a fourth aborted once it was airborne. All total, four B-17Cs and eight B-17Es departed for Hawaii.

The long flight was uneventful, and they had no trouble locating the island. Capt. Richard H. Carmichael called the tower at Hickam Field, but the reply was garbled and could not be understood. Shortly afterward a flight of fighter aircraft was spotted and the crews on the B-17s thought they were coming out to greet them. Suddenly, the fighter aircraft attacked the Fortresses and the pilots had to take immediate evasive action. They had flown right into the Japanese attack on Pearl Harbor on December 7, 1941!

Lt. Robert H. Richards tried to land his B-17C at Hickam, but he encountered so many Japanese attacks he aborted the landing and headed out to sea. He finally attempted a downwind landing at Bellows Field, but came in too fast and ran off the runway into a ditch. Zeroes then repeatedly strafed the aircraft and left it in an unflyable condition. Three of the crew were wounded.

Capt. Raymond T. Swenson managed to land his aircraft at Hickam, but a strafing Zero hit the flare box in the middle of the aircraft and it burned in two. The crew got out safely except for Lt. William R. Schick, the flight surgeon traveling with them, who was mortally wounded.

The four other aircraft of the 38th Reconnaissance Squadron managed to get down safely at Hickam.

The 88th Reconnaissance Squadron met much the same opposition as the 38th. Captain Carmichael and Lt. Harold Chaffin passed up Hickam and landed at a small auxiliary field at Hal-eiwa. Lt. Frank P. Bostrom tried to get in at Hickam, but finally gave up and flew to the northern part of the island where he landed on the Kahuku golf course. Two more Fortresses finally got in to Hickam safely between Japanese attacks. The last Fortress was reported to have originally landed at Wheeler Field, but it later wound up at Hickam. Fortunately, only two B-17s out of the flight of twelve were destroyed.

Of twelve B-17Ds already stationed at Hickam Field, five were destroyed in the attack by the Japanese.

At Clark Field in the Philippines nineteen B-17s were still on the base. A number of Fortresses had been sent south to Del Monte on Mindanao for safety. When news of the attack on Pearl Harbor came on December 8 (Philippine time), Col. Eugene Eubanks was called in for a conference with Gen. Douglas MacArthur, leaving Maj. David Gibbs in charge at Clark. Lt. Hewitt Wheless had taken off earlier that day on a reconnaissance mission over Formosa to investigate the Japanese build-up. Shortly after the alert there was a report of approaching enemy aircraft, so Gibbs ordered the B-17s into the air.

The most puzzling question that has mystified everyone is why MacArthur didn't order a strike on Formosa by the B-17s once he learned of the attack on Pearl Harbor. It has been said that he,

A line-up of B-17Ds at Port Moresby, New Guinea, on their way to the Philippines in September 1941. Wallach

Capt. Colin Kelly, who became America's first World War II hero when he saved his crew over the Philippines. He stayed at the controls of the crippled B-17 until his crew could bail out. Kelly died in the crash. USAAF

like the US administration, was waiting for the Japanese to make the first move. Likewise, Gen. Louis Brereton, commander of the Army Air Forces in the Philippines, was awaiting the return of his reconnaissance aircraft and no one ordered the strike.

Once the Fortresses were low on fuel Major Gibbs had them land, and then told them to go to lunch and await orders at their aircraft. Three crews were ordered on a photo mission over Formosa, and they were readied for takeoff. As the three B-17s began their takeoff roll, the first bombs began to fall on Clark Field. All three of these Fortresses were destroyed on the field. Few of the B-17s had been damaged by the bombing, but then the Zero fighters came down to strafe. When they had finished, twelve B-17s were destroyed and five were damaged. When Lieutenant Wheless returned from Formosa and another B-17 that had been on patrol over the eastern side of the island of Luzon landed at Clark, they were the only two serviceable B-17s left at the base.

The next morning, some of the B-17s from Del Monte came up to Clark and were sent out in an attempt to find a Japanese task force heading for Luzon, but failed to find it. Lieutenant Wheless took off from Clark Field in an attempt to bomb the invasion fleet, but an electrical failure forced him to abort the mission.

B-17s of the 19th Bomb Group flew the first American bombing missions of the war on December 10, 1941. Capt. Cecil Combs led a flight of five Fortresses attacking the Japanese invasion fleet in Lingayen Gulf. They dropped loads of 100lb bombs and reported hits on a transport.

Four B-17s that came up from San Marcelino landed at Clark Field to be bombed up to attack the Japanese invasion fleet. Maj. Emmett O'Donnell and Lt. George E. Schaitzel took off with loads of eight 600lb bombs, but Capt. Colin Kelly and Lt. G. R. Montgomery were forced to depart with partial bomb loads because of an air raid alert.

Major O'Donnell dropped his bombs on enemy vessels off Vigan north of Lingayen Gulf, but got no hits. Lieutenant Montgomery headed for Vigan and he, too, missed with all of his bombs. However, Montgomery returned to Clark, got another load of bombs, and returned to the Vigan area where he got hits on a Japanese transport.

Captain Kelly had only three 600lb bombs aboard, but went north to Aparri where a second enemy invasion force was landing. His first two bombs missed, but a third got a direct hit on an enemy cruiser. Kelly's crew reported the ship sunk.

As Kelly headed back to Clark, his Fortress came under attack from Japanese Zeros. They started a fire in the bomb bay and killed engineer-gunner Sgt. J. W. Delehanty. The enemy fighters continued to make passes at the bomber and started a fire in a wing tank. The B-17C that Kelly was flying was not equipped with self-sealing tanks. Kelly stayed at the controls until all of his crew could bail out. By this time, Kelly was too low to bail himself out and the aircraft exploded. Kelly's body was found near the wreckage with an unopened parachute.

With the rapid fire victories of the Japanese, the American public was desperate for something that would boost their morale. Capt. Colin Kelly would become its first hero. News releases told of his B-17 bombing and sinking of a Japanese battleship. He then saved the lives of all his crew by his self-sacrifice, for which he was posthumously awarded the Distinguished Service Cross and was lauded by President Franklin Roosevelt.

The last real Philippine bombing mission by the 19th Bomb Group was flown on December 14 against enemy shipping in Legaspi Bay. Six B-17s were assigned to the mission. Lt. James Connally was to lead the mission, but he blew a tire. Lt. Lee Coats then took over the lead, but was forced to abort because of engine trouble. He was soon followed by Lieutenant Ford, who also experienced engine trouble. Lieutenant Wheless also had engine trouble, but dropped down in altitude and was able to get his bad engine running again.

Lt. Jack Adams dropped his bombs on enemy shipping and was immediately jumped by six Zeros. He sought cloud cover, but the Zeros hung on. Two of his engines were shot out and two crew members were wounded. Adams successfully crash-landed his Fortress in a rice paddy on Masbate. Adams got out of the Philippines, but his crew were pressed into service as infantrymen.

Lt. Elliot Vandevanter made three bombing runs over the enemy shipping, but was unable to see the results. He returned to Del Monte without incident. Lieutenant Wheless was intercepted by Zeros before he got to his target. Two of his gunners were wounded and his radio operator, Private First Class Kellin, was killed. Wheless' bombardier dropped the 600lb bombs and Wheless went into evasive action. He managed to land his badly damaged aircraft on a small strip at Cagayen, flat tires and all.

With the loss of two more B-17s, the 19th Bomb Group had been reduced from thirty-five to fifteen B-17s. All of the surviving Fortresses were located at Del Monte, but now that the enemy had discovered the base it was imperative that they be moved. A strafing raid cost the group another B-17 before they began their departure for Australia on December 17. The few missions that the surviving Fortresses would fly in the Philippines would be flown from Batchelor Field in Australia, and staged through Del Monte.

The loss of the Philippines was now inevitable, and the surviving bombers, plus a handful that had arrived with the 7th Bomb Group, took up the fight in Java. By the end of December, the ma-

The crew of B-17 Daylight Limited, *which had to crash-land in Mareeba after an August 26, 1942, mission to Milne Bay.* Wallach

The famous B-17D Swoose *on its way home. It flew bomb missions with the 19th Bomb Group and became Gen. George Brett's air-* craft. *It was named for half-swan, half-goose, as it was rebuilt from two different B-17Ds.* Wallach

A B-17E at Charleville, Australia, in 1942 after the Philippines and Java had been lost to the rapidly advancing Japanese forces. Giroux

The Aztec's Curse *was flown by Capt. W. E. Chambers of the 26th Bomb Squadron during the Guadalcanal campaign.* Chambers

jority of bombers were in Java where they flew a limited number of missions against the enemy invaders, but with little success. It was too little too late to combat the overwhelming forces of Japan. By the first of March 1942, it was all over in Java.

The few aircraft that survived Java retreated to Australia. Bombing missions were then flown against new targets by the 7th and 19th Bomb Groups. The enemy was in New Guinea and had established a formidable base at Rabaul on New Britain. The missions flown by the handful of B-17s were more of a nuisance to the enemy than any real hindrance. The primary object was to delay the Japanese until American reinforcements could be brought to the Pacific.

The onslaught in the Pacific was turned back with a victory at the Battle of the Coral Sea on May 9, and then the American victory at Midway on June 7 put a new complexion on things. A new air commander arrived in the southwestern Pacific who would, through the years, lead the new Fifth Air Force to victory. His name was Gen. George Kenney. Reinforcements began to arrive via the 11th Bomb Group, and the 43rd Bomb Group was activated. At last a small stream of B-17Es began to arrive.

One of the more impressive missions against Rabaul was assembled and flown on August 7, 1942. A force of fifteen B-17s was slated for the mission. It would consist of nine Fortresses from the 93rd Bomb Squadron and six from the 28th and 30th Bomb Squadrons. The mission was under the command of Lt. Col. Richard Carmichael.

Numbers of aircraft from the 93rd Bomb Squadron gradually were depleted before the mission even began. One B-17 crashed on takeoff from Seven Mile drome base outside Port Moresby, New Guinea. Two more were forced to abort the mission with engine trouble shortly after takeoff. In the end, Maj. Felix Hardison led the mission with six 93rd Bomb Squadron B-17s. The "tail end Charlie" position was flown by Capt. Harl Pease, who had begged his way onto the mission, although the aircraft he was flying was plagued with electrical troubles and four engines that were long overdue for overhaul.

The bombers were forced to skirt some bad weather, but on arrival over Rabaul they found the target in the

Capt. (later Maj.) W. E. Chambers, pilot of The Aztec's Curse. *Chambers won two Silver Stars during the Guadalcanal campaign.* Chambers

Smoke rises from a target in the Solomons as The Aztec's Curse *returns from a mission.* Chambers

open. As they swept over the area from an altitude of 22,500ft they were attacked by some twenty Zero fighters. Despite the attack, the bombers continued to drop their loads while their gunners downed several enemy interceptors. In about 20 minutes the Fortresses made their way to cloud cover–except for the aircraft flown by Captain Pease, which had fallen behind the formation.

As it struggled along, Pease's aircraft had number two engine out. Then the flaming bomb-bay fuel tank dropped and the B-17 went down in flames with both inboard engines out and enemy fighters still swarming around their victim. The official report stated that the aircraft crashed in flames and that Captain Pease and crew were killed. For his exceptional gallantry in action, Captain Pease was post humously awarded the Medal of Honor.

Years later, it was determined that Captain Pease and his crewman, Sergeant Czechowski, had managed to parachute out of the flaming Fortress and had been taken prisoner by the Japanese. A Catholic priest who had

A Japanese warship under attack from B-17s during the Guadalcanal campaign. Chambers

A Japanese Zero comes in for attack on a B-17 during the Guadalcanal campaign. Chambers

American contemptuous humor illustrated by this nose art on a Pacific B-17. Giroux

been interned by the Japanese vividly remembered Pease and Czechowski who were in the prison camp with him until October 8, 1942. At that time, they were taken out for a so-called "work detail" and never seen again. Undoubtedly, they were executed by the enemy.

On August 7, 1942, the same day as the mission to Rabaul, US Marines landed on Guadalcanal in the Solomon Islands. B-17s that would support this campaign flew from an advanced base at Espiritu Santo in the New Hebrides chain. One of the Fortress pilots was a young Alabaman named Capt. W. E. Chambers of the 26th Bomb Squadron, 11th Bomb Group, who flew an aircraft named *The Aztec's Curse.*

Chambers flew one of his more successful missions on August 25. He reported: "Jap task force reported off Malaita Island . . . I led a flight of three. We arrived at point of contact and a Jap destroyer started shooting at us. We went a little farther and saw a large transport burning [it had been attacked by dive-bombers] and a cruiser moving in slowly to pick up survivors. Best target we could find, so made a run on him at 9,000ft, dropped 500lb bombs. Got three direct hits and several near misses. The explosions completely covered the ship. The crew was in an uproar, yelling back and forth on the intercom. No fighter opposition, thank goodness . . ."

Japanese records show that they lost the destroyer *Mitsuki* to B-17s on that day.

Chambers and crew would not be so lucky on the mission of October 4. By this time, the Fortresses frequently were using Guadalcanal as an advanced base. Chambers related: "The *Aztec Curse* took off at 0300 on a striking mission to Buka, flying number two position in a five-ship formation. The weather was pretty bad and flying night formation was hell. The flight hit a front just after daylight about fifty miles from the target and had to turn around. We flew right over two Japanese task forces, but the antiaircraft did no damage. Then we were attacked by twelve Zeros. They fell in line about 2,000ft above us and about five miles off to the left, between us and the sun, which had just come up, and peeled off one at a time. They came in from the front a little below us and then up, right through the formation. The first one came through and tried to half-roll back out, but misjudged his distance and crashed into the number five man in our formation. Both planes went down.

"The next one made the same attack, and I thought he was going to ram the lead ship. He just missed and stalled right over our formation on his back. All four of our ships were shooting at him and he was so close, I could see large pieces of metal and fabric coming off his engine and wings. As he fell, he started to burn. The pilot must have been dead because he had been firing all the time he came in and as he went down, I could still see lines of tracers coming from his guns.

"The rest came in, but did not attempt to come through the formation; they came in fast, took a quick shot, and then half-rolled out under the formation. The ball turrets got two more, one in flames and the other with one wing cut completely off. Number three ship had one engine shot out, but remained in formation. Two men jumped from the number five aircraft, but were machine gunned by the Zeros as they floated down. We landed at Cactus [Guadalcanal] at 0935. I don't think I have ever been so tired in my life."

Chambers flew another successful mission on October 15. Nine Fortresses took off from Espiritu Santo to attack Japanese troops landing on Guadalcanal. As Chambers recalled: "We found fourteen Japanese ships right in the harbor with four transports in near the shore landing troops. One transport had been torpedoed by a Navy PBY and was burning. Watched the second element make its run on a warship out in the bay. It scored several near misses and silenced some AA guns. I led my element around to the land side away from the ships and made a bombing run on one of the transports. Three Zeros attacked us while we were on the run, coming up underneath in frontal attacks and half-rolling away. Our ball turret gunner, Garvy, got the first one as he rolled out underneath us. The second one came in very close, so close I could see the flashes from all his guns and see tracers going into our right wing. As he rolled over on his back, Carter, our navigator, got in a good burst, and the whole plane seemed to burst into flames. During this time, Myers, our bombardier, dropped his bombs and the wingmen followed suit. We scored several hits and the

transport was burning as we headed home. As we hit the ground on landing, the plane started pulling to the right. The tire on that side had been hit and was flat . . ."

As Chambers continued his tour, he saw more and more of his fellow crews fall victim to the Japanese fighters. Soon the crews spent most of their time on Guadalcanal where their sleep was interrupted nightly by air raids, and all fell victim to malaria and dysentery. Still, they struck at Japanese shipping and bases day after day.

On one mission to Rabaul, the Fortresses ran into a storm so vicious that they had to fly on instruments for two and a half hours. As Chambers related: "I did a small amount of praying, and we finally broke out about fifty miles from the target. We arrived in the vicinity of Rabaul harbor, but could not find it on account of cloud cover and darkness. I started circling, waiting for daylight. All at once we were right in the middle of about forty searchlights, with AA bursting all over the place. I ducked in the clouds and lost them. I saw two large transports right together through a break in the clouds and made a run at 8,500ft. The AA was heavy, so I had to duck in a cloud before I could see the results of the two 1,000-pounders that Myers dropped . . . On the way back, I had

Gen. Douglas MacArthur's Flying Fortress, which was fitted out as a plush transport and aptly named Bataan. Chambers

to fly through the storm again . . . We broke out of the storm just before we reached the mountains, but arrived at our field to find it closed in and raining like hell. I had to land because of gas, so I came in over the field at 100ft downwind, made a 180 degree instrument turn, and made an instrument approach by compass. Was lucky and hit it right on the nose. Saw the ground 50ft above it and sat her down. Had ten minutes of gas left and I was worn out. I slept for a while, then went out and got skunk drunk."

After several months of flying missions under trying conditions, Chambers and his crew were finally relieved. As he summed it up at the time: "I think my combat flying is over. Out of fifty-four missions we have been on, we have flown *Curse* on at least forty-five. She has always gotten us back. There are sixteen crews out of thirty-eight left in the group and there is only one other crew that hasn't had a man injured. My crew is still intact and are the best bunch of fellows on earth. Our score stands at nine Zeros shot down, one cruiser sunk, two transports and one

Maj. Jay Zeamer (left) and Lt. Joseph R. Sarnoski (right) both won Medals of Honor on their mission to Buka in the Solomons on June 16, 1943. Despite serious wounds, they completed a vital photo-reconnaissance mission. USAAF

tanker sunk, and we had hits on other transports with the results unknown . . . The last time I saw the *Curse,* she was on Guadalcanal with her tail broken off. She's a grand ole lady and I wish I could bring her back to the States with us."

As time passed, the Fortresses in the Pacific were being replaced by Consolidated B-24 Liberators. Gen. Ira C. Eaker of the Eighth Air Force in England wanted the B-17s, and Gen. H. H. Arnold, commander of the Army Air Forces, agreed to give them to him.

One group that continued to fly the old Fortresses up to the bitter end in the Pacific was the 43rd Bomb Group. It was on one of their last B-17 missions that

the action of two crewmen merited the Medal of Honor for both. On June 16, 1943, Capt. Jay Zeamer and his crew volunteered to fly a photo mission to Buka strip on Bougainville in the Solomon Islands. The crew was about ten miles from Buka when they were intercepted by about twenty Zeros. In the nose, bombardier Lt. Joseph R. Sarnoski downed the first attacking Zero while Sgt. John J. Able in the top turret took care of another. However, the Fortress had taken hits that disabled the oxygen system. Zeamer had to take the aircraft down from 28,000ft in a hurry.

As he pulled out of his dive, Zeamer's B-17 was attacked once more head-on. The Fortress pilot had gotten the armorers to install a fixed gun in the nose of the aircraft, which Zeamer could fire from a button on his yoke. As the Zero came in with guns blazing, Zeamer opened up and shot it down. At about the same time, the B-17 was hit in the nose with 20mm fire. Zeamer was

wounded in the legs, so the copilot, Lt. John Britton, had to take over the rudder pedals.

The explosion of the 20mm shell had thrown Lieutenant Sarnoski back into the passageway under the flight deck, but Sarnoski called out that he was okay and went back to his gun. As another Zero came in, Sarnoski blazed away at it and then dropped to the floor, dead from a stomach wound.

The air battle raged for 40 minutes, during which time the Buka strip was photographed and five Zeros were downed by the crew. As the B-17 crew made their way back to base they were in dire circumstances. The pilot and copilot were both wounded, their radio was shot out and the operator wounded, and the top turret was still manned but the engineer was wounded. From time to time, Zeamer would pass out from loss of blood. Despite his wounds, engineer-gunner Sgt. John Able came down from his turret and stood behind the pilots and helped them fly the plane.

After almost three hours, the Fortress neared its destination. By this time, Sergeant Able had gotten the pilots to come around enough that they were able to land the aircraft with Lieutenant Britton on the rudder pedals and Captain Zeamer on the yoke. In their dazed condition they made a downwind landing, and with a crew of wounded men they were all fortunate to survive.

Zeamer and Sarnoski were both awarded the Medal of Honor, and each member of the crew was given the Distinguished Flying Cross.

By late 1943, just about all of the B-17s were gone from the Pacific and it became a theater of B-24 bombers. However, the B-17 had been there at the start and had done a tremendous job under appalling odds. From the very beginning, Boeing's Flying Fortress let the enemy know it had a most worthy opponent.

Chapter 4

England–The Daylight Bombing Experiment

America had stationed observers in England since the outbreak of World War II to report on the events transpiring in the conflict. Officers of the US Army Air Corps were on station during the Battle of Britain, and had followed closely the fortunes of the RAF's bombing campaign against Germany. When the United States entered the war following the attack on Pearl Harbor, the influx of American personnel in England was immediately stepped up, and planning began on what the mission of the Army Air Corps would be in the European Theater.

In February of 1942, General Eaker and a small staff went to England to prepare the groundwork for what would become the US Eighth Air Force. At that time the only thing they could accomplish was to negotiate for bases, set up logistic sites, and confer with RAF personnel regarding their operations and the associated facets that were necessary to begin bombing operations.

In April 1942, Gen. Carl "Tooey" Spaatz was appointed commander of American Air Forces in Europe, and he immediately requested that the new Eighth Air Force, which was in training in the southeastern United States, be assigned to England. His request was readily approved by Gen. H. H. Arnold, chief of staff of the US Army Air Forces, and the wheels of progress began to grind. Eighth Air Force headquarters

was established at High Wycombe in Buckinghamshire, about thirty miles from London. Construction was begun on bases that would house the American units and in some cases, permanent RAF stations were slated to be turned over to the Americans.

The first unit selected for assignment to England was the 97th Bomb Group, which was training in Boeing B-17Es at Sarasota-Bradenton Airport in Florida. The unit was slated to get in 125 hours of flying time and 50 hours of instruction for ground echelon within six weeks. This was all being accomplished on a base that was still under construction and was sadly lacking in aircraft operations facilities. The 97th received overseas orders on May 12, 1942, and seven days later, the ground echelon boarded trains for their port of embarkation, Fort Dix, New Jersey.

The troops had a short stay at Fort Dix and boarded the former cruise liner *Queen Elizabeth* on the night of June 3. The unescorted ship made the trip in only six days and on June 9, the group boarded trains for their initial station in England at Polebrook.

The aircrews had to wait while the B-17s underwent engine changes and other modifications before they were ready for the flight over the Atlantic. By the last day of May the crews were at Presque Isle, Maine, awaiting their departure. Then their plans were changed:

the Japanese bombed the Aleutian Islands in Alaska. The 97th Bomb Group plus the 1st Fighter Group, which had been scheduled to accompany the bombers overseas, were rushed to the West Coast. By the end of the month it had been decided that the attack on the Aleutians was a decoy to draw US forces away from Midway Island. The Fortresses of the 97th and the P-38s of the 1st Fighter Group headed back to Presque Isle.

Overseas movement of the air echelon began on June 26, and by July 27 the aircraft of the 97th were on station in England. Four aircraft were forced to land on the ice because of bad weather, but no personnel were lost.

From the beginning of planning for bomber operations over Europe, the RAF did its utmost to convince the Americans that daylight bombing would not be successful. They had tried it early in the war but were forced by heavy losses to switch to bombing under cover of darkness. They were satisfied with their night bombing program, and welcomed the Americans to join them in the nocturnal skies. Generals Spaatz and Eaker were both confirmed disciples of daylight precision bombing and felt that the American bombers were sufficiently armed and possessed capable performance to allow operations against targets on the Continent with reasonable losses. The Norden bombsight was de-

Fortresses lined up for takeoff on a mission over the Continent in the early days of daylight bombardment. USAAF

A Luftwaffe fighter pilot's view of a Fortress formation from his head-on attack position. USAAF

signed for pinpoint bombing, which was impossible at night, and failure to use such a weapon would be folly. Regardless of RAF objections, the Army Air Forces would have a go at daylight precision bombing.

Now that the 97th Bomb Group was on station, it was imperative that they be made ready for operations. This was difficult, however. The pilots had little instrument time, which was necessary in penetrating the English weather for assembly and letdown. And they had little experience flying formation, and tight formations were essential for their defense against Luftwaffe fighters. Navigators had no experience over Europe, and both navigators and radio operators needed to learn British communications procedures. The aerial gunners had no firing experience nor proper training for repelling enemy attack. The Luftwaffe fighters, however, and the antiaircraft batteries over the Continent were well trained and experienced. It was the greatest challenge that American aircrews ever faced.

August 17, 1942, marked the first mission by the B-17s of the Eighth Air Force. The target was the Sotteville marshaling yards in Rouen, one of the largest and busiest in France. Twelve Fortresses took off with Col. Frank Armstrong, commander of the 97th Bomb Group, and Maj. Paul Tibbetts in the lead aircraft. Gen. Ira Eaker was aboard the lead aircraft in the second flight, *Yankee Doodle,* which was flown by Lt. John P. Dowswell. A flight of six other B-17s was airborne to fly a diversionary route over the English Channel.

The first aircraft was airborne at 1526 hours and the formation sighted its first antiaircraft or flak over St. Valery. From an altitude of 23,000ft the bombers in vees of three dropped forty-five 600-pound bombs and nine 1,100-pounders. A few bombs hit about a mile short of the target, but the majority smashed into the assigned area. General Eaker reported, "A great pall of smoke and sand was left over the railroad tracks."

As the bombers turned off the target they encountered more flak and at Ypreville, the Luftwaffe put in an appearance where they were intercepted by the British Spitfire escorts. One Focke-Wulf Fw 190 made a turn into the formation where it received a burst from the ball

A B-17F is from the 401st Bomb Squadron, 91st Bomb Group. Mary Ruth *failed to return from a mission on June 22, 1943.* USAAF

turret guns of Sgt. Kent West. The Fortresses arrived home safely, with little damage.

The 97th was out again on August 19 when twenty-two B-17s bombed Abbeville Drucat airdrome in northern France. A number of aircraft were destroyed on the ground, and the airfield was put out of commission for a time while British commandos raided Dieppe. The next morning, RAF Spitfires escorted a dozen Fortresses to the Longureau marshaling yards, where they attacked an assemblage of 1,600

Fortresses from the 322nd Bomb Squadron, 91st Bomb Group over English cloud cover. Note the mottled paint. USAAF

A B-17F under attack from a Messerschmitt Bf 110, which can be seen at six o'clock high. USAAF

An Eighth Air Force Fortress streaming smoke from the number four engine nears a ditching position. Air-sea rescue saved many aircrew from the English Channel. USAAF

cars and seventeen engines. At least fifteen hits were scored on the target.

The first of many tragedies plagued the 97th when it flew to Rottendam on August 21. Twelve Fortresses took off, but four were forced to abort the mission because of mechanical troubles. The remaining aircraft were 16 minutes late for rendezvous with the escort fighters. When the formation reached the Dutch coast the bombers were recalled. The bombers' Spitfire escort soon had to depart, after which the bombers were attacked by twenty to twenty-five German fighters.

As a result of the fighter attacks, things were getting perilous in a Fortress named *Johnny Reb*. The tail gunner had gotten some hits, but in the top turret one of the guns had jammed. One of the waist gunners had a blob of ice in his mask and was trying to fire his gun with one hand and clear the mask with the other. In the nose, the navigator had fired at a crossing fighter when a burst of cannon fire tore through the windshield on the flight deck. Copilot Lt. Donald A. Walter was fatally wounded and pilot Lt. Richard S. Starks suffered from plexiglass splinters. As he struggled for breath, Lieutenant Starks managed to call for help and got bombardier Lt. Edward Sconiers and engineer-gunner Sergeant Allen to come up and assist.

Lieutenant Sconiers managed to get the dead copilot out of his seat, and replaced him at the controls. The pilot instructed Sconiers, while Sergeant Allen did his best to aid the wounded men. The Fortress dropped out of formation, but managed to make it home safely despite the loss of two engines.

On September 6, the 301st Bomb Group flew its first mission when it accompanied the 97th back to the Sotteville marshaling yards. The following day, the 92nd Bomb Group joined in and the Fortresses took their first losses. The Luftwaffe fighters initiated their deadly head-on attacks on the B-17s by sections and downed two of them—one from the 92nd Group and one from the 97th. The 97th also brought home one dead gunner and three wounded crew members.

October 9 marked a historic point for VIII Bomber Command. The 306th Bomb Group flew its first mission, and the Fortresses were joined by the 93rd Bomb Group in B-24s to mark the first time more than 100 American bombers joined in operations. However, this would mark the last mission of the 92nd Bomb Group for some months, as they would become a training unit for incoming bomber crews.

October 21 proved to be the 97th Bomb Group's final mission with the 8th Air Force (the group would depart for North Africa in early November to support the American invasion there) when the 97th, 301st, and 306th Bomb Groups took off to bomb the submarine pens at Lorient, France. The 301st and 306th returned early, however, because of solid overcast over the English Channel. The 97th Group plowed on and broke out over the target at 17,500ft. The enemy was taken by surprise, and the Fortresses let go thirty 2,000lb bombs of which twenty-one hit within 1,000ft of the target. Workshops and floating docks were destroyed, but the bombs failed to penetrate the submarine shelters' thick cement covering.

As the B-17s turned off the target they were attacked by thirty-six German fighters. First hit was the Fortress of Lt. Francis X. Schwarzenbeck. As the B-17 went down, the crew continued to blaze away at the enemy fighters when they should have been bailing out. Two enemy fighters were seen to fall to their guns. The bombardier and three gunners survived. Two other Fortress crews were lost in the fight. The mission to Lorient marked the heaviest loss to any bomber group to date.

Missions continued against the U-boat installations along the French coast through October and into November. The 301st Group flew its last mission from England on November 8, and then departed for North Africa. This left the 8th Air Force with only the 306th and the 91st Bomb Groups, the latter of which had flown its first mission the previous day. These two groups would be joined by the 303rd and 305th Bomb Groups on November 17. These four B-17 units would carry the load until May 1943.

A mission to St. Nazaire, France, on November 23 brought about a sharp fight with the Luftwaffe, and one crew set quite a record as they were singled out by Fw 190s from Jagdgeschwader 2 (JG 2). The targeted Fortress was the 306th Group's *Banshee* and was flown by Lt. William J. Casey. In a 12 minute

Hell's Angels *from the 303rd Bomb Group was the first B-17 to complete twenty-five missions.* USAAF

Fortresses of the 96th Bomb Group beginning to leave contrails over a spotty undercast. USAAF

S/Sgt. Maynard "Snuffy" Smith receives his Medal of Honor from Secretary of War Henry Stimson. USAAF

running fight with the Focke-Wulfs, his crew downed seven enemy fighters. As noted by the 306th historian, "Parley D. Small, the tail gunner, got the first at 1328 hours at 400 yards with the pilot bailing out.

"Waist Gunner Reginald Harris hit one at 200 yards at 1334; the plane went into the water with no escape for the pilot.

"Joe Bowles in the ball turret scored at 1335, destroying the attacker at 50 yards as the plane broke into flames.

"Engineer Wilson Elliott caught one at two o'clock high and saw it disintegrate in the air at 200 yards.

"At 1338 Harris got his second at 100 yards; the pilot bailed out.

"Bowles hit his second, catching the fighter as it zoomed towards his ball turret. He used only 70 rounds of ammuni-

tion and watched the plane hit the water.

"Allan Meaux in the waist got his at 1340; the plane fell out of control and plunged into the sea."

Lieutenants A. G. Smith, bombardier, and Walter Leeker, navigator, were both wounded, but Casey managed to bring them all home intact.

The mission to Romilly-Sur-Seine on December 20, 1942, really stirred up the Luftwaffe. They rose in great numbers on the route in and even more so on the route out. One crew that was heavily involved in the fight was that of Lt. Bruce Barton of the 91st Bomb Group, who was flying a B-17 named *Chief Sly*. He was flying the right wing of Capt. Ken Wallick, who was leading the strike against the airdrome south of Paris, one of the deepest penetrations the bombers had made.

The weather was beautiful, and the bombers assembled and headed out for the target with great expectations. Soon after they crossed the Channel, however, they ran into fighters. Barton stated: "Focke-Wulf 190s—world of them. I watched them circle around and make their attacks, but never did get worked up because they didn't seem to be shooting at me. I guess my crew was a bit excited, for they had never seen so many fighters. The pressure was lifted when they all agreed over the intercom that one of the waist gunners had shot down a fighter . . ."

The Fortresses of the 91st Bomb Group went over the target where there was little flak and made a good bomb run. The group had lost two B-17s in the fight inbound, but now the enemy had disappeared, the formation was good, and visibility was excellent. About this time, the fighters returned.

As Barton saw it: "Yes, they were out to our right. The sky was black with them. Then they began their attacks. It seemed as though they were all coming in off our right wing. One behind the other they came—all shooting. At first I thought they were all coming straight for us, but they broke and picked on the group below and ahead of us. That group really caught hell. The fighters were flying right through the formation, shooting everything they had. I sat up above and watched it as though I was in the balcony of a theater seeing a movie. Two fighters went down flaming; a B-17 ex-

Capt. Robert K. Morgan and the crew of Memphis Belle *are congratulated on the completion of their combat tour. They were the first Eighth Air Force crew to do so.* USAAF

ploded in mid-air; another dropped behind on fire and parachutes began to pop out of it. It was a great show, but it left a sunken feeling inside of me.

"Then they started on us! I was too busy flying a tight formation to see much of what was going on. It seemed as though every gun on our ship was firing all the time. I glanced over once to see a Focke-Wulf break away only a few feet off our right wing tip. It had a big yellow nose and I could see the pilot sitting there. I turned back and stuck my wing closer into my leader as we held a mean formation. The gunners were clocking fighters in from everywhere and occasionally they would report one going down.

"I saw one coming in straight ahead underneath and called for the ball turret man, S/Sgt. Myron Srsen, to get him. He

got him all right, for I watched the tracers going straight into the cockpit. Then the plane burst into flames. I couldn't watch the fighters while flying, so I let my copilot, Lt. Arthur Reynolds, watch out for them. Several times he grabbed the yoke and pushed it down quickly as the bullets of the enemy passed over our heads.

"We only got a few scattered holes out of the fray, but the worst was yet to come. Wallick's lead ship got hit badly. One of the engines was burning, and the plane was vibrating badly. He couldn't stay in formation under such conditions, so he gradually began to drop behind and down. I saw nothing to do but stay on his wing and give him as much protection as possible . . ."

Barton continued: "I could see the English Channel in front of us as we be-

gan to get hit. The attacks were still coming from the right so we got the worst of it. First it was holes in the wings and scattered holes in the fuselage. The tail gunner was hit in the face as a 20mm shell burst in front of him. Then bullets ripped into our number three engine and we lost it entirely. Then number four engine started smoking from a hole in the oil line.

"I was still in formation with Wallick when something hit the tail knocking a hole three feet wide and eight feet long—which threw us tumbling out of formation. It took the strength of both of

41

us in the cockpit to pull the vibrating plane out of the dive. Just then another burst caught us in the right wing, cutting the aileron control loose and jamming the aileron in the up position, tending to pull us to the right into our dead engines. We let one fighter slide in from above, which almost got us. His bullets raked across the cockpit and top turret. They missed me by inches and Reynolds said, 'They got Hare.' Technical Sergeant Hare, our top turret gunner, looked like he had been hit, for we saw his knees bending. Actually, he was not hit, only tailing the plane overhead with his guns, this bending his knees. He had had a close call . . . Shortly thereafter he ran out of ammunition, but continued to operate the turret so the fighters around us wouldn't know he was through."

Barton sighted some clouds several thousand feet below and headed for them, but six Fw 190s accompanied him. Barton added, "I had always heard that in such a case one should turn into the attacks. I think the hardest thing I ever had to do in my life was to make myself turn the battered plane into the fighters that were headed toward us. I closed my eyes, hoping it would work. And it did. They missed with their shots. After that, it was easier to evade their attacks."

As Barton neared the clouds, he straightened out. That was a mistake; another fighter was able to make a pass and his bullets shattered the nose of the aircraft and wounded the navigator, Lt. Paul Burnett, in the leg. Limping along, Barton managed to make England and bring his battered Fortress down in a cabbage patch.

It was during this period that a man whose name would become synonymous with strategic bombing came to the forefront. The man was Col. Curtis LeMay, commander of the 305th Bomb Group. He was a veteran B-17 pilot from the early days at Langley Field, Virginia, and perhaps no one knew the capability of the aircraft more than he. The first

change that he inaugurated in his unit was the formation. He favored a system whereby two or three squadrons flew in a stepped-up formation of eighteen aircraft. These aircraft were staggered into three-plane elements within the group to form a box formation, thus giving aircraft mutual protection support and forming up well for pattern bombing.

The second thing that LeMay did was to eliminate evasive action on the bomb run. Bombing results from the early missions largely had been poor. LeMay knew the major reason for this was that most of the aircraft were using evasive action to evade enemy flak right up to the final seconds before the bombs were dropped. He sat down and calculated from an old artillery manual the rate of fire, distance, and so on, and found that the odds against being hit at bombing altitudes were favorable. From that day on, the Fortresses in LeMay's unit flew straight and level from the initial point through the bomb run, regardless of the time elapsed. This theory caused much unrest with the crews, however, and many felt that to follow LeMay's orders would be suicide.

The test came on January 3, 1943, when LeMay led his 305th Bomb Group against St. Nazaire. They used their staggered formation and held straight and steady on the bomb run. The group suffered no losses during the 9 minutes before bombs away. The bombing was effective, and it also proved that an excellent pattern could be covered using the lead bombardier method whereby all other bombardiers dropped their bombs

This ball turret took a direct hit right in the view plate. USAAF

when the lead aircraft did. It would be only a short time before the other groups in the 8th Air Force adopted LeMay's tactics.

January 27, 1943, marked the first mission of 8th Air Force heavy bombers against Germany. The target was the naval base at Wilhelmshaven. Four groups of B-17s were dispatched to the target, and fifty-five dropped their loads. Only one Fortress was lost, even though the Luftwaffe put up every type of fighter they had available. The Battle of Germany had begun!

Chapter 5

Air Battles over the Reich

The initial mission against Germany proper brought a new complexion to the air war over Europe. With the buildup of American bomber forces in England, the Luftwaffe came under tremendous pressure not only from Air Marshal Hermann Goering, but also from Adolf

Lt. William R. Lawley, who won the Medal of Honor by bringing his wounded crewmen home on February 20, 1944. USAAF

Hitler to protect the Fatherland from bombardment. Reinforcements were brought in for the fighter forces in the West, and tactics were developed to combat the bomber formations. The year 1943 would find the bomber formations of the Eighth Air Force fighting not only to complete their missions and to prove daylight bombing a success, but before it was over, the crews themselves would be fighting for their very existence.

Up to this point, the majority of B-17s used by the 8th Air Force were F models, which were very similar to the early E models. The main visible changes were the new plexiglass nose and the paddle-blade propellers. Many other changes had been made, however, including new electrical and oxygen systems and a new and more powerful Wright R-1820 engine that developed 1,380hp under emergency conditions. Many of the new modified F models were fitted with the new "Tokyo tank" fuel cells in the outer wing sections.

Additionally, a number of field modifications were made. With the head-on attacks by German fighters, which had been initiated by Luftwaffe ace Oberst Egon Meyer of Luftwaffe fighter group II/JG 2, the lack of nose armament had become apparent. Many of the bomb groups had come up with various modifications in the plexiglass nose where two guns could be fitted, while others had fitted the nose section with "cheek"

guns. Later F-model B-17s were fitted with cheek gun positions at the factory.

The crews also suffered from the extreme cold at high altitudes over northwestern Europe. The outside temperature at 25,000ft was often 40–50 degrees below zero Fahrenheit. The open waist windows sent sweeping frigid air across the gunners, and back to the tail position. The gunners in the rear of the aircraft nearly froze. The radio operator, with an open hatch above his position, fared no better. The first baby blue electrically heated suits may not have been perfect, but they were a real godsend to all crew members. The other great innovation was the introduction of flak suits. These vest-like protectors contained quilted steel plates that were effective against shrapnel and fragments from explosive 20mm fire. The flak suits were supplemented by steel helmets with steel earflaps that were worn particularly while the aircraft was on a bomb run. Later, the gunners were blessed with the installation of plexiglass waist windows and plexiglass radio-room hatches.

As losses began to mount among bomber crews, the men began to bemoan their fates. How many missions would they be subjected to before they would be relieved from combat? As their numbers began to dwindle, it didn't take a genius to figure that the odds were against *any* of them making it, even when the combat tour was set at twenty-five missions. As the air war continued over Germany and US losses rose, the morale sunk even further. But early in 1943 more hope and determination existed among the troops.

On February 4, 1943, the bombers were slated to strike at Hamm, Germany, but weather prevented it, so Emden was struck as a secondary target by some of the Fortress groups. The Luftwaffe was up in strength, and for the first time, twin-engine fighters made their appearance. Five Fortresses were lost, one of them colliding with a Focke-Wulf 190.

This mission was significant for one crew of the 91st Bomb Group. The crew of Lt. William J. Crumm, which flew *Jack the Ripper,* completed their eleventh and final mission that day. They had been selected to return to the United States and instruct new units in the operations of the 8th Air Force bombers. Upon their return, they wrote a manual that would serve as an invaluable tool for crews who would be going to England to join in the fight over northwestern Europe.

On March 4, 1943, four groups of B-17s set out to bomb the marshaling yards at Hamm, in the industrial Ruhr region of Germany. After they formed up and headed out on course for the target, they encountered heavy clouds. The Fortresses plowed on toward the target. As conditions grew worse, all but one of the groups turned back for England: The 91st Bomb Group continued eastward. The lead navigator reported that they had crossed the coast and then the weather broke and the skies were clear. With sixteen B-17s still in formation Maj. Paul Fishburne chose to continue on to the target.

The Fortresses of the 91st put eighty 1,000lb bombs on the target, but in the course of the mission, they encountered a Luftwaffe force of over one hundred fighters. The enemy pilots swarmed around the B-17s like bees and pressed their attacks in so close that the Fortress crew could see their faces. Four bombers fell to Luftwaffe guns, while several others barely made it home.

The most notable survival story was that of Capt. George Birdsong and his crew. They were so determined to make the mission, they had rushed back to their base and loaded up in another aircraft named *Stormy Weather* when their

A Fortress *comes off a target that is still in the process of trying to cover itself with a smoke screen.* USAAF

"Bombs away" from Devil's Daughter *of the 95th Bomb Group.* USAAF

306th Bomb Group Fortresses wound up and ready to go. Loaded down, this was always a moment of truth. 306th BG Assn.

A most unusual tiger tail design on a Fortress from the 306th Bomb Group. 306th BG Assn.

own aircraft had engine trouble while forming up for the strike. They were hit by German fighters before they got to the target and on the initial attack, the oxygen tank under the pilot's seat was hit and knocked out. This started a fire which top turret gunner T/Sgt. Eugene Remmel and navigator Lt. Ernie Miller managed to get under control. Yet, the flight deck was still so full of smoke that Birdsong couldn't even see his copilot next to him.

Captain Birdsong's aircraft made the bomb run. The bombardier called, "Bombs away," not knowing that the bomb bay doors had not opened. As they came off target, one of the German fighters hit them with 20mm fire. Number two engine was hit by one shell, then Lieutenant Miller was painfully wounded by the second, and a third shell came through the cockpit windshield, seriously wounding the copilot and sending a glass fragment into Birdsong's eye.

Sergeant Rummel managed to lift the copilot off the controls and carry him to the radio room for first aid. Then another fighter attack came and knocked out number three engine. Birdsong had both surviving engines at full throttle while trying to see through the blood flowing down his face. *Stormy Weather* lagged behind, but managed to stay with

The B-17 Little Audrey *flew with the 306th Bomb Group.* 306th BG Assn.

the formation out over the North Sea. As they crossed the water, the crew discovered that they still had their bombs aboard. Then they had to reinstall the safety pins, for the Fortress had let down too low for the bombs to be salvoed.

Birdsong brought the B-17s in to Bassingborn only to discover that the brakes were inoperable. The aircraft went off the end of the runway, through a fence, across a road, and then through a field of Brussels sprouts. At this point, the crew jumped out of the aircraft, bringing their wounded with them. Torn and bloodied, they had made it home!

For their successful lone strike against Hamm, the 91st Bomb Group was awarded a Distinguished Unit Citation.

It was on a mission to Vegesack, Germany, to bomb U-boat yards on March 18 that a member of VIII Bomber Command would win the command's first Medal of Honor. Lt. Jack Mathis was a bombardier in the 303rd Bomb Group aboard a B-17 named *The Duchess*. While the aircraft was on the bomb run it was hit by flak, but as the navigator noted, Mathis didn't seem to pay any attention to the interruption. He stayed at his bombsight and called out, "Bomb bay doors open."

The navigator related: "On the bomb run, flak hit us. We were seconds short of the bomb release point when a whole barrage of flak hit our squadron, which we were leading. One of the shells burst out to the right and a little below the nose. It couldn't have been over 30ft away when it burst. If it had been much closer it would have knocked the whole plane over.

"A hunk of flak came tearing through the side of the nose. It shattered the glass on the right side and broke through with a loud crash. I saw Jack falling back toward me and threw up my arm to ward off the fall. By that time, both of us were back in the rear of the nose—blown back there I guess, by flak burst. I was sort of half standing, half lying against the back wall and Jack was leaning up against me. I didn't know he was injured at the time.

"Without any assistance from me, he pulled himself back to his bombsight. His little seat had been knocked out from under him by flak and he sort of knelt over the bombsight. He knew that as bombardier of the lead ship, the re-

Raunchy Wolf *was a B-17F from the 551st Squadron, 385th Bomb Group.* USAAF

The B-17F Liberty Belle, *serial number 42-30096, flew with the 544th Squadron, 385th Bomb Group.* USAAF

Hoosier Hot Shot, *B-17G serial number 42-38006, flew with the 91st Bomb Group, Eighth Air Force.* USAAF

Another 91st Bomb Group B-17G, Pist'l Packin' Mama. USAAF

The B-17 Betty Lou's Buggy *of the Eighth Air Force's 91st Bomb Group.* USAAF

sults of the whole squadron might depend on his accuracy. And he didn't let anything stop him. Part of my job as navigator is to keep the log of the flights, so I looked at my watch to start timing the fall of the bombs. I heard Jack call out on the intercom, 'Bombs . . .' He usually called it out in sort of a singsong. But he never finished the phrase this time.

"I looked up and saw Jack reaching over to grasp the bomb bay door handle to close the doors. Just as he pushed the handle, he slumped over backwards. I caught him. That was the first indication that anything was wrong. I saw that his arm was pretty badly shot. 'I guess they got you this time old boy,' I remember saying, but then his head slumped over and I saw that the injuries were more serious than just some flak in the arm. I knew then that he was dead. I closed the bomb bay and returned to my post."

Lt. Jack Mathis had made the supreme effort to get back to his bombsight in order to enable his squadron to put their bombs on target.

April 17 marked the fiercest opposition that the Fortress crews had experienced to date. One hundred fifteen B-17s from four bomb groups were dispatched to strike the Focke-Wulf 190 plant at Bremen, Germany. With the 91st Bomb Group leading, the bombers began to encounter enemy fighters just past the Frisian Islands. The fighter attacks were coordinated, with head-on attacks against four to six enemy aircraft at a time. They went after the bombers throughout the route in, and even attacked through the flak over the target. It was reported that Junkers Ju 88 twin-engine aircraft dropped some sort of aerial bombs on the B-17 formations from above. Bombing results were reported as being good, but sixteen aircraft were lost out of the leading combat formation. The 91st Bomb Group lost six aircraft, while the 306th Bomb Group lost ten.

In addition to the fighter attacks, the 306th Bomb Group reported they encountered the heaviest concentration of flak they had ever seen. The Eighth Air Force flak officer's report stated: "The intensity of the flak was probably the most severe that has ever been experienced by this wing, and the huge volume of smoke that overhung the target area acted as a very real deterrent, causing many members of crews to feel that it would be an impossibility to fly in the area without suffering damage."

Capt. William J. Casey, leading the 367th Bomb Squadron of the 306th Bomb Group, had his aircraft *Banshee* raked over by fighters and his crew fought valiantly, but the deteriorating condition of the aircraft forced Casey to head his plane back to land as his one remaining engine was running away. During the repeated fighter attacks and the final pass by a twin-engine fighter, the five crewmen in the back of the bomb bay were all killed. At 23,000ft the men up front began leaving the plane, planning to open their chutes immediately so that the high winds aloft might blow them over land in the Frisian Islands. All made it, although they landed close to water and were captured almost immediately.

Lt. Maxwell Judas, the only 368th Bomb Squadron plane to make it home, was hit hard on the bomb run by fighters and as he turned off the target, all of his squadron disappeared. Unable to maintain altitude, Judas was forced to descend to 500ft. He nursed his aircraft back across the North Sea with about an engine and a half, flying all the way to Thurleigh at 105mph indicated airspeed.

In *Old Faithful*, Capt. Pervis Youree traveled down the bomb run with two engines feathered and the top turret shattered after encountering a Luft-

Fickle Finger of ? *was B-17F serial number 42-3335 of the 385th Bomb Group, Eighth Air Force.* USAAF

The Vibrant Virgin, *a B-17F, serial number 42-30275, was assigned to the 548th Bomb Squadron, 385th Bomb Group.* USAAF

Stars and Stripes, 2nd Edition *was a B-17G assigned to the Eighth Air Force's 385th Bomb Group.* USAAF

waffe welcome. Youree also had to take his plane down on the deck, and flew 200 miles at wave-top heights with one engine. Lt. Leroy Sugg, the copilot, held together the control cables for the number three engine with his hands. With full power on one engine, Youree was able to make 115mph indicated airspeed. The crew busily jettisoned everything, including the ball turret.

The 306th Bomb Group mission report by Maj. John L. Lambert included the following: "On the way in from the coast some forty E/A in string formation flew parallel to our formation, level and about 2,000 yards to the left. Attacks were withheld until we were on the bombing run, when there were heavy attacks . . . The 306th Group fell out of column to the left, with resulting concentrated head-on attacks . . . Dozens of E/A sailed right into and through our formation, rolling over and diving as they passed through. This was the period when heaviest losses were sustained."

A mission to the U-boat pens at St. Nazaire, France, marked the second event that would bring a Medal of Honor to a B-17 crew member. Sgt. Maynard

H. "Snuffy" Smith was flying his first mission as a crew member assigned to the ball turret. The aircraft belonged to the 306th Bomb Group and was flown by Lt. L. P. Johnson. As the Fortress came off the target and headed for home it was hit by fighters, causing serious destruction and setting fires in the aircraft.

Smith related the events from that moment: "My interphone and the electrical controls to my turret went out, so I hand-cranked myself up and crawled out of the turret into the ship. The first thing I saw was a sheet of flame coming out of the radio room and another fire by the tail wheel section.

"Suddenly the radio operator came staggering out of the flames. He made a beeline for the gun hatch and dove out. I glanced out and watched him hit the horizontal stabilizer, bounce off, and open his chute. By this time the right waist gunner had bailed out over his gun and the left waist gunner was trying to jump, but was stuck half in and half out of his gun hatch. I pulled him back into the ship and asked him if the heat was too much for him. All he did was stare at me and I watched him bail out the rear door. His chute opened okay.

"The smoke and gas were really thick. I wrapped a sweater around my face so I could breathe, grabbed a fire ex-

tinguisher, and attacked the fire in the radio room. Glancing over my shoulder at the tail fire, I thought I saw something coming and ran back. It was Gibson, the tail gunner, painfully crawling back, wounded. He had blood all over him.

"Looking him over, I saw that he had been hit in the back and that it had probably gone through his left lung. I laid him down on his left side so that the wound would not drain into the right lung, gave a shot of morphine, and made him as comfortable as possible before going back to the fires.

"I had just got started in this when this Fw 190 came in again. I jumped for one of the waist guns and fired at him. As he swept under us I turned to the other waist gun and let him have it from the other side. He left us for a while so I went back to the radio room fire again.

"I got into the room this time and began throwing out burning debris. The fire had burned holes so large in the side of the ship that I had just tossed the stuff out through them. Gas from a burning extinguisher was choking me, so I went back to the tail fire. I took off my chute so I could move easier. I'm glad I didn't take it off sooner, because later I found that it had stopped a .30 caliber bullet.

"I fired another burst with the waist guns and went back to the radio room with the last of the extinguisher fluid. When that ran out I found a water bottle and a urine can and poured these out.

"After that I was so mad, I urinated on the fire and finally beat on it with my hands and feet until my clothes began to smolder. That Fw 190 came around again and I let him have it. That time he left us for good. The fire was under control, more or less, and we were in sight of land."

Johnson brought the aircraft in for a landing at Predonnock but as he let the tail wheel down and slowed, the fuselage began to crack at the trailing edge of the wing and finally crumpled to a standstill.

Another amazing B-17 survival story took place on May 15 in a Fortress named *Old Bill* that belonged to the 305th Bomb Group. The Fortresses had taken off to bomb Wilhelmshaven but when the target was found not to be visible, the formation headed for Heligoland on the coast. *Old Bill* was flown

B-17G from the 385th Bomb Group. The letter in the box denoted that the aircraft came from the 3rd Bomb Division. C. B. Rollins

by Capt. William D. Whitson, along with his regular crew, who had brought the aircraft overseas with the original contingent.

Enemy aircraft were encountered, and on one of the first passes, the oxygen system was shot out. Whitson had no choice but to dive the aircraft down from 25,000ft to an altitude where the crew could breathe. Not only had they lost their oxygen, but Whitson had been wounded in the leg.

Whitson went to the rear to check for damage and get some portable oxygen bottles. When he returned to the flight deck he found his copilot, Lt. Harry L. Holt, almost unconscious for lack of oxygen. Once Holt was revived, Whitson returned to the rear to have his wounds treated.

Shortly after Whitson returned, the aircraft was attacked by some twenty German fighters. As the Focke-Wulf 190s made their head-on passes they shot through the cockpit windshield, seriously wounding Holt and hitting Whitson for the second time.

The plexiglass nose was completely shot away and navigator Lt. Douglas Venable had been killed. The bombardier saved his own life by throwing himself flat when he saw the German fighters blazing in at his level.

Shell fragments had splintered the top turret and wounded engineer-gunner T/Sgt. Albert Haymon in the head. Although blood streamed down, Haymon operated the turret and guns with an emergency hand-crank until the crank jammed.

The tail gunner, T/Sgt. Kenneth Meyer, was firing away at the enemy fighters with vigor. He claimed three destroyed in rapid order. In the ball turret, S/Sgt. Edgar Nichols kept firing despite his wounds, and hit two fighters. Right waist gunner Sgt. John Breen downed another.

Once the top turret was no longer operative, Sergeant Haymon left it to as-

Formation view from the tail gunner's seat. Copilots on the lead aircraft often took this position to report on the unit's formation. C. B. Rollins

Madam Shoo Shoo *was one of the attractive nose art girls that flew with the 385th Bomb Group.* C. B. Rollins

Pfc. Ruby Newell was elected the most attractive WAC in England, and this 385th Bomb *Group aircraft was named after her.* C. B. Rollins

sist radio operator T/Sgt. Fred Brewak in moving Lieutenant Holt back to the radio room. Then Haymon went forward again and took over the copilot's seat.

Sergeant Meyer ran out of ammunition and went up to the waist for more. When it was expended, he returned to the waist and manned one of the guns there until the fighter attacks ceased. At that time, Meyer went up and replaced Haymon in the copilot's seat.

Although he was wounded, bombardier Lieutenant Barrall went up to the flight deck where he helped Captain Whitson with his wounds and gave him a shot of morphine for the pain. He then returned to the nose. Despite the tremendous blast of air through the missing plexiglass, Barrall manned the cheek gun and managed to put telling shots into a Messerschmitt Bf 210 that came to finish off *Old Bill.* Following this encounter, Barrall went back to the flight deck and took over the controls in the copilot's position.

The rear of the aircraft was a mess. Bullet and flak holes had riddled the interior. Of the eleven men who were aboard *Old Bill* only two had not been wounded, Sergeant Meyer and right waist gunner Sergeant Breen. Overall, the balance of *Old Bill* was not good. The right wing was buckled and its hydraulics were shot out. Regardless, Whitson brought the Fortress in for a successful, wheels-down landing at its home base at Chelveston.

On examining the shot-up bomber on the ground, the group flight surgeon was heard to say, "Not a damn thing in there but blood and empty cartridge cases."

For their outstanding action that day, the crew of *Old Bill* became the most decorated aviators of the 303rd Bomb Group. Captain Whitson and Lieutenant Barrall each received the Distinguished Service Cross, and other crew members received eight Silver Stars and seven Purple Hearts.

May 17, 1943, was a triumphant day for Capt. Robert K. Morgan and several of his crew members of the 91st Bomb Group. They became the first Eighth Air Force bomber crew to complete a tour of twenty-five combat missions. Flying in their Fortress *Memphis Belle,* they had beaten the odds and now they were slated to return to the United States for a War Bond Tour. From there,

Fortresses of the 95th Bomb Group en route to a target in Norway. USAAF

they would visit various bases where new crews were being trained for combat in the Eighth Air Force.

The *Memphis Belle* had completed only twenty-four missions on May 17 when its skipper and several other crew members finished up their tour, so it was up to another pilot to see the valiant craft through its twenty-fifth mission. The honor went to Lt. C. L. Anderson and crew, who took the *Memphis Belle* to Kiel on May 19, 1943. Although *Belle* was not the first to complete a tour, the bomber would receive the lion's share of publicity for the feat on its return to the United States. The honor of being the first B-17 to complete twenty-five missions went to *Hell's Angels* of the 303rd Bomb Group, which returned from its twenty-fifth on May 14, 1943.

On May 27, 1943, the 8th Air Force introduced a new weapon when it struck at the submarine pens at St. Nazaire. The new aircraft was the Boeing YB-40, a heavily armed version of the B-17. The new Fortress was armed with the conventional top turret, ball turret, and tail guns, but there were several new additions. A Martin twin-gun power turret was installed in the radio room, each waist installation was fitted with twin .50 caliber guns that were hydraulically boosted, and a chin turret with twin .50s was installed under the plexiglass nose. The latter turret would become standard on B-17Gs in late 1943. The aircraft arrived without the cheek guns in the nose but these were installed before combat, bringing the total number of .50 caliber guns aboard to sixteen. The ad-

vised total ammunition load was 11,200 rounds. The additional guns and ammunition brought the total weight of the YB-40 at takeoff to some 10,000lb more than a loaded B-17F.

A dozen of the YB-40s were assigned to the 92nd Bomb Group and would fly not only with the 92nd, but on occasion would be used by other bomb groups in their formation. From its first mission to St. Nazaire, the aircraft was not a success. The plane carried no bomb load, so when the B-17s in the formation dropped their bombs, the YB-40s—still laden with heavy guns and ammunition—could not keep up. Ammunition feed re-

A 385th Bomb Group comes home to roost. Operations officers are out by the flight control trailer to check in the birds. C. B. Rollins

An olive drab Fortress teams up with a shiny new silver sister aircraft from the 306th Bomb Group. 306th BG Assn.

quired modification. Although the aircraft was tested under various conditions, the only real advantage that it brought about was the chin turret. By July of 1943, the YB-40 would be history.

A mission to Kiel on June 13, 1943, proved to be disastrous for the 4th Bomb Wing which was composed of the 94th, 95th, and 96th Bomb Groups. The 95th would suffer its highest loss of the war when ten of its Fortresses fell, and the 94th would lose nine. The 96th was fortunate to get out with only three losses. All total, twenty-two aircraft in sixty attacks were lost, or about 30 percent.

The wing was led by Brig. Gen. Nathan Bedford Forrest, grandson of the famed Civil War Confederate Cavalry general, who had come direct from Washington to take over a combat wing. Rather than fly the staggered formation that had been adopted by the other 8th Air Force bombers, the 4th would fly a flat, wingtip-to-wingtip formation over the target, as decreed by General Forrest. The general also had instructed that the gunners use a new type of oil for their guns which supposedly would prevent their freezing.

General Forrest flew in the copilot's seat of the lead aircraft with Capt. Harry Stirwalt as pilot. The formation moved across the North Sea and then began to make its penetration toward the Kiel shipyards. At that moment, hordes of enemy fighters began to appear. The Bf 109s and Fw 190s came in waves from head-on and did their utmost to close to the point that they could break up the formation.

As the Fortresses made their bomb run, the attacks continued. One after another, B-17s began to fall. The aircraft on which General Forrest was flying dropped its bombs and then went down. Only two men survived of the thirteen men aboard; General Forrest was not one of them.

A number of B-17s went down because many of their guns were frozen. It was not unusual for half the guns of one of the 95th Bomb Group's aircraft to be unserviceable because of the new type oil that had been used. Those who *could* fire did their utmost to turn back the Luftwaffe fighters. As the Fortresses fought their way over the North Sea they dropped down to about 800ft, but still were attacked over and over by Luftwaffe pilots. One German fighter collided with one of the B-17s which in turn collided with another B-17. All three aircraft crashed into the sea. In addition to the ten aircraft lost on the mission, the 95th Group had one B-17 crash-land upon reaching England.

To the crews of the 94th Bomb Group, the attacks of the German fighters seemed suicidal. Pilots reported that they had to take violent evasive action to keep some of the fighters from crashing into them. The group came under especially heavy attack as they rallied off the target. Six of their nine aircraft losses came in the target area. Maj. Louis Thorup managed to get his shot-up Fortress over the North Sea with one engine out. There he was attacked by a flight of four Bf 109s, one of which made a pass that knocked out another two engines and shot off the entire left stabilizer. Thorup managed to stay aloft a few more miles and set the plane down in the sea. Fortunately, the crew was rescued eleven hours later.

The final analysis of the mission was that the abandonment of the staggered formation had been a fatal mistake. It caused the bombers to be strung out, sacrificing defensive fire power. Debriefings by all three groups revealed innumerable errors in both the planning and execution of the mission.

A mission to Hamburg on July 25 brought about sharp defensive action from the Luftwaffe and cost the 384th Bomb Group seven aircraft, nearly half of the fifteen that were lost by the 1st Bomb Wing. The 379th Bomb Group lost two B-17s, but had one come home through the concerted effort of crew members of a Fortress named *Judy Bea*.

The pilot of this aircraft was Lt. Willis Carlisle, a big, strapping 200-pounder. His copilot was a little wiry guy by the name of Lieutenant Bigler, whom he called "Big." Though they fought and swore at each other, Big refused to take a crew of his own and stayed on to fly with Carlisle.

As the B-17s approached the target, they came under attack from fighters. On one of the initial passes, Carlisle was hit and killed by a burst of 20mm fire. The fire that killed Carlisle knocked out the oxygen system on the right side of the flight deck. Carlisle slumped over and fell against Lieutenant Bigler. Realizing that he might pass out from lack of oxygen, Bigler trimmed the plane and

by holding the pilot off with one hand, he kept the bomber in formation with the other hand. After making the bomb run, Bigler called for help over the intercom.

When Lt. Joe Glazer, the bombardier, arrived, Technical Sergeant Tyler, the top turret gunner, was holding the pilot off the controls. Glazer switched the oxygen control for Bigler to emergency, but it was out. He then stripped off the pilot's mask and put it on Bigler. By this time Tyler was turning blue, so Bigler gave his walkaround bottle to him and sent him back up to the top turret to ward off fighter attacks.

Glazer was getting weak trying to hold Carlisle's body off the controls, so he had to get down on the catwalk to find an oxygen outlet that worked. Then one of the waist gunners came forward with four bottles and Glazer took them and returned to the flight deck. The pilot's body then slumped over and the aircraft went into a steep dive. Before Tyler and Glazer could remove the pilot's body from his seat, they had dropped to 8,500ft and oxygen was no longer necessary.

Glazer settled down in the pilot's seat, and he and Bigler brought the Fortress home.

For a similar act of courage, F/O John C. Morgan won the Medal of Honor on July 26, 1943. Morgan was flying as copilot with the 92nd Bomb Group on a B-17 named *Ruthie II* en route to bomb Hanover when the aircraft was attacked by Focke-Wulf 190s. When the fighters made their first pass, pilot Lt. Robert L. Campbell had his skull split open by enemy fire. Immediately after being hit Campbell slumped over the controls, grasping the yoke tightly. Morgan seized the controls and doggedly fought to keep the plane in formation while he tried to keep the pain-crazed pilot off the controls with the other hand. Desperately, Morgan called for help, but the intercom was shot out. When he received no response he assumed that the majority of the crew must have bailed out.

At the same time that the pilot was hit, the top turret gunner fell from his position down into the nose with his arm all but severed. The navigator realized that the man would quickly die without medical attention. The nose hatch was opened, and with great difficulty the navigator managed to push the gunner out with his parachute unfurled in his

A copilot's view of a feathered prop on the number four engine. Note the oil streaks back over the nacelle. USAAF

arms. Miraculously, the canopy opened and the gunner was later reported to be taken as a prisoner of war.

Meanwhile, Morgan continued to fight off the efforts of the pilot as he struggled to stay in formation. Rather than take a chance to run for home in the face of heavy enemy attacks, Morgan chose to fly on with the group. After two hours during which *Ruthie II* completed the mission with the rest of the B-17s, Morgan was finally discovered by navigator Lieutenant Koske, who helped remove the mortally wounded pilot from his seat and into the nose of the aircraft.

Weather and a new weapon by the Luftwaffe spelled disaster for a number of 8th Air Force Fortresses on July 28. The target was Oschersleben, but an appreciable number of the 4th Bomb Wing B-17s aborted the mission when layers of high clouds menaced the formations and several aircraft became separated from their units. Also spelling trouble for the bombers were the Fw 190s and Bf 110s that were equipped with rockets. These sizeable missiles were carried in tubes under the wings of the enemy aircraft and weighed about 250lb. They carried a 21lb warhead that had a preset range of about 1,200 yards, which was outside the range of the .50 caliber guns on the B-17s. One of the missiles hit a 385th Bomb Group Fortress which in turn crashed into two other B-17s in its formation; all three aircraft went down to their destruction.

Other Fortress formations were broken up in their attempt to avoid the missiles and wend their way through the clouds. The 96th Bomb Group came under very heavy attack during this period and lost a number of its aircraft, including its lead ship, before it reached the German coast. Most of the crew members who were forced to bail out or ditch in the sea were lost.

Some of the 96th Fortresses formed on the rear of the 94th Bomb Group which fought its way on in to the target, the Focke-Wulf assembly plant, at Oschersleben. As one of the 96th crew members recalled going in from the initial point of the bomb run, "Fighters were pressing home savage attacks. A Fort broke out in flames, across all four engines. I saw five chutes open. A German fighter exploded—a ball of orange flame hanging in the air. Another Fort twisted out of control, an engine burning, its tail sheared off . . . "

The 96th Bomb Group returned to base at Snetterton to find seven of its aircraft missing. The 4th Bomb Wing lost fifteen of its Fortresses on the mission.

August 17, 1943, is a date that will live forever in the annals of aerial warfare. It was on that date that 8th Air Force flew its historic dual mission to Regensburg and Schweinfurt. Regensburg was the home of the Messerschmitt factory, manufacturers of the vaunted Bf 109, and Schweinfurt was the location of three ball-bearing factories, the essential components of everything mechanical in the Third Reich. To eliminate these centers would cut deeply into German aircraft and armament production. If the two plants could be completely destroyed, it could shorten the war in Europe.

The missions had been in the planning stage for some time, and the planners knew that strikes so deep into Germany without fighter escort would bring with it heavy casualties in the bomber force. In order to minimize losses, yet en-

able the missions to be flown, a plan was formulated that would send the 1st and the 4th Bomb Wings against the targets simultaneously. The plan called for the Regensburg force—which would be provided with P-47 Thunderbolt escort—to cross the coast of Holland at approximately 0830 hours. The Schweinfurt force would be 15 minutes behind them. It was contemplated that the Regensburg force would draw the majority of fighter opposition, thus reducing the hazards for the Schweinfurt force. To further confuse the Luftwaffe, the Regensburg force would turn south and continue on to bases in North Africa. This should string out the Luftwaffe, and make attacks against the Schweinfurt force minimal as they did their bombing and returned to England.

Unfortunately, the operation did not go as planned. On the morning of August 17, weather did not cooperate. The staff of VIII Bomber Command debated canceling or postponing the operation, but finally made a decision that would prove lethal to the crews aboard the B-17s. The Regensburg force would take off as scheduled, while the Schweinfurt force would not get airborne until over three and a half hours later!

Col. Curtis LeMay led the Regensburg force, flying in the lead aircraft of the 96th Bomb Group. Its B-17s began to get off the ground at 0621 hours. The bombers formed up and headed out across the English Channel. They were provided with escort by the 353rd and 56th Fighter Group P-47s. There was some interception by the Luftwaffe, but no great damage was done until the Thunderbolts ran low on fuel and were forced to break off the escort and return to England.

Once the P-47s left, the Luftwaffe began their attacks in earnest. They not only used the head-on attack, but also came in from every angle. Some came straight down on the combat boxes, diving all the way from the high squadron to the low. Twin-engine Messerschmitt Bf 110s and Junkers Ju 88s sat out of .50 caliber range and fired rockets into the formation. The historian of the 100th Bomb Group reported the air battle as follows:

"It happened ten miles southwest of Antwerp. The Germans came in fast. The Fortresses turrets ground in azimuth and elevation, and short bursts

stitched through the sky. From the initial moment of near-terror until the assault ceased two hours later, more than two hundred attacks were pressed against the Hundredth. There was desperation in the air as the Luftwaffe piled in and slugged it out. They seemed to anticipate the route, and later, many men confessed that they felt sharp fear of the formation being caught and trapped. As the aircraft crossed into the Reich proper the attacks seemed to increase in intensity. The group rocked under the constant pressure of individual fighter attacks from every clock position. It would scarcely have helped had the men known that the struggle was still not anywhere near its peak. Forts and fighters lit the sky with a series of brilliant explosions and the debris-cluttered air seemed to hold nothing but death and the realization that death was inevitable.

"A couple of Jerry twin-engine jobs stood off to the side as though sitting in on a wake and sent word to their friends further up the road to prepare a hot welcome for the invaders as they drove deeper into the land.

"The B-17s shook with the fury of their .50s as the gunners became inured to destruction. Ammunition ran low in many ships and belts were transported from one position to another. Outside the windows, parachutes descended in swaying patterns and slow motion, an odd contrast to the swift and jagged geometric patterns of aircraft parts that plummeted down. It was impossible to keep track of any near order of events. The entire flight became a kaleidoscopic dream of nightmarish quality, a scene in ugly colors of smoke, fire and the yellow, red and black nosed enemy etched against the incongruously peaceful blue backdrop of the sky."

Of the twenty-four Fortresses that were lost on the mission to Regensburg, nine of them that fell were from the 100th Bomb Group. Also hard hit on the mission was the 390th Bomb Group, which lost six aircraft.

It was, no doubt, fortunate that the Regensburg force turned south, for the Luftwaffe would have been ready to intercept them once more on the way home. The B-17s journeyed down to North Africa where they landed, but much to their chagrin they found that

there was little there to welcome them or assist them with their damaged aircraft.

The Schweinfurt force did not become airborne until after 1100 hours. They, too, had two groups of Thunderbolts escorting them in, but when the escort departed, the Luftwaffe, which had already done extensive damage that day, was fully alert and waiting for them.

The Luftwaffe appeared just before the Fortresses reached Eupen where they were to have rendezvoused with the Thunderbolts of the 4th Fighter Group. The P-47s did not appear, and Focke-Wulf 190s of I/JG 26 attacked the low squadron of the 91st Bomb Group.

Lt. Don Von Der Heyde's B-17 was hit and went down spinning. Only two men would survive.

The real battle began when the Luftwaffe attacked the 381st Bomb Group. S/Sgt. Kenneth Stone, a ball turret gunner in the lead ship, reported the following: " . . . Our fighter escort left us near the German border, and we entered southern Germany protected now only by our own guns. Ten minutes after our fighter escort had turned back, enemy formations appeared from out of the clouds. There were over a hundred: Messerschmitt 109s, Focke-Wulf 190s, and Messerschmitt 110s. I watched them circle our group, sizing us up. They separated and formed in flights of fifteen abreast about 5,000 yards in front of our plane.

"The first flight came in head-on with their 20mm guns blazing. I fired at the plane nearest my position and gave

Sunrise for a maintenance crew. These men knew no limits to which they would not go to get their Fortress airborne. 306th BG Assn.

him a short burst. Four more flights came in head-on and scattered through our formation. Lieutenant Painter and Captain Nelson, who were flying behind us as deputy leader, fell out of formation and left the group with one engine blazing. The crew bailed out. Three more planes dropped out of formation, and parachutes billowed from them. Fighters were going down right and left. The Fortress gunners were deadly accurate. The plane of my former copilot, Lieutenant Darrow, had one engine knocked out, but managed to keep up with the remaining formation.

"The enemy fighters finally departed for their bases to refuel and prepare to meet us on our way back to England. Our group had already lost four planes. As we approached the target we were met by flak. The German gunners put up a barrage over the target, and we had to fly straight through the flak. This proved to be disastrous to some planes. Our bombardier, Lieutenant Hester, opened the bomb bay doors and dropped our deadly cargo. I watched the bombs plummet down and hit the target. The ball-bearing plants were well plastered with bomb hits, and smoke rose high and fast.

"Our only thought now was to get back safely to our base. About fifteen minutes after leaving the target, enemy fighters were sighted coming in towards our right. They again attacked head-on, five abreast. This method of attack was new to us and was very effective. Campbell, our radio operator, asked permission to leave his radio to fire his gun; it was okay with Captain Briggs. Our right wing man, Lieutenant Jarvis, had his number three engine hit by enemy guns and it caught fire. The waist gunner waved to us as they dropped out of formation. Chutes were all over the sky—white ones and the brown chutes of enemy fighter pilots.

"Sweat was running down my face even though the temperature was thirty degrees below zero. I was afraid that we would never see England again; the odds were too much against us. I saw more fighters—miles to the right—and heading our way. I began praying to God and asking him for courage to see this through. The fighters came closer and closer and began attacking the pride of the Luftwaffe. Our escort had finally arrived . . . Hallelujah!"

Also being shot to pieces in the lead formation was the 91st Bomb Group. They managed to hold themselves together for the first 15 minutes of the attacks; after that, they were downed one by one. Amazingly, the lead aircraft flown by Lt. Col. Clemens Wurzbach, the group commander, survived.

Thirty-six B-17s from the 1st Bomb Wing were lost that day, including

96th Bomb Group Fortresses taxi out for take-off turns en route to another mission over Europe. Ethell

eleven from the 381st Bomb Group and ten from the 91st Bomb Group. This, coupled with the Regensburg losses, brought a total of sixty Fortresses lost in the attacks. Although gunners on the bombers claimed 288 enemy fighters destroyed, they actually downed twenty-one. Escorting P-47s are credited with fourteen enemy fighters, and RAF Spitfires got another seven.

It was thought from the strike photos that the Messerschmitt factory at Regensburg was completely destroyed. After digging through the wreckage, however, the Germans found that most of the machine tools were undamaged, and the factory was reconstructed. The Germans officially estimated that some 800 to 1,000 fighters were lost as a result of the raid, which was equivalent to six to eight weeks' production. Damage at Schweinfurt was even less, but it did prompt the manufacturers to begin doling out ball-bearing production to small manufacturers scattered across Germany. This made it impossible for the Allies to put a complete halt to production.

In the massive air battles that took place in 1943 it is usually related, particularly in unit histories and such, that the fighters encountered were either the "Abbeville Kids," "Goering's select group of aces," or "Goering's yellow-nose elite." While the Luftwaffe fighter units were very good, none of these descriptions is accurate. The group usually referred to as the Abbeville Kids consisted of the fighters of JG 26, which was based on the French coast in the Abbeville area. While the pilots in this unit in 1943 were largely veteran combat aviators, they were not all high-scoring aces nor were they picked by Goering for this unit or for any other fighter wing for that matter. The German fighters that were encountered during 1943 were largely from JG 1, JG 2, JG 3, JG 11, and JG 26. A Jagdgeschwader could be composed of up to twelve squadrons, and the squadrons were usually three to a group. However, not all JGs in action in the West were composed of all three groups at this time. During the summer of 1943, the Luftwaffe pulled in ZGs (wings of twin-engine Bf 110 destroyers) to aid in the defense of the Reich. When necessary, twin-engine night fighters from the NJGs (night-fighter wings) were pressed into service.

The Eighth Air Force did not attempt another strike deep into Germany until September 6, 1943, when it set out on a maximum effort to strike the SKF instrument bearing plant at Stuttgart. Gen. H. H. Arnold was in England on an inspection trip and, undoubtedly, General Eaker wanted to show him that the Eighth Air Force still could successfully penetrate and bomb a target deep in the Third Reich.

The 96th Bomb Group set out leading its wing and once France was crossed without fighter opposition, it was felt that it would be a particularly good mission. When they reached the German border, however, a front of clouds appeared. The Germans surrounded the target area with smoke pots, further obscuring the target. On the first bomb run, the target was not visible, so the bombers swung around through the flak for a second bomb run. Then the Luftwaffe decided to put in its appearance.

The 388th Bomb Group was picked by the German fighter pilots to receive their undivided attention. More than one hundred fighters attacked the group, which desperately repelled attack after attack for an extended period of time. The first heavy attack consisted of fighters forming up two or three miles in front of the bombers and then coming in level from eleven o'clock to one o'clock. For the first 5 minutes, the attacking fighters assumed a traffic pattern attacking mostly from the left at eleven o'clock. They trailed each other in, slightly stepped up, at about twenty-second intervals. At 300 to 400 yards the fighters would start their roll and make their pass at the lead squadron. After the low squadron of bombers was eliminated, the traffic pattern was shifted over to the right. Some attacks were pressed as close as fifty to seventy-five yards.

The 388th Group lost eleven of its Fortresses on the mission and suffered one crew member killed and two seriously wounded on the aircraft that returned.

The lead squadron of the 303rd Bomb Group led the 41st Combat Wing, with Brig. Gen. Robert F. Travis, new wing commander, in the lead aircraft. When the wing arrived and found the target covered by clouds and smoke, it began to orbit. Many of the Fortresses were low on fuel by this time, so it was imperative that they drop their bombs

and head for England. Even so, Travis kept leading the formation through steep banks to one side and then the other, making it impossible for some of the aircraft to maintain formation. Some were forced to salvo their bombs to keep up. When bombs were finally dropped, it was a known fact that many of the B-17s did not have enough fuel left to return to England.

Twelve B-17s were forced to ditch in the English Channel with 118 crew members being picked up by air-sea rescue. Two other Fortresses crash-landed in England. Four badly damaged bombers made it to Switzerland, and one crashed in a Swiss lake. All in all, the mission had been an expensive fiasco.

September 1943 saw the arrival of the first B-17Gs in the Eighth Air Force. The engines were a newer and more powerful modification, and there were numerous minor changes made in the aircraft that improved its overall performance. The two most important new features on the G model were the chin turret, which originally had been introduced on the YB-40, and staggered waist windows that were covered with plexiglass. These additions and modifications gave the nose of the aircraft the firepower that it had needed for so long, and the improved waist windows cut the chilling winds aloft in the rear of the aircraft that had resulted in so many severe cases of frostbite. Additionally, the oxygen hoses and communication leads for the waist gunners were placed on their respective sides of the fuselage and no longer did the gunners have tangled lines coming down from the ceiling of the fuselage, nor were they bumping rears constantly, which tended to frustrate action on either side.

Several other innovations were introduced to the 8th Air Force during this period. For some weeks, several Fortresses had been assigned to the new 813th Bomb Squadron. This unit was formed to indoctrinate crews using British H2S radars that allowed accurate blind bombing when the target was obscured by clouds or smoke. Initially, the radar sets were installed under the Fortresses' nose, but the radar was installed in place of the ball turret, in a retractable housing, in later aircraft. This set, called "Mickey" by the Eighth Air Force crew members, was used in radar bombing of targets from the fall of 1943

on. The crews from the 813th Bomb Squadron, called "Pathfinders" or "PFF," went from one unit to another performing their duties.

Other innovations that came to light during the fall of 1943 were "window" and "carpet." Window consisted of strips of tinfoil about 1/16in wide and 11in long. These strips were dropped from the Fortresses beginning at the initial point of the bomb run. They tended to appear as thousands of targets on the

Royal Flush *from the 401st Bomb Squadron, 91st Bomb Group takes off from Bassingborn on November 3, 1943, en route to Wilhelmshaven.* USAAF

German radar screens, and often confused the radars that aimed the flak batteries.

Carpet was an airborne transmitter that could be used to jam ground radar frequencies. This was another attempt to reduce the effectiveness of the flak batteries which were beginning to take a higher toll of the bombers.

The Pathfinder crews of the 813th Bomb Squadron took on their first task on September 27, 1943. Two B-17s were assigned to the 1st Air Division and two to the 3rd Air Division's to accompany the bombers on a mission to Emden. The mission was not really successful, though, as one of the Pathfinders assigned to the 1st had his radar go out and the 1st Air Division second aircraft had its radar set hit by flak on the way to the target. One of the 3rd Air Division operators found his radar faulty, so the crew did not go on the mission. The other aircraft made the mission and marked the target, which was cloud covered. The target was bombed, but later reconnaissance photos showed that most of the bombs had hit wide of the mark.

October 8 found the Fortresses on their way to Bremen. The 3rd Air Division went in over the North Sea, followed by the B-24s, which veered off to bomb Vegesack. The 1st Air Division attacked Bremen after overflying Holland. Clouds caused several formations to bomb targets of opportunity. Those that did fly over Bremen encountered some of the heaviest flak of the war. The 100th Bomb Group, after encountering fighter attacks before the bomb run, was hard hit by flak and lost several of their aircraft to the barrage. All total, seven of the 100th's B-17s failed to return from the mission.

All of the units participating came under very heavy attack from Luftwaffe fighters. The 381st Bomb Group was particularly hard hit, losing seven of their B-17s to Focke-Wulf 190s before they reached the target. One of the 381st's aircraft that did get home that day was *Tinker Toy*. This Fortress had come under heavy attack by enemy fighters. On the first run, the fighters put 20mm shells in the pilot's side of the

Mechanics hard at work getting the engines of Boss Lady *ready for another mission.* Ethell

cockpit and decapitated Lt. William J. Minerich. Copilot Lt. Thomas Sellers took over the controls.

At the same time, the nose had been blown off the aircraft and the bombardier and navigator fought fighter attacks in the freezing blast. A second fighter pass hit Lieutenant Sellers in the arm and left him flying with one arm. The navigator came up and assisted Sellers in bringing the aircraft home.

October 9 saw VIII Bomber Command perform one of the most successful diversionary missions in its history. All three air divisions started out across the North Sea, and the German controllers were at a loss to determine their destination. It seems they decided that all were destined for Anklam, the home of the Arado aircraft factory. This proved to be the destination of the 1st Air Division, but the majority of the 3rd Air Division went on to strike the Focke-Wulf factory at Marienburg while other 3rd Division B-17s went to Gdynia and the B-24s of the 2nd Air Division went to Danzig.

The missions were carried out at medium altitudes of 11,000 to 16,000ft, for it was known that there was no heavy flak concentration at Marienburg. The 3rd Division did an excellent job of bombing there, and damage to the Focke-Wulf plant was extensive. The Fortresses of the 1st Air Division also did a good job at Anklam, but they certainly accomplished their job of getting the fighters off the Marienburg bombers, for they ran into the fight of their lives.

A number of single-engine fighters were encountered after the B-17s crossed the Danish coast and some losses were suffered. It was after the bombs had been dropped and the formations were on their way home that the massive attacks took place. First, there were twin-engine Bf 110s, Bf 210s, Ju 88s, and even Dornier Do 217s standing off to fire their rockets in the bomber formations. The 91st and the 351st Groups took the brunt of the attacks, each losing five aircraft on the mission. Some formations were under attack for as much as three and a half hours. The crews of the 91st Bomb Group considered the attacks "their Schweinfurt."

October 10 marked the first time that the bombers of the 8th Air Force had ever been given a civilian target. The aiming point was the center of Munster,

Germany. The city was a railroad hub and it was thought that by striking at the city, many rail workers would become their targets and the rail system in the Ruhr valley would suffer accordingly.

Sixteen groups of B-17s took off en route to the target with the 13th Combat Wing of the 3rd Air Division consisting of the 95th, 100th, and 390th Bomb Groups leading. P-47s escorted the bombers up to the point that they were 9 minutes from Munster. Due to ground fog on their base, the relieving Thunderbolts were not able to make their rendezvous. This spelled disaster for the lead wing.

As the Fortresses pushed on, they faced the greatest concentration of Luftwaffe fighters they had ever encountered. On their first pass they concentrated on the 100th Group which was flying low group in the wing. On the first pass, eight to ten enemy fighters went directly through the Fortress formation from twelve o'clock level. The first attack took three B-17s out of the 100th Group formation. From then on, the enemy continued to barrel through the lead groups in waves while their twin-engine fighters stood off to the side and rear and lobbed their rockets into the bombers.

As they came off the target the 100th Group Fortress, *Sexy Suzy, Mother of Ten,* piloted by Lt. William Beddow, collided with a Bf 109. The crew members only knew that something had hit the left wing and everything was on fire. Four of the crew members managed to bail out of the inferno. Lieutenant Beddow did not survive.

This collision spiraled into a second Fortress, *Sweater Girl,* which went down as a result of the crash. Its six survivors bailed out to become prisoners of war.

Of the 100th Group's aircraft that came off the target, a few of the remaining aircraft dove for the deck in a vain attempt to escape the fighter attacks and run for home. None of them made it. The only survivor of the thirteen 100th Group B-17s was *Royal Flush* being flown by Lt. Robert "Rosie" Rosenthal. Although one engine had been knocked out, his aircraft bombed the target and then became the target of numerous fighter attacks. The number three engine was hit and had to be feathered, and the oxygen system was almost completely destroyed. Lieutenant Rosenthal

managed to bring the aircraft back home on two engines and put it down in a gathering fog.

While the 100th Group had lost twelve aircraft, the 390th had lost eight and the 95th Group of the 13th Wing lost five. The Luftwaffe decided to knock out the lead wing and they just about did it. The bombing destroyed large sections of the city and knocked out its electrical system completely. The intensity of the air battle is indicated by the high claims made by the crew members of the Fortresses. The B-17 crews claimed 183 enemy aircraft destroyed on the mission. German records show that only twenty-four of their fighters went down that day.

October 14 would become another fateful day in "Black Week" for the Eighth Air Force. The mission was the second attempt to knock out the ball-bearing factories at Schweinfurt. The official publication *The Combined Bomber Offensive* stated: "All told more than 300 enemy aircraft participated in the battle and these made 700 separate attacks on the bombers during the principal fight.

"The first enemy maneuver was to attack from the front at very close range with a screen of single-engine fighters firing 20mm cannon, and machine guns. Following this screen were a number of twin-engine fighters in formation, firing rockets from projectors suspended under the wings. The rocket-firing craft began their attacks at a distance and did not come in nearly so close as the single-engine fighters. The Fortress formations were subjected to great numbers of rocket projectiles.

"After the single-engine fighters had made their initial assault, they refueled and returned to the battle, this time attacking from all directions in an attempt to confuse the gunners in the heavy bombers. Then followed the second effort of the enemy twin-engine fighters, which attacked principally from the front and rear.

"The rocket-firing craft seemed to concentrate upon a single combat wing until their ammunition was exhausted. After these maneuvers, all enemy fighters centered their attention on the bombers that had been crippled by the organized attacks . . . "

The 305th Bomb Group was the hardest hit that day en route to Schweinfurt, losing a quarter of the total lost

by the Eighth Air Force, fifteen out of eighteen planes. "I watched from my left window as the 305th, flying low and to our left, away from the other groups, lost one plane after another," related Capt. Charles Schoolfield, leader of the 306th Bomb Group formation. "First they got the last plane and then chewed up through the formation until they almost completely destroyed it."

In the fury of the assault it was difficult for Schoolfield, as the group leader, or Lt. Curtis L. Dunlap, flying as tail gunner and formation observer, to keep track of what was happening. When the shooting slackened, Schoolfield was shocked to learn that he had only five planes left. The 306th birds huddled together for mutual protection as they came down the forty-second bomb run, tailed only by the 92nd Bomb Group. The 306th dropped its 1,000lb

bombs, and sixteen of them landed within in a 1,920ft circle.

Having bombed on a heading of forty-five degrees, the planes came around to the left and headed west on a withdrawal route that took them south of Paris and then north toward England. Schoolfield's badly damaged plane staggered along as the leader. At one point, with a fire in the number three engine, Schoolfield had actually pushed the alarm bell switch, but nothing happened, so he gave up thoughts of bailing out and tried to keep the plane flying.

Later, Maj. Gen. Orval Anderson, in conversation with Schoolfield, said that the withdrawal route had been his idea; both agreed that had the withdrawal been along the line of penetration, the casualties would have been much more than the sixty lost by the Eighth Air Force. This represented 20 percent of

Knockout Dropper *is another illustration of the varied art on Eighth Air Force noses.* Ethell

the planes taking off in the raid. In the annals of warfare, and particularly to those who met an unwanted fate on October 14, the day will be known forever as "Black Thursday." Indeed, it was for the ten 306th crews who gave their all on the mission.

Of the one hundred men who did not return to Thurleigh that afternoon, thirty-five died on the mission or later of wounds. Sixty-five went to prison camp.

The 305th Bomb Group led by Maj. Charles G. Y. Normand had its troubles as was observed by Captain Schoolfield. Over Frankfurt, twin-engine Bf 210 fighters appeared astern and again lobbed rockets. By now, the 364th Bomb

Squadron had lost all seven of its airplanes. Still, the enemy attack picked up in intensity. Soon all four 366th Bomb Squadron planes, flying the high squadron, fell to the flak and the fighters.

Major Normand watched in horror as plane after plane was shot down. The sky was filled with burning aircraft and the parachutes of the men that had escaped from them. As the remnants of the group turned on the initial point for the bombing, Normand's bombardier called for a separate bomb run. He didn't know that only three planes were left in the formation and one of them was on fire.

Lt. Raymond Bullock flew the aircraft that was on fire, a Fortress named *Sundown Sal*. The B-17 had been hit in the left wing by a 20mm shell, which started the blaze. Bullock held the B-17 in formation until the bombs were dropped. Immediately after the bomb run, he left the formation and told his crew to bail out. All became prisoners.

In the final tally for the 305th Bomb Group, the 364th Squadron lost all seven of its aircraft; the 365th Squadron lost two; and the 366th Squadron lost four. Two 365th planes returned. Of the 130 crew members lost, thirty-six had been killed. The 87 percent loss for the day left the group devastated.

The assessment of damage at the target was originally stated to be total destruction. Unfortunately, this was not true. While considerable damage had been done, in no way did it put the Germans out of the ball-bearing business. However, the damage forced the Germans to speed up the dispersion of the industry to the countryside.

The loss of sixty bombers on the mission further swelled the loss figure for October. In all, the Eighth Air Force lost 176 B-17s during this month. Bomber crew morale hit a new low. Never did they think that they would be asked to fight their way to the target and back under such overwhelming opposition. Of course, it was hurting the Luftwaffe as well, but many of their pilots were recovered and back in the air the following day. The one thing that the American Fortress crews had proven beyond a doubt was that they had the guts to

A colorful formation of B-17s over England. Defensive positions can be clearly seen. Ethell

press on to their targets regardless of the odds. They were never turned back by the enemy!

There was little comfort for the bomber crews in the message that Chief of Staff Gen. H. H. Arnold released to the press following the Schweinfurt mission. The message read: "Regardless of our losses, I'm ready to send replacements of planes and crews and continue building up our strength. The opposition isn't nearly what it was, and we are wearing them down. The loss of 60 American bombers in the Schweinfurt raid was incidental."

If the opposition wasn't nearly what it was, the crews of the Fortresses felt they must have been hallucinating!

To further compound the odds that the bomber crews had to face, by November 1943 the Luftwaffe had reinforced its fighter aircraft strength in the west to 800. The good news was that drop tanks for the Thunderbolts were finally beginning to become more available, and two groups of P-38 Lightnings arrived. The P-38 would never become the victor that it was in other theaters because its performance suffered in the extreme cold of northwestern Europe, but it could provide deep escort. The best news was that the P-51 Mustang would arrive in England in December. This aircraft, with its superb performance, could also go all the way with the bombers regardless of the target. The days of Luftwaffe superiority were definitely numbered.

The Eighth Air Force made some forays into Germany in November and completed a long mission to Norway during the month, but enemy opposition was negligible. Most of the missions over Germany encountered bad weather and used PFF bombing if the bombs were dropped.

December also got off to a slow start, but it did find the P-38s aloft. On December 5, the P-51s got in the picture when the 354th Fighter Group escorted the bombers to targets in France. The next sharp action with the Luftwaffe came on December 16 when the bombers went to Bremen. The 96th Bomb Group put up thirty-six B-17s in an A Group and a B Group, but all was not fated to go well for the men from Snetterton that day.

The A Group fared the better of the two groups, but lost two B-17s to a mid-air collision. It happened over the North Sea, and there were only two survivors.

The B Group was hit by fifteen Focke-Wulf 190s that came roaring out of the sun. The first two B-17s went down following an attack on an aircraft that had an engine shot completely loose from its wing. The engine fell down on the aircraft below, and before it was all over the two Fortresses became tangled and fell together.

As the bombers became scattered the fighters jumped on them individually, and three more were downed, making a total of five B-17s downed by the Luftwaffe. As the bombers came home they lost another Fortress, one of the most historic aircraft in the group.

Fertile Myrtle III had led the Regensburg mission with Colonel LeMay at the controls, and had led the 3rd Air Division to Schweinfurt on October 14. It came back over England from the Bremen mission badly shot up, with all control surfaces damaged and a number of control cables severed. The fin was slashed and there were a number of large holes in the fuselage and wings. The pilot, Capt. Tom Kenny, gave the order and the crew bailed out. *Myrtle* crashed near Norwick.

The bombers went back to Bremen on December 20, and it was on this mission that a second enlisted crew member on a B-17 won the Medal of Honor. The 303rd Bomb Group entered heavy flak over the target, and *Jersey Bounce Jr.* was hit and left the formation. Number one engine was on fire, but the pilot, Lt. John Henderson, and instructor pilot Capt. Merle Hunderford, who was flying copilot, managed to roll the aircraft into the wing and blow out the fire.

Then the fighters began to attack. One came in from six o'clock and got in a telling burst that seriously wounded the tail gunner, Sgt. George Buske, and also put shrapnel in the legs of Sgt. Forrest Vosler, the radio operator. Vosler says that he went over to his chair and sat down, but decided that was not the thing to do and got back up and manned his machine gun.

Fighters continued to fly their attacks with the gunners fighting them off and apparently scoring good hits and perhaps downing some of them. Vosler had a twin-engine fighter come in from the rear so close he could see the pilot's face. A good burst from his guns and the German pilot dove down and went beneath the Fortress.

Then a 20mm shell went into the radio room, followed down the side of Vosler's gun, and exploded, showering Vosler with shrapnel. He was particularly hard hit in the eyes and face. Blinded in one eye and bloody all over, he felt that his time had come but Vosler went over to his radio table and apparently went into a state of shock for a time.

By this time, the pilots had the B-17 down on the deck, and the able crew members were throwing out everything they could to lighten the load. The wounded tail gunner had been brought forward to the radio room and Vosler sat at his radio, blinded, but able to carry out emergency procedures on his set. As soon as the Fortress was over water, Vosler began sending out SOS signals. They were acknowledged, and air-sea rescue services were put in motion.

The aircraft was ditched not far off the coast of England and all the men except the pilots went out the radio hatch. The tail gunner, still unconscious, was put out on the wing. While boarding the dinghies the tail gunner almost slipped into the sea, but the nearly blind Vosler grabbed the unconscious gunner and held on until he could be placed in the raft. Only then did Vosler get in the dinghy.

The entire crew was picked up by a ship shortly thereafter and taken back to England. Vosler and the tail gunner were sent to the hospital. Vosler was later returned to the United States for treatment. He remained blind for a time, but once the damaged right eye was removed, he began to regain sight in his other eye. For his fortitude and devotion to his job and assistance to his crew, though critically wounded, Vosler was awarded the Medal of Honor.

As 1943 came to a close, the Eighth Air Force could look back on its accomplishments with great pride. It had proved that daylight bombing could be successful. Although the Luftwaffe had taken its toll and October 1943 had proven to be such a bad month, the crews on the bombers continued to fight their way through. If their claims for enemy fighters destroyed had been true, there would have been no Luftwaffe left to oppose them. Yet, they had cost the enemy hundreds of their best trained pilots and aircraft. They had forced the Luftwaffe to move a number of its fighter units from the Eastern Front where they were desperately needed, and from the Mediterranean where Germany had lost North Africa and Sicily, and had seen Italy invaded. At the beginning of 1943, only four B-17 units were in operation. By the end of 1943 there were eighteen Fortress units operating, plus the B-24s of the 2nd Air Division. Instead of 100 heavy bombers ready to launch an offensive in January 1943, the Eighth Air Force could put over 600 aircraft aloft in January 1944.

The Eighth Air Force would soon grow to the extent that it could send more than 1,000 bombers and another 1,000 fighters to escort them to any target in Germany. The daylight bombing offensive was ready to dominate the skies over northwestern Europe.

Chapter 6

Big Week, Big B, and Beyond

January 6, 1944, brought a momentous announcement to VIII Bomber Command. Lt. Gen. Ira Eaker, who had commanded the Eighth Air Force since its inception, was to be relieved of his command and would be replaced by Lt. Gen. James H. Doolittle, who had been air commander in the Mediterranean. Gen. Carl "Tooey" Spaatz was named commander of strategic bombing in Europe and would command not only Doolittle, but also General Eaker who would take over as commander of the air forces in the Mediterranean. VIII Bomber Command would cease to exist, and bombing activities would be commanded directly by General Doolittle.

For some time, the bombers of the Eighth Air Force had been trying to launch a deep penetration into Germany and it was deemed that January 11 would be a good day. The 1st Air Division was slated to strike the Focke-Wulf plant at Oschersleben and aircraft facilities at Halberstadt. The 3rd Air Division was to strike at Brunswick and Osnabruck.

Leading the 1st Division was the 303rd Bomb Group, and division commander Brig. Gen. Robert Travis was in the lead aircraft. The formations were assembled and were out over the Channel and over the enemy coast on schedule. General Travis reported: "The fighters started their attacks at the Zuider Zee despite our fighter escort and came

at us in bunches. Our first attacks were four Fw 190s, the next was thirty Fw 190s, the next was twelve, and they just kept coming. They attacked straight through the formation from all angles without even rolling over. They came in from all sides and it was quite apparent that they were out to stop the formation from ever reaching the target."

As usual, the single-engine fighters came in from head-on and came to within seventy-five yards of the Fortresses before they broke away. As the fight became more heated, collisions also occurred that resulted from the Luftwaffe pilot pressing his attack too close, or perhaps he had been killed or wounded in his attack and his aircraft just kept coming until it smashed into one of the B-17s.

Somewhere in the vicinity of Dummer Lake, General Travis reported that the weather was deteriorating rapidly over England, so the mission was being recalled. The 2nd and 3rd Divisions turned back, but the 1st Division was so close to the target that Travis ordered them to continue the mission. Unfortunately, the escorting fighters received the recall and many of them turned and headed for home while the 1st Division Fortresses continued eastward.

The enemy fighters continued to come at the lead formation. Amazingly, General Travis' aircraft *The Eight Ball* did not go down, although the aircraft

surrounding it did. The Focke-Wulfs got the Mickey radar aircraft on the first pass and then took out the leader of the second element and his wingman from the lead squadron. Leading the 1st Division, the 303rd Bomb Group's bombs struck the target well and apparently did extensive damage, but the intense air battle cost them eleven aircraft lost and most of those that did return suffered damage.

The rest of the Fortresses of the 1st Combat Wing also took heavy losses, with the 381st Bomb Group losing eight aircraft and the 91st Bomb Group losing five. One of the 381st B-17s was lost in a collision with an enemy fighter.

Although many of the escorting fighters turned back when the recall was sounded, others remained in the combat area. The outstanding event of the day was the performance of Maj. James H. Howard flying one of the new P-51 Mustangs of the 354th Fighter Group. He found the 401st Bomb Group under heavy attack and entered the fight alone. For over half an hour he battled all types of enemy aircraft and no doubt saved the Fortresses from a number of losses. The crew in the B-17s would confirm six enemy aircraft destroyed for him, but Howard would only accept credit for three. For his feat he was awarded the Medal of Honor.

The 3rd Division, which was headed for Brunswick, received its recall but in

Previous Page
This aircraft from the "Bloody Hundredth" Group came home with its tail almost completely shot off. USAAF

view of the fact that the lead groups were only twenty-five miles from the target when it was received, flight leader Maj. Louis G. Thorup of the 94th Bomb Group decided to proceed. The 94th was initially unable to identify their target so they did a 360 degree circle and then went in and bombed. As they came off the target, eighteen Messerschmitt Bf 110s set up out of range and began firing rockets into the formation. Hits were scored on several Fortresses, and these damaged bombers

were forced to leave the formation; then they were attacked by Focke-Wulf 190s.

Both the 94th Bomb Group and the 447th Bomb Group that accompanied them were under heavy attack for over an hour. The 94th lost eight of its B-17s while the 447th lost three.

The Eighth Air Force lost sixty B-17s for the day, and many of those returning would never fly again. The intensity of the air battle that day is indicated by the fact that the bomber crew members claimed 210 enemy aircraft destroyed. Actual Luftwaffe losses for the day were only thirty-nine, with thirty-one claims being made by the fighter escort.

The 94th Bomb Group took off on February 10, 1944, en route to Brunswick, and once more the Luftwaffe was

waiting. The B-17s were attacked an hour from the target by a force of at least 150 Luftwaffe fighters, and as usual the attackers performed effectively with their head-on passes by single-engine fighters and rockets from the twin-engines. The B-17s were under attack for about two hours—from the Zuider Zee on the way in, to the Zuider Zee on the way out.

One veteran crew that didn't make it home that day was that of Lt. Don Anderson in *Good Time Cholley III.* Just before the initial point they were hit by 20mm shells between number three and

71

A beautiful profile photo of a B-17G at sunset over England. 306th BG Assn.

four engines. Fire broke out and the Fortress was forced to leave formation. Both waist gunners and the ball turret gunner were wounded. Anderson hit the bail-out bell and the navigator, bombardier, and top turret gunner bailed out. Meanwhile, two of the gunners were

looking after Sgt. Rex Smith who had been badly wounded. Anderson dropped down to 500ft and got the fire to die down, and decided to make a run for home.

However, Lady Luck was not with them. A stray Bf 109 appeared on the scene and although the wounded gunners did their utmost, the Fort was sprayed with fire from one end to the other. Anderson immediately told the crew they would have to bail out, but

then discovered that Smith was not able to do so.

Anderson and his copilot, Lt. Al Capie, began looking for a landing site. Just as they lined up on a field, another stray fighter came along looking for the cripple and once more the wounded gunners were engaged. This time, Sgt. Carl Evans was wounded and Sergeant Kremper was hit for the second time. The enemy fighter left the scene smoking, just before Anderson set down the

Fortress. All aboard were taken prisoner shortly after landing.

Once more, the Luftwaffe had taken a heavy toll of the B-17s of the 3rd Division. Twenty-nine out of 169 bombers dispatched had been lost for a 17 percent loss. Although 466 fighters had been launched, most of them missed their rendezvous which contributed heavily to the loss of the bombers.

For some weeks Gen. Carl Spaatz, commander of US Strategic Air Forces in Europe, had been planning a joint offensive in conjunction with the RAF against the German aircraft industry. The Eighth Air Force from England and the Fifteenth Air Force from Italy would strike the enemy installations during the day while the RAF would bomb them at night.

After weeks of waiting, the weather finally cleared sufficiently for what was to become known as "Big Week" to begin on February 20. The Eighth Air Force sent out over 400 B-17s from the 1st Bomb Division and 300 from the 3rd Bomb Division against aircraft factories and component plants in Germany. The 2nd Bomb Division of B-24s was also dispatched against similar targets. The Fifteenth Air Force was to have bombed

Regensburg at the same time, but icing conditions over the Alps prevented their mission.

Although cloud conditions prevented some targets from being bombed, the Fortresses did strike at Tutlow and Rostock in northeastern Germany and also at Leipzig, Oschlersleben, and Bernburg. More than 800 escorting fighters were in the air, and bomber losses fell accordingly. Most memorable about these missions was the fact that three Medals of Honor were awarded for deeds performed that day by Fortress crew members.

One of the B-17s that bombed Leipzig was flown by Lt. William R. Lawley of the 305th Bomb Group. His troubles began over the target when bombardier Lt. Harry G. Mason was unable to get the bombs to release. Then, just as they came off the bomb run, they were hit by fighters in a head-on attack. A 20mm shell exploded on the flight deck, killing the copilot instantly and wounding Lawley in the face. While fighting to pull the aircraft out of a dive after the copilot fell forward on the controls, Lawley saw that he had an engine on fire. With a full bomb load and a fire

Chow-Hound was one of the better known Fortresses from the 322nd Bomb Squadron, 91st Bomb Group. It failed to return from a mission over France on August 8, 1944. US-AAF

on board an explosion was imminent, so Lawler rang the bail-out bell.

It was then that Lawler learned that he had eight wounded men aboard, including himself. He managed to get the aircraft on an even keel and sent Mason back in the bomb bay to see what could be done about getting the bombs to drop. As both men worked desperately to remedy the situation they were again attacked by enemy fighters. Lawley managed to get the fire out in one engine and then the other while Mason managed to salvo the bombs. Although wounded, the gunners fought off the attack.

When Mason came out of the bomb bay he went back to his guns in the nose. After the fighters had been driven off, he went back to the flight deck where he found Lawley all but unconscious from the loss of blood. He immediately took over the controls and set the aircraft on course for England. It proved to be a long, slow flight on two engines, but Ma-

Previous page
Princess Elizabeth poses with the crew chief of Elizabeth's Own, *a B-17 named in her honor. The Fortress was assigned to the 423rd Bomb Squadron, 306th Bomb Group.* 306th BG Assn.

son made it. He spotted the small fighter field at Redhill and knew he would have to put down the Fortress there. He shook Lawley back to consciousness and Lawley took over. Through a supreme effort, Lawley managed to keep the aircraft under control, even though a third engine sputtered and died.

Ground crewmen service the oxygen system on one of the Fortresses of the 306th Bomb Group. 306th BG Assn.

Lawley told Mason to feather the propeller on the engine, and then on the final approach the last engine caught

96th Bomb Group B-17s leave England to head into heavy cloud cover. USAAF

fire. Miraculously, Lawley set down the aircraft as fire trucks and ambulances sped to the scene. Lawley was awarded the Medal of Honor and Mason the Silver Star.

Also in a 351st Bomb Group Fortress over Leipzig were navigator Lt. Walter E. Truemper and engineer-gunner Sgt. Archibald Mathies. A vicious fighter attack killed their copilot and gravely wounded their pilot. The bombardier hit the bail-out bell and went out the nose hatch, but most of the crew stayed aboard to see what had happened.

Truemper and Mathies managed to get the copilot's body out of his seat and the two of them took turns flying the aircraft. Although neither had any pilot training, they managed to bring the B-17 back to their home base where all of the crew bailed out except Truemper, Mathies, and their wounded pilot. The group commander told Truemper and Mathies to bail out but they refused to leave their skipper, who was still alive. Colonel Romig and Major Ledoux, tower officer of the day, took off in another B-17 and contacted Truemper on the radio. Twice they tried to talk the men through to a field landing, but failed. They then took them to Molesworth, but failed again. Finally, Colonel Romig decided to take them to a large field in the countryside. This time the approach was better but as they fought the controls, they came in nose-down and crashed. The aircraft burned, and all three men died in the crash. Truemper and Mathies were both awarded the Medal of Honor posthumously.

Overall, the losses for the Eighth Air Force were light for the number of aircraft that had been dispatched. Only thirteen B-17s were lost and the escorting fighters had done their job well, claiming sixty-one German fighters destroyed.

The following day, Eighth Air Force took advantage of the good weather and bombed Diepholz, Brunswick, and other targets of opportunity. The bombing at

Nine O Nine was one of the most famous B-17s with the 91st Bomb Group. It flew well over a hundred combat missions. Havelaar

Diepholz was successful, and Brunswick was bombed using PFF techniques. There was little Luftwaffe resistance and the Fortresses lost only twelve for the day.

Bombers were in the air for the third straight day by February 22, but the weather was so poor that the 3rd Division was prevented from forming up properly so they were recalled. The 1st Division formed up and went to Bernburg, where they bombed the Junkers factory.

The mission was costly to some groups, particularly the 306th Bomb Group which lost seven aircraft. The Luftwaffe took advantage of the bombers whenever the escort was not present. Although Mustangs saved them several times, the German fighters stayed away and as soon as they saw P-51s departing, they appeared. Twice, Lt. Col. Robert Riordan turned the formation into the attacking fighters, causing them to break off their attacks.

The 381st Bomb Group lost six aircraft on its mission to Bunde. Although there was now a fighter escort they, too, found that once there was any sort of a time gap when the fighters were not there, the Luftwaffe came in. They were greatly moved by the determination of the German fighters. When they got after one individual Fortress, the Germans would not let up until the B-17 went down. One of their B-17s had its tail section shot completely off.

The 1st Division lost thirty-eight B-17s, primarily to fighter attacks.

Weather caused the cancellation of missions on February 23, but the Fortresses were out in force again on February 24. This time, the primary targets were Schweinfurt and Rostock. The 1st Division put 238 B-17s over Schweinfurt, with good results. Only eleven B-17s were lost. On the 3rd Division's strikes at Rostock the bombing was largely effective and only five Fortresses were lost. It is possible that the primary reason the B-17s fared so well was that the 2nd Division B-24s took heavy losses from the Luftwaffe at Gotha, and the Fifteenth Air Force encountered heavy fighter opposition at Steyr, Austria, that same day.

The final day of Big Week, February 25, was not without its problems and losses. The 3rd Division struck Regensburg, and the 1st Division went to Augs-

The crew chief gives his aircraft, Miss Patricia, *of the 306th Bomb Group, a final onceover at the end of the day.* 306th BG Assn.

A nice formation of Fortresses from the 401st Bomb Squadron, 91st Bomb Group. Havelaar

Beautiful formation shot of 306th Bomb Group B-17s over England in 1945. 306th BG Assn.

burg. The 96th Bomb Group picked up high tail winds aloft and found itself over the target 40 minutes early. This caused them to miss the rendezvous with the escort, and the enemy fighters took advantage of the situation. The group lost four aircraft on the mission.

One of their B-17s that did come home made it the hard way. In a sudden blazing attack *The Saint* was hit by an Fw 190 that shot up the flight deck. The copilot was killed instantly, and the oxygen system was shot out. Lt. Stan Peterson, navigator, spent the next few hours going back and forth over the aircraft collecting walk-around bottles to keep the pilot going.

The 306th Bomb Group went to Augsburg to bomb the Messerschmitt Bf 410 plant on February 25. They encountered intense and accurate flak over Saarbrucken, which caused the formation to break while taking evasive action. This was the break the German fighters wanted. They dove to the attack and downed two Fortresses before they could close up the formation. A third B-17 was lost over the target to flak.

During Big Week, the Eighth Air Force lost ninety-seven B-17s. Coupled with the B-24 losses, the figure totaled 137. The Fifteenth Air Force, with B-17 and B-24 losses combined, lost eighty-nine aircraft. These American losses were quite high, but the Luftwaffe losses were also high. Their twin-engine units were all but wiped out by the escorting American fighters. Over 33 percent of the single-engine fighter force

was lost, taking with them 17.9 percent of the single-engine fighter pilots.

The damage to German aircraft plants was considerable as well. However, the Allies never seemed to realize how swift the recovery rate was in Germany. Through the use of slave labor, most damaged plants were back in production in a few weeks. Second, the enemy continued to scatter its production facilities over the countryside. Many small towns had factories turning out aircraft components. In truth, the manufacture of German single-engine fighters increased monthly almost up to the end of the war in Europe.

Ever since the US Army Air Forces began striking deep into Germany, all of the crews were on edge, wondering when they would be given the opportunity to strike at the heart of the Third Reich—Berlin. The order came down on

March 3, but once the bombers formed up and headed out, they encountered weather that was so bad they had to turn back. A few struck targets of opportunity on their return.

Crews were briefed for Berlin again on the morning of March 4. More than 500 B-17s were dispatched. As they neared the enemy coast, most formations began to make 180 degree turns, heeding a recall to base. One formation continued to fly on toward Germany. The 95th Bomb Group, led by Lt. Col. Harry G. "Grif" Mumford, ignored the radio calls and continued to climb to get over the weather. Colonel Mumford and copilot Lt. Al Brown figured that if they aborted and returned on the same inbound route, they would probably be

mauled by enemy fighters, so they might as well take a chance on getting to the target.

The formation included 95th Group B-17s and a few from the 100th Group. The Fortresses climbed to 29,600ft to get above the clouds. They had not seen the ground since leaving England, but on reaching Magdeburg they began to get a few breaks in the clouds and were able to continue their run to the target through dead reckoning. Enemy flak was encountered and then a formation of Bf 109s was sighted. To the delight of the B-17s' crews, a formation of P-51 Mustangs came in to drive them off.

As the Fortresses approached Berlin, they began to encounter heavy flak. One shell came up through the B-17 being

A 306th Bomb Group Fortress at rest on its hardstand. The 306th was one of the old-timers of the Eighth Air Force. 306th BG Assn.

flown by Lt. William Reis; it bored a 6in hole in the floor and then blew a 3ft hole in the top as it burst. It knocked one waist gunner back against the ball turret without hurting him, but it blew the other waist gunner completely out of the aircraft.

As the B-17s came down to the bomb run it was found that the bomb bay doors on the lead aircraft were frozen shut. In order for the formation to bomb, it was necessary to use the radar navigator on the Pathfinder aircraft to work

Note the short Cheyenne tail on this 306th Bomb Group B-17G. It gave the gunner more room and a new sight. 306th BG Assn.

in conjunction with Lt. Forrest Flagler, the bombardier in the lead ship. When the navigator on the Pathfinder aircraft told his bombardier, Lt. Marshall Thixton, to drop, Lieutenant Flagler fired a flare to tell the formation to let their bombs go. The bombs dropped on Berlin!

During their run, the bombers were attacked by enemy fighters and a few B-17s were damaged. As they turned westward and began their letdown, the B-17s took stock of events. Four 95th Group aircraft had fallen to the enemy, and the 100th Group had lost one. In all, twenty-one 95th Group and eight 100th Group B-17s made it through to Berlin.

On his return to base, Colonel Mumford did not know whether he would be court-martialed or rewarded for hitting the capital of Germany. When the Fortresses landed, a number of "big brass" and press awaited them. To Mumford's amazement he was decorated with the Silver Star, and Lt. Al Brown received the Distinguished Flying Cross from General LeMay in the briefing room.

The B-17s did not fly the following day, but on March 6, every bomber that could get in the air was sent to Berlin. This mission would prove to be the biggest air battle over Germany during World War II.

On the morning of March 6, 504 B-17s plus 226 B-24s escorted by 800 fighters set out to bomb Berlin. The 1st Air Division led the sixty-mile procession, followed by the 3rd Division with the

2nd Division bring up the rear. As the bombers thundered toward the target, the Luftwaffe Bf 109s and Fw 190s were assembling over Lake Steinhuder. The vanguard of the leading bombers had passed when Hauptman Rolf Hermichen led his Messerschmitt fighters to intercept. As he maneuvered his force into position, he noted that there were only eight escorting Thunderbolts to the front of the Fortress wing that he was closing on; the balance of the escorts in the area were to the south with the main bomber stream, which had flown off course.

The unfortunate wing that met the onslaught was the 13th Combat Wing composed of the 95th, 100th, and 390th Bomb Groups. The Fortresses of the 100th Group were led by Maj. Bucky Elton, who reported that they were vi-

A mixed formation of painted and unpainted B-17s from the 91st Bomb Group forms up over cloud cover. USAAF

B-17Gs from the 323rd Bomb Squadron, 91st Bomb Group. The aircraft in the foreground

failed to return from a mission to Nuremberg on November 2, 1944. USAAF

ciously attacked at 1159 hours by an overwhelming number of enemy fighters. They came in head-on through the 13th Wing.

After the first attack, Elton looked up and was stunned to see six of the high squadron's planes on fire in formation, long trails of fire streaming from their engines. When the fighters came back, all six of these aircraft fell out of formation. This attack took place over Haseluenne, a small German town northeast of Lingen.

In the first plane hit, both the pilot, Capt. David Miner, and copilot were killed in the initial pass and the nose was shot away. The balance of the crew bailed out as quickly as possible.

Lt. Zeb Kendall's aircraft exploded with all the crew lost, and Lt. Sherwin Barton and his crew bailed out of their flaming B-17. Lt. Dean Radtke's Fortress had two engines out and a fire in the bomb bay when his crew bailed out.

The fifth aircraft to fall from the high squadron was piloted by Lt. William Terry, and nicknamed *Terry and the Pirates*. Most of the controls were shot out and the aircraft went into a spin.

A 367th Bomb Squadron Fortress over England. The triangle denoted the 1st Bomb Division. 306th BG Assn.

This 398th Bomb Group Fortress apparently had a landing gear collapse when it came in.
USAAF

Only three men were able to get out because of the centrifugal force of the spin.

Lt. Samuel Barrick in *Barricks Bag* had two engines out. Barrick salvoed his bomb load and managed to drop down out of formation and fly to Sweden, where the crew was interned.

In the low squadron, Lt. George Brannan had his right wing and two engines on fire when he ordered the crew to bail out.

Six men from Lt. Merril Rish's *Spirit of '44* bailed out when the entire aircraft became enveloped in flames. The fuselage broke in two at the radio room and threw two men out. The navigator was also blown out of a gaping hole.

Lt. Coy Montgomery was killed, but not before he managed to get his crew out. Also on fire was Lt. Robert Kopel's *Going Jessie*. Only three crew members survived.

The box of twenty B-17s was led by Capt. Jack Swartout, whose B-17 had collided with a Focke-Wulf 190 in the initial attack. Only a spar held on what was left of the rudder, but Swartout managed to get the aircraft down low and fly it back to England.

The lead was taken over by Lt. Edward Handorf, who managed to get the remnants of the formation over Berlin.

Unfortunately, Handorf's bomber was hit by fighters on the way home. A Bf 109 came in low from one o'clock and ripped the B-17 with 20mm fire. The wing tanks caught on fire, and only two men got out of the aircraft before it exploded.

Following the initial attack by fighters, Lt. John Lautenschlager's *Half and Half* developed a fire in the bomb bay. The bombs were salvoed and Lautenschlager proceeded to get his crew out of the aircraft before he trimmed it to fly without a pilot at the controls so he could bail out. He got out just before the Fortress exploded. All survived except the radio operator whose parachute failed to open.

Lt. Albert Ameiro's aircraft blew up shortly after the initial attack. One of the waist gunners was blown clear to become the only survivor.

Bigass Bird II fell with its tail on fire after the pilot, Lt. William Murray, was killed by 20mm from the fighter attack. Seven of his crew survived.

Lt. Celesta Harper had his oxygen system shot out and put his aircraft in a steep dive. He overstressed the aircraft, but managed to pull out and go home on the deck.

Lt. Mark Cope's aircraft was shot up badly but he, too, got down on the deck and scooted for home.

Lt. Frank Granack's aircraft was hit by flak over the target. This forced him out of formation and then the fighters came in. When they were through, he had only one good engine. With numbers three and four smoking, Granack trimmed up the aircraft and had his crew abandon the aircraft.

Thirty B-17s from the 100th Bomb Group had gone out from Thorpe Abbots that morning. Only half of them would return home, and of those aircraft that did survive, many were badly damaged.

A few minutes following the massive attack by single-engine fighters over Haseleunne, a second massive attack force was assembled. III/ZG 26 leader, Maj. Hans Kogler, assembled up a formation of so called "destroyer" aircraft composed of Messerschmitt Bf 110s and Bf 410s, all of which were carrying rockets. In the sky above them were seventy-two single-engine fighters which provided escort for the striking force.

At 1230 hours, Kogler got word from the group controllers to take his force from Magdeburg, where they had assembled, to intercept the lead groups of bombers, which was made up of the 1st and 94th Combat Wings. Just as the destroyer aircraft were positioned to attack they, in turn, were attacked by the escorting P-51 Mustangs. These fighters from the 4th and 357th Fighter Groups struck just as the Bf 110s began to fire their rockets from 1,000 yards behind the bomber stream.

At that moment the Bf 109s and Fw 190s of the destroyer escort force readied themselves to dive down to the rescue. However, the 354th Fighter Group, also in P-51s, arrived on the scene and climbed up into them. The destroyer formations were broken up by the Mustangs and many of the Bf 110s were shot down. Soon after, a massive dogfight began between the P-51s and the Bf 109s and Fw 190s of the destroyer escort force. The battle raged all over the sky while the B-17s plodded on to the target.

Eight Fortresses fell to the destroyer aircraft, and another three were destroyed in collisions caused by evasive-maneuver attempts to get out of the rockets' line of fire. Sixteen Bf 110s and Bf 410s were shot down, along with four P-51 Mustangs.

The 388th Bomb Group of the 45th Combat Wing was the last Fortress unit in the procession. The 388th had put up thirty-three aircraft for the mission to comprise an A Group, and the lead and low squadrons of a B Group, which was filled in by the 452nd Bomb Group.

As the 388th Group historian recorded: "Approximately 15 to 20 Fw 190s were first met on the route in to the target in the vicinity of Dummer Lake. The attacks, which started at 1200 hours, lasted until 1220 hours, were mainly directed at the groups ahead. No serious enemy attacks were again encountered until the formation was again in the same area on the return route. Here the same numbers of Fw 190s plus several Bf 109s pressed home vicious, daring attacks for 30 minutes. It was from these encounters that six of our aircraft were lost. The seventh was lost when one of our crippled ships collided with it. Attacks were from all clock positions but mainly from 10 to 2 o'clock high, with the enemy aircraft coming in line abreast and diving through the formation. Two to six enemy aircraft in line astern would also attack from the nose high. Crew members report that the 20mm cannon which were used exclusively fired both incendiary and time-delay shells. Many bombers shot down were observed to burst into flames immediately after the attacks by the enemy fighters.

"Inaccurate scattered flak was encountered from Amsterdam, Quakenbruck and Vechta. In the Berlin area an intense barrage was seen over the center of the city. Over the outskirts of the capital flak was continuous following, accurate and intense.

"Lt. B. K. Land's crew had several instances of conduct beyond the call of duty . . . Aircraft 9076 was flying number three position, lead element, low squadron, was violently attacked by enemy fighters at 1200 hours on the route to the target.

"In one attack by an Fw 190 the ship was racked by 20mm shells which knocked out an engine, damaged rudder and controls, hit oxygen lines, thereby forcing the plane to return alone. In this attack Sgt. Sartin was fatally wounded. The left waist gunner, Sgt. H. E. Kellner, was wounded but continued on his guns and is credited with destroying the attacker. The tail gunner, Sgt. C. S. Momeyer, was badly wounded in legs and face but continued at his guns while the attacks persisted and is credited with damaging an enemy aircraft in a later attack. He later crawled back to the

A Fortress from the 452nd Bomb Group begins its long earthward fall. USAAF

Two crewmen from a stricken B-17 free-fall before pulling their ripcords. USAAF

83

Rare view from the ball turret gunner's position. He saw everything looking up from his cramped, suspended quarters. USAAF

waist to assist the wounded waist gunner. Lt. Land brought the plane back safely, receiving excellent fighter escort until near the coast."

None of the three primary targets for the mission was hit effectively. Only the Genshagen aero engine plant was hit at all. The Erkner and Klein Machnow plants escaped completely. Very little damage was done to any military plants, and the most damaging effect was the fact that all industrial plants had to be shut down for several hours.

In the violent air battles, sixty-nine American bombers were felled along with eleven escorting fighters. This was far less than the 108 bombers and twenty fighters claimed by the Germans. By the same token, the bomber crews claimed ninety-seven enemy fighters while the escort claimed eighty-two. The total German loss was actually sixty-six aircraft.

As for the bomber crews, it had been a long mission, and the hell that many of them lived through that day would never be forgotten. For those most drastically affected, a post-mission event at Thorpe Abbots, home of the 100th Bomb Group, tells it best. Lt. Bob Shoens land-

ed his *Our Gal Sal,* which was one of the survivors of the 13th Wing's B Group that had lost ten of its fifteen B-17s. As he taxied to his hardstand, Shoens saw the squadron commander standing there waiting for them. "He was crying," Shoens said. "We were stunned to learn that we were the only aircraft of the squadron to return to the field and only one of four to make it back to England. What do you say, what do you do when your squadron commander is crying and wants to know what has happened? You do the same."

The bombers returned to Berlin on March 8. This time, the 45th Combat Wing was to lead, with the 96th Bomb Group in the forefront. The Luftwaffe had other plans for them. They attacked just as the 3rd Division was passing Hanover, and damaged the PFF aircraft to the extent that it was forced to abort.

The 96th Group was hard hit. When the PFF aircraft aborted, Lt. George Pond took over the lead. No sooner had he pulled into his new position when his aircraft was hit by oncoming fighters. The initial attack knocked out number two, three, and four engines, destroying most of the instrument panel and setting the aircraft on fire. Pond and his crew bailed out.

The second Fortress shot out of the formation was flown by Capt. Norman Thomas. After being badly damaged on

the first pass and forced out of formation, Thomas' B-17 was ganged up on by enemy fighters who didn't let up until the crew was forced to abandon the shot-up bomber.

Lt. Don Kasch was killed and his copilot broke his arm during the vicious attacks. Their aircraft went down on fire as crew members took to their parachutes.

A fourth B-17 was lost to fighters near Magdeburg, and a fifth B-17 was lost before they arrived at the initial point when its engine fire spread to the entire aircraft.

Lt. Clark Ross attempted to abort the mission after his B-17 had been badly damaged by fighters. The oxygen system and the intercom were out, so Ross dove down to a lower altitude for survival. However, fighter attacks continued, killing the bombardier and wounding the navigator in the face.

The copilot went back beyond the bomb bay to get the crew out of the aircraft. The two waist gunners were trying to help the badly wounded ball turret gunner out of his turret, and get a parachute on him. Hurriedly they jury-rigged the ripcord and pushed him out the fuselage door. Unfortunately, his parachute tangled with the horizontal stabilizer and then he fell.

After having attempted to help the ball turret crewman, the two waist gunners got to the door to bail out. As Sgt. Frank Ford stood in the door with his hand on the ripcord, he caught a blast of 20mm fire and was killed.

The 388th Bomb Group of the 45th Wing was also hard hit, losing five of their Fortresses to fighters. The Eighth Air Force lost a total of thirty-seven bombers on the mission, twenty-eight of them B-17s.

The B-17s went back to Berlin on March 9 and 22, suffering a minimum of losses while the Luftwaffe licked its wounds after losing 56.4 percent of its single-engine fighters and 22 percent of its single-engine pilots during the previous month.

The Fortresses took heavy losses again on April 11 when they journeyed out over the Baltic Sea to bomb targets in northern Germany. The primary target for the 3rd Division B-17s was Arnimswalde, but bad weather forced most of the Fortresses to hit Politz and Rostock. The 96th Bomb Group went to Ro-

Smoke screen or no, the formation of B-17s heads on in to the target. USAAF

stock, but was hit by large numbers of enemy fighters over the Baltic Sea and lost eleven B-17s.

Of their losses, two managed to ditch successfully, and survivors were picked up by the Germans. Another aircraft lost managed to make it to Sweden, where they received a fighter plane escort into the field and were interned.

On April 11, another member of the Eighth Air Force earned a Medal of Honor. This time it was a 305th Bomb Group pilot who would be honored for his ordeal in getting his Fortress back to England. Lt. Edward S. Michael piloted a Fortress named *Bertie Lee,* after his wife. Michael was a veteran with more than twenty-five missions to his credit.

Lieutenant Michael was part of a formation bound for Stettin loaded with incendiary bombs. Michael's bomber was the left aircraft in the high squadron element, a very exposed position.

The 305th had picked up some flak near Brunswick where *Bertie Lee* had received a pretty good hit in the wing. As they journeyed, they saw the Luftwaffe rip through a B-24 formation and then come back to hit the 305th Group northeast of Brunswick.

Two head-on passes by the Focke-Wulf 190s put four 20mm shells into the aircraft. One hit below the windshield and exploded in the cockpit. A fragment wounded Lieutenant Michael in the leg. This shell and another destroyed most of the instrument panel and severed the throttle controls to two of the engines, forcing the lieutenant to pull out of formation.

The radio operator then reported to Michael that the bomb bay was on fire. Michael told Lieutenant Leiber, the bombardier, to get rid of the bombs. He got no response and was not aware that Leiber's intercom was shot out. Lieu-

tenant Michael hit his salvo switch, but the bombs did not drop. Sergeant Phillips got out of the top turret, went into the bomb bay, and attempted to release the bombs, but they would not go.

The Fortress went into a spin and lost 3,000ft before Michael leveled out. The fighters came in again and did further damage. Phillips was already wounded, and the second attack knocked out his aircraft's chin turret. Lieutenant Leiber was firing away at the chin turret when an explosion knocked him back with the turret controls in his hands.

With many of the controls shot out, the bomb bay on fire with hung-up thermite bombs, and visibility all but nil from hydraulic fluid all over the wind-

A close-up of a 96th Bomb Group Fortress, a modified F model that has been fitted with a chin turret. USAAF

Bombs fall away from a Pathfinder aircraft of the 457th Bomb Group. Note the radar an- *tenna suspended where the ball turret would be. USAAF*

shield, Lieutenant Michael gave the bail-out order. Most of the crew bailed out.

As they let down with little visibility, Michael thought that he and copilot Lieutenant Westberg were the only crew aboard. They were down to about 2,500ft when Michael told Westberg to bail out. Each insisted that the other go first and when that got nowhere, Michael went back again to try to get the bombs out. When this failed, he returned to the cockpit and told Westberg they would have to go. As they dropped down to the nose hatch there sat the bombardier, Lieutenant Leiber. They told him to go, and he pointed to his parachute pack which was shredded by 20mm fragments. Michael offered Leiber his parachute, but he refused.

Lieutenant Michael went back to flying the aircraft manually and told Leiber to try the bombs again. He did, and by pulling and pulling he finally salvoed the bombs. Leiber then went back to the nose and fought off a fighter attack with the navigator's guns. Then they were hit by flak again and Michael dropped down to about 75ft, pulling up for houses and trees.

When they were finally out over the English Channel, Lieutenant Michael got the Fortress up to 3,000ft. Then another enemy fighter showed up and made passes from the rear where they had no guns. Michael turned and skidded to get out of the line of fire, and for no reason the fighter finally pulled off and went home.

Lieutenant Michael came in over the first landing field he could find and made a beautiful belly-landing. Weak from the loss of blood, Michael was taken to the hospital where he spent several weeks. He was awarded the Medal of Honor for his feat, and both Lieutenants Leiber and Westberg won Silver Stars.

On April 13, the B-17s experienced some of the heaviest fighter attacks that they had encountered for some weeks. The bombers went after targets at Schweinfurt and Augsburg. Thirty-two B-17s were lost. The 384th Bomb Group took the high losses with nine of their aircraft not returning.

Bombers were sent back to the Berlin area on April 18. The 94th Bomb Group was led by Maj. Lew Weimer, and Col. Charles Dougher was flying his first mission as 94th's commanding officer.

The weather was good until the Fortresses reached the target area. The 94th and the 385th Bomb Groups continued toward their targets, plowing through the weather. Most of the other bomb groups on the mission turned away from the bad weather and searched for targets of opportunity, and most of the escorting fighters followed. This gave the Luftwaffe the opportunity to come after the 94th Group which was without fighter protection. Some forty to seventy enemy fighters came roaring into the formation as a group, not as flights or in small numbers as they had been doing. The lead B-17 flown by Major Weimer was hit and fell out of formation shortly after they attacked. In the initial onslaught, eight bombers and two PFF aircraft were either shot down or fatally damaged.

As three of the crew members recalled, "We noticed a light brace of flak which diverted our attention and while so occupied, the fighters hit with a shocking suddenness." He went on: "They hit us in a bunch and then they were gone . . . the Luftwaffe appeared frantic and desperate without regard for caution. It seemed as if it was their last stand for survival."

The 94th Bomb Group lost eight B-17s while the entire B-17 force from the 1st and 3rd Divisions lost seventeen aircraft for the day.

The 306th Bomb Group had one of its worst days on April 24 when it flew in the low group of the B force bombing an aircraft assembly and repair center at Oberpfafenhofen, in southern Germany.

The unit lost its first B-17 shortly after crossing onto the Continent when Lt. Walter Peterson's aircraft was hit by flak. Number four engine was on fire when the Fortress pulled out of formation. Three chutes blossomed before the aircraft blew up.

Enemy fighters played cat and mouse for about an hour and a half before they decided to play the game in earnest. When they did come, the attacks were fierce and relentless. The demise of the 306th Fortresses occurred as follows: Captain Stolz's B-17 had three engines hit; Stolz salvoed the bombs and made it to Switzerland on two engines. Lieutenant Ebert's aircraft lost two engines and went to Switzerland. Lieutenant MacDowell was killed in the fighter attack; with number three

The B-17G Milk Run Special. 306th BG Assn.

and four engines out, the copilot ordered the crew to bail out. Lieutenant Ramsey's B-17 lost two engines and had a fire going; the crew abandoned the aircraft. Lieutenant Tarr's aircraft was hit by fighters; Tarr ordered his crew to abandon aircraft, and it exploded after the crew had cleared the aircraft. Lieutenant Schwedok's B-17 lost two engines; he salvoed his bombs, and went to Switzerland. Lieutenant Coughlin's crew lost five men to the fighters before they hit the silk. Lieutenant Biggs' aircraft was on fire, and number three and four engines were shot out; the crew parachuted and the aircraft blew up. The last to go was Lieutenant James, who was checking out a new aircraft commander. The new pilot, Lieutenant Vander-Marliere, was wounded in the initial attack and was pinned against the aircraft when he first bailed out. He finally fell clear and the parachute opened successfully.

The 1st Bomb Division lost twenty-seven Fortresses, with the 306th Bomb Group absorbing ten of the losses.

The bomber crews of the Eighth Air Force regarded the 100th Bomb Group, which had become known as the "Bloody Hundredth," as the hard-luck group among them. By the middle of May, the aircrews from the 96th Bomb Group would argue the point. They lost six B-17s on March 8 at Berlin and then eleven at Rostock on April 11. Their mission to Brunswick on May 8 cost them ten Fortresses. Then on May 12, they went to Zwickou, Czechoslovakia, and lost a dozen aircraft when their wing was cut to pieces by the Luftwaffe.

Things did not get off normally for the 96th on May 8. Rather than use their usual eighteen-ship formation, Group commander Col. James Travis insisted on using a new fourteen-aircraft formation that he had come up with. The group was airborne in two sections, an A Group and a B Group.

The first thing that went wrong was when the lead PFF aircraft was forced to abort the mission because of troubles in the aircraft's oxygen system. Lt. John White took over the lead of the A Group in his PFF aircraft. Then a time foul-up ensued when the 96th Bomb Group ar-

A formation of Fortresses from the 381st Bomb Group with a P-51 Mustang for escort. USAAF

rived at its rendezvous too early and encountered a B-24 formation which forced the 96th north of their course. After the Liberators moved on, the 96th could never get itself into the bomber stream with the 3rd Division where it belonged.

German fighters attacked in the Dummer Lake area. Some thirty to forty single-engine fighters roared in, closing to near ramming, before they broke and went downward. Three of the 96th's B-17s went down on the first attack. Lt. Charles Birdsay's aircraft went down under a swarm of fighters. Lt. Harold Eye's B-17 lost its number two engine and had its left wing on fire when he gave the order to abandon ship. Two men bailed out before Eye decided to

crash-land the stricken plane; Eye and his copilot died in the crash. Lt. James Kirkpatrick's aircraft blew up. There was only one survivor.

Lt. George Sterler assumed the lead of A Group. Eight of his aircraft dropped their bombs on a B-24 outfit's PFF markers. On withdrawal, the 96th was hit once more in a furious encounter with a formation of Focke-Wulf 190s.

Lt. Harold Niswonger's aircraft was hit in the number three engine and a fire started. His copilot and radio operator were both wounded. Niswonger rang the bail-out bell, and then he and the engineer-gunner went back to help the radio operator. Niswonger's B-17 then exploded after being rammed by an Fw 190, which probably had a dead pilot at the controls.

Lt. John White, who had led the A Group to the target, had his Fortress riddled on the withdrawal attack and hit the bail-out bell after the aircraft burst

into flames. Some of the crew got out before the aircraft exploded.

Lt. George Sterler, who had led the B Group to the target, went down in flames as well. Also victims of the second attack were Capt. Milton Shoesmith who crash-landed and saved all his crew, and Lt. Frank King who lost his rudder and stabilizer, yet managed to crash-land his aircraft after five of his crew bailed out. This act saved a wounded man, but cost King a leg. The tenth Fortress to fall was flown by F/O Leo Green. All the crew bailed out except for the tail gunner, Sgt. Harry Shirley, who was still blazing away at the fighters even though he was seriously wounded in both feet. Shirley was blown out of the aircraft and survived to receive a post-war Distinguished Service Cross for his action.

A Fortress named *Reluctant Dragon*, flown by Lt. Jerry Musser, made it home to Snetterton that day. The aircraft was badly damaged, and one waist gunner had been killed. After six of the crew bailed out, Musser, along with the engineer, T/Sgt. Leon Sweatt, and the bombardier, Lt. John Flanyak, managed to bring the ship in to roost.

The crews of the 96th Bomb Group were still reeling from their losses on May 8 when they were briefed for what would be the first mission of the new campaign to destroy Germany's sources of energy. The Eighth Air Force dispatched nearly 900 bombers escorted by over 700 fighters to strike oil targets.

The 96th was assigned an oil plant at Zwickou, Czechoslovakia. Once more, fourteen-plane formations were used and twenty-six B-17s were dispatched. The mission went well until about noon, when a big gaggle of Bf 109s and Fw 190s, accompanied by a few Bf 410s, decided to concentrate on the 45th Wing. Before it was over, the men of the 96th and 452nd Groups would classify this mission as their Ploesti.

The German attacks were flown in three continuous sweeps. After making their passes, the enemy regrouped about 2,000 yards from the bomber formation and then came back in. Each assault lasted three to four minutes. A navigator's log from the 96th Group shows that the attacks came at 1210, 1224, and 1230 hours. After each pass, three or four fighters would linger to catch any cripples that fell out of formation.

On the first attack the leader and deputy leader of A Group were knocked out as well as the leader of B Group. Capt. James Knupp, A Group leader in the PFF aircraft, went down with his right wing cut off at number four engine and on fire. Col. Marcus Lemley, commander of the 339th Squadron, was aboard. Only Captain Knupp and the radio operator survived. The deputy leader of A Group, Capt. Jack Link, and all of his crew except for the navigator were lost.

Lt. Tom Moore flying the lead and PFF aircraft for B Group had six officers aboard. When the first attack transpired, the nose was blasted with 20mm fire. Moore and Lt. Richard Thompson were both killed. The regular copilot on the crew, Lt. Vic Johnson, flying the tail position, bailed out. There were no survivors in the nose of the aircraft.

The Fortresses flown by Lts. Robert Simmons, Robert Lewis, and Harold

The B-17G Toggle Tessie. 306th BG Assn.

Tucker all went down in flames. Lt. Herb Moore, flying a PFF aircraft, tried to take evasive action when another B-17 blew up, and Moore's B-17 collided with the B-17 flown by Lt. Art Hon. The bombardier and navigator on Moore's ship were killed, as were all the men in the nose of Hon's B-17.

Lt. Charles Filer had three engines shot out before he gave the bail-out order. The left wing of Lt. Wilford Kin-

man's aircraft started to burn, and his crew bailed out. Lt. Bob Laurie's aircraft was possibly hit by a falling Bf 109. Only two men survived.

Lt. Jerry Musser, who had nursed *Reluctant Dragon* home on May 8, didn't make it back from this mission. His navigator and radio operator were killed in the fighter attack, and the ship was damaged so severely that Musser crashlanded it in enemy territory. The rest of the crew survived, but Musser suffered a mangled hand in the crash.

The 96th Bomb Group suffered twelve losses, but the 452nd Bomb Group took fourteen losses in the fighter attacks. One of the 452nd Fortresses that made it back that day was flown by Lt. Milan "Mike" Maracek. As he recalled: "The Fortress over us exploded and a body of a crew member came tumbling and crashed into the nose of our ship. The force of the impact sheared off the glass nose, ripped out our nose guns, and the shattering glass threw our navigator and bombardier back five feet and threw them against the step going up to the cockpit. Both men were wounded. The navigator was hit in the stomach by flying metal and the bombardier received a gash over his eyes from a piece of flying glass.

"One Fw 190 raked the ship with bullets from the nose to the tail. A shell hit the top turret gunner in the side of his head and he died instantly. Bursting at the left waist window, another shell exploded and blasted the glass window and metal frame to pieces. A metal screw from the frame embedded itself in the gunner's nose. The right waist gunner received a wound over one of his eyes, the ball turret gunner was hit in the head, and the tail gunner was injured in the back."

Despite their wounds, the living gunners remained at their posts and kept scanning the skies for fighters. The radio operator, S/Sgt. Dwight Miller, went from one to the other administering first aid. Miller said he just tried to keep them conscious, although some were getting weak from the loss of blood.

The aircraft continued on the bomb run, then dropped its load and headed for home. The oxygen system was knocked out, so the crew took turns using a walk-around bottle. The bomb bay doors refused to close. With the nose shot out and the bomb bay doors open, the aircraft was not able to keep up with the others and had to leave formation. Maracek took the Fortress right down

A B-17G of the 96th Bomb Group at rest. An ever-alert ambulance sits in front—standard fare on airfields. Ethell

90

on the deck and hoped for the best. Two engines failed, and then a Bf 109 appeared. The left waist gunner gave the Messerschmitt a burst and the fighter departed.

The Fortress *Lady Stardust II* managed to avoid most of the flak along the coast, but when it reached the English Channel, it couldn't quite make it all the way home. The pilot ditched and the nine survivors were rescued from the sea.

Beginning in May 1944, the bombers of the Eighth Air Force began to fly numerous tactical missions to set the stage for the invasion of the Continent. These missions were directed at marshaling yards, bridges, and any sort of transportation target that would prevent the Germans from reinforcing their positions on the Normandy peninsula where the invasion would take place. Airfields were also prime targets. One thing that the bombers had accomplished was to drive the Luftwaffe from its bases in the occupied countries in order to defend the Reich. When invasion did come, there were few German fighters based in France.

On D-day, June 6, 1944, the bombers of the Eighth Air Force flew more than 1,700 sorties in support of the invasion. There were bombers continuously over tactical targets behind the beachheads. The greatest reward for the crew members was the fact that they were supporting the ground forces, and that losses to the bombers were minimal in these tactical strikes.

The most exciting event for the bomber crews of the Eighth Air Force after D-day was the first shuttle mission to Russia. The units were to take off from their English bases, bomb targets en route, and continue on to land at bases in Russia. From there they would bomb targets in the Balkans and land in Italy. From Italy they would bomb targets en route back to England.

Two bomb wings participated in the mission: the 13th Wing composed of the 95th, 100th, and 390th Bomb Groups, and the 45th Wing composed of the 96th, 388th, and 452nd. The planes flew the first leg of the mission on the morning of June 21, and they all bombed their tar-

The radio room and ball turret were wrecked on this Fortress, but it still came home. US-AAF

gets with good results. Then they continued on across Poland and into Russia.

The 13th Wing landed at Mirgorod while the 45th Wing landed at Poltava. There they were entertained by the Russians with food and drink. A good time was being enjoyed by all at Poltava when the air-raid alarm sounded. Unknown to the Americans, a German reconnaissance plane had followed the bomber stream to Poltava and flown back to report their landing ground. That night, two bomber units composed of Junkers Ju 88s came over, marked the field with flares, and began to bomb it. The Russians had few antiaircraft guns, so the Germans bombed for more than two hours as they devastated the bomber force on the ground.

When the survey was made the next day, two Americans had been killed and six wounded. Of the seventy-three B-17s on the field, forty-seven had been completely destroyed, two were good only for cannibalization, fifteen were repairable within seven days or more, and only nine were repairable within one day. American commanders were disgusted that they had been so poorly protected by the Russians, but all had the utmost praise for the common Russian soldiers, men and women who had done their utmost with their limited antiaircraft weapons to drive away the German bombers and later, to fight the many fires.

The remaining American aircraft on Russian bases were immediately disbursed and personnel were moved around. Repairable aircraft were worked on, and a task force was mounted to fly a mission en route to Italy. They finally took off on June 26, bombed an oil refinery at Drohabycz, Poland, and continued on to Italy.

The hundreds of Fortress crew members who were stranded in Russia had to be flown out by Air Transport Command. They were picked up from the Russian bases and sent back to England by way of Tehran, Cairo, Benghasi, and Casablanca.

The oil campaign continued throughout the summer of 1944. While the bombers of the Fifteenth Air Force out of Italy continued to strike at the main source of oil supply, the Romanian refineries at Ploesti, the Eighth Air Force bombed the synthetic oil refineries that were clustered primarily in central Ger-

Waist ripped wide open and ball turret is gone from this miraculously returned 351st Bomb Group B-17. USAAF

many. As the attacks continued, the buildup of antiaircraft defenses continued. Flak became a major factor in bomber survival as the flak batteries became more proficient and radar tracking enabled them to fire with great accuracy.

The 100th Bomb Group ran afoul of the flak batteries at the Leuna oil plant at Merseburg on July 29, 1944. As the A Group came in from the south, they ran into a barrage of extremely heavy flak. In the next few minutes, the low squadron of the lead group lost five out of six B-17s. The high squadron lost one aircraft to the barrage.

The B Group's lead aircraft, flown by Capt. Joe Zeller, was hit in the Tokyo tank just after bombs away. The aircraft burst into flames immediately, and the crew bailed out. A second Fortress in B Group was badly damaged and had to ditch in the North Sea. Fortunately, the crew was rescued by German ships.

All total, fifteen B-17s were downed over Merseburg that day, with the 100th Bomb Group losing eight aircraft.

One sighting that had been made on July 29 and a combat that ensued brought further evidence that the Luftwaffe was ready to put some new weapons into the air. An escorting fighter encountered a Messerschmitt Me 163, a rocket-powered interceptor capable of being launched from the ground and making brief, but very destructive attacks with 30mm cannons. The Me 163 encountered on July 29 was on a test flight. It was attacked by an American escort fighter, which put some telling hits into it before it screamed earthward.

Following the invasion of France, the bombers flew many tactical missions supplying Free French forces arms to combat the Germans behind the lines. One of these missions saw a copilot flying as a formation observer in the tail. Sometimes it got hot back there!

On July 14, 1944, Lt. C. B. Robbins, Jr., of the 385th Bomb Group, was flying the tail gunner's position on a mission to Valance, France. As Robbins told the story: "On this particular mission we were to lead the low group to take arms to the Free French in southern France. We were the lead ship, the group command officer took my seat and I, as copilot, was assigned to the tail as formation control target.

"This was my second trip to drop tubes of arms. I recalled what a beautiful sight [it was] to see the thousands of colored parachutes floating to the earth landing in open fields and the Free French running out to pick them up in their trucks and haul them away. I thought I would take some photographs of this wonder sight. However, about the time I was getting my camera out one of the waist gunners called over the intercom saying there were Bf 109s at about three o'clock coming down the bomber stream. As we had a lot of jovial comments about fighters, I replied, 'Let's cut all the crap, you guys, there is no such thing as fighters way down this far in southern France.' As I looked back over my shoulder, much to my surprise, there were Bf 109s coming down the bomber stream. They made a turn to the right and started to make a pass at our number six ship in the lead squadron.

"Naturally, I grabbed the twin .50 calibers in front of me and aimed at the first fighter, had it in my sights, and pulled the trigger. Nothing happened. I forgot to take the safety off.

"By the time the second ship came through, I was smart enough to take the safety off and fired at him. He was a good distance away, but at least I heard the rattle of guns.

"I took a shot at the third one, too, and missed, but I was really holding the trigger down. Then I noticed I had followed the Bf 109 down through our formation and was firing very close to one of the ships in our formation.

"Then another Bf 109 came through and by that time I had shot up all my ammunition or jammed the guns. Shows you how good a gunner I was. After the 109s, we went on in at tree-top level and dropped our parachutes and came on home. It was a total of about nine hours and thirty minutes on that flight.

"There was some discussion from one crew back at debriefing that they had checked their plane on the hardstand and it looked like they had received some hits from machine guns rather than from the 20mm of the 109s in their left wing, and they were wondering if anyone knew or saw any other fighters during the attack. Not to make confessions about my gunnery ability, I made no comments."

The threat that was most feared by the Eighth Air Force was the Messerschmitt Me 262. This was a new fighter powered by two jet engines that provided enough thrust to give it an 80–100 mph speed advantage over the P-51 Mustang. It was also heavily armed with 30mm cannons, and its fire on the bomber stream could be lethal. With its rate of closure, there was no way that the escorting fighters could stop its attacks. The only solution for the American fighters was to locate the bases of the jets and attack them on takeoff or landing when they were at a decided disadvantage.

The summer of 1944 saw two more shuttle missions to Russia by the B-17s. A force of seventy-six Fortresses escorted by Mustangs bombed the Focke-Wulf factory at Gdynia, Poland, en route to Russia on August 6. They flew one mission out of Russia and then departed for Italy on August 8. This time there was no air raid, and all went well for the American fliers.

The final shuttle to Russia began on September 11 when seventy-five Fortresses and their escort attacked an armament plant at Chemnitz en route to their bases in the east. They stayed a very short time, departing on September 13 en route to Italy on their way home.

On September 11, when one formation of B-17s had gone to Russia, the balance of the 3rd Division attacked other oil targets. The 100th Bomb Group was cruising along en route to Ruhland when, as the group historian recorded, "at 1205, unheralded and with no alarm on VHF, the Luftwaffe hit with everything it had, when three waves of enemy aircraft came deceptively from out of the sun to completely overwhelm the trailing and unprotected low group of the 100th C formation in a frontal attack, to tear the 350th Squadron apart and at the same time knock the six planes in the lead element out of formation."

Captain Giles, whose aircraft had its wing tips burning and breaking up, ordered his crew to bail out. Lt. Joseph Raine, who was flying on Giles' left wing, had his aircraft blow up; Raine and four of his crew were killed. Lt. Albert Trommer's B-17, flying Giles' right wing, was downed with only four survivors. Lt. Harold Taylor had been directly behind Giles; he did a wing-over with gas tanks afire, righted his aircraft, and tried to make a crash-landing—but all of the crew except the waist gunner were killed.

Two other Fortresses out of the same formation were hit and tried to make a run for home, but both were caught and shot down by fighters in their attempt.

The low element of C Group was also badly hit and lost three of its number quickly. Lt. Wesley Carlton's B-17 was hit, and only the navigator and copilot survived. Both of Carlton's wingmen also went down, with only seven survivors off the two crews.

Two Fortresses were shot out of the high element, making a total of eleven aircraft lost by the 100th Bomb Group in a very brief encounter. There was a twelfth aircraft lost on the mission. Lt. Raymond Heironimus' Fortress survived the first attack, but pulled up in a stall and spun down to 6,000ft. At that point the radio operator bailed out. The pilot set course for France and had hoped to make it to Paris, but finally had to set down in a turnip patch close to the front lines.

The following day, the Luftwaffe once more violently opposed missions against oil targets. The 306th Bomb Group was busy bombing Ruhland. The routing called for the 40th Bomb Wing, of which the 306th was a part, to fly to the north of Berlin, past the city defenses, and then turn south to Ruhland. As the Fortresses passed north of Berlin it

A 388th Bomb Group B-17G above England. The fact that the ball turret guns are pointed downward indicates the gunner is out of the turret, or just about to get in. Ethell

was noted that some of the formations ahead were turning too close to Berlin, and were getting in the flak there. The 306th lead got off to the left, hoping to miss the antiaircraft fire. Before they got clear, two Fortresses were hit. Lt. John W. Sasser, leading the high group, had two engines shot out immediately, so he lost altitude, with his group following him down.

The low group, which was trying to get out of the flak, nearly collided with another group that came barging in

from their right and caused the formation to break up.

The 306th Bomb Group historian states: "At this moment about twenty-five Fw 190s jumped the disorganized planes. The entire attack did not last more than five or six minutes, but accounted for seven planes from the 306th Group, one of which crash-landed in England. The lead group of the 40th A Combat Wing which hung together solidly was not attacked and reports attacks on other groups as being from 5 to 7 o'clock high, level and low by enemy aircraft flying four to six abreast. The lead group lost one aircraft to flak.

"The low group reports that about twenty-five Fw 190s came from 11 o'-clock high firing at the group to their left and made one pass, then turned and

came at the low group from 6 o'clock low in five waves of three and four aircraft each. They half rolled beneath us and fell away steeply. The low group lost five aircraft to fighters, one of which crash-landed in England.

"The high group was attacked by seven to eight fighters and lost one to flak. Two planes of the high group tagged on to the lead, while the remaining planes of the high and low, with a few stragglers from the group which was responsible for breaking up the 40th A CW formation, struggled together into group formation and pulled clear as P-51s came to their rescue."

Maj. Robert Farwell had been leading the high squadron of the lead group when his aircraft was hit by flak. With a fire in the nose, he ordered his crew out. Lieutenant Sasser, who was leading the high group when he was hit by flak, tried to get out and away, but was caught by enemy fighters and forced to crash-land. Only three of his crew survived the landing.

When the fighters came, Lt. Earl Barr's B-17 had two engines on fire when he ordered bail-out; Lt. Paul Bailey's B-17 had one engine on fire and another fire in the radio room before he ordered the crew to bail out; Lt. Lewis White had his aircraft shot to pieces and his tail gunner killed before the crew parachuted; Lt. Charles Wegener flying *Umbriago* had all his aircraft's controls shot out and an oxygen fire before he ordered his crew to bail out; *Belle of the Blue* with Lt. Daniel Gates at the controls was completely on fire in the rear when it went down; and the aircraft flown by Lt. Marvin Freeman was shot in two by the Focke-Wulfs.

The 351st Bomb Group was also hard hit on the mission, losing six of their Fortresses to Focke-Wulf 190s.

More than one thousand bombers were launched by the Eighth Air Force on September 28 to bomb oil targets in the Third Reich. One of the units en route to Magdeburg was the 457th Bomb Group. Since their entrance into combat in February 1944, the group's losses had been light and they had been lucky.

The group's luck ran out on September 28, however, when they were attacked by some fifty Bf 109s and Fw 190s just before their bombers turned on the initial point. The fighters came in low from four to nine o'clock, attacking the rear of the bombers. In a period of 12–13 minutes six aircraft were damaged badly enough to fall out of formation. From that point on, these six aircraft came under constant attack until they were abandoned by their crews. Two of the Fortresses were seen to explode.

As the Eighth Air Force moved into the fall of 1944 the numbers of B-17s increased. In the summer of 1944, it had been decided that the number of operational Fortresses would be increased. Over a period of two months or so, five B-24 units were converted to fly B-17s. The groups so changed were the 486th, 487th, 490th, 493rd, and finally the 34th, which became operational in B-17s on September 17, 1944. This gave the Eighth Air Force a total of twenty-six

Fortress groups, which meant that a maximum effort by the bombers could put more than 1,000 B-17s aloft!

Strikes at Berlin continued. Although many of the missions to the German capital no longer brought Luftwaffe attacks, there was always the possibility that it could happen. On October 6, the 385th Bomb Group suffered its highest loss of the war while flying a strike to Berlin. All eleven aircraft of the high squadron were shot down. The Luftwaffe amassed a formation of approximately seventy-five fighters, and sent them down in waves from five to seven o'clock high. By concentrating on the one unit, they managed to overwhelm the massed gun defenses of the bombers. Observers recall that in seconds the sky was marked with five B-17s exploding and five more smoking badly.

The following day, the bombers of the Eighth Air Force were out continuing their attacks on oil targets. The 94th Bomb Group's B Group was doing well until about 12 minutes before reaching the initial point. Suddenly fifty to sixty enemy fighters emerged out of high cloud cover. Single- and twin-engine attackers were scattered in disarray as they came in from the rear. In waves of eight and ten aircraft, they closed to attack. After firing at close range they split up, peeling off left and right with a few going under the formation and executing a split-ess.

The B-17 gunners fired for all they were worth In a very short period of time, the escorting fighters arrived, but it was too late. Nine aircraft were either missing or in the process of going down.

Most of the Fortresses that were hit either exploded or went down in flames. One B-17 had its whole tail section shot off. Lt. Julius Loesing and his copilot managed to regain control of their Fortress after it went down in a spin, and they crash-landed the battered bomber in a field. Once the dust settled, it was found that all the crew had survived except the waist gunner who apparently had been killed in the fighter attack.

Lt. R. E. Kennedy rang the bail-out bell on his Fortress when it was badly hit by the fighters. The aircraft was enveloped in smoke, and it began vibrating badly. Three of the crew bailed out immediately. Suddenly, the smoke cleared and Kennedy decided to see if he could

keep the aircraft flying. He managed to stay in the air long enough to reach a field in Belgium, where he landed safely.

While fighter attacks continued to be sporadic, there was no lack of flak. The 351st Bomb Group attacked the synthetic oil plant at Politz that day and lost seven of their B-17s to flak. The lead plane, flown by Lieutenant Colonel Glawe, left the formation with two engines feathered and a large hole and fuel leak in one wing and went to Sweden. Before the day was over Glawe and his crew would be joined by three other Fortresses crews from the 351st, whose aircraft had also suffered extensive flak damage.

Lt. Einer Peterson had headed for Sweden after losing an engine and having his fuel tanks holed. As he fell behind the formation, a second engine stopped because of lack of fuel. Then as Peterson's aircraft crossed Bornhalt Island in the Baltic Sea it was hit again by flak and lost a third engine. Peterson prepared to make a crash-landing in a field. As he got ready to set down, he sighted a number of people in front of him digging potatoes. He pulled up to avoid the potato pickers, which caused him to run out of room to land in the field. The B-17 smacked into a clump of trees, and only two of the gunners survived the crash.

The primary target on November 2, 1944, was the Merseburg-Leuna synthetic oil plant. Over 1,000 bombers were to strike at the target, and this was one day that the Luftwaffe put up its maximum force to intercept them. However, more than 900 American fighters were airborne to escort the bombers, so the Luftwaffe had to carefully select its point of interception.

The 91st Bomb Group lost one Fortress to an electrical fire before the initial point. Upon arrival over the target it was found to be socked in, so bombing was done by PFF. Flak was not heavy over the target. Just after the formation pulled off the target, it was hit from the rear by a bevy of Focke-Wulf 190s. They came in four abreast at six o'clock level and split-essed after making their passes.

The 91st lost ten aircraft to the Focke-Wulfs, two to flak, and one had to crash-land on its arrival in England.

The 457th Bomb Group, flying along with the 91st, was also hit by Fw 190s.

The severity of the combat was described by one of the gunners in the 457th: "The first two waves came in wiping out most of our box, but most of them were wiped out, too. The plane I was tracking and shooting at went over our tail and tore his left wing on the rear dorsal fin of our left wingman. I saw that our left wingman was also on fire behind his number three engine and just about then he peeled off and down. I swung my guns around to five o'clock again as the pilot, using evasive action, dropped the plane about twenty-five to fifty feet, leaving an Fw 190 shooting over us at a spot we had just vacated.

"The next plane that I fired at went over the top of us and straight down in front of our nose. At about that time Fw 190s were falling all around us as the third and final wave started to come in. They were more broken up than the first two waves because some of them were picking out stragglers as they fell out of formation.

"As I brought my guns back to six o'clock two more fighters were coming in close to our tail, one at five o'clock and the other directly on our tail somewhere under us. I could hear the ball turret gunner firing away. I started firing at the one at five o'clock, and the radio operator was firing at him, too. He started to smoke as he fell off to the right, and down under our belly he burst into flame. The other one lost his prop and blew up about twenty-five feet from our tail."

It is likely that the 91st and 457th Bomb Groups fell victim to the Focke-Wulf 190s from two assault groups of the Luftwaffe, IV/JG 3 and II//JG 4. With a total of sixty-one Fw 190s, they claimed some thirty B-17s around noon that fateful day. However, they lost thirty of their own aircraft, with seventeen pilots being killed and seven wounded.

A Fortress from the 447th Bomb Group with Lt. Robert E. Femoyer aboard as navigator was another aircraft that was severely damaged by flak on the mission to Merseburg. When the B-17 was damaged, Lieutenant Femoyer was severely wounded in the back and in the side by shrapnel. Although he was in extreme pain and weak from the loss of

A formation of B-17s forms up for a mission over England. Ethell

blood, he refused to take a shot of morphine. Femoyer refused any assistance, for he wanted to be able to navigate his crew home safely. He asked to be propped up on the floor where he worked with his charts and instruments until he directed his Fortress over the English Channel. Only then would he take the shot of morphine.

The aircraft made it back to England and to a safe landing. Femoyer was

removed from the B-17, but died shortly thereafter. He was posthumously awarded the Medal of Honor.

Two additional Medals of Honor were posthumously awarded to members of a Fortress crew for their performance on a mission to Saarbrucken, Germany, on November 9. Lt. Donald J. Gott was the pilot and Lt. William E. Metzger, Jr., was the copilot of a B-17 from the 452nd Bomb Group that was

Excellent photo of radar bombing by the 306th Bomb Group. Note the markers that the Pathfinder has just released to denote the target for the aircraft following. 306th BG Assn.

severely damaged by flak. Three of the engines had been damaged and number four was streaming fire as far back as the tail assembly. Some flares in the cockpit had ignited and with hydraulic

Naughty Nancy *graces the nose of a B-17G in England.* Ethell

fluid present a more severe fire was imminent.

The radio operator's arm had been severed below the elbow and the engineer-gunner was painfully wounded in the leg. A tourniquet was placed on the radio operator's arm. They had no static line to bail out the radio operator, so the two pilots conferred and decided to try to make it to Allied-held territory once the bombs were away. After dropping the bombs, they immediately set course for friendly territory. Upon arrival, Lieutenant Gott had Lieutenant Metzger see that the rest of the crew bailed out. Once this was accomplished, Metzger came back up to assist Gott in a crash-land-

ing. When they were only about 100ft in the air on their approach for landing, the Fortress exploded. All three men aboard were killed.

On New Year's Eve, 1944, the 100th Bomb Group set out to bomb Hamburg, Germany. The weather was beautiful, so rather than have the entire formation salvo on the lead bombardier, it was decided that each squadron would bomb individually. This concept proved tragic, however, for shortly after the initial point, the Fortresses were hit by swarms of Bf 109s and Fw 190s. The spacing out left them much more susceptible to enemy attack and the Luftwaffe took advantage of it.

A number of the Fortresses were hit by flak over the target and succumbed to these damages while others were damaged by flak and then came under attack

from fighters as they tried to flee for home. Two B-17s collided after leaving the enemy coast.

The majority of the enemy aircraft attacking the 100th Bomb Group were from II/JG 30, an assault group. All total, the 100th Group had twelve B-17s fail to return of which probably six fell to the fighters. Their attackers had eight pilots killed and three wounded.

The year 1945 saw the bombers of the Eighth Air Force reign supreme over Germany. They continued to strike at oil targets, communications installations, and airfields. The Luftwaffe got several jet units into operation, but never was able to have enough aircraft serviceable to really make a difference. The most successful unit was JG 7, which brought down a number of bombers during its career. Then in the spring of 1945 the select unit JV 44, commanded by the former chief of the German fighter forces, General Adolph Galland, got into combat. This unit was largely manned by Knights Cross winners who were very high scorers. Some of these aces got a number of victories flying the Me 262, yet the jet unit very seldom had over a half-dozen aircraft in service at one time.

In March 1945 Air Marshal Hermann Goering had organized the Sonderkommando Elbe group which was composed of volunteer pilots who would fly attacks in Bf 109s and press them to the point that they were committed to ram the bomber if they could not shoot it down. Both the Sonderkommando and the jets made a great effort on April 7, 1945, when the B-17s went after industrial targets in central Germany.

The intelligence report of 1st Air Division for that day states: "After a lapse of several weeks during which conventional single engine enemy aircraft have largely been non-active partners in the air war and even when encountered have shown little fighting spirit, today, in excellent flying conditions, the German Air Force put up a force of some 115–130 single engine enemy aircraft supplemented by more than fifty jets. From all reports it appears that this was a desperate attempt on the part of the enemy and although the enemy aircraft fought aggressively and made determined efforts to get through to the bombers, Allied losses were comparatively light while more than half the enemy force was destroyed or damaged. Signs of desperation are evidenced by the fact that enemy pilots deliberately rammed the bombers, bailing out before their planes went in the bomber formations and making fanatical attacks through a murderous hail of fire. Tactics were thrown to the wind and attacks were made from all positions, mainly in ones and twos. A few attempts were made to draw off fighter escort but the P-51s and P-47s were not fooled and did a good job of dispersing and destroying enemy aircraft.

"Reverting to this old policy of attacking in the area of Dummer and Steinhuder Lakes, the enemy met the leading groups of the first force at 1230 hours with some 105–120 Bf 109s, Fw 190s and 30 plus Me 262s flying between 18,000 and 30,000ft. Of these only some 45–50 single engine enemy aircraft and 15 jets managed to approach the bombers, destroying eleven. The B-17s claim 26 enemy fighters destroyed . . . "

One of the gunners that was successful that day was T/Sgt. Weaver L. Reckland of the 388th Bomb Group. Weaver related: "I got a Me 262 on the seventh and probably the only reason I shot it down was that the tail gunner had called to tell me a fighter was coming up fast on us from six o'clock. I was top turret gunner and we were under heavy fighter attack. I realized that unless he banked under us he'd have to come up in front of us. I turned my twin .50s around to one o'clock and waited a few seconds and sure enough he pulled up in front. He was in a steep climb at about one o'clock and not more than 300–400ft range. It was a dead straight shot and all I had to do was frame him in my sights and pull both triggers, keeping my turret tracking him on up until he trailed smoke. He spun into the ground without the pilot ever getting out. I didn't see the plane go but the copilot, ball turret, tail gunner, and waist gunner did and verified him for me."

On April 25, 1945, 307 B-17s were dispatched to Pilsen, Czechoslovakia, to bomb the Skoda armament plant. The bombs were aimed visually, and many strikes on the target were observed. Six B-17s were shot down by accurate flak. This marked the last combat mission of the B-17 Flying Fortresses of the Eighth Air Force. For thirty-two months, the famous aircraft had rained destruction over every possible target in northwestern Europe. With a force that had grown from the fledgling dozen B-17s that journeyed to Rouen, France, in 1942, it had culminated in a force of more than 1,000 Fortresses that dominated the daylight skies over Germany.

Chapter 7

North Africa and the Mediterranean

The 97th Bomb Group, pioneer bomber unit of the Eighth Air Force, became a pioneer in the new Twelfth Air Force in North Africa. They became involved early on when on October 19, 1942, Gen. Mark Clark and four of his staff climbed aboard a 97th B-17 flown by Maj. Paul Tibbetts, Jr. They flew to Gibraltar from whence General Clark and his colleagues made a secret mission to Algeria. Upon their return, they were flown back to England.

On October 29, six Fortress crews from the 97th flew to southern England for another top-secret mission. One waist gunner was dropped from each crew and was replaced by the crew chief. Baggage racks and seats were installed in the aircraft, while only the top turret, ball turret, and one nose gun received a small quantity of ammunition.

On the morning of November 5, 1942, the command staffs of the African invasion loaded aboard the 97th Bomb Group B-17s. Passengers were Gen. Dwight D. Eisenhower and his staff, Gen. Kenneth Anderson and his staff (to command the British First Army), and Gen. Mark Clark and his staff. Five B-17s took off in a heavy rain that morning for Gibraltar. One aircraft was delayed because of trouble with its hydraulic system. It departed two days later and near Cape Finisterre, the Fortress was attacked by three German fighters. Copilot Lt. Thomas Lohr was wounded and the

aircraft received minor damage. Aboard the B-17 was Gen. James E. Doolittle, new commander of the Twelfth Air Force.

Once the first landings were made in Operation Torch—the invasion of North Africa—on November 8, the 97th stood ready to bring the commanders into the theater. On November 9, General Clark and his staff were transported to Maison Blanche airfield at Algiers. General Doolittle took off in another B-17 destined for Oran. As the aircraft carrying General Clark was landing, a formation of twenty Junkers Ju 88s attacked the airfield. The Fortress turned off the end of the runway as bombs began to fall. One stick of bombs missed the B-17 by less than 100ft. Other B-17s en route to the airfield had to circle for an hour. The passengers all credited the American Spitfires in the area with defending the base and making their landings possible.

On the afternoon of November 16, the 97th Bomb Group under the command of Major Tibbetts led the first combat mission by B-17s in North Africa. The six Fortresses arrived over their target, Sidi Ahmed airdrome at Bizerte, Libya, and found it covered by clouds. They dropped down to 7,500ft and dropped their bombs on the hangar line. One B-17 suffered damage to its wing by intercepting fighters, but all returned safely.

Two more missions were flown by the 97th from Maison Blanche, both of them striking at El Aouina, outside of the city of Tunis, Tunisia. General Doolittle flew as an observer on one of the missions.

The Luftwaffe struck back on the nights of November 20 and 21. They made several runs across the airfield at Maison Blanche, dropping demolition and delayed-action bombs. The 97th lost a B-17 in each attack. It was decided that there were too many American aircraft on Maison Blanche, so the units were to be dispersed.

On November 22 the 97th Bomb Group was moved to Tafaraoui, seventeen miles southeast of Oran, Algeria. There they had a hard surfaced runway and several hangars. The base appeared to have great potential—until the rains came. There were no taxiways or hardstands for the bombers, so the aircraft sunk in the mud. Gasoline came in five-gallon cans, which made refueling the bombers a time-consuming chore because the B-17F carried over 2,200 gallons of fuel. The gasoline from the cans also had to be filtered through a chamois to remove water. Once the mud came and bombs were loaded, the wheels of the Fortresses sunk deeper and deeper in the muck.

The 301st Bomb Group joined the 97th at Tafaraoui in late November, and the two groups began to team up on

A Fortress of the 2nd Bomb Group, Twelfth Air Force, undergoing maintenance in North Africa. USAAF

their mission. Both groups went to Bizerte on November 28, and both experienced their first losses in North Africa. They were intercepted by Luftwaffe fighters that were very aggressive, and both groups lost two B-17s each. Lt. Robert Maher of the 301st Bomb Group made his bomb run on three engines. As he descended after the bomb run, his Fortress was pounced on by six Bf 109s that made constant attacks until the aircraft crashed into the sea and exploded. At the same time, four Bf 109s followed Capt. John Bruce off the target. Shortly thereafter, four parachutes emerged from the B-17, and it exploded.

In mid-December the 97th Bomb Group moved two squadrons to Maison Blanche and two to Biskra. The 301st Bomb Group also moved two of its squadrons to Biskra, but was forced to leave two at Tafaraoui. Regardless, the units operated under difficult conditions, and morale was low. Most of the fliers lived in tents, food was poor, and maintenance problems were legion. The engines and all operating parts on the aircraft were quickly eaten up by sand. Parts were hard to come by as well, for it seemed that B-17 units were on the end of the supply pipeline.

It had originally been planned that the Fortresses would be primarily strategic bombers. It did not work out that way in North Africa. They were constantly in demand as tactical bombers to strike at enemy troop and supply concentrations, airfields, and ports. B-17 units also continued to endure enemy air raids. Biskra was raided twice in January 1943, and some casualties were suffered.

The 97th participated in two missions against the French naval base at Ferryville, Libya, ten miles southeast of Bizerte, that were quite effective. On the first mission on January 8 they were intercepted by Luftwaffe fighters, but were able to put their bombs right on target. Five French vessels—a subma-

One of the most famous B-17 photos of the war. This Fortress from the 97th Bomb Group was ripped open by a Bf 109, yet it still made it home. USAAF

rine, a sailing vessel, a tug, an aircraft tender, and a patrol vessel—were destroyed or damaged beyond repair.

An attack on Bizerte in January was intercepted by fifteen Bf 109s, and the Fortress of Capt. Fred Dallas, Jr., seemed to get the most attention. A burst of flak had already knocked out the number two engine when the fighters came in. They immediately knocked out the communications system from the flight deck to the nose. The bomb bay doors were shot up, preventing them from closing, and the controls to the flaps were out.

Waist gunner Sgt. Elmer L. Burgher had been hit in the thigh by a piece of flak and he could only get up by pulling himself up on the gun as the occasion required. The ball turret was out of commission, and gunner Sgt. Edward Leary had been wounded in the left hand and shoulder.

The fighters began working on the Fortress and soon it became the center of their attention. Number three engine was hit and caught fire, but the fire was put out by diving the aircraft. Sergeant Leary now took over the waist gun from the wounded Sergeant Burgher. As the next attack came in from the rear, the tail gunner, the engineer, and radio operator all fired away but all took wounds from the fighter. The tail gunner was hit by a 20mm cannon shell, the radio operator got fragments in his knee, and a freak shot brushed the top turret gunner and severed the upright support of the turret, making it inoperative. On the same pass Captain Dallas was hit in the chest area by three machine gun bullets; all entered from the rear, went through his body, and struck the aircraft's instrument panel. Unbelievably, none touched a vital organ and he continued to fly the aircraft.

In the nose, the bombardier manned the guns while the navigator, Lt. Marvin Kay, worked to set a course that would take them to the Allied lines via the shortest route. With the Fortress down

El Diablo, *a veteran Flying Fortress of the 99th Bomb Group in Italy.* USAAF

This 99th Bomb Group aircraft is just coming in from a mission to France with number one engine still burning. USAAF

to about 1,000ft, Captain Dallas ordered all the crew except the copilot into the radio room for a crash-landing. With only one engine functioning properly, no flaps, bomb bay doors open, ball turret guns down, and wounded aboard, the pilot bounced the ship off a couple of sand dunes to slow his progress and then set the craft down in the sand. The tail section broke off and the copilot's elbow was dislocated, but all survived.

A mid-air collision on February 1 between a B-17 and a German fighter over the Tunis dock area became the subject of one of the most famous photographs of World War II. An enemy fighter attacking a 97th Bomb Group formation went out of control, probably with a wounded or dead pilot. It crashed into the lead aircraft of the flight, ripped a wing off the Fortress, and caused it to crash. The enemy fighter then continued its crashing descent into the rear of the fuselage of a Fortress named *All American,* piloted by Lt. Kendrick R. Bragg, of the 414th Bomb Squadron.

When it struck, the fighter broke apart, but left some pieces in the B-17. The left horizontal stabilizer of the Fortress and left elevator were completely torn away. The vertical fin and the rudder had been damaged, the fuselage had been cut approximately two-thirds through, the control cables were severed, and the electrical and oxygen systems were damaged. Although the tail swayed in the breeze, one elevator cable still worked, and the aircraft still flew—miraculously!

The aircraft was brought in for an emergency landing and when the ambulance pulled alongside, it was waved off for not a single member of the crew had been injured. No one could believe that the aircraft could still fly in such a condition. The Fortress sat placidly until three men climbed aboard through the door in the fuselage, at which time the rear collapsed. The rugged old bird had done its job.

The 301st Bomb Group was called upon to fly tactical missions on February 14 after the American ground forces had been routed by the Afrikakorps at Kasserine Pass. The 301st Bomb Group flew two missions the next day, one against an airfield and the second to strike at a German panzer division.

When the Fortresses arrived, the area was cloud covered. Most of the B-17s bombed to the east, but one squadron went down below 5,000ft to strike at the road along the pass. They destroyed a number of German tanks in the process.

In mid-February, the 97th Bomb Group moved to Chateaudun, Algeria, from which it would operate for quite some time. The 301st Bomb Group moved to its new base at Constantine, Algeria, on March 5. From their new bases, the two B-17s groups not only continued their tactical support of the US Army in North Africa, but they also began crossing the Mediterranean to bomb targets in Sicily, Sardinia, and Italy. The two bomb units that had become the 5th Bomb Wing in January were reinforced in March by the arrival of the new 99th Bomb Group.

The 301st Bomb Group ran into some sharp action on March 22 when they hit the docks at Palermo, Sicily. They were attacked by German fighters before they got to the target, but the enemy did little damage. As the 301st B-17s went over the target, the flak was accurate, but the Flying Fortresses dropped their bombs right on target. As they moved along after bombs away, the entire formation was rocked by a tremendous explosion. Their bombs had hit an ammunition ship.

As the 301st came off the target, they were hit by fighters once more. One Fortress had a fire going and Lt. James Hair's aircraft was hit in the fuel tanks. Fire immediately broke out, and his aircraft exploded at 19,000ft. Lt. Harbour Middleton's aircraft had been hard hit by fighters and knocked out of formation. Another Fortress then did a 360 degree circle and let down to protect him. This would later become a court-martial offense—to break formation to help a friend.

Middleton managed to limp in with his damaged aircraft, another example of excellence in B-17 design and construction. Two of the B-17's engines were out, but the amazing thing was that the fire from the fighters had severed the aircraft's right wing spar as well as its main longitudinal girder.

The 301st Bomb Group flew an outstanding mission on April 6. Thirty-three B-17s were airborne to attack a convoy fifteen miles off Bizerte, Tunisia. One aircraft aborted the mission, but the balance successfully dropped their bombs from 9,000 to 12,000ft. Those at the lower altitude met heavy flak and were attacked by twenty to thirty Bf 109s. Two Fortresses were heavily damaged and nine crew members were wounded. One of the wounded crewmen was responsible for the great success of the mission. Lt. Hyman Goldberg was hit by flak shortly before the bomb run. Although in great pain, he had a fellow crewman brace him so he could man his bombsight and release the bombs. His bomb run was highly successful: a 6,000–8,000-ton ship took a direct hit and blew up, and another vessel was left in flames. For the outstanding success of the entire mission, the 301st Bomb Group was awarded a Distinguished Unit Citation

The 301st and the 97th Bomb Groups teamed up on April 10 to attack two 10,000-ton Italian cruisers, the *Gorizia* and the *Trieste*, which were anchored at the port of La Maddalena, Sicily. Sixty B-17s set out to bomb the ships and hit them with 1,000lb bombs from 19,000ft. The 301st got twenty hits on the *Trieste*, and the ship quickly sank. The 97th Bomb Group got good hits on the *Gorizia,* but with its 9in armor, it was only damaged.

In April, the 5th Bomb Wing was joined by the 2nd Bomb Group which further increased the Flying Fortress strength in the Mediterranean. The 2nd Group would fly its first mission on May 3, 1943.

As the Allied ground forces forced the Afrikakorps to retreat into Tunisia, the Allied air forces cut off the German supplies coming from Sicily and Italy. The Fortresses continued to pound the ports, destroying the supplies that the enemy needed so badly.

Also targeted by the Fortresses were the airfields in Sicily, Sardinia, and Italy. On March 31 the 97th Bomb Group bombed Decimomannu and Nonserrato airfields in Sicily. In a 30 minute running battle with enemy fighters, the bomber crew claimed nine destroyed while no bombers were lost. More than one hundred enemy aircraft had been destroyed on the ground at Decimomannu. Gen. Carl Spaatz flew along on the mission as an observer.

The last African target was struck on May 5, when the Fortresses bombed the port of Tunis. German flak was still

B-17s of the 97th Bomb Group in heavy flak. The vee formations of the Fifteenth were unlike those of the Eighth Air Force. USAAF

strong, and a number of the B-17s were damaged. However, heavy damage was done to the docks, and eight small craft were sunk.

The bombing campaign against Sicily got under way on May 9, when 140 B-17s, making up the bulk of the attackers, bombed the docks at Palermo. Not only was the flak heavy and intense, but the bombers were attacked by a variety of fighters as they came off the target. No Fortresses were lost, but many of them came home with flak damage.

The B-17s nearly got Field Marshal Erwin Rommel on May 11, when they bombed Marsala, Sicily. Rommel was wounded and his aide was killed. A large number of German troops were also killed in the attack. Luftwaffe fighters intercepted the American bombers, and both the 2nd and 97th Bomb Groups lost two B-17s.

On May 25, strikes began against Messina, Sicily, on the eastern terminus of the island, which was only a few miles from the Italian mainland. Most of the flak guns that had been withdrawn from North Africa had set up at Messina, and it was the most heavily defended city in the Mediterranean at that time. It was later learned that on one of the bombing raids on Messina, the Italian cargo-carrying submarine *Romolo* was destroyed.

The Flying Fortresses were also striking at targets in Italy during this period. On May 28, a bombing mission to Leghorn sunk the Italian cruiser *Bari*. At the same time, the 99th Bomb Group hit an oil storage tank, which sent smoke rising to 10,000ft.

On June 5, the 5th Bomb Wing went after the remnants of the Italian fleet in the harbor at La Spezia, Italy. The battleships *Littorio* and *Roma* were both damaged, and the *Vittorio Veneto* was severely damaged. Although the flak was heavy and intense, none of the B-17s were shot down.

The 5th Bomb Wing continued to pound all the Axis airfields in the area in preparation for the invasion of Sicily. However, before the latter could be accomplished, the island of Pantelleria had to be neutralized. This small, rocky island was fortified with an airfield and some coastal guns that could be a real thorn in the side of an invasion fleet if they were not taken out. In the air efforts to knock Pantelleria out of the war, the B-17 groups flew 679 sorties and dropped 2,000 tons of bombs on the island. On June 11, the Italian comman-

This 2nd Bomb Group B-17 is undergoing some major repairs in North Africa. USAAF

der of the island surrendered. This was the first time that any objective had been conquered by air power alone.

The B-17s continued striking at airfields and coastal gun emplacements on Sicily up to the day of the invasion on July 10, 1943. Even after the invasion, the Fortresses continued to pound the dock installations at Messina. They also bombed numerous targets in Italy during July, the most notable being the city of Rome. The San Lorenzo marshaling yards were the targets in a city where the bombardiers had to be most cautious to avoid civilian and religious areas.

While the Fortresses continued to fly missions supporting ground forces in Sicily the big question that arose at the end of the Sicilian campaign was, why were the B-17s not used more at the straits of Messina where the German

Army left the island to retreat to Italy? Thousands of fighter and medium bomber sorties were flown through the flak-riddled skies over the area, but B-17s flew only 121 sorties while 100,000 German troops and 10,000 vehicles escaped.

With the fall of Sicily on August 11, 1943, the Fortress groups began systematic bombing of primarily transportation centers in Italy in preparation for the invasion of Italy. The city of Foggia, which in due time would become the hub of Fortress airfields, was a primary target in the attempt to stop all rail traffic to the south.

Foggia was bombed by the 5th Bomb Wing on August 19, 1943. Extensive damage was done to transportation facilities, and the electric power station was knocked out.

A very successful mission was flown against Luftwaffe bases around Foggia on August 25. One hundred fifty P-38 Lightnings took off and set course to the east toward Greece. The Fortresses then

took off and began to gain altitude. The American mission planners knew that the Germans had to be fully alerted to an attack and would be preparing for takeoff. As the Lightnings, which had dropped down to less than 500ft to avoid radar detection, neared the coast of Greece, they turned and headed westward. Coming in with the sun at their backs, the P-38s came in strafing at minimum altitude in three waves. Destruction and chaos reigned! As flames rose and pandemonium predominated, the Fortresses arrived and dropped their bombs. As a result of the mission at least forty-seven Luftwaffe aircraft were destroyed, many Luftwaffe pilots were killed or wounded, and a large number of ground installation targets were destroyed.

The bomber crews of the 5th Bomb Wing were aware that the invasion of Italy was imminent, particularly after they were briefed to bomb the headquarters of Field Marshal Albert Kesselring, the German commander in Italy, on the morning of September 8. One hundred and thirty B-17s bombed the headquarters at Frascati, a city east of Rome. The Luftwaffe rose to challenge the Fortresses, but the bombing caused great damage and the loss to the B-17 force was minimal.

Two hours after the bombers returned to their bases in North Africa it was confirmed that the US Fifth Army under the command of Gen. Mark Clark had invaded Italy at Salerno. Italy surrendered the same day, but the German forces fiercely defended the Italian peninsula.

The balance of the month of September 1943 saw the B-17s flying a number of tactical missions in support of the US Fifth Army. Bridges and troop concentrations were the primary targets. Heavy flak was still experienced around marshaling yards and other rail targets.

Several strategic missions were slated for the Fortresses in October, but most of them were not achieved because of bad weather. The bases in North Africa were mired in mud. When the bomber forces did get airborne, they experienced cloud-covered targets. The crews of the Mediterranean were not blessed with radar bombing aids, and their bombing attempts suffered.

Chapter 8

Fifteenth Air Force

On November 2, 1943, the four B-17 groups of the 5th Bomb Wing and two B-24 units of the Ninth Air Force were combined with two fighter groups from the Twelfth Air Force to form the new Fifteenth Air Force, which would become the strategic air force in the Mediterranean.

The new force wasted no time getting into action. On November 2, seventy-four B-17s and thirty-eight B-24s, escorted by seventy-two P-38s, set out on a 1,600-mile roundtrip to bomb the Messerschmitt factory at Wiener Neustadt, Austria. The Luftwaffe hit the first wave of bombers over the target with a force of eighty to one hundred fighters.

The second wave, composed of two B-17 groups, came in 45 minutes later. This formation was attacked by some forty-five enemy fighters. The concentrated attacks on the 301st Bomb Group cost them four B-17s. All went down in flames from the fury of the attacks, and all were from the 32nd Bomb Squadron. Two other B-17s were lost on the mission, but bombing results were good.

Two days later, ninety-five Fortresses set out to bomb the Bolzano Railroad Bridge. The formations encountered fighter attacks from some thirty-five to forty enemy fighters and lost five B-17s on the mission. Because of bad weather, only about one-third of the force bombed the bridge.

The rest of the month of November saw the Fortresses bomb targets in France, and a few missions were flown against tactical targets in Italy. The weather continued to be a big problem, and many aircraft had to abort most of their missions.

In December 1943, all of the Fortress groups moved from North Africa to Italy. Some of the moves were good; others resulted in mud problems that wouldn't be solved until January 1944.

A mission to attack the docks at Piraeus, Greece, on January 11 was marred by a tragic number of mid-air collisions. The weather was bad, limiting visibility to a few feet beyond the wing tips of the B-17s. The Fortresses of the 301st Bomb Group attempted to get some space between squadrons as they journeyed toward the target. At about that time, two B-17s from the 97th Bomb Group flew almost head-on into the 301st Group formation. One of them clipped the wing of the 301st leader's aircraft, apparently after having collided with another aircraft. One B-17 in the lead element exploded, as did two in the second element. Five B-17s from the 301st Group were lost as well as the two from the 97th Group.

The most miraculous escape was that of Sgt. James Raley, tail gunner on one of the affected aircraft. The tail was cut off Raley's B-17 in the collision and his tail section fluttered to earth, coming

to rest in a clump of pine trees. Raley was not fully aware of what had happened until he opened his bulkhead door. Of the forty-seven 301st crew members who were in the planes that collided, ten survived. Eight of them evaded capture in Greece and returned to Italy.

Sgt. Thomas Huffman, waist gunner in one of the 97th Group B-17s that was involved in the collisions, managed to get his parachute pack snapped on as the aircraft broke up. The chute had just opened when it came to rest in a tree. He and two others were picked up by Greek underground partisans and taken back to Italy. They were the only survivors of the two 97th Bomb Group Fortresses.

The Fifteenth Air Force flew an extraordinary mission on January 30. Fifth Bomb Wing Fortress formations took off to bomb Luftwaffe fields in the Udine area of northern Italy. They knew they would be picked up on radar and that the German forces would be getting ready to intercept. Meanwhile, sixty P-47s of the 325th Fighter Group took off and sped northward on the deck, hoping to slip into the fight undetected.

The Thunderbolts got in the midst of the German fighters just as they were getting airborne and claimed thirty-six aircraft shot down for the loss of two P-47s. At that moment the Fortresses swept over the four German airfields and bombed them, destroying another

eighty aircraft on the ground. Their escorting P-38s shot down eight enemy fighters for the loss of a single P-38. All total, the Americans claimed the destruction of 142 Luftwaffe aircraft for the loss of five B-17s and three fighters.

The Fortresses also had to do quite a bit of tactical bombing during late January 1944 to support the American landing at the Anzio beachhead in Italy.

The B-17s of the 5th Bomb Wing flew their initial mission in the controversial bombing of Monte Cassino, Italy, on February 15. While ground-force leaders were of the opinion that the Germans were using the Benedictine Monastery as an observation post, its military value was debatable, and there was much discussion about whether it was really necessary to destroy such a valuable religious shrine. Nevertheless, early that morning, four B-17 groups put 142 aircraft in the air and dropped 354 tons of bombs on the monastery. It was deemed that the destruction was absolute, but such was not the case. Most of the treasured items survived, and the Germans continued to occupy the premises for another two months.

For several months, Allied planners had wanted to put into effect a plan code-named "Argument" that would bring about coordinated strikes against German fighter production. The Eighth and Fifteenth Air Forces would strike at the enemy's facilities by day and the RAF by night. Finally, planners were informed that beginning about February 19, the Continent should enjoy a few days of good weather.

As mentioned previously, these strikes in late February 1944 became known as Big Week. The RAF started things off on the night of February 19–20 when they struck targets at Leipzig, Germany. The following day the Eighth Air Force hit targets in the Leipzig area while the Fifteenth Air Force was scheduled to bomb Regensburg. Once more, weather got in the pic-

B-17 from the 342nd Bomb Squadron, 97th Bomb Group arrives in Russia on the first shuttle mission. USAAF

ture as the Fifteenth was forced to abort the mission. The most difficult obstacle for the Fifteenth in bombing Germany and Austria was getting over the Alps.

The Fifteenth got in on the act on February 22 when they got through to Regensburg. Liberators made up the first wave, and they absorbed the bulk of the Luftwaffe attacks. The Fortresses came in on the second wave, but only the

This 2nd Bomb Group Fortress came home with its radio room all but missing. USAAF

Welcome to Vienna. This target's defenses were second only to Berlin's. A Fifteenth Air Force Fortress challenges the barrage. US-AAF

97th and 301st Bomb Groups were able to bomb the primary target. Five Fortresses were lost on the mission.

On February 23, the B-17s were turned back because of weather, but all forces were up in strength the following day. The Fifteenth Air Force launched 151 Fortresses, along with 172 escorting fighters to attack the Daimler-Puch aircraft component plant at Steyr, Austria. Once more, weather got in the picture

and a number of the bombers were forced to abort. Rendezvous with the escorting fighters didn't come off either, and the Fortresses paid the price.

Only eighty-seven B-17s from three groups got through to Steyr and dropped 261 tons of bombs. More than one hundred German fighters intercepted the bombers. The 97th Bomb Group led the way to the target and dropped its bombs to good effect. The 2nd Bomb Group came under attack at 1215 hours at about twenty miles north-northwest of Fiume, Italy, and the attack continued for an hour. Then some P-38s arrived and the Luftwaffe left, but not before the 2nd had taken tremendous losses. Four-

teen of their B-17s fell to the attackers.

The 2nd Group historian recorded: "The attacks were made all around the clock, high, low and level and came in as close as fifty yards, singly, in pairs, four, six and eight at a time, using V-formations as well as abreast formations. Some of the twin-engine fighters stayed out of range and fired rockets, after which they came in for an attack, while other single engine fighters dropped aerial bombs. One group of fighters would attack, after which they would go out of range, re-form and come back in. In the meantime the other groups of fighters would be attacking, so there was a continuous attack on the bomber formation.

They picked on the second wave and literally picked them off like ducks. The only time the attacks let up at all was while the bombers were going through flak . . . Enemy pilots were experienced and aggressive."

The 429th Bomb Squadron of the 2nd Group was spared, probably because it was in the lead. The 20th Bomb Squadron lost two planes, the 49th Bomb Squadron lost seven, and the 96th Bomb Squadron lost five. The 97th Bomb Group got out unscathed and the

301st Bomb Group lost three Fortresses on the mission.

February 25 marked the last day of Big Week, and on that day the Fifteenth Air Force went back to Regensburg. The 2nd and 99th Bomb Groups led the Fortresses, followed by the 301st and the 97th Bomb Groups. The Fortresses had trouble with the weather from the time they formed up. The formations passed low over the Adriatic Sea, and enemy ships in the area reported their presence. Before the bombers reached

Crewmen have just exited a Fortress over the aircraft factory at Wiener Neustadt, a part of the Vienna, Austria, complex. USAAF

their target, they spotted the Luftwaffe force at seven o'clock. The enemy fighters immediately went after two straggling bombers, and then concentrated their fury on the 301st Bomb Group. Well over a hundred fighters began their attack near Fiume, Italy, and came in from astern in waves of up to twenty air-

craft. These fighters were responsible for all of the thirteen Fortresses lost by the 301st Bomb Group on the mission. Most of the unfortunate bombers were hit in the engines, starting fires from which a number of the aircraft exploded, or causing them to straggle from the formation where they were pounced upon and finished off.

One Fortress managed to make it back to Anzio beachhead, where it ditched just offshore. Another B-17 managed to make it home even though it had suffered an engine fire and other extensive damage in addition to having six of the crew bail out.

The 2nd Bomb Group, which had suffered such severe losses the previous day, had only been able to put up ten B-17s for the mission, but they struggled through even though they lost three of their number to German fighters.

This mission ended Big Week. There had been considerable damage done to the German fighter aircraft industry, but at most only a few weeks' production was lost. Perhaps the most damage was done to their existing fighter force. German records indicate that during Big Week, 198 single-engine fighters had been lost.

Weather continued to hinder Fifteenth Air Force bomber operations in March 1944, and most of the missions were tactical attacks against rail targets. The B-17s did fly a hotly opposed mission on the eighteenth of the month when they went after the airfields in the Udine area of northern Italy. Over forty enemy fighters came up to intercept the bombers, and they managed to down seven of the Fortresses. Assessment of the bombing indicated that at least fifty enemy aircraft had been destroyed on the ground.

The 5th Bomb Wing was reinforced in the spring of 1944 with the arrival of two additional B-17 groups: the 463rd and 483rd Bomb Groups. The 463rd Bomb Group flew its first mission on

Operations from Italian bases were very dusty and the steel-planking runways didn't help the situation. Here a B-17 from the 99th Bomb Group kicks up the dust. USAAF

March 30, 1944, and the 483rd Bomb Group flew its initial mission on April 12, 1944. This gave the 5th Bomb Wing a total of six groups with which to attack strategic targets.

The month of April saw a number of Fortresses bomb the ball-bearing plant at Steyr, Austria. Through an operations slip-up, the 97th Bomb Group lead aircraft pilot and group commander, Col. Frank Allen, flew the mission without a copilot. The mission was successful, but the 97th lost three B-17s in a running fight with enemy fighters. This mission also marked the first use by the Fifteenth Air Force of the tinfoil strips known as window to confuse enemy radar.

The mission to Gyor, Hungary, on April 13 developed into a most unusual event for the 97th Bomb Group. Lt. Lawrence G. Moore returned from the mission alone, his crew having bailed out over enemy territory. It all began when a short circuit in the electrical system started a fire in the oxygen system. With smoke filling the aircraft and all the fire extinguishers expended, Moore assessed the situation and called for his crew to bail out. Ammunition was exploding and the men needed no urging. Moore had headed the aircraft back toward the Adriatic Sea and put it on autopilot after the last of his crew abandoned the B-17. When Moore dropped down by the nose hatch to depart, he saw the cause of the fire and pulled the oxygen line away from an arc of fire and

Sunny Italy and a 463rd Bomb Group Fortress at rest on its hardstand. Ethell

the flames subsided. Although his hands were severely burned, Moore went back up on the flight deck and began to run through the controls to see if the fire would continue to diminish. As the fire continued to wane, Moore settled down in the cockpit and headed out over the Adriatic, hoping no fighters would show up. From this point he only had one problem: he needed to transfer some fuel. So he put the Fortress back on autopilot, went back in the bomb bay, made the transfer, and went back to the cockpit to fly the aircraft in to Bari, Italy.

B-17 from the 97th Bomb Group showing considerable wing damage from flak. USAAF

At long last, the 5th Bomb Wing put radar bombing into effect on April 15. From the amount of oil smoke that penetrated the cloud cover over Ploesti, Romania, there could be no doubt that some of the oil refineries and storage facilities had been hit using the new Mickey aircraft.

A mission to Wiener Neustadt, Austria, on May 10 cost the 97th Bomb Group its commander, Col. Jacob E. Smart. The B-17 in which he was flying took a direct flak hit in the bomb bay and exploded. The loss of the lead aircraft on the bomb run caused a poor bombing pattern. Several other group Fortresses were seriously damaged, but no more were downed.

Also on the mission was the 463rd Bomb Group, which was attacked by forty to fifty German fighters just as it

came off the bomb run. There had been good fighter escort up to the initial point for the bomb run, but as they came off the run, there was no escort. The gunners of the new Fortress group put up quite a fight, but seven of their B-17s were shot down.

The 463rd Bomb Group was hard hit again on May 18, but not before they bombed their target. They were the only group from the 5th Bomb Wing that was not stopped by the weather that day, and they successfully bombed the Romano-Americano oil refinery at Ploesti using Pathfinder aircraft. Five minutes after bombing the target, about a hundred enemy fighters attacked and engaged the B-17s in a running fight for over 15 minutes before the P-38 escort arrived on the scene. Seven of the Fortresses fell victim to the Luftwaffe fighters.

During June 1944 the 301st Bomb Group tried its hand at AZON, or "Azimuth only," bombing. The AZON technique made use of radio-controlled 1,000lb bombs that could be steered in to the target—sort of a primitive version of today's "smart" bombs. The plane carried a radio control box, a radio receiver, and an antenna. The bombs were equipped with a set of ailerons on the tail fins, a gyro stabilizer, and a flare. A few seconds after the bomb dropped, a flare fired from the tail of the bomb, enabling the bombardier to follow it down. The gyros were designed to keep the bomb from rolling while the bombardier controlled the path of the bomb with a radio control box mounted next to the bomb sight.

Six aircraft and crews that had been trained in the use of the AZON bomb joined the 301st Bomb Group in April of 1944. These crews would fly a number of missions with the group from April through July, but the bombs were never as accurate as their designers hoped they would be. There were a few successes on bridges and viaducts, but not enough to warrant full-scale use of the weapon. It was finally decided that the weapon would work better from medium altitudes, so the program was turned over to B-25 units.

On the morning of June 2, 1944, three groups from the 5th Bomb Wing—the 2nd, the 97th, and the 99th—took off on their first shuttle mission to Russia. Flying in the lead 97th Group aircraft was Gen. Ira C. Eaker, commander of the Mediterranean Allied Air Forces. Lockheed Lightnings provided escort to the bombers that bombed Debreczen, Hungary, en route. No flak or fighters were experienced, but the ceiling continually decreased as the force flew eastward. By the time the Fortresses arrived at Poltava, Russia, rain was coming down steadily.

The Americans were treated royally by the Russians during their stay at

This 463rd Bomb Group B-17 lost its entire nose to flak over the target, but continued to fly for a short while before going down. USAAF

Poltava. General Eaker was rushed off to Moscow to report on the mission, but his men couldn't have been treated better. There was ample food and drink, and the Russians even put on a couple of musical shows for the aviators.

On the morning of June 11, the Americans took off on their return to Italy. More than one hundred B-17s bombed the airfield at Facsani near Bucharest, Romania, where a number of enemy aircraft were destroyed on the ground. One 97th Bomb Group B-17 was lost to enemy fighters when it lost an engine and couldn't keep up with the formation.

As summer continued, the primary target for the Fifteenth Air Force was the oil refinery complex at Ploesti, Romania. Defenses for the area constantly increased. By the end of the campaign against the complex, it possessed 558 guns and more than 2,000 smoke generators that were capable of covering the entire area in less than 40 minutes.

The raid on Ploesti of June 23 included all six groups of B-17s from the 5th Bomb Wing. The defenses were put into action promptly. Forty-plus single-engine fighters hit the Fortress formation before they arrived at the target area. When the bombers did get to the complex, it was covered with smoke and the flak barrage was hot and heavy.

A 97th Bomb Group Fortress flown by Lt. Edwin O. Anderson took a direct

117

A 2nd Bomb Group B-17 gets airborne in Foggia, Italy. Ethell

hit in the right wing while on the bomb run, shattering the control surfaces and ripping a fuel tank loose. The bomb run was completed with one engine out. As the B-17 emerged from the flak, it was immediately pounced on by enemy fighters. The tail gunner, Sgt. Michael J. Sullivan, was wounded by a 20mm shell that ripped through his position.

Sullivan's intercom was out, so he crawled up to the waist where the gunners picked him up and took him into the radio room. There Lt. David R. Kingsley, the bombardier, administered

first aid. As Sullivan recalled: "I was pretty banged up, and my chute harness was ripped off by 20mm cannon shells, and as I was in a daze and shocked, I couldn't see what was going on in the ship. I crawled out of the tail after I was hit. My waist gunners gave me first aid but couldn't stop the flow of blood that was coming from my right shoulder. They called up Lieutenant Kingsley and he gave me a tourniquet to stop the flow of blood.

"Finally the blood was stopped, but I was pretty weak. So then Kingsley saw that my parachute harness was ripped, so he took his off and put it on me. As I was laying in the radio room, he told me that everything was going to be all right

as we had two P-51s escorting us back to our base. We were still about 500 miles from home and the ship was pretty badly shot up. Finally, our escorts, the P-51s, were running low on fuel, so they told our pilot that they would have to leave and asked if we could make it. Our pilot thought he could and they left.

"As soon as they were gone, we were then attacked by eight Bf 109s who came out of the sun and started making passes at us. Finally, after about a fifteen-minute fight, we were told by the pilot to get ready to bail out as our ship was pretty well shaking apart in the air and most of our guns were knocked out. You see, that was the third group of enemy fighters to hit us that day.

A head-on view of Fortresses outbound from their Italian bases to bomb a target in the Balkans. USAAF

"As soon as the bail-out bell was given, the rest of the gunners bailed out. Lieutenant Kingsley then took me in his arms and struggled to the bomb bay where he told me to keep my hand on the ripcord and said to pull it when I was clear of the ship. Then he told me to bail out. I watched the ground go by for a few seconds and then I jumped. Before I jumped, I looked up at him and the look he had on his face was firm and solemn. He must have known what was coming because there was no fear in his eyes at all. That was the last time I saw Kingsley, standing in the bomb bay."

Kingsley ran into copilot Lieutenant Symons as he went forward in the bomb bay. He asked where the pilot was, and went forward to the flight deck. As Symons bailed out he almost hit Lieutenant Anderson, who had just bailed out the nose hatch. Perhaps Kingsley was searching for a spare parachute that should have been aboard. The men parachuting downward then noted the weird maneuvers of their Fortress. Anderson thinks that Kingsley did his best to try to crash-land the B-17, but with only one engine going it proved to be too much for him. At last, it corkscrewed into the earth.

For his self-sacrifice, Lieutenant Kingsley was posthumously awarded the Medal of Honor.

The 5th Bomb Wing attacked Memmingen airdrome on July 18, 1944. Because of bad weather forty-four B-17s aborted the mission and twenty-seven others hit a railroad bridge in Italy on the way home. Only seventy-nine Fortresses hit the primary target. The 483rd Bomb Group arrived at Memmingen alone and went on to bomb the airdrome there, which was a center of jet fighter production. An overpowering force of some 125 German fighters attacked them while the fighter escort had to take on another 100. In a 20 minute fight all the way to the initial point, fourteen 483rd Fortresses were shot down. The remaining twelve went on to bomb the target.

B-17s from the 483rd Bomb Group with gear down for landing return from another mission over the Balkans. USAAF

Two shiny Fortresses from the 99th Bomb Group over the snow-capped Alps. The mountain beauty disguised a mighty obstacle that the bombers had to challenge. USAAF

The 5th Bomb Wing went after the aircraft factory at Wiener Neudorf on July 26, and everything went wrong for the 301st Group. For some reason, the fighter escort didn't make the rendezvous, but seventy-five to one hundred enemy fighters showed up prior to the initial point. The enemy continued to attack even while the Fortresses were on the bomb run. As they came off the run, the B-17s encountered a huge cloud that only served to spread the formation. As the bombers broke out of the cloud, the fighters hit again. The 301st lost eleven B-17s in the fight.

Most of the Fortresses went down in flames, and there was one mid-air collision. Of the 109 crew members who went down that day, forty-six survived.

The Fifteenth Air Force shifted its mission emphasis on August 12 to preparing for the invasion of southern France. On that day it sent all of its heavy bombers to strike gun positions. On the following day, another strike was mounted. The invasion came on August 15, and the 5th Bomb Wing was assigned targets along the beach between the Toulon and Cannes.

A very successful mission was flown to Ploesti on August 18. The target was the Romano-Americano refinery. The German defenders put their smoke generators to work, and it was originally thought that the target would be covered. The wind shifted, however, and the smoke dissipated, allowing the 97th Bomb Group, which led the mission, to hit the target dead center. Only three B-17s were lost on the mission, but the

B-17s from the 97th Bomb Group on the way to strike marshaling yards at Linz, Austria. Most welcome is the presence of the contrailing P-38s above them. USAAF

A B-17 from the 483rd Bomb Group goes down in flames over the target in Yugoslavia. USAAF

123

bombers left oil smoke towering up above 15,000ft.

August 19 marked the last mission to Ploesti. Soviet forces occupied the area on August 22. From April 5 through August 19, the 5th Bomb Wing hit Ploesti a total of fifteen times. The Fortresses flew 1,774 effective sorties against the targets there and lost forty-five B-17s.

The 2nd Bomb Group had a rough mission to Morovaka, Czechoslovakia, on August 29. The Luftwaffe caught their formation when the escort was not there and downed nine of the Fortresses. The entire 20th Bomb Squadron went down on this raid.

The 5th Wing went to Blechhammer North at Gleiwitz, Germany, oil refineries on September 13, and the 97th Bomb Group received its highest loss for one day when heavy, intense flak hit the lead aircraft at bombs away: Five Fortresses were lost and one was so badly damaged that it had to land on the island of Vis off the coast of Yugoslavia on the way home. Altogether, ten B-17s fell to the very accurate Blechhammer flak batteries.

In October, the 5th Bomb Wing started sending out "lone wolf" missions. These consisted of small numbers of aircraft for night raids on various strategic targets. These Pathfinder radar-equipped Fortresses primarily were to serve as nuisance raiders more than anything else. They kept the enemy flak forces at their posts, and kept civilians in air raid shelters through a great portion of the night. During 627 bomber sorties by the Fifteenth Air Force to the end of the war, seventeen bombers were lost, which was a rather high percentage, particularly for the damage they did. Very few sorties of this type were flown in 1945.

Bad winter weather took its toll of mission days during January and February 1945. Most of the missions that were flown during this period were tactical strikes in Italy. The strategic missions got going again in March with missions to Austria, Germany, and Hungary. A mission to Ruhland, Germany, got a heated response from the Luftwaffe, which cost the 483rd Bomb Group six B-17s.

On March 24, 1945, the 5th Bomb Wing went all the way to Berlin. One hundred sixty-nine B-17s, escorted by 289 fighters, made the long trip, and the Fortresses dropped their bombs on the Daimler-Benz tank works. A number of Messerschmitt Me 262 jets were seen on the mission, and one Fortress fell to the guns of a jet. All total, nine B-17s did not return from the mission, which ran over nine hours.

The Third Reich was on its last legs, and Allied air power dominated the German skies. By April, the B-17s of the 5th Bomb Wing had just about run out of targets. The majority of their strikes were tactical missions to northern Italy in support of ground troops.

The Fifteenth Air Force—an outfit that the Eighth Air Force had called "minor leaguers"—had done a "major league job" on the targets in southern Europe. The Fifteenth made great strides in knocking out Axis oil production by their attacks on the Ploesti complex, as well as the attacks on Blechhammer and other synthetic-oil targets. The aircraft factories of Regensburg and Vienna felt the full fury of their bombs while targets such as Budapest, Munich, and Brux were also on the Fifteenth's strike list. Additionally, they had a big job to perform in doing the tactical bombing of many targets in Italy, France, and in the Mediterranean as a whole. Regardless of the task, the B-17 Flying Fortress had done its job as well in the south as it had in flying from England.

Chapter 9

Shot Down–A Personal Remembrance

"Time to go." The most dreaded words that could come to a bomber crew member were spoken in the darkness of an Italian morning. It meant that I had to crawl out from under mosquito netting and join my fellow gunners sitting on the edge of the folding cots that graced our pyramidal tent home. An early morning cigarette was ritual before we gathered our flying gear from under the cots and stumbled along toward the lights that marked the entrance to the mess kitchen.

Once we had picked over the "rubberized" pancakes with the watery ersatz syrup and downed a welcome, warm cup of coffee, we went out to board the trucks that would take us down to the group headquarters area for briefing. We were still relatively new members of the 340th Bomb Squadron of the 97th Bomb Group. We had only joined this historic unit in early August 1944, but we had really flown our rear off in the few weeks since arrival. My first two missions had been to the oil refineries at Ploesti, Romania, so I knew that we definitely were in for no picnic in this theater of operations.

As we sat and squirmed in the smoke-filled briefing room, we anxiously stared at the covered map on the platform, wondering what our destination would be. A loud "Ten-Hut!" brought the room to attention, and "At ease" brought thuds of bodies dropping their rears

back on the noisy steel stools that once had been a part of bomb cases.

The Fifteenth Air Force was in the midst of an oil campaign, so it was not surprising that when the cover was pulled from the map, the long red cord stretched near its limit to come to rest far up in the northeastern quadrant. "Men, your target for today is the Blechhammer South synthetic oil refinery near Gleiwitz, Germany," stated our group commander, Col. Nils Ohman. "This is another important oil target, and it is imperative that we knock it out." Further briefing went over routes, weather, possible enemy fighters, and I recall something more clearly having to do with "intense and accurate flak."

Following briefing, we boarded the truck once more and were taken to the equipment shack where we picked up our heated suits and parachutes. I recall being most chagrined over the fact that my nice, new parachute pack for my chest harness was not given to me. Instead, I was given a pack that was rather dirty and showed signs of abuse. Instead of arguing with the man behind the counter, I figured what the heck, I won't need it anyway. Little did I know!

We then trucked out to our individual aircraft. We were once again deposited on the hardstand of a shiny B-17G known only by the last three digits of its serial number "166." We did not have assigned aircraft in our unit; we

flew in whatever aircraft was assigned to us. However, we had been trying to get a mission in on 166 for two days prior to this September 13, 1944, meeting. On September 11 we got off in it. Once we were airborne, our assigned copilot became quite ill, and we were forced to bring him back to base. The following day we reported to 166, only to have the mission canceled because of bad weather over the target area.

On this particular morning, all seemed to be going well. I wiped down and checked out my waist gun, plus one of the cheek guns and one of the chin turret guns in the nose. Other little chores were taken care of, and there was time for a last smoke before we boarded the aircraft for taxying. Engines were started, and one by one the Fortresses in the area began to pull out on the steel taxi strips and begin the procession of roaring engines and screeching brakes as they maneuvered toward the end of the runway.

As we moved along, suddenly there was a blowing of a horn alongside, and we noted the operations officer in his jeep was signaling us to stop. As we braked to a stop, a man jumped from the jeep and ran to the waist door. We opened the door and let him in. He told our radio operator to go with the operations officer. Our radio operator had been reassigned to the lead aircraft at the last moment, and we were brought

The author's crew just before departing Drew Field, Florida, for Italy. Their fates in combat are in parentheses. Front row, from left: Lt. Bruce Knoblock, pilot (POW); Lt. Glen Tiffany, co-pilot (completed combat tour); Lt. Lee Cooning, navigator (POW with another crew); Lt. W. "Ted" Hill, bombardier (KIA with another crew). Back row, from left: Sgt. Olis Henley, tail gunner (POW); Sgt. V. D. Smith, radio operator (KIA with another crew); Sgt. Roy McFaddin, ball turret gunner (POW); Sgt. Walter Brand, engineer-gunner (POW); Sgt. William Hess, waist gunner (POW). Not in photo: Sgt. Charles Collar, waist gunner (POW).

The telegram that was sent to the author's father when he was missing in action.

the radio operator from the spare aircraft. This last-minute switch was to cost our radio operator his life.

Once we were airborne, we began to jockey for position in the formation. We were flying deputy lead in the squadron, which put us on the leader's right wing. We began our long climb to altitude and headed out over the Adriatic Sea. At 12,000ft, we went on oxygen and tested our guns. I pulled the charging handle a couple of times and triggered a short burst aimed down at the sea. The aircraft vibrated as the various guns were fired and the smell of gun powder permeated the air.

The trip to Blechhammer was a long one, and once over enemy territory, our visual sweep of the skies became more intense. After a time I sighted contrails high above us. As they came closer, I could recognize the silhouettes of P-51 Mustangs, our escort. There was certainly nothing more beautiful to bomber crew members than the essing flight maneuvers of four "Little Friends" against a beautiful blue sky. I often wondered how such a beautiful setting could preface a scene of death and destruction.

After a time, the contrails of our Little Friends turned away and we knew that we must be about to reach the initial point of our bomb run. As the aircraft in our formation maneuvered into position for bombing, I heard someone over the intercom say, "Target dead ahead. Damn, look at that flak." I turned off the power to my heated suit so all available electrical current could go to the bombsight and associated circuits. Although it was probably forty degrees below zero outside, sweat always seemed to pop out and my mouth became very dry. I snapped on my quilted steel flak vest, plopped the steel flak helmet down on top of my flying helmet, and set my eyes on the lead aircraft as its bomb bay opened. As soon as the lead plane dropped its bombs ours would go, too.

The flak was there, very intense and right in on us. It seemed that we were in a cloud of black puffs that were drawing closer all the time. There was a sinister beauty in these explosions against the sky—until you knew what they could do. Tensely, I glued my eyes to the lead ship and thought, it has to be any second now. Wham! "What the hell?" I cried out, and felt myself falling. The next moment, I found myself on the floor and

FIFTEENTH AIR FORCE
Office of the Commanding General
A. P. O 520

19 October 1944

Mr. Cas G. Hess
Box 638
Laurel, Mississippi

Dear Mr. Hess:

I regret to inform you that Sergeant William N. Hess, 18210045, has been missing in action since September 13, 1944, when the B-17 on which he was an aerial gunner failed to return from a daylight bombing mission to Blechhammer, Germany.

After successfully reaching the target intense and accurate anti-aircraft fire was encountered the result of which disabled Bill's aircraft. Only two parachutes emerged from the descending bomber. I sincerely hope that Bill was able to bail out. You may be sure that if additional information about him is received it will be forwarded to you promptly by The Adjutant General, Washington, D. C.

Bill has done a commendable job while he was with this air force. In recognition of his capable participation in operational flights he has been awarded the Air Medal. His many friends here wish me to extend deep sympathy to his family at this time.

Very sincerely yours,

N. F. TWINING
Major General, USA
Commanding

The letter that always followed up the missing status from the Fifteenth Air Force commanding general.

Fortress from 340th Bomb Squadron, 97th Bomb Group. USAAF

heard a hissing noise somewhere above me. Had we blown up? I was in a daze and everything seemed smoky or foggy. Slowly, I pulled myself up.

I looked at my side of the waist, which was a shambles; the plexiglass was gone, above the window was a large hole that a man could stick his head through, and two more holes were in the armor plate below the window. All around the window were a score of holes through the aluminum skin. Then as I looked above, I saw that the hissing was

coming from an oxygen line that had been shot out. My steel helmet was on the floor with a dent in it big enough for my fist, and as I looked down in front of me, some of the steel plates from the flak vest fell on the floor. The canvas holding it together was shredded.

I looked out the window, and the scene was one of devastation. There were still black blotches of flak everywhere. The wing of a B-17 fluttered down with both propellers still turning. Several parachutes drifted down through the flak and debris. Then I looked at our wing and got a real sinking feeling in the pit of my stomach. The number one engine had taken a direct

hit. The propeller looked as if it had been in a crash-landing, with all three blades bent back. The number two engine had taken a hit in the oil tank and the wing was covered with oil. The wing, itself, was full of holes and fuel streamed back in a white vapor.

We started to make big circles in the sky, losing altitude. The other waist gunner looked at me in dismay. He later told me that he looked at me on the waist floor and wouldn't look back, for he knew I had to be dead. The ball turret gunner was out of his turret and the tail gunner came forward. The latter reported that we had a hit in the tail and apparently some of the control cables were ripped apart in the rear. Our skipper, Lt. Bruce Knoblock, desperately tried to set a course south for Romania, which had just been overrun by the Russians, but he didn't have the controls to do so.

Then came the words "you walk back from this one." The copilot was sent back to see that the rear of the aircraft was cleared. One by one, the gunners went out the fuselage door. They told me to snap on my pack and bail out. Still in a daze, I went over and sat down on it. They got me up and in the door. I looked down at my ankles and then I was out. Don't know if I jumped or was pushed, but I have always figured the latter was probably true.

There was one thing about it: there was no sensation of falling. I remember seeing the aircraft going away from me and I pulled the ripcord. What a shock. As I swung under the canopy, I began to think, this isn't really so bad. Then, the risers popped up on me, hitting me under the chin, and I thought I had fallen out of the harness. Now, that was scary.

As I swung down, I began to see people running around on the ground. Then, TWANG! Hell, somebody was shooting at me. I looked and saw the parachutes of my other crew members now and noted where my friend, the engineer-gunner Sgt. Walter Brand, was coming down and planned to try to join him. Then all of a sudden the ground seemed to be coming up fast, and I was

falling right into a tree. I went crashing down the side of a large tree, taking off several limbs on one side before my canopy caught in the tree. I wound up like a kid in a swing, with my heels barely touching the ground. I couldn't have planned such an easy landing.

I got out of the harness, took off my flying boots, and put on my GI shoes, which I always tied on my harness ring. I was in a small patch of woods, so I got down in a ditch and covered my Mae West life preserver and my boots under some leaves. Cautiously moving in the woods, I came to a sudden stop when I heard a terrific roar. As I looked up I saw two Focke-Wulf 190s roar overhead. They were out looking for us in our crippled B-17. As I moved along once more, I heard TWANG! I was still getting shot at. I hugged the bottom of a ditch and moved along cautiously. Finally, I came to a road. Across it was about 100 yards of open field, but beyond that was a virtual forest. If I had been able to get into the forest , perhaps I could have evaded.

I waited a few minutes in a ditch alongside the road and decided I would make a run for it. Warily, I stepped out on the road and when I was about halfway across I heard TWANG! TWANG! I looked to my right and there, just coming around a bend in the road from the patch of woods that I had left, came three German soldiers, two with rifles and one with a machine pistol. For me, the war was over.

When these pictures were made at gunnery school, they jokingly were referred to as "MIA photos." Many of them became just that. USAAF

Chapter 10

Prisoner of War–A Personal Remembrance

Stalag Luft IV, where over 9,000 aerial gunners from the Eighth and Fifteenth Air Forces were held.

Following my capture by German troops, I learned more of the fate of my crew and the final status of our aircraft. I was taken to a cluster of buildings that housed the German headquarters of some sort of armored unit. When I was taken into one of offices, I was heartened to see the majority of my crew sitting there on the floor. The navigator who had been flying with us that day was quietly bleeding on the floor. He had been shot through the armpit coming down in his parachute. The Germans claimed that they thought we were Russian paratroops coming down!

That night we were taken to a German air base in Krakow, Poland. There we spent three days up on the third story of a building overlooking the airfield.

It was quite unusual to observe enemy Messerschmitt 109s and Focke-Wulf 190s leaving the field early in the morning to fly to advanced bases on the Eastern Front and then to return late in the evening. Somehow, the word must have gotten out about us, for many Poles came by our building late in the afternoon and would gaze up at us sitting in the windows and nod their heads.

The nine of us and four guards were taken down to the station one afternoon and put on a train going west. For several days we went across Germany, made a few changes, and observed many cities that had been heavily bombed. The one scare that we had was during a train change one afternoon. We were out on the platform with our guards when a German officer who was minus a leg came down to stare at us, and then the civilians began to stare at us. I got behind the big guard with the machine pistol and stayed there.

We arrived in Frankfurt, Germany, late one night and walked to Dulag Luft, which we were to learn was interrogation center for Allied aviators. There we were placed in solitary confinement cells that contained a cot and a stool and nothing else. I was so worn out that I slept the entire first day that I was there. It was only on the second day that I began to wonder if I would spend the rest of the war in the cell. We were given ersatz coffee in the morning and some black bread and margarine during the day, and that was about it.

Finally, on the third day, I was taken before the interrogator. When I told him only my name, rank, and serial number, he pulled out a large folder with 97th Bomb Group on the cover and began to tell me much more about the unit than I knew. He then wanted to know what a German boy like me was doing bombing the Fatherland. They had really hit the jackpot with the crew that I went down with; we had Hess, Knoblock, Wagge, Anderson, Brand (shortened from Brandt), and Henley.

Following that day, I was put in a regular stockade and reunited with my crew. The next day, we boarded a train that took us to another Dulag Luft, a transit camp. There we received a small POW kit that contained socks, underwear, toilet articles, and so on, which came through the Red Cross. We also got our first decent meal since capture.

Right after the meal, however, the air raid alarm sounded and Wetzler, the city near the camp, was bombed.

Late that afternoon, we enlisted men were gathered up for shipment out to a permanent camp. We bid our skipper good-by, and were taken down the road to Wetzler. Because of the bombing that day, we had a double guard, but the civilians were busy cleaning up and putting out the fires that were still burning. Rocks and curses came our way, and we had our first experience at being treated as "Luft Gangsters" and "Terror Fliegers." We were put in box cars, about thirty men on one end and four guards on the other, and told that we would be leaving that night. Meanwhile, rocks continued to bounce off the sides of the cars.

Our journey lasted four days and five nights, and we prayed for rain. Even though our cars were marked "POW" on the top, we were right behind the engine, and the balance of the train was made up of cars full of munitions going to the Eastern Front. We had the rails bombed out in front of us once, but fortunately ran into no strafing Allied fighters. Thank the Lord, he did let it rain on us most of the journey.

We traveled to Pomerania, in northeast Germany, and were unloaded at Grosstychow and taken to Stalag Luft IV. When we arrived, we were assembled before the headquarters building. When I looked up on the flagpole and saw the Nazi banner, the full realization came to me that I was a prisoner of the Third Reich. There was no mama, no papa, no Uncle Sam that was going to look after me in this place. From that day forward, the sight of the United States' "Old Glory" has had a special meaning for me.

Our stockade was not ready, so we were scattered in various barracks in A Lager. The room that I was placed in was filled with some of the oldest RAF prisoners in Germany. They were primarily sergeant pilots who had been shot down very early in the war. Before they came to Luft IV they had been in Luft VI, which was near Danzig. Here were men that had never seen a B-17 or B-24, from which most of the American POWs had exited.

After about a week or so, we were placed in the new stockade, C Lager. The barracks were large, prefabricated,

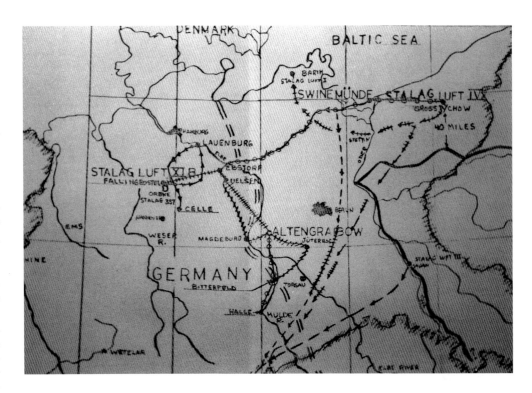

The top route, from Stalag Luft IV to Stalag XIB, was that followed by the author during his incarceration. O'Donnell

and not very well put together. We had about thirty men in each room and initially had no stove for heat and no bunks. We were issued one GI wool blanket and one German blanket. We had to team up with a partner to make a mattress consisting of the two German blankets stuffed with straw. We got no stove until the snow began to fly, and we got the bunks shortly before we had to evacuate the camp. Our German ration consisted of a bowl of kohlrabi soup at noon and a few boiled potatoes in the evening. These rations were supplemented by Red Cross parcels that were designed for a parcel a man per week. We got half parcels when I arrived at Luft IV, and this diminished to quarter parcels before we departed.

With little to do in the camp, we got to know our roommates real well. We soon knew their life histories, their ambitions, and their likes and dislikes. With the low-calorie diet, there was unbelievably little talk of females. The favorite pastime was listing menus of food the men wanted on their return home. All food was priced in cigarettes which were received in the Red Cross parcels. Most of us got about two packs a week.

The most exciting event we had in our room happened on a dark and cold winter evening. We had to place heavy wood blinds over the windows before

dark for blackout purposes. That night, one of our blinds blew off and the guard in the tower opened fire with his machine gun through the window. How thirty of us got through the door so quickly I'll never know. Miraculously, no one got hit.

On February 6, 1945, we were told to get our meager belongings together because we were being moved. The Russians were close enough that we could hear the artillery, and we had hopes of imminent liberation. Early that morning we were marched out to the front of the camp and given a Red Cross parcel each. Then we began a march that would be nothing but a trek of misery, starvation, and sickness. More than 8,000 men started out; some of them would not make it to the day of liberation, and many of them would suffer the throes of frostbite and dysentery before the end of the road.

We traveled northward to the port of Stettin, and I will never forget crossing the bay at Swinemunde and seeing a German U-boat coming in from the Baltic Sea with all the crew aligned on the deck. German Marines were busy

An older and hopefully wiser author after his return from POW camp.

building fortifications, and the whole area was a mass of activity.

Some days later, I had my little pack of possessions stolen and this left me with no changes of underwear or socks. Walking in snow and mud kept my feet wet. With the cold at night, it was not long before I fell victim to frostbite. This, coupled with a severe case of dysentery, made life miserable. I struggled along with a "sick party" who were often hauled in wagons pulled by oxen. How wonderful it would have been to be walking instead of freezing in the wagons!

At one point, those of us in the sick party were reunited with the marching columns and all were placed in box cars, about sixty to seventy men in each car. Most of the men were sick, practically all suffering from dysentery, possessing all but no food. We were transported to God knows where, and denied water or the opportunity to get out of the cars at any time. With only a box for dysentery, the air was stifling. It was reported that some of the men died during these four days, but I never knew of the deaths.

A number of men escaped during the days on the march, but this was extremely dangerous. All Germany was an armed camp and anyone caught without proper papers in any area would be shot at once. Many German soldiers were deserting, and this made the situation worse. Any of them who were caught were executed on the spot. It was reported and later confirmed that Hitler issued an order for all Allied aviator prisoners of war to be executed. Fortunately, cooler and more frightened heads in the Luftwaffe prevailed and the order was never seriously considered.

In late March 1945 our sick party was placed in Stalag XIB, an international camp at Falling Bostel, Germany, which was about fifty miles north of Hanover. There we had an assortment of prisoners from every country imaginable. The majority of the men that we were placed in the stockade with were British paratroops who had been captured following the fiasco at Arnhem, Holland.

Liberation finally came on April 16, 1945, when the British 7th Armored Division "Desert Rats" overran our area. There were only about 300 fellow Americans in the camp, but we had a wonderful time celebrating our freedom with the men from many nations.

I was flown to Brussels, Belgium, and then returned to American control at Namur, Belgium. We traveled to Camp Lucky Strike at Le Havre, France, from which we departed for the United States.

Chapter 11

Postwar

Regrettably, most B-17s went to the desert at Davis-Monthan Field in Tucson, Arizona, or other installations where World War II aircraft went to await the cutter's torch. Fortunately, there were some that were purchased and were to see long lives in various uses. The US Army Air Force and the later US Air Force used some of the B-17s in air-sea rescue service. These aircraft carried large rescue boats mounted on the belly of the aircraft so they could be dropped to maritime-disaster victims.

In civilian service, a few were converted to private corporate transports, but more were used as mapping aircraft or fire bombers. Quite a number of Fortresses were active in firefighting activities up until the 1970s.

At this late date, just about all of the surviving B-17s are museum items, some static and some still flying. There are a number of beautifully restored Fortresses still flying on the air show circuit.

Texas Raiders *is the B-17G that is the pride and joy of the Confederate Air Force. It is on the air show circuit annually.* R. Gill

Thunderbird *belongs to the Lone Star Air Museum located in Galveston, Texas, and is one of the most beautifully restored B-17s around.*

Sentimental Journey *belongs to the Arizona Wing of the Confederate Air Force and is beautifully restored.*

An air-sea rescue RB-17 at Nisawa, Japan, in 1949. Thompson

Memphis Belle *undergoing repairs in Memphis, Tennessee, in 1986.* Thompson

Static-display B-17G at Eighth Air Force Museum, Barksdale Air Force Base, Louisiana. Bardwell

The pride of the Arizona Wing at rest at its home base. The aircraft is widely known on the air show circuit.

Thunderbird *from the Lone Star Air Museum features the markings of a historic Fortress from the 303rd Bomb Group.*

Texas Raiders *taxis in following another successful air show.*

Appendix I

B-17 Specifications

Designation	No. Built	Wingspan	Length	Height	Engines	Top Speed	Cruise	Range
Model 299	1	103'9"	68'9"	15'	P&W 750hp	236mph	140mph	3,011mi
Y1B-17	13	103'9"	68'9"	15'	WR-1820	239mph	175mph	2,430mi
Y1B-17A	1	103'9"	68'9"	15'	WR-1820	271mph	183mph	-
B-17B	39	103'9"	67'10"	15'	WR-1820	286mph	-	3,000mi
B-17C	38	103'9"	67'10"	15'	WR-1820	300mph	227mph	3,400mi
B-17D	42	103'9"	67'10"	15'4"	WR-1820	318mph	-	2,540mi
B-17E	512	103'9"	73'9"	15'4"	WR-1820	-	226mph	3,300mi
B-17F	3,405	103'9"	74'9"	19'2"	WR-1820	325mph	160mph	4,420mi
B-17G	8,680	103'9"	74'4"	19'2"	WR-1820	302mph	160mph	3,750mi

Appendix II

B-17 Flying Fortress Serial Numbers

Y1B-17	36-149 thru 36-161	B-17F-DL	42-2964 thru 42-3482		44-85492 thru 44-85841
Y1B-17A	37-369	B-17F-VE	42-5705 thru 42-6204	XB-40	41-24341
B-17B	38-211 thru 38-223	B-17G-BO	42-31032 thru 42-32116	YB-40	42-5732 thru 42-5744
	38-258 thru 38-270		42-97058 thru 42-91407		42-5871
	38-583 and 38-584		42-102379 thru 42-102978		42-5920 and 42-5921
	38-610		43-37509 thru 43-39508		42-5923 thru 42-5925
	39-1 thru 39-10	B-17G-DL	42-3483 thru 42-3563		42-5927
B-17C	40-2042 thru 40-2079		42-37714 thru 42-38213	TB-40	42-5833 and 42-5834
B-17D	40-3059 thru 40-3100		42-106984 thru 42-107233		42-5872
B-17E	41-2393 thru 41-2669		44-6001 thru 44-7000		42-5926
	41-9011 thru 41-9245		44-83236 thru 44-83885		
B-17F-BO	41-24340 thru 41-24639	B-17G-VE	42-39758 thru 42-40057		
	42-5050 thru 42-5484		42-97436 thru 42-98035		
	42-29467 thru 42-31031		44-8001 thru 44-9000		

Appendix III

World War II B-17 Combat Units

Pacific

Group	Squadrons	Period
19	14, 28, 30, 92, 435	Dec. 1941 to late 1942
7	9, 11, 22, 436	Dec. 1941 to late 1942
11	26, 42, 98, 431	Dec. 1941 to late 1942
43	63, 64, 65, 403	Feb. 1942 to Sep. 1943
5	23, 31, 72, 394	Dec. 1941 to late 1942

Eighth, Twelfth and Fifteenth Air Forces

Group	Squadrons	Period
97	340, 341, 342, 414	Aug. 1942 to May 1945
301	32, 352, 353, 419	Sep. 1942 to May 1945

Twelfth and Fifteenth Air Forces

Group	Squadrons	Period
2	11, 49, 91, 429	Apr. 1943 to May 1945
99	346, 347, 348, 416	Mar. 1943 to May 1945

Fifteenth Air Force

Group	Squadrons	Period
463	772, 773, 774, 775	Mar. 1944 to May 1945
483	815, 816, 817, 840	Apr. 1994 to May 1945

Eighth Air Force

Group	Squadrons	Period
91	322, 323, 324, 401	Nov. 1942 to May 1945
92	325, 326, 327, 407	Sep. 1942 to May 1945
94	331, 332, 333, 410	May 1943 to May 1945
95	334, 335, 336, 412	May 1943 to May 1945
96	337, 338, 339, 413	May 1943 to May 1945
100	349, 350, 351, 418	Jun. 1943 to May 1945
303	358, 359, 360, 427	Nov. 1942 to May 1945
305	364, 365, 366, 422	Nov. 1942 to May 1945
306	367, 368, 369, 423	Oct. 1942 to May 1945
351	408, 409, 410, 411	May 1943 to May 1945
379	524, 525, 526, 527	May 1943 to May 1945
381	532, 533, 534, 535	Jun. 1943 to May 1945
384	544, 545, 546, 547	Jun. 1943 to May 1945
385	548, 549, 550, 551	Jul. 1943 to May 1945
388	560, 561, 562, 563	Jul. 1943 to May 1945
390	568, 569, 570, 571	Aug. 1943 to May 1945
398	600, 601, 602, 603	May 1944 to May 1945
401	612, 613, 614, 615	Nov. 1943 to May 1945
447	708, 709, 710, 711	Dec. 1943 to May 1945
452	728, 729, 730, 731	Feb. 1944 to May 1945
457	748, 749, 750, 751	Feb. 1944 to May 1945
34*	4, 7, 18, 391	Sep. 1994 to May 1945
486*	832, 833, 834, 835	Aug. 1944 to May 1945
487*	836, 837, 838, 839	Aug. 1944 to May 1945
490*	848, 849, 850, 851	Aug. 1944 to May 1945
493*	860, 861, 862, 863	Sep. 1944 to May 1945

* These units entered combat as B-24 groups. Converted to B-17s in months shown.

Other Eighth Air Force B-17 Units

36th Bomb Squadron (radio countermeasures squadron), 1944-1945

5th Air Sea Rescue Squadron, 1944-1945

3rd Air Division Headquarters Flight, 1944-1945

1st Air Division Headquarters Flight, 1944- 1945

Appendix IV

Notable B-17 Survivors

Notable B-17 Survivors

Model	Serial	Location
B-17F	41-24485	Mud Island Museum, Memphis, Tennessee. Memphis Belle static display.
B-17F	42-29782	Museum of Flight, Boeing Field, Seattle, Washington. Static display.
B-17G	42-32076	USAF Museum, Wright-Patterson AFB, Ohio. Shoo Shoo Baby static display.
B-17G	44-83575	Bob Collings/Collings Foundation, Stowe, Massachusetts. Flies as 231909, Nine-O-Nine.
B-17G	43-38635	USAF Museum, Castle AFB, California. Displayed as 38635, Virgin's Delight.
B-17G	44-6393	USAF Museum, March AFB, California. Displayed as 230092, Second Patches.
B-17G	44-8543	Dr. William D. Hospers/B. C. Vintage Flying Machines, Ft. Worth Texas. Flies as 48543 Chuckie.
B-17G	44-83512	USAF Museum, Lackland AFB, Texas. Displayed as 483512 Heavens Above.
B-17G	44-83514	Confederate Air Force, Mesa, Arizona. Flies as 483514, Sentimental Journey.
B-17G	44-83546	Military Aircraft Restoration Corporation, Chino, California. Loaned to March AFB Museum, California.
B-17G	44-83684	Planes of Fame, Chino, California. Displayed as 483684, Picadilly Lily.
B-17G	44-83785	Evergreen Equity, McMinnville, Oregon. Flies as 483785.
B-17G	44-83872	Confederate Air Force, Midland, Texas. Flies as 483872, Texas Raider.
B-17G	55-83884	Eighth Air Force Museum, Barksdale, AFB, Louisiana. Displayed as 38289, Yankee Doodle II.
B-17G	44-85599	Dynes AFB Museum, Abilene, Texas. Displayed as 48559.
B-17G	44-85718	Lone Star Flight Museum, Galveston, Texas. Flies as 238050, Thunderbird.
B-17G	44-85740	EAA Aviation Foundation, Oshkosh, Wisconsin. Flies as 85740, Aluminum Overcast.
B-17G	44-85778	Warbirds of Great Britain, Bournemouth, England. To fly as Sally A.
B-17G	44-85784	B-17 Preservation Trust, Duxford, England. Flies as 24485, Sally B.
B-17G	44-83559	UAAF Museum, Offutt AFB, Nebraska. Displayed as 23474, King Bee.
B-17G	44-83563	National Warplane Museum, Genesco, New York. Flies as 297400, Fuddy Duddy.
B-17G	44-85228	USAF Museum, Pima County Air Museum, Tucson, Arizona. Displayed as 231892, I'll Be Around.
B-17G	44-85829	Yankee Air Force, Willow Run, Michigan. To fly as 485829, Yankee Lady.

GREAT AMERICAN BOMBERS OF WWII

B-24 LIBERATOR

Frederick A. Johnsen

*For Sharon, who provides
the healthy counterpoint to my
aviation passions.*

Preface

Understand right from the start, I've been an unabashed fan of Liberators and Privateers since I was a small boy.

It's difficult to analyze these things. Maybe it all started with a childhood fascination with an old Revell B-24J model kit of dubious accuracy. Perhaps it was the "Victory at Sea" footage of the air war in the Pacific, accompanied by the symphonic strains of "Beneath the Southern Cross" as outbound Liberators passed graceful palm trees. However it started, my love of the Liberator was fed by those remarkable *National Geographic* wartime photo stories, and tales of air combat with Messerschmitts related by the genial landlord of the house my family rented in the late 1950s.

As I grew older, I devoured the news accounts of the finding of the B-

Bent but amazingly intact, the ghostly Lady Be Good *fired the public's imagination when the lost B-24D was found by oil prospectors in the Libyan desert in 1959. In 1962, the US Air Force invoked its procedure for property disposal by advertising to sell* Lady Be Good *to the highest bidder. There were no takers.* US Air Force Museum Collection.

24D *Lady Be Good* in Libya. Stories about Ploesti gripped my attention. This was high adventure for a boy. But the more I sought out every shred of information about my favorite aircraft, the more I heard stories about the Liberator's supposed inferiorities to the B-17, or how Liberators were unwanted guests in the European Theater of Operations.

And yet, the Liberator had its staunch partisans: crew members who wouldn't let the Lib take a slur in conversation many years after the end of their wartime association with B-24s; historians who extolled the versatility of the Liberator airframe. These voices were raised in defense of this nearly extinct, obsolete heavy bomber.

And therein lies a major reason for my ongoing passion for this airplane—the people who lived and died by it. If early B-24s in the Pacific were not sufficiently defended from head-on attacks, American aviators devised a power turret to remedy the problem, exercising that wonderful Yankee ingenuity found on either side of the Mason-Dixon Line. When the war in Europe and the Middle East was far from a foregone Allied victory, American aviators climbed aboard stout B-24Ds and weaved among smokestacks to bomb

vital oil refineries from rooftop level in a daring mission that was certain to claim many of their lives. When the comforts of home were thousands of miles from the South Pacific, Americans in B-24s brought these comforts a bit closer by taking the necessary ingredients aloft, where atmospheric refrigeration allowed ice cream to be churned high above the steaming tropics. And when paint and brushes were put in the hands of squadron artists, American aviators used the broad flanks of the Liberators and Privateers to create the definitive examples of warplane nose art.

We Americans pride ourselves in having a can-do spirit. That spirit emerges in the tale of the Consolidated B-24 and PB4Y bombers.

Browse with me through Liberator archives in this volume. Sure, we've heard from those who criticized aspects of the B-24, sometimes with good cause. But that only adds depth to the story of the most heavily produced American military plane ever, and the upbeat flight crews, ground crews, support people, and engineers who took the B-24 into battle and emerged victorious.

—*Frederick A. Johnsen*

Technical Notes

If you've ever worked around a major Air Force aircraft production run, you know that what "the book" says is not always the way it really is. The deeper we delve into the history of more than 18,000 Liberators and Privateers, the more variables we find. Effort has been made to use reliable documentation to explain many quirks and changes in Liberator production. But in the crush of World War II events, some things didn't get done by the book. They didn't even get *entered* in the book. Use the information in this volume as a guide to the wonderful world of B-24s and their kin, but keep light on your feet for anomalies that may still show up in Liberator research. Be wary of anyone who professes to know everything about B-24s, for Liberators were in service in too many arenas at once for anybody to keep an omniscient eye on them all. And friends, with this volume I've uncovered and corrected some errors I, and other writers, inadvertently allowed into print earlier. It is ironic that we get more accurate in some aspects of the complex B-24 story as more years elapse, even as we lose more of the precious first-person memories of the Liberator years each time a veteran dies.

Acknowledgments

The list of people who have generously helped build my B-24 research files is continually growing. The naming of those who had a hand in the materials presented in this book must start off with Peter M. Bowers, whose unselfish lending of photos from his vast collection provided a meaty nucleus for this book. Thanks, Pete.

Others who have helped, over several decades, include: Rick Apitz, Rhodes Arnold, David Gale Behunin, Steve Birdsall, the Confederate Air Force Museum, Convair-General Dynamics, Jim Dilonardo, Johnny Dingle, Jeff Ethell, Bob Etter, Wayne Fiamengo, Tom Foote, Charlie Glassie, Jr., Chet Goad, A. B. Goldberg, Carl Hilde-brandt, William G. Holder, Ben Howser, Albert W. James, Larry Jaynes, Mr. and Mrs. Carl M. Johnsen, Kenneth G. Johnsen, Don Keller, Jim Kiernan and Sharon D. Vance Kiernan, Keith Laird, Fred LePage, the Liberator Club (and especially Bob McGuire), Al Lloyd, Al Lomer, Ray Markman, Jim Masura, Dave Menard, Allan Metscher, Bill Metscher, Bill Miranda, Louis Mladenovic, L. M. Myers, Thomas K. Oliver, Earl Otto, Dennis Peltier, Milo Peltzer, Bob Richardson, Bill Riepl, Rockwell International (and Gene Boswell), the San Diego Aerospace Museum (and Ray Wagner and George Welsh), Walter Schurr, Victor D. Seely, Ted Small, Glen Spieth, Ivan Stepnich, Carl A. Stutz, David Tallichet, Herb Tollefson, Orville Tosch, University of Washington Aeronautical Laboratory (and Professor William H. Rae, Jr.), US Air Force Museum, US Navy office of history, Bill Willard, and Charles F. Willis, Jr.

Documentation compiled since the 1940s by US Air Force historians unlocks riddles, and adds much to the biography of the Liberator. The Air Force can be proud of its half-century of diligent historical record-keeping.

Motorbooks' aviation editor Greg Field fostered this project. I like to think he knows a good thing when he sees one.

Chapter 1

Pedigree

New Ideas

The B-24 Liberator (Consolidated Aircraft Co. Model 32) was that company's reply to a US Army Air Corps suggestion that Consolidated establish a second production line to turn out more Boeing-designed B-17 Flying Fortresses. To speed a mock-up of its own heavy bomber design into readiness for Air Corps inspectors, Consolidated engineers borrowed the untried Davis wing from the Model 31 flying boat proposal, along with the Model 31's huge twin-tail assembly. (The wing was named for its inventor David R. Davis.) In a late-war issue of *Aviation* magazine, J. H. Famme, Consolidated's chief design engineer at San Diego, said, "Ease of production was one of the main considerations in selecting this wing design." According to Famme, the front and rear wing spars were widely spaced "to provide maximum room for fuel cells of sufficient capacity to insure the greater range specified by the Army Air Forces [AAF], and also to provide clearance for main landing gear wheels."

On March 30, 1939, signers inked the contract for a mock-up wind-tunnel model, and one prototype XB-24 airplane. Exactly nine months later to the day, the XB-24 was supposed to be completed. In actuality, the prototype first took to the air on December 29, 1939, more than a month early.

The Davis Wing

By the time the XB-24 first left the runway, the Davis wing had flown (on May 5, 1939) on the prototype Model

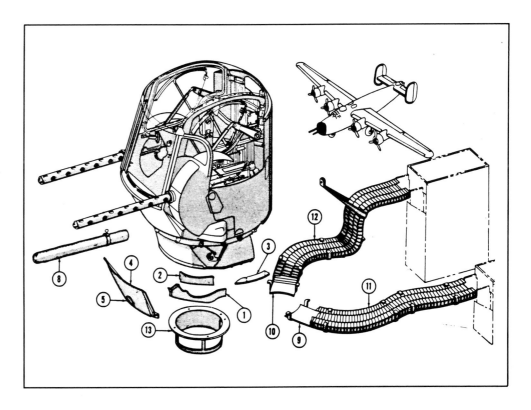

The oldest surviving Liberator is the LB-30B flown by the Confederate Air Force. Frederick A. Johnsen

Motor Products Corp. (MPC) nose and tail turrets refined the basic Consolidated design with streamlining, more glazing, and gently curved armor glass.

Gun mounts were symmetrical. Externally mounted ammunition cans fed all the nose and tail turrets.

Prototype XB-24 (39-556) set the basic form of all Liberators to follow, even as metamorphosis embellished the line. Peter M. Bowers Collection

When fitted with turbo-supercharged versions of the R-1830 engine, and other refinements, the prototype XB-24 was renumbered 39-680, and redesignated XB-24B. A salient feature of the sole B-model was the use of characteristic wide oval nacelles on the stubby airframe of the prototype. Propeller spinners were tested. San Diego Aerospace Museum

31, and engineers were enthusiastic about the performance edge it gave. Now the B-24's fortunes were tied to the abilities of the Davis high-lift airfoil. Although, as if still not unanimous in their confidence, Consolidated engineers ran a wind-tunnel test on the Davis airfoil only days before the XB-24's first flight. Two wings were compared in this test, in the University of Washington Aeronautical Laboratory (UWAL) wind tunnel, between December 21 and 26. One of the 1/12 scale wings used the Davis airfoil; the other employed a more traditional National Advisory Council on Aeronautics (NACA) 230 series airfoil. Both wing models used the same planform as did the XB-24, and earlier the Model 31, with an aspect ratio of 11.6. This was a high ratio—a feature that minimized some components of drag, contributing to the efficiency of the wing.

The wind-tunnel results showed Davis' wing promoted a laminar airflow over a greater portion of the chord (from leading edge to trailing edge of the wing) than did the NACA section. This gave the Davis wing a lift advantage: Lift increases with an increase in pitch (angle of attack) of the wing, up to the point where the airflow separates from the wing and aerodynamic stall occurs. The data for the Davis wing confirmed that it enjoyed increasing lift at increasingly higher angles of attack up to the stall point with a smaller drag penalty than did the NACA wing.

Perhaps most telling was a graph plotted at airspeeds between 150 and 250mph, and a theoretical altitude of 10,000ft. The graph showed that the Davis wing gave 150mi greater range than did the NACA wing at 150mph, with that benefit dwindling to 40mi extra range for the Davis wing at 240mph. The Davis wing had the range.

As designed, the B-24 wing was intended to incorporate rubber deicer boots that physically altered their shape enough to slough off ice in flight. Later, Convair introduced a new hot-air exhaust heat anti-icing system. The exhaust heat system necessitated ducting and double-skin sections to conduct heated air to the leading edge surfaces. On Liberators so equipped, air heated by exhaust gases was piped through the leading edges of flight surfaces, as well as into the compartments of the pilots, radio operator, bombardier, tail gunner, and top turret. Other crew members still relied on electrically heated clothing. The heat exchangers for this system were located in the engine exhaust stacks just ahead of the turbosuperchargers. Outside air passed through the heat exchangers before flowing through the aluminum tube ducting to locations where needed. The

Flight-test crew members flashed V-for-Victory signals to mimic that given by Gran'pappy *painted on the nose of the XB-24B. The first Liberator outlived* the war as a test and transport aircraft, finally being scrapped in 1946. San Diego Aerospace Museum

Trading on its options, the AAF gave six of its seven ordered YB-24s to the British, to wait for more advanced production Liberators. That makes this the sole true YB-24, number 40-702. Orthochromatic film altered the appearance of the national star insignia tones. Peter M. Bowers Collection

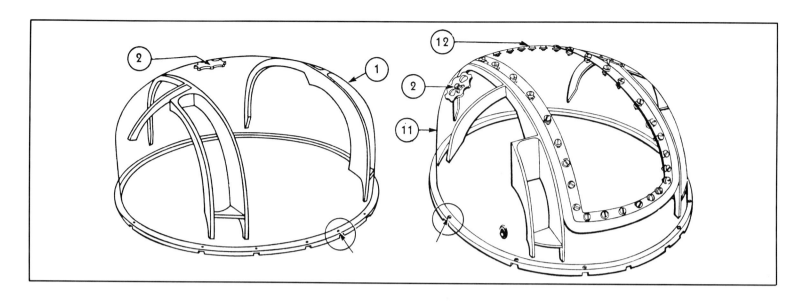

Two types of Martin top-turret Plexiglas domes graced B-24s. Photographs taken well into J-model and Privateer production still show the old-style dome (left). When the K-13 and other computing gunsights were introduced, the dome was redesigned with a replaceable center Plexiglas sighting window with a constant-radius curvature to facilitate accurate sighting. This resulted in the so-called "high hat" dome (right).

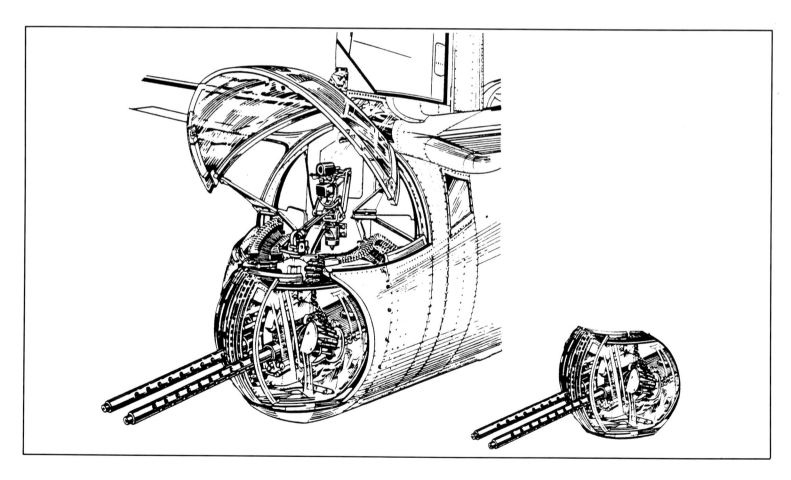

Promising tests were made with Bell power boost twin .50cal gun mounts set into modified greenhouse B-24D noses. The Bell unit adapted for this use was designed as a tail gun emplacement on the Martin B-26 Marauder, as depicted. Problems of supply, and the anticipated introduction of the B-24N, thwarted this modification.

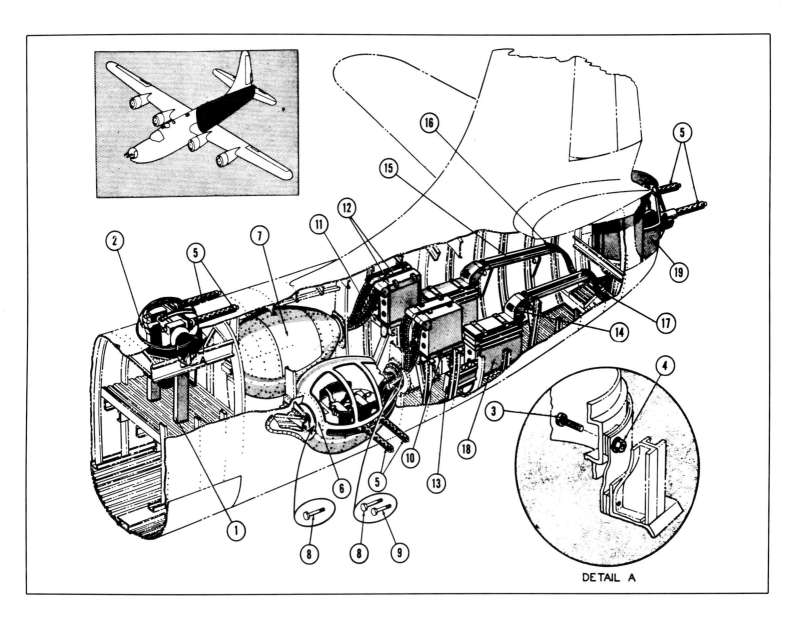

DETAIL A

ducting, according to the *Aviation* design analysis, was covered with sheet asbestos.

Consolidated's honeymoon with the Davis wing did not signify a break with traditional NACA thinking. The airfoil section of the B-24's vertical fin-and-rudder set used NACA 0007 cross section; the horizontal tail surface cross section was NACA 0015. The elevators of the B-24 had 30deg of up travel, and 20deg of down travel; the twin rudders had 10deg of movement either side of center.

And a Box to Put It In
The fuselage of the B-24 was designed as a semi-monocoque shell reinforced with Z-section stringers, and transverse beltframes and bulkheads.

Beltframes were generally 18in apart. The longitudinal Z-stringers were typically spaced about 6in apart, but were grouped closer where needed for more strength. Longerons were used only to carry loads around openings like the bomb bays and access doors, or other places where the strength of the skin-and-stringer construction was interrupted. Convair designer J. H. Famme called the B-24's shape a four-sided modified eliptical fuselage.

Liberator Roll Call
As B-24 development progressed, major and minor variants included the following:

XB-24 (Air Corps serial number [s/n] 39-556): First B-24; gross weight 41,000lb.

Page from the Privateer Illustrated Parts Catalog reveal details of construction and interior furnishings. In the aft fuselage, micarta ammunition boxes mounted in pairs fed the twin .50cal machine guns of each ERCO blister turret. Other boxes fed the tail turret.

YB-24 (Air Corps s/ns 40-696–702 assigned, but all except 40-702 were delivered to the British as LB-30A): Gross weight raised by 5,300lb above that of XB-24.

B-24A (Air Corps s/ns 40-2369–2377): First US production variant; .50cal guns replaced .30cal weapons; gross weight raised to 53,600lb.

XB-24B (Air Corps s/n 39-680): Renumbered prototype XB-24 with new engines using the characteristic oval cowlings of subsequent Liberators.

B-24C (Air Corps s/ns 40-2378–2386): Nine aircraft which might have been B-24Bs, but were called C-models with the addition of a Martin top turret and twin .50cal guns in the tail. The C-model was nearly three feet longer than earlier B-24s, and was similar in appearance to the first USAAF combat-ready B-24, the D-model.

B-24D (AAF s/ns 40-2349–2368; 41-1087–1142; 41-11587–11938; 41-23640–24311; 41-24339; 42-40058–41257; 42-72765–72963; 42-63752–64046): Number of this model built was 2,738 aircraft. D-models served in combat in Europe and the Pacific; need for increased frontal defensive firepower led to field and depot modifications with a B-24 tail turret mounted in the upper nose. Gross weight up to 60,000lb.

B-24E (AAF s/ns 41-28409–28573; 41-29007–29008; 42-6976–7464; 42-7770; 41-29009–29115; 41-64395–64431): Visually similar to B-24D; used different propeller; most were built under contract by Ford Motor Co. at Willow Run, Michigan. Knock-down kits of Ford E-models also were assembled by Douglas Aircraft Co. at Tulsa, Oklahoma, and Consolidated Aircraft Co. at Fort Worth, Texas.

XB-24F (AAF s/n 41-11678): Converted from a B-24D, retaining its original s/n; tested hot-air deicing system.

B-24G (AAF s/ns 42-78045–78474): Built by North American Aviation Incorporated in Dallas, Texas. After first 25 with D-style greenhouse, the G-models introduced Emerson nose turrets following the style already introduced on Ford B-24H models.

B-24H (AAF s/ns 41-28574–29006; 42-51077–51225; 41-29116–29608; 42-50277–50451; 42-64432–64501; 42-

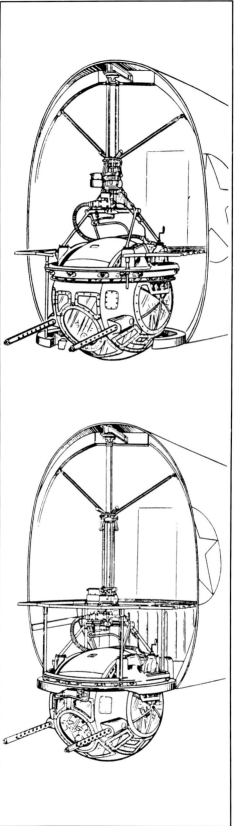

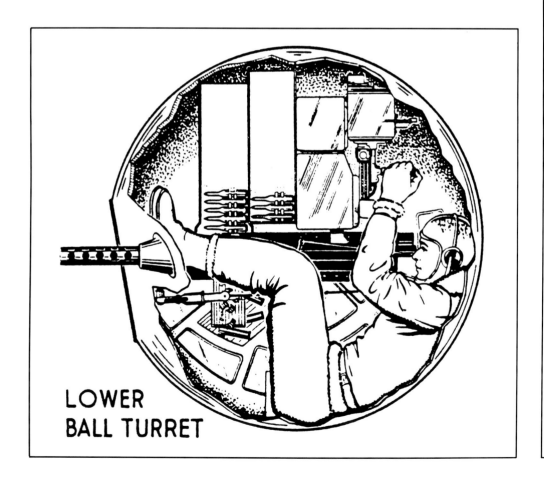

LOWER
BALL TURRET

Cutaway drawing from a World War II armaments catalog shows ball turret *gunner in place, with internal ammo cans in his turret.*

The B-24's ball turret shown in the retracted and extended positions.

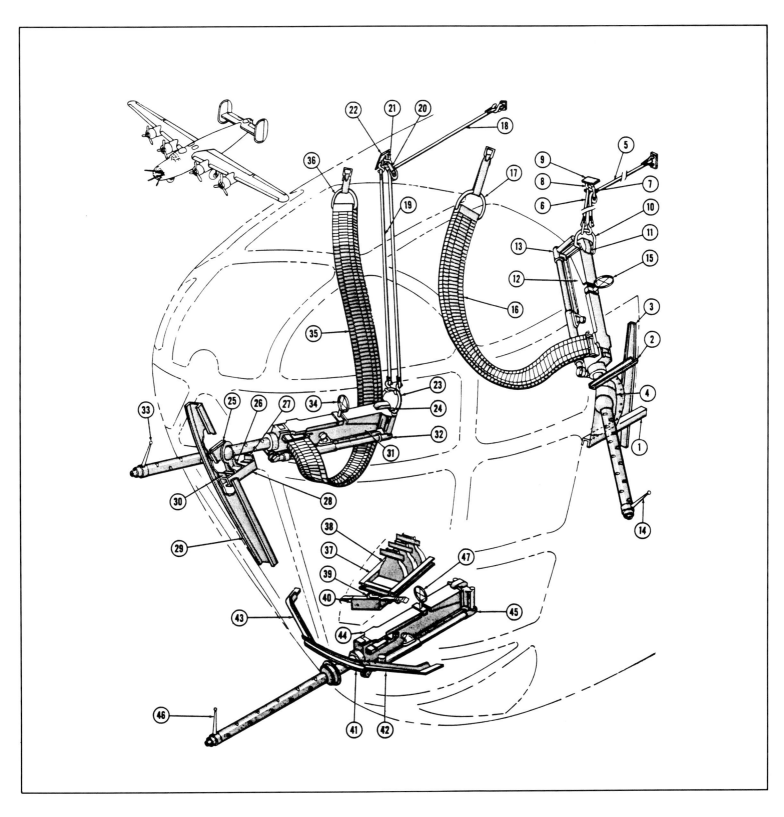

Greenhouse B-24s like the benchmark D-model were typically fitted with three .50cal nose machine guns in K-4 sockets, one in the lower nose, and one in each cheek. These used E-11-type recoil adaptors and C-19 mounts to attach the weapons to the sockets. Flexible feed chutes gave the guns more staying power than did small ammo cans that were quickly expended, sometimes requiring a one-sided lull in the middle of a gun-battle as the B-24 gunner swapped cans. In the greenhouse nose, the long, triangular bombsight window was made of laminated safety glass, much like car windows of the vintage.

Early British Liberator with short nose and gleaming natural aluminum propellers. Six British LB-30As were short-nose YB-24s placed in the hands of the British; twenty similar Liberator I models were known at Consolidated as LB-30Bs. Peter M. Bowers Collection

The pug-nose B-24A carried large flags proclaiming America's neutrality before the entry of the United States into World War II. The AAF's B-24As pioneered long-range air routes during the uneasy period prior to American participation in the conflict. The neutrality markings and insignia are painted over British-style camouflage. US Air Force via Jeff Ethell Collection

7465–7769; 42-52077–52776; 42-94729–95503): Built by Douglas, Convair Fort Worth, and Ford. *B-24I:* Not assigned.

B-24J (AAF s/ns 42-50452–50508; 42-64047–64394; 42-99736–99935; 44-10253–10752; 44-44049–44501; 42-50509–51076; 42-51431–52076; 42-95504–95628; 44-48754–49001; 42-51226–51430; 42-72964–73514; 42-99936–100435; 42-109789–110188; 44-40049–41389; 42-78475–78794; 44-28061–28276): Considered the definitive nose-turret B-24; gross weight was up to 65,000lb, from the XB-24's gross weight of only 41,000lb, for an increase of 12 tons over the prototype!

XB-24K (AAF s/n 42-40234; modified from B-24D): First AAF B-24 with a single tail; fitted with nose turret and updated equipment. Improved performance would lead to order for refined variant as B-24N. (Since Ford built the N-models, some confusion surrounds the sole K-model, which historian Allan Blue says was actually a Consolidated project at San Diego.)

B-24L (AAF s/ns 44-41390–41806; 44-49002–50251): Featured lightweight

tail gun installation; the Eighth and Fifteenth Air Forces had difficulty standardizing on combat-capable features needed in B-24s, and hoped to iron out differences in L-model.

B-24M (AAF s/ns 44-41807–42722; 44-50252–51928): Last regular production B-24 model; late B-24Ms introduced a knife-edge canopy design.

XB-24N (AAF s/n 44-48753) and YB-24N (AAF s/ns 44-52053–52059): Single-tail Liberator with new nose and tail turrets, incorporating weight savings and more useful nose compartment for bombardier, navigator, and gunner. Improved performance over earlier models. Order of 5,168 production B-24Ns was canceled when European war ended.

B-24O: Not assigned.

XB-24P: Testbed made from B-24D s/n 42-40344.

XB-24Q (AAF s/n 44-49916): Converted B-24L used as test bed by General Electric Corp. (GE) for radar-directed B-47 tail turret.

C-87 (AAF s/ns 42-107249–107275; 43-30548–36027 [including 3 C-87A models with 10 berths]; 44-

The last B-24A built for the AAF (40-2377) in latter-day garb, with late-1943-style national insignia and natural-metal finish not typically seen until 1944. Peter M. Bowers Collection

39198–39298; 44-52978–52987 [other C-87s and C-87As were included in B-24D s/n sequences]): The C-87 was a remarkable production adaptation of the Liberator bomber into a viable transport, used around the world during the war. Typically, about 20 passengers and a crew of five could be carried in a C-87. More than 280 C-87s were built.

C-109 (converted from B-24s): Carried gasoline in special fuselage tanks, which could be pumped into ground storage tanks for later use. B-24 found favor for this task due to great range. Its huge tankage of volatile gasoline lent the nickname *C-One-Oh-Boom,* which may be largely undeserved.

AT-22 (five converted C-87s): Flying classrooms for flight-engineer training; later redesignated TB-24.

British Liberator II (LB-30) introduced the lengthened nose typical of subsequent B-24s (2ft, 7in longer than previous models), plus a slightly deeper aft fuselage that faired the horizontal stabilizer differently than on earlier Liberators. The 139 Liberator II/LB-30 bombers were the only Liberator series fitted with Curtiss Electric propellers instead of Hamilton Standard Hydramatics. Long prop domes of Curtiss Electric are visible on this 1941 view of Liberator II number AL543. Peter M. Bowers Collection

F-7 (photo reconnaissance variant converted from B-24Hs): F-7A and B were converted from B-24Js; carried cameras in bomb bay, or nose; saw service in the Pacific.

XB-41 (AAF s/n 41-11822): Converted from a B-24D, and intended as a large "escort fighter" for B-24 formations. Featured Bendix chin turret, two dorsal turrets (one elevated), and double waist guns. Developed in parallel

with XB-40 B-17 variant; XB-41 did not see combat or production status.

The US Navy desired Liberators for patrol missions. In a give-and-take trade, the Navy released its hold on Boeing Aircraft Co. assembly lines at Renton, Washington, in trade for a part of the San Diego Liberator production run, and the antisubmarine mission previously held by the USAAF. The first Navy Liberators, designated PB4Y-1, were similar to B-24Ds. Later PB4Y-1s were built with a round Engineering and Research Corp. (ERCO) bow turret, following some of the greenhouse versions that the Navy modified with the ERCO turret.

Though working independently of USAAF studies, the Navy also realized a single fin and rudder could enhance Liberator performance. The Navy answer was the PB4Y-2 Privateer, with a tail taller than the XB-24K, and a fuselage lengthened by more than seven feet. Naval designations for C-87 variants were RY-1 and RY-2; cargo version of the Privateer was RY-3, which

almost went into production for the AAF, as well as the C-87C. US Navy s/ns for Liberators and Privateers were as follows:

PB4Y-1 (Navy Bureau of Aeronautics numbers [BuNo.] 31936–32287; 32288–32335; 38733–38979; 46725–46737; 63915–63959; 65287–65396; 90132–90271; 90462–90483): Twin-tail Navy Liberator patrol bombers.

XPB4Y-2 (BuNo. 32086; 32095–32096): Prototypes converted from B-24Ds.

PB4Y-2 (BuNo. 59350–60009; 66245–66324): Gross weight 65,000lb; two top turrets, twin-gun power ERCO waist blisters; some carried Bat glide bombs on underwing stations.

RY-1 (BuNo. 67797–67799).

RY-2 (BuNo. 39013–39017).

RY-3 (BuNo. 90020–90021; 90023–90059): Single-tail transport variant similar to Privateer.

Navy Liberators and Privateers survived in postwar service longer than USAAF versions. PB4Y-1Ps were used

for photography. By 1951, the few Dash 1s still in service were redesignated P4Y-1P, along with Privateer P4Y-2, P4Y-2B (Bat bomb carriers), P4Y-2S antisubmarine patrollers, and P4Y-2K target drones. The Privateer even entered the new military unified nomenclature of 1962 when the remaining Privateer drones in Navy service received the basic designation P-4; their drone status and model letter designated them QP-4B.

The British used many Liberator models, including some RY-3 single-tail transports. Early short-nose Liberator I models were followed by Liberator IIs and LB-30s. LB-30 was a Consolidated designation for a land bomber, originally being produced for France, but diverted to England when France fell. Consolidated used the designation LB-30A to signify the six YB-24s transferred to the British, and LB-30B to denote the similar Liberator I. When the

This classic Consolidated B-24D publicity photo still had the aircraft's tail number censored. This D-model was fitted with deicer boots covering nearly all the exposed edges of the vertical stabilizers.

United States entered the war in December 1941, a number of LB-30s (British Liberator IIs with longer noses than previous variants) were taken

163

The first Liberator assembled at Consolidated's Fort Worth, Texas, factory was D-model 41-11705, made of subassemblies shipped from the San Diego, California, Consolidated plant.

over by the USAAF. These were hybrid Liberators, employing an aft location for the top turret which was a four-gun (.303cal) Boulton-Paul turret on British LB-30s, and a Martin two-gun .50cal turret on the American LB-30s.

LB-30s saw combat in the 7th Bombardment Group in the Pacific in 1942. USAAF LB-30s also bombed in the Aleutians and patrolled the Panama Canal Zone. When not serving as bombers, some LB-30s were set up for regular transport runs in the Pacific, ultimately receiving many C-87–style modifications. Some of these converted bombers outlived the war to become civil transports and freight haulers.

Line-up of Liberators at Fort Worth includes desert-sand examples in three positions nearest camera, followed by two early Navy PB4Y-1s, another AAF B-24D, and some bombers with mismatched olive-drab and desert-sand vertical tail components. Second row of planes in upper right of photo includes C-87 Liberator Express transports. Ivan Stepnich Collection

A red-cowled B-24D being marshaled on the ramp for parking. US Air Force via Jeff Ethell Collection

Wash's Tub, *a well-decorated early D-model, returned to the States after combat, eventually being scrapped at Spokane, Washington.* US Air Force

US Navy RY-1 was a C-87A equivalent, with 10 sleeper berths and R-1830-45 engines instead of the -43s of straight C-87s. Peter M. Bowers Collection

North American-built B-24Gs at the factory flightline near Dallas, Texas, show details of fuselage bulkhead immediately behind nose turret. Irregularly scalloped gray paint on undersides of fuselage and engine nacelles is different from Consolidated's straight feathered demarcation. North American Aviation

The North American B-24G, although the lowest-letter B-24 with a factory nose turret, actually received nose turret later in its production life than did the B-24H. Waves in camouflage demarcation on this North American example tends to be less regular than those used on Ford-built B-24s. North American Aviation

Ford B-24H (42-7718) shows scalloped fuselage paint, with straight nacelle demarcation curving up to wing juncture. This plane is fitted with enclosed waist window mounts. Peter M. Bowers Collection

Natural-metal B-24J-145-CO on the ramp at San Diego shows old-style disappearing nosewheel doors and MPC nose turret. The antiglare panel stops mid-astrodome. Convair

This view of a B-24J from Fort Worth highlights the high-aspect-ratio Davis wing. The anti-glare panel extends all the way to nose turret. Peter M. Bowers Collection

The sole XB-24K was a Consolidated San Diego single-tail test bed using components from a Douglas B-23 vertical tail and, later, a C-54 horizontal tail. Originally, the conversion was performed on B-24D 42-40058. Later in 1943, the single-tail aft fuselage was removed and grafted on a vastly updated B-24D, featuring a nose turret and other new components, and carrying number 42-40234, generally acknowledged as the definitive XB-24K.

B-24M-31-FO shows late-production features—knife-edge windscreen, hooded turbo-superchargers, and large, rectangular navigator windows. Peter M. Bowers Collection

XB-24N was a harbinger of sporty single-tail Liberators that never got into large-scale production by war's end. Armament updates replaced traditional nose and tail turrets with new gun emplacements. R-1830-75 engines were used. Peter M. Bowers Collection

Navy RY-3 shows openable waist window on right side of fuselage; on left side, cargo doors took up this area. Liberator Club

Chapter 2

Calendar of Combat

Information from the official US Air Force *Combat Chronology: 1941–1945,* compiled by Kit C. Carter and Robert Mueller, illuminates the Liberator's war. The following details characterize AAF B-24 operations. Virtually daily, somewhere in the world, between Pearl Harbor Day and VJ-Day, Liberators plied their craft. The following highlights are just that— highlights. Additional B-24 operations took place; those excerpted here provide an overview of the Liberator at war. AAF B-24s were a huge part of the overall air armada that contributed to the downfall of the Axis around the world. As the B-24s carried the war to the enemy, so did many other warplanes, sometimes in concert with the Liberators. The Air Force log frequently attributes aircraft to their numbered air force, rather than individual bomb groups or squadrons. The chronology often accommodates the mixed B-24 and B-17 operations (especially of the Eighth Air Force) by merely referencing HBs—heavy bombers—for a day's missions, inadvertently obscuring what

role the ever-present B-24s played in that bomber force. Herewith is a diary of the war of the B-24s:

The first American Liberator combat loss was a ground casualty at Hickam Field on December 7, 1941. It was a B-24A, s/n 40-2371.

In early 1942, LB-30s carried the war to the Japanese as Fifth Air Force (AF) crews tried in vain to thwart a Japanese convoy approaching Java on February 27. Bombing results were not a significant factor in the Battle of Java Sea, and by March 1, the American heavy bombers flew their last mission from Java. The next day, three of the LB-30s joined five B-17s in evacuating the last 260 soldiers from Jogjakarta— the last airstrip on Java still under Allied control. Japanese troops were about 20mi away as the LB-30s roared off the runway.

On June 4, 1942, a B-24 was missing after Eleventh AF attacks on a Japanese carrier force in the Aleutians. The Japanese presence in these Alaskan islands was timed to coincide with the enemy's attack on Midway. The following day, two Eleventh AF LB-30s joined other bombers and fighters in a search for the Japanese fleet that did not find the ships. On the night of June 6–7, General Tinker, commander of the Seventh AF, led a flight of LB-30s from Midway to bomb

Wake. The Liberator carrying Tinker appeared to stall and crash at sea. On June 8, a lone LB-30 flying armed patrol found Japanese naval units in Kiska Harbor in the Aleutians. By June 11, the Air Force chronology listed five B-24s in the Eleventh AF arsenal being dispatched to bomb Japanese targets at Kiska, along with an equal number of B-17s. The bombers made low-level attacks on two cruisers and a destroyer; antiaircraft fire downed one of the B-24s. The other four Liberators were chased by four Japanese fighters back to Umnak, until American fighters drove the enemy away. The next day, one of the B-24s in Alaska joined six B-17s in a return engagement over Kiska Harbor that left one Japanese cruiser damaged and a destroyer burning.

Halfway around the world, spanning the night of June 11–12, 1942, 13 B-24Ds of the HALPRO (for Halverson Project) Detachment under Col. Harry A. Halverson rose from Fayid, Egypt, to drop bombs in the first attack on the Romanian oil fields of Ploesti. A dozen of Halverson's Liberators made the bomb run at dawn. The Liberators recovered at scattered locations in Iraq, Syria, and Turkey, the latter country impounding the four B-24s that entered Turkish airspace. Damage to Ploesti was light, but the tone was set

Jerk's Natural *was a 93rd BG B-24D that spent considerable time away from England in North Africa, where RAF-style fin flashes were used. The black ring around the star probably was used to dull a yellow ring applied to Allied aircraft during the earlier Operation Torch in North Africa. The star was dulled with gray paint to diminish its visibility at a distance. Medium green blotching was applied to some olive-drab B-24s to break up their lines. The survival of original World War II color photography is due almost exclusively to durable Kodachrome films of that era.* US Air Force via Jeff Ethell Collection

for future combat by Americans in Liberators in the Middle East. Three days later, seven HALPRO B-24Ds were joined by a pair of British Royal Air Force (RAF) Liberators, and torpedo-laden RAF Beaufort twin-engine bombers as they attacked the Italian Navy east of Malta. The B-24s claimed damage to a battleship and a cruiser.

That same day, two Eleventh AF B-24s and three B-17s were forced to abort their intended bombing of Kiska because of weather. (The AAF record for the Aleutians reveals the worst possible weather for sustained flying operations. Weather aborts, and aircraft lost in weather, abounded in this far-northern battlefield. The Liberator crews—and their compatriots in the Eleventh AF—gallantly fought a little-

known war, and deserve recognition for their pluck in the face of cold, ice, fog, snow, rain, and wind during most of the year.)

On June 18, 1942, one LB-30 and four B-24s made up the Liberator component of an eight-ship heavy bomber force that struck Kiska Harbor from high altitude. As the Liberators and Fortresses left Kiska, they tallied one enemy transport ship blazing and sinking, with another damaged. One of the B-24s crashed in the water; some of its crew members were rescued.

Nine of the HALPRO B-24Ds arrived over Bengasi Harbor, Libya, at night on June 21 after RAF Wellington bombers illuminated the target area with flares and incendiaries. In North African operations in 1942 and 1943,

Its 90th BG bomber days over, B-24D Pug Nose flew transport runs with its top turret deleted. Lee Bushnell Collection

American and British airpower worked closely. AAF planes quickly adopted the RAF-style fin flash of red, white, and blue as an Allied recognition feature; on twin-tail aircraft including Liberators, the flash appeared on the insides as well as the outsides.

Throughout June and July, Eleventh AF B-24s and LB-30s, often operating with B-17s, launched bombing missions against targets including Kiska. Weather pre-empted some sorties.

Seventh AF LB-30s staged through Midway the night of June 26–27, and bombed Wake Island. For the first half of the initial year of war for the United States, Liberator bombing missions were almost exclusively performed by small groups of planes in Alaska, North Africa, and the Central and South Pacific. The B-24 as mass strategic weapon was yet to be realized.

On the night of June 29–30, AAF B-24s bombed Libya's Tobruk Harbor. When one of the Liberators was lost, the first US combat casualties in the Middle East occurred.

The Fourth of July 1942 saw deadly pyrotechnics in the Mediterranean as B-24s attacked a convoy the night of July 4–5, flaming one tanker. More B-24s visited enemy shipping in Bengasi Harbor that night.

The build-up of American forces in North Africa and Alaska in 1942 prompted some late logistical switches. The 404th Bomb Squadron (BS), its B-24s already painted desert sand for North Africa, was dispatched to the Alaskan Theater instead, arriving on July 8. Crews called these Liberators Pink Elephants because of the hue of the desert-sand paint.

On July 9, 1942, six Liberators in the Mediterranean, on their way to

shipping targets, were jumped by enemy fighters. One B-24 was shot down, and the other five returned without bombing their objective. It was a lesson that would become clear in every theater: No matter how well gunned, B-24s (and B-17s) were vulnerable to fighter attacks.

On July 11, Japanese seaplane fighters attacked four B-24s taking off for a Kiska strike. These Liberators persisted without loss, and bombed a Japanese cruiser with unobserved results.

The HALPRO B-24s were redesignated the Halverson BS on July 17. Along with the 9th BS, which had 19

Battle-scarred B-24D of the Liberandos cruises past Mount Vesuvius, Italy.

B-24s and nine B-17s, these Liberators then formed the 1st Provisional Group on July 20, 1942, still under the command of Col. Harry Halverson at Lydda, Palestine. As the summer of 1942 unfolded, AAF Liberator combat operations continued primarily in the Middle East and Alaska. Harbor bombing—whether at Tobruk and Bengasi, or Kiska—saw B-24s and an occasional Alaskan LB-30 being employed to support the objectives of surface forces. On August 21, B-24s from two squadrons intercepted an enemy convoy southwest of Crete. Liberator crews claimed two ships probably sunk. Enemy fighters picked off a straggling B-24, which then ditched at sea. Liberator operations were launched almost daily in this period. The Alaska sorties continued to suffer a high number of aborts due to weather and mechanical problems.

On September 6, an Eleventh AF B-24 on armed reconnaissance patrol over Tanaga sank a Japanese mine layer and strafed a tender, as well as tents and buildings on shore. The majestic heavy bomber could pinch-hit on the deck, too.

During the nights of September 16–17 and 19–20, B-24s ranged to Greece to attack shipping in this German-held country. Late in September, the 90th Bomb Group (BG), a pioneer of Pacific B-24 operations, paused in Hawaii to fill a void in the force of heavy bombers deemed necessary for the protection of the islands.

On September 25, the Eleventh AF put up nine B-24s for bombing and a tenth for photography as part of a formation including B-17s and P-39 and P-40 escorts. This marked the Eleventh's first combined American-Canadian mission as Royal Canadian Air Force (RCAF) Kittyhawks joined the armada. The number of B-24s in Alaska grew during 1942 to afford the Eleventh AF the opportunity to launch a total of 14 B-24s plus one LB-30 recon plane on September 27. Though small by later European Theater of Operations (ETO) air-war standards, this force represented gathering momentum in Alaska. The next day, a B-24

and an LB-30 bombed installations on Attu. Over Bengasi on October 6, two B-24s went down as heavy, accurate flak, and fighters, challenged the Liberators.

Because the Eighth AF ultimately operated vast fleets of B-24s and B-17s, many notations in the Air Force combat chronology only list the number of heavy bombers dispatched, without calling out specific types. The first notation for the Eighth specifically citing use of B-24s was on October 9, 1942, when Liberators participated in the first American mission in which more than 100 bombers were sent from England to bomb the Continent. Five targets in France were hit by the combined forces.

The Tenth AF used B-24s on October 21, 1942, for the first heavy bomber mission over China, and the first AAF bomb strike north of the Yangtze and Yellow Rivers. The Liberators were part of the India Air Task Force (IATF). They staged through Chengtu, China, and bombed coal mines at Linhsi. As conceived, the mission was to bomb nearby power stations and pumps in order to flood the mines, denying their output to the Japanese. The bombing did not succeed in flooding the coal mines, but did damage the target area. As described in the Strategic Bombing Survey for the Pacific war, Japan was resource-poor, and dependent upon its conquered territory for materials, including coal, to drive its wartime economy. Hence, an ongoing emphasis on interrupting the flow of raw materials to Japan had deliberate consequences on Japan's war-making capability.

United States Army, Middle East Air Forces (USAMEAF) activated the Liberator-equipped 376th BG at Lydda, Palestine, on October 31, 1942. The 376th replaced the 1st Provisional Group, and was placed under the original group's commander, Col. George F. McGuire. At first, the 376th was envisioned as part of an English-American air force that would be dispatched to the Caucasus to help the Soviet Union. But that idea was not realized, and the 376th stayed in the Middle East. On November 7, the 376th began the move from Palestine to Egypt.

Two days later, Gen. Carl Spaatz acknowledged to Gen. Dwight D.

Eisenhower that any more air force build-ups in North Africa must of necessity erode build-ups in England, because no other theaters had force levels considered reducible. That same day, the Eighth AF launched an experimental attack by B-24s and B-17s from reduced altitudes on the submarine base at Saint-Nazaire, in occupied France. Twelve Liberators, bombing from 17,500–18,300ft, sustained but little flak damage, while 31 B-17s flying at 7,500–10,000ft suffered three shootdowns and 22 planes damaged. Low-level heavy bomber attacks on German submarine bases were not pursued after this. (Ultimately, the U-boat threat would be neutralized on the high seas, often by Liberators.)

On November 12, 1942, the US-AMEAF was dissolved and replaced by

the Ninth AF. The next day, the 98th BG arrived in Egypt from Palestine, to bolster Ninth AF Liberator assets, as Tobruk fell to the British Eighth Army. In the hard-fighting Fifth AF, on November 17, 1942, a lone B-24 bombed the Japanese-held Rabaul wharf area as Liberators added their might to the fight for the South Pacific.

On November 20, IATF B-24s of the Tenth AF bombed the Mandalay marshaling yards as these B-24s stepped up their campaign against Japanese targets in Thailand and Burma. By November 23, 1942, Eighth AF crews reported a noticeable shift in enemy fighter tactics as the fighters perceived the B-24s' and B-17s' relatively weak defenses against frontal attacks. The fighters began more head-on attacks instead of attacks from the rear.

The 93rd BG fielded olive-drab B-24Ds in European combat, as this 1943 photo depicts. US Air Force via Jeff Ethell Collection

(Ultimately, this would precipitate an ongoing struggle to add power nose turrets to B-24s and B-17s, as well as heavy cockpit armor, especially in the Eighth AF, where Liberators and Fortresses were often fitted with thick slabs of armor glass in the cockpit. Some Eighth B-24s clearly showed the application of external bolt-on armor plating on the fuselage beside the cockpit area.)

On December 4, 1942, the Ninth AF sent B-24s in the first attack by American bombers on Italy. The Italian fleet and docks at Naples reeled from

177

Overcast on November 24, 1944, did not stop this Eighth AF B-24 from releasing a stick of 12 bombs over Europe. US Air Force

the bomb tonnage. Hits were claimed on a battleship, among three or four ships struck, as well as harbor targets and a railyard. The next day, Fifth AF B-24s bombed the Japanese airfield at Kavieng on New Ireland, northeast of New Guinea.

A year after the Japanese attack on Pearl Harbor, three squadrons of B-

24s from the 93rd BG arrived in North Africa from England to add to the Twelfth AF inventory.

On December 8, 1942, B-17s and a lone B-24 of the Fifth AF attacked six Japanese destroyers bringing troops to reinforce the Buna-Gona beachhead, which was then under Allied ground assault. The six destroyers were discouraged by the heavy bombers and turned back for the Japanese stronghold at Rabaul. It was a textbook example of how prewar planners thought heavy bombers would be employed; in actual combat, such routs of warships

were infrequent. (Five days later, B-17s and B-24s intercepted a convoy of five Japanese destroyers again steaming for Buna with reinforcements; this time, the heavy bombers did not deter the enemy convoy.)

By December 12, the Ninth AF's Bomber Command exercised operational control over RAF Liberators as they attacked the Naples dock area. The operational control of these RAF Liberators would be common through the end of 1942. On December 14, the Eighth AF's inspector general reported that the diversion of Eighth AF assets to equip the Twelfth AF in North Africa (as with the B-24s of the 93rd BG) was seriously hindering Eighth training and combat programs.

On December 21, single-ship Fifth AF B-24 strikes against Japanese shipping and barges north of Finschhafen, New Guinea, and in the mouth of the Mambare River, as well as near Cape Ward Hunt, reflected local doctrine that led to the use of Liberators individually in the Pacific far more than over European targets.

December 22 was a harbinger of a dreary future for Japanese forces when the Seventh AF launched a remarkable 26 B-24s against Wake Island, bombing the night of December 22–23 after staging through Midway, from Hawaii. A dozen Tenth AF B-24s bombed docks, a railway station, an arsenal, and a powerplant at Bangkok on December 26. Three days later, the same-size B-24 formation from IATF attacked shipping around Rangoon, in southern Burma.

On the last day of 1942, Ninth AF B-24s and RAF Liberators bombed docks and shipping at Sfax, Tunisia, with good effect. That same day, in the South Pacific, Fifth AF B-24s, operating singly, bombed the Japanese-held airfield at Gasmata, New Britain, and attacked shipping in Wide Bay and Saint George Channel. Meanwhile, six Eleventh AF B-24s, protected by an escort of nine P-38s, attacked Kiska Harbor, hitting two cargo vessels. Six Japanese fighters intercepted the B-24s and P-38s; one enemy plane was listed as a probable kill. The first full year of war for the AAF drew to a close with Liberators on several fronts.

The best plans of the AAF could be undone by weather. On January 2, 1943, the Eighth AF sent four radar-equipped B-24s on a "moling" intruder mission to harass the Germans. The idea was to use cloud cover that made mass bombing unfeasible (in the days before advanced radar-bombing and radio-bombing techniques), by having the moling B-24s alert enemy air-raid crews north of the Ruhr Valley, in northwestern Germany, thus causing an expenditure of German activity to meet a nonexistent threat above the clouds. However, this mission and two more attempts in January were thwarted when clear weather over the

target area allowed the Germans to see that there was no serious bomber formation.

In the Pacific, the takeover of Buna Mission on January 2 by Australian and American forces exemplified what would follow: repeated air strikes, many by B-24s, to prepare a site for ultimate land invasion.

On January 5, the Ninth AF sent the 93rd BG's B-24s against Sousse Harbor, Tunisia, when the primary target—Tunis—was obscured by clouds. That night, RAF Liberators from 160 Squadron, under Ninth AF operational control, revisited both harbors. On January 16, the Ninth AF B-24s bombed Tripoli Harbor and town, and RAF Liberators from 178 Squadron struck at Tripoli's Benito Gate and a road junction.

On January 20, Tenth AF B-24s, on the largest mission in the theater to date, flew reconnaissance that revealed new railway construction by the Japanese between Thailand and Burma. The Tenth AF gained more Liberator crews when the 492nd BS, new to combat, borrowed four B-24s and one crew from the 436th BS, with which to mount a nine-plane strike against Rangoon docks.

As January 1943 closed, the Seventh AF applied increased pressure in the Central Pacific. After six B-24s dropped 60 bombs on Wake on January 25, the Seventh sent out three Liberators the next day from Funafuti in the Ellice Islands to fly photo reconnaissance over Tarawa, Maiana, Abemama, Beru, and Tomama, in the Gilbert Islands. Over the lagoon at Tarawa, the B-24s attacked a merchant ship.

By February 8, the Tenth AF was able to put up 18 B-24s to hit Rangoon rail facilities. On February 12, the unit loaded seven B-24s with the first 2,000lb blockbusters used in the China-Burma-India (CBI) Theater of Operations. The blockbusters failed to damage the Myitnge Bridge. A dozen other Tenth B-24s returned to Rangoon the same day.

The Thirteenth AF's 424th BS, part of the 307th BG, first sent its B-24s into combat February 13, 1943, in an attack on Buin and on shipping in the Shortland Islands that turned deadly when Japanese fighters ripped into the Liberators' light fighter cover,

destroying half of the B-24s and three escorting fighters. The next day, nine B-24s with light fighter protection again attacked Buin. Again, stiff Japanese fighter opposition downed two B-24s. The cumulative loss of five Thirteenth AF B-24s in two days prompted a halt in all their daylight bombing missions until adequate fighter escort could be provided.

Tenth AF B-24s pressured the Japanese on the night of February 22–23 when 10 Liberators mined a section of the Gulf of Martaban in southern Burma. A force of 24 B-24s and RAF Liberators flew a diversionary strike against Rangoon and Mingaladon airfield.

On March 2, the Fifth AF regimen of single-plane B-24 strikes was altered for the Battle of Bismarck Sea. B-17s and B-24s attacked a 16-ship Japanese convoy comprised of equal numbers of transports and destroyers steaming from Rabaul toward Huon Gulf. First bombed north of New Britain, the convoy was last bombed that day between New Guinea and New Britain. By day's end, half the transports were sunk or sinking, according to AAF reports. The next day, the heavy bombers were joined by other American and Australian planes and US Navy PT boats. By the end of day two, all eight transports had been sunk and airpower had demolished half the destroyers, as well as a large part of the Japanese fighter planes covering the convoy. On March 4, Allied planes continued bombing remnants of the convoy in Huon Gulf, thereby closing the Battle of Bismarck Sea as a decisive defeat for the Japanese. This marked the last try by the Japanese to use large ships to reinforce positions on Huon Gulf. Though not strictly a B-24 action, Liberators took part.

On March 6, the Eighth AF launched 15 B-24s on a diversionary attack on a bridge and U-boat facilities at Brest, France, while a main force of heavy bombers attacked a power plant and other targets at Lorient. (When Germany proper was bombed, American planners discounted the value of bombing German power plants because of the largely erroneous assumption that Germans could shunt power over redundant systems to restore electrical energy to any section of the country af-

Picturesque mosaic of European farm fields underlays smoky ribbons from marker flares dropped by an Eighth AF B-24. Kiernan Collection

fected. In reality, German officials expressed concern that the Allies would destroy an electrical system that often had insufficient redundancy.)

B-24s bombed Rabaul on March 11. The AAF in the Pacific, including the available and growing number of B-24s, attacked the problem of strategic targets differently than did their European counterparts. The tenuous reach of Japanese supply lines made attacks on shipping and individual bases take on a greater strategic significance than that in Europe.

On March 15, Liberators of Fifth AF units and Australian warplanes attacked targets on Dobo, in the Arol Islands, and Wokam. Joint US-Australian operations would continue, sometimes involving Liberators operated by both countries' air forces.

During this period, Tenth AF B-24s repeatedly bombed bridges and viaducts in the CBI; Fifth AF Liberators went after shipping and airfields, and Ninth AF B-24s revisited Naples and other targets useful to the impending Allied invasion of Sicily and Italy, including ferries and harbor installations at Palermo and Messina. The plucky Eleventh AF continued to launch against targets including Kiska.

Indicative of the build-up of B-24s, the Eleventh AF was able to muster 16 B-24s on April Fool's Day 1943, against Kiska. The large (for Alaska) group of Liberators joined B-25s and P-38s in attacking ships, camps, and the beach area. The next day, 18 more B-24s launched sorties against Kiska, while four Liberators bombed the runway on Attu. (The previous day, preparations were ordered for Operation Landgrab—the Allied invasion of Attu.) By April 15, the Eleventh mustered 23 B-24s, launching from Adak to strike Kiska.

The Thirteenth AF sent three B-24s on harassing strikes against Kahili airfield in Bougainville in the Solomon Islands on April 10. Just as the Japanese sent single-ship night bombers over American airfields, the AAF sent B-24s, often at night, and often alone and spread several hours after the previous solo B-24, to bomb Japanese airfields. Reasons were many: The harassing strikes deprived enemy personnel of rest; they cratered runways, to temporarily slow operations and necessitate expenditure of manpower; they destroyed aircraft and enemy equipment; and they forced the Japanese to commit some resources to antiaircraft protection.

On April 11, a Ninth AF B-24 went down on a mission over Naples Harbor. Intense flak and fighting took a toll of the formation, while the B-24's gunners claimed three enemy fighters downed.

Factories formerly used by Ford and General Motors Corp. in Antwerp, Belgium, were the target of 65 Eighth AF heavy bombers on May 4. A mixed group of 34 B-17s and B-24s were successful in their feint toward the French coastline, drawing more than 100 German fighters—more than half the enemy fighters in the area—aloft. Many of these fighters drawn away from the main bomber force were unable to interfere with its mission.

As American forces were establishing their landing on Attu in the Aleutians, the Eleventh AF sent a single B-24 on May 11 for use as an air-to-ground liaison plane, while B-24 supply-dropping sorties were flown in support of the troops. Poor weather obscured some B-24 bombardment missions, and one B-24 dropped leaflets over Attu. A May 15 mission to bomb Wake by Seventh AF B-24s from Midway netted mixed results: seven B-24s bombed Wake, four aborted, and seven others failed to find the target. Twenty-two Japanese fighters attacked the bombers. One B-24 was lost, and B-24 gunners claimed four Japanese planes shot down.

On June 4, six Eleventh AF B-24s followed a Navy Ventura bomber and made a radar-bombing run over North Head, in the Aleutians. The Eleventh continued to use other B-24s as air-to-ground liaison aircraft in the theater.

When the US War Department diverted the 389th BG from England to North Africa on June 7, the Eighth AF lost another building block in its strategic plan. The 389th subsequently was to play a role in the famous August low-level mission against Ploesti's oil refineries in August.

On June 26, the 93rd BG's Liberators left England for North Africa, in anticipation of heavy bombardment requirements for the invasion of Sicily and the low-level Ploesti oil refinery raid. The next day, the Eighth AF's 44th BG took its B-24s to North Africa as well, as the 201st Bomb Wing (Provisional) was attached to the Ninth AF in the Mediterranean, for operations between July 2 and August 21.

Seventh AF Liberators continued long-range missions in the Central Pacific. On June 28, 1943, a bombing mission by Seventh units dwindled from attrition. Of 19 B-24s launched from Hawaii, one crashed at an en route stage stop at Palmyra, to the south. Of the 18 Liberators reaching the forward staging base of Funafuti, two were released from the mission because of engine trouble. When two more of the B-24s crashed as the bombers were taking off from Funafuti, eight more B-24s were grounded following the second crash. This left a force of only six B-24s

A grateful 449th BG airman poses in the flak hole in the left wing of his B-24 in Italy after a nearly fatal mission. Chet Goad Collection

aloft for the mission to bomb Nauru. Two of these aborted, and two more did not find Nauru because of a weather front. At last, only two B-24s of 19 dispatched from Hawaii actually bombed Nauru, with unobserved results.

On July 8, Fourteenth AF units put aloft 22 B-24s, escorted by 13 P-40s, to attack shipping, docks, and a cement works at Haiphong in French Indochina. Nine B-24s returned to Haiphong two days later, and three were in the vicinity again on July 11.

The Ninth AF, bolstered by B-24s sent down from England, launched about 80 Liberators to drop bombs on the marshaling yards at Naples on July 17. One B-24 was shot down, and several others received damage as a result of stiff fighter challenges. The B-24 gunners claimed 23 enemy fighters.

On July 18, 21 B-24s from Thirteenth AF units joined P-40s, P-38s, and about 140 Navy and Marine dive-bombers and fighters in a thorough attack on Japanese facilities at Kahili. Fifteen of the Liberators went after the Kahili airfield, bombing antiaircraft emplacements, runways, and revetments.

In the Mediterranean, the Ninth AF flexed its Liberator strength by launching more than 100 B-24s on July 19. They bombed railyards at Littoria, in central Italy, and a nearby airfield. On the flight home, railroads at Orlando and Anzio were bombed too. Effective Italian railroads—a success for

Benito Mussolini's regime—were significant targets in the Italian bombing campaign. As the war in Italy progressed, everything from P-47 fighter-bombers to B-24s were employed to stop the trains from aiding the Axis war effort.

The climactic push against the Japanese base at Munda in the Solomons on July 25 involved the heaviest air attack to date in the South Pacific. Included in the American air armada were Thirteenth AF B-24s and some remaining Pacific B-17s. Later that day, 10 more B-24s, with escort, bombed Bibolo Hill. The ground assault on the area opened the same day.

The cadence of the war, prosecuted by determined Allies, delivered bases closer to the shrinking Japanese perimeter as the last half of 1943 unfolded. Signaling the acquisition of closer airfields was the Seventh AF's last mission against Wake to be launched from Midway, on July 26. During this strike, eight B-24s bombed an oil storage area. About 20 Japanese fighters attacked the Liberators; a possible sighting of a German FW 190 among the attackers most likely was in error. Rumored to be in Japanese service, and even given an Allied code

The 718th BS of the 449th BG put B-24s over the Alps. Plane nearest camera has lightweight tail gun emplacement. Chet Goad Collection

name, FW 190s do not appear to have actually been used by Japan, according to historian Rene Francillon.

Fighter pilots flying P-47 Thunderbolts handed the Luftwaffe a surprise on July 30, 1943, as the Americans escorted Eighth AF bombers when German fighters attacked over Bocholt. This was a deeper penetration than the Luftwaffe was accustomed to, and was made possible by the auxiliary gas tanks the P-47s carried. The advent of long-ranging escort fighters would enable B-24s and B-17s of Eighth AF units to carry the war deep into Germany.

On the last day of July 1943, AAF Liberator operations included a nine-plane mission by Tenth AF B-24s to lay mines in the Rangoon River.

August 1, 1943, was the fateful date of Operation Tidal Wave —the minimum-altitude strike by 177 Ninth AF B-24s against Romanian oil refineries at Ploesti. Noncombat attrition be-gan over water on the long flight to Romania, and accelerated dramatically when the bombers came under fire over land. Ultimately, 54 Liberators and 532 aviators were lost on this mission, but significant damage was registered on the refineries, despite navigational mix-ups that saw some targets bombed by more B-24s than briefed, and others less heavily hit.

The increasing tempo of the American war effort was manifested in Alaska on August 4, when the Eleventh AF logged a one-day record of 153 tons of bombs dropped on Kiska. The mixed force of attacking planes included a total of 25 B-24 sorties in at least two groupings.

Pressure on the German war machine increased on August 13 when 61 B-24s launched the first Ninth AF raid on Austria, bombing an aircraft factory at Wiener-Neustadt. The Ninth returned the next day, intent on destroying Bf 109 fighters before they could be completed.

In Alaska, on August 13, 1943, an Eleventh AF B-24 flew a "special" reconnaissance mission, according to the official AAF history. The next day, it launched two B-24s on radar ferret and reconnaissance flights. Ferrets were specially instrumented aircraft that probed enemy installations.

On August 15, American and Canadian troops invaded Kiska. An eerie silence greeted the Allies—the Japanese took advantage of the frequent Aleutian fogs to evacuate their garrison.

The Ninth AF sent 86 B-24s to bomb an area of the city, and airfields, at Foggia, Italy, on August 16.

The wandering 44th, 93rd, and 389th BGs brought their B-24s back to England from the Mediterranean in time to resume Eighth AF operations on September 8.

Ranging out from Canton Island in the central Pacific, Seventh AF B-24s on September 8 fired their machine guns at a Japanese flying boat, but no visible damage could be discerned.

The war in the Far East caused its share of attrition. On September 15, 1943, four of five B-24s attacking a Haiphong cement plant were shot down by an enemy fighter force estimated at 50 aircraft. The surviving B-24 claimed 10 enemy fighters downed by its gunners.

War in the Mediterranean demanded more heavy bombers, so Gen. Dwight Eisenhower requested that the Eighth AF send the veteran 44th, 93rd, and 389th BGs back. Their return to the Med occurred on September 16.

When American commanders wanted to prevent Japanese attacks on US installations at Baker Island and in the Ellice Islands by taking the Japanese at Tarawa out of the fight, 24 Seventh AF B-24s, rising from Funafuti and Canton Island, bombed multiple targets in the Gilbert Islands on the night of September 18–19, as part of a coordinated Army-Navy attack.

The Ninth AF launched its last mission from North Africa, on September 22. It was a B-24 strike on Maritsa and Eleusis airfields. The bomb groups of IX Bomber Command subsequently were assigned to the Twelfth AF in the Med. The Ninth AF emerged as a tactical air force in England, established on October 16. The Twelfth was willing to expand the B-24s' repertoire, and sent Liberators on a low-level raid to bomb Italian bridges on October 19.

On October 25, more than 60 Fifth AF B-24s bombed Rabaul, claiming about 20 airplanes destroyed on the ground. Between 60 and 70 Japanese fighters contested the Liberators' presence, and B-24 gunners claimed more than 30 shot down in a running gun battle. The volume of this day's Rabaul strike was a far cry from the small efforts mounted in the beginning of the year.

On November 1, 1943, the Fifteenth AF was activated in Tunis, under Gen. James "Jimmy" Doolittle's command. The Fifteenth took up the strategic bombardment role in the Mediterranean, launching B-24s and B-17s the next day to Wiener-Neustadt.

Armistice Day, November 11—a day commemorating the end of World War I, and symbolizing world peace—was greeted in 1943 by a busy slate of B-24 operations around the world. Six Fourteenth AF B-24s bombed the Burma Road, causing a punishing landslide. Twenty-eight B-24s from Fifteenth AF units attacked the Annecy ball bearing plant and a viaduct at Antheor, both in southern France. Meanwhile, Fifth AF B-24s bombed Lakunai airfield, and the Thirteenth joined planes from the Fifth AF, US Navy aircraft carriers, and the Royal Australian Air Force (RAAF) in an attack on Rabaul Harbor—the first Rabaul strike for elements of the Thirteenth. In the central Pacific, the Seventh AF was on the receiving end of an attack as Japanese bombers hit the Nanumea airfield, damaging or destroying several planes including one B-24.

On November 15 and 16, the Fourteenth AF persisted in strikes on the Hong Kong-Kowloon areas. When bad weather on November 15 kept 15 Liberators from bombing, five more hit docks at Kowloon. The next day, 11 B-24s, with a pair of B-25s and four P-40s, returned to the Kowloon docks, keeping up the pressure because shipping was the key to Japanese survival.

A telling entry in the AAF chronology for the last day of November 1943 chronicled a force of 200 Eighth AF heavy bombers that aborted their mission because of cloud formations which made it difficult for the bombers to form up over England, and which, according to the Air Force chronology, required "flying at altitudes not feasible for the B-24s included in the mission." (As detailed in another chapter of this

book, the increasing weight of B-24s equipped for combat in the European environment levied a penalty in altitude performance.)

On the third of December, Fifteenth AF B-24s bombed Rome.

After the withdrawal of Japanese forces from the Aleutians, Liberator activity in Alaska diminished. But on December 8, three Eleventh AF B-24s flew an armed recon mission, while that night, another B-24 sent on a photo mission over Kasatochi Island turned back with mechanical problems.

December 13, 1943, was the first time the Eighth AF put up more than 600 heavy bombers on a single mission, when a total of 649 B-17s and B-24s, out of 710 originally dispatched, dropped bombs on German port areas at Hamburg and Bremen, and subma-

Fifth BG B-24s depart smoking refineries at Balikpapan. Jack Hayes Collection

rine yards at Kiel. Also for the first time, P-51 Mustang fighters escorting the bombers reached the limit of their escort range.

The night of December 19 reverberated with the engines of 20 B-24s sent by Tenth AF units to bomb newly expanded docks in Bangkok. Substantial damage was claimed.

On December 21, eight Seventh AF B-24s from Nanumea conspired with four Navy PB4Y-1s on a photo mission over Kwajalein Atoll in the Marshall Islands. (Sometimes, the battle order called for the AAF B-24s to bomb the target, keeping enemy defenses occu-

B-24s of the 5th and 307th BGs attack a Japanese surface fleet in Brunei Bay in northern Borneo on November 16, 1944. Intense, long-range flak downed several Liberators; warship near bottom center of photo is illuminated by its own muzzle blasts reflecting off the water. Jack Hayes Collection

pied, while the Navy patrol bombers photographed enemy installations from slightly farther away, relatively unhindered.)

The official history highlighted a Fifth AF mission by B-24s the night of December 23–24, in which the Liberator crews harassed Japanese forces at Cape Gloucester by dropping small bombs, hand grenades, and beer bottles. (The use of empty beer bottles was not limited to this one particular B-24 mission. Some crews found they could drop empty beer bottles that would whistle as they fell, creating the illu-

sion of a bomb in flight. When no explosion resulted, the crews reasoned, the enemy would be wary of delayed-action bombs; a cheap way of stretching limited resources.)

Christmas Day 1943 saw the Fifth AF mount a mission of about 180 B-26s, B-25s, A-20s, and B-24s against Cape Gloucester, continuing bombing pressure on that target as an ongoing pre-invasion softening, under way for days. The day after Christmas, the US 1st Marine Division landed at the cape.

Over Italy on December 28, 17 unescorted B-24s from Fifteenth AF units were jumped by about 50 fighters before reaching their target: the marshaling yards at Vicenza. Ten B-24s were shot down. Several B-24s salvoed their bombs over the target area. The Liberators claimed 18 fighters shot down. That same day, in the central Pacific, the Seventh AF exemplified island-hopping by staging B-24s out of Tarawa to hit Maloelap. Not too much

earlier in the year, Tarawa itself was the target of the Seventh Liberators.

On the last day of 1943, a year that saw B-24 strength swell in all theaters where they were used, the Fourteenth AF launched 25 Liberators against the Lampang railroad yards. Large fires and many secondary explosions were noted.

Activation of the 868th BS, working directly under XIII Bomber Command, took nocturnal, radar-equipped Snooper SB-24s out of the domain of the 5th BG effective January 1, 1944. Snoopers flew night interdiction missions against targets including Japanese shipping.

The Eighth AF sent more than 570 B-17s and B-24s over Germany on January 11. Electronics-equipped Pathfinder aircraft in the formation included, for the first time, B-24s. This textbook European strategic bombing mission was contested by 500 German fighters; 60 heavy bombers went down.

Single B-24 armed recon sorties bombed Maliai, Vunakanau, and Lakunai on January 18, 1944. The growing strength of the Fifth AF B-24 bomb groups manifested itself January 19 when 57 Liberators bombed Boram, while 17 more hit Amboina and Halong, and two more claimed hits on a freighter near Aitape. Sixteen Tenth AF B-24s bombed an encampment at Prome, Burma, on January 22. The Seventh AF kept up a program of bombing Kwajalein after staging through Tarawa during this period in the war. Fifteenth AF B-24s took the war to enemy marshaling yards and other transportation targets in Italy during this time.

Bombing by the light of flares dropped by other B-24s, 19 Liberators of Thirteenth AF units attacked the Japanese-held airstrip at Lakunai late in the evening of January 25. Forty-three Eighth AF B-24s, using Gee-H blind-bombing equipment for the first time, bombed a V-weapon site at Bonnieres on January 28. Gee-H was more accurate than the older H2X system, but was tethered to a 200mi range for its homing beacon.

On January 29, with American invasion troops heading toward the Marshall Islands, Seventh AF B-24s kept up day and night attacks on Maloelap, Jaluit, Aur Atoll, Wotje, and Mille. The next night, they kept up all-night air strikes against Kwajalein, readying for the invasion of that atoll on the last day of January by US Army and Marine troops. On the first of February, the Seventh AF deployed B-24s to hit beach defenses on Kwajalein to aid the American troops fighting there. On February 2, 1944, Fifteenth AF B-24s bombed a radar station at Durazzo in northern Albania. Spitfires escorted the Liberators over Italy.

Eleventh AF B-24s joined P-38s and Navy aircraft to fly cover missions for Navy destroyers and light cruisers retiring after bombarding the Kurabu Cape-Musashi Bay areas. The planes then photographed and attacked Paramushiru and Shimushu in the Kuril Islands.

The 454th BG's B-24s became operational with the Fifteenth AF on February 8, 1944, bringing the total of heavy bomb groups in the Fifteenth to 10. The 455th and 456th B-24 groups added their strength to the Fifteenth when they went operational on February 18. Two days later, Fifteenth AF B-24s bombed enemy troop concentrations at the Anzio beachhead.

On February 14, 1944, the Seventh AF put up more than 40 B-24s of the 11th and 30th BGs, launching from Makin and Tarawa, and striking Ponape Island during the first Seventh AF raid in the Caroline Islands. Two of the B-24s bombed the alternate target at Emidj Island.

During February, the Eighth AF B-24s repeatedly bombed German V-weapon sites. Additionally, Eighth B-24s struck other targets. On February 24, 238 Liberators bombed an airfield and factory at Gotha, suffering a loss of 33 B-24s. A combined force of 680 B-17s and B-24s from the Eighth bombed aircraft factories at Regensburg, Augsburg, and Furth, as well as a ball bearing producer at Stuttgart on February 25. The attacks were launched in concert with a Fifteenth AF raid on Regensburg, and significant attacks by the RAF on Schweinfurt and Augsburg the nights of February 24–25 and February 25–26, respectively. The two European strategic bombardment forces—the Eighth and Fifteenth AFs—continued to set the pace for massive deployments of B-24s against strategic daylight targets.

On February 26, XI Bomber Command (Air Striking Group TG 90.1) was directed to perform armed photo recon missions in the Kurils by day or by night, as weather permitted in the harsh northern regions.

In the Pacific, the presence of substantial numbers of B-24s was sometimes a wearying signal to the Japanese that another Allied invasion was at hand. On February 28, 1944, 23 Fifth AF B-24s and 39 A-20s bombed Hansa Bay, New Guinea. About 20 other Liberators bombed the nearby Awar and Nubia airfields. A mixed group of B-25s and B-24s hit Momote, Lorengau, and other targets in the Admiralty Islands in preparation for the Allied landing.

Entries for early March 1944 continued the almost daily use of Liberators on varied fronts. The harsh Alaskan environment forced nine Eleventh AF B-24s to turn back to Shemya, in the Aleutians, from a search for enemy shipping on March 3, as heavy icing and squalls thwarted the Liberators. Two days later, obstructive cloud conditions caused many aborts in a 219-plane Eighth AF B-24 mission to bomb airfields in France. Alternate targets were bombed by the remaining B-24s. On March 11, 34 Eighth B-24s bombed the V-weapon site at Wizernes, using blind-bombing techniques be-

A 5th BG B-24 conformed to the drainage ditch beside the runway in this mishap. Sharp pieces of runway coral could puncture tires, leading to results similar to this. Harvey Davison Collection

cause of a thick overcast. The next day, 52 Eighth AF Liberators again used blind-bombing techniques to bomb the V-weapon site at Saint-Pol/Siracourt. On March 9, while approximately 300 B-17s bombed Berlin, Eighth AF B-24s numbering 158 laid bombs on other targets, including Hannover, Brunswick, and Nienberg.

Seventh AF B-24s operated out of Kwajalein for the first time on March 11, 1944, on the first raid from the Marshall Islands against Wake. Four days later, the Seventh again capitalized on its positioning at Kwajalein to send B-24s on its first mission against Truk Atoll, striking Dublon and Eten Islands in a predawn raid that also saw alternate targets at Oroluk Anchorage and Ponape Town hit.

As March 1944 wore on, Thirteenth AF B-24s added their weight to repeated strikes on Rabaul.

March 15 saw the contested area around Monte Cassino, in central Italy, bombed by a mixture of more than 300

The Goon *immortalized a nemesis of Popeye, and flew combat over China. The plane is B-24D number 41-24183.* US Air Force via Jeff Ethell Collection

Fifteenth AF B-24s and B-17s, supporting the US Fifth Army. On March 17, bombs from more than 200 Fifteenth AF B-24s whistled down on Vienna and targets of opportunity, as P-47s and P-38s provided escort cover. That same day, Fifth AF Liberators continued their campaign against Wewak, New Guinea. Two days later, the Fifth launched 130 aircraft, including B-24s, B-25s, A-20s, and P-38s, to attack and nearly annihilate a Japanese supply convoy trying to make it from Wewak to Hollandia; at least five ships were sunk.

About 650 Eighth AF B-24s and B-17s attacked the Berlin vicinity on March 21, while 56 Eighth B-24s went after the V-weapon launch facility at Watten. That same day, the Thirteenth AF put up 22 B-24s to bomb Vunakanau airfield. The pattern for B-24 attacks in the Pacific in this era showed a willingness to deploy large formations when called for, or to use small groups or single Liberators on less dense targets, sometimes at night, contrary to doctrine in place over Europe.

On March 25, six Fourteenth AF B-24s dropped bombs on a motor pool and fuel dump at Mangshih in western China, taking out a large portion of the target area.

In the spring of 1944, Allied troops were pressed in by Japanese forces in the Imphal Valley in India. The situation called for drastic measure, including rushing C-47 units from Italy to India to help airlift supplies to the surrounded garrison. On March 26, 1944, three Tenth AF Liberators and an equal number of B-25s bombed Japanese troops along the Imphal-Tiddim Road.

An increasing number of Fifteenth AF heavy bomb groups led to the largest attack by that Air Force to date, on March 28, when almost 400 B-24s and B-17s bombed marshaling yards at Verona and Mestre, and railroad and highway bridges at Cesano and Fano. None of the heavy bombers were lost, while their gunners, and excellent fighter escorts, claimed 12 enemy fighters downed for the loss of five American fighters. The following day,

an even larger Fifteenth AF total, still hovering around 400 B-24s and B-17s, bombed marshaling yards at Turin, Bolzano, and Milan.

While the Fifteenth AF set and broke records in Italy, the Tenth AF continued to slug away at Japanese-held targets, putting up a dozen Liberators to bomb the Victoria Lake area near Rangoon on March 29. That same day, B-24s of the Thirteenth AF's 307th BG made the first daylight raid on Truk Atoll, when they hit the airfield on Eten Island. The complex mission staged from Munda through Torokina for arming and Nissan for refueling. Unescorted, the B-24s made claims for 31 Japanese interceptors destroyed, as well as about 50 aircraft on the ground. Two of the Long Rangers' Liberators were casualties on the mission.

March 30 saw the Fifth AF flex its increasing muscles with a show of more than 60 B-24s, backed up by about 90 P-47s and P-38s, conducting the first large-scale daylight raid on Hollandia. Airfields and fuel dumps were targeted. The fighter screen protecting the B-24s claimed 10 kills that day. The Fifth sent more than 60 Liberators back to Hollandia the next day, continuing a familiar pattern of pressure on Japanese strongholds.

On the first of April 1944, heavy clouds covered the path of 438 B-24s and B-17s sent by the Eighth AF to bomb Europe's largest chemical complex at Ludwigshafen in southern Germany. The 192 B-17s in the lead force abandoned the mission over the French coast in the face of the clouds. The second force's 246 B-24s became dispersed as they pressed the attack. Liberators numbering 162 bombed targets of opportunity at Pforzheim and Grafenhausen; another 26 B-24s inadvertently bombed Schaffhausen, in neutral Switzerland, and Strasbourg, France, mistaking them for German towns.

On April 3, a trio of Fourteenth AF B-24s sowed mines in Haiphong Harbor.

The Fifteenth AF sent 334 B-24s and B-17s to bomb Ploesti and other targets on April 5, 1944. Enemy fighters and antiaircraft shot down a total of 13 of the mixed heavy bombers. That same day, the Tenth AF sent 13 B-24s to bomb the railroad in Burma from

Moulmein to Kanchanaburi, destroying three bridges and damaging several more. Tracks and railroad cars also suffered under the B-24 attack.

On April 10, the Fifth AF put about 60 B-24s into the air to team with American destroyers, bombing Hansa Bay, and concentrating on antiaircraft positions and airfields, setting the stage for subsequent raids by a variety of Fifth AF warplanes on days to follow.

The Eleventh AF sent three Liberators to photograph and bomb Matsuwa Island on April 11; two of the B-24s turned back while the third bombed Matsuwa's runway area. Two days later, three Eleventh Liberators again visited Matsuwa and Onekotan Islands. The next day, three B-24s added Paramushiru Island to the list while again flying armed recon over Matsuwa and Onekotan.

April 15 saw yet another Fifteenth AF attack on Ploesti, Bucharest, and Nish, with a large mixed group totaling 448 B-24s and B-17s. The inaugural Seventh AF raid on the Mariana Islands was an April 18, 1944, B-24 mission in which B-24s escorted US Navy photo recon aircraft investigating Saipan.

Inclement weather forced the recall of Fifteenth AF bombers on April 21; of 17 bomb groups originally dispatched, seven groups did not receive the recall signal. More than 100 B-24s ended up over Bucharest and Turnu-Severin. Of 150 friendly fighters sent out as escorts, more than 40 rendezvoused with the unrecalled B-24s, and engaged about 30 enemy fighters. The other fighters, not meeting up with bombers to escort, attacked about 40 enemy fighters. When the day was over, the fighters and B-24s claimed 35 aerial victories for the loss of 10 American warplanes.

The Fifteenth and Eighth AFs interacted on April 24, when more than 520 Fifteenth AF B-24s and B-17s, escorted by more than 250 fighters, attacked Bucharest and Ploesti, occupying many enemy fighters. At the same time, the Eighth sent 716 B-24s and B-17s over a variety of German targets. Even with Fifteenth AF pressure, the Luftwaffe concentrated 250 fighters on the Eighth AF fleet. The Eighth lost a staggering total of 39 B-24s and B-17s on this day.

The Seventh AF launched its first mission against Guam on the night of April 24–25 when Kwajalein-based B-24s, staging through Eniwetok Atoll, struck Truk and Guam. On the last day in April, the Seventh mustered 41 Kwajalein-based Liberators to bomb a variety of targets at Wake Island.

The Tenth AF put more than 30 B-24s over Mandalay, Maymyo, and Yenangyaung's oil facility on May Day 1944, as the Thirteenth sent out 24 B-24s over coastal guns at Borpop; the Thirteenth Air Task Force sent some Liberators to bomb Woleai and Eauriprik Islands; and the Eighth AF launched a mixed fleet of 328 B-17s and B-24s to hit various marshaling yards in Western Europe. The Eighth continued its pressure on V-weapon sites during this part of 1944, often employing B-24s for the task.

The cost of running a strategic bombing campaign included the expense of launching 851 Eighth AF B-24s and B-17s on May 4, 1944, bound for Berlin and Brunswick, only to have all but 48 bombers—B-17s—recalled due to heavy cloud conditions. The toll in gasoline, maintenance, and wear-and-tear was phenomenal in an air war that often used vast quantities of resources in the effort to destroy other vast quantities of resources.

The Fifteenth AF continued to break its record for the number of heavy bombers launched when, on May 5, more than 640 B-24s and B-17s attacked marshaling yards at Ploesti and troop concentrations and the town of Podgorica in southwestern Yugoslavia. More than 240 fighter sorties supported the heavies. That same day, the Fourteenth AF dispatched 11 Liberators to bomb the docks and shipping at Haiphong, Indochina.

B-24s of the Seventh AF escorted Navy photo recon aircraft on a raid over Guam on May 6. The B-24s bombed Guam from 20,000ft, hitting two Japanese airfields and a town area before proceeding to Los Negros to prepare for their return to home base. Four Japanese interceptors were claimed by the B-24s' gunners.

On May 9, 1944, the Eighth AF began a deliberate offensive against Luftwaffe airfields at Saint-Dizier, Robin-

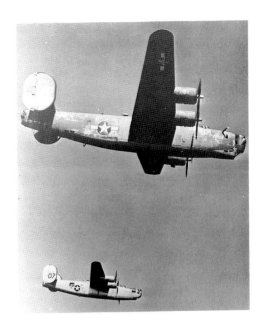

Arctic Eleventh AF B-24s from Shemya, in the Aleutians, attacked Japanese targets. Plane nearest camera has Oklahoma City Air Depot-style nose-turret modification. Steve Mills Collection

son, Thionville, Juvincourt-et-Damary, Laon/Athies Laon/Couvron, Lille, Nivelles, Saint-Trond, and Florennes, as well as some marshaling yard targets, to keep the Luftwaffe reeling in the face of the impending Normandy invasion. A mixed fleet totaling 797 B-24s and B-17s carried out these opening strikes.

The 485th BG of the Fifteenth AF was declared operational on May 10, using its Liberators to realize the Fifteenth's planned operational strength of twenty-one heavy bombardment groups, some of which flew B-17s. That same day, the Eleventh AF in Alaska directed its component units to focus on bombing and photographing specific targets instead of running general recon sorties in the cold Aleutians.

The Eighth AF went after German transportation with a series of marshaling yard strikes carried out by B-24s on May 11, 1944. Of the Liberators launched, 164 hit targets at Mulhouse, Epinal, and Belfort, while 24 went after secondary marshaling yard targets at Chaumont, and 66 Liberators bombed Orleans/Bricy and other targets of last resort. Five B-24s went down in the early afternoon missions.

This 493rd BG B-24 appears to have the s/n on its tail abbreviated to the last five numerals (52496). The plane probably is a B-24H, which would have the prefix 42- to the s/n, with the 2 appearing on the tail with the last five digits. Jeff Ethell Collection

On May 12, about 730 B-24s and B-17s—the largest Fifteenth AF heavy bomber force used in one day—ranged over a variety of targets including German headquarters at Massa d'Albe and Monte Soratte. More than 250 fighter sorties supported the heavies. The next day, the Fifteenth continued interdiction support for ground forces with a mixed fleet of about 670 B-24s and B-17s. Such raids showed a flexibility in utility of heavy bombers, and blurred the classic distinctions between strategic and tactical bombardment.

The fist of power in the Pacific saw a large force of 53 Seventh AF B-24s from Kwajalein join B-25s and Navy planes in attacking Jaluit on May 14. On May 17, more than 100 Liberators controlled by the Fifth rumbled over antiaircraft positions on Bosnik, Sorido, and Mokmer, along with supply areas and airfields on Noemfoor. Still other Fifth B-24s bombed other targets that day as the available force of Liberators grew in the Pacific.

The pressure on Ploesti's oil refineries continued on May 18, 1944, when the Fifteenth sent nearly 450 B-24s and B-17s, the majority under fighter escort, to hit those oil refineries, as well as marshaling yards at Nish and Belgrade. That same day, over the cold Kurils, an Eleventh AF B-24 on weather reconnaissance hit a Japanese plane.

The Fourteenth AF sent two B-24s on a May 19 sweep of the ocean south of Hong Kong, where they seriously damaged two freighters. The next day, 13 Liberators of the Fourteenth AF went back to attack shipping south of Hong Kong, claiming two motor launches destroyed and several larger vessels damaged. Three bombers were lost at sea that day.

In the spirit of interservice cooperation, which sometimes led to Pacific AAF B-24s flying diversionary bomb strikes to aid Navy recon aircraft, Navy fighters escorted a pair of Thirteenth Liberators as they attacked a launch and barges northwest of Rabaul on May 20, 1944. In the Tenth AF, on May 21, a solo B-24 bombed the northwestern part of Mandalay.

Clearing weather favored the launching of about 550 Fifteenth AF B-17s and B-24s on May 22 to strike communications and transportation targets and military sites in central and northeastern Italy.

Combined totals for Eighth AF heavy bombers lost in raids on May 24 was 33. During these missions, more than 400 Liberators attacked French airfields at Orly, Creil, Melun, and Poix. Pre-invasion targeting by the Eighth continued to punish the Luftwaffe on the ground. The next day, the Eighth put up a mixed grouping of 859 B-24s and B-17s, in four distinct forces, to bomb marshaling yards, airfields, and coastal batteries in France and Belgium, for the loss of only four bombers—two to flak and two to unknown causes.

May 26 saw nearly 700 Fifteenth AF B-24s and B-17s bomb French marshaling yards at Lyon, Saint-Etienne, Nice, Chambery, and Grenoble.

The remoteness and harsh weather endured by the Eleventh AF revealed itself repeatedly in mission summaries. On May 25, only one of two B-24s launched to reconnoiter and bomb in the central Kurils made it; the second aborted due to equipment failure. The next day, both Eleventh B-24s sent out on an armed photo mission over Shimushu turned back with mechanical problems.

The Fourteenth AF dispatched several B-24s on May 29, with two claiming a 250ft freighter sunk off Hainan, while three Liberators bombed the town of Wanling, and seven B-24s struck areas along the vital Burma Road. Also on May 29, the Fifth AF sent Liberators against Japanese troops and defense areas during the first tank battle of the Southwest Pacific, fought on Biak Island, west of Parai. Other B-24s bombed airfields nearby at Babo and Timoeka. B-24s of the 13th Air Task Force, under Fifth AF control, attacked Woleai and other nearby islands in the Carolines.

Seventh AF B-24s, returning from Los Negros after an earlier shuttle bombing mission, hit Ponape on May 30, as two other forces of Seventh AF Liberators rose from Kwajalein to bomb Wake and Truk.

On the last day of May 1944, the Fourteenth AF logged 27 Liberator sorties when thirteen B-24s set fires in the town of Lungling in western China, and fourteen Liberators bombed the warehouse area at Lashio in central Burma. Meanwhile, Fifth AF B-24s and other aircraft continued their relentless pressure on Wewak and Hansa Bay.

Between June 2 and 5, 1944, the Eighth AF used heavy bombers to neutralize transportation and airfields in northern France. Additionally, it implemented a feint known as Operation Cover, consisting of a series of attacks on coastal defenses, especially in the Pas de Calais area, in an effort to deceive the Germans about the location of the impending Allied invasion of France, and take attention away from Normandy.

Low clouds impacted the weather that drastically curtailed Fifteenth AF operations on June 3. Nonetheless, 36 Liberators managed to bomb the waterfront area at Ormis while 38 more B-24s dropped bombs on the port and west part of Split, Yugoslavia.

The night of June 4, Japanese forces on Truk felt the blast of bombs from Seventh AF B-24s, which staged through Eniwetok to accomplish their mission.

On June 6, 1944—the day of the Normandy invasion—the Eighth AF reached its top strength when the 493rd BG's B-24s became operational, giving a total of 40 heavy bomb groups. (Later, the 493rd converted to B-17s.) On that day the fledgling 493rd lost two Liberators in a collision on their first mission, in support of the invasion. The following day, Liberators of the 34th BG, returning to their base at Mendlesham after more post-invasion strikes, were pounced on by infiltrating Me 410 fighters. Four Liberators went down in the fray.

On June 14, four Eleventh AF B-24s flew an extensive photo recon mission above the central and northern Kurils. About 20 Japanese fighters pressed an attack, with three of the fighters suffering damage. The Fourteenth AF put up 24 Liberators on June 15 to cause serious damage to a warehouse area of Canton. Meanwhile, the Far East Air Force (FEAF) was formed, with jurisdiction over the activities of both the Fifth and Thirteenth.

Poor weather impacted some Eighth heavy bomber missions in the days following the Normandy invasion. On June 17, hundreds of heavy bombers managed to bomb targets in northern France. The fleet of 273 Liberators took advantage of a favorable break in the weather to bomb several airfields and targets of opportunity. Antiaircraft fire snatched one Liberator from the sky.

By June 20, the Eighth was realigning many planes to more strategic targets in the pursuit of victory over the Germans, as 1,257 B-24s and B-17s bombed 14 strategic targets in northern Germany. Target lists included synthetic oil plants, oil refineries, a military vehicle factory, and an ordnance depot for tanks. This same morning, another force of 130 Eighth AF B-24s bombed 10 V-weapon sites in the Pas de Calais region.

Also on June 20, the Tenth AF sent five B-24s, carrying fuel, to Kamaing in northern Burma, followed by six B-24 fuel sorties two days later, and 12 B-24 gasoline missions on June 23. (The ability of the Liberator to carry useful quantities of fuel led to the creation of specialized C-109 tanker variants, used to bring gasoline to areas where it was urgently needed, both in the CBI Theater and on the European continent.)

The cauldrons of Ploesti, Giurgiu, and Nish boiled on June 23, 1944, when the Fifteenth AF sent more than 400 B-24s and B-17s, with escorting fighters, to those targets. Opposition was fierce and accurate—more than 100 American planes were shot down that day, while the heavy bombers' gunners and the escorting fighters claimed 30 enemy aircraft destroyed.

While the crew and planes of the Fifteenth were suffering staggering losses on June 23, the Fourteenth put up 20 Liberators to bomb the docks at Hankow in central China. On June 24, 334 B-24s were launched by the Eighth to a variety of targets in France, including railroad bridges and landing strips. Of 288 escorting fighters, some later peeled off to strafe ground targets, adding to the carnage.

On June 25, 1944, the Eighth AF used its heavy bomber assets flexibly, attacking targets that often were bypassed, and using the cover of darkness in an unusual switch to night bombing. In the morning, while B-17s were launched to their targets, 107 Eighth B-24s hit French airfields at Bourges and Avord. By midday, 153 B-24s were bombing 17 electrical power and transformer stations in an effort to disrupt the flow of electricity to V-weapon sites. Sixty-four B-24s, thwarted by cloud cover over their primary aiming points, bombed a variety of last-resort targets including airfields at

Nuncq and Peronne. That night, a fleet of 300 B-24s and B-17s was sent to bomb seven railway bridges and two airfields near Paris.

A V-weapon supply site at Saint-Leu-d'Esserent drew attention from 40 Eighth AF B-24s on June 27, while 51 more Liberators bombed railyards and an airfield nearby at Creil. Five of the B-24s succumbed to flak.

July 1944 began with Fourteenth AF B-24s nocturnally planting mines in the river near Canton. FEAF Liberators bombed the airfield at Namlea and hit shipping around the Amboina-Ceram-Boeroe region, while other FEAF B-24s softened up Japanese facilities on Noemfoor Island in anticipation of the Allied landings there. Still other FEAF B-24s on armed reconnaissance bombed targets on Peleliu and Yap. The Seventh AF sent B-24s staging through Eniwetok to hit Truk the night of July 1–2, and the Eleventh launched four B-24s against southern Shimushu and Kurabu Cape, where the Liberators used radar to bomb through overcast. It was a busy first of July for Liberator crews in the Pacific.

On July 5, Fifteenth AF Liberators had the opportunity to work with Eighth AF B-17s when the Fortresses flew a return leg of a shuttle mission (England–USSR–Italy–England), and attacked the railyard at Beziers in concert with the Fifteenth B-24s. Meanwhile, the Fourteenth put up 22 B-24s to bomb a supply and ammunition depot at Canton, and five B-24s to mine Shanghai Harbor.

Flight after flight of Eighth AF B-24s—231 in all—dropped bombs on the dock facilities of Kiel, Germany, the morning of July 6. In the Pacific, Seventh AF B-24s economized on shuttle missions by staging through Eniwetok to bomb Truk the night of July 5–6, and repeating that target during daylight hours on the sixth. The Seventh AF repeated this scenario of night bombing at Truk, followed by other raids the next day, during the nights of July 7–8, 9–10, 11–12, and well into July.

On July 12, the skies rumbled with the roar of more than 420 Fifteenth AF B-24s as they attacked rail targets in southeast France. (In little over a month later, the invasion of southern France would occur.)

Airmen congregate by a 458th BG B-24. Some of the men use the handy bicycles so evident at English airfields. Jeff Ethell Collection

During the evening of July 14, 93 Eighth AF Liberators bombed airfields at Peronne and Montdidier; about 40 more heavy bombers failed to drop their ordnance when blind-bombing equipment did not work. No bombers were lost in this effort. That same day, FEAF B-24s pressured Yap, a FEAF Liberator target of continuing interest during this period.

A massive effort of 571 Eighth AF B-24s bombed German equipment and troop concentrations, to support a

British Second Army assault in the vicinity of Caen in northern France. The RAF furnished 90 Spitfires as escorts for the Liberators.

During mid-July, the Fourteenth AF repeatedly sent groups of as many as 25 Liberators to bomb the Chinese city of Changsha.

As FEAF B-24s again pounded Yap on July 21, opposing Japanese fighters dropped startling, but largely ineffective, phosphorous bombs among the Liberator formation. In the fierce air battle, the Liberators claimed seven fighters shot down.

The Fifteenth's B-24s frequently went after petroleum and synthetic oil plants during this period, as on July 23, when 42 Liberators bombed the Albanian oil refinery in Berat.

July 28 was not favorable for many Eighth AF Liberator operations. As many as 111 B-24s were sent to bomb Brussels targets, but were recalled because of 100 percent cloud cover over the targets; 180 B-24s that were sent to bomb targets in France were similarly recalled because of heavy clouds. That same day, FEAF sent four squadrons of Liberators against targets on Woleai Island, while other FEAF B-24s bombed Laha, Cape Charter, and airfields around Manokwari and Babo, among others.

The Eighth AF sent July 1944 out with a bang, launching well over 1,000 heavy bombers against an array of targets on the thirty-first of the month. Three fighter groups escorted 447 B-24s beyond the Dutch coast as the Liberators went after a chemical works at Ludwigshafen, and the southwest portion of Mannheim. Airfields at Laon/Athies and Creil were hit by 85 more B-24s. At the end of the day, the Eighth counted its heavy bomber losses at six B-24s on the Ludwigshafen mission, and 10 B-17s over Munich.

On the first of August 1944, bad weather limited the Fifteenth AF to some recon missions, while the Eighth experienced numerous aborts because of the unfavorable weather over Europe. On August 3, 23 Fourteenth AF B-24s bombed the town of Yoyang (also called Yochow), a port in central China.

The neutralization of Iwo Jima by the AAF kicked off with a Seventh AF B-24 mission—the first to be launched from Saipan in the Marianas—on August 10, 1944, even as the Seventh's other Liberators from Kwajalein hit Wotje. Taking advantage of Saipan, the Seventh AF dispatched B-24s from there on August 12 to bomb a seaplane base, an airfield, and shipping at Chichi Jima.

On August 12, the Eleventh AF put up four B-24s and two F-7A photo recon Liberator variants over Paramushiru and Shimushu. The Liberators attacked enemy shipping in Higashi Banjo Strait as well as a runway and buildings on Suribachi. Japanese fighters rose to the attack; the Liberator crews returned with claims of three kills and 13 other Japanese planes either probables or damaged.

On August 14, the Fifteenth AF sent 540 B-24s and B-17s to bomb gun emplacements in Toulon and Genoa as Operation Dragoon—the invasion of southern France—neared its D-day. The next day, the Fifteenth launched its first mass night heavy bomber raid, sending 252 B-24s and B-17s in a predawn takeoff, to pound the beaches near Cannes and Toulon. This bombing was timed to be immediately ahead of the kick-off of Operation Dragoon.

The Seventh AF sent B-24s from Saipan to bomb Yap on August 20. This marked the beginning of a four-day Saipan-to-Yap bombing spree by Seventh Liberators.

Accurate Japanese antiaircraft fire discouraged a lone Eleventh AF B-24 from dropping bombs during a recon mission over Shasukotan, Onekotan, and Harumukotan Islands on August

25. The next day, the Eleventh sent three B-24s to Kashiwabara's staging area early in the morning, setting several fires. Seven more Eleventh AF B-24s bombed a fuel dump, docks, piers, and boats while on a mission to Kashiwabara and Otomari Cape. Again on August 27, the Eleventh went on the warpath, sending five B-24s to bomb and photograph Kashiwabara in two raids.

September 1944 opened with more than 50 Liberators sent by FEAF to bomb the airfields at Sasa, Matina, and Likanan. Other FEAF Liberators, failing to reach their original target on Mindanao, bombed Beo.

On September 2, the Tenth AF launched an even two dozen B-24s, hauling fuel to Kunming. Two days later, with heavy rain thwarting most combat operations in the Tenth AF's area of responsibility, 24 B-24s carried 32,000 gallons of fuel to Kunming. The next day, 21 Tenth Liberators again flew fuel to the city, a service they kept up daily through September 12. Then, on September 15, the Liberators flew fuel to Liuchow, when 13 B-24s formed an aerial pipeline. Liuchow continued to be the destination for several more days that month.

As land battles raged in European, the Eighth AF engaged in unorthodox missions including one on September 8 by 100 B-24s toting supplies to the battle area.

Also on September 8, the Fourteenth AF sent 18 Liberators to attack five rail bridges in Indochina, at Giap Nat, Dui Giang, Hue, Trach, Duc Tho, and Quang Tri. The bridge at Quang Tri was knocked out. Three other Fourteenth B-24s claimed a destroyer sunk south of Hong Kong that day.

The Fifteenth AF launched 45 B-24s, escorted by Mustangs, flying supplies to Lyon, France, on September 10, 1944. The next day, when poor weather inhibited many other operations, it sent 54 Liberators on another supply run to France, and again on September 12. The capacity and range of the B-24 came into play increasingly for critical transport duties during this period in the war. On September 15, while other Fifteenth AF B-24s and B-17s bombed targets including airfields and a submarine base, 53 of their aircrew flew a supply mission to southern France.

Twenty-four Fifteenth AF Liberators also began evacuating aircrew who had formerly been imprisoned in Bulgaria. The men, now free in Cairo, were flown to Bari.

September 16 saw 54 Fifteenth AF B-24s again on the supply run to southern France; the next day, bad weather thwarted all but eight of 54 B-24s tasked for a similar mission. On September 17, the Fourteenth AF put up 29 B-24s to bomb Changsha—a large number of Liberators in this theater of operations.

Nearly 250 B-24s, emblazoned with group colors of Eighth AF units, took along close to 200 escorting fighters on a sweep into the Netherlands to airdrop supplies to the First Allied Airborne Army on September 18, 1944. The Germans were deadly with their flak—16 Liberators and 20 escort fighters went down as a result.

Gasoline was vital to the onrushing Allied forces in Europe. The Eighth sent 80 Liberators carrying gas to France on September 21, then more than 100 the next day, and more than 150 the next. By September 28, the number of Liberator gas sorties totaled around 200.

Whether in demand by the Allies, or the object of attack to prevent its use by the Axis, petroleum was essential to the war effort. On the last day of September 1944, FEAF-directed B-24s bombed Japanese-held oil production facilities at Balikpapan, Borneo—called the Ploesti of the Pacific. FEAF Liberators returned to Balikpapan on October 3, and again on October 10 and 14.

The Seventh AF continued paying calls on persistent targets in the central Pacific. On October 4, it sent Liberators from Saipan to attack shipping west of Iwo Jima, and to bomb airfields, buildings, a radio station, and area targets on Pagan, Marcus, and Iwo Jima. Meanwhile, other Seventh AF B-24s from the Marshalls dropped bombs on the airfield at Moen.

FEAF B-24s roared over Mindanao to bomb Zamboanga on October 7; escorting P-38s exercised by hitting seaplanes, shipping, and targets of opportunity in the area.

Also on October 10, four B-24s of the plucky Eleventh AF were forced to abort a strike aimed at Kashiwabara

Bombs await loading and mating with fins for this 460th BG B-24 in Italy. Tailored covers protected glazed areas of the B-24 on the ground. Jeff Ethell Collection

because of weather. Two days later, the Eleventh got three B-24s off to bomb airfield and shipping targets around Matsuwa and Onekotan. On October 12, four Eleventh AF B-24s bombed and photographed targets at Kashiwabara.

Twenty-eight B-24s were part of a force including 33 P-51s and 18 P-40s dispatched by units of the Fourteenth AF to bomb White Cloud airfield and shipping near Hong Kong on October 15; two Fourteenth B-24s also bombed Amoy that day. Strafing was executed by a lone Eleventh AF B-24, attacking a freighter off Shimushiru on October 16. The following day, the Eleventh AF put up seven B-24 sorties—a sizable number for Aleutian operations. These Liberators flew cover for a naval task force.

FEAF's main effort for October 17, 1944, was a strike by nearly 60 B-24s on barracks, shore targets, and oil installations on Ilang and northern Davao Bay in the Philippines.

A lone radar-equipped Snooper SB-24 dispatched by the Seventh AF

dropped bombs, at Iwo Jima, the night of October 20–21. On October 21, 28 Seventh AF B-24s from Saipan bombed Iwo Jima, continuing the pressure on the Japanese there. It was a busy period for Seventh Liberators—2 more B-24s bombed Yap that day, in the first American air strike launched from Guam.

Successes in the ongoing Allied prosecution of the European war diminished the need for covert supply-dropping Carpetbagger B-24s, as major portions of France were retaken from German forces. On October 22, the 492nd BG and its Carpetbagger B-24s, which had been under control of VIII Fighter Command, were reassigned to 1st Bomb Division for employment as an anomalous (for the Eighth AF) night-bombing group. A remaining Carpetbagger squadron would continue to resupply underground forces in Scandinavia, the Low Countries, and Germany, until VE-Day.

On October 28, FEAF Liberators struggled with bad weather to bomb the airfield at Puerta Princesa in the Philippines. The night of October 28–29, FEAF B-24s bombed the dock area at Wilhelmina.

Weather dismantled a major Fifteenth AF operation on October 29, when only 35 B-24s of a force of more than 825 heavy bombers, dispatched

with fighter escort, bombed marshaling yards at Munich. The other bombers aborted missions to a variety of targets. During October 30–31, three Fifteenth AF Liberators bombed Klagenfurt marshaling yards; most other Fifteenth missions were canceled by bad weather, including a force of 174 B-24s sent to bomb Yugoslavian targets, but forced to abort due to the weather.

The first day of November 1944 saw weather relax enough for about 320 Fifteenth AF B-17s and B-24s to bomb an ordnance factory, diesel works, and marshaling yards at Vienna, as well as a tank factory, marshaling yards, and targets of opportunity in southern Germany, Hungary, Yugoslavia, and Austria. On that same date, FEAF Liberators bombed Philippine airfields at Cebu City, and targets at Alicante, Negros Island, Philippines, and supply dumps at Del Monte. Del Monte had been a frantic B-17 base in the dark days of December 1941, when Japanese fortunes were on the rise; now, B-24s were carrying the war back to the Japanese occupiers of that field. Also on November 1, the Seventh AF sent eight B-24s from Guam to attack Japanese shipping northeast of Iwo Jima. Twelve more Seventh AF B-24s escorted Navy photo planes over Iwo Jima, Haha Jima, and Chichi Jima. These B-24s bombed airfields, a warehouse, and shipping, and may have created a diversion to allow the photo planes to work without being attacked.

The tempo of the European liberation accelerated, prompting an order on November 2 for the Liberator-equipped, leaflet-dropping, 406th BS to increase its size. The activities of this unorthodox squadron would continue through May 1945.

The Fifteenth AF, unwilling to be stifled by bad weather, adapted an attack method that was tried on November 3 with 46 B-24s and B-17s, flying without escort, against a Vienna ordnance depot, Moosbierbaum oil refinery, marshaling yards at Munich, an aircraft factory at Klagenfurt, the railroad near Graz, and the towns of Innsbruck and Graz. The bombers abandoned the typical European strategic formation to attack individually, relying on cloud cover for protection. In addition to those bombers carrying out this hide-and-seek raid, 30 more heavy bombers had to abort when clearing weather—usually a boon—proved to be a bane to this method of attack.

The Eleventh AF launched six B-24s to bomb an airfield, structures, and offshore shipping at Kurabu and Suribachi on November 4.

The Fifteenth launched the largest operation against a single target during World War II on November 5, 1944, when 500 B-24s and B-17s bombed the Vienna/Floridsdorf oil refinery, while 10 more heavy bombers bombed about 20 scattered targets. They were escorted by 198 P-51s and 139 P-38s. Meanwhile, the Fifteenth sent 42 more B-24s, with protective fighters, on a tactical mission to bomb troop concentrations at Mitrovica and Podgorica, Yugoslavia.

On November 5, four Eleventh AF B-24s dropped bombs on Matsuwa and Onekotan; three other Eleventh Liberators bombed Kataoka naval base, igniting fires and drawing seven Japanese fighters into battle. The B-24s claimed one enemy fighter destroyed.

Beginning November 6, and continuing through December 24, Seventh AF B-24s on Saipan logged 24 missions in which they sowed 170 mines in several anchorages used by the Japanese throughout the Bonin Islands.

It was back to traditional tactics, if not traditional strategic targets, for Fifteenth Liberators on November 8 when 34 B-24s managed to bomb troop concentrations at Mitrovica, Prijepolje, and Sjenica; 70 other Liberators had to abort when clouds obscured targets.

Iwo Jima reverberated under the concussions of bombs from 27 Saipan-based Seventh AF B-24s on November 10; a half-dozen other Seventh Liberators from Angaur Island struck at Koror the same day. The following day, freshly arrived P-38s escorted 29 Seventh AF B-24s back to Iwo Jima, to bomb airfields.

On November 15, the Fifteenth AF launched a gaggle of 80 B-24s and B-17s to make runs including single-bomber sorties on a variety of targets. Two intercepting fighters challenged four Eleventh AF B-24s November 17 over Suribachi airfield. Damaged, one of the Liberators made a forced landing on Soviet Kamchatka. On November 21, not waiting for diplomatic clearance to be granted, an Eleventh AF B-24

air-dropped provisions to the stranded crew.

On November 20, the Fifteenth sent 92 B-24s to bomb Sarajevo's railyards, as well as rail bridges at Zenica, Doboj, and Fojnica, as other Fifteenth Liberators and Fortresses bombed targets ranging from an oil refinery at Blechhammer to a variety of weather-dictated alternates in Czechoslovakia, including the town of Zlin.

On November 22, the Fourteenth AF sent 22 Liberators to bomb Hankow. That same day, FEAF B-24s hit targets including a nickel mine in the Kendari area, and small shipping in Brunei Bay. This followed a celebrated Brunei mission by Thirteenth AF B-24s on November 16, during which Japanese battleship heavy guns successfully downed three Liberators while the B-24s were still nearly 10mi distant and approaching.

The first true long-range-escort mission by the Seventh AF's new P-38 fighters came on November 22, when 22 of the twin-engine fighters escorted a like number of Seventh AF B-24s from Saipan on a mission against airfields on Moen and Param. On November 23, 81 Fifteenth AF B-24s attacked road and rail bridges near Zenica Brod and Doboj. Meanwhile, 13 of the Fifteenth AF's B-24s and B-17s dropped supplies in Yugoslavia.

The Eighth AF's 36th BS, a former Carpetbagger clandestine B-24 outfit, became an electronics countermeasures unit, and began daily operations November 25, 1944, as a screen for the regular bomber formations. In this role, the Liberators of the 36th Squadron protected the Eighth AF's primary VHF and fighter-to-bomber communications from interception by the Germans during the assembly portion of missions. An increase in flak batteries around German military and industrial areas soon forced the 36th BS to use its radar countermeasures skills and equipment to assist the regular bomber force—a welcome aid that continued through the end of the European war. (Suppression and confusion of enemy radars remains a key ingredient in modern warfare, as was deftly shown in Desert Storm.)

Mass Eighth AF heavy bomber raids on November 26 put more than 1,000 B-24s and B-17s aloft, escorted

by the strength of 15 fighter groups, as the heavies pounded several targets. Enemy fighter opposition was estimated at about 550 aircraft. Combined heavy bomber losses were more than 35—25 of them to fighters. American fighters claimed more than 100 air victories that day.

On November 27, the Seventh AF made a strong showing, launching 24 B-24s from Saipan to hit Iwo Jima. Then, 29 more B-24s, from Guam, flew another strike against Iwo Jima, and yet another 25 B-24 sorties were logged by Seventh AF crews from Angaur, bombing Del Monte airfield. The next day, the Seventh's activities included a return to Iwo Jima by 21 Saipan-based Liberators, and a nocturnal Snooper B-24 mission against Iwo on November 28–29.

The last day of November 1944 saw heavy Liberator action in parts of the Pacific as Far East Air Force sent B-24s on major strikes against Malimpoeng and Parepare, as well as Legaspi airfield, Matina airfield, and four other airfields on Halmahera in the Moluccas. Meanwhile, in Seventh AF territory, 23 B-24s from Saipan bombed an airfield on Iwo Jima; eight Guam-based Liberators escorted photo planes over the Kazan and Bonin Islands, bombing Haha Jima in the process; 37 Seventh AF B-24s from Angaur bombed Legaspi airfield (the target also hit by FEAF B-24s the same day); and during the night of November 29–30, two Seventh AF B-24s from Guam and Saipan had bombed an airfield on Iwo Jima during Snooper missions.

In December 1944, with thoughts of a white Christmas far from home, Eighth AF crews put forth continued effort to end the war. On December 2, about 275 of its heavy bombers hit German railyard targets at Bingen, Oberlahnstein, and Koblenz-Lutzel, as well as a rail line and four targets of opportunity. More than 150 heavies aborted due to heavy clouds. About 100 enemy fighters were encountered that day, and eight B-24s over Bingen succumbed to the Luftwaffe.

On December 3, five B-24s were sent by the Fourteenth AF to deliver delayed-action bombs near the Pengpu Bridge. On the same day, the Fifteenth sent a mixture of 14 B-17s and B-24s to air-drop supplies over Yugoslavia; on

P-51s move in with silver B-24s of the 458th BG. Jeff Ethell Collection

December 4, 14 B-24s and B-17s dropped supplies over northern Italy where partisan activity was in progress.

Pairs of FEAF B-24s sought targets of opportunity near Langoan and in northern Borneo on December 5. On December 6, the Eleventh AF sent four B-24s to bomb Suribachi airfield, recording hits on the runway and batteries. One of the B-24s received damage from Japanese antiaircraft fire. The same day, an Eleventh AF B-24 on a weather sortie force-landed in the Soviet Union.

On the third anniversary of the bombing of Pearl Harbor on December 7, two Fourteenth AF Liberator crews claimed the sinking of a cargo ship in the South China Sea. FEAF B-24s commemorated Pearl Harbor Day with bombings of Japanese installations at Malogo, Masbate, and Legaspi. Meanwhile, over Europe on December 7, the Fifteenth AF launched 31 B-24s and B-17s on predawn raids against marshal-

ing yards at Salzburg, Klagenfurt, Villach, and Lienz, as well as targets in Wolfsberg, Spittal an der Drau, Mittersill, Sankt Veit in Defereggen, and Trieste.

On December 8, 1944, B-24s and B-29s teamed up as 89 Seventh AF Liberators joined about 60 Twentieth AF B-29 Superfortresses, as well as US Navy cruisers, in a bombardment of Iwo Jima airfields, to reduce Japanese air raids launched from Iwo against American air bases in the Marianas. P-38s flew escort for the bombers. December 10 saw a Fifteenth AF congregation of more than 550 B-24s and B-17s, sent to bomb petroleum targets in Germany, recalled because of overcast weather.

On December 17, 1944—41 years since the Wright brothers' first flight—nine B-24s from the Fourteenth AF dropped bombs in the area of Camranh Bay in south Indochina; meanwhile, the Seventh AF sent 26 B-24s from Guam and 24 more from Saipan to pound Iwo Jima. The Fourteenth sent 33 B-24s to bomb barracks and administrative buildings at Hangkow on December 18. The night of December 18–19, four Seventh AF Snooper B-24

missions were launched from Guam and Saipan against stubborn Iwo Jima.

FEAF launched B-24s, B-25s, and fighter-bombers against a total of 10 airfields, mostly on Negros and other sites in the central Philippines, on December 21. The next day, FEAF B-24s as well as RAAF Liberators were on sorties against Japanese targets. On December 24, FEAF B-24s bombed historic Clark Field in the Philippines, while three Fourteenth AF Liberators claimed the sinking of a tanker in the South China Sea.

Christmas 1944 was no holiday from war as FEAF B-24s dropped bombs on airfields at Sasa, Mabalacat, Sandakan, and Jesselton, and a dozen Seventh AF B-24s rose from Saipan to continue punishing Iwo Jima. Seventh AF Liberators from Guam and Saipan continued night strikes against Iwo Jima on December 25–26. A lone Eleventh AF B-24 dropped bombs on Kataoka on December 29.

On the last day of 1944, four Fourteenth AF Liberators claimed a freighter sunk and another damaged off Hainan Island. FEAF ended the year by sending B-24s and B-25s to bomb airfields in the central Philippines, on Luzon and Mindanao. Other FEAF Liberators went after Ambesia airfield, Dili, and various targets throughout Halmahera Island. The Seventh AF's December 31 contribution included launching 19 B-24s from Guam to strike Iwo Jima airfields during the day. Ten additional Seventh heavies flew individual harassment raids stretched over a 6hr period during New Year's Eve and into the new year.

FEAF welcomed the new year with raids including a January 1, 1945, Liberator operation against Clark Field. P-38 Lightnings provided escort cover. Through January 3, 1945, bad weather kept Fifteenth AF B-24s, along with other combat aircraft, on the ground for five days, and limited activities to some P-38 recon sorties. On January 4, the bombers were out in force; next day, only one B-24 bombed the Zagreb railroad sidings as 69 others aborted because of complete cloud cover at the target.

January 5 saw three Seventh AF B-24s provide navigational escort for seven P-38s that strafed Iwo Jima.

That same day, the Seventh sent 22 B-24s to bomb Iwo Jima in morning and afternoon raids. Still other B-24s acted as airborne artillery spotters during a naval bombardment of Chichi Jima and Haha Jima. The first use in the Eleventh AF of H2X equipment for radar bombing took place January 9 when four Liberators hit Suribachi Bay airfield. On January 13, FEAF B-24s attacked Japanese troop concentrations at San Juan, Del Monte, Muzon, and San Vicente in the Philippines. (At least one unit, the 5th BG of the Thirteenth AF, employed a spotter plane—a revamped Douglas A-24 Dauntless—to assist during troop bombing missions by 5th BG B-24s in the latter period of the Pacific war.)

The Tenth AF sent a dozen B-24s on January 15 to bomb a Japanese troop concentration and supply area at Mong Ngaw. Meanwhile, FEAF B-24s continued bombing targets in the Philippines that day, while 12 Seventh AF Liberators from Saipan persisted in hitting Iwo Jima. Hong Kong shook under the bombs from 29 Fourteenth AF B-24s on January 18, 1945.

Returning from an unsuccessful recon of Kurabu airfield January 18, one of three Eleventh AF B-24s made a forced landing in the Soviet Union on the return trip. The next day, another flew a radar ferret mission over Shimushu and Onekotan. Two other Eleventh B-24s raided Onekotan and Matsuwa.

On January 18, the 15th Special Group (Provisional) was organized in the Fifteenth AF. The next day, this group received control of the 859th (B-24) and 885th (B-17) BSs, with which to air-drop supplies over France, Yugoslavia, and Italy. By March 1945, the 15th Group was redesignated the 2641st Special Group (Provisional). As such, its units were attached to the Twelfth AF for operational control, while remaining in Fifteenth AF's sphere of administrative control.

On January 22, 1945, FEAF B-24s, escorted by P-38s, dropped bombs on Heito airfield in the first major Fifth AF raid on Formosa. Other B-24s under FEAF control-bombed barracks in the Cabaruan Hills, gun emplacements by Manila Bay, and Fabrica airfield the same day. Meanwhile, the Seventh AF, in an archetypal rendition of its ongoing Iwo Jima campaign, sent 20 B-24s from Guam to hit Iwo Jima's airfields on January 22, followed by eight B-24s flying individual strikes against the airfield during the night of January 22–23.

Eleventh AF B-24s waded into contested airspace January 23, with one Liberator performing a recon sortie along the east coasts of Onekotan and Matsuwa, and four more striking Kakumabetsu cannery, and targets on Paramushiru. Eight to 10 Japanese fighters intercepted—1 B-24 was lost, and B-24 gunners claimed two victories over the fighters.

Corregidor came under repeated FEAF B-24 attacks in late January 1945.

For nine days, ending with improved weather January 31, Fifteenth Liberators and other warplanes were unable to bomb. During the nights of January 29–30 and 30–31, some Fifteenth AF B-24s were able to drop supplies in northern Italy.

The first and second days of February 1945 saw the Seventh AF contribute to the attack on Corregidor by dispatching 20 and 22 B-24s, respectively, from Angaur for that purpose.

On February 1, Fifteenth AF B-24s and B-17s numbering 300 attacked a variety of targets; a half-dozen Fourteenth AF B-24s raided shipping off the coast of Indochina, where the Liberator crew claimed one cargo vessel sunk and a patrol boat damaged. On February 2, the plague of bad weather closed down Fifteenth AF bombing operations again, although one B-24 and one B-17 managed to drop supplies in northern Italy.

Fighters escorted 25 Fifteenth AF B-24s on a supply drop mission to Yugoslavia on February 5. That same day, the heaviest attack to date on Corregidor was carried out by 60 FEAF B-24s. On February 7, six Liberators of the Eleventh AF, sent to bomb Kataoka, aborted their mission when all the B-24s accidentally dropped their bomb loads before the bomb run.

The night of February 10–11, the Fifteenth AF conducted a B-24 supply mission to Yugoslavia. On the eleventh, FEAF Liberators kept up an almost continuous attack on Corregidor throughout the day. Corregidor and Iwo Jima rated repeat attention during this period. On February 13, FEAF B-24s kept up the pressure on Corregidor, with a sizable portion of the Liberators bombing coastal gun emplacements, and scoring direct hits on several batteries.

When weather permitted, the Fifteenth continued sending fleets of B-24s and B-17s out to pound targets in Austria and elsewhere in the region. The Eighth AF, making a deliberate effort to convert some bomb groups from B-24s to B-17s, also continued pressure on the Reich as 1945 aged.

B-24s were again part of the FEAF mixture attacking Corregidor in the early daylight hours of February 16, followed later in the day by amphibious and airborne landings. Also on February 16, the Seventh AF launched 42 B-24s to hit Iwo Jima; total cloud cover over the island forced the recall of the Liberators. Again on February 18, 36 Seventh AF B-24s from Guam had to be recalled from a planned strike on Iwo Jima because of weather.

On February 19, a coordinated air campaign in the Pacific saw about 150 B-29 Superfortresses attack Japanese targets in the hopes of drawing fighters away from Iwo Jima, as US Marines launched the invasion of Iwo. Meanwhile, the Seventh AF sent 44 B-24s from Saipan to bomb Iwo. Fourteen of these Liberators dropped bombs on bivouac areas, defensive positions, and storage areas about an hour before the 4th and 5th Marine Divisions made their amphibious invasion at 9am on the island's southeast coast. The other 30 Liberators had to abort their invasion tasks because of mechanical problems, cloud cover, or reaching Iwo Jima too late to safely make a bomb run.

On February 22, FEAF sent 100 Liberators to bomb Japanese troop concentrations northwest of Fort Stotsenburg, while other B-24s bombed supply areas near Baguio, and still others hit Tarakan and Labuan airfields. Liberators would be frequently employed tactically to disrupt troops in the campaign to retake the Philippines.

On February 23, 1945, US Marines hoisted the American flag on the summit of Iwo Jima's Mount Suribachi. That night, seven B-24s from the Seventh AF assets on Guam flew Snooper raids against neighboring Chichi Jima and Haha Jima. Even with the Stars

This 450th BG B-24 in Italy carried the yellow fuselage band typical of Liberators in the 47th Bomb Wing. F. Bamberger via Dave Menard and Jeff Ethell Collections

and Stripes flying atop Iwo Jima's high ground, parts of the island remained in fierce Japanese possession. On February 25, nine Seventh AF Liberators from Guam bombed Japanese mortar- and rocket-launching positions, and blockhouses, on the northwest part of Iwo Jima. Nine Liberators returned to Iwo Jima February 27 to attack fortifications, artillery positions, and mortar sites on the northern part of the bitterly contested island.

During the latter part of February 1945, Fourteenth AF B-24s frequently swept over the Gulf of Tonkin, attacking freighters.

In Europe, 102 Fifteenth AF Liberators were launched against tactical targets in Yugoslavia on February 26. The B-24s and their fighter escort had to be recalled when clouds completely obscured the objectives. The month ended with a February 28 strike by Fifteenth P-38s and P-51s on an enemy airfield at Bjelovar, where the intruding American fighters destroyed a German-held B-24 and P-38, removing

them from any advantageous use by the enemy.

March 1945 roared in like a lion for the Eighth AF, dispatching one of its signature armadas of 1,153 B-24s and B-17s to bomb eight marshaling yards in southwest Germany, along with two targets of opportunity. Nine P-51 fighter groups provided close escort to the heavy bombers.

Also on March 1, the Fifteenth revisited Moosbierbaum oil refinery and other targets with more than 630 B-24s and B-17s. On March 6, the long bombing assault on Iwo Jima, followed by furious ground fighting, allowed the Seventh AF to land 28 P-51s and a dozen P-61s on the ravaged island.

Fourteenth AF Liberators, numbering 34 and supported by 21 P-51 Mustangs, attacked Shihkiachwang on March 8. That same day, Seventh AF B-24s continued a pattern of bombing Susaki airfield. On the ninth of March, the Eighth AF sent more than 1,000 B-17s and B-24s against an array of six marshaling yards, a big tank factory, and a castings plant in Germany. Five fighter groups flew close escort and three more patrolled the area. That same day, the Eleventh AF sent three B-24s on a shipping search that did not find enemy action.

On March 11, a day on which Seventh B-24s continued their repeated

bombings of Susaki airfield, P-51s used their newly won base on Iwo Jima to launch attacks of their own on Susaki. The island-hopping strategy continued to serve the AAF. (A last attack on American installations on Iwo Jima would be launched by the Japanese March 26; by 8am that day, the capture and occupation phase of the Iwo campaign was considered complete.) On March 15, FEAF B-24s supported US ground forces on Luzon with an attack on a Japanese headquarters area at Baguio; A-20s and P-38s also participated.

A navigational error produced a record mission for a pair of Eleventh AF B-24s on March 16, 1945. The Liberators, on a photo mission to Matsuwa, actually ranged 130mi south of the island—the deepest penetration of the Japanese home islands by the Eleventh to date. The two bombers turned north again, photographed Matsuwa, and bombed Shimushiru, with unrecorded results.

On March 17, FEAF B-24s pounded Formosan airfields in quantity, while other FEAF Liberators bombed the beaches at Panay before Allied landings there on the following day. FEAF Liberators also bombed Japanese troops on Mindanao.

March 21 saw 90 Eighth AF B-24s form up to bomb Mulheim an der Ruhr airfield, under the watchful eye of friendly fighters. The Eighth sent 235 B-24s to drop supplies to Allied forces in the assault area east of the Rhine River at midday on March 24. The Liberator proved effective in this airlift operation, using its great range, armament, and capacious bomb bays to accomplish tasks contemporary airlift planes could not match. (Some air-drop modified European B-24s had sirens installed to warn friendly personnel of an impending release of supplies overhead, veterans recalled.)

On March 28, Fourteenth AF B-24s bombed Haiphong and Hanoi docks and Bakli Bay barracks; meanwhile, Seventh AF B-24s paid a visit over the Japanese stronghold at Truk.

While a half-dozen Eleventh AF B-24s bombed Kataoka naval base on March 29, a solo Eleventh AF Liberator flew a sophisticated radar ferret mission along the Paramushiru coast.

As March 1945 drew to a close, the month's war diaries showed AAF Liberators around the world were employed against the Axis in a variety of roles. The Fifteenth AF sent Liberators to bomb marshaling yards and oil facilities, while other Fifteenth B-24s dropped supplies to partisans. The Eighth also used Liberators against transportation targets, and as air-drop planes to support far-reaching ground forces. Pacific B-24s continued the formula of putting recurring pressure on Japanese airfields and strongholds, while FEAF B-24s went tactical in a series of missions that either directly bombed Japanese troops in the Philippines, or attacked enemy supplies, support, and transportation links.

The continuing emphasis placed by the Fifteenth AF on strangling German transport in northern Italy resulted, on April 8, in a 500 plane B-24 and B-17 effort against bridges, viaducts, and marshaling yards feeding into Brenner Pass. A power-generating dam also was targeted for the heavies that day.

As tactical objectives demanded airpower, the vast armada of heavies permitted B-24s and B-17s to fill tactical needs, as on April 9 when 825 Fifteenth AF Liberators and Fortresses, working closely with the British Eighth Army, bombed gun positions and other forward military targets southeast of Bologna, immediately west and southwest of Lugo. That same date, over the Philippines, FEAF B-24s and fighter-bombers supported Allied ground forces on Central Cebu and Negros. The next day, April 10, 648 Fifteenth AF B-24s and B-17s again supported the British Eighth Army by bombing machine-gun nests, artillery positions, and infantry defenses along the Santerno River. This was the largest number of Fifteenth AF heavies attacking targets on a single day to date. Also on the tenth of April, FEAF Liberators again supported ground forces, in central Cebu in the Philippines.

On April 10, the Eleventh AF, in a coordinated effort with US Navy planes, sent seven B-24s carrying napalm with which they bombed Kataoka naval base. FEAF Liberators bombed the Taikoo docks in Hong Kong and storage areas in Canton on April 13, while other FEAF B-24s bombed airfields at Tainan and Okayama. Still more FEAF-controlled B-24s bombed the Davao area.

The Fifteenth AF broke its old record, and set its wartime high, on April 15, 1945, by sending 1,142 escorted B-24s and B-17s in two major efforts—830 heavy bombers supporting the US Fifth Army in the vicinity of Bologna, and 312 heavies bombing rail bridges and ammunition supplies and production. This was the largest war effort in a 24hr period by the Fifteenth in terms of the number of fighters and bombers dispatched and attacking, and in terms of bomb tonnage released.

Six Eleventh AF B-24s radar-bombed Kataoka naval base April 16, and one more Eleventh AF Liberator flew a radar ferret sortie that day.

In mid-April, the Fifteenth AF sent B-24s and B-17s several times to bomb in support of Army ground operations near Bologna; other Fifteenth B-24 operations during that month attacked bridges and transportation to block German withdrawal from northern Italy. On April 21, 18 Guam-based Seventh AF B-24s dropped their bombs on Marcus. FEAF B-24s ranged out to Saigon's naval base on April 23; other FEAF Liberators flew a shipping sweep over Makassar Strait that day.

The Eighth AF sent about 275 B-24s to bomb a transformer station near Traunstein, Germany—not normally a high-priority target because the Allies overestimated German electrical redundancy capabilities—on April 25. The Liberator force also had marshaling yard targets to attack that day.

April 26 saw 107 B-24s from the Fifteenth AF bomb a motor transport depot at Tarvisio, as well as several marshaling yards that were targets of opportunity. Other Fifteenth AF Liberators and Fortresses aborted bomb missions to northern Italy because of bad weather.

By April 27, 1945, the flow of replacement B-24s, as well as B-17s and P-51s, to Eighth AF units had ceased. A previous authorization of 68 planes per bomb group was pared back to its original level of 48 heavy bombers. Victory was imminent.

Six Eleventh AF B-24s returned to Kataoka naval base April 27, this time dropping fragmentation bombs. Another Alaskan B-24 attacked Minami Cape, and one more flew a solo radar ferret mission.

May 1, 1945, saw FEAF B-24s support Australian landings on Tarakan Island. Meanwhile, the Seventh AF sent 16 B-24s from Guam to bomb the airfield on Marcus, while 10 Liberators bombed air installations on Param. During the night, nine more Seventh B-24s flew individual Snooper strikes over airfields on Param and Moen.

By May 2, 1945, Soviet forces were in complete control of Berlin. Offensive European B-24 operations were at an end; the final Fifteenth AF bombing mission of World War II turned out to be a 27-plane B-17 effort May 1 against the Salzburg, Austria, station and marshaling yards.

On the third of May, 1945, the Indian 26th Division occupied Rangoon, signaling the end of the Tenth AF's war against the Japanese in Burma. That same day, FEAF B-24s bombed Saigon, striking at oil storage areas and a boatyard, the latter sustaining considerable damage. The next day, the FEAF Liberators returned to inflict heavy damage on Saigon oil installations.

May 5, 1945, a dozen of the Seventh AF B-24s rose from Angaur to bomb Koror; on that same date, a solo Eleventh AF B-24 flew a weather sortie over the Kurils. On May 7, 1945, the German high command unconditionally surrendered all land, sea, and air forces at Reims, France, effective May 9. On the ninth, the first bomb group of the Eighth to be redeployed after the cessation of hostilities began its departure from Old Buckenham in England to the United States. It was the B-24-equipped 453rd BG: the only bomb group departing by ship.

Because radar returns uncovered considerable Japanese shipping activity between Paramushiru and Shimushu, on May 9 a dozen Eleventh AF B-24s radar-bombed through overcast in an effort at thwarting the operation. Another B-24 flew a radar ferret mission over Paramushiru and Shimushu.

On the ninth of May, the Seventh AF sent 29 Liberators from Guam to bomb Param and Moen, in three forces, over a 6hr period.

May 10 saw the Eleventh AF and US Navy Fleet Air Wing Four conduct

By late July 1945, veteran European Theater B-24s were undergoing overhaul at Spokane, Washington, for possible Pacific deployment.

their heaviest and most successful joint mission to date. A dozen B-24s bombed shipping targets at Kataoka naval base, and flew photo recon over Paramushiru on the return trip. Sixteen Eleventh AF B-25 Mitchell medium bombers also hit targets that day; one B-25 and one B-24 made forced landings in the Soviet Union. On May 15, the Eleventh sent 13 B-24s to bomb the Kashiwabara-Kataoka area; the Liberators claimed one ship destroyed and another taking a direct hit. Japanese antiaircraft fire punched into two of the B-24s, one of which limped to a forced landing in the Soviet Union. Eleventh Liberators flew other strikes as May progressed.

On May 20, FEAF B-24s bombed Piso Point, and Seventh AF Liberators from Guam attacked a Japanese air operations building on Marcus. The ensuing days of May were sprinkled with Pacific B-24 missions, like a 26-ship attack on the Marcus airfield and environs by the Seventh AF B-24s on May 24; FEAF B-24s pounding railyards and rolling stock east of Saigon at

Muong Man and Phan Rang on May 27 and 28; and a large force of more than 100 FEAF Liberators attacking Kiirun and several other towns on Formosa on May 29. FEAF ended May with several days of B-24 efforts using about 100 bombers to execute.

On June 2, FEAF B-24s struck the Pontianak airfield, and Tarakan and Labuan Islands. Pontianak harbored a wooden-boat industry useful to the Japanese, and its airfield provided at least rudimentary defense, as Navy Liberator crews learned when challenged there. The third of June, a lone Fourteenth AF B-24, with two P-51s as escorts, damaged a bridge north of Shihkiachwang.

Three years after the Japanese had launched serious air attacks against American installations in the Aleutians, the Eleventh AF sent 11 B-24s to radar-bomb the Japanese at Kataoka naval base on June 4, 1945. The ongoing dependency of Pacific combatants on ships was underscored by a June 7 attack by two dozen Seventh AF B-24s on a boat repair basin on Aurapushekaru Island.

On June 9, the Eleventh AF sent six B-24s and eight B-25s to work with US Navy surface and air units attacking the Kurils. The Liberators did not score results that day, half of them jettisoning their bomb loads.

An Eleventh B-24 flew the theater's longest mission, lasting 15.5hr, and having a round-trip distance of 2,700mi, on June 19. This shipping search mission took the Liberator as far as Uruppu Island. Turning north, the B-24 dropped bombs on a small convoy 25mi southwest of Shimushu Bay, sinking one vessel, damaging another, and torching two more.

For 19 days running, from June to July 1, 1945, FEAF Liberators bombed parts of the Balikpapan oil refinery complex and especially its defenses, in the time-honored Pacific tradition of pulverizing a target with relentless bombings prior to an invasion. Australian forces made amphibious landings on Balikpapan on July 1; FEAF B-24 attacks there continued to accumulate after the landings, at least as late as July 9, the date Australian and Dutch forces completed their encirclement of Balikpapan Bay. On July 8, FEAF B-24 attacks included some RAAF Liberators bombing warehouses at Donggala.

The securing of Okinawa allowed the Seventh AF to put B-24s there; on July 9, 43 Liberators left Okinawa to bomb Omura airfield while another B-24 hit the airfield on Kikai Island. The next day, 43 Okinawa-based B-24s bombed Wan and Sateku airfields on Kikaiga Island. From July 11–14, FEAF B-24s pounded troop concentrations on Negros Island, supporting Allied troops with these tactical operations. As FEAF B-24s gained footholds closer to their targets, they stretched their war to China, as on July 18 when a gaggle of bombers and fighters paid a visit to the Shanghai area. The biggest and most successful Eleventh mission of the month came on July 20, when eight B-24s bombed hangars and revetments on Matsuwa airfield.

The Fifth AF shared in the use of Okinawa, as more than 100 of the Fifth's FEAF-controlled B-24s launched their first strike from Okinawa to hit the Chiang Wan airfield north of Shanghai on July 24.

On July 26, FEAF Snooper B-24s ranged over several targets including the docks at Pusan, Korea. On that same date, seven Eleventh AF B-24s used incendiaries in a successful raid on Kataoka naval base. As the Liberators departed their target, smoke pyres rose almost a mile in the air. Moderate enemy antiaircraft fire was inaccurate over Kataoka, to the relief of the B-24 crews.

A fleet of more than 60 Fifth and Seventh AF B-24s, under FEAF direction, bombed the marshaling yard at Kagoshima on July 27. That same day, other FEAF Liberators from the Thirteenth AF bombed an airstrip north of Pontianak. On July 28, about 70 FEAF B-24s bombed Japanese shipping at Kure, and claimed direct hits on a battleship and an aircraft carrier. Meanwhile, over Negros Island, FEAF Liberators continued to support ground forces engaging the Japanese.

July 29 saw B-24s from Okinawa, as well as other aircraft under FEAF control, hit targets in the Japanese home islands, including conventional attacks by Liberators on Nagasaki. Other FEAF Liberators bombed a pocket of Japanese resistance south of Fabrica, on Negros Island. On the last day of July and again the first day of August, FEAF B-24s returned in force to Japan, around Nagasaki. Other targets hit by these Liberators on July 31 included Sasebo naval base.

On August 6, the day the atomic bomb was dropped on Hiroshima, FEAF Liberators continued their conventional attacks on Japanese resistance pockets on Negros Island. Two days later, in a move some American planners thought was opportunistic, the Soviet Union declared war on Japan. FEAF B-24s over Honshu bombed Iwakuni airfield on August 9, the day an atomic bomb was dropped by a B-29 over Nagasaki.

Through August 13, Pacific B-24s continued bombing missions. The Eleventh AF launched its last combat mission on that date, when a half-dozen B-24s radar-bombed Kashiwabara's staging area, leaving behind towering columns of smoke. That same date, FEAF B-24s and B-25s flying out of Okinawa pounded Japanese shipping in the waters by Korea and Kyushu, as well as in the Inland Sea.

On August 21, days after the August 15 cessation of offensive action against Japan, two Eleventh AF Liberators attempted to photograph the Soviet occupation of the Kurils, but were thwarted by cloud cover. Four more of its B-24s aborted a photo mission to

Paramushiru and Shimushu because of weather; this latter mission was successfully completed on August 23. On the twenty-fourth, Eleventh AF B-24s again failed to photograph the Soviet occupation of the Kurils because of clouds.

The stage was being set for the Cold War as two Eleventh AF B-24s flew a high-altitude photo recon mission of Paramushiru and Shimushu on September 4, 1945, and encountered Soviet fighters. (Liberator historian Rhodes Arnold says Eleventh AF B-24s were confronted by Lend-Lease P-63 Kingcobras in Soviet markings on at least one occasion.) On September 6, all further Eleventh AF missions of a wartime nature were canceled.

This chronology of the Liberator's war cannot detail every mission by every B-24; nor can it relate all the courage, ingenuity, and suffering that went into these massive Liberator efforts around the world. But it does show the rise and fall of the Axis, and the continuing rise of the USAAF, pushed ahead in no small part by the successes enjoyed by Liberator crews, from late 1941 well into 1945.

Chapter 3

Submarines and Repatriates

The AAF Stalks a Submarine

A year into the war, an AAF anti-submarine B-24D under the umbrella of VIII Bomber Command left its English base at St. Eval, at 8:45am on the last day of 1942. The stout Liberator was part of the 1st Antisubmarine Squadron, in an era when the AAF claimed these long-ranging missions for its Liberators. Exactly 5hr, 1min later, as the lone Liberator droned over the waves at 1,000ft, a radar return suggested a surface ship was 8mi distant, and 30deg to the right of the Liberator's heading of 270deg. The Liberator's pilot took up the trail toward the radar echo, and when 4-1/2mi distant and 750ft above rough seas, the bomber crew saw a fully surfaced submarine. A check of coordinates put the sub at 51deg, 20min north; 20deg, 58min west.

The U-boat's decks were awash, and the B-24 crew could discern no wake behind the submarine. The Liberator attacked from the right of the sub,

and slightly to the rear, roaring in at 200mph and only 175ft overhead. Using the bombing intervalometer, the Liberator crew loosed nine British-made Torpex 250lb depth charges with 16ft between each. The charges were fuzed to detonate at a depth of 25ft— shallow enough to hurt a surfaced submarine, and deep enough to inflict damage even if the vessel began to submerge. The attack was executed 3min after the initial radar contact.

The B-24 crew looked for signs of a successful drop. They estimated the first three bombs in trail exploded 50ft, 34ft, and 16ft short of the submarine's exposed conning tower. Depth charges four and five straddled the conning tower; number six overshot the conning tower by about 20ft, and the rest ex-

Highly polished B-24J-CF of the Pima Air Museum awaited replacement Plexiglas when the photo was taken in 1990. As a British Pacific war veteran, this Liberator was configured differently than its European counterparts, which were more heavily armored. Frederick A. Johnsen

Old Bessie, *a greenhouse B-24 of US-AAF's 18th Antisubmarine Squadron, was photographed with an aircrew at* Langley Field, Virginia, in 1943. Albert W. James Collection

One of the Eleventh AF's LB-30s, probably AL602, came to grief on a stream bank, its Davis wing's structural integrity faring better than the crumpled fuselage. Rick Apitz Collection

ploded in the sea beyond the embattled U-boat. The crew praised the precision of the intervalometer in stitching such a precise line of destruction; the submarine was caught in the middle of the string of depth bombs. Now the submarine began to submerge; Liberator crew could see markings on the still-exposed portion of the conning tower, but these were indecipherable in the quick pass

202

over the enemy vessel. Up in the nose, the B-24's navigator hosed the sub with a .50cal barrage lasting 25 rounds. This early B-24 lacked a lower ball turret, so a tunnel gunner squeezed off another 25 rounds at the German submarine.

Perched in his Consolidated tail turret, behind a flat slab of armor glass, the rear gunner said he saw a "long, dark slim object at least 15ft in length rise up with the geyser of water" as the depth charges detonated. The tail gunner cut loose with 40 rounds at the object, which he later said looked like a photo he was shown of the damaged stern of a submarine. As the Liberator turned off of its bomb run, the

left waist gunner reported an oil slick in the area of the attack. A minute and a half after the attack, the B-24 passed over the spot and dropped a marine flare marker, but it failed to ignite. For the next 8min, the Army bomber lingered over the scene of the attack, although nothing of the vessel could be seen. By then, the oil slick was about 600ft wide, and seemed to issue from a geyser-like source.

Submarine crews were known to eject oil and even debris from their submerged craft to simulate their own demise, in the hope of lulling attacking aircraft into leaving the scene. The Army B-24 crew tried a trick of their own, leaving the vicinity of the attack by flying west, into the wind for 30min, and then returning, with a tail wind, for 20min until their Liberator was supposed to be over the spot. Radar did not indicate the sub had surfaced, and the crew was unable to pick up any sign of the oil discharge on the cold sea.

An hour and a half later, another plane cruised the area, having heard the first Liberator's radio report of the attack. The second aircrew reported seeing an oil slick four miles long and a quarter mile wide. Evidently the strike camera of the first Liberator fogged over, as photography of the attack was unusable.

The intelligence report of this high-seas confrontation caught the essence of lonely sea-search missions by Liberator crews over the North Atlantic. Seas in turmoil spat foam into clammy skies as solo B-24s sought out the enemy. Vigorous low-level bombing runs, punctuated by geysers from the Liberator's gunners, could often lead only to a

speculative victory as the U-boat slipped beneath the waves, taking with it the secret of its survival, or its demise. This crew had more reason to believe they succeeded than some; the magnitude of debris and oil gave credence, even though the harsh elements conspired to deprive this Liberator crew of photographic proof of victory.

Bred for Britain, Saved for Uncle Sam

The Liberator IIs built for the British, but retained by the AAF as LB-30s for American use, outlived much newer Liberators during the course of the war. Liberator historian Allan G. Blue, writing in the Spring 1970 volume of the *American Aviation Historical Society Journal*, said 51 Liberator II/LB-30 variants were retained for American use.

According to Blue, the conversion to American use (and LB-30 nomenclature) included the installation of typi-

cal B-24 style Martin top turrets on the Liberator IIs, albeit in a unique location amidships instead of immediately behind the cockpit. His research fur-

Sometimes, bomber pilots got a chance to buzz like their fighter-pilot compatriots. Rooftops near Carlsbad Caverns, New Mexico, reverberated from this low pass. Don Douglas Collection via Peter M. Bowers

Feathered outboard props suggest this was a taxiing accident, with worrisome consequences for the forward fuselage of this B-24 at Walla Walla Army Air Base in southeastern Washington state. Evelyn Howard Collection

A Ford B-24H converted to TB-24H-25-FO standard to train B-29 Superfortress gunners with remote-sighting weapons. Two dorsal B-29 gun turrets, two ventral turrets, and tail guns with radar were serviced by nose, side, tail, and dorsal central fire control gunners' sighting stations. Don Douglas via Peter M. Bowers

ther showed 15 of the LB-30s were rushed to the Philippines and Java by the 7th BG to bolster the strength of the embattled 19th BG, with 12 of the Liberators actually reaching Java. A handful of others went to Alaska and Hawaii, a few were absorbed into cargo and transport duties, and 17 were sent to defend the Panama Canal against a possible Japanese carrier-borne attack.

The Java LB-30s suffered high attrition, according to Blue, with no fewer than seven being written off during the early months of 1942. Another succumbed to a Japanese air raid while parked at Darwin, Australia. Survivors of Java joined a late arrival, number AL573, in flying patrol missions for which their great range suited them.

Meanwhile, Alaska operations utilized LB-30s numbers AL602, AL613, and AL622 out of Kodiak. One of these,

AL613, survived the harsh Alaska combat environment and returned to Convair in 1944 for rebuilding as a transport version.

In the months before American entry into World War II, some defense planners in this country quietly voiced concern over the vulnerability of the Pacific side of the Panama Canal to attack. To avoid the specter of direct US government intervention in Latin America, Pan American Airways cooperated by seeking use of airfields in the region. Ostensibly, improvements were made to fields including Guatemala City, while a newly created Co. sought permission from Ecuador to build an airstrip on the Galapagos Islands. Ultimately, a grouping of bases in several countries in the region gave sufficient locations from which to launch Pacific search missions.

Some of the repossessed Liberator IIs were fitted with ASV radar of British design. When coupled with the Liberator's great range, radar made the LB-30s viable sea-search patrollers. The 6th BG operated the Canal Zone's LB-30s, dispatching them to various fields in the search network.

As their Latin American patrols droned on, these LB-30s did not routinely roar out and sink enemy ships. Yet they fulfilled an important obligation in the aerial defense of the interests of the United States for a two-year period until the old bombers were rotated home in 1944. Just as the Japanese were forced to allocate a greater portion of their air forces to home defense after the stunning Doolittle Tokyo raid on April 18, 1942, so was the United States obligated by sound judgment to scan the approaches to the Panama Canal. The availability of the far-ranging LB-30s with radar plugged this gap, and allowed newer, more combat-ready Liberators to enter the fray in the overseas fighting fronts.

At least six of the LB-30s returned from Panama during 1944, when American production allowed their replacement by newer B-24s. Consolidated's Nashville, Tennessee, facility served as a modification center for these early Liberators. When the aircraft emerged, they were virtually C-87 Liberator Express transports, although their early ancestry showed in the circular cowlings they retained. Convair

rebuilt another LB-30 at its main San Diego, California, plant, and the seven early Liberators flew transport runs with Consairways, a contract service operated over the Pacific by Consolidated for the Air Transport Command (ATC).

The LB-30s were first cleaned with solvent before being completely rebuilt. Paint stripper was applied to cause the camouflage coat to blister and peel from the aluminum skin of the Liberator. About 2,000ft of metal hydraulic, vacuum, and gas lines were removed and replaced with new duraluminum tubing. After the paint stripper had attacked the finish of the Liberator, an air hose was used to blow the flaky coating from the skin. Removal of the 175lb coat took an estimated 50hr. The subsequently polished aluminum skin improved performance, and was said to diminish radio static interference.

New replacement wiring was housed in conduit for greater protection. This was in deference to civil aeronautics requirements, and probably helped the postwar civilian marketability of the LB-30s. New control cables replaced the existing strands. An AAF historian documenting the project said the original control wires to the tail had been routed along the sides of the fuselage. These were redi-

The 446th BG in England flew Lazy Lou *until it became a battle casualty.* Jeff Ethell Collection

rected overhead, which was said to make maintenance easier, while getting the cables out of harm's way when loading cargo up against the sides of the fuselage.

Instruments and cockpit controls were inspected, and overhauled or replaced as needed. Then, before the bomber configuration was altered to transport form, the fuselage and wing were jigged and measured with a transit to see if they were still in proper factory alignment. If a hard landing or other strain had twisted or sprung the airframe, it was realigned, and all critical dimensions were measured for accuracy.

The glazed greenhouse bombardier's station was replaced with a streamlined aluminum cap that opened to access a forward cargo hold capable of carrying 1,600lb. The stubby aft end of the fuselage was faired with a streamlined cone to diminish drag, now that machine guns were no longer needed there. All crew members of the converted transports worked on the flight deck, with the navigator and radio operator located aft of the pilots. A

Arrays of 16mm movie projectors were used with an Emerson nose turret, left; a K-7 waist-gun mount with K-13 gunsight, center; and an MPC turret, right, for gunnery training at Tonopah Army Airfield, Nevada, in 1945. The trainers, probably part of the Jam Handy system, incorporated means to score students' tracking skills against filmed fighter attacks. Harvey Herr manned the waist gun in the photo, with Ken Maisch on the microphone. Central Nevada Historical Society, Harvey Herr Collection

bunk was added to provide relief for alternating crew members during long flights.

The salient task in converting these bombers to transports was the construction of an aluminum "canoe" with 17 bulkheads and 19 stringers, skinned in aluminum, to replace the bomb bay doors, bulkheads, and catwalk keel, which were removed from the jigged Liberators. To further beef up the integrity of the fuselage, skin sheets 0.040in thick were removed from parts of the fuselage sides and replaced with material 0.064in thick. Into these thick skins, seven windows were cut on each side of the fuselage.

Some of the fuselage bulkheads were removed and replaced with stronger structure. Stout longeron members were added to the upper and lower structure of the aft fuselage to carry loads around the large cargo door opening being installed. A compartment toilet was added in the aft fuselage.

A floor with attach points for 23 removable airline seats was installed. With the ability to carry this many passengers, the life-raft capacity was doubled from two to four. Additional life-raft compartments were built into the upper fuselage in sections about 2x4ft cut into the structure.

While the refurbishing was taking place, some structure including the outer wing panels and the stabilizer were beefed up to match the increased strength of later-model production B-24s. The bomber-style self-sealing rubber fuel cells were removed, and the wing cavity was sealed to make an integral fuel tank. Four new Pratt & Whitney engines were mated to the modified LB-30s.

Upholstery in two-tone tan and white further diminished the plane's resemblance to a bomber. Soundproofing material was attached to metal members still visible inside the fuselage, and leather seats added a sumptuous look.

When released to Consairways, these Liberator airliners still belonged to the USAAF, and retained their original British s/ns for identification. After the war, LB-30s showed up in civil service with operators including Morrison-Knudsen Construction, which flew two LB-30s in Alaska. As of this writing, one of the Morrison-Knudsen Liberators that was damaged on landing at a remote Alaska strip is a candidate for restoration.

The first Morrison-Knudsen LB-30 at Anchorage, Alaska, in the last half of 1952. Wayne Edsall Collection

Chapter 4

Problems and Solutions

Going to Waist

When B-24Ds roared into combat, their waist gunners braved frigid wind blasts through huge open windows with low sills. Gunners swung their weapons into position on a movable post that held a fork mounting an E-12 or similar recoil adaptor cradling the gun. This prevailed well into Liberator production, when closed waist windows, still mounting a single gun each, were introduced. The first enclosed waist windows on AAF Liberators were modifications to existing aircraft. Some of these used K-5 gun mounts with E-11 recoil adaptors. Soon, the coffee-can-shaped K-6 mount, with an E-11 recoil adaptor, became the choice for enclosed B-24 waist-gun positions on production airplanes. The ultimate late-war B-24 waist window set-up used a geared K-7 mount (similar in appearance to the K-6), connected by cables with a K-13 computing gunsight and the purpose-built E-13 recoil adaptor.

At Wright Field, in Ohio, a chart of armament and bomb installations on AAF planes as of August 1, 1945, logged armament changes as they were

In-flight view through the open waist window of David Tallichet's restored B-24J over Utah, July 1980. Frederick A. Johnsen

introduced on the assembly lines. These tables are helpful mileposts for Liberator waist armament, although changes made after Liberators left the factories (likely including after-the-fact conversions of some B-24s to K-7 mounts), could alter these statistics somewhat.

According to the monthly armament installation chart, San Diego-built B-24Ds up to the Dash-25 block did not come equipped with waist guns as built. After the addition of .50cal machine guns in open waist windows, the next San Diego assembly line change in waist armament came when enclosed windows housing K-6 gun mounts were introduced on B-24M-10-CO machines. This was immediately followed at San Diego by K-7 computing waist mounts in closed windows, beginning with B-24M-15-CO Liberators.

Fort Worth B-24s used open waist-gun mounts until the advent of the B-24H-20-CF introduced closed waist windows with K-6s (although some former Indian Air Force [IAF] B-24J-CFs have open waist windows).

At Ford Motor Co., the first 30 E-models did not list waist armament as factory equipment; open waist guns then prevailed until K-6 mounts in closed windows entered production at the B-24H-20-FO. Next change at Ford saw K-7 mounts introduced beginning with B-24M-10-FO bombers. The handful of B-24Ns built by Ford before production was terminated also used the computing K-7 waist-gun mount.

At Douglas Tulsa, the first eight kit-built B-24Es did not list waist armament; beginning with the B-24E-10-DT, open waist guns were carried. Beginning with Tulsa's first B-24H-20-DT, K-6 mounts in closed windows were used, until the end of the Douglas production run. North American's Dallas assembly plant started building G-models with open waist windows, and never changed through the relatively short life of the North American production run.

Setting Sights and Changing Models

The AAF's *Monthly Chart—Armament and Bomb Installations* suggests some North American nose-turret Liberators were to have been designated B-24Hs unless their Sperry S-1 bombsights and A-5 autopilots were replaced with Norden M-9 bombsights and C-1 autopilots, at which time these aircraft were to be classified as B-24Js. Since North American production totals and block numbers do not indicate construction of H-models, this substitution of bombsights and autopilots is assumed to have taken place. Some Ford, Douglas, and Convair Fort Worth, H-models also were listed with the ability to be counted as J-models with this same bombing equipment conversion.

This view looking forward in the waist of a 5th BG B-24 (probably a J-model) shows crowding that could occur with both gunners swinging into action simultaneously. On open-waisted B-24s, hatches swung up and latched inside the fuselage. Gun mounts in the photo used E-12 recoil adaptors. Wind deflectors located outside the fuselage ahead of each waist window could be extended into slipstream to provide a buffer for the gunner. Deflectors can be seen through the windows in the photo, extended for action. Edward I. Harrington Collection

Project Yehudi

Slang flourished throughout World War II. If Kilroy was the name scrawled on walls and crates worldwide to signify that he was everywhere, his opposite was Yehudi, described by a wartime research organization as "the little man who wasn't there." With a sense of humor, the Louis Comfort Tiffany Foundation's classified wartime project to make a B-24 invisible was code named Project Yehudi.

Brig. Gen. Harold M. McClelland, director of technical services for the AAF, described a problem facing sea-

search patrol bombers: A B-24 might acquire a surfaced enemy submarine on radar, and home in for the kill. But even a white-bellied Liberator would be rendered as a dark silhouette against the sky, visible to the watch posted in the submarine's conning tower. This would enable the submarine to crash-dive, as sailors jammed in the bow of the boat to hasten its descent to safety. If the Liberator could be rendered invisible until it was within two miles of the submarine, General McClelland said, a depth-charge attack could be made before the enemy boat submerged.

Researchers came up with a radical proposal: "If the plane could always approach the submarine in such a manner as to present the same head-on aspect, concealment might be possible by placing lights along the leading edge of the wings and in the fuselage section. It is known from data on the visual acuity of the human eye that, at a distance of two miles, individual lights are indistinguishable as such if their spacing is less than about four feet. If, by means of suitable reflectors, the light from each lamp is confined to a narrow beam visible only from the deck of the submarine, the most economical use of power is achieved."

The AAF said a sea-search bomber could hold such a constant course with a deviation of less than 3deg. Researchers responded, "Even a bomber as large as a Liberator could be made to match ordinary sky backgrounds with a power consumption of less than 500 watts."

The Louis Comfort Tiffany Foundation of Oyster Bay, New York, was given this project as part of its camouflage field studies already under way. A hashed-together 2in board studded with flashlight bulbs was placed on a rooftop 900ft from an observation point, where the Tiffany scientists estimated it represented the wing of a bomber two miles distant. A transparent blue pigment in linseed oil was painted over the lamps to "convert the spectral energy distribution of the tungsten lamps to approximately that of daylight," according to the report. On September 26, 1942, as General McClelland watched, the plainly visible board faded from sight after the lights were switched on, and adjusted to optimum intensity. The Yehudi Principle, as Tiffany workers called the phenomenon, worked! Even when silhouetted with a white card reflecting full sunlight, the test bed could be rendered invisible.

Now the Tiffany scientists were anxious to make a full-size B-24 vanish using the Yehudi Principle. The use of an actual Liberator was not practical for this next set of tests, so two 100ft tall towers were erected on the Tiffany estate, to suspend a full-size frontal silhouette of a B-24, with its 110ft wingspan and barrel-shaped fuselage cross section. From the opposite side of Oyster Bay, a two-mile observation distance was achieved. A curious construction project ensued, and by the end of January 1943, the two steel towers stood out against the horizon. Acreage was cleared of growth to enhance the view from across the bay.

A local carpenter built a B-24 head-on silhouette in six sections which were taken to the hilltop test site and mated. A defective suspension cable soon destroyed this model, and a theatrical scene-maker performed a unique wartime contribution by constructing the replacement silhouette. The form of the B-24 could be lowered with a pair of winches to cradles on the ground.

The upper half of the steel towers was painted white to reduce contrast with the sky. When elevated to its viewing position, the B-24 effigy on the hilltop was 235ft above sea level. The first time Tiffany engineers raised the silhouette in position, volunteer airplane spotters several miles away reported an approaching four-motor bomber!

Tiffany experimentors came up with the proper arrangement for the lights, as well as the proper color tint. They counseled the AAF, "Many blue glasses and blue plastics [for tint filters] transmit freely at the long wavelength end of the spectrum. When used with incandescent lamps, this high red transmittance would make red goggles an effective counter-measure." As the thickness of the Liberator's Davis airfoil increased near the wing root, the spacing of the lights diminished to provide more coverage. Typically, 16 lamps were placed along each wing, for a total of 32, with 10 more in a grid in the nose. Engineering data suggested the amount of power required to match the brilliance of any type of sky behind the Liberator.

Several demonstrations were made, the most successful of which took place on the unusually clear afternoon of February 19, 1943. Against a blue afternoon sky, the full-size Liberator shape and its two supporting towers stood out starkly. According to a Tiffany report, "...When the lights on the silhouette were turned on, the Liberator model became invisible to the observers at the Observation Post, two miles distant. The model's wingspread of 110ft occupied more than half the space between the two steel towers, so the observers had the special advantage of knowing exactly where to look. Nevertheless they were unable to detect even the barest outline of the silhouette, although they could discern the one-inch steel cables that acted as guy-wires for the support of the towers." Oyster Bay police dispatched patrol cars to keep traffic moving near the lookout point when Yehudi tests were in progress. The Yehudi effect could be discerned from the road for a stretch of about 300ft near the overlook point.

Work began quickly on a B-24 at Wright Field that was fitted with lights to prove the mock-up's soundness. Dur-

ing May 1943, the ghost Liberator began flights from the airfield. As could be expected, the first missions were not effective as the technicians zeroed in on the proper light alignment. Then, on an overcast day, the Yehudi B-24 made a successful disappearance, according to the test report summary. A later test on a sunny day was less than successful, however, because the color filtration of the lamps on the Wright Field Liberator had different spectral characteristics than the filters used by Tiffany.

The lightweight B-24 tail gun emplacement had narrower spacing between guns than on powered tail turrets. This is the mount introduced on some B-24Ls. Inside the Plexiglas enclosure, the flat window may be armor glass for gunner's protection. Harvey Herr Collection

The test bed B-24 suffered a landing accident following the less-than-perfect sunny mission, and was sent to a repair hangar. While the bomber was

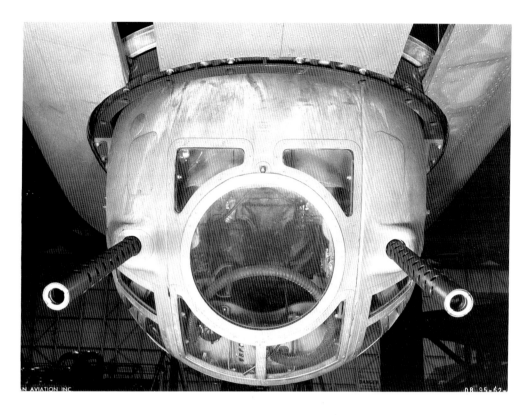

The B-24's ball turret retracted into the fuselage, with slots for each gun. The circular gunner's sighting window was two discs of laminated safety glass with an air space between the two. This window was not armor glass. Both guns in the photo have barrels removed. The barrel and internal breech parts could be extracted to the rear of the gun, leaving the perforated cooling jacket and receiver shell in place. North American Aviation

still grounded, the AAF and the Navy reached an agreement whereby all sea-search duties were turned over to the Navy, and Project Yehudi was canceled, but the Navy used the knowledge gained to hide an experimental Grumman TBF Avenger torpedo bomber in January 1944. The post-Yehudi summary said, "In these flights, two identical planes flying side by side approached the observers over a pre-determined course. Although the conventional TBF was spotted at 12mi, the Yehudi plane closed the range to 3,000 yards before being observed." Navy enthusiasm included an order to equip a squadron of Avengers with the Yehudi mechanism.

The inventors at Tiffany said a dark, saturated blue paint on portions of the plane exposed to enemy observers might be the best compromise color for ease of illumination. They also devised a plot showing an approach to a submarine in a crosswind. Rather than crabbing into the wind, which would defeat the head-on effectiveness of the Yehudi gear, the plan was to fly an arc, with the lights always aimed at the submarine as a result.

The use of binoculars by submariners could reduce the effectiveness of the Yehudi camouflage, but the extremely reduced field of view produced by binoculars hampered overall aircraft spotting chores by making it difficult to scan the sky effectively. The Tiffany report said, "It was stated as part of the original project assignment that the use of this camouflage measure would be fully justified if its only result was to require that enemy lookouts use binoculars continuously." And should the submarine switch on radar to locate a Yehudi-equipped Liberator, that radar signal could lead the bomber back to the sub.

Arming the Liberator

The AAF Proving Ground Command conducted tests generating reams of documentation on B-24 armament ideas. In the balmy climate of Florida's Eglin Field, tests ranged from proof of validity for items later seen on many production Liberators, to bizarre one-shot attempts that did not bear fruit.

On April 18, 1942—the day Jimmy Doolittle's crews bombed Tokyo in carrier-launched B-25 Mitchells—a B-24C 40-2384 touched down at Eglin Field for use in lower turret tests. Only nine C-models were built before the assembly lines settled on the D-model for mass production, and it was to be expected that the odd C-models would be used for miscellaneous purposes like testing, instead of being mixed in with an operational group of B-24Ds.

The first B-24 test flown at Eglin Field used B-24C number 84 to examine a modified Bendix lower turret using an amplidyne drive, and other changes. Bendix devised versions of a lower turret that appeared in early B-24s and B-25s in the ventral position. Both planes soon deleted the turret, due at least in part to gunner sighting difficulties. Similar Bendix lower turrets showed up again as chin installations in the XB-40 and XB-41 bomber escort versions of the B-17 and B-24; ultimately, a version of the Bendix turret found a niche as the chin armament on production B-17G Flying Fortresses.

Flexible Nose Gun Mounts

Liberator 84 also tested flexible machine-gun mounts in the nosepiece. Ultimately, many B-24Ds entered combat with a socket in the right side of the greenhouse for a .50cal gun, and another socket in the left side of the nose installed in a new window located between the edge of the greenhouse and the existing small navigator's side window. Subvariants show up in photos of B-24Ds in service with the cheek windows, with the left side window sometimes having a horizontal metal web just above the K-4 gun socket. The Eglin testers suggested the cheek windows could quickly be converted for either .30 or .50cal guns, at the discretion of individual commanders who might want to forego the bulk of big .50cal weapons. In service, the .50's wallop was preferred, and small .30cal guns as B-24 cheek armament showed up chiefly in the Pacific to bolster the frontal firepower of Liberators already fitted with power nose turrets. A few photos of B-24Ds in stateside use reveal evidence that newer K-5 cylindrical gun mounts were put in some cheek windows, although it is not established whether this K-5 cheek variant ever saw combat in B-24s.

The AAF *Monthly Chart—Armament and Bomb Installations* indicates cheek windows as San Diego factory equipment first appeared on B-24D-25-CO Liberators, beginning with s/n 41-24220. Multiple nose guns remained standard on San Diego D-models thereafter. Consolidated's Fort Worth plant installed cheek guns from the first B-24D-1-CF assembled there, serial 42-63752. Fort Worth also rolled out externally similar E-models from Ford-supplied kits, all of which had cheek gun installations. However, the first Liberator actually assembled at Fort Worth carried a San Diego s/n and no cheek mounts, since it was made of B-24D-CO parts shipped from the home base in California. Douglas' Tulsa, Oklahoma, B-24 assembly line began its Liberator production run with B-24E-1-DT number 41-28409, part of an eight-plane production block with only one nose gun. Subsequent Douglas greenhouse E-models, beginning with B-24E-10-DT number 41-28417, carried cheek mounts.

E-models assembled by Douglas and Convair Fort Worth represented knock-down kits produced in the Ford plant, and assembled at the other factories as Liberator multi-factory production got under way. When North American began producing B-24s in Dallas, Texas, the initial product was a greenhouse-nosed B-24G-NT in a production run of 25 aircraft, starting with s/n 42-78045 and ending with 42-78069. These few greenhouse G-models had cheek gun mounts, soon replaced on the Dallas assembly line by Emerson nose-turret production Liberators, still listed as B-24Gs. (Chronologically, according to Liberator historian Allan Blue, the honor of producing the first production Liberator with a nose turret actually went to Ford, with the B-24H. The G-model was built only by North American at Dallas, and introduced the nose turret after Ford had done so.)

When Ford began assembling Liberators, the first two blocks, totaling 90

aircraft, did not carry cheek windows, but the extra cheek armament appeared beginning with the first B-24E-10-FO number 42-7066.

As can be seen from tracking cheek gun installations on greenhouse Liberators, early mass production of B-24Ds and Es is convoluted, and requires more than a cursory check of s/ns if the true origin of each airframe is to be ascertained. This is because both the Consolidated San Diego factory and the new Ford assembly line produced kits that were assembled by new factories operated by Douglas in Tulsa and Consolidated in Fort Worth, until these new Tulsa and Fort Worth lines were completely established as production facilities. Evidence suggests these knock-down kit planes carried whatever features were standard at the time, on the production lines where their components were made originally.

Testbed B-24C number 84 also received a Sperry retractable ball turret, which tested satisfactorily before going into production on late D-models. This B-24C also tested a 46in diameter experimental Emerson pressurized turret in the retractable ball turret location. In this turret, the guns were partitioned off from the gunner's capsule, enabling the gunner to fly in pressurized comfort. It was the operational ceiling of 25,000 to 27,000ft in combat B-24s and B-17s that made the pressurization feature of limited value, and the idea was not pursued, even though summaries indicate the Emerson unit performed satisfactorily.

El Toro (Bull of the Woods) *showed application of armor glass windscreen and side cockpit windows, plus bolt-on armor plate, used on many Eighth AF B-24s to protect pilots from deadly fighter attacks.* Jeff Ethell Collection

Another test examined a K-5 gun mount in the waist of a B-24C. The K-5 comprised two cylinders, one set inside the other at 90deg. One of the cylinders could pivot for elevation, the other for azimuth. The gun's cooling jacket slipped through an opening in the inner cylinder. The B-24C waist window was glazed over with Plexiglas, and the K-5 was set in a rectangular frame within the Plexiglas. The closed window greatly increased waist-gunner comfort by keeping out wind blast. The testers recommended installing K-5s as standard on all B-24s, and testing them on B-17 waists as well. K-5 gun mounts did show up on a number of B-24 and B-17 waist-gun installations on combat bombers, usually characterized by a heavy ribbing to the window area.

A different B-24C (40-2386) incorporated an early version of the GE remote sighting system under development for the pressurized B-29. The use of a B-24C in this test was simply an expedient because actual B-29s were unavailable; the sighting system was not intended for Liberator production. "Picking up the target with the periscopic sight of the lower sighting station proved very difficult, and effective tracking was impossible," wrote a reviewer of the test data. In early 1943, the GE system returned to Eglin for more tests aboard the same B-24C. Bugs remained: "The pedestal sight as installed in the B-24C would not permit smooth tracking in azimuth, elevation and range," the AAF concluded. The armament testers at Eglin requested three actual B-29 Superfortresses be sent to them for testing. One would have the GE system for centralized fire control; one would carry a Sperry system; and one would revert to locally controlled turrets. (Ultimately, the GE system prevailed in the B-29, with variations showing up in the P-61 Black Widow and A-26 Invader.)

Opinion from England, December 1942

Christmas 1942 saw three travelers from the United States touring wartime England, gathering information based on the early combat experiences of B-17 and B-24 crew members. Their trip report, filed in January 1943, carried home observations about the suitabilities of B-24Ds then in combat with the fledgling Eighth AF. The three were Colonels L. C. Craigie, M. S. Roth and J. F. Philips of the Air Materiel Command (AMC).

The combat-tested 44th BG furnished feedback on Liberator operations in the ETO. First comment in the report was a telling one: "The most serious shortcoming of the B-24 is the lack of forward fire. The installation of two hand-held guns is decidedly inadequate. Because of the narrow fuselage it is extremely difficult for the two guns to be used at the same time. They have found that the ammunition containers supplied for these front guns were inadequate."

The 44th BG's engineering officer "expressed himself as being very well pleased with the B-24 as a plane, and the [Pratt & Whitney] 1830 as an engine—because there was very little maintenance trouble that could be attributed to the airplane or the engine."

New B-24Ds arrived at the 44th BG from the United States with insufficient numbers of walkaround oxygen bottles, the AMC interviewers learned, "The last [B-24D] they got had four bottles in it. The airplane was tagged for a crew of six, which is a crew in the de-

signed gross weight of the airplane." No matter that a B-24D actually used a crew of nine or 10; it hit its posted design gross weight, with the addition of combat equipment, when carrying only six crew members, so that is how it was configured. The Liberator would forever battle staggering increases to its actual gross weight, and ramifications were surfacing as early as December 1942.

Crews quickly learned of a deficiency in the fire interrupter mechanism of the Martin top turret, the AMC report noted: "The interrupter on the top turret does not permit the guns to fire down in the space between number two and three props [the two inboard engines]. The interrupter cam cuts straight off from the top of number two to number three, about where the prevalence of head-on attacks are. This has got to be modified to permit the guns to fire straight ahead between the props." (For the low-level Ploesti mission of August 1943, some of the B-24Ds were modified to allow the top-turret guns to fire ahead and down, to suppress flak guns at tree-top height.)

Heads or Tails: Eglin Tests Emerson Turret

The early comments of the fact-finders in England echoed universal concerns about frontal armament on Liberators. An Eglin test proved the merit of the Emerson nose and tail turret in the D-model, which showed up in production first on the noses of B-24Hs, Gs, and many subsequent Liberators. The Emerson did not catch on as a tail turret for production Liberators.

Tests in 1943 showed two fixed forward-firing .50cal guns could be effective in suppressing ground targets such as antiaircraft guns during low-altitude attacks. The big B-24 could be maneuvered nimbly enough to bring the guns to bear. However, the B-24 could not maintain the necessary glide angle—about 20deg—to keep the .50cal slugs from skipping off water, or from failing to penetrate a submarine hull. A 37mm cannon was rejected as less satisfactory than the fixed .50s. In practice, fixed forward-firing guns had been installed already in 1942 in the HALPRO Detachment B-24Ds which flew a preliminary low-level Ploesti mission, and in the Pacific some Ma-

rine and Navy PB4Y-1 and later PB4Y-2 crews experimented with field-mounted 20mm cannons for low-level strafing. (One Privateer crew member remembered the cannons improvised onto his PB4Y-2 shattered the glass in the instrument panel gauges during a test-firing.)

The problem of inadequate forward firepower in the B-24D was well known, and members of the 90th BG pioneered efforts to mount a Consolidated tail turret in the nose of a Liberator. At the request of the Antisubmarine Command, Air Service Command, and the Seventh AF (located in the Pacific, where many B-24 nose-turret mods took place), a standard Consolidated tail turret was mounted in the nose of a B-24D. A twin-mount .50cal installation in the tail replaced the power turret on the test plane; test waist gun and ventral gun mounts were tried on this plane also. The results confirmed the desirability of a nose turret, although the Emerson or Motor Products Corp. (MPC) models were requested as superior to the Consolidated turret. The testers found the hand-held twin-mount gun installation in the tail less effective than a true tail turret because of scant protection for the gunner, smaller field of fire, and lack of good balance. They recommended its use "only on missions where the saving of weight in the tail position was absolutely necessary." (Photos show that a number of B-24Ds in Pacific combat did incorporate a hand-held open-air tail emplacement, but this was not a factory option. Later, the B-24L introduced an enclosed lightweight hand-held tail armament as an alternative to the heavy power turret.)

By 1943 the B-17 was testing a K-6 enclosed waist-gun mount, and this was recommended for the B-24 waist as well. The K-6 used the K-5's principle of two cylinders at right angles for elevation and azimuth. But the K-6 enlarged the size of the whole mount, and incorporated heavy steel coil springs on either side of the mount to balance the gun (as some K-5s had also done). The entire K-6, including the springs, was contained inside the outer cylinder, which was about the shape and size of a coffee can. This cylinder, with openings for the gun, was mounted on the waist windowsill, nested into a snug cutout in a Plexiglas window. When the cylinder rotated in azimuth, it maintained contact with the window cutout, baffling the harsh slipstream from the outside. Ultimately, K-6s began appearing on B-24 waist windows.

A test M-4 gun mount with another 37mm cannon aimed by a GE pedestal sight in the nose of a B-24D at first looked promising when runs were made against a tow target at close range and low relative speeds. When a Culver PQ-8 target drone was used to make head-on attacks on the Liberator, report reviewers said "the longer ranges and higher relative speeds completely destroyed . . . accuracy." A sophisticated computing sight, possibly with ARO (Air Range Only; a radar range-finder) was also urged for this cannon mount.

Other tests tried Briggs retraction mechanisms for the Sperry ball turret, and then a Briggs version of the turret itself. Meanwhile, other testers wanted to replace the ball turret entirely, and tried several hand-held gun mounts, which had a restricted view compared with the 360deg view from a ball turret suspended beneath the plane. (Nonetheless, some Pacific B-24s employed hand-held guns in place of the turret. At Eglin, a weight savings of 750lb was estimated for one of the test designs. Data does not show what the Pacific Liberator crews achieved in weight savings or gunnery effectiveness, but photos reveal the Pacific Liberators so modified for the 5th BG had enlarged windows cut in the lower fuselage to aid the belly gunner in scanning for targets. Similar installations appeared on some stateside training B-24s.)

Jamming and vibration problems with some Consolidated turrets in action led to a modification of the basic Consolidated tail turret by MPC. The MPC unit tested at Eglin incorporated provisions for hand-operating the guns and the turret itself in case of a loss of turret power; a revised ammunition feed system; and a hydraulic jack for azimuth drive, and gear drives instead of cables. With a few modifications, the MPC turret got a thumbs-up from the Eglin testers, and MPC variations proliferated on production Liberators, as nose and tail turrets. The MPC and Consolidated turrets can quickly be

distinguished from the Emerson nose turret by the slightly canted angle of the main window in front of the gunner on the MPC and Consolidated versions.

Emerson turrets were installed in the nose and tail of a test B-24D, which also sported a Briggs retractable ball turret, Martin top turret, and hand-held waist guns. This Liberator was tested with bomb loads up to 8,000lb, and at weights up to 65,000lb. According to an AAF historian reviewing this plane's test data, it was found to be "very stable, pleasant, and easy to fly." The Proving Ground Command went so far as to call the B-24D in this configuration the best operational heavy bomber tested up to the summer of 1943.

Rockets Slow Bombs' Travel—at a Price

A test reported in January 1944 was the use of external and internal rails attached to modified, outward-opening rear bomb bay doors on B-24D 42-40830. The installation was designed for use with VAR (Vertical Antisubmarine Rockets), or 16 60lb Mark XX bombs. The use of bombs with rocket motors was devised so the thrust of the rocket would cancel the forward speed of a normal gravity bomb, thus imparting a true vertical drop to the bomb. This was considered desirable

A B-17G style chin turret was tested on Lil' Texas Filley *in 1944, complete with B-17 style bombardier's seat.*

for antisubmarine warfare missions. According to a test summary, "On the first mission the B-24D was loaded with 16 Mk6 inert bombs equipped with Mk2, 7V-12 motors. The first salvo of four exterior bombs blew the front bomb bay doors all but completely free of their tracks so that they had to be roped and secured from the catwalk before landing." By late 1943, the Navy had taken over antisubmarine duties, and the recommendation came from AAF channels to hand over all vertical-bombing data to the proper authority, and discontinue its testing in the AAF.

A 1943 test placed external bomb racks inboard of the engines under the wings of a B-24D. From D-7 bomb shackles, 1,600, 2,000, or 4,000lb bombs could be carried. Slinging a pair of 4,000lb bombs, the B-24D lost about 25mph to increased drag; this diminished to 20mph with the 2,000lb bombs, and about 12mph with empty racks. On a test flight to 25,000ft with an 8,000lb external bomb load, the struggling Liberator took 1hr, 22min to reach altitude, when it should have made it in 36min, 30sec without the

The B-24J/B-17G hybrid produced an aircraft with roomy nose accommodations and intolerable performance. Peter M. Bowers and Victor D. Seely Collections

drag of the external load. The racks were not recommended for production.

Cold-Soaking the B-24

Extreme low temperatures were sought for two B-24Ds, a B-24E, and a B-24H sent to Ladd Field, Fairbanks Alaska Territory, during the winter of 1943–1944, to see if the Liberator was functioning satisfactorily for use at extremely low temperatures. (The use of aircraft parked at low temperatures is more complex than for aircraft departing temperate climates and entering low temperatures in flight, and then returning to temperate conditions on the ground. On the ground in cold climates, cold-soaking occurs, rendering some fluids and normally pliable materials stiff or solid.)

The Liberators in this Alaska test were operated at ground temperatures as low as minus 46deg F., and at flight temperatures as low as minus 62deg F. The testers concluded that the B-24 was not as satisfactory as was the B-17 for operation at subzero temperatures.

XB-41 Frontal Armament Raises Dilemma

In 1943 tests of the XB-41 escort fighter version of the B-24D, the Bendix chin turret was found to be satisfactory, but not as desirable as the Emerson nose turret. Herein lay a conflict: For gunnery, the Emerson was preferred; for bombardier access and

some other flight characteristics, the Bendix chin installation would be revived in tests later on.

Eglin testers quickly discarded M-5 power twin waist-gun mounts of the XB-41 because they could not be operated in the event of a power loss, and had an inferior field of fire. With the dual waist guns discarded in favor of single mounts, and with some form of nose turret on the way for production B-24s, the escort-ship XB-41 offered only the additional two guns from a second Martin top turret, plus a much higher load of ammunition, than a standard B-24 bomber variant could offer. Because the high-ammo load could slow the XB-41 down after the bombers it was supposed to escort had dropped their bomb loads, it was deemed operationally unsuitable, especially when it couldn't contribute to the total number of bombs on target.

Test personnel at Eglin suggested using the XB-41 airframe to develop a four-gun nose turret instead. Tests showed the XB-41 was about 15mph slower than a regular B-24, and could only attain 22,000ft. An AAF test summary explained, "In level flight, the XB-41 used considerably more power to stay in formation with the B-24, resulting in excessive consumption of gasoline. In addition, the airplane was unstable and had a dangerously high center of gravity." In a comparison formation test with a B-17F bomber, the XB-41 became increasingly unstable and was very difficult to maneuver above 21,000ft. (The companion YB-40 escort variant of the B-17 made it into combat with the Eighth AF where it was also discarded for some of the same reasons, including slowness with a full ammo load.)

Hurrah for the H-Model!

Another Eglin test showed the B-24H to equal the B-17F in speed, with the H-model Liberator superior in range and bomb load.

A report from February 1944 tested K-6 gun mounts in enclosed waist windows on two B-24Js. One installation was made at the St. Paul, Minnesota, Modification Center, and the other by Ford at Willow Run, Michigan. The St. Paul version protruded outward, and centered the mounts on the bottom of each sill. The Willow Run set-up was flush except for a small portion of the K-6 cylinder, and was staggered with the K-6 to the aft of the left window, and to the forward part of the right window, to give the gunners more clearance inside. Installations much like the Willow Run version appeared on combat B-24s. Another Eglin report suggested that crowding in the waist could be eliminated by carrying only one waist gunner, to alternate between windows. This does not seem to have found favor in combat, however. (Both the B-17 and B-24 suffered from cramped quarters for two waist gunners moving about in combat. During B-17G production, the Flying Fortress' answer to the problem was to stagger the entire window openings to give the gunners clearance. On B-24s, the windows remained directly opposite each other while only the gun mounts were staggered within the windows, as described.)

Still not content with the MPC version of the Consolidated tail turret, a further metamorphosis saw the advent of the Southern Aircraft Corp. (SAC) improvement, called the SAC-7. The SAC-7 saved weight and provided a good field of fire.

Another revival of the Bendix chin turret, this time on a B-24J, resulted in mediocre ceilings and overheating engines, so the idea was dropped. Also revisited was the carrying of external bomb loads under the wings of a B-24J, which met with results more dismal than the early external bomb load tests.

Making the B-24J Look Like the B-17G

The dissatisfaction with cramped quarters in the noses of turret-equipped Liberators led to one of World

War II's most bizarre surgeries. The complete forward fuselage of a B-17G Flying Fortress was grafted to a B-24J. According to an AAF test summary, the massive splice job resulted in an operationally unsuitable airplane. Three test missions were flown: one at low altitude for speed calibration and general aircraft familiarization, and two with full military loads at high altitude, including 8,000 and 6,000lb of bombs. The findings: "The operational performance of this aircraft is poor in all respects." The hybrid Liberator with the Fortress nose lacked directional and longitudinal stability, especially at altitude. It had a disappointing service ceiling of only 18,000ft—murder over a defended target. A very damning aspect was the notation that this nose installation "increases the already excessive basic weight of the B-24J."

Acknowledging the basically good crew comforts of the B-17 nose, the report said, "The visibility for the bombardier and navigator is excellent," adding that working room in the nose compartment for the navigator and bombardier was adequate.

Making the B-24 Combat-Ready Again

The combat evolution of the B-24 was a series of armament and armor additions to meet ever-increasing enemy threats. As a result, late-war Liberators (especially configured for European combat) were cumbersome and overweight compared to earlier ships.

This metamorphosis was of concern at the highest levels in the AAF. In January 1945, Lt. Gen. James H. Doolittle, Eighth AF commander, wrote Lt. Gen. Barney M. Giles, Chief of Air Staff, "It is my studied opinion that no minor modifications will make the B-24 a satisfactory airplane for this theater [the ETO]." General Doolittle started out sympathetic to the B-24 in his letter to General Giles. "The original B-24 would carry a greater bomb load [8,000lb against 6,000lb] than the B-17. It would carry this load farther and was faster. Upon being put into operations in the ETO, it was found that the armament and armor of the B-24 were inadequate and in order to operate without prohibitive losses it was necessary to make emergency modifications immediately. These modifications con-

sisted, among other things, in a formidable nose turret which together with the other additions substantially increased the weight, reduced the aerodynamic characteristics and although increasing the fire power, eventually unacceptably reduced the overall utility of the aircraft. The load carrying capacity was reduced to 5,000lb for long range high altitude operation, which is 1,000lb less than the B-17."

While hard statistics for the two heavy bomber types are elusive due to a host of variables, Doolittle's letter revealed a trend toward loading up the B-24 with armor and armament at the expense of performance.

General Doolittle described another Liberator phenomenon: The lengthening of the nose, which occurred way back with the British Liberator II, was aggravated with the installation of a nose turret that protruded above the original fuselage contours. Additionally, the extra weight and drag of the turret and other additions led to slower speeds, which forced the wing to be flown at a higher angle of attack, further raising the nose in flight. With a long nose high before the pilots, vision was less than optimum, and General Doolittle said this "has been the cause of frequent collisions."

Increased gasoline consumption and reduced speed gave the heavy Liberators a radius of action less than the B-17's, Doolittle told Giles. (In lighter configurations, Liberators in the Pacific excelled as long-range champions until the advent of the new B-29 Superfortresses.) General Doolittle's letter said the modifications to B-24s had the effect of putting the center of gravity aft, degrading longitudinal stability. "The addition of the nose turret re-

Sugar Baby, *flying with one camouflaged gray replacement bomb bay door, displayed yellow bottom edges to its bomb doors common on Eighth AF B-24s later in the war. This may have been a quick-reference marking to determine when bomb doors were open, since they conformed to fuselage sides and were less visible than hinged B-17 doors.* Jeff Ethell Collection

duced directional stability and the B-24 became harder to fly," Doolittle added. "Spinning out of the overcast is much more common than with the B-17 and it is not as steady a bombing platform."

The degraded aerodynamics and heavy weight of the B-24 reduced the Liberator's service ceiling, Doolittle wrote, "until now it is difficult to hold a good formation, with load, above 24,000 feet. The B-17 can be flown as readily under similar conditions, in formation, at 28,000 feet. That means flak losses, over the same territory, would be substantially greater in the B-24."

Bad aerodynamics and weight problems aside, Doolittle opined: "Perhaps the greatest handicap to bombing efficiency in this airplane is the space restriction for bombardier and navigator in the nose and the interference with their forward vision resulting from the present nose turret. It must be pointed out that about 75 percent of our missions failures are the result of poor navigation and that inaccurate navigation through specified corridors has substantially increased our flak losses. To find and destroy small targets from high altitude, both the navigator and bombardier must have adequate forward vision."

The experimental Bell chin gun mount tested by the Eighth AF in 1944 used B-24H number 42-7580, and the upper portion of a B-24D style greenhouse nose. Lack of sufficient parts to quickly implement this change on a wide scale, plus anticipated introduction of the B-24N, helped retire this promising innovation. Ivan Stepnich Collection

Several problems tended to revolve around this contention. Both the Eighth and Fifteenth AFs agreed B-24s from the factory were operationally unsuitable. Each of these two European air forces had differing bombing requirements, and hence differing approaches, to the proper way to configure the Liberator for combat. A common practice with many types of American combat planes was to build the basic aircraft at the factory, and fly it to a modification center to install the latest field requirements before sending the plane overseas. The planes destined for the Fifteenth AF in Italy were different than those used by the Eighth out of England. By late 1944 and into 1945, the number of B-24 modification centers was dwindling as B-29 modifications demanded shop space. The Eighth and Fifteenth AFs tried to reconcile their different requirements to create a standard operational B-24, using the late-war L-model as the standard.

The Eighth AF needed more types of instrument bombing equipment in the nose of the plane. The Fifteenth AF had some rough airstrips that could tear up radomes mounted in the ball turret location if they were allowed to protrude slightly below the fuselage contour, which the Eighth did not consider a problem. But both air forces agreed the Liberator needed to provide the bombardier and navigator more visibility up front. The outward manifestation of this was the proliferation of enlarged and bulging windows on the sides of the noses of late B-24s. (In December 1944, a navigator returning from the ETO, and a stint in the 454th BG, told an AAF Air Intelligence Contact Unit that such extra windows were vital. The alternative was grossly inefficient, and placed an additional navigator in combat peril: The 454th BG sometimes put two navigators in the nose of a Liberator, one at the navigator's table and a second in the nose turret; the second had better visibility than the table-bound navigator.)

General Doolittle argued that the requirements of the Eighth AF were more specific than those of the Fifteenth because of the greater amount of instrument bombing equipment carried in Eighth AF Liberators. He suggested it would be easier to configure

Fifteenth AF B-24s from the Eighth master copy than the other way around. In his January 1945 letter to General Giles, General Doolittle predicted: "It is believed that a study by the Fifteenth AF of the latest nose arrangement being delivered to the Eighth AF, will indicate minor changes on Block 16 [of B-24L-FO aircraft] production which will meet the requirements of both theaters and result in a single standard design pending the advent of the chin turret."

The chin turret—on production B-24s—was an experimental Eighth AF modification which General Doolittle embraced as the best way to cure the Liberator's perceived ills. The installation was not a rewarmed Bendix chin, first flown on the experimental bomber escort XB-40 (B-17 variant) and XB-41 (B-24 version). Rather, the Eighth AF modification used a Bell power boost twin .50cal unit from a Martin B-26 tail emplacement, situated below the modified greenhouse nose characteristic of B-24Ds. This chin turret, and the experimental Emerson Model 128 nose ball turret, promised to allow top contours of the Liberator's nose to return to an unbroken line, to reduce drag and enhance pilot vision. These two turrets also gave the bombardier and navigator greater working room and a better view than available in conventionally turreted Liberator noses.

The test bed converted by Eighth AF engineers in 1944 was a war-weary B-24H nicknamed *Hap Hazard*. The Emerson nose turret and the bombardier's station were removed, and the upper two-thirds of a B-24D nose grafted on, with the B-26 tail gun emplacement faired in beneath this. Ivan Stepnich, who served as a pilot and engineering officer on this project after flying combat with the 44th BG, remembered the engineers were so eager to test fly the product they neglected to clean up myriad aluminum filings in the nose compartment left over from the modification process. Since the Plexiglas fairing around the guns was normally facing aft on a B-26, it had gaps that allowed air to ram in when it faced forward on the nose of *Hap Hazard*. The result, Stepnich said, was a shower of floating aluminum bits, like chaff, in the cockpit as the wind blasted the metal flakes airborne. Cleaning the plane, and installing zippered boots over the gun slots, cured that problem.

General Doolittle said the Bell boosted chin turret was superior to the proposed production Emerson ball turret planned for the single-tail B-24N. This opinion was based on photos of the Emerson installation, which showed it to offer poorer visibility than the Bell boosted variant, while providing "no improvement in space available in the nose for personnel and for the special equipment required here for navigation and instrument bombing," according to Doolittle.

A report circulated by Headquarters, US Strategic Forces in Europe, in 1944 touted the Bell boosted gun nose, but acknowledged its introduction to existing Liberators could be hampered by a shortage of B-24D nose greenhouses to graft on to newer fuselages, some of which varied due to different manufacturers. At the time of the report, the Bell power boost units for the hand-held guns were in short supply, with the Ninth AF taking priority to get grounded B-26 Marauders back in action. Gen. Henry H. "Hap" Arnold sent a message in October 1944 to Generals Carl Spaatz and Jimmy Doolittle in Europe, explaining that tests and production of the Bell modification kits would require an extra six months, by which time B-24Ns (with Emerson 128 nose turrets) were forecast to be ready, although the N-model ultimately was not ready for service by then. Arnold asked Doolittle and Spaatz, "Do you still desire kits for Chin Gun installation instead of the present nose turret in your B-24 airplanes, considering the delay involved?"

Ultimately, the B-24N was to have been the answer, but orders for 5,168 single-tail N-models were dropped after victory in Europe was achieved in 1945. When Liberator production ended on May 31 of that year, one XB-24N and seven YB-24Ns had been produced.

The Emerson 128 turret was tested in 1944 at Eglin Field in B-24G number 42-78399. It was an electric ball turret installed in the nose, replacing the standard Emerson nose turret at a weight savings of 210lb. The 128 ball used a K-11 gunsight, according to AAF reports, and provided a 120deg frontal cone of fire protection for the Liberator. The turret collected its own

spent shells and links rather than spilling them overboard as did some Liberator armaments. The retention of the shells and links was a way to protect aircraft in tight formation from suffering damage from flying debris. Especially in a tight javelin-down formation, with successive waves of bombers below and behind those preceding them, foreign-object damage from shells was a real problem.

The Emerson 128 had a unique ability to be centered and fired by the Liberator's copilot in emergency situations, according to AAF papers. Upon completion of the Eglin tests on July 19, 1944, testers in Florida said the Emerson 128 was "superior to any nose armament installation in a B-24 type airplane previously tested by this command."

In 1944, the AAF investigated ways to give the loaded B-24J a higher operational ceiling. It rejected a suggestion that the gross weight be restricted to 60,000lb, which would cut into the B-24J's fuel or bomb loads. The promise of improved performance in the XB-24N was the cause of the rejection. "It is believed that the XB-24N will show a marked increase in operational ceiling over the B-24J airplane," wrote Col. Jack Roberts in a report under the banner of Gen. Hap Arnold's office as commanding general of the AAF. Among items approved for introduction in the Liberator line was the Emerson 128 nose ball turret "in all production B-24s as soon as the turret becomes available." In practice, this effective armament was fitted to only a few test airplanes before production ceased.

Eighth AF modifications, including add-on armor plating and bulging navigator window over the old-size window frame, kept Dinky Duck *upgraded for combat.* Jeff Ethell Collection

Other improvement tests on B-24s were discouraged late in 1944, to give emphasis to the single-tail B-24N program. The N-model was held in high regard as the answer to many operational problems. Its engines were Pratt & Whitney R-1830-75s fitted with hooded B31 turbo-superchargers. The Dash-75 engine produced about 150hp more than previous versions of the 1830. The hood, planners hoped, would increase speed by about 6mph, and was visible beneath the engine nacelle.

The cockpit of the B-24N was redesigned with a knife-edge windscreen, which also showed up on late-production Ford-built B-24Ms. This windscreen afforded the pilot and copilot better visibility. Pilot and copilot overhead escape hatches were requested for this configuration as well.

While this redesigning was under way, the top turret in late Liberators was anchored more securely in an effort to reduce the tendency for upper turrets to rip loose and plunge forward to the flight deck in crashes.

There's a sense of disappointment that the sporty B-24N did not achieve production and never had a chance to strut its stuff—but this let-down is ameliorated by the reason the B-24N was never mass-produced: overwhelming Allied victory!

Chapter 5

Warpaint

Paint and markings on Liberators and Privateers provide seemingly endless variations and mutations. Some trends emerged, and can be of use in sleuthing information from photographs. On camouflaged Liberators, deep, uniform scallops between the gray undersides and the olive uppers are hallmarks of a Ford paint job. Less-uniform scallops mark early camouflaged North American G-models. Straight, yet feathered, demarcation between gray and olive were typical of Consolidated-built Liberators.

In the decades since World War II, historians and collectors of nose art photography have endeavored to catalog the specific identities, squadrons, and serials of decorated B-24s. For a variety of reasons, errors creep into the body of information available. Sometimes, aviators with box cameras meandered off their own flightline and into a neighboring group area to take snapshots. In the years following the

Records indicate Virgin Abroad *was a B-24M-15-FO, number 44-50941, serving with the 529th Squadron of the 380th BG in 1945. Because airpower was massed at some locations later in the war, some confusion occasionally arises over ownership of particular aircraft photographed at specific locations.* C. M. Young Collection

end of the war, that excursion to a neighboring bomb group gets forgotten, and all the planes in the photos become melded erroneously into one unit. Efforts have been made to cross-reference most of the nose art photos in this volume. If any errors still exist, hopefully other mistakes have been rectified.

Dedicated B-24 nose-art researchers find it valuable to check multiple publications on the topic; sometimes, a distant full-plane shot in one book complements a nose art close-up in another, allowing an artist, or modeler, or restorer to render a complete version of the intended subject B-24.

Color as Plain as Black and White

How many times have you heard someone say, "I'll believe it when I see it in black and white"?

In the case of vintage aircraft photography, "black and white" has many shades of meaning, as the accompanying photos reveal. One of the tasks of the curator, model builder, artist, aircraft restorer, and historian is to recreate the colors of the past, often with limited access to full-color photography.

The difficulty of the task can be compounded by the use of two radically different types of black-and-white films in the 1930s and 1940s. Orthochromatic film has a very low sensitivity to light in the visible red portion of the

spectrum. Thus it was ideal for box cameras where a small, circular red window on the back of the camera revealed the number of the negative being exposed. Orthochromatic film can also be processed in a darkroom with red safelights without damaging the image.

A disadvantage to orthochromatic film is its lack of natural-looking shades of gray when printed. Because red objects do not expose the film emulsion, they are rendered clear on the negative, and subsequently show dark on the positive print. To a degree, other colors that have a red component also are rendered darker than natural.

Panchromatic film is sensitive to the entire visible spectrum. Its disadvantage is the need to handle it in total darkness for processing. The big advantage to panchromatic film is the natural way it renders shades of color in terms of blacks, grays, and whites.

Yet another factor enters the picture: filtration. Color filters placed in front of the camera lens alter the way black-and-white films record images. Even with panchromatic film, the use of a yellow filter will render blue skies darker than they would appear with no filter.

The task of sorting out colors in black-and-white prints has intrigued aviation historian and author Peter M. Bowers. These shades are described in the book *United States Military Air-*

Million $ Baby *color Kodachrome was obtained after detailed analysis of various black-and-white photos yielded probable color scheme for this Liberator, which was number 44-50768 of the 43rd BG. See text to determine how accurate the reading of the black-and-white photos was.* Jeff Ethell Collection

Photo 1 *of* Million $ Baby *shows tones typical of panchromatic film. See chapter text for complete analysis of the color information these black-and-white photos impart.* Al Lomer Collection

craft since 1908, *authored by Bowers and Gordon Swanborough. Bowers and Swanborough say orthochromatic film renders reds dark, yellows quite dark, and blues fairly light. With the advent of panchromatic film, reds were lightened, blues darkened, and yellows could almost appear white, especially if the popular yellow K2 filter was used to snap up the sky definition.

Dana Bell's book Air Force Colors, Volume I, 1926–1942 asserts that light blue appears so dark when photographed on panchromatic film that it may resemble olive drab.

Let's apply what we know of film characteristics and aircraft markings to the accompanying three photographs of a B-24 Liberator nicknamed Million $ Baby, photographed on Ie-Shima in the Pacific in 1945. The photos are so remarkably different in the way they represent the colors of the bathing suit that one might assume the plane had been repainted. But the truth probably lies in the realm of pan and ortho films, and filters.

Photo 1 probably was made with panchromatic film. A clue is the medium shade of the fire extinguisher hatch, located immediately above the woman's raised knee. This hatch was painted red at the factory, providing one reliable color reference as an anchor for further research. The line curving down from her lowest sandal is a snubber mark for towing, to serve as a guide for the maximum turning angle of the nosewheel. It typically was painted black. Expect the antiglare panel on top of the fuselage to be olive drab.

Notice how the red fire extinguisher hatch appears much darker in Photo 2 and 3. This is a clue that they were shot on orthochromatic film. It is logical to expect the woman's painted lips to be red. And they appear the same shade as the red fire extinguisher hatch in all three photos. Similarly, one might suppose the large bow around the woman's neck is red with black shading. Note how the bow is a light shade in the first photo, where it matches the red fire hatch, and the bow is darker in the second and third, where it still matches the red fire extinguisher hatch, which also is rendered darker in appearance.

222

The panel behind the *Million $ Baby* lettering also seems to mimic the shade of the fire extinguisher hatch, and may also be red. Since orthochromatic film makes little distinction between red and black, the shadow shading on the lettering is obscured in both Photo 2 and 3, if indeed they are orthochromatic, and the panel is red.

The woman's hair color matches the basic shade of her bathing suit in all three photos, turning darker in the second and third. In the panchromatic Photo 1, the hair and bathing suit are light. All these clues indicate the hair and suit are yellow. (Even if the suit looks dark in Photo 3! That's the magic of orthochromatic film.)

The floral designs on the bathing suit may be blue since they appear lighter on the ortho prints (Photo 2 and 3) than on the panchromatic print (Photo 1). Similarly, the large sun hat appears to retain the same tone value as the floral pattern; the hat, too, may be blue.

The sandals change hue in the photos, and are not the same as the hat or swimsuit colors. The sandals are darker in the orthochromatic prints and lighter in the panchromatic print. This might mean they are brown with a high red pigment content. (In the panchromatic Photo 1, the sandals do not have exactly the same tonal value as the fire extinguisher panel, which probably rules out true red for the sandals.)

In the first and second photos, the aircraft data block stenciling can be seen in part of the letter N and the dollar sign. This indicates the lettering was left unpainted, to allow the natural aluminum finish of the B-24 to add shine to the name. The serial appears to be 44-50260; the identifiers FO visible in the original photo in the dollar sign confirm this is a Ford-built Liberator, which matches that s/n. The serial was assigned to a B-24M built at Willow Run, Michigan.

Sleuthing with these three photos has produced a likely composite of the color scheme of this elaborate artwork:

Red: Lips, bow, and sign background

Yellow: Swimsuit and hair

Blue: Floral design on swimsuit and hat

Brown: Sandals

Photo 2 of Million $ Baby *renders some shades, like the red fire extinguisher hatch, dark. This suggests it was made with orthochromatic film.* Tom Foote Collection

Photo 3 of Million $ Baby *could also be from orthochromatic film, with different filtration than Photo 2.* Al Lomer Collection

Flesh tone: Skin

Black: Shadow detailing and outlines

Natural aluminum: Lettering

(Note: This analysis was made with only black-and-white photography to evaluate. Subsequently, a color photo was obtained, and is published in this volume. Refer to it to check the validity of this tonal evaluation.)

The Squaw *was a D-model of the 98th BG that survived the August 1, 1943, low-level Ploesti mission. It was photographed on a promotional tour at Fort Worth, Texas, in 1943. Some patched bullet holes appear to have been painted pale blue and others yellow, in color photos of* The Squaw. *Group emblem and map of the plane's mission history were painted on opposite side of forward fuselage. US Air Force*

Desert-sand B-24D displays national insignia on both wings, with yellow surrounds and RAF-style fin flashes on both sides of vertical fins. Exhaust has started to smudge the wing behind the engines. Style of individual plane number 84 on tail and nose suggests this Liberator flew with the 376th BG. Gerry Furney Collection

The 397th BS in Panama used the considerable talents of PFC William M. Carter to adorn many LB-30s and B-24s with artwork like that on Jungle Queen (AL-640). Jungle Queen served the 6th BG until November 1, 1943, when the group was disbanded; the Panama Liberator squadrons then came under 6th Bomber Command. Jungle Queen was adorned on both sides of the cockpit, with the pose reversed. Data block stenciled beneath cockpit on left side reads: U.S. ARMY LB-30 AC NO. AL-640. Ted Small Collection

The Stud Duck *adorned 397th BS LB-30 AL-634*. Ted Small Collection

Tiger Lady, *a 6th BG (later, VI Bomber Command) LB-30 that carried number AL641, according to the records of pilot Ted Small. White underbelly blended with wing undersurface, and dropped* down ahead and behind wing. Similar rise in white can be expected at horizontal tail. Ted Small Collection

Princess Sheila *was 6th BG LB-30 number AL-639, according to Panama veteran Ted Small.*

Lettie Jo, *another 6th BG LB-30, carried number AL-632.* Ted Small Collection

Peace Offering *may be B-24M-10-FO number 44-50811 of the 529th BS of the 380th BG in the Pacific.* C. M. Young Collection

Bull O' The Woods *bears evidence of an earlier painted-out name—possibly Diablo. According to 397th BS pilot Ted Small's records, this aircraft was LB-30 number AL-583 in service over Panama.* Ted Small Collection

Blonde Blitz *was 6th BG LB-30 number AL-628.* Ted Small Collection

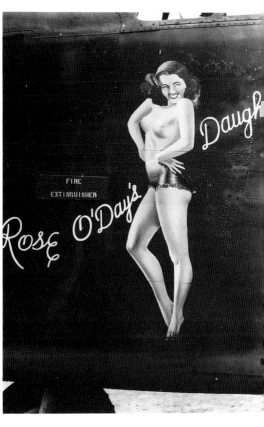

Miss Anabelle Lee *was a B-24 assigned to the 397th BS, in Panama. The last* three digits of its s/n probably were 957. Ted Small Collection

Rose O'Day's Daughter *was a B-24 assigned to the 6th BG in Panama, and decorated on both sides. Last three digits of s/n probably were 961.* Ted Small Collection

Night Mission *artwork appeared, in mirror image, on both sides of the fuselage of this 6th BG B-24D, number 42-40891. One panel of this artwork was* cut from the bomber as it was scrapped, and is preserved by the Confederate Air Force. Ted Small and Peter M. Bowers Collections

Bail-out Belle *was a B-24D (s/n 42-72951), probably assigned to the 529th BS of the 380th BG in the Pacific. The art appeared in mirror image on both sides of nose, and remained after the plane's camouflage paint was stripped to bare metal. When a Hawaii Air Depot nose turret was added, the .50cal cheek gun port was skinned over. A machine gun ball socket was installed in the navigator's window. Lee Bushnell and Larry Jaynes Collections*

Some color deterioration cannot hide the beauty of Lucky Strike, *which may be B-24M-5-CO 44-41876 of the 530th Squadron of the 380th BG in 1945.* C. M. Young Collection

Sure Pop *was B-24D-CO-130 s/n 42-41073, assigned to the 90th BG, and probably the 319th BS. Extreme discoloration shows where nose-turret addition caused new olive paint to be added over its faded coat.* Larry Jaynes Collection

Gus' Jokers *was the last B-24M-1-CO (44-41848), and flew with the 31st BS of the 5th BG. Dark background with last three digits of s/n in white on forward fuselages of 5th BG B-24s gave way in 1945 to the last four digits being painted directly on the aluminum sides of the forward fuselages. C. E. Larsson and Albert W. James Collections*

Booby Trap *carried the smiling skull of the Fifth AF's 90th BG on Pacific mis-* *sions. Its s/n may be 44-40193. Dennis Peltier and Larry Jaynes Collections*

C-87 number 44-39229 in the CBI showed a replacement cargo door with a piece of national insignia differently placed than on the rest of the plane. Oily exhaust smudged the lower curve *of the vertical fin. This photo is one of many taken under crude field conditions by aviation historian Peter M. Bowers, who, as an AAF officer, used discarded aerial film that he trimmed* *in the darkroom to fit 616 size film spools when his limited supply of film ran out. Peter M. Bowers Collection*

An unnamed bulldog adorned a British Liberator in India.

V Grand, *the 5,000th Convair San Diego B-24, was autographed by Consolidated Vultee workers before going off to war with the Fifteenth AF. This B-24J-195-CO twice made emergency landings on the island of Vis, in the Adriatic Sea, between Italy and Yugoslavia. She probably served with the 454th BG. In service,* V Grand *received Fifteenth AF-style enclosed waist windows with K-5 gun mounts, but retained the wind deflectors. General Dynamics, Herb Tollefson, and Charlie Glassie Collections*

Pistol Packin' Mama, *one of the most popular of all B-24 nose art names, adorned this Fifteenth AF example in Italy. Additional windows have been added in the nose; wavy camouflage demarcation suggests this is a Ford-built Liberator.* Charlie Glassie Collection

Stateside AAF camouflage testing included this bewildering repetition of Liberators on Liberators, in an effort to confuse enemy fighters long enough to ruin their aim. Peter M. Bowers Collection

A scaly, grinning creature adorned this Eighth AF B-24, which had add-on cockpit armor glass. The Emerson A-15 nose turret is an early model with front Plexiglas extending all the way to the bottom of the turret. Al Lloyd Collection

Chapter 6

Join the Navy

Protecting the Sea Lanes

Antisubmarine missions often were characterized by long hours of tedious overwater flying, where great range and reasonable speed were desirable traits in an aircraft. The US Navy found range, if not speed, in its strut-braced PBY Catalina seaplanes and amphibians.

But the province of heavy bombardment airplanes remained with the Army Air Corps. The slick new Davis wing, tried by Consolidated first on the experimental Model 31 flying boat for the Navy, found a home on the Army's Model 32 Liberator. When the Air Corps gained acceptance for heavy bombers in the 1930s, the idealized mission involved flying out to sea to meet enemy ships, and sinking them before they could attack the United States. In the minds of AAF planners, land-based heavy bombers as antisubmarine weapons were logically the AAF's obligation and turf. American policy limited the Navy's use of land-based planes. Inroads in this provincial plan were made with amphibious PBY-5A Catalinas, and with Lockheed Hudson twin-engine land-based bombers requisitioned by the Navy in October 1941. The Navy got into the land-based

bomber business with the Hudsons plausibly because the use of seaplanes for America's Neutrality Patrol from Newfoundland and Iceland was threatened by winter icing conditions on the water. George F. Poulos, who served as operations officer and executive officer of Navy PB4Y-1 squadron VB-103, was well acquainted with the early politics involved in antisubmarine duties. Writing in the Spring 1991 *Briefing* of the International B-24 Liberator Club, Poulos recalled that Gen. George C. Marshall proposed a Coastal Air Command for the AAF, to have domain over Liberators and other landplanes in maritime usage, when the Navy urged development of naval antisubmarine squadrons of landplanes. "This disagreement was consistent with the basic differences that existed between the Navy and the Army organizational concepts," Poulos said. "The Navy believed that the *function* was the primary basis for organization, whereas the Army operated on the theory that the *weapon* should be the prime organizational consideration." In other words, the AAF figured if the mission demanded a Liberator, an AAF crew would fly it. But the Navy believed if a largely maritime mission required a special landplane, that landplane should be given to the Navy to do the job right.

Perhaps it was the breakthrough in range and speed of the Liberator itself that encouraged the Navy to rethink

its classic reliance on waterborne patrol bombers, and pursue faster landplanes. The trackless ocean could be monitored with long-legged, land-based Liberators. In the early months of American combat in 1942, the faster speed of aerodynamically streamlined land-based patrol bombers paid dividends when the Navy's PBO-1 Hudsons sank two U-boats because the Hudsons could close to attacking range faster than the lumbering Catalinas. The Catalinas could be seen on the horizon by surfaced submariners, who had more time to crash-dive than they did with the Hudsons on the prowl. Other problems dogged the seaplanes, particularly when engaged by enemy fighters, during which the survivability of a slow seaplane was considered less than that of a faster landplane bomber.

As early as February 1942, the Navy asked for a share of B-24 production deliveries to bolster naval antisub patrols. But the AAF was not easily persuaded to give up that mission—or a portion of its B-24 Liberator heavy bombers—in the struggling months of the first year of war. The Navy had an asset coveted by the AAF: The Boeing factory on the south shore of Lake Washington, at Renton, Washington, was earmarked for production of PBB-1 Sea Ranger patrol seaplanes. This plant was ideal for construction of the new B-29 Superfortress for the AAF. Even while arrayed against the com-

An early greenhouse PB4Y-1 over England, 1943. National Archives

Wing-mounted radar antennas aided this early US Navy PB4Y-1 in finding ships and surfaced submarines. Peter M. Bowers Collection

mon Axis enemy abroad, the Navy and AAF bartered shrewdly with one another at home. Chief of Staff George C. Marshall agreed, on July 7, 1942, to cleave off part of Consolidated's Liberator production to meet Navy needs. The Navy also was given a share of Mitchell and Ventura production. The AAF was pleased to get the Boeing Renton plant when the Navy declared the Sea Ranger moot, thereby freeing up shop space and R-3350 engines for the B-29 assembly line to be created there. To further enhance production of the Liberators the Navy and AAF both wanted, the Navy agreed to limit its orders for Catalinas, also built by Consolidated in San Diego, to minimize interference with Liberator production.

The Navy had its own nomenclature for aircraft during World War II. All Navy Liberators were built as PB4Y-1s, whether delivered with a B-24D greenhouse nose, the Navy's ERCO bow turret, or, in some instances, the Emerson nose. All Privateers were delivered as PB4Y-2s. (Some acquired the designator PB4Y-2B to indicate they were fitted for slinging Bat glide bombs under their wings.) By 1962, the American services adopted a universal nomenclature for aircraft by which the few remaining Privateers in Navy service were redesignated basically P-4, and more narrowly, QP-4B, as drone aircraft.

By August 1942, Navy PB4Y-1 Liberators were reality. On November 5, 1942, the first Navy Liberator to sink a U-boat recorded this feat while operating out of Iceland.

A year would pass, in which the AAF also flew B-24Ds on antisubmarine patrols. Not until August 1943 did the AAF agree to disband its own Anti-

submarine Command, putting this specialized mission squarely in the hands of the Navy. The AAF antisubmarine squadrons would phase out gradually as the Navy was able to replace them. According to George Poulos' account, the AAF's 479th Antisubmarine Group's 19th Squadron departed Dunkeswell, England, on September 7, 1943, to join up with the Eighth AF. The AAF's 6th Squadron left Dunkeswell on September 22, and two days later, Navy squadron VB-103 moved to Dunkeswell from St. Eval. The Army's 22nd Squadron departed St. Eval on September 28, but the AAF's 4th Squadron continued to patrol the Bay of Biscay until October 31, 1943. By then, a third Navy Liberator squadron was ready to join 103 and 105 squadrons, according to Poulos.

Some swapouts of bombers occurred, as the Navy inherited radar-equipped antisubmarine Liberators from the AAF in place of some of the Navy's early PB4Y-1s, which lacked

To comply with aspects of Portuguese neutrality so they could use the Azores during World War II, some VB-114 PB4Y-1s curiously carried dual US and British markings. This example, BuNo. 32205, carried a Leigh searchlight under its right wing. Propeller hubs and blades out to the diameter of the cowling sometimes were painted white to blend with the nacelles. Donald C. Higgins via Liberator Club Collection

Not all nose-turret PB4Y-1s used ER-CO bow turrets; some, like PB4Y-1 BuNo. 38894, flew with AAF-style Emerson nose turrets instead. This aircraft came from the second-to-last batch of San Diego B-24Js, and carried Navy tri-color camouflage. Peter M. Bowers Collection

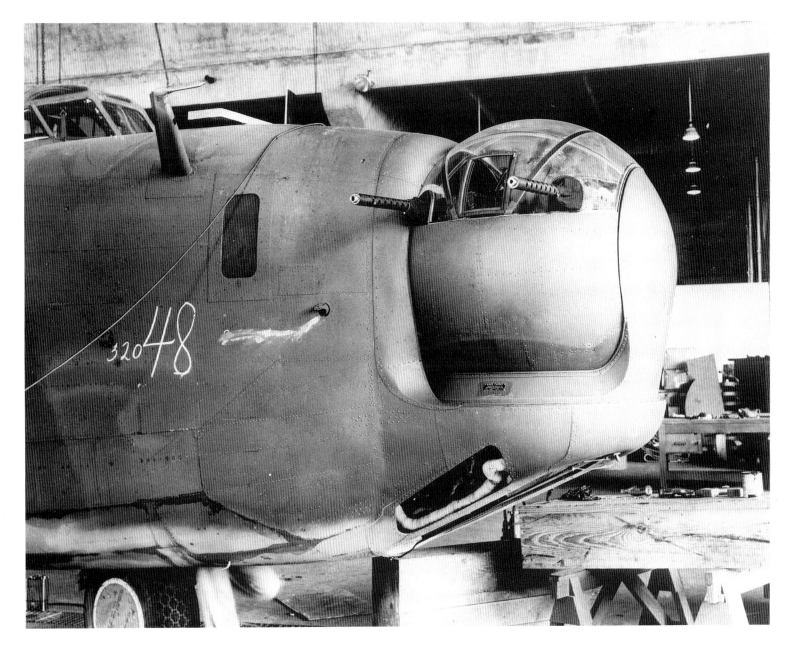

This former AAF B-24D, redesignated PB4Y-1 number 32048, received an ERCO bow turret installation at North Island Naval Air Station in May 1943. Chuck Hansen Collection

the electronics needed to find subs beyond visual range.

Typically, Navy PB4Y-1 Liberators were built by Consolidated in San Diego; when single-tail Privateers were introduced, all of these sophisticated PB4Y-2s were San Diego products.

During World War II, the Navy dabbled in transport Liberators, flying three C-87s with R-1830-45 engines as

RY-1s, and five more with R-1830-43 powerplants. A transport version of the Privateer, designated RY-3, flew briefly with the Navy and Marines, but slipped out of service quietly in postwar years. Fewer than 40 RY-3s were built for the Navy and Marines; some saw service with the RAF.

Navy Nose Jobs

The Navy soon acknowledged the need for improved frontal firepower in its PB4Y-1s, and grafted ERCO (Engineering and Research Corp.) spherical turrets to some of its greenhouse PB4Y-1s. These were the same bow turrets designed for the PBB-1 Sea

Ranger the Navy gave up in favor of getting a share of landplane production runs. A test contract for equipping a combat squadron of PB4Y-1s with ERCO bow turrets was let in the summer of 1942, as the Navy wasted no time in upgrading its Liberators. Results were favorable, and combat losses of ERCO-equipped Liberators were said to diminish.

After removing the greenhouse, a protruding lip containing the turret ring was mounted and faired into the fuselage contours. Shallow quarters for the bombardier below the large turret included a large, flat optical aiming window, usually bracketed by two small scanning windows. Later PB4Y-1s and PB4Y-2 Privateers used larger, more effective scanning windows.

The ERCO Model 250SH bow turret had an upper surface of Plexiglas held in place by metal straps; the clear portion could be removed for emergency escape. The two .50cal machine guns in the turret were rigidly mounted; the entire ball, encasing the gunner, was moved by hydraulic pressure in azimuth and elevation to track targets. The door to the turret served as a padded backrest for the gunner. Spent shells and links were collected internally, with links falling into zippered canvas bags beneath each gun, while the empty brass gathered in an internal compartment in the lower front of the turret, accessible from the outside following a mission.

Some Navy records indicate some PB4Y-1s and later PB4Y-2 Privateers were ferried, minus ERCO bow turrets, from the Consolidated San Diego factory to nearby North Island Naval Air Station, also in San Diego, for the turret installation. Photos accompanying this text show an early PB4Y-1 receiving its ERCO turret at North Island. However, a footnote in the PB4Y-2 Privateer parts catalog says: "Airplanes 59433 to 66324 inclusive furnished with dummy nose fairing forward of station 9.1 and instal[lation] of nose-turret structure and turret accomplished at Litchfield Park [Arizona] as a Navy modification." This series of Privateers, starting with BuNo. 59433, may correspond with those Privateers receiving ERCO bow turrets. Photos of Privateers with Consolidated/MPC-style nose turrets generally depict aircraft with lower BuAer numbers. The basic aircraft manufacturers were constantly playing catch-up with modifications. Sometimes, to keep production moving at an even pace, it was simpler to complete an aircraft with a known deficiency, and send it immediately to a modification center for update, than it was to create turmoil in the basic assembly process by trying to insert all the newest changes at the factory.

Navy Combat

The November 1942 sinking of a U-boat was followed by years of diligent combat flown by Navy and Marine aviators in PB4Ys. War and weather were

During a Bay of Biscay patrol, US Navy PB4Y-1 pilot Charles F. Willis, Jr., buzzed a downed example of his German equivalent, a cracked-up Focke-Wulf Fw 200, somewhere in Spain. Charles F. Willis, Jr., Collection

In the January chill of 1944, Charlie Willis' PB4Y-1 found and sank this German submarine from an altitude of 100ft. Charles F. Willis, Jr., Collection

Blue Belle *flew photo recon for Navy squadron VD-5 when this photo was taken on Iwo Jima early in 1945.* San Diego Aerospace Museum

quick, unforgiving teachers to the new Navy crews, some of whom were veterans of Pacific Catalina combat. VB-103 launched Liberators from Argentia, Newfoundland, beginning in May 1943, escorting convoys to mid-Atlantic. Veteran George Poulos recalled: "On June 23, while en route to rendezvous with a convoy, Lt. H. K. Reese reported a radar blip and came through a very heavy overcast to investigate. No further messages were received. My search of the area the next day, in perfect weather, uncovered three huge icebergs. We all learned from this incident and . . . when investigating an isolated radar blip in bad weather we always allowed a five degree offset on the radar scope until we had visual contact."

As a footnote to the history of the Vought F4U Corsair fighter, it was while escorting PB4Y-1 Liberators of squadron VP-51 on a daylight shipping strike over Kahili, Bougainville, that the gull-wing Corsair first saw air-to-air combat on February 13, 1943.

The summer of 1943 did not pay out in submarine contacts for the crews of VB-103. Evidently the escort carriers were being so successful that the U-boats were prompted to haunt different waters. On August 15, 1943, VB-103 departed Argentia for St. Eval, England, arriving two days later. AAF antisubmarine B-24D squadrons at Gander also departed for England during this time.

Over the North Atlantic and the Bay of Biscay, Navy Liberators in distinctive white-bottomed, high-sided camouflage did their best to scrub the cold sea clean of German submarines. PB4Y-1s occasionally asserted themselves in unlikely air-to-air combat against their four-engine Luftwaffe counterpart, the FW 200 Kondor. During the summer of 1943, the Luftwaffe began launching twin-engine fighter variants of the Ju 88 to seek out Allied patrol planes like the PB4Y-1s. To this threat, the British responded effectively with sweeps by Bristol Beaufighters and deHavilland Mosquitoes.

On occasion, PB4Y-1 crews out of England were engaged by Messerschmitt Bf 109 fighters. The big Davis wing, skillfully flown, could foil the attacks of a lone Messerschmitt by turning the fighter's higher wing loading against it in tight maneuvering. If the Luftwaffe pilot attempted to follow the Liberator into the turn, the fighter risked a stall. At low altitude over the icy waves, such a stall could prove fatal to the fighter. This gave the Bf 109 pilot a dilemma, for if he broke off the turn, he lost his shot at the Liberator. If the lone PB4Y-1s of the Navy lacked the umbrella of combined firepower that their AAF counterparts enjoyed in mass formations, the solo Navy bombers at least had the freedom to maneuver in the open sky to shake off their attacker.

The Marines took greenhouse PB4Y-1s into Pacific combat with squadron VMD-254. Some of their Liberators packed a fixed cannon in the nose—Marines aren't shy about using firepower in combat.

It was the fall doldrums when Navy squadron VPB-108 came to the Pacific in 1943, to fly in the campaign to take the Gilbert Islands. Beginning November 17, the Liberator crews of VPB-108 mocked weather that grounded other planes. They soon began exercising their Yankee ingenuity. They flew their PB4Y-1s on the deck, downwind, at top speed, and under radar detection height and then popped up to 150ft to drop bombs by eyeball. Lt. Frank W. Ackermann in *Pistol Packin' Mama* tried the trick out, against Mille, in the Marshall Islands. Strafing down one side of the island, Ackermann circled the harbor and claimed a supply ship sunk by two bombs. Squadron accounts say he flew 15ft above the Mille runway, as his gunners strafed everything of value. Six Japanese fighters engaged his Liberator— two went down, one was damaged, and the rest failed to bring Ackermann down. Lt. Richard B. Daley repeated the trick three days later, flying *Nippo Nippin' Kitten* to Jaluit Atoll. Among targets Daley's crew claimed that day were two fuel storage tanks, a landing barge filled with troops, and a Kawanishi H8K Emily flying boat, resting on the water. The pace was set. The squadron moved in about a month to position themselves for the battle of the Marshall Islands.

In January 1944, Lt. Comdr. Edward Renfro, skipper of VPB-108, led 10 Liberators on a palm-shaking run over Kwajalein. The surprise element

was so effective only one enemy gunner fired back on the first pass, only to be silenced by a gunner in a PB4Y-1. The bold attack inflicted damage on the Japanese garrison—and was staged as a diversion to permit two camera planes access to low-oblique photography of Kwajalein useful in subsequent major attacks.

Two VPB-108 Liberators hung in the air 19hr to reach Wake Island, and return, on February 28, 1944. They dropped 500lb bombs from less than 100ft.

Relieved at Eniwetok by VPB-116 on July 10, 1944, VPB-108 was reformed on September 20 that same year at Alameda, California, this time with new PB4Y-2 Privateers.

The first bombing mission against Iwo Jima by landplanes was a July 14, 1944, strike by Navy PB4Y-1 Liberators of VB-109, flying out of Saipan. The distinctions between AAF and Navy targets, and aircraft, were blurring as the dictates of combat set the pace.

In October 1944, the Navy revised its nomenclature for bombing squadrons. Multi-engine bombing squadrons that had been signified by *VB* combined their terminology with patrol squadrons, that had been *VP*, to form the single designation *VPB*, used for the remainder of the war.

On May 13, 1945, the Navy put up what was to have been a mixed three-plane formation of two PB4Y-1s and

Ranging out from Whidbey Island Naval Air Station in Washington state, Privateer 59604 sported mottled paint scheme applied to some PB4Y-2s. View shows paired antennas under nose for scanning either side of plane's line of flight.

one single-tail PB4Y-2, loaded with incendiaries for the destruction of the Pontianak, Borneo, shipyard, according to mission participant R. L. Wolpert. The performance advantage of the Privateer prompted its crew to bomb early, leaving a fire licking at the shipyard when the two PB4Y-1 Liberators of VPB-111 arrived on scene. Wolpert, copilot on one of the Liberators, noted

Privateer Tortilla Flat *served in VPB-106, surviving combat before returning to Camp Kearney, near San Diego, for training use. Sharkmouth appears to have "gums" in red, and pinstriped outer lips and spaces between teeth in black.* David Behunin and John Dingle Collections

his plane received a few hits from the alerted enemy. A lone Mitsubishi Ki-51 Sonia, packing two wing-mounted machine guns and probably equipped with a flexible machine gun in the rear cockpit, gamely attacked the two Liberators. No doubt to the surprise of the Japanese pilot, the Liberators returned the attack, as Wolpert's pilot peeled off and went after the Sonia in a banking shallow dive! The dogfight might have looked arthritic compared to a full-blown duel between front-line fighters, but the slow Sonia and the big PB4Y-1s slugged it out for about a half hour, Wolpert recalled in the Fall 1989 *Briefing* of the International B-24 Liberator Club. "It was only because there were two of us and one of him that we finally got that Sonia," Wolpert said. "Fact is, at one point near the end, he damned near got both of us. We had him at the apex of a loose 'V' formation when he performed a perfect Immelman and came back between us. We were so intent on our target that we both turned

in on him simultaneously and a head-on collision was averted only by what I have always believed was a miracle."

Tall Tail

With the Navy's foot squarely in the door of Liberator production, it is not surprising a Navy-encouraged derivative of the Liberator took form on Consolidated drawing boards. Many ingredients combined in this process: Consolidated already had in mind field-of-fire improvements for Liberator gunners that a single tail could provide. Independent of Navy studies, the AAF and Consolidated pieced together the B-24ST (Single Tail) and XB-24K (essentially one program using spliced airframes and a tall tail from a B-23 Dragon bomber). The AAF test plane began flying in March 1943; the Navy ordered three prototype single-tail variants of its own on May 3 of that same year.

Both the AAF and Navy variants enjoyed benefits of improved stability and handling from the single-tail configurations. But the route to Privateer production was not the same path the AAF followed in its single-tail Liberator projects. The Navy wanted a long-range radar search plane. To house the secret electronics suite of the Privateer, a fuselage extension of seven feet was spliced into the three prototypes ahead of the wings, as PB4Y-1s numbers 32095, 32096, and 32086 were dissected to become the first Privateers.

The basic Privateer form was comparison-tested with a standard greenhouse PB4Y-1 model in the University of Washington wind tunnel. Configuration changes included tests with the large ventral radome (located in the new fuselage plug) extended for operation, and with bulging side gun blisters, evoking images of "form follows function" engineering. The single tail of the model was an early version; on production Privateers, it was heightened still more. The wind-tunnel model was also tested in a hybrid form—lengthened and studded with protuberances like a Privateer, but retaining the twin tails of a Liberator.

Consolidated's San Diego plant delivered all three XPB4Y-2 prototypes with twin tails, even though the single tail was an integral part of the plan. The lengthened bombers flew first in

September, October, and December 1943 as they were sent to the Navy. Later that year, all three returned to San Diego for Consolidated's installation of the original short single tail. The Navy took the revised XPB4Y-2s again on February 2, 1944. The first two prototypes kept standard B-24 engine nacelle packages; the third prototype introduced the vertical oval shape, minus turbo-superchargers, that would characterize production Privateers.

The first version of the single tail was inadequate. After examining some expedient fixes proposed by Consolidated designers, the Navy decided the best answer involved new engineering for a still taller tail, to top out at a stunning 29ft, 1-5/8in above the tarmac.

The tail increase delayed deliveries of Privateers, but resulted in a better airplane, generally liked by crews.

The three XPB4Y-2 prototypes carried Consolidated nose turrets, replaced on early production Privateers by similar MPC turrets that made the noses of the first Privateers look strikingly like a contemporary B-24 Liberator. The definitive Privateer nose was the ERCO bow turret installation as applied to later Navy PB4Y-1s.

Equipping the Privateer

The Norden bombsight, so central to AAF strategic bombardment, found little favor with the Navy, since anti-shipping strikes were more successful at low altitudes, where the Norden's abilities waned. According to a document produced by Navy historian Lee Pearson in 1974, "Up until early 1944, the Norden sight was installed in all new patrol planes and torpedo bombers. . . . Regulations also required that bombsights be in the aircraft whenever they were transferred. De-emphasis of the Norden sight began early in 1944 when the requirement that it be transferred with the aircraft was dropped. In February and March of 1945, the requirement for its installation was also cancelled." Nonetheless, Navy bombers including Privateers sometimes retained the stabilizer portion of the Norden bombsight equipment, which could be used as an autopilot or to stabilize a Privateer for radar bombing.

Some Privateer pilots used visual cues at low altitude, and bombed with-

out bombsights, and in some cases, without a bombardier aboard.

Though enemy submarines gave impetus to the Navy's original desire

for Liberators, by the time Privateers left the United States for Pacific action, the probability of encountering a friendly submarine largely precluded

Miss Sea-duce *followed a common Pacific practice of allowing nose art to en-* *croach on plane numbers.* Jim Masura Collection

Sailing low over a wood-paneled station wagon is a PB4Y-2 at Whidbey Island Naval Air Station, Washington.

Privateer 59640 was photographed in September 1946 with JATO (jet-assisted takeoff) bottles attached on the fuselage ahead of and behind the bomb bays. Warren Bodie via Peter M. Bowers Collection

antisubmarine missions in Privateers. D. A. Rosso, Jr., who served as a radio-radar-countermeasures aircrewman on Privateers in VPB-124, told historian Pearson: "We did not do ASW [antisubmarine warfare] per se. If a sub was on the surface, we would treat it as any other surface target." Rosso recalled that his Privateer did not have mag-

netic-anomaly-detection (MAD) gear, or sonobuoys, to aid in finding submerged submarines.

Rosso recalled using ASG radar—referred to as George gear—(and probably superceded by AN/APS-2 equipment) for searches: "I can remember getting landfalls on Okinawa at 90 to 100mi consistently when returning from missions."

A Navy airborne radar countermeasures manual covering World War II applications glibly says: "The designers of RCM [radar countermeasures] installations in naval aircraft have made an effort to provide a lay-out which will help you operate the equip-

ment with the maximum comfort and to produce the maximum inconvenience to the enemy." RCM components were designed in standard module sizes of about 10in wide by 8in high and 22in deep, or in half-size cases that were only 5in wide. This facilitated swapping out RCM components to change the suite to meet differing tactical situations.

The Navy manual describes a typical PB4Y-2 radar installation: "RCM search installations are somewhat more elaborate on the large patrol planes. Typical of these is the PB4Y-2 which carries a direction finder and a microwave search receiver, in addition to the usual AN/APR-1 receiver and AN/APA-11 pulse analyzer." Additionally, Privateers carried a selection from the following RCM equipment allowance for the PB4Y-2:

AN/APR-1 search receiver

AN/APR-2 recording search receiver

AN/APR-5A microwave search receiver

AN/ARR-5 communications search receiver

AN/ARR-7 communications search receiver

AN/APA-10 panoramic adaptor

AN/APA-11 pulse analyzer

AN/APA-17 direction finder (high frequency)

AN/APA-24 direction finder (low frequency)

AN/APA-23 recorder attachment

AN/APA-3S panoramic adaptor

AN/APT-1 jamming transmitter

AN/APQ-2 jamming transmitter

AN/APT-5 jamming transmitter

The antenna array under the nose of a Privateer typically included four pairs of antennas for search and jamming. Each pair was located to scan opposite sides of the Privateer's path; hence a similar row of antenna bumps occurred on the left and right (port and starboard) sides of the lower nose. The array included: AS-124/APR, for receiving signals between 300 and 1,000 megacycles; the AS-67/APQ-2B, for use with the AN/APQ-2 transmitter listed above; the AS-125/APR, for use with the AN/APR-5 receiver for signals in the 1,000–3,000 megacycle range; and the AT-53/AP, for receiving signals between 100 and 300 megacycles.

Since each side of the nose antenna array covered only that side of the Privateer's flight, the RCM manual instructed: "It is necessary to switch from side to side when searching an area in which signals may come from any direction." An antenna switch was provided the operator, the manual said, so that "a flip of the wrist will connect the search receiver to any desired antenna or direction finder." Coaxial cables ran from each antenna to a patchboard, where short jumper cables were used to connect the most-used antennas to the antenna selector switch for the needs of a particular mission. For receiving signals below 100 megacycles,

the PB4Y-2 was equipped with AT-54/AP stubs that could be switched with the AT-53 or AT-52 stub antennas that can often be seen behind the four paired antenna bumps.

Privateer Combat

VPB-106 took a dozen new PB4Y-2 Privateers through Hawaii and out into the Pacific for combat, leaving late in 1944. They flew a mixed group of bombers, some with the early MPC nose turret, and some with the later standard ERCO bow unit. The squadron lost one Privateer to Japanese fighters over Singapore. There was nothing the second PB4Y-2 in the two-plane formation could do as fire burned through the right wing, sending the stricken bomber inverted into the sea. Three other PB4Y-2s of VPB-106 simply failed to return from patrol.

VPB-108, champions of low-level Liberator attacks in the central Pacific, returned to the fray on April 4, 1945, in PB4Y-2 Privateers. That day, Lt. Comdr. Robert C. Lefever made a glide-bombing and strafing attack on antiaircraft positions at West Ngatpang. The Privateers of VPB-108 based out of Peleliu, and then Tinian and Iwo Jima. Early in May 1945, three of 108's Privateers joined six planes from VPB-102 in a strike on Marcus intended to thwart rumored Japanese attacks staging through there, to hit the American

PB4Y-2 Privateer V521 shared ramp space with several other Navy patrol planes. Jeff Ethell Collection

anchorage at Ulithi. Three of the VPB-102 bombers arrived first, and when the three Privateers of VPB-108 roared in, Japanese defenses were primed. Lieutenant Commander Muldrow and crew went down in a Privateer shedding pieces, and one complete engine, before crashing into the sea. Somehow, five men survived, and were rescued by the US Navy. Muldrow was not among the fortunate.

A closing act for Privateers of VPB-102, 108, 109, 116, and 121 was flying barrier patrols to keep Japanese recon planes and kamikazes from damaging the Third Fleet as it sailed nearer to Japan.

On August 11, 1945, after two atom bombs convinced the Japanese to seek peace, but scant days before a ceasefire, two Privateers of VPB-121, flown by Lt. Comdrs. J. B. Rainey and T. G. Allen, cruised near the coastline of Honshu, south of Tokyo and Yokohama. Nearing the end of their mission and about to turn for base, the two Privateers were bounced by a half-dozen Japanese fighters. Even with the Privateers' impressive firepower, Rainey's blue bomber was downed in a matter of

Characteristic Privateer cowling used cooling inlets of different sizes on top and bottom, instead of the side-to-side symmetry of the B-24/PB4Y-1. Frederick A. Johnsen

Bearing modified cockpit and B-25 engine packages as used on Super Privateer civilian fire bomber conversions, the US Naval Aviation Museum's Privateer looked like this in February 1992, on outdoor display at the museum's Pensacola, Florida, site. This is the first Privateer to enter a museum collection.

seconds. Allen's P4Y-2 took hits and limped home with a wounded tail gunner. The tragedy occurred on VPB-121's last mission of World War II.

Chapter 7

Liberators in Postwar Service

Though an American bomber first and foremost, Liberators served other countries during and after World War II. Most obvious is the use of Liberators, way back to the prewar Liberator I, by the RAF. RAF Liberators included greenhouse D-model equivalents, on through nose-turret models. (The world's current supply of Fort Worth-built B-24Js is attributable to RAF Liberators left behind in India in the late 1940s.)

Along with the RAF, the RCAF, RAAF, and South African Air Force all flew Liberators during World War II.

Turkey impounded a HALPRO B-24D, 41-11596, and ultimately received others before war's end.

Nationalist China acquired B-24s, including some M-models. In the Cold War years, the Nationalist Chinese also operated dark-blue PB4Y-2 Privateers.

The French Navy used some of its PB4Y-2s to bomb Indochina; others served in French colonial North Africa.

In Honduras, Privateers minus armament served the armed forces.

Tinted red, white, and blue water cascaded from the tanks of Hawkins and Powers Privateer air tanker number 127 during a demonstration at the Reno National Championship Air Races, September 1975. Frederick A. Johnsen

Most celebrated among the postwar users was the Indian Air Force (IAF). Hindustan Aircraft Industries rebuilt Liberators of various models after the RAF disabled them and abandoned them in country. India flew B-24Js, Ls, and Ms, as well as at least one C-87. The Indian Liberators served as maritime recon aircraft as late as 1968, fitted with turrets also rebuilt in India.

Nazi Germany captured B-24s and tested them for defensive strengths and weaknesses.

After the War

The end of World War II quickly put B-24s out of business in the AAF. For bombardment, masses of B-29s were available, with B-36s and jet B-47s on the horizon. For transport, C-54s, C-82s, and bigger purpose-built transports were in the inventory or on the way. For training, proficiency, and utility purposes, there was an almost universal rejection of the B-24 in the postwar Air Force in favor of docile B-17s, or B-25s. The few B-24s remaining in service after V-J Day typically flew tests, either for atmospheric research or as platforms for new radar defenses or jet engine trials.

The US Navy treated its Liberators and Privateers differently. While putting postwar dollars into new carriers and new aircraft for the carriers, the Navy retained Privateers to aug-

ment P2V Neptunes in patrol work. PB4Y-1s continued to serve in Navy photo mapping squadrons well into the 1950s. It may have been economics—the Navy had less access to an abundance of large airframes than did the Air Force, and could ill afford to dispose of all its Liberators and Privateers.

In 1949, VP-61 earned a flying safety award for keeping its six PB4Y-1P (*P* designated Photo) Liberators flying for 5,000hr without an accident. "It is one of the few units in the armed services still using Liberators," noted a story in the March 1949 *Naval Aviation News*. For the two years prior to the award, VP-61 extensively photo-mapped Alaska, including 68,000 square miles of the slope of Alaska, to be used in oil exploration in Naval Petroleum Reserve Number Four. Mosaics taken by the cameras in VP-61's Liberators also enhanced the accuracy of US Geological Survey maps of Alaska. These blue Liberators carried K-17 6in focal-length cameras, K-18 24in focal-length cameras, and Fairchild CA-8 cartographic cameras.

Mapping Kodiak Island in 1947, crews learned they needed to hone their level-flying skills to an incredible degree to afford the cameras the most uniform platform for consistency. Tilting of the wings could throw a photo's accuracy off. During 1948, VP-61 practiced its skills over the Imperial Valley of California before returning to tackle Alaska again. VP-61 was given credit for vital contributions to a federal program of surveying Alaska's resources.

Records kept by the Navy indicate the last squadron use of twin-tail Liberators was with VJ-62, flying P4Y-1P (the *B* was deleted from nomenclature) aircraft on May 31, 1956.

The Navy did not preserve any of its PB4Y-1s. One surplus Navy greenhouse Liberator was flown to Troutdale, Oregon, in the years following World War II. Its intended purpose—becoming a gas station ornament—was accomplished by a different entrepreneur using a new surplus B-17G, so the tri-color blue Navy Liberator was sold to California-Atlantic Airways of St. Petersburg, Florida, eventually winding up in Bolivia, according to Bob Sturges, whose Columbia Airmotive Co. was involved with negotiations on the Liberator.

Navy patrol squadrons continued to fly radar-studded Privateers in the 1950s pending replacement, typically by P2V Neptunes. Postwar Privateer squadrons in the US Navy included VP-22, VP-23, VP-24, VP-25, VJ-2 (called "hurricane hunters"), VP-772, VP-9, and VP-871 (the latter three flying Korean War combat missions).

Eye of the Storm

Squadron VP-23 gained fame as hurricane hunters before VJ-2 took the duty in Florida. In 1950, *Naval Aviation News* detailed the procedure VP-23's PB4Y-2s used to breach hurricanes: "The usual procedure is to circumnavigate about 30 miles out from the center with surface winds of 60 knots commencing in the southeastern quadrant." When the Privateer crew estimated their position to be due north of the eye of the storm, as 60 knots of wind beat against the plane, it would penetrate the storm. As the dark blue bomber progressed toward the eye of the spiraling hurricane, dramatic decreases in barometric pressure accompanied increases in wind speed. Depending on how much the Privateer was being tossed by the hurricane, actual entry into the eye of the storm was at the pilot's discretion, according to the published account. Once the eye was picked up on the radar scope, actual penetration was no longer necessary. The eye of the storm could be picked up from 15 to 20mi away, and sometimes as far as 30mi away.

Anytime the storm got too violent, the Privateer could exit by making slow, flat rudder turns to the right, while holding attitude and altitude. The turn to the right for escape was held until the wind "is just abaft the starboard beam, making course adjustments to keep it there until out of

Their combats over, Liberators in various Eighth AF group markings awaited scrapping at Albuquerque (Sandia), New Mexico, in 1946. Don Alberts Collection

Badger Beauty, *awaiting its fate in a boneyard in Albuquerque, New Mexico, in 1946, showed evidence of a Ford-*style antiglare panel in flat black—not all B-24s had olive green antiglare paint. Don Alberts Collection

This tiger-faced Eighth AF B-24 with red Emerson nose turret spent its final days in a scrapping field at Kirtland Army Airfield, Albuquerque, New Mexico, after World War II. Don Alberts Collection

Turkish markings on the rudders indicate new ownership for this B-24. Faint overpainted patches on vertical stabilizers probably hide RAF-style fin flashes used in the Mediterranean by AAF B-24s in 1942–1943. This aircraft may be Halverson Detachment B-24D 41-11596, nicknamed Brooklyn Rambler, which landed in Turkey after the early Ploesti mission of June 11, 1942. Interned by the Turks, the crew took Brooklyn Rambler back in a bold escape. The Turkish government protested, and the B-24 was given back to Turkey, without the crew, following some repairs that were made to the plane in Eritrea. Herb Tollefson Collection

British Liberator II modification resembled US LB-30/C-87 conversions, but had distinct round portholes. New-style deicer boots were added by the time of the photo (July 1946). Peter M. Bowers Collection

Commando, Winston Churchill's aircraft, was the second Liberator II built (AL504). Consolidated's Tucson, Arizona, modification center altered Commando in 1944 with a single tail, cargo doors, and fuselage extension, creating a virtual RY-3 that retained its original powerplant packages. It is said that Churchill never flew in the modified Commando. Peter M. Bowers Collection

heavy weather or turbulence," the account related.

Flare for Korean Combat

Six years after flying solo shipping sorties against the Japanese, PB4Y-2s went to Korea to help thwart communist expansion to the south. VP-772 started flare-dropping missions on June 12, 1951, according to Allan G. Blue's *The B-24 Liberator*. The flares they dropped illuminated targets for Marine night fighters. VP-9 joined the flare runs, as communist traffic increasingly moved at night. Marine fighter-bombers attacked what the Privateers illuminated. A chute was placed over the rear ventral hatch, from which flares were slipped on orders. More than 150 flares could be carried in the bomb bays of the blue Privateers. The flares were set to ignite at a predetermined altitude, sometimes specifically requested by the attack pilot to match personal preferences. The great range of the Privateer meant one flare-dropper could loiter to service several fighter-bombers in turn, as they expended their ordnance. This sometimes put the Privateers over hostile territory for as much as 4–8hr, said to be the longest duration any American combat planes spent over enemy areas in Korea.

Reserve Privateers

Naval Reserve squadron VP-981 was taking on Privateers at Naval Air Station (NAS) Seattle by December 1952. Other Reserve squadrons acquiring Privateers in this era are listed in the chart:

Naval Air Station	Tail Code Letter
Seattle, WA	T
Glenview, IL	V
Memphis, TN	M
New York, NY	R
Miami, FL	H
Olathe, KS	K

Last Loss?

A Nationalist Chinese PB4Y-2 allegedly used to resupply guerrillas was shot down by Burmese fighters in 1961, records indicate. This must rank as the last combat loss of an American-made heavy patrol bomber of the World War II era.

Red Tails in the Sunset

The last Privateers in US Navy service were the rich red QP-4B drones used at the Pacific Missile Test Center (PMTC), Point Mugu, California. On January 18, 1964, the one Privateer remaining in the Navy was downed in a missile test, according to an account in

Called Liberator C-IX, this RY-3 (JT973) was photographed in an RAF livery on November 4, 1947. The British received 26 of the 33 RY-3s built. *British RY-3 numbers were JT973, JT975-998, and JV936. Peter M. Bowers Collection*

IAF B-24s served as late as 1968, and provided a wealth of nose-turret Libera- *tors for museums and warbird collections. Indian Air Force*

B-24M 44-51228 in post-1947 star configuration. Used for ice research, 228 went on permanent display at Lackland AFB, Texas, at the end of its career in the early 1950s—the last Liberator in US Air Force service. Later Ford knife-edge canopy and modified nose contours are visible. Peter M. Bowers Collection

P4Y-1P number 65356 (the B was deleted from nomenclature when this photo was taken) served into the 1950s. Hooded turbo-superchargers are evident. Peter M. Bowers Collection

Privateers of VP-871 prepared to leave snowy Atsugi, Japan, for nocturnal combat flare missions over Korea that could sometimes last 12hr. The squadron flew almost 1,000 sorties over Korea for an eight-month period in 1951–1952. James Tiburzi Collection

the *Missile*, the newspaper for PMTC. The story said the Navy was down to two Privateers by mid-December 1963. Known by the call signs Opposite 31 (sometimes nicknamed *Lucky Pierre*) and Opposite 35 (sometimes known as

US Coast Guard P4Y-2G number 66302 flew postwar search missions with scanners' seats in modified nose, waist, and tail locations. Number 66302 later entered the civilian market as fire bomber number N2871G, operated by Hawkins and Powers Aviation as Tanker 121. Peter M. Bowers Collection

This red Privateer target drone, BuNo. 59872, spent its final days at Point Mugu, California. Jim Morrow Collection

Clyde), the red drones occasionally flew manned transport runs out to the PMTC airstrip on San Nicholas Island when the regular C-54 was down for maintenance.

On December 18, 1963, Opposite 31 went airborne on a NOLO (No Live Operator) drone mission from San Nicholas. Point Mugu's test squadron, VX-4, fired missiles at the red Privateer as its remote operator maneuvered between 500 and 1,000ft in altitude to evade the armaments hurled at the QP-4B. San Nicholas was packed with

258

spectators that day. To their vocal delight, Opposite 31 continued to fly even after receiving a direct hit from a missile that ripped into a starboard bomb bay door. According to the published account, the last fighter attack on the test program that day launched a missile that cut the right wing off the Privateer, which rolled over and splashed down in the Pacific in a shower of sea foam.

Civilianizing the Warplane

Liberators and Privateers were examined for their civil aviation potential after the war. In addition to the former Navy PB4Y-1 ferried to Oregon, and later sold into South America, several LB-30s, C-87s, and converted B-24s made it into the civilian market. LB-

30s (see chapter 2 for more details on the LB-30) flew passengers and freight for several companies in various parts of the postwar world. Stripped of armament and armor plate, and not required to hold formation at 22,000ft or more, civilianized Liberators worked well.

In the 1950s, a commercial aircraft broker in southern California advertised several LB-30s for sale. At least two B-24s are thought to have flown as cargo haulers in Bolivia up to the 1960s, and a few seldom-photographed Liberators plied the 1950s skies between American airports in an era before warbird spotters tracked all such movements.

Privateers found a home with firefighting companies. The PB4Y-2s could

carry more retardant than could B-17s. From the late 1950s to the present— 1993—Privateers have fought fires in the United States. By the 1970s, the survivors of this dangerous peacetime profession had been upgraded to "Super Privateer" status with Wright Double Cyclone engines and nacelles from B-25 Mitchell bombers replacing the Pratt & Whitney R-1830s and their characteristic long, oval cowlings. The R-2600 engine packages add performance at altitude, which can be critical to a Privateer in the mountains on a hot day, when the air thins out, with much the same effect as rarified air at high altitude.

Civilian Privateer Tail Numbers

Following is a compilation of many of the known civilian Privateers flown in the United States. Details about the aircraft are provided where known:

N6813D, BuNo. 59876: Former US Coast Guard plane. Airframe less engines, in peeling white paint, was parked at Grass Valley, California, in the late 1960s, with spray booms attached to wings; the aircraft was later flown out and operated as a fire bomber by Hawkins and Powers Aviation, Greybull, Wyoming, as tanker No. 125 on fire contracts in the western United States, including Alaska. It was

Hawkins and Powers Aviation's Tanker 124, modified over the years with Coast Guard-style nose, clear-view canopy, and B-25 engines and nacelles, was poised for firefighting duty at Boise, Idaho, in the summer of 1989. Frederick A. Johnsen

ditched off the north end of Vancouver Island in 1975 while returning from Alaskan fire duty. It was later rebuilt for static display by the Yankee Air Museum, Willow Run, Michigan.

N6816D: Operated by Wenairco of Wenatchee, Washington, as a fire bomber in the 1960s and later sold, al-

Clipped wing tips housed cameras to record performance of missiles launched at this red P4Y-2K drone at Point Mugu, 1962. Final designation of Privateer drones was QP-4B. Sommerich via Peter M. Bowers Collection

though kept in Wenatchee. Painted white with red trim, and nicknamed *Moby Dick;* later stripped to bare aluminum with orange and white trim. It was assigned tanker No. 42. The aircraft was destroyed on the Wenatchee (Pangborn Field) runway by fire in 1972.

N6884C (two PB4Y-2s): First Privateer carrying this civil registration was BuNo. 66284, which crashed in the

summer of 1959. Second Privateer to carry N6884C registration was BuNo. 59701, which was painted aluminum with yellow trim in late 1960s, with tanker No. 84 on tail; acquired by Hawkins and Powers Aviation, Greybull, Wyoming, it was upgraded to Super Privateer engine configuration and had an F-86 canopy placed vertically as its nose cap to improve lower frontal visibility for pilots. Assigned tanker No. 127, this aircraft is still in service as a fire bomber as of 1992.

N7682C: Sold surplus with turrets intact; disposition unknown.

N7962C, BuNo. 59882: Hawkins and Powers Super Privateer; tanker No. 126. Still active as fire bomber in 1993.

N2870G, BuNo. 66304: Hawkins and Powers Super Privateer. Written off in a landing mishap in Ramona, California.

N2871G, BuNo. 66302: Hawkins and Powers Super Privateer, Tanker No. 121. Still active as of 1993.

N2872G, BuNo. 66300: Hawkins and Powers Super Privateer; tanker No. 124. Still active as of 1993.

N7620C, BuNo. 66260: Hawkins and Powers Super Privateer. Still active in 1993.

N3191G: A fire bomber seen at Medford, Oregon, in late 1960s, it had early application of flat-sided increased-view canopy. Assigned tanker No. 85, it reportedly crashed in Diamond Lake, Oregon, and was scrapped.

The formative years of American fire bombers found PB4Y-2, registration number N3739G, sharing dusty Arizona ramp space with warbird classics including a TBM, a B-25, and B-17F number N17W in the late 1950s or early 1960s. As of this writing, Privateer N3739G, former BuNo. 59819, is part of the Lone Star Flight Museum in Texas, while B-17F N17W is in the collection of the Museum of Flight, Seattle, Washington. Ken Shake

Air Tanker N6813D got a new lease on life as a static display under restoration by the Yankee Air Museum at the Willow Run, Michigan, airport. Todd Hackbarth Collection

N3739G, BuNo. 59819: Converted to fire bomber in early 1960s at Prescott, Arizona, by Flight Enterprises. It was sold to SST Inc. in 1967 and has been operated since 1975 by T and G Aviation, Chandler Field, Arizona. It flew as Tanker No. 30 before being sold in early 1991 to the Lone Star Flight Museum, Galveston, Texas.

Preserving Liberator Lore

Time has seen increasing efforts to memorialize B-24 and PB4Y aircraft.

There was a time when you could count the preserved Liberators in the United States on the fingers of one hand, and still have three digits unemployed. The Air Force Museum at Wright-Patterson Air Force Base (AFB), Dayton, Ohio, had the foresight to save a combat-veteran B-24D, while Lackland AFB, near San Antonio, Texas, put on display a modified B-24M. Other hulks and pieces remained, but for many years, these two Air Force displays were the only efforts to preserve Liberators. The Pima Air Museum in Tucson, Arizona, doggedly raised money in the 1960s to ferry an IAF B-24J to Tucson as a centerpiece of the then-new museum near Davis-Monthan AFB. Meanwhile, in Texas, fliers who live the good-ol'-boy lifestyle with finesse bought a mongrelized LB-30, initially bedecked it with a Confederate flag, and flew it as part of the tongue-in-cheek Confederate Air Force (CAF), who still operate this oldest surviving Liberator variant as of this writing.

The success of the Pima museum effort at retrieving a former IAF B-24 was repeated for the Canadian National Aeronautical Collection in Ottawa, this time with an L-model. The cost of acquisition and recovery of Liberators would only increase, yet the passion to do so climbed at an even faster rate. Aircraft fancier David Tallichet ob-

Smoke rushed away from the engines as they were started on David Tallichet's B-24J-95-CF number 44-44272 at Bayview, Washington, in May 1977 during filming of a movie about Navy PB4Y-1 pilot Joe Kennedy. For many years, Tallichet's B-24J was the only flying B-24 in true bomber configuration. Frederick A. Johnsen

Bearing latter-day nose art, this B-24M underwent a remarkable restoration at Castle AFB, California, for display in the Castle Air Museum. Frederick A. Johnsen

tained in India a twin to the Pima B-24J, which he flew back to the United States. Tallichet also bought two former Canadian B-24Ds that had been dismembered in such a way that their restoration was deemed not feasible. The cockpit section of one of these went to the March Field Museum near Riverside, California, and later to a blossoming air and space museum in Virginia. The characteristic greenhouse from the other was mounted on the nose of the CAF Liberator.

Liberators were in vogue as rare collector items in the 1970s and 1980s. The RAF acquired another former IAF machine, and yet another of the re-

markably preserved Indian Liberators was shipped to England by a private buyer who later sold it to Bob Collings in Massachusetts. Under the umbrella of the Air Force Museum Program, Barksdale AFB, Louisiana, secured a slumbering hulk of a Ford-built B-24J in Oklahoma, and sling-loaded it to Louisiana beneath a Skycrane helicopter. Two J-style Liberator nose and cockpit sections were re-imported from Canada by collector and dealer Bruce Orriss. One went to Barksdale as a source of parts, and the other was refurbished in Michigan for display in the state historical society museum in Lansing, where it bears testimony to Ford's role in producing quantities of B-24s in that state during World War II.

A sleeper among the resurrected Liberators was the M-model shipped from Bolivia in 1981 for inclusion in the Castle Air Museum at Castle AFB,

Atwater, California. Civilianized many years ago and used as a freight hauler, this Liberator was converted back to bomber status by 1989. Also in the 1980s, Hawkins and Powers Aviation partially restored a languishing PB4Y-2 Privateer, and traded the result to the Navy for inclusion in the naval aviation museum at Pensacola, Florida.

A Privateer fuselage once displayed in the old Ontario Air Museum in southern California was scrapped when the museum was forced to vacate its Ontario airport site, and moved to Chino, California, according to museum director Ed Maloney. A B-24D cockpit and nose formerly employed as a movie prop, with removable fuselage panels, wound up in the storage collection of the National Air and Space Museum at Silver Hill, Maryland. The author purchased the partial cockpit of a PB4Y-2 drone for restoration as a portable museum display, and in Tennessee, the entire fuselage of a Liberator is undergoing refurbishing for static displays around the country.

And the list may not end here—museum groups already are pondering the feasibility of recovering an LB-30 crash-landed by Morrison-Knudsen Construction in Alaska in the 1950s, and a Privateer that slipped beneath the surface of Lake Washington near Seattle in that same decade. Rumors persist of at least one more Liberator to be had from a private owner outside the United States.

From a forlornly discarded and forgotten remnant of the war, the Liberator has recovered lost status to become a key element in several displays and museums in North America and abroad.

Liberators—and significant portions thereof—have been adopted by the following museums and individuals:

Surviving Liberators

Variant	Serial	Comments
Liberator I	AM927	Flown by CAF, Midlands, Texas
B-24	D-160-CO 42-72843	On display in Air Force Museum, Dayton, Ohio; nicknamed *Strawberry Bitch*
Liberator	HE807(India)	On display in RAF Museum, England
B-24	JKH191 (India)	Owned by Bob Collings, Stowe, Massachusetts
B-24	J-90-CF 44-44175	On display in Pima Air Museum, Tucson, Arizona
B-24	J-95-CF 44-44272	Owned by D. Tallichet; put in various museums
B-24	J-25-FO 44-48781	Eighth AF Museum, Barksdale AFB, Louisiana
B-24	L-20-FO 44-50154	Canadian National Museum, Ottawa, Ontario
B-24	M-5-CO 44-41916	Castle Air Museum, Atwater, California
B-24	M-20-FO 44-51228	Display, Lackland AFB, Texas
PB4Y-2 (P4Y-2G)		For static display by Yankee Air Museum, Willow Run, Michigan; former fire bomber
PB4Y-2	59819	Under restoration for flight (R-2600s) by Lone Star Flight Museum, Galveston, Texas
PB4Y-2		On display at Naval Aviation Museum, Pensacola, Florida; B-25 engine nacelles; modified canopy
PB4Y-2 cockpit 59759		Under restoration by the author
PB4Y-2 forward fuselage		Under restoration by Ron Sathre, Union City, California

Chapter 8

Eye of the Beholder

A half-century after its combats, the B-24 needs no excuses, and owes no apologies. Nor do the people associated with these aircraft. The men and women who built and flew Liberators and Privateers remember that time in their lives with a sometimes-frightening clarity and candor; a disarming truthfulness that remains after the years of story-telling embellishments and hindsights are washed away by the tears of remembrance.

What follows is the product of interviews conducted in 1992 with those who knew the Liberator and its kindred aircraft; a human history.

Ivan Stepnich, Pilot, 66th and 67th BSs, 44th BG

"I think you had to learn the secret of the B-24," Ivan Stepnich explained. And that secret, celebrated by many Liberator pilots and questioned by others, was "what they called 'being on the step.'" B-24 pilots who believed in the plane's "step" said it was necessary to climb several hundred feet above intended cruising altitude in a loaded B-24, and then drop the nose to pick up speed and establish a proper angle of attack for efficient cruising. Merely

Carl Stutz was radio operator on Playmate, *B-24J number 44-40791 in the 494th BG in the Pacific in 1945. Larry Davis Collection*

climbing to altitude and leveling off in a heavy B-24 was said to result in a nose-high mushing flight with attending bad traits ranging from reduced forward visibility to general sluggishness. Engineers and pilots may argue whether the step premise is valid, but one thing is evident: by visualizing the step concept, and flying accordingly, some B-24 pilots were able to trim and operate their Liberators more efficiently.

Ivan Stepnich was moved from B-17 training to B-24s at Gowen Field, Idaho, in the summer of 1943. Finishing up at Pocatello, Idaho, Stepnich and his crew were routed as replacements to Camp Shanks, New York, where they boarded the converted luxury liner *Queen Elizabeth* for the voyage to the United Kingdom in the fall of 1943. Pressed into service as a troop ship, the ocean liner's plumbing had some emergency wartime concessions, and hot showers were taken with salt water. Lieutenant Stepnich shared a stateroom with several other men. He commented, "As an officer it wasn't too bad for me." Days were spent in the large ship's auditorium, where many card tables saw heavy use hour after hour.

Train rides through Scotland and England carried Stepnich and crew from the *Queen Elizabeth* to a transition field at Chedington. He still did not know to which combat group he

and his crew would be assigned. The orders came for the 44th BG at Shipdam. The 44th was the oldest AAF Liberator bomb group, highly experienced, and woven into the fabric of the mighty Eighth AF.

From the start, Stepnich's plane was *P-Bar,* both as a radio call sign and an unofficial nickname, because the individual letter *P,* underlined with a bar, was this B-24's identifier within the 44th BG system of markings. *P-Bar* was either a B-24H or B-24J. Stepnich flew his bomber routinely at 19,000–21,000ft over Europe, with Eighth AF B-17s going higher. The lower Liberators sometimes bore the brunt of antiaircraft hits. "The closer you are to the flak, the more accurate it is," Stepnich explained. And the fighter opposition was "the best there was." The Luftwaffe, taking advantage of early-morning conditions which had the B-24s facing the eastern rising sun, would make head-on attacks out of the sun. "Before our gunners could even pull the triggers, they [the German fighters] were gone. Then we'd see the unlucky ones go down." As sobering as the sight of falling B-24s was, Stepnich and the rest of the 44th BG plowed ahead, gradually getting accustomed to the deadly routine. "We were regularly hit with flak and fighters," he added.

Stepnich took pride in his airmanship, and attentively flew as briefed to achieve a smooth form-up over Eng-

Liberator crews learned they could slow their tricycle-gear B-24s by unfurling parachutes from the waist windows if they anticipated brake loss. This Douglas-built B-24H flew with the Eighth AF's 466th BG. Jeff Ethell Collection

land. Following the briefed headings and altitudes through the often-overcast English skies was important. "Everybody had to fly it just right or you could have a mid-air," he said. As the winter of 1943 bore down on the crews, flying in the already-cold upper

atmosphere, Stepnich was pleased to find the electrically heated flying clothing worked as advertised.

During Stepnich's combat flying, the number of missions needed for completion of a tour was raised from 25 to 30. He logged a mission on February 25, 1944, that nearly cut his combat career short. *P-Bar* was part of a formation dispatched across France and into Germany to drop bombs on an aircraft plant at Furth, near Nurnberg. The Initial Point (IP) was made with no undue problems, and the target was bombed from only 18,000ft, with a true

airspeed of 185 knots. Navigator G. R. Henriet's flight plan logged bombs away at 1403. As *P-Bar* and the formation turned left off the target, Henriet wrote: "Good hits all over. . . Lots of fires."

Then came one burst of flak immediately abeam *P-Bar,* puncturing the Liberator from nose to tail and cranking it over sideways as Stepnich wrestled the big bomber back to level. The tail gunner was hit in the shoulder, while up front, Stepnich and his flight engineer each caught flak from the one burst. The oil-fed propeller governor on

No. 3 engine was damaged, and that engine was shut down but windmilling because the governor could no longer feather the blades. This added drag to the stricken Liberator and contributed to a staggering loss of altitude, compounded by a flak-weakened No. 2 engine that gave about half power. Punctured hydraulics, strange noises, and faltering powerplants held Stepnich's attention as he initially tried to maintain his briefed exit route back to England. *P-Bar* lost 10,000ft before stabilizing only 8,000ft over a very hostile Germany. At a point southeast of Wurzburg, Stepnich turned south, because neutral Switzerland was closer than trying to run clear across the rest of Germany and enemy-occupied France at 8,000ft, alone. Southwest of Heilbron, 37min after bombs-away, Stepnich knew he could never get the injured *P-Bar* high enough to cross the mountains into Switzerland. He took up a new heading westward, laboring across Germany and France.

During *P-Bar*'s ordeal, one German fighter pressed an attack, but broke it off. Other enemy fighters were seen in the air, but did not engage the lone aircraft. Stepnich set up westward headings based on his navigator's advice. The route was south of that flown by the rest of the group, and that may have helped spare *P-Bar* from attacks aimed at the large group of B-24s. The crew began jettisoning guns and ammunition over the English Channel to further lighten *P-Bar*; they had to keep the weapons while over enemy territory in case they were spotted. A fighter field on English soil, too short for a Liberator and with uphill terrain at the far end of the runway, was Stepnich's only alternative to ditching.

Nursing a damaged B-24 back to England on little more than two engines, with gas running low, it was natural for Ivan Stepnich to hoard altitude. On final approach to the short fighter strip, he realized the bomber was still too high, and would consume too much of the precious runway if he tried to land from this height. Stepnich initiated a go-around, over the protests of his copilot and flight engineer, both of whom feared *P-Bar* was about to run out of gas. Stepnich prevailed, preferring to take his chances on the fuel remaining rather than pile up into the

hill at the end of the runway. His gamble paid off. Unknown to the crew at the time, one of the B-24's main tires was destroyed by the flak burst, and this may have saved the plane and crew as they jammed the damaged Liberator into the cramped fighter strip. The useless wheel dragged the B-24 to a stop before running into the hill. Afterward, the flight engineer measured only about 40 gallons remaining in the limping Liberator's tanks. Old *P-Bar* was repaired, but Stepnich doubted it ever saw combat again. But Ivan Stepnich and crew went to war soon—in a replacement *P-Bar*.

Ivan Stepnich flew with finesse, and fully embraced the B-24 Liberator. Unlike some Liberator pilots, Stepnich enjoyed formation flying most of all: "That was a thing of beauty," he said. The customary stiffness of the B-24's controls may have aided his formation technique because the stiffness prevented overcontrolling. "You had to exert plenty of positive force and therefore you didn't overcorrect," explained Stepnich.

His 30 missions finished, Stepnich went to Eighth AF headquarters as an engineering officer, where he worked on a war-weary B-24H nicknamed *Hap Hazard*. This B-24 was the test bed for a revised nose with a boosted twin .50cal gun mount made by Bell in a

Same art as on Playmate, *but a different artist rendered this version of a Varga girl as* Shoo Shoo Baby, *B-24H number 42-95197 of the 446th BG, Eighth AF. Nicknames and pieces of pin-up art were repeated on B-24s and other warplanes throughout the US-AAF.* Doug Remington Collection

modified B-24D greenhouse. Stepnich, by then a captain, was on the crew that flew the test bed back to the United States for inspection by AAF and factory officials at sites like Wright Field.

Mercer R. "Ray" Markman, Pilot, 759th BS, 459th BG

"All I remember is a great big cross going by my side . . . the biggest black cross I'd ever seen!" Lt. Ray Markman saw the flash of German insignia as a Bf 109 roared past his Liberator's cockpit after making a head-on pass that left Markman's ball turret gunner dead in his turret, and the B-24's No. 2 Pratt & Whitney engine shot out. It was Markman's first mission as a new pilot in the Fifteenth AF, April 23, 1944. "That's when you realize they're playing for keeps," he commented. The target was a Messerschmitt plant at Bad Voslau, Austria.

With one engine out and a full load of bombs, Markman's B-24 lost alti-

Ray Markman, left, inspected a German 20mm slug that lodged in his B-24. Ray Markman Collection

tude, its bomb bay doors already open in anticipation of impending bomb release. All eyes were on the lead bombardier; when he dropped, the rest of the formation would drop. Markman faced a new peril as he struggled to keep up with the formation: If he slipped back as he lost altitude, the bombs of a Liberator still at formation altitude could smash into his crippled B-24. Gamely, Markman tried to keep his B-24 directly under the hole in the sky where he had been before the fighter attack. He flew between 100 and 200ft beneath the rest of the formation. Bombs fell all around his Liberator, and his bombardier toggled his bombs in time.

With an incapacitated ball turret jammed in the extended position and one engine shut down, Markman could not hope to stay with the lightened formation as they turned away from the target area. He and his crew were alone, over enemy-annexed Austria, heading for the Adriatic Sea as quickly as their slowed bomber would allow. Occasionally, lone P-38 Lightning fighters, dispatched on other sorties,

would form up with Markman and offer a few minutes' protection before accelerating on to their assigned duties.

Markman landed the crippled B-24 back at his airstrip in Italy with the damaged ball turret extended, its gunner still entombed inside. He instructed other available crew members to be as far forward in the plane as possible once a safe touchdown was achieved, to keep the low-slung B-24 from rocking back and dragging the ball turret on the runway. Markman, his bombardier, and navigator were aboard this Liberator with other experienced men from different crews. For him and his crew members, it was a stark baptism of fire.

When Ray Markman was assigned to the Fifteenth AF, he needed to accomplish 50 mission credits to complete a tour of duty. Most missions earned one credit; lengthy, difficult, and dangerous missions could earn two credits. It took him 37 passes over targets to amass 50 mission credits and complete his tour.

Markman's first mission was a taste of things to come. Later, on June 9, 1944, as part of a formation bombing an airfield at Munich, Germany, his camouflaged B-24 was singled out by a lone Bf 109 for a persistent stern attack. With hundreds of Liberators to

choose from, it seemed to Markman the German fighter pilot could only see his B-24 that day. The Messerschmitt's 20mm shells frequently flew over and past the B-24, seemingly whizzing through the Liberator's propeller arcs sometimes. One slug lodged in the nose but did not explode; others punched holes in the bomb bay area until the fighter drew close enough for the tail gunner to swap bullets with the German, sending the fighter peeling away streaming light smoke—not enough to confirm a kill.

On the return from Munich, Markman's crew tied parachutes to the waist-gun mounts to slow the damaged B-24 on landing, since its hydraulics—and brakes—were damaged in combat.

The persistent Fifteenth AF attacks on Ploesti's oil refineries included a high-altitude effort on July 15, 1944, that put Markman's Liberator as tail-end Charlie behind the rest of the 459th BG. Pilots dreaded this slot for two reasons: The last bombers were open to stern attacks, and it required far more maneuvering and gasoline to stay in place in the group. The last plane in formation was like the tip of a cracking whip, needing exaggerated movement and acceleration to hold its position, as the planes ahead amplified any perturbations felt by the lead bombers.

Leaving the target area, Markman's formation was momentarily dispersed by a surprise flak barrage. The formation leader had been setting a cruise speed about 5mph faster than normal already, and when Markman advanced his throttles further to regain his place in the formation, all four R-1830 engines began to vibrate and complain. Once again, Ray Markman had no choice but to watch the rest of the formation accelerate and run off ahead as his weakened Liberator lagged back.

Once clear of Yugoslavia, the crew began jettisoning guns and ammunition over the Adriatic. Fuel consumption was a concern as the B-24 descended. Ten miles out from his home field, he received radio landing instructions. Still the Adriatic Sea loomed large ahead and beneath the Liberator. Down to about 2,000ft, the bombardier went aft to jettison the waist windows in preparation for ditching. The left waist hatch got away from him in the slipstream and embedded itself in the horizontal stabilizer, acting as a speed brake for the lame bomber.

All four engines were cutting in and out, delivering fitful power. Markman figured he was only two or three miles from shore, and maybe six miles from the runway, when he knew he had no choice but to ditch. Fishing boats loomed in the windscreen as he maneuvered to avoid them. He cut all four throttles to avoid a surprise burst of power at the last minute from the erratic engines that could yaw the plane dangerously. He leveled out and then dragged in tail-low. Water probably hammered up through the opening where the retracted ball turret nested, ripping the turret free of its mounts and punching it through the right side of the fuselage. The top gunner, seated for ditching in the aft fuselage, may have been carried out with the careening ball turret; he was never found. There was no skipping or planing atop the water; the Liberator slammed to a halt, nose low, but floating. The tail section was broken and hanging down at an angle from the waist.

Stunned, Markman started to make his way from the cockpit. Somehow, he figured he scrambled through the windscreen, but the sequence of events was blurred. He found himself underwater, and pondering drowning, until he opened his eyes in the salt water and saw he was near the Number Two engine. Markman hoisted himself up on the prop dome of that engine and surveyed the wreck topside. An Italian fishing boat neared the floating Liberator, and he slipped back in the water to make sure all the crew was out of the B-24. He found his bombardier, dazed by the crash, still seated in the tail section where he had assumed his ditching position. Markman repeatedly called to the bombardier to leave the fuselage via the gaping hole torn by the ball turret in the right side of the fuselage. The drama of the precariously floating Liberator heightened the tension as the still-groggy bombardier finally heeded his call and abandoned the plane for the Italian boat. Everybody but the unfortunate top-turret gunner had survived.

Aboard the boat, the crew members removed soaked flight jackets and boots, which Markman noticed the boat

crew quietly putting away, never to be seen again by the bedraggled fliers. The men transferred to a British torpedo boat, which took them to shore.

Not until a 1992 reunion with his flight engineer did Ray Markman learn why some events of the ditching were unclear in his memory: The engineer, seeing his preoccupied pilot emerge from the sea with a bleeding gash on his forehead, administered a morphine shot that Markman was unaware he had received until 48 years later!

Over a month later, after a stay in the hospital, and time off for rest and recuperation, plus a trip north to the fighting front as a sightseer aboard a B-25, Ray Markman again hoisted a B-24 into the air on a mission August 20. He hadn't lost any of his finesse with a B-24 in the time he was away, but he remembered, "I was a little nervous about flying over water. It took a few missions for me to get over that."

The airfield where Ray Markman lived and flew was in an Italian wheat field. The British provided antiaircraft guns for protection, although an inbound Do 217 bomber manned by Yugoslavian defectors was never shot at; it crash-landed nearby after circling until it ran out of gas. The nearest town was Cerignola, in the Foggia area. The officers of his crew shared a tent, and his enlisted aircrew shared

Ray Markman's first combat mission, in Leila Nell, *resulted in this muscle-powered engine change.* Ray Markman Collection

another, remodeled with wooden walls made from crates. Every morning at about 3:30 a jeep driver, honking the vehicle's horn, ambled through the living area waking those crew members who had a mission—and distracting everyone else.

Ray Markman was unusual among B-24 pilots—before joining the AAF in 1942, he worked for Consolidated Aircraft in San Diego, building Liberators.

Markman said the thing he liked least about the B-24 was "the flight deck was awfully crowded."

What Ray Markman liked most was the dependable Pratt & Whitney engines, and the unusually comfortable design of the rudder pedals, with cradles for the heels of the feet. He also liked the tricycle gear, which he said made the B-24 easier to land than tail-wheel aircraft.

Louis Mladenovic, Chetnik, Yugoslavia

"We couldn't talk; I imagine they were pretty well shook up," Louis Mladenovic recalled. Mladenovic had just helped rescue and hide members of a B-24 crew from the German patrol that was looking for them. Gradually communications improved, and the fierce Chetniks proved to be loyal friends, willing to take great risks to guide the Liberator aircrew back to safety.

The Chetniks were legendary in Yugoslavia as mountain people who defied the Turks centuries before Nazi Germany invaded Yugoslavia. In 1941, Louis Mladenovic shed his Yugoslavian Army uniform and blended back into the fabric of his hometown of Kragujevac after the German takeover. That July, the Nazi regime executed 3,000–4,000 Yugoslavians in the nearby town of Krajlevo, including Mladenovic's sister and the third-grade class she taught. The first week of October, the Germans rounded up thousands of people in his home town and began randomly counting off their hostages in groups of 100 people. One group was set free; the next executed; and on through the captives in a fiendish math exercise intended to terrorize the citizenry. Mladenovic had missed the round-up; now his father urged him to leave Kragujevac, to escape the fate of his sister, or of his younger brother, a watchmaker's apprentice, who was shipped to Germany as forced labor in an aircraft instrument factory.

Louis Mladenovic went to live with an uncle for about six or eight months, where he learned about the Chetniks' armed resistance to the German occupation. After local Chetnik leaders were convinced he would not betray their cause, Mladenovic joined forces with them near Boljevac in the late summer of 1942. When asked why he chose to fight the Germans, his answer was succinct: "Why did they kill my young sister for no reason?" Instructed in the ways of train bombing by British commandos who parachuted in to teach the hardy Chetniks, Mladenovic was part of a unit of 80 resistance fighters in his region. About 200 local citizens additionally took up arms at night to bolster the Chetnik forces.

Sometimes Mladenovic hiked past the locust trees, and higher beyond the oaks and maples, into open sheep meadows and up to the rocky top of a 10,000ft mountain where he could watch the incredible Fifteenth AF armada winging toward Ploesti repeatedly in the spring of 1944. One such sunny mountain day, he sat back and tallied 350 American heavy bombers before he stopped counting them all. At this height, the constant roar of the bombers shook the earth, and caused rocks to loosen and roll downhill.

When not awe-struck by the armada, Mladenovic and his colleagues fought an ongoing war of attack and sabotage against the occupying Germans throughout this period.

Into this melting pot of Yugoslavian patriots parachuted B-24 pilot Thomas K. Oliver and eight members of his crew on May 6, 1944. Oliver, who paid homage to his own superstition by always carrying a slip of paper with his estimated time of arrival back at base, was surprised when that talisman whipped out through the cockpit window as he taxied out for takeoff that day. Later, Oliver recalled, "I remember the flight engineer saying, 'We didn't need that, did we?' I bravely said 'No' and on we went." The B-24 that day was not Oliver's usual mount, which had been nicknamed *The Fighting Mudcat*. The replacement ship would not outlast the day. After successfully bombing the Campina marshaling yards near the Ploesti oil fields, Oliver and his 459th BG compatriots took flak and fighter damage as the lead group for the Fifteenth AF that day. "Shortly after 'bombs away' No. 3 engine was losing oil pressure," Oliver recounted. "I tried to feather it, without success.... The prop governor had been hit and was hanging by one bolt. The drag and vibration forced us to slow down and lag behind the formation."

Now No. 3 engine seized after losing all oil. "The vibration was horrendous," Oliver explained. "The right wing shook in a sine wave pattern as though one took one end of a rope and tied it to a tree, and then gave a good shake to the other end." Suddenly the propeller began free-wheeling, probably with the failure of the overwrought reduction gear. "Things went more smoothly for a while," Oliver said. But then No. 4 engine began registering a drop in oil pressure. With no desire to repeat the problems of the runaway engine, Oliver feathered No. 4 while he still had engine oil pressure available to drive the feathering mechanism.

"With two engines dead on the same side we threw out guns, flak suits . . . anything to reduce weight," he remembered. Holding 8,000ft of altitude, Oliver figured he could limp home, as his navigator charted a course away from known flak batteries.

The crippled Liberator, much lower than normal and chugging over unfamiliar parts of Yugoslavia, chanced upon the town of Bor where a copper and gold mine had its output guarded by a German antiaircraft battery not charted on the navigator's maps. One shell set fire to the B-24's No. 2 engine, and perforated the bomb bay doors like the holes in a salt shaker. The only choice was parachuting from the plane. "As I tumbled through the air I remember saying to myself that even if the parachute didn't open, I was no worse off than when I was in the plane."

Oliver landed in the midst of a Serbian picnic celebrating the annual summertime return of the Chetniks to the mountains—a legendary event dating back to the time of the Turks. The B-24 crashed with a brilliant explosion on a hill near Bogovina, about 20 or 25mi distant from the mine at Bor.

As German armored vehicles raced toward the scene of the crash, Louis Mladenovic and his fellow Chetniks, aided by local farmers, safely hid nine of Oliver's crew. Crashing shortly after noon, the Liberator aircrew were dangerously close to being apprehended by the Germans by about 4pm. "I picked up two" of the crew members, he recalled. "We had them all together after two or three days."

The next day, May 7, 1944, another stricken B-24 swooped over the leafy trees and open fields of northeastern Yugoslavia, looking for a place to forceland. "The second plane, we saw him coming down. . . . As the crow flies it wasn't three kilometers from the other one," Mladenovic said. The pilot managed to put the Liberator down safely enough to spare his entire crew of 10. The left wing was destroyed in the crash-landing. (Records indicate the 454th BG lost two B-24s on that date; this may be the origin of the second B-24 downed in Mladenovic's area.)

After both crews were sheltered by the Chetniks, a knowledgeable member of the second crew—almost certainly a gunner—volunteered to take the Chetniks back to the wreck to strip out the waist guns and ammunition for continued use against the Germans on the ground. Wrecks were dangerous for Yugoslavians to visit because of German prohibitions. At night, aided by flashlights, the American and about 10 Chetniks returned to the crash and carted off the two .50cal waist guns, in their E-12 recoil adaptors and yokes. Six full ammunition boxes were packed away from the wreck as well. Back in the relative safety of the Chetnik hideout, the American taught his protectors how to clean and service the big Browning machine guns. A local blacksmith welded tube tripods to mount the guns, which were then packed into battle on the X-frame saddles of horses. The guns rode on the horses' backs in the crook of the X-frame, with ammunition boxes tied to the sides of the saddle frame. Ring-and-bead gunsights intended for framing Messerschmitts in flight were now used against German mortar and machine gun positions.

Eventually, the B-24 aircrews were smuggled out of Yugoslavia. Some crossed the Adriatic in fishing boats bound for Italy; others scrambled aboard C-47s that landed on an improvised sod airstrip tamped out by the Chetniks on a hilltop. Oliver returned to his base in Italy 96 days after parachuting from his B-24. As he entered the C-47, Oliver and many other crew members being evacuated tossed their shoes back, as a token of appreciation, for use by the strapped Chetniks in their continuing guerrilla war against the Germans.

Louis Mladenovic was commander of a machine-gun group that used one of the B-24 weapons for three or four pitched fights with the Germans before expending all the ammunition. He said the authoritative report of the big .50cal got the Germans' attention. "We used [the B-24 guns] mostly against the other machine guns and mortars. . . We cut the trees with them," Mladenovic said.

Even though the aircrews had long been passed from friend to friend in Yugoslavia, the Germans evidently had bad information that Mladenovic's Chetnik outfit still harbored the Americans in August 1944. On August 16 the Germans engaged the Chetniks, possibly in search of the Americans,

and possibly because (as he remembered it) some Chetniks had shot a Luftwaffe fighter pilot as he wafted to earth in his parachute. Armored German vehicles supported the attack on the Chetniks, which began about 7pm and lingered until about 4am the next morning. As gun crew captain, Mladenovic warned his gunner manning the .50cal to keep his head down. When next he looked over at the gunner, he saw the top of his head blown away by a German bullet. Mladenovic took up firing with the B-24 gun until the last round was shot.

Out of ammunition, Mladenovic ran from the now-useless weapon. He thought he felt a tug at his British-style uniform jacket, but there was no pain to tell him a German bullet had hit him in the back, passing between his ribs and exiting his chest. He continued running about 200ft before he noticed blood and foam spouting from his chest. At that point, he collapsed—far enough from the battle to be left for dead by the Germans. A Chetnik subsequently propped Mladenovic on a horse and assumed he was dead, taking him to a farmhouse for burial. In the cellar of the rural home, Mladenovic stirred, to the surprise of the occupants. Local women soaked cloths in homemade brandy and bound his chest. It was the only medication he received for his wound. Seven days after being shot, Louis Mladenovic, walking with a stick for a crutch, carried a British grease-gun automatic weapon as he was once again on the run with the Chetniks.

Nearly 50 years after he helped save American Liberator crews from capture, Louis Mladenovic, living in the United States, succeeded in contacting Thomas Oliver, the pilot of the first B-24 involved. In a very tangible way, the B-24 touched the life of Louis Mladenovic in Yugoslavia.

Ted Small, Pilot, 397th BS, 6th BG

"My opinion of what made the B-24 reliable was the Pratt & Whitney engines," commented Ted Small. Small's tour in Liberators began right out of multi-engine school, and before he had time for any formal B-24 phase training. He was already in Tucson to begin Liberator pilot training when he was

picked to be a copilot in the Canal Zone's 6th BG. In May of 1943, Small joined up with the 397th BS, learning the ropes from the right seat of the unit's weary old LB-30s.

Small found the LB-30 to be a mixed blessing. Lighter than subsequent B-24s, the LB-30 enjoyed a performance edge in some phases of flight. But wear-and-tear had taken their toll on the LBs. Unlike later B-24s, the LB-30s were not fitted with a gasoline "putt-putt" power unit. Instead, the LB-30s relied on the strength of two batteries for start-up electrical power. The added power drain imposed by the use of Curtiss Electric propellers was a source of problems. "We had a terrible time with the Curtiss Electric propellers on the LB-30s," Small recalled. When the batteries gave out at the end of the runway, the loss of electrical power allowed the brakes on the electric propeller assemblies to relax, causing the prop blades to go out of pitch.

Small was philosophical about flying well-worn LB-30s: "We felt bad to have such poor airplanes, but we felt the guys in actual combat needed the good ones more than we did." Parts were scarce, and a local depot in the Canal Zone was not high on Small's list for turning out reliable overhauled parts—including the vaunted Pratt & Whitneys, which sometimes had to be replaced multiple times before a good overhauled powerplant could be found. Gasoline leaks in the wing tanks eventually grounded all the squadron's LB-30s until the depot could fix them.

Ted Small spoke with genuine emotion as he recalled bailing out of a burning LB-30 on July 15, 1943, over Panama. It was a flier's nightmare; after aborting a radar search mission because No. 1 engine was not producing power, and being chewed out for returning to base when the problem could not be duplicated on a ground check of the LB-30, copilot Small and five other members of the crew reboarded the old bomber for a test hop, in anticipation of returning to base for the rest of the crew if the hop proved the plane was okay. The test showed the balky engine still was not developing proper power, and as the pilot headed the LB-30 on downwind leg of the landing pattern, the engine began to burn.

Ted Small smiled for the camera as he posed with a 6th BG LB-30, The Groundhog. *Note the sea-search mottling on sides and undersurfaces that may consist of white sprayed irregularly over neutral gray, although the background color under the white has not been positively identified. Upper surfaces on LB-30s in Panama typically were mixed patterns, probably consisting of olive drab or medium green and dark earth.* Ted Small Collection

Fire extinguishers only caused the blaze to falter momentarily before blistering back to life. The electric prop would not feather. The pilot climbed as the problem unfolded, affording the aircrew an altitude of about 900ft from which to bail out.

Seemingly unrelated chance events strung together to save Ted Small's life that hot July day over Rio Hato's airfield. Earlier, his parachute got soaked with water, rendering it unusable. Ex-

tra parachutes were in the waist of the Liberator, left by the other crew members still waiting on the ground. Small recalled how his pilot told him to go back and jump with one of the spare chutes, which is exactly what the young lieutenant, along with three other crew members, were able to do. One of the men who jumped died because his parachute burned. The survivors all left from the waist of the LB-30. Up front, for reasons Ted Small can never know, his pilot did not leave the cockpit even after telling him to do so. When the burning Liberator crashed, the pilot and radio operator were still in their seats. Small still wondered as of this writing if the pilot thought he could save the burning bomber and land it. But the circumstances were aerodynamically unhealthy—the dead engine was on the left wing, and the traffic pattern was a left turn onto final approach, which could have proven disastrous to a Liberator with shy power on the wing inside the turn.

Small and the other survivors were grounded a couple days while an officer conducted a brusque investigation of the mishap, and the men held funerals for their fellow crew members.

Soon Ted Small was flying again, first as a copilot whenever the brass needed him to fill that seat on VIP flights, and then as the first pilot for his old crew mates.

The 6th BG (and VI Bomber Command after November 1, 1943) had the charter of providing long-range bombing power in the event an enemy fleet dared approach the Panama Canal. Almost as a secondary role, the Liberators of the 6th assisted the US Navy in patroling both the Pacific Ocean and the Caribbean—the former for signs of a Japanese fleet and the latter for the very real threat of German submarines.

The old LB-30s had a Bendix radar that Small disdained for being hard on the eyes of the operator. Later B-24s in Panama had newer radars. During spikes in U-boat activity in the Caribbean, these AAF Liberators helped the Navy patrol the area. It was on one such mission that Ted Small had his only probable enemy contact. "I had one disappearing radar contact," he recalled, saying the radar echo—or the submarine it probably represented—was not visible by the time the Liberator made its run over the water at 500ft. The next day, a Colombian destroyer sank a submarine in that area, Small was told.

When patrolling Pacific approaches to the Panama Canal, Small and the rest of the 6th crews on those missions would fly from Baltra in the Galapagos Islands, and then to San Jose, Guatemala, where they remained overnight. The next day, they would fly the leg back to the Galapagos. Sometimes, two Liberators launched, doubling the swath of observation. Another track took the 6th BG from Galapagos to overfly a part of Peru about 400mi distant, then swinging back north and recovering at Baltra.

In 1944, B-24Ds began supplanting the tired LB-30s. These were followed by J-models and some Ford-built B-24Ms that the crews called "Tin Lizzies" in reference to their auto-maker ancestry.

Ted Small, originally an enlisted AAF radio operator after joining up on December 17, 1941, passed exams to enable him to become a flying cadet, and thence a commissioned officer and pilot. Not long after the war, while on a 30-day leave back in the States, Small was offered separation from the service rather than his projected return to Panama. He settled back into the peaceful, if vigorous, agrarian lifestyle near Walla Walla, Washington.

But Ted Small never shed his interest in the Liberators that he knew so intimately for more than two years in the cockpit, down in Central America's largely overlooked war zone.

Carl A. Stutz, Radio Operator, 867th BS, 494th BG, Seventh AF

"I didn't know how to boogie-woogie or anything, but I knew radio," recalled Carl Stutz. Sergeant Stutz built a crystal radio when he was 12 years old, and excelled in math and science in high school. That, he believed, helped propel him into the AAF instead of the regular Army when he was drafted out of high school in 1943.

As an enlisted radio operator, Stutz saw double duty, as right waist gunner on the B-24J nicknamed *Playmate.* The 494th BG was the last Liberator bomb group formed, rumbling into combat in November 1944. By early 1945, after

receiving B-24 crew training at Muroc, California, and crewing a brand-new B-24M from Hamilton Field, near San Francisco, to Hawaii, Stutz and his crew found themselves flying combat in an older, yet reliable, B-24J when their brand-new bomber was taken in Hawaii. Stutz said his crew was flown to Palau in ATC C-54s and C-46s in stages, to begin racking up a string of 26 combat missions before the Japanese surrender in mid-August 1945 cut short this crew's career as Liberator warriors.

Stutz' crew was given B-24J number 44-40791, with a fetching Varga girl lounging on the left side of the nose. His crew added the name *Playmate.* Unlike some crews, Stutz flew all his combat in that one B-24, piloted by Lt. James Fair.

The 494th bombed targets in the Philippines from the Palau Islands before taking up residence at Yontan, on newly occupied Okinawa.

On a typical mission, would pretune the B-24's tube-radio receivers and transmitters for optimum signal. He knew this to be an art. "If you pulled too much [power on the liaison radio transmitter] the plate on the tube would get red. . . . If you mis-tune a transmitter, it just melts down inside," he explained. Once tuned, the command radio receivers could be operated by the pilot, who had "coffee-grinder" control cranks for tuning frequencies as needed. Stutz' office was in the forward fuselage, just behind the copilot's seat. The command radio and radio compass gear were located aft of the wing.

For the first part of a mission, Stutz stayed at his radio post. On flights in a noncombat area, like the ferry flight to Hawaii, he made position calls hourly, based on coordinates furnished by the navigator. This helped plot the location of the B-24 in the event of its disappearance. In combat, he maintained radio silence except for those missions in which his was the lead crew. Then it was his responsibility to send off a coded strike assessment, using the Morse key, as soon as the target was hit. The bombardier would provide the assessment data, including an estimate of the percentage of bombs on target.

Typically, each mission had a zone in which fighter opposition could occur. As *Playmate* entered this zone, it was Stutz' responsibility to leave his radio post and occupy the drafty right waist-gun position. But his combats in 1945 did not yield any duels with enemy fighters. Sometimes, the lack of expected enemy aerial opposition prompted the Liberators to fly unescorted. Mustang fighters were available if hostile air action was anticipated. "We had about 30 P-51s with us on some missions," Stutz recalled. "They would not let a B-24 shoot down a fighter if they were around. They wanted to get credit for it, and we sure appreciated it. . . . A fighter never did get in to us."

Sergeant Stutz did face flak, especially over parts of the Philippines like Zamboanga. "When you can hear them, they're close," he added.

Records from Stutz' missions show that *Playmate* typically bombed from altitudes ranging between 9,000 to 12,000ft—suicidal over Europe, but feasible against some Japanese-held targets. These low altitudes precluded the need for anyone to be on oxygen.

Overall, Stutz said his combat tour "was the smoothest 26 missions."

David Gale Behunin, Tail Gunner, VPB-106

"The first time I opened up, I couldn't believe the damage I was doing to that ship," recalled Dave Behunin. Behunin was comfortable and competent in the Consolidated (MPC) tail turret of his lanky PB4Y-2 Privateer. As part of Navy squadron VPB-106, he saw the war backward, as it reeled beneath his '4Y-2 and disappeared, sometimes in a hail of tracer fire.

"Our primary goal was weather reporting and keeping track of major [Japanese] ship movements," Behunin explained. They were barred from attacking major warships because of the vessels' competent defenders and massive firepower, but, said Behunin, "If we wanted to we could take out the picket boats." The pickets radioed American movements back to Japan, and sinking them deprived the Japanese of some of their early-warning capability.

Behunin's crew, usually flying their beloved *Tortilla Flat,* as their Pri-

275

David Gale Behunin saw the war from the tail turret of the Privateer called Tortilla Flat. *David Behunin Collection*

vateer was nicknamed, readily engaged picket boats in mast-top attacks. Through 46 combat missions, mostly in this shark-mouthed aircraft, Behunin said he found the picket boats well-armed and well-manned, but poorly trained. The fiercely grinning Privateer only took one hit from a picket boat, when a cannon shell—possibly 20mm—punched through one of the solid-aluminum Hamilton Standard propeller blades.

Behunin recalled anxious moments on his first picket-boat attack. Scanning the sky behind the Privateer from a leisurely 3,000ft over the blue waves, Behunin became aware of the impending fight as the bomber's nose dipped and power was applied for more speed. The dive could be unnerving to a green gunner, not able to see what the pilots could up front. He looked up through the clear canopy of his power turret—up past the tall tail of his Privateer—and was astonished to see all calibers of bullets, running out of energy high in their trajectories, spinning lazily

and tumbling as they flew over the plane. Intercom silence did not reassure Behunin at this point. How could all these rounds miss the big bomber? Were the pilot and copilot already dead, and was he riding a doomed Privateer? "I thought the damn plane was going to fly into the water," he recalled. Just then, Behunin caught sight of .50cal ammunition links whipping beneath the Privateer, as he felt the chattering shudder from the plane's forward guns, and he knew someone was still fighting up front at least.

A new and deadly sound reached Behunin's ears: He could discern the reports from guns on the picket ship as they fired desperately at the Privateer. He figured a ship's bridge was its command center; knock out the bridge, and the ship could only function haphazardly at best. As soon as the Japanese picket boat slipped into the view from his gently curved armor glass, he laced tracers into the bridge. He remembered his surprise at watching the bridge disintegrate in an eroding barrage of .50cal rounds, wood and glass splintering and flying through the air. He kept firing until his tracers dropped short into the sea, signaling the end of his guns' range.

Pontianak, Borneo, was home to a Japanese shipyard for picket boats. Made largely of wood, the ship facility was ripe for incendiaries when Behunin rode in to attack the place in May 1945. Flying upriver to reach Pontianak, the pilot kept the Privateer down near the water. "We flew low enough up the Pontianak River that we could look under the jungle canopy," Behunin explained. There, hidden from view, were Japanese ships which the Privateer gunners strafed even as they roared upriver to their primary target. The treetop Privateer war over Borneo was not without peril. In some locations, the Japanese anticipated Privateer run-ins by placing high-explosive charges in the treetops, to be detonated in the path of an onrushing bomber.

Aviators often acknowledged superstition, especially as a combat tour drew to a close. Eager to survive and rotate home, the crew would cling to favorite sunglasses, or other talismans, as good-luck charms, vital to their continued success in avoiding death in combat. Behunin's replacement crew was already on base at Palawan in the Philippines, and he and the others were anxiously awaiting their release to go home. "By this time, we were all getting pretty superstitious," he explained. A combat mission to Borneo came up. The replacement crew, instead of taking the combat run, opted for a familiarization flight of the area, leaving one more flight over hell to Behunin's crew. It was too ominous; thoughts of dying in Borneo rolled over the crew like storm-driven squalls.

The reality was upbeat as Behunin and crew survived what turned out to be their last combat mission, landing at Palawan and wandering in to hear a radio report of the Japanese surrender. It was August 15. The war was over. Everyone had .38cal revolvers; some had Thompson submachine guns. Down to the beach went celebratory aviators of VPB-106, firing any weapon at hand. "We'd shoot, and shoot, and shoot on the beach," he remembered, marveling that nobody was killed by a stray bullet of celebration.

Behunin liked the Privateer the first time he saw one at Camp Kearney, near San Diego. After one stateside ditching in a storm, and 46 combat missions in the reliable "two-by-four," he felt his initial faith in the plane was well warranted.

Bill Willard, Bombardier, VPB-102

"I remember when we'd fly out of Iwo we'd pass a squadron of Bettys heading toward Iwo and we'd waggle our wings at each other and keep on going," Bill Willard recalled. Willard joined up with VPB-102 in early 1945. Trained on PB4Y-2 Privateers, which he helped ferry to Tinian, he was disappointed when his crew was given a used Liberator in VPB-102 instead. "We were upset," he recalled, saying the Liberators were beat-up, compared to the tight new Privateers they had just ferried to the combat theater.

Although he was classically trained on the Norden bombsight, the Nordens were taken away about the time he got into combat because the work was low altitude. His new sighting apparatus was an effective but inglorious set of crosshairs on the bombsight window, christened the Rat Trap. Willard perfected his Rat Trap bombing by dropping leftover ordnance for practice during the return legs of patrol sorties. His use of a whale for a target met with swift official disapproval, so other objects were sighted through his aiming window.

Willard's PB4Y-1 typically staged out of Iwo Jima for about two weeks at a time, flying prearranged sector patrols lasting 12–16hr each. Some of the sectors were hot with enemy action; others were safely, boringly, thankfully cold. It was while launching out of Iwo to begin sectors that Willard and crew would sometimes see inbound Japanese bombers. The Liberator crew wanted to light in after the Japanese bombers, but was denied permission to do so. "We'd call back [to base to radio the presence of the Japanese formation], and they'd be waiting for them with P-51s."

The taking of Iwo Jima bypassed fortified Chichi Jima and Haha Jima. One of the tasks of Willard and his PB4Y-1 crew was to patrol the skies aproaching these two Japanese garrisons, to make sure no supply ships got in. "We were always looking for ships." And, in a war without benefit of satellite coverage, the Navy Liberators and Privateers provided updated weather information about conditions encountered on patrol.

Initially, Willard's Liberator carried a lower ball turret. This was swapped for a radome later. After the sensitive Norden bombsight was taken away, the crew installed a fixed 20mm cannon in the nose. Willard avoided being down there when it was in use. His tours into the hot sectors raised fighters, which only sometimes proved willing to engage the blue bomber. Three Japanese planes—Willard thinks they were a Jake and two Zeros—fell before the gunners on his Liberator.

Sometimes tasked to fly air-sea rescue missions, Willard and crew would orbit over ditched crew members—sometimes from B-29s returning from bombing Japan—until friendly submarines could effect the snatch. The effects of seapower impressed him on one air-sea sortie that took his Liberator close to Japan in the waning days of the war. "We were in Tokyo Bay and saw a P-51 go down. They [the Japanese] sent a PT boat after the pilot," Willard related. As the big Liberator readied to attack the boat and intervene on behalf of the downed fighter pilot, a US Navy submarine broke radio silence, and told the bomber to stay out of the fracas. As Willard watched in fascination, the submarine split the sea and surfaced, as deck gunners scrambled to get the range of the enemy boat. A few rounds from the sub's cannon was all it took to target the patrol boat and send it under. The pilot was plucked safely from the sea by the submarine.

Culminating Bill Willard's combat career was a mission over the decks of the USS *Missouri* on September 2, 1945, as the treaty ending World War II was being signed. "We took pictures of MacArthur and all of them right on the deck," Bill recalled with a gleam that cut through nearly five decades. Liberators saw the war begin, and they participated in a massive umbrella of airpower over the war's end in Tokyo Bay.

Chapter 9

No Higher Tribute:
Liberator Crew Medals of Honor

If there's a hierarchy in aviation, pilots enjoy accolades beyond those bestowed on other aircrew members. In a 10-person B-24 roaring over a flak- and fighter-infested target, all are heroes, sometimes placed in harm's way by the decisive actions of a pilot who later is honored for his leadership of the crew under fire. The following is a complete list of AAF and Navy Liberator and Privateer fliers who received the Medal of Honor, America's highest tribute, for bravery. These recipients' individual acts of heroism should not be minimized, nor should the gallantry of the other nine crew members aboard their fated Liberators.

Addison E. Baker

The cauldron of Ploesti yielded a group of Medals of Honor, conferred on fliers who steeled themselves to grim odds of survival, and pressed on stoically. Lt. Col. Addison E. Baker led the 93rd BG into the target area on the low-level mission of August 1, 1943. Oil refineries were at stake. Oil to fuel the Third Reich—and over which Germany would be forced to expend finite re-

The restored B-24J All American, *commemorating Liberator aviators, toured Tacoma, Washington, in June 1992.* Frederick A. Johnsen

sources defending against American attacks.

Addison Baker's dark olive-drab B-24D, blotched with medium green edging the wings and tail to hide the strikingly straight lines of the Liberator, sported the nickname *Hell's Wench.* It now carried an additional marking; the vertical fins sported British-style red-white-and-blue fin flashes, since the Americans were flying in skies defended by British gunners as they departed and returned to their North African airstrips. But mistaken identity and overzealous British gunners were far from Baker's thoughts as his B-24 roared to Ploesti at minimum altitude, to preserve surprise as long as possible.

Compound calamities and errors led mission navigators to remove their aircraft from the ponderous Ploesti formation before it cleared the Mediterranean. An overland error led the Liberators toward Bucharest, Romania, alerting more Axis defenses than necessary. Around Baker, his anxious 93rd BG watched as the formation headed in what many of them thought was the wrong direction. Baker made an eloquently simple decision as the smoke from Ploesti's stacks smudged the sky 90deg to the left. He turned *Hell's Wench* toward the refineries, breaking from the formation and taking the crews of his Traveling Circus, as the 93rd BG was nicknamed, directly to the target. Ploesti was not going as

planned, and Baker felt obliged to lead the Traveling Circus there, if no other bomb group made it. Some of the Circus' Liberators were down to 20ft above the Romanian countryside as phony haystacks toppled to expose antiaircraft guns. Turret gunners aboard the dark Liberators swapped fire with artillery troops on the ground. When they could, crew members glanced about, able to see pilots in other cockpits concentrating severely on flying, eyes straight ahead, as the big B-24s bucked in the wakes of the bombers ahead of them.

The Liberators screamed at 245mph, way in their emergency power setting range, and the crew wondered how long the Pratt & Whitneys could take the urgent abuse. A Traveling Circus bomber took a belting hit in its bomb bay; fire torched back behind the plane possibly three times its length. Few bailed out as the stricken plane's pilot traded airspeed for altitude to afford them the opportunity to jump. The flaming B-24 stalled and burned on the outskirts of a Romanian village as Addison Baker plowed ahead with the remaining members of the 93rd BG glued to his tail. Baker's heading was not as briefed because of the earlier mix-up in navigating. He and his copilot knew the group was dutifully roaring into battle right behind them, counting on their leadership to fill the vacuum left when one mission navigator crashed

Unbelievable boiling pyres rose higher than the Liberators that caused them over Ploesti, Romania, on August 1, 1943. Courage, both documented and unnoticed, was demonstrated in the bucking B-24s that day. US Air Force via Peter M. Bowers Collection

and his back-up dropped from formation.

Survivors of the low-level Ploesti mission reported seeing flak guns from 20 to 105mm in size. It was a large-bore gun, according to the citation for Addison Baker's Medal of Honor award, that fired the shell that punctured Baker's B-24 and set it afire, low over Romania. Only about three miles from the refinery complex when strick-

en, Baker's Liberator was over wheat fields smooth enough to afford a reasonable chance of surviving a forced landing. Unwilling to leave his task before seeing it to completion, Baker ignored his own best chance for survival and held to his course, leading the 93rd BG to its refinery target. Others in the formation saw more than one hit on *Hell's Wench*. Still, Baker held course, leading his Traveling Circus toward the gap between two smokestacks over the refinery after clipping a barrage balloon cable that set the captive gas bag free. Crews in other Liberators reported the flight deck engulfed in flames; still *Hell's Wench* barreled ahead, on Addison Baker's determined course. Once the refinery was reached, *Hell's Wench* staggered for altitude, gaining about 300ft as some of the crew

bailed out. Baker's bomber began falling off on its right wing tip, narrowly missing another B-24 before impacting the ground. None of his crew, including those who bailed out, survived Ploesti.

Addison Baker, while flying a B-24 Liberator, contributed a powerful lesson in selfless leadership that August day over Ploesti.

John L. Jerstad

Maj. John L. Jerstad flew as Addison Baker's copilot in the 93rd BG B-24 nicknamed *Hell's Wench* over Ploesti's oil refineries on August 1, 1943. Former Missouri high school teacher Jerstad had enough missions behind him to avoid participation in Ploesti, but he volunteered to go. When Baker and Jerstad turned *Hell's Wench* and the rest of the 93rd BG toward the target area and away from the mistaken 376th BG's heading, *Hell's Wench* pointed the way over the heaviest antiaircraft defenses of the area. The heavy-bore hits on *Hell's Wench* appeared inevitable. Ploesti veterans from other Liberators have said they believe no one human could have held the stricken, flaming *Hell's Wench* on course for so long, adding evidence of Jerstad's contribution to the success of the mission. Major Jerstad's volunteerism was highlighted as a trait worthy of emulation, in the citation that posthumously gave him the Medal of Honor for his stoic heroics in a B-24D.

Lloyd H. Hughes

Second Lt. Lloyd Hughes climbed into his 389th BG B-24D on August 1, 1943, and prepared for the impending inferno of Ploesti. The 389th's briefed Ploesti target refinery involved the longest flying of any of the sites the Liberators would hit. This Campina complex was also believed less heavily defended than some of the other refineries. The newer D-models of the 389th tanked more fuel than some of the earlier D-models of the other bomb groups. Extra weight, including ball turrets on some 389th Liberators, also made them slower than the others. So it was natural to send the longest-ranging Liberators to the farthest target refinery, and likewise logical to send these slower B-24s to the target with the lightest antiaircraft defenses.

But Campina was a blazing inferno by the time Hughes' B-24, part of the last formation, approached the target. Accurate groundfire punctured fuel tanks in the bomb bay and the left wing, sending gasoline spewing aft from the Liberator in dangerous streams. At this time, Hughes could have elected to leave formation, to afford his crew a chance to belly the bomber in, or possibly bail out. Ahead, flames from the damaged refinery leaped into the air higher than the altitude of Hughes' B-24.

Knowing the danger his leaking B-24 posed, Hughes held course and roared over the refinery. The gasoline fountain rushing from the B-24 ignited from the towering refinery fires, and other fliers saw Hughes finally attempt a forced landing after dropping his

bomb load. It was too late for landing; the rapidly developing fire consumed the Liberator, which crashed even as it appeared Hughes was trying, to the very end, to set it down in a river bed. Three men survived the crash; one of these died later. Hughes' posthumous Medal of Honor citation said he flew the Ploesti mission "motivated only by his high conception of duty which called for the destruction of his assigned target at any cost . . ."

Leon W. Johnson

Col. Leon W. Johnson commanded the 44th BG, and led his group to Ploesti on August 1, 1943, from the copilot's seat of the B-24D nicknamed *Suzy-Q*. The 44th Group was part of the Ploesti armada that stretched out behind the leaders, falling farther back as Johnson decided to stay with the other lagging groups. A tedious frontal penetration over mountains at the border of Greece ate up more time for the 44th and the other trailing groups as they spread out to accommodate the lower altitude penetration through the clouds, required by some B-24s of the accompanying 98th BG which lacked oxygen for high altitude.

When some of the first B-24s neared the target area, while Leon Johnson's 44th BG was still distant, some wrong turns were made, and an impromptu salvaging of bomb runs saw another group hit Johnson's prearranged target refinery. Johnson's combat equation changed radically as antiaircraft gunners were primed by the earlier bombers overhead, and as delayed-fuze bombs from the earlier B-24s posed an imminent threat to the low-flying 44th BG, as did fires raging from the first Liberator attacks on Johnson's target. Intense smoke obscured parts of the refinery as Colonel Johnson led the way. The 44th was credited with totally destroying what remained of their target refinery in the Ploesti complex. Col. Leon Johnson survived to receive his Medal of Honor.

John R. Kane

Col. John R. "Killer" Kane emerged from Ploesti, and North Africa, a figure in airpower folklore—the quintessential hard-driving group commander who led by example. His 98th BG, known as the Pyramiders, made North

Africa their backyard, even as they looked forward across the Mediterranean to an expanded war. Texan Kane earned his Medal of Honor on August 1, 1943, over Ploesti when he led the third, and largest, element of Liberators over the target. Part of the Ploesti force that was detained by weather en route, Kane's Pyramiders arrived over their assigned target only to find it had already been damaged by an earlier group gone astray. Kane faced gunners already practiced in tracking the low-flying Liberators of the first bomb group as they passed overhead. A train, packed with flak guns, audaciously ran along tracks parallel to the group's flight path, pouring fire into the low B-24s.

Kane's B-24D, nicknamed *Hail Columbia*, punched into boiling, flame-laced smoke clouds over the Astro Romana refinery. This was the single most important target of the Ploesti complex, now reeling from the delayed-action bombs of the earlier group who passed this way in the confusion of battle. Flak clunked into the No. 4 engine of *Hail Columbia*, and Kane feathered the prop. Bombs rippled out of the deep bays of his B-24, and Kane pressed on, as other Pyramiders less fortunate rode their desert-sand B-24s into the ground, slamming into the Astro Romana complex. Kane's Liberator would not make it back to Libya that day, limping as far as Cyprus before setting down out of necessity.

Operation Tidal Wave, the low-level Ploesti mission that swept over the Romanian countryside like a rolling wave, produced more Medals of Honor than any other single air action.

Horace S. Carswell, Jr.

The Liberator's Pacific war frequently involved single-plane shipping strikes. On October 26, 1944, Maj. Horace S. Carswell, pilot, and his crew hoisted their B-24 into the sky and nosed out for the South China Sea, going it alone, at night. A convoy of 12 ships, shepherded by at least a pair of destroyers, steamed into the night oblivious to Carswell's approach. The trade-off was stark: Fly too high, and turning ships could wheel out of the way of falling bomb; fly too low, and risk death in withering antiaircraft fire thrown up by the ships. At 600ft, Car-

Destined to earn the Medal of Honor in a B-24, Leon Vance held his daughter, Sharon D. Vance, beside the Liberator bearing her name, before he departed the United States for combat. Sharon D. Vance Kiernan Collection

swell's heavy bomber made its first run unchallenged. A near miss was registered on one of the ships. Carswell circled for another pass over the now-alerted Japanese. The gauntlet was horrific. Even as the crew claimed two direct hits on a tanker, AA (antiaircraft) fire halted two of the B-24's engines and slowed the output of another. Carswell's copilot reeled from wounds. The B-24 sank toward the sea, hy-

draulics damaged and a gas tank holed. The citation honoring Major Carswell said he demonstrated a "magnificent display of flying skill" in checking the descent in the dark, and putting the B-24 into a faltering climb, chugging away from the convoy and toward the China coast. Landfall was a godsend for the crew, who could bail out and expect to survive this harrowing night. One man then learned the worst: His parachute was ripped by flak over the convoy, and was now a useless bundle of fabric.

Carswell's choices were few, and tough. While he ordered the rest of the crew to jump to safety, he remained at his seat in the cockpit, determined to crash-land the bomber in the dark if

need be to save his stranded crew member who had no parachute. The noble attempt ended abruptly against a mountainside, in a fireball. Major Carswell was honored for his selfless initiative with a posthumous Medal of Honor shortly after the end of the war. The Air Force further acknowledged Texan Horace Carswell by naming Carswell AFB in Fort Worth after this native son.

Leon R. Vance, Jr.

Oklahoman Leon Vance is remembered as a big man who embraced life with gusto, excelling in athletics and enjoying a hard-driving poker game. In wartime interviews, he showed a soft facet to his character, proudly naming his B-24H after two-year-old daughter Sharon Drury Vance. But it was not in his beloved *Sharon D.* that Lt. Col. Leon Vance would earn the Medal of Honor.

On June 5, 1944, in preparation for the D-day invasion, Vance led the 489th BG against coastal positions near Wimereaux, France. The mission was part of the choreography intended to keep the Germans guessing where the invasion would land. As mission commander, Vance stood on the wide Liberator flight deck behind and between the pilot's and copilot's seats. The route in to Wimereaux was devoid of German fighters, but filled with antiaircraft fire. Vance counted just 10sec to the target gun emplacements when accurate flak knocked out three of the B-24H's engines. The olive-drab Liberator struggled on, leading the 489th successfully to the drop on one engine. Fateful flak then exploded just outside the cockpit of the B-24, killing the pilot and almost cutting off Vance's right foot. It was hopeless to try to hold formation in a damaged Liberator with only one engine, and a ragged right elevator.

While the copilot flew the Liberator, another crewman constricted a tourniquet around Vance's leg above the nearly severed foot. Crew members raced to stave off fuel leaks, purging gasoline through the open bomb bay doors. More flak rocked the doomed Liberator. The battered bomber continually lost altitude on its return journey across the English Channel, and Vance struggled to fly the aircraft from the floor near the copilot's seat, and ordered the rest of the crew to bail out over England. By now, the Liberator was descending through 12,000ft in a pure glide; the last of the Pratt & Whitneys was dead, but windmilling, unable to feather.

Vance did not assess the gravity of his wounds at the moment. His grievously injured foot, still attached to his leg, was entangled in armor plating, preventing him from getting up from the cockpit floor. "I couldn't take my hands off the controls to get my leg loose, because the ship would have stalled," he recalled later in a hospital in England. Lying on his stomach to reach the control wheel, Vance heard intercom chatter that led him to believe his wounded radio operator remained in the waist of the Liberator, unable to bail out. In fact, other crew members assisted the injured man in jumping from the descending bomber. Now Vance prepared to ditch the Liberator in the sea, the safest of the poor options available to the crippled flier. Like the competitor he was, Leon Vance kept thinking, devising, and performing in the best interests of his crew and himself all the way down, never resigning himself to an uncontrolled crash, despite his own dire predicament.

Vance used his parachute pack as padding to prevent head and neck injuries from the shock of ditching deceleration. Impact with the water tore the Martin top turret loose, and several hundred pounds of armored gun turret hurled forward to pin Colonel Vance in the cockpit. "It was lying across my back, and I was under about six feet of water," Vance recalled. "I figured that was the end of the line for me." Vance held his breath as he performed what he acknowledged was an odd act: He released the safety harness of the dead pilot beside him. Just as Vance felt his lungs would burst, something within the Liberator exploded and hurled him, amputated from his right foot, to the surface. He dragged himself over the wreckage in an attempt to reach the waist where he still believed his radio operator was trapped, but at last Leon Vance's heroic strength gave out. Marshaling just enough energy to pull the lanyards allowing his Mae West life preserver to inflate with carbon dioxide gas, Vance was in the water when a British rescue boat snatched him some 50min later.

Vance convalesced well in England, and was dispatched back to the United States late in July aboard a Douglas C-54 Skymaster transport that was lost en route. Vance AFB in Oklahoma was named in his honor.

Bruce Avery Van Voorhis

Hailing from the lumber port town of Aberdeen, Washington, Bruce Van Voorhis joined the Navy in Nevada. He commanded Navy squadron VPB-102 on July 6, 1943, during the battle for the Solomon Islands. As a PB4Y-1 plane commander, Van Voorhis volunteered for a risky single-ship bombing mission against a Japanese installation on Greenwich Island. Urgency attended the mission, deemed vital to staving off a Japanese attack of American positions.

Van Voorhis launched his Liberator in darkness, without escort, on the 700mi journey to Greenwich. Winds varied capriciously en route; visibility was low and terrain treacherous as Van Voorhis wended his way to the enemy installation, which he reached to the accompaniment of antiaircraft bursts blooming around his PB4Y-1. As Japanese warplanes engaged the Liberator in combat, one was shot down. The enemy planes caused Van Voorhis to seek the relative safety of lower altitude, which denied the fighters three-dimensional freedom to execute sweeping attacks. The Navy flier set up six attacks on the base, and was credited with destroying the vital radio installation on Greenwich, as well as other facilities and three more enemy aircraft—seaplanes on the water. It was the blast from his own bombs that felled Van Voorhis' low-skimming Liberator. His mission was a sacrificial bid to thwart the enemy; against incredible odds, his chance of survival was dubious. He died in the wreck of his PB4Y-1, and the Navy singled out Lt. Comdr. Bruce Avery Van Voorhis as the only Liberator or Privateer airman in their service to earn the Medal of Honor.

Donald D. Pucket

Donald D. Pucket flew a 98th Bomb Group B-24 on a high-level bombing run over Ploesti on June 9, 1944, when flak rocked the Liberator. Handing the bomber over to the copilot, Lieutenant Pucket tended wounded crew members first, and then assessed the condition of the damaged B-24. With two engines producing power, chances of returning home were poor, so Pucket called for the crew to abandon the bomber. Because three of the men aboard could not bail out, Lieutenant Pucket stayed with them and tried to fly the crippled Liberator to a crash landing. A third engine stopped, and the bomber crashed. For his selflessness, Donald Pucket was posthumously awarded the Medal of Honor.

Appendix 1

Liberator and Privateer Training Bases

The following list represents sites in the United States where some aspect of training involving Liberators or Privateers took place at some period during World War II. Training missions changed during the war; Army airfields like Ephrata and Walla Walla, Washington, at various times hosted B-17s and B-24s. Due to the ever-changing training doctrine during the war, this list may not reflect every site where B-24s were employed in training, but it represents a core of that effort.

Alamogordo AAF, New Mexico
Barksdale AAB, Louisiana
Biggs AAF, Texas
Bruning AAF, Nebraska
Camp Kearney, California (US Navy)
Clovis AAB, New Mexico
Davis-Monthan AAF, Arizona
Ephrata AAF, Washington
Fort Myers, Florida
Gowen AAF, Idaho
Kearns AAF, Utah
Liberal AAF, Kansas
Lowry AAB, Colorado

March AAF, California
McCook AAF, Nebraska
MacDill AAF, Florida
Mountain Home AAB, Idaho
Muroc AAF, California
Pocatello AAF, Idaho
Pueblo AAF, Colorado
Salt Lake City AAB, Utah
Sioux City AAB, Iowa
Tonopah AAF, Nevada
Walla Walla AAB, Washington
Wendover AAF, Utah

Descriptive Bibliography

Much has been written about the B-24—the most-produced American warplane. The following bibliography goes beyond titles and publishers to characterize the nature of these volumes. Some are out of print. They all contribute something to the fabric of the Liberator story—a story too vast for any one book to encompass.

Arnold, Rhodes. *The B-24/PB4Y in Combat—The World's Greatest Bomber.* Reserve, New Mexico: Pima Paisano Publications, circa 1990.

One of the staunchest defenders of the B-24, Arnold played a role in acquiring and flying a B-24J from India to Tucson, Arizona, in 1969 for the Pima Air Museum. Arnold's unabashedly pro-Liberator book is significant for its detailed treatment of Eleventh AF operations, and its table of combat losses that may help other historians unravel the fates of lost Liberators. Arnold also incorporated a list of Liberator nose art names, matched to s/ns or units wherever known. This isn't a beginner's B-24 book, or a sweeping Liberator biography to answer all questions about the bomber. But it is a delightfully quirky addition to any serious B-24 historian's bookshelf.

Birdsall, Steve. *Log of the Liberators.* New York: Doubleday, 1973.

Here's a good one for the human-interest side of the B-24 story. Birdsall blended his crew narratives with just enough AAF and Navy history to flesh out a readable biography of the Liberator. Not too technical; very personal and personable.

———. *The B-24 Liberator.* New York: Arco, 1968.

The old Arco Famous Aircraft series of softbound books filled a need in the 1960s for inexpensive, photo-laden reference works on planes including the Liberator. Birdsall marshaled a good group of photos, coupled with his trademark—human-interest narratives about the men who served in B-24s. Birdsall did not set out to write a nuts-and-bolts B-24 book with this volume; he did create a very readable set of vignettes.

Blue, Allan G. *The B-24 Liberator.* New York: Charles Scribner's Sons, 1975.

Allan Blue's hardback biography of the B-24 is a must-read. Blue goes into great detail on construction changes and modifications, and demystifies some Liberator myths and question marks. Includes capsule histories of numerous Liberator combat units, and contains many tables and appendices of production data and serials.

Bowman, Martin. *The B-24 Liberator, 1939–1945.* Norwich, England: Wensum Books, 1979.

Bowman's book is at its best when treating crew reminiscences anecdotally, and when covering British and Commonwealth Liberators—this book gives an interesting view from across the pond.

Davis, Larry. *B-24 Liberator in Action.* Carrollton, Texas: Squadron-Signal Publications, 1987.

Number eighty in the ongoing line of Squadron-Signal aircraft monographs, Larry Davis' effort is an easy-to-use reference when building a B-24 or PB4Y model. A cache of photos and some generally well-executed color renderings by Don Greer make this an inexpensive addition to a B-24 library.

GREAT AMERICAN
BOMBERS
OF WWII

B-29 SUPERFORTRESS

Chester Marshall

Foreword

In the pages that follow, Chester Marshall takes you on a fascinating journey chronicling the great World War II B-29 bomber program. With anecdotes, accurate historical coverage, pictures, and personal recollections, he guides you through the evolution of the B-29 from a troubled beginning to a very successful combat airplane.

Chester and I were in two different arenas during the war. He was in the military, and I was in a civilian industry, heavily involved in experimental flight tests of the no. 1 XB-29, which continued through the end of World War II. Chester has integrated these two perspectives and many other facets of the B-29 program, and the result is an outstanding story.

The B-29 was radical for its time and its development was unique for many reasons. It was conceived of in an atmosphere of great urgency to do a job that no other airplane could do: to effectively bomb an enemy from very distant bases. Its gestation period was plagued by changing requirements, and it was severely criticized and subjected to pressure to move faster.

Robert M. Robbins, a Boeing experimental test pilot, poses by The Flying Guinea Pig, *the first prototype B-29 built, known as no. 1 XB-29. As aircraft commander, Robbins accumulated more than 400hr on no. 1 XB-29.* Boeing Archives

By the time of its birth—the first flight of the no. 1 XB-29 was on September 21, 1942—this urgency had greatly intensified to meet the threat of Japanese forces ravaging the Pacific. The need was so great that firm orders had already been placed and production initiated for 764 B-29s. It was recognized as a necessary fly-before-buy program so that assembly lines could begin production as soon as possible.

The urgency had grown "white hot" by the time the troubled flight test program was only five months old. Orders had increased to 1,600 airplanes and the massive production effort was now rapidly accelerating and beginning to swell assembly lines. However, only two XB-29s had flown and, due to many problems, fewer than 35hr and only thirty-two flights had been possible in those five hectic months. There were lots of problems and questions but as yet few solutions or answers. When the no. 2 XB-29 crashed and its entire crew was lost on February 18, 1943, the already-troubled program was in even more desperate straits. The no. 1 XB-29 was grounded indefinitely until reasons could be found for the accident and safety measures taken in it and the other B-29s in production.

Many changes resulted from the accident investigation. It took more than three months of intensive effort

before the next B-29 in the "infant" program was ready to fly, on May 29—and it, too, nearly crashed because the aileron control cables were crossed! After that, almost all of the truly serious flight test crises were behind us. High-priority engineering and developmental flight testing continued throughout the war to further improve the airplane and increase its capability. Much of this flight-testing involved the engines, which, although greatly improved, were always troublesome.

Early-production airplanes of late-1943 and early-1944 were built by dedicated but mostly inexperienced people from all walks of life who had been quickly trained. In addition, numerous changes had to be retrofitted in "finished" airplanes, a job normally assigned to experienced mechanics, who now were spread very thin. The resulting problems led to the "Battle of Kansas" to correct discrepancies in already-delivered airplanes.

In the China-Burma-India (CBI) theater, the B-29 was troubled but its effectiveness was improving. The program matured fully in the Mariana Islands, reaching its awesome combat potential as it destroyed the war-making capability of industrial Japan and decimated the will of that nation's people to continue fighting. It brought World War II to an end just two-and-one-half months before the planned invasion of the Japanese homeland, an invasion that was expected to cost five million US casualties.

The B-29 program started "behind the eight-ball" with extreme requirements and too little time. Problems were solved and capability was increased, and despite persisting engine troubles, the resilience, toughness, and survivability of the B-29 endeared her to most of her crews. It was the second-largest World War II industrial program in scope and dollars. Only the Manhattan Project was bigger—and that program's product, the atomic bomb, still had to be delivered by B-29s to abruptly terminate the war.

The Boeing B-29 Superfortresses were the Air Force's mainstay immediately after World War II. They were the first to go into battle at the onset of the Korean War as the youthful, vigorous jet age was beginning to evolve and propeller-driven combat airplanes were becoming obsolete. Many of the Superfortresses that escaped being melted down into aluminum pots and pans were converted to tankers for refueling the new short-range jets. Others were used in the experimental atomic drops at the Bikini Atols in the Pacific and in the lifting of the X-1 experimental airplane to altitude on its way to breaking the sound barrier for the first time in the history of aviation.

This unique story of the B-29 program is graphically told by Chester Marshall. I'm sure you'll find it fascinating.

—Robert M. Robbins
Boeing Experimental Test Pilot on the no.1 XB-29

End of the road for The Flying Guinea Pig.
At Boeing scrap yard, about May 1948.
Bob Robbins

Acknowledgments

Professional writers, historians, and aviation buffs came to my assistance when they learned I was writing this book. I'm grateful to them all, especially Wilbur Morrison, Tom Britton, Bill Hess, and Warren Thompson, for helping me accumulate photographs, color slides, and historical facts about the B-29. I also thank Josh Curtis, a young aviation enthusiast who is dedicated to helping preserve the history and to keeping the memory of the famed World War II airplane alive for his and future generations.

I thank the people at Boeing Aircraft Co. for their help, valuable information, and pictures—especially the gracious assistance of both Marilyn A. Phipps, the archivist specialist at the Boeing Historic Services, and Bob Robbins, a former experimental test pilot at Boeing and command pilot of the no. 1 XB-29, the first Superfortress built.

I am also indebted to the wing and group historians in the old 20th Air Force who sent information and pictures, among them Bill Rooney, Denny Pidhayny, Larry Smith, and Fiske Hanley. I deeply appreciate the invaluable information given me by Lt. Gen. (Retired) James V. Edmundson, Maj. Gen. (Retired) Earl Johnson, Maj. Gen. Winton Close, and Maj. Gen. Henry Huglin.

I am grateful to Robert C. Tharratt, Albert E. Conder, and Ray Brashear for information, photographs, and slides pertaining to the B-29 Superfortress between wars and during the Korean War. Ray Ebert, 73rd Wing historian, opened up his collection of pictures for use in this book, as did Carl Dorr and Harry Mitchell. And many thanks to John V. Patterson, Jr., a former Boeing employee who furnished me with many contacts.

And, finally, I want to say thanks to my wife, Lois, who encouraged me while I toiled to finish this manuscript.

The following individuals contributed first-person anecdotes or described episodes from their combat experiences; the number-letter combination to the right of each name represents the unit in which the person served:

Cleve R. Anno, 29th BG
Stephen M. Bandorsky, 504th BG
Jake Beser, 509th Composite Group
Ray Brashear, 499th BG
Charles G. Chauncey, 9th BG
Arthur Clay, 6th BG
John Cox, 499th BG
Russell Crawford, 444th BG
Harry Crim, 7th Fighter Command
Harold Dreeze, 73rd BW
Clyde Emswiler, 498th BG
Richard Field, 73rd BW
Jack Grantham, weather observation
Ray "Hap" Halloran, 499th BG
Jim Handwerker, 19th BG
Fiske Hanley, 505th BG
George Harington, 315th BW
Allen Hassell, 499th BG
Ed Hiatt, 499th BG
Carl Holder, 9th BG
Edwin L. Hotchkiss, air-sea rescue
Elmer Huhta, 500th BG
Murry Juveluer, 498th BG
Victor King, AS GP
William Leiby, 19th BG
Norman Lent, 3rd PRS
Roger Marr, 16th BG
Glenn McClure, 500th BG
Hal McCuistion, 315th BW
Jack McGregor, 497th BG
Robert W. Moore, 15th FG
Warren G. Moss, 498th BG
Jim O'Donnel, 499th BG
James O'Keefe, 40th BG
Fred Olivi, 509th Composite Group
Van Parker, 19th BG
Edward Perry, 462nd BG
Sture Pierson, 498th BG
Stubb Roberts, 468th BG
Gerald Robinson, 498th BG
William Roos, engineering
Mary Thomas Sargent, Red Cross
Daniel J. Serritello, 444th BG
George A. Simeral, 29th BG
Lawrence S. Smith, 9th BG
Chuck Speith, 498th BG
Wilbur N. Stevens, 509th Composite Group
Jim Teague, training
Kelcie Teague, 314th BW
Rudy L. Thompson, 462nd BG
Robert D. Thum, 549th Night Fighter Group

Introduction

As war clouds gathered in Europe during the late-1930s, there was great concern among US military leaders because of the strong isolationist mood prevalent throughout the country. People in high places were extolling a hands-off policy, lest we make Hitler angry at us. A war was the last thing we needed, they said.

America had struggled for most of the decade to throw off the shackles of the Great Depression, and it was hard to find funds to keep the military services supplied with even enough necessary equipment to maintain a ghost of an army or navy. Lack of funding plus myriad restrictions imposed by Congress delegated our armed services to a defensive role only. As late as 1938, when Maj. Gen. Henry H. ("Hap") Arnold became its chief, airplanes in the Army Air Corps were not allowed to venture beyond 100mi from our shores.

Arnold was a long-time believer in strategic bombing, and thought the Air Corps should be in a position to carry out such an offensive undertaking if faced with a shooting war. He had many friends in the Air Corps—including Gen. Frank Andrews, Col. Oliver Echols, Col. Carl Spaatz, and Maj. Bill Irvine—who were also strong advocates and agreed that the country needed a fleet of long-range bombers.

By early-1939, General Arnold was able to convince the soon-to-retire Army Chief of Staff, Gen. Malin Craig, that there was an urgent need to set up a board to study types of long-range bombers which were needed, he suggested, for the defense of our hemisphere. Under these pretenses, a board was formed in May 1939, headed by Gen. Walter Kilner. Other members of the board included Col. Carl Spaatz, Arnold's top assistant; Charles Lindberg, America's favorite aviation hero; and two other officers. It took only one month for the board to draft its first report, recommending, among other things, the development of long-range bombers.

The Kilner report was delivered September 1, 1939—coincidentally, the last day of General Craig's tenure as Army Chief of Staff and ironically, on the same date that Hitler's goose-stepping Army and dive-bombing Air Force attacked Poland. World War II was underway in Europe. Things would never again be the same.

The Air Corps luckily found a friend in the new Army Chief of Staff, Gen. George C. Marshall. His firm decisions, especially those pertaining to long-range bombers, were instrumental in moving the Air Corps to a higher level of responsibility and toward a self-sustaining operational Air Force.

In November 1939, General Arnold stepped up his efforts to get approval from the War Department to let contracts for a very long-range, very heavy, four-engine bomber. On December 2, 1939, he got the green light to proceed. Capt. Donald Putt, an Air Corps test pilot and engineer at Wright Field, Ohio, was given the task of writing a "statement" of requirements for a super-bomber. Putt was well qualified for the job and knew first-hand what was needed: He had been in the flight testing program at Wright Field for several years and in the mid-thirties had participated in the flight-testing of the Boeing B-17, the first of which crashed while he was testing it.

On January 29, 1940, the Air Corps requirements document requesting a heavy, four-engine airplane that could fly at a speed of 400mph, with a range of at least 5,333mi carrying a maximum bomb load of 1 ton, was sent to four airplane manufacturers, resulting in four Air Corps mission-design-series designations: B-29, Boeing Model 345; B-30, Lockheed Model 51-81-01; B-31, Douglas Model 332F; and B-32, Consolidated Model 33. For various reasons, Lockheed and Douglas dropped out of the running, and Boeing and Consolidated-Vultee were declared winners of the competition.

Boeing was considered way ahead of Consolidated. Its design teams were familiar with four-engine airplanes, having experimented with various concepts of long-range, heavy bombers since 1939. Their experiences with both the unsuccessful huge, underpowered XB-15 and the very successful B-17 led to the development of the Model 322, the design they hoped would win the competition. They had experimented with several versions, one of which was a pressurized B-17 with tricycle landing gear. After selecting Wright Aeronautical's 2,200hp R-3350 twin-row radial engines to power their design, they came up with specifications that they designated Model 341. This was the model Boeing submitted to Wright Field, but to make it more combat-ready, the model was modified later and designated the Model 345.

This is the story of that airplane, World War II's premier bomber—about the people who designed and built it, and those who suffered through its development. The Boeing B-29 Superfortress was indeed the forerunner of today's modern Air Force bomber fleet. Many of the innovative ideas incorporated in the B-29 more than fifty years ago are still in use.

Fifi is the last of the flying B-29s. This grand warbird is operated by the Confederate Air Force. Glenn Chaney

Chapter 1

Birth of the Boeing B-29 Superfortress

The Air Corps requirements document found its way to Boeing Aircraft Co. president Philip Johnson on February 5, 1940. Within three weeks, Boeing's Model 341 was submitted to Wright Field's Col. Oliver Echols.

Because of Boeing's interest and experience in building four-engine airplanes, company officials for years had maintained a close, cordial relationship with Air Corps leaders. They were so convinced that, sooner or later, very long-range bombers would be built that Boeing used company funds to conduct experiments and construct mock-ups before Congress ever approved any appropriations for such a project. Such men as Edward Wells, Claire Egtvedt, and Wellwood Beall had advance knowledge of the Air Corps' super-bomber hopes and plans. The gamble was about to pay off for Boeing.

Fortunately, at the same time that the Air Corps was requesting bids for its new bomber, the British were giving the War Department the inside scoop on the German Luftwaffe— warning that Allied airplanes needed better crew protection, self-sealing fuel

The forward pressurized section, which was occupied by two pilots, the bombardier, the flight engineer, the navigator, and the radio operator, are shown ready for the assembly line. Boeing Archives

tanks, and more defensive armament. Though Boeing had a contract to build three prototype XB-29s, these revelations caused Boeing to change some of the specifications in its Model 341. Among the changes were the addition of armor plating and heavier guns which increased the weight of the airplane from 97,700lb to about 105,000lb. This new Model 345 was the prototype from which the B-29s were built.

Boeing Receives First Appropriation

Boeing's Model 345 was judged to be superior to the others submitted, and the company was appropriated $85,000 for further study and wind tunnel tests. On August 24, 1940, Boeing received $3,615,095 to build two prototypes. The contract for this appropriation was not signed until September 6, and was amended on December 2 to include a third prototype.

About the time Boeing received the original contract, both Lockheed and Douglas pulled out of the competition and Consolidated received a similar contract to proceed with development of its XB-32. This decision meant that two super-bombers would begin development simultaneously with hopes that at least one of the two would live up to expectations.

By mid-1941, the Germans had violated the Neutrality Act by sinking

two American ships. President Franklin D. Roosevelt acted immediately, calling upon the War Department to step up production requirements and to "shoot if necessary" if the Axis nations continued violations against the United States.

A committee of Air Corps officers, headed by Col. Harold L. George, prepared an "air plan" in August 1941 in response to the president's urgent call for action. The plan was called "Air War Plan Division—1" (AWPD-1). Serving with George were Lt. Col. Kenneth Walker, Maj. Haywood S. Hansell, Jr., and Maj. Lawrence Kuter. Among other radical changes in the future role of the Air Force, the plan stressed the urgent need for very long-range heavy bombers should strategic bombing be necessary.

General Marshall sided with General Arnold and the plans committee. He approved the plan with the remark, "This plan has merit," but the approval did not come easy. Some of Marshall's staff thought the plan would counteract the traditional role of the Air Corps, that of a secondary mission of aiding the Army in a combat situation.

Many in the Air Force considered the Marshall decision in August 1941 as the turning point in the Air Force's future. It was, they say, the real "birth of the United States Army Air Forces (USAAF)" The name change from Air

Boeing's Model 345 from which the B-29 Superfortress was built. Boeing Archives

The no. 1 XB-29 at Boeing Field, Seattle, in September 1942 before the first test flight by chief test pilot Eddie Allen. Bob Robbins

Corps to USAAF took place June 20, 1941.

To give the USAAF and General Arnold a more authoritative position in the War Department's chain of command, the Chief of Staff made Arnold his Deputy Chief of Staff for Air of the United States Army. This was a tremendous improvement in the struggling Air Corps' hopes for a strong Air Force. The decision also gave assurance that more appropriations would come quicker for the development of the B-29 Superfortress.

Building of the Superfortress Begins

As 1940 came to a close, a mockup of Model 345 was inspected and given final approval, along with an order from the Air Force to build a third prototype and a fourth airframe for static tests. The design engineers sent the first engineering drawings to the Boeing shop in Seattle on May 4, 1941, calling for the completion of the first B-29 to be no later than August 1942.

On May 17, 1941, Boeing received a conditional contract from the Air Force to build 250 B-29s. The "condition" asked that the company expand its Wichita, Kansas, facilities, where the much-needed Stearman trainer was produced, to meet demands for the production of the B-17 Flying Fortress, along with a quota of B-29s.

As the plant expansion at Wichita proceeded and production at Boeing's home plant in Seattle geared up to a giant undertaking, the Japanese pulled their sneak attack on Pearl Harbor. With the country now at war, the Air Force wasted no time in upping the order for more B-29s, even though not a single B-29 had been built at that time. More than nine months would come and go before one would leave the ground for the first time. On January 31, 1942, Boeing's "conditional" contract for the original 250 airplanes was not only signed but was amended to increase the number to 500 airplanes, plus $53 million for spare parts for the B-29s.

The Wing

The new bomber was revolutionary in so many ways that designers were faced with extreme challenges as specifications changed. The huge wing

presented one of the greatest challenges. A search for a suitable wing by Boeing's chief aerodynamicist, George Schairer and flight-test pilot Eddie Allen was unsuccessful. The wing had to have low drag at cruising speed and good high-speed and stall characteristics. Finally, Wellwood Beall, Boeing's chief engineer, decided that Boeing should develop its own wing. After eight different designs and thousands of hours of work, the excellent Boeing "117" wing was developed.

What made the new wing so successful was the size of its flaps. They were the equivalent of one-fifth the area of the entire wing, which allowed the aircraft to take off and land at a lower speed than it would have if it had conventional wings and flaps. George Schairer was credited with being the father of the huge wing.

Self-sealing fuel tanks were installed in the inboard wing structure. At the time, the two wing spars were the longest and heaviest Duralumin extrusions ever used in a production aircraft. Development of the Boeing "117" wing was a major contribution to the success of the B-29.

Pressurization

Pressurization of large areas in the new bomber presented the design-

ers with more challenges. Faced with the problem of maintaining pressurization while opening bomb bay doors in order to drop bombs, designers came up with a unique solution by connecting two pressurized sections with a 40ft tunnel large enough for men to crawl through. The tunnel had a diameter of 34in and was located at the top of the fuselage above the two bomb bays.

The two pilots, the bombardier, the navigator, the flight engineer, and the radio operator were located in the forward section, and the central fire control gunner, two side gunners, and the radar operator were located in the mid-ship section. The tail gunner position was pressurized by two 6in pipes connected between the central section and the tail gunner. Between these two sections was an unpressurized part of the aircraft where the oxygen bottles were stored. Also in this section was a gasoline-operated auxiliary generator, called the "putt-putt." This auxiliary unit had to be started and its power placed on-line with the main electrical system before the engines could be started or the bomb bay doors raised. It also had to be started before landing.

The Americans were not the first to incorporate pressurization in their

The various sections of the Superfortress, produced separately, are shown here at the Boeing-Wichita, Kansas, plant. Boeing Archives

combat bombers. The German and English air forces had experimented with pressurizing cockpits of combat aircraft, but none were as sophisticated or could accommodate large areas as the B-29 Superfortress could.

A pump located under the floorboard in the radar room which dispensed supercharged air to the pressurized areas in the B-29 maintained the equivalent of an 8,000ft altitude when flying at 30,000ft. With the development of the B-29, for the first time in American aviation history, a combat crew could be comfortable at high altitude.

Remote-Controlled Gunnery System

The development of a remote-controlled defensive gunnery system for the B-29 put the aircraft in a class of its own. Four companies competed for the contract to develop this innovative system, including Bendix, General Electric, Sperry, and Westinghouse. With its retractable turrets and periscope sights, the Sperry system

The B-29B is shown at the Renton, Washington, plant, in its final assembly. The B-29B was a modification of the A-model in which all gun turrets and the remote controlled firing system were removed. Only the tail gun position remained. The deletion of the turrets added about 10mph to the B-29B's speed. As the air war against the Japanese cities progressed, fighter opposition became almost nil, so the defensive weaponry was no longer needed. This plane was used in the 315th BW and the 509th CG. The 315th BW flew most of their missions at night against Japanese fuel dumps and oil refineries, with great success. The 509th CG was the atomic bombing group. Boeing Archives

won the original contract. After experimenting with the system on the first three XB-29 prototypes, however, the contract was given to General Electric because General Electric's system featured stationary turrets and computerized sights.

There were five gun positions: upper-forward, upper-aft, lower-forward, lower-aft, and tail. The bombardier and each gunner except the tail gunner could aim and fire two turrets simultaneously. Each of the turrets except for the upper-forward turret and the tail gun position mounted two .50cal machine guns. A 20mm cannon was mounted in the tail position. The cannon was later removed because most of the Japanese fighter attacks came from the front, and two extra .50cal machine guns were incorporated in the upper-forward turret.

The system developed by General Electric was a computerized and flexible system that gave control of turrets to more than one gunner. Each of the gunners had primary guns, but could operate two turrets at the same time if necessary. The central fire control gunner, located in the central gunner's section, sat in an elevated seat between the two side gunners. Since he had a better overall view by looking through a plexiglass blister, he controlled the master gunnery panel. He could also flip a switch and assign turrets to gunners who had a better view of an attacking plane, thus increasing firepower where needed.

Mounted gun sights were at each of the gunner's position, about 1ft high with the reticule sight near the top. The gunner gripped it by two round knobs about the size and shape of oversized iced tea coasters. The sight swiveled horizontally at the base, and the upper section rotated in elevation by forward and backward twisting of the wrists. The sighting mechanism included an incandescent light source that sent a pattern of dots upward through a lens from inside the sight. This pattern struck a piece of clear glass set at a 45deg angle in the center of the part of the sight the gunner looked through. The image appeared as a circle of bright red-orange dots with one dot in the center. The right-hand sight knob rotated independently of the left-hand one. By twisting this knob back and forth through a few degrees, the gunner could make the circle of dots shrink in on the center dot or expand to fill the sight. There was a dial on the back of the sight with which to set the wingspan of the attacking aircraft. The right-hand knob also had a metal flap on it which was spring loaded to hold it out at a 30deg angle. This was the action switch. Unless it was held down by the palm of the hand, the turret would not activate.

With the computer switched on, a target could be tracked smoothly. Gyroscopes scanned the enemy plane's wing tips, and those electrical signals were sent to the turret, allowing it to lead the target and to elevate the guns to compensate for range from the target. When correct data, such as air speed, altitude, and so on, were fed into the computer system, the gunners' bursts of fire were significantly more accurate than those fired from conventional turrets.

Central fire control gunner Kendal Chance, member of the author's crew, explains how he directed fire at multiple attacking planes: "Since I had an overall better view of attacking planes, I used the in-plane intercom to direct the fire. If I had a better shot advantage, I would take control of two guns and fire them simultaneously. Each of the other gunners could fire two guns also, except for the tail gunner."

The gun sights included a deadman's switch; if a gunner were knocked out of action, his turret automatically was assigned to the gunner with secondary control. To prevent a gunner from shooting parts of his aircraft when tracking a target, a switch would cause firing to stop momentarily while passing scanned parts of his own aircraft.

There were a few instances of gunners' blisters blowing out after being hit by shrapnel or bullets. Crew members were instructed to wear oxygen

A graphic picture of side blister of Superfort, showing how gunner sights and fires by remote control at target. Albert Conder

masks while over the target area because of the danger of losing pressurization while under attack.

Though this turret system was complex, it was maintainable under combat conditions.

B-29 Radar Units

Another first for the Superfortress was that each of the B-29s that went to combat had a radar unit installed, and each crew of eleven members included a radar operator trained to aid the navigator in navigating and locating the target. If the target were covered with overcast or the weather were extremely bad, the targets were located by radar. During the incendiary raids on Japanese cities, the radar units were helpful in preventing collisions by B-29s merging on the same target area during extremely bad weather. Most of the B-29s were equipped with the AN/APQ-l3 radar equipment developed by Bell Telephone Laboratory and the Massachusetts Institute of Technology (MIT) Radiation Laboratory. The radar antenna for this unit was a 30in hemispherical radome located between the bomb bays and protruding below the fuselage a couple of feet.

Later in the war, a new and more efficient radar unit was developed. It was also developed by MIT's Radiation Laboratories and Bell Telephone and was called the AN/APQ-7 Eagle radar unit. Western Electric Co. actually built both radar units.

The Eagle unit was used primarily by the 315th Bombardment Wing (BW) at North Field at Guam, in its campaign of precision attacks on oil fields and fuel targets. Most of these highly successful missions were carried out at night. The Eagle antenna was wing-shaped in a housing installed underneath the forward section of the fuselage. It spanned 17ft, had a 31in chord, and was about 8in thick.

As war in the Pacific progressed, the AN/APN-4 Loran system was also used by the B-29s. This was a long-range navigation aid that helped navigators determine their plane's position by means of Loran signals broadcast from known positions. When Iwo Jima was captured, a Loran signaling station was installed on Mount Suribachi,

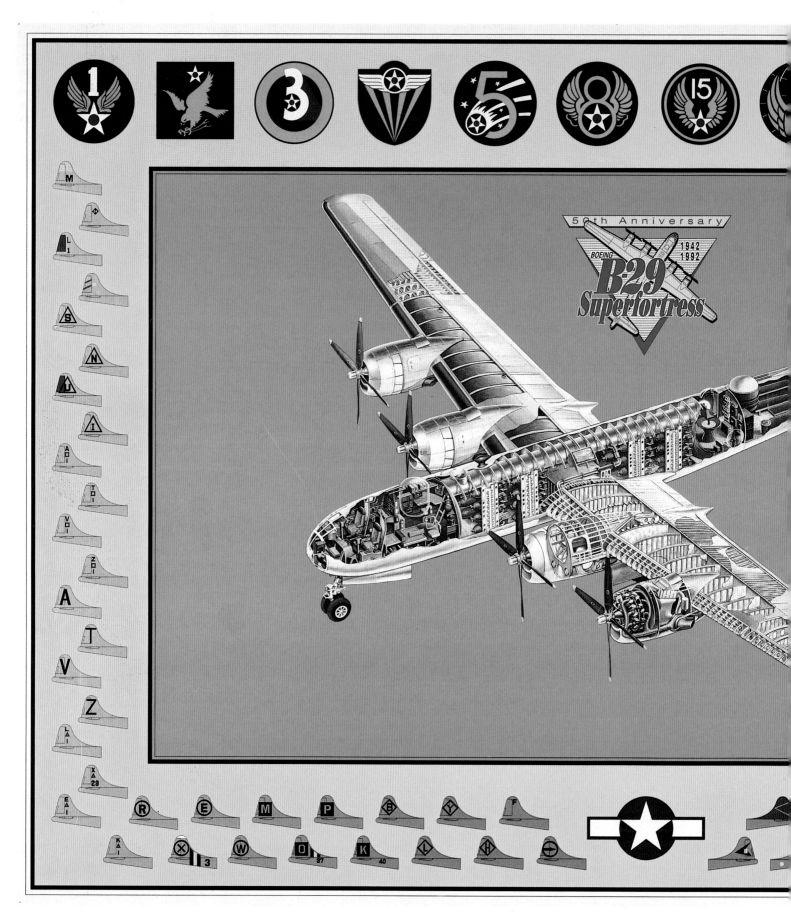

50th Anniversary
1942 1992
BOEING
B-29
Superfortress

further assisting navigators regardless of the weather. Philco built the AN/APN-4.

Late-model B-29s carried the AN/APN-9 Loran system, which was an improved version of Loran equipment, built by RCA.

Boeing's refined Model 345 was submitted to Wright Field on May 11, 1940. Model 345 would be powered by four Wright 2,200hp R-3350 twin-row radial engines (also refined). Four retractable (later stationary) turrets mounted twin 50cal machine guns and a tail turret held twin 50cal machine guns and a 20mm cannon (which was later removed). Three pressurized compartments—a forward section, a mid-section, and a tail gun section—were connected by a tunnel over the two bomb bays. Its landing gear was tricycle, with double wheels all around. The specs for this model called for a 5,333mi capability carrying 1 ton of bombs and a maximum bomb load of 16,000lb. It would carry a twelve-man crew.

A final production program for the B-29s was decided on at a meeting of military and industrial representatives in February. Boeing-Wichita would have the responsibility of production and assembly of the B-29s. In a plant yet to be erected, Bell Aircraft Co. would build B-29s at Marietta, Georgia. Two other plants would build the super-bomber, but the companies and locations were shuffled around before production actually began: Boeing at Renton, Washington (just north of the Seattle headquarters), took the place of North American Aviation in Kansas City, in a swap with the Navy, and Glenn L. Martin Co. at Omaha got the job of producing B-29s when Fisher Body was asked to concentrate on the P-75 fighter plane.

Wright Aeronautical Corp. received an order to triple its production of engines on the original order in April. The giant R-3350 engine would become one of the major headaches from day one because of excessive overheating. Many modifications were made to correct the problem—the en-

This cut-away shows the three pressurized compartments for crew members. Boeing Archives

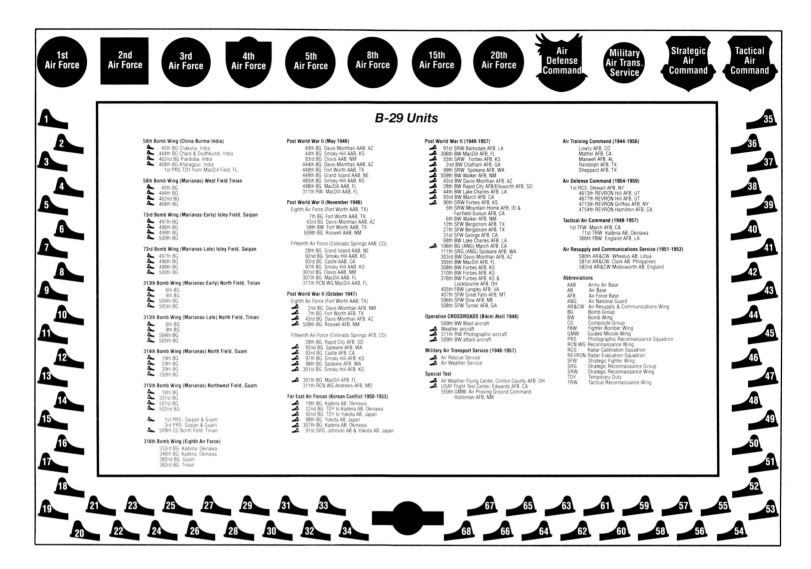

B-29 Units

gine nacelle was redesigned and the baffling shortened to reduce drag when opened to allow more air to the engines—but the problem remained.

One of the reasons for this overheating was the material used to build the engine crankcases. Engineers first used magnesium because it was lighter than aluminum and could yield a ratio of 1lb weight in an engine to produce 1hp, a ratio that was considered ideal in helping to reduce overall weight of the huge aircraft. The magnesium proved to be problematic, however, getting much hotter than aluminum under sustained use and causing the engine to crack. Another engine problem was the oil pumping system, which did not feed oil to the top cylinders; this was the reason for so many "swallowed" valves. A swallowed valve meant having to shut down the engine and feather the propeller.

To those first assigned to the B-29 program, these problems were very frustrating, and some tried in vain to be transferred to B-17 units. An early assignee to the B-29s was M/Sgt. Russell Crawford, who served as crew chief on one of the first seven Superfortresses, designated the YB-29 and built at the new Wichita plant. Assigned to the 468th Maintenance Squadron, 444th Bombardment Group (BG), 58th BW, Crawford had this to say about the early B-29s: "I learned about the mysterious bugs and gremlins that filtered into and around the early B-29s before the USAAF even ran the acceptance check on them. Rumors floated around that the rise and fall of the tide in the nearby Pacific Ocean affected the construction of the aircraft during the building of the first three prototypes at the Boeing no. 1 plant in Seattle. I was crew chief of one of the first seven YB-29s to come off the assembly line at the new Boeing-Wichita plant. Like most people associated with the Superforts at first, I lived through the frustrations and disappointments as we tried to iron out the kinks."

Flight Tests Begin

In early September 1942, the first XB-29 was rolled out of the assembly shed for its first taxi tests. A few days later, Eddie Allen and crew boarded no. 1 XB-29 for a series of more serious taxi tests. He almost got the airplane airborne three times during the faster taxiing, bouncing it into the air about 15ft each time, then settled her down on the runway, as his confidence surged.

Edmund T. Allen, affectionately known as "Eddie," had the reputation of being the most experienced and possibly the best test pilot in the United States. He learned to fly after joining the Air Service in 1917, and became a flight instructor and taught advanced acrobatics. During World War I, he was sent to England to learn about British aircraft flight-testing techniques. After the war, he became a test pilot for the National Advisory Committee for Aeronautics, and then for two years flew World War I De-Havillands as an air mail pilot for the Post Office Department until the department got out of the flying business in 1927. He then worked for various airlines and manufacturers as a pilot and a free-lance test pilot.

On April 26, 1939, Eddie Allen became Boeing's first and only director of aerodynamics and flight research, a position that gave him the opportunity to influence the research, testing, and development of several aircraft, especially the B-29. Allen surrounded himself with some of the best brains in the business, including Al Reed, chief of flight testing and chief test pilot, who was in charge of the Flight Research Department; and MIT-educated and renowned aerodynamicist George Schairer, who was responsible for developing the Boeing "117" wing. (The large high-lift wing flaps on the "117" allowed takeoffs and landings to be made in reasonable distances with the smallest wing surfaces, greatly reducing drag and, thus, maintaining the speed of the aircraft. The fuselage, nacelles, fairings, and other equipment were also designed to produce a minimum of drag.)

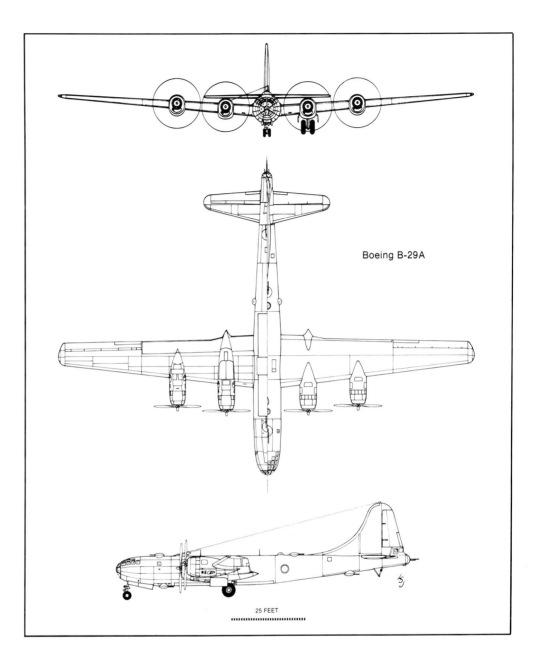

Boeing B-29A

25 FEET

"She Flies!"

With satisfactory taxi testing completed and after 1,400,000 man hours spent on Model 345, the wind tunnel tests, the research, and the development work done by Eddie Allen and George Schairer and their people finally paid off. On September 21, 1942, no. 1 XB-29 taxied out onto the runway at Boeing Field in Seattle. Eddie Allen was in the pilot's seat and Al Reed occupied the co-pilot's seat. At various stations in the aircraft were eight more members of the flight test crew, each ready to monitor and record specific readings and observations during the flight.

The takeoff was uneventful. Allen climbed to 6,000ft and made the lateral, directional, and longitudinal stability and control checks. Everything that should be checked on a first flight was satisfactorily accomplished in 1hr, 15min.

As the engines were shut off, Allen told the waiting crowd of co-workers, "She flies!"

The day after Allen's first flight, Capt. Donald Putt, now an Army project officer, took the no. 1 XB-29 up for a short flight. Upon landing, Putt declared, "She's easier to fly than the B-17." He could claim the distinction of being the second man to test-hop the

XB-29 and the first USAAF man to fly it.

Soon after the first two flights, though, troubles began to plague almost every flight. It seemed that Murphy's Law was originated to apply to the B-29 program: If something bad could happen it usually did! Allen was able to get only 27hr in the air out of twenty-three flights by December 1942. During the first three months since the first flight, sixteen engines had to be changed, nineteen exhaust systems had to be revised, and twenty-two carburetors had to be replaced. There were many other problems, including governor and feathering diffi-

culties with the four-blade Hamilton Standard propellers, which caused runaway engines.

Allen and his crew had trouble accumulating enough data with such short flights, which averaged just a little over 1hr. Half of the flight was usually spent fighting mounting odds trying to get back to the field.

One bright spot was the fact that the B-29's performance and handling qualities were excellent. Other than the rudder boost being removed, no significant aerodynamic changes were ever made.

On December 30, 1942, no. 2 XB-29 was ready for its initial flight. Allen was at the controls for this flight also. Engineers had cleared three of the engines for a maximum of 35hr flying time. Trouble erupted early, and Allen elected to discontinue the flight and return to the field. Six minutes from the field, fire broke out in the fourth engine and soon the smoke in the cockpit was so thick that Allen could hardly see the ground. Luckily, the crew made it in and the fire was put out on the ground.

Fires continued to haunt the B-29s. Boeing engineers reported that at least part of the cause was a faulty engine fuel induction system—a charge denied by Wright. It was fifteen months before there was positive proof that the R-3350 was susceptible to induction system fires, and that these fires would escalate rapidly and become uncontrollable magnesium fires, which then destroyed the evidence of the original fire's origin. The proof

came during a routine test flight of no. 1 XB-29 on March 24, 1944, while Boeing test pilot Robert ("Bob") Robbins was feathering the engines: a fire started in the fourth engine. Fortunately, he was able to get the engine feathered and the fire extinguished before the fire spread beyond the induction system and became an external fire.

More tests were needed on no. 2 XB-29 and no. 1 was out of commission until modifications were finished—so the engines from no. 1 were removed and put in no. 2. Everyone at Boeing, especially Eddie Allen, was anxious to get the problems solved and testing behind them.

Disaster in Seattle

At 12:09pm, February 18, 1943, with Bob Dansfield flying as co-pilot and nine crew members aboard, Eddie Allen took off in no. 2 XB-29 on a flight that resulted in the most shocking air accident anyone could remember. The entire B-29 program, on which so much hope was riding, was placed in jeopardy, instantly.

Eight minutes into the flight, the first engine caught fire. The engine was routinely shut down and the props feathered. All aboard thought the fire was out, but Allen decided to abort the flight and return to the field. At 12:24pm, the radio operator reported the plane's altitude as 1,500ft about 4mi from the field. At this time, no one suspected that the fire was still alive, but it had spread into the wing section front spar. Allen was making a routine landing pattern when the raging fire was discovered.

At 12:25pm they had just completed turning onto the base leg and had just crossed the heavily populated west

shore of Lake Washington. At that time, ground witnesses heard an explosion that sounded like a loud backfire and saw a piece of metal fall from the airplane. About this time, the radio operator, who could see into the forward bomb bay and the wing center-section spar, yelled to Allen, " You'd better get this thing down in a hurry. The wing spar is burning badly."

In a desperate effort to get the airplane on the ground, Allen turned on final approach at an altitude of 250ft. Three crew members jumped from the burning plane, but they were too low to the ground for their parachutes to open and they died when they hit the ground. At 12:26pm, just 3mi from Boeing Field, no. 2 XB-29 crashed into the Frye Meat Packing Plant, killing all aboard and about twenty in the building. Allen and the others aboard were killed instantly.

Bob Robbins summed up the tragic accident and aftermath: "The flight test team that Eddie assembled and trained was decimated, devastated, and demoralized. Some of its members would probably never completely get over his loss—but they did put the pieces back together and continued to fight the battles and get the answers as Eddie would expect them to."

The third prototype XB-29 made its initial test flight on June 16, 1943. The next month, Boeing made its first delivery to the USAAF, which included seven of the YB-29 service test series from the Wichita plant.

Gen. K. B. Wolfe's Special B-29 Project

The tragic crash of no. 2 XB-29 caused ripples up the chain of command all the way to President Roosevelt, who was already unhappy with the lack of progress being made in the airplane's development. He had promised Generalissimo Chiang Kai-shek an early deployment of the giant aircraft in the hopes of bolstering US-Chinese relations. He wanted B-29s on the way to India by the end of 1943.

After the tragedy, there were more investigations. General Arnold was eager to find the causes of these fires and steer the super-bomber away from ensuing political upheaval. Somebody had to come up with something real soon to quick-start the project, find some solutions, and get the B-29s rolling off the assembly line and headed for combat—or else.

Senator Harry S. Truman, who had made a name for himself as the head of a Congressional Investigating Committee that had exposed fraudulent overcharging and other violations in defense acquisitions, even looked into the troubles associated with the B-29 program. His committee's report stated that, "Quality had run second to quantity in building engines for the Superfortresses," and placed blame for substandard or defective engines equally on Wright Aeronautical Co. and the USAAF for applying too much pressure on the engine-building company to speed up production.

General Arnold had called on some of the most experienced pilots in the USAAF, including Brig. Gen. Kenneth B. Wolfe, Col. Leonard ("Jake") Harman, Col. Haywood ("Possum") Hansell, and Col. LaVern ("Blondie") Saunders. As trouble continued to mount and with time running out, something had to be done—and done quickly—to move the B-29 program forward.

And something did happen! A bombardment project officer at Wright Field came up with what turned out to be the solution to getting the B-29 project rolling. Colonel Harman, who worked with the B-29 project and had even flown in a B-29 with Eddie Allen, was the man who came up with the bright idea. Harman wasted no time in going over his plan with his boss, General Wolfe.

Harman's idea was that the B-29 program needed a "special project" tag with teeth in it. This special project would exercise full control over every-

Left to right: Bob Robbins, co-pilot; Jim Werner, flight-test project pilot; and Jim Fraser, flight-test project pilot. Bob Robbins

thing pertaining to the B-29 program. In other words, a single command would have full control for flight tests, production, modifications, and the selecting and training of combat crews. The idea was so unique that General Wolfe thought it would not only work, but could be sold to the top people in Washington. "Write what you just told me down on a piece of paper," he told Harman, "and we'll take a trip up to Washington and see what General Echols thinks of the idea, before going to General Arnold."

Echols read the proposal, studied it for a while, and handed it back to Harman. "Take it down the hall and show it to General Arnold," he said. "I like the idea and I think he will!"

Colonel Harman had the proposal neatly typed with a place for General Arnold to sign above his name if he approved it. After the general read the proposal, he also studied it for a minute or so, and then said, "Why can't somebody else do something for

me like this? Yes," he said, "I think it will work." He signed the paper.

The short proposal developed into what was called "The K. B. Wolfe Special B-29 Project." As the project got underway under the leadership of General Wolfe and Colonel Harman, things began to improve noticeably. Although the gremlins and bugs would continue to hamper the engine performances and other setbacks would occur, the B-29 Special Project could claim considerable responsibility for getting the giant bombers through the assembly lines, to the modifications centers, and ready for combat. Also, crew members from across the country, if they were thought to be B-29 combat crew material, were brought into the program.

Chapter 2

Three-Pronged B-29 Battle Erupts

The beginning of 1943 brought with it three distinct "battles" not pertaining to the "hot" war, but all associated with the B-29 Superfortress program: battle of the political decisions, battle to eliminate setbacks in production of the B-29, and the "Battle of Kansas," in which all hands pitched in to make the Superfortress ready for combat and to train combat crews and ground crews to maintain the planes in combat.

After the January 1943 Casablanca Conference, President Roosevelt made a decision to inform Generalissimo Chiang Kai-shek that all possible aid would be sent to prevent the Japanese from taking over China. Japan's army had cut off all land-deployed help to the USAAF by capturing Burma. Normally, supplies to China came over the Burma and Lido Roads, but now they would have to be flown in. Both Army Gen. Joseph Stilwell and USAAF Maj. Gen. Claire L. Chennault, newly appointed head of the 14th Air Force in China, were trying to exert pressure on the president to initiate this plan. They and Chiang

Jacob Beser, standing before the atomic bomb-carrying Superfortress at Tinian Island, was the only man to fly in the strike plane on both atomic missions: in the Enola Gay *to Hiroshima and* Bock's Car *to Nagasaki. Jake Beser*

Kai-shek wanted the B-29s sent to China so that they could begin and maintain an air offensive against Japan.

General Marshall was cautious because he realized the enormous problems that would develop from trying to supply bombers in China from bases in India before each bombing raid could take place. He thought the war in Europe, at this stage, would suffer if transport planes were taken from that theater and moved to the CBI theater. Major decisions had already been made with Allied forces to win the war in Europe before turning full force on Japan.

President Roosevelt still insisted on getting help to Chiang Kai-shek. He suggested sending up to 300 US bombers, not necessarily B-29s, to China.

Service Tests Begin

In the meantime, General Arnold had more or less staked the future of the USAAF on the early deployment of the B-29s against Japan. He depended heavily on the K. B. Wolfe Special B-29 Project to get this done.

The Wolfe Special B-29 Project had been given top priority in men and material, second only to the secret "Manhattan Engineer District Project." General Wolfe used this priority treatment to request the transfer of the Accelerated Service Test Branch

(ASTB), headed by Col. Abraham Olsen from Wright Field to Smokey Hill Army Air Field in Salina, Kansas. The new Boeing-Wichita plant, with orders to produce fourteen YB-29s that were to be tested and used for USAAF acceptance checks, began rolling planes off the assembly line in June 1943. On June 27, Colonel Harman flew the first service-test YB-29 at the Wichita field. Because Smokey Hill had extra-long, 10,000ft runways, built especially for one of the first B-29 groups for combat training, Harman decided that the service testing be done there, rather than at the shorter field at the Wichita plant.

The high priority of the Special B-29 Project allowed General Wolfe to choose the top aides who worked for him at Wright Field when the 58th BW was organized on June 1, 1943. He chose Colonel Harman as his deputy and General Saunders, who had commanded a B-17 group and served as group commander of the 11th BG in the South Pacific early in the war, to direct the B-29 crew-training program.

On August 14, 1992, many B-29 veterans gathered at Boeing Field to commemorate the fiftieth anniversary of the first flight of the B-29. Lt. Gen. James V. Edmundson, US Air Force (Retired), related an interesting account of his first encounter with the B-29: "I first met the B-29 in the sum-

A Superfortress from the 331st BG, 315th BW, proudly flies overhead. Many of those who fought to take the Mariana Islands, to make the B-29 operation possible, rest below at Guam. Josh Curtis

The Maj. Robert Goldsworthy crew pose in front of their new B-29 at Herrington, Kansas, before flying it to Saipan in October 1944. Goldsworthy, center, was shot down over Tokyo in December 1944, and remained a POW until the war ended. He remained in service after the war and retired as a major general. Hurth Thompkins

mer of 1943. After returning from the South Pacific in the spring of that year, I was assigned to Washington. Blondie Saunders had been promoted to brigadier general and was also assigned to the Pentagon. One day, he called me into his office and told me that he was involved in the B-29 program. He told me to grab an airplane and make a quick trip around the States to see how many of the old 11th Group troops I could find and how many of them would like to go back to war.

"I went out to Bolling Field and was assigned an airplane that, I guess, in this company should remain nameless. If I told you that it was shaped like one of General LeMay's cigars, had almost no wings at all, and was built in Baltimore, you'd be able to guess what kind of an airplane had been issued to me.

"Anyway, I toured the country in my flying cigar and ran into a bunch of

the old 11th Group troops. I couldn't tell them where we would be going or what we would be flying. I could tell them that General Saunders would be going with us, and virtually to a man, they volunteered. I told them to sit tight and within a couple of weeks they would be getting orders assigning them to the 58th BW in Marietta, Georgia, and I'd see them there.

"The 58th BW, under the command of General K. B. Wolfe, with General Blondie Saunders as director of operations, had its headquarters in an old farmhouse in the back acres of the base at Marietta. There was a big hangar on the flight line where a YB-29 was safely hidden when it wasn't flying. The ramp was full of those little, twin-engined, cigar-shaped birds—B-26s! There, I said it!

"During those early days in Marietta, as my old 11th Group buddies came driving in to report for duty, they would have to phone me from the gate in order to get on the base. I'd take them for a tour around the ramp loaded with B-26s and they were not bashful about asking me just what in the hell I'd gotten them into. I'd say something about not letting anybody talk you into volunteering for any-

thing. It went over like a lead balloon. When we'd just about reached the point where they were ready to tear me limb from limb, I'd take them inside the hangar where they got their first look at that great big, beautiful YB-29. It was fun to watch their eyes light up. Since Jake Harmon had just checked me out in that YB in July, I was real proud of her.

"It isn't often realized what a big contribution the troops from Blondie Saunders' old 11th BG made to the early B-29 program. Of the sixteen squadrons in the 58th BW, eight were commanded by guys from the 11th BG. And others were scattered through the four groups in key staff positions."

Boeing and the USAAF were very congenial during the stepped-up testing program. The plan was for the USAAF to evaluate the airplane's speed, range, and engine cooling. Boeing ground crews would maintain the airplanes, and military pilots would teach Boeing flight personnel so that the company could build a staff to fly the B-29s as they rolled off the production lines.

General Wolfe was named commander of the newly formed 58th BW, VH (the VH designating "very heavy" aircraft), with headquarters in Marietta, Georgia. Along with the ASTB, Wolfe and his skeleton staff moved the 58th headquarters to Smokey Hill. One of Wright Field's brightest project officers was Maj. Vic Agather, who went to India with the 58th BW to help with maintenance as combat against Japan got underway.

Brig. Gen. "Rosey" O'Donnell (left), 73rd BW commander at Saipan, chats with Maj. Gen. Curtis LeMay (right), commander of the 21st BC after January 1945. Hurth Thompkins

A 9th BG Superfortress showing the group's insignia. Al Browne/Josh Curtis

Of the engine-fire problems, Major Agather said, "We had long since determined the troubles went back to the original design by Wright Aeronautical. Because a lighter-weight material was used to build the engine crankcases, the magnesium which was used rather than a heavier material such as aluminum, resulted in getting hotter, and when used on a sustained basis, it eventually exploded, or would swallow a valve, causing engine failure and, in most cases, fires.

"To correct this problem would require a redesign, and time had run out for any such delay. Consequently, we did patchwork, such as shortening the length of baffles and installing cuffs on the base of each propeller blade to increase airflow to exhaust valves."

Trained Mechanics Brought In

At Smokey Hill Army Air Base, USAAF-trained mechanics were brought into the B-29 program to assist in the ASTB testing of the YB-29s. John Mitchell was one of the USAAF mechanics. He recalls some of the things that took place during those days: "A Captain Morris was the engineering officer from Wright Field in charge of mechanics and support personnel. These people were drawn from all over the USAAF. For the most part, they were as new to the B-29 as the plane was new to the USAAF. The manufacturers of the airframe, engines, and other components sent technical representatives to lend assistance, but these men also had to learn the details of the equipment as testing proceeded.

"Slowly, the problems were mastered and by the end of the service test program, the ASTB produced the most highly trained and skilled B-29 mechanics and technicians then in the USAAF."

General Arnold personally selected the commanders of the four groups that made up the 58th BW, VH, which was activated on June 1, 1943. Four huge airfields with wide runways about 10,000ft long were built in Kansas to accommodate the new airplanes. Col. Lewis Parker was Arnold's choice to command the veteran 40th BG, to be located in Pratt, Kansas. To head the 462nd BG at Walker Field in Victoria, Kansas, was Col. Richard H. Carmichael. At Great Bend, Col. Alva L. Harvey would head the 444th BG, and Col. Howard F. Engler was named to head the 468th BG at Smokey Hill.

During the ASTB testing, Colonel Olson checked out Colonel Parker, who took a YB-29 to Pratt Army Air Field, and began setting up the 40th BG. Within three weeks, he had received two more B-29s. Colonel Harvey took the next three production planes to Great Bend to begin training the 444th BG. Harvey had served as B-29 project officer at Boeing Aircraft Co. and was moved to Wichita early in 1943, before assuming command of the 444th BG. Engler's 468th BG received the next three production B-29s from Wichita, and Carmichael took the next three for his 462nd BG at Walker Field.

Colonels Harvey and Parker were sent to England to observe the 8th Air Force combat operations and as observers to participate in a few combat missions. Parker's plane was shot down on his fifth mission and he sur-

vived the war as a German prisoner of war. Colonel Harvey returned to the States after five missions over Europe. He was the senior group commander of the 58th BW.

As future crew members were selected to fly and maintain the B-29s in combat, various schools were set up around the country. At Harvard, MIT, and Boca Raton, Florida, men were trained to operate the new AN/APQ-13 radar set that would be aboard each B-29. Wright Field set up a school to familiarize ground crew with the R-3350 engine. Gunners had to be taught how to operate the innovative new remote-controlled gunnery system, and the maintenance crew had to be taught how to maintain the pressurization system.

The author's first encounter with the B-29 Superfortress went something like this: The date was June 26, 1943. It was graduation day for about 200 aviation cadets of Pilot Class 43-F at Blackland Advanced Twin-Engine School in Waco, Texas. I was still more or less floating on Cloud Nine, having just received my new second lieutenant bars and, best of all, a pair of silver pilot's wings, when my flight instructor, Pilot Officer Donald Laver of the Royal Air Force (RAF), stopped by our table while we ate lunch in the officers' club. After lunch, we would get our assignments, preceded by a much-awaited two-week leave, before reporting to our new flying assignments; then after a much-awaited two-week leave, we would report to our new flying assignments.

Pilot Officer Laver was a product

Another B-29 crew poses in front of their new plane before heading to Guam. Pictured is crew no. P10 of the 60th BS, 39th BG, 314th BW. Elmer Jones, shown left, standing. Elmer Jones

Ground crewmen repair T-Square-44 Patches, s/n 42-24624, of the 498th BG, after a Japanese Zeke fighter strafed it on a retaliation raid on Saipan, November 24, 1944. This Superfortress still has the 20mm cannon in the tail. Josh Curtis

of America's Lend-Lease agreement with England in reverse. He was one of the many RAF pilots loaned to the USAAF to assist in training much-needed pilots to man the many bombers, fighters, and other aircraft rolling off the assembly lines of factories across the country. I considered it a special honor to have been one of his students. Laver wasted no time in giving me a hint of what was to come at the upcoming meeting.

"Mister 1, eh, I mean Lieutenant Marshall," my former instructor began. As he stood there beside our table, my mind pictured him as the perfect RAF pilot, in his royal blue uniform and well-trimmed mustache, reminding me of the newsreels or a movie portraying one of the few who Prime Minister Winston Churchill proudly told his nation about: "Never in the history of civilisation have so many owed so much to so few." He was, of course, talking about the heroics performed by the outmanned RAF pilots during the Battle of Britain when they defeated Marshal Goering's highly touted German Luftwaffe. "Have you had any mechanical engineering training in civil or military life?" Laver continued.

I was somewhat baffled at the question. "No sir," I replied immediately. The fact that I had completed an aircraft mechanics course at Chanute Field in 1941 before entering the aviation cadet program never crossed my mind. I asked him why the question at this time.

"Well," he said, "I heard a rumor that a few of you fellows will be assigned to some kind of special project, and I think your name is on that list."

"What kind of project?" I quizzed, as my pulse picked up.

"Nobody knows," he said. "Sounds like some sort of interesting experimental project, though. I wish I could tell you more, but I'm sure you will find out shortly!"

At the assignment meeting, the officer went through the list alphabetically, announcing assignments. As each name was called out, the recipient left the room after collecting his orders, which included a two-week leave. Most names called out were going to B-17 or B-24 transition school and a very few to fighters or instructor school. Bomber pilots were needed most at this time to carry the stepped-up air war to Germany.

Eleven of us were left seated in the near-empty room when the names and assignments were all called.

"O.K. fellows," the captain said, "You have been pegged for a special project and our orders are to hold you here at Blackland until we receive word about your new assignment."

That was it. Nobody knew anything! No leave, no word, no nothing—that's how it was for the next four days. The order finally came on July 1: We would clear the field, catch the 6:00pm train for Salina, Kansas, to become part of the K. B. Wolfe Special B-29 Project. The assignment was the most disheartening news we'd received since entering the cadet program. We would be enrolled in the first class of B-29 flight engineer school at Smokey Hill Army Air Field!

Beginning July 1, 1943, newly commissioned pilots gathered at Smokey Hill. We soon learned that all were former GIs who had completed airplane mechanics or specialty school before entering pilot training. It seemed that General Saunders, General Wolfe, or somebody had come up with the big idea that "These bright young men who had survived airplane mechanics school and also pilot training would be ideal people to become the third pilot aboard the new Super-

Joltin' Josie, *the first B-29 to land in the Mariana Islands on October, 12, 1944. Aboard were Brig. Gen. Haywood Hansell, commander of the 21st BC, and Maj. Jack Catton and crew.* Josh Curtis

Dauntless Dotty, *piloted by Bob Morgan of Memphis Belle fame, led the first B-29 raid on Tokyo, on November 24, 1944. Later, Dotty crashed into the sea on takeoff at Kwajalein Island en route to the United States just prior to the end of the war.* Warren Thompson

fortress, with primary duty of flight engineer." Having not yet even seen a B-29, we learned that the flight engineer would ride facing aft behind the pilots, monitoring a huge panel of instruments.

We crashed through the flight engineer course, saw our first B-29 later that month, but that's about all. No hands-on instruction was available,

but we did graduate. There would be no "washing out" and we were scattered among the four Groups that were forming in the new bases in Kansas. I went to Colonel Carmichael's 462nd BG at Walker Field. So far, to most of us flight engineer-pilots, the K. B. Wolfe Special B-29 Project was like cold water splashed in our faces. Had it not been for the pretty little "Rosie the Riveters" who were building the B-29s down at Wichita, our morale would have been much lower.

Fall weather in Kansas that year came on like a lion. B-29s began to trickle to the four bases. Before the airplanes could be delivered to the bases, however, they had to go to a modification center. In addition to Wright Field and others, a huge center for modifying the B-29s was opened in Birmingham, Alabama, where more than 9,000 people were employed to accelerate the changes to be made.

Before the real "Battle of Kansas" got underway, policy makers changed courses again to get better-qualified people to man the flight engineer seats. All of the pilot-flight engineer (FE) officers were shipped out to Roswell, New Mexico, to go through B-17 transition and rather than releasing us for a combat unit in Europe, we were held over to join the 73rd BW

Lucky 'Leven *carried some of the best nose art over Japan, but then orders came down in April 1945 banning "girlie" art. Lucky flew with the 498th BG, 73rd BW, Tinian Island.* Warren Thompson

that would follow the 58th BW as they vacated the bases in Kansas. Ground crew chiefs or experienced mechanics were given the jobs of flight engineers.

Also changed was the original plan for the newly formed 20th Bomber Command (BC). Originally, the 20th BC would include both the 58th BW and 73rd BW, which was also formed in June, and would go to the CBI theater. General Wolfe was made commander of the new bomber command and Colonel Harmon took over the job of commanding the 58th BW. The 73rd BW became the initial wing of the 21st BC, and the 58th would join the CBI theater and go into combat under the Matterhorn plan. Under this plan, the B-29s would be based in India, with forward bases in China. The 20th BC would supply its own planes for combat missions against Japanese targets, by flying bombs and extra gas across the Himalayan Mountains to bases in China. To accumulate enough of each to complete one combat mission, a B-29 would have to take about seven trips across the mountains.

Chapter 3

Ready or Not, the 58th Bombardment Wing Heads for India

In late November 1943, the Matterhorn plan was approved; Generalissimo Chiang Kai-shek promised to build bases in China, and the British agreed to provide bases in India. The decision to use the B-29s against Japan was never in real doubt, but there was much haggling when it came to how they should be used.

As the B-29s moved closer to overseas debarkation, theater commanders clamored for a piece of the action. Gen. Douglas Mac Arthur thought all the B-29s should be placed under his command, but others wanted to divide the lot. Gen. Claire Chennault, 14th AF commander in China, all but demanded that some of the Superfortresses be sent to him. Generalissimo Chiang Kai-shek wanted some and so did British Admiral Lord Louis Mountbatten. Even the US Navy wanted some for long-range reconnaissance flights.

Birth of the 20th Air Force

General Arnold and the Air War Plans Division found all of the requests for B-29s totally unsatisfactory. Brig. Gen. Haywood S. Hansell, Jr., recalls his part in these developments: "As a member of the Joint Plans Com-

Every crew was anxious to have its bomber named and illustrated properly. This B-29 flew with the 468th BG, 73rd BW, Saipan. Ken Rust

mittee, I got permission from General Arnold to approach Adm. Ernest Joseph King with a proposal for unified command of the B-29s.

"I pointed out to Admiral King a similarity between the command problem of the B-29s and that of the US fleet units who were temporarily based in the various ports, but the operational command of those fleet units resided not at the local base level, but at the top echelon of the Navy. Admiral King was a member of the Joint Chiefs of Staff (JCS) and commanded the US fleets, regardless of where their components were located. Base area commanders were responsible for the administrative and logistical support of fleet units and for the defense of the bases, but they did not have operational command. Unity of command of combat units was needed in the area of concerted combat.

"'The B-29 command problem was very similar,' I told the Admiral. 'Would it not be reasonable to solve it in a similar manner by providing unity of command at the highest level, and charging base commanders with administrative and logistical support and base defense? Top command could be vested in the JCS, with General Arnold as executive agent and commander of the B-29 force. Theater commanders could be charged with support, but not operational command.' Admiral King

said simply, 'I could find such an agreement acceptable.'

"Gen. George C. Marshall agreed. Thus was born the 20th Air Force, with Gen. Hap Arnold as its commander. The date was April 4, 1944."

Although the decision to concentrate the B-29s under JCS control made possible the development of the concerted bomber offensive against Japan, it did not mark the close of the argument from the theater field commanders. They continued their efforts to gain control of the B-29 units in their own areas. General MacArthur's headquarters was especially insistent and coupled its requests with personal letters from Gen. George Kenney to Arnold contending that B-29 operations out of the Mariana Islands against the Japanese home islands were militarily and technically unfeasible. At this time, plans had been formulated for the Navy, with Marine and Army troops, to invade the Marianas and to prepare one of the islands, Saipan, with a suitable base from which B-29 combat missions could be launched against targets in Japan.

With the activation of the 20th AF to operate under one commander and reporting only to the JCS, General Arnold, the new 20th AF commander, named General Hansell his chief of staff, responsible for the day-to-day activities of the 20th BC. He was assist-

The 20th AF patch insignia.

ed by Operation Deputy Col. Cecil Combs.

B-29 combat training continued at the Kansas bases as 1943 faded into history. There were still many bugs to be ironed out, as the battles continued. About 600 Boeing employees from the Wichita plant were sent to the B-29 bases in Kansas to try to solve the problems before the airplanes were sent overseas. Crews trained for combat flying B-17s. The bitterly cold Kansas winter was no help; mechanics had to work outside in freezing weather, because the hangars were not large enough for the B-29s. In the meantime, by December, the Bell plant in Georgia and the Renton plant were turning out B-29s ready to be modified, and the Omaha plant would be ready to start up by mid-1944.

General Wolfe Goes to India

In addition to training problems plaguing the B-29 program, General Arnold was deeply concerned with the quality and progress of bases being prepared in India and China. As 1943 ended and with President Roosevelt

breathing down his neck, he ordered General Wolfe to round up his 20th BC staff and check those bases. Wolfe arrived in India in January, and in early February reported that he had met with Generals Chennault and Stilwell and members of their staffs, as well as other key figures.

In India, existing airfields the British had used were brought up to B-29 standards. The southern Bengal area was chosen for the base area, because it was fairly safe from Japanese attacks and not far from port facilities at Calcutta. Wolfe decided on the Ganges plains about 70mi west of Calcutta to build the four bases, one each at Kharagpur, Chakulia, Piardoba, and Dudkhundi, and Kharagpur for his headquarters.

The Chinese bases were built in the Chengtu area, mostly using thousands of peasants who broke up stones and transported them by hand to build the runways. Washington accused the Chinese of greatly overcharging for this work, but they got the work done.

When the Dudkhundi base was finished and ready to accept the 444th BG, the personnel saw little improvements over the base they left. Years later, one of the aircraft commanders

of Colonel Harvey's group, Winton R. Close, had this tongue-in-cheek assessment of conditions at Dudkhundi: "In 1944, Dudkhundi was a little, rural village about 40mi northwest of Calcutta, India. It was not a very attractive place. In the dry season, it was flat, ugly, dirty, dusty, and hot. During the monsoon season, it was flat, ugly, dirty, and muddy. During the months of April through August—part of the dry season—it would become so hot in the middle of the day that one could not touch the aluminum skin of the B-29 without getting burned.

"It was not a nice place at all. The water supply was suspect, so we drank slightly diluted chlorine from Lister bags. There was no ice. There was no beer. The only distilled liquor came from Calcutta. Its brand name was Carew's. We called it Carew's Booze for combat crews. It came in three flavors: gin, rum, and whiskey. All three tasted exactly the same. The only difference was the coloring used in each: no color for gin, a light tinge of yellow for rum, and a sort of dark tan for whiskey."

Colonel Carmichael and his 462nd BG settled at Piardoba, and both the 468th BG and the 20th BC headquartered at Kharagpur. Each of the four groups of the 58th BW were now in India and anxious to get on with the task of bombing Japanese targets. They were assigned forward bases in China, from which the mission against Japan proper and other targets on the Chinese mainland, would originate. The 40th BG would operate out of Hsinching, China, the 444th BG from Kwanghan, the 462nd BG from Kiunglai, and the 468th BG from Pengshan.

When new combat crew members got their first look at the giant B-29 Superfortress, they were amazed at its size. It was a beautiful airplane. Weighing in at about 100,000lb empty, its gross load with fuel and bombs, plus the crew, increased to almost 140,000lb on missions to Japan during the low-altitude fire raids. This was about 20,000lb more than original specifications called for. The original design was for a total gross load of 120,000lb.

The airplane's wingspan was just short of 142ft from wing tip to wing tip, and from nose to tail, it measured 99ft. There were four remote-con-

A Superfortress in India. Note the guard at the front of the plane. Josh Curtis

trolled gun turrets, one forward on top of the fuselage and aft on top, with the same alignment on the bottom of its fuselage. Each turret had two .50cal air-cooled machine guns. The tail gunner's position also had twin .50s and originally contained a 20mm cannon (later removed). Broomsticks were installed after the cannon was removed, to make it appear to an attacking fighter that the cannon was still there. Two extra .50cal guns were later incorporated into the top forward turret. During World War II, 3,965 B-29s were built at an average of $600,000 each.

Denny D. Pidhayny, historian and recording secretary of the 58th Bomb Wing Association, quotes General Arnold in a fascinating story of how one of the most famous B-29s of World War II got its name: "On January 1, 1944, I was going through the Boeing Airplane Plant at Wichita, Kansas (where the giant new airplanes were being produced), looking over the B-29s as they were assembled. When they told me how many B-29s they planned to complete that month, I walked back down the line and picked an unfinished aircraft just a little beyond that goal. I wrote my name across the fuselage and said, 'This is

the plane I want this month.' The Superfortress I wrote my name on became known as the *General H. H. Arnold Special*.

"Needless to say, the Boeing people met that goal and shortly thereafter, Gen. [William S.] Knudsen, in an impressive ceremony, accepted the plane for the government. The crew that came to fly the plane to combat became known to everybody at the Boeing plant, and when the *Special* reached the Far East, the factory employees followed with pride each mission as closely as they could.

"Assigned to the 468th BG, 58th BW, which deployed to bases in India to begin combat operations against the Japanese via forward bases in China, the *General H. H. Arnold Special* began its sixteen-mission combat tour of duty on June 5, 1944. The mission was the first shakedown B-29 mission in combat. The target was the railway shops at Bangkok, Thailand.

"Mission number sixteen, and the final one for the *General H. H. Arnold Special*, took place on November 11, 1944. Flying from a forward base in the Chengtu area, the target was the Omura Aircraft Factory on Kyushu, one of Japan's home islands. While over the target, the pilot reported that

his airplane was low on gas. That was his last message.

"Later, intelligence learned the crew landed the *Special* at the Vladivostok Naval Air Station in Siberia. They were escorted on the last leg of their flight by ten Russian fighter planes, and then interned until their release by Iran on February 2, 1945."

General Arnold's promise to President Roosevelt that the B-29s would be headed to India by March 1, 1944, fell short this time by fewer than three weeks. Col. Frank Cook, a former Wright Field production engineering officer, took the first B-29, one of the original fourteen YB-29s built at Boeing's Wichita plant, off on a mission planned to confuse the Axis intelligence spy-ring en route to a newly enlarged base in India. The idea was to make it appear that the giant new bomber would be used in the European theater, rather than against the Japanese. Colonel Cook's flight plan took him on a criss-cross flight across the Atlantic. Within an hour after landing in England, a German reconnaissance plane recorded the arrival.

A mechanic removes the cowling on the huge R-3350 radial engine. Chuck Spieth

A formation of 462nd BG B-29s on their way to a target. Marshall

Neither the Germans nor Japanese were fooled by the ploy. They knew about the development of the long-range B-29, and the Japanese had long since determined that the Superfortresses would be stationed at the larger bases in India and in China, from which they would attempt to attack Japanese targets. The airplane was inspected by Generals Eisenhower and Doolittle, before Cook took off for India. He landed at the Karagpur base on April 6. His B-29 was not the first, but the second, B-29 to reach India.

First to Reach Bases in India

Brig. Gen. Blondie Saunders and Col. Jake Harman departed Kansas on March 25, leading a stream of brand-new B-29s to their overseas bases in India. Their first stop was Presque Isle, and from there they flew to Gander Lake, Newfoundland. Each leg of the journey into the unknown was briefed before departure to the next destination, which in itself was confusing to some of the crew members. After Gander Lake came Marrakech, French Morocco, then Cairo, Egypt, and on to Karachi. Leaving Karachi, Saunders and Harman landed at the Chakulia base on April 2, 1944. Theirs was the first B-29 to reach the theater from which they would begin combat against Japan. General Wolfe and aides were on hand to greet them.

Saunders also pioneered the route over the Himalayan Mountains to the forward base of Kwanghan at Cheng-tu, China. He was met by Chinese dignitaries and Maj. Gen. Claire Chennault, commander of the US 14th AF, which was based in China. More than 75,000 Chinese laborers were also there when the Superfortress landed, all shouting "Ding hao," or "Congratulations." Crews from the 40th BG were among the first arrivals and, as commander of the 40th BG, Colonel Harman assumed command of the advance echelon.

The climate change from a cold environment to the suffocatingly hot and dry desert played havoc with the troubled R-3350 engines. At one point during the deployment, after several planes were lost due to engine failures, General Wolfe wired General Arnold and insisted that a better engine cooling system still had to be developed before the B-29s could possibly be combat ready. At this point, all B-29s were grounded en route to overseas bases and more field modifications were made on cowl flaps and crossover oil tubes were installed from the intake to the rocker box of the top cylinders on both rows of the twin engines. After this modification, the flights resumed, and by May 8, 130 B-29s had arrived at the Indian bases.

Since the Dudkhundi base was not yet ready to receive it, the 444th BG was routed temporarily to another British base at Charra, where steel matting was used to extend the runways for the B-29s. The Group arrived at Charra on April 12.

First Enemy Attack, First Injury

One of the major concerns General Wolfe had with his attack force now at bases in India lay with getting supplies across the Himalayas to the forward bases in China. Since no transport planes were available, the solution was to use the B-29s to fly the extra fuel and bombs over the "Hump" and store them at their forward bases until enough supplies were accumulated for a bombing raid on a Japanese target.

It was during one of these Hump supply trips that the B-29s' first attack by Japanese fighters and the first B-29 crew member injury took place. On April 26, 1944, shortly after the B-29s started arriving in the CBI theater and two days after the India-to-China supply run was initiated, the Superfortress piloted by Maj. Charles Hansen and transporting fuel was attacked by six Japanese Oscars. After staying out of range for 15 or 20min, one of the enemy planes suddenly whipped out of formation and twisted toward the B-29. During the attack, Sgt. Walter W. Gilonske was injured, becoming the first B-29 crewman in World War II to receive injuries from an enemy attack.

The enemy attack lasted about 25min before the Japanese broke off.

A weapons carrier loaded with 2,000lb high-explosive bombs. Chuck Spieth

One of the airplanes left the scene smoking as a result of fire from the tail gunner's position. Major Hansen and his crew were credited with two historical "firsts" in the B-29 offensive against Japan.

Bill Rooney, who edits the quarterly publication *Memories* for the 40th BG, tells an interesting story of President Roosevelt's introduction to the Boeing B-29 Superfortress: "On February 20, 1944, Col. Walter Lucas [aircraft commander in the 40th BG] and his crew, plus two crew chiefs, were dispatched to Washington, DC, in B-29 no. 42-6303. They were to land at Bolling Field. As far as can be determined, no reason was given to the crew for making the flight. Bolling Field, at that time, had four runways, the longest of which was 6,000ft. Colonel Lucas landed the airplane and was met by none other than Gen. H. H. Arnold himself. It was learned then that the purpose of the flight was to show the B-29 to President Roosevelt.

[Considering that the cost of the B-29 project was more than the atomic bomb project—$3 billion compared to $2 billion—this was a significant occasion.]

"General Arnold met each member of the crew and had each one brief him on his duties. The following day, February 21, between 4:00 and 4:30pm, the President came to Bolling Field and visited the plane. His chauffeur drove the limousine to the front of the plane. The President did not leave the car, but he gave the giant bomber a close scrutiny. Accompanying the President were his daughter, Anna, and her two children, Eleanor and Curtis. They did get out of the car and inspected the plane. The President flashed his famous smile at the crew members as he left."

Chapter 4

20th Bomber Command Poised for Combat

With 120 Superfortresses in India by May 8, 1944, ready and anxious to get the show started, General Wolfe and his staff wasted no time preparing plans for the first strike against Japanese targets.

The B-29s, each with an extra engine aboard, had made the long trip from the States with some difficulty, losing five planes en route, but otherwise arriving in fair condition. There had been a few cases where plexiglass bubble blisters protecting gunners operating remote-controlled gun turrets blew out due to climatic changes. The engine overheating problem was not yet conquered.

Ground personnel were already in place when the combat crews arrived, and the crew complement had been standardized in all four groups, each with four squadrons. (The 58th BW was the only wing to have four squadrons per group.) By October 1944, three squadrons became standard.

As the 58th BW prepared for its first mission, a major decision had been made to change plans for the 73rd BW, now training at the vacated Kansas bases. The 73rd would be sent to Saipan as the initial wing of the

Appropriately named Censored. *This aircraft flew with the 444th BG, 58th BW, Tinian Island.* Ken Rust

21st BC. American forces planned to attack and capture Saipan, located in the Pacific about 1,500mi south of Tokyo, by July 1944.

The crew complement in the B-29s consisted of eleven men. Five were officers—the aircraft commander, pilot, bombardier, navigator, and flight engineer—and six were enlisted men—the central fire control gunner, left and right gunners, tail gunner, radio operator, and radar operator. This crew configuration was the same in the 73rd BW. By mid-1944, the flight engineer ranks had been opened to enlisted men. Some of these men were among those who had replaced the pilot-flight engineer officers back in 1943. Also, some of these enlisted men were offered a commission, and a few received commissions after having been given the rank of flight officer. Later in the war, because of the highly classified electronic equipment, such as high-tech radar and the new navigational aid Loran, the crews had one or two more officers.

First B-29 Raid Was to Bangkok

The 58th BW commander, Brig. Gen. Blondie Saunders, led the first B-29 combat mission against a Japanese target on June 5, 1944, one day before another memorable occasion, that of the second front invasion of Europe by Allied forces led by Allied Supreme Commander "Ike" Eisenhower. Sched-

uled for a strike—or a "shakedown mission," as some called it—against the Makasan Railway Yards at Bangkok, Thailand were 112 B-29s, ninety-eight of which proceeded toward the target; only seventy-seven made it to the target area.

The mission, with a nighttime takeoff, involved a 2,261mi round trip, the longest bombing mission yet of World War II. It was a daylight attack from 23,000ft altitude. Only forty-eight planes were able to bomb the target, and five of the bombers were lost to mechanical problems. None were lost to enemy action.

The nighttime takeoffs really woke up the base. One-hundred or more B-29s taking off, which lasted almost 90min, literally shook the earth, as witnessed by Sgt. Mary Thomas of the Red Cross, stationed with the 22nd Air Depot, 20th BC, at Kharagpur. She remembers how it was when the big bombers woke her up, to go on a prowl: "The 'basha' where the Red Cross girls lived was down near the end of the 2mi-long runway, and when they began revving up the engines on the B-29s, not only could you hear the sound, but the ground reverberated as well.

"I would grab my flashlight, tie a scarf around my head, and run out between the buildings, hoping the sound of my boots would scare away the snakes. I didn't have time to worry about the panthers they said lived in

Bombs spew from the bomb bays of the 497th BG over a target in Japan. Chuck Spieth

the nearby jungles. I just wanted to get to the place where the big silver planes stopped before they turned out on the runway. I could see the aircraft coming one behind the other down the taxi strip as they left the herring-boned side ramps.

"Where men were still working on planes, there were big, hazy patches of light from the lamps mounted on top of tall metal stands that could be wheeled to where they were needed, but as the planes approached the end

of the runway, it was all dark except for the little lights on their fuselages. From where I stood, the blisters were all dark. I couldn't see the faces of the crew members, but I knew they were there.

"I did as the men had asked after they learned I always came out to watch the night takeoff. I held the flashlight under my chin and made the "Ding Hao" sign with my right hand, my thumb pointing up. Sometimes, the gunners would reply by making a cross with their lights inside the blisters. While the pilots checked the magnetos, I walked around under the plane and down the other side, waving to the right gunner, as well.

Then I'd dash under the tail and back to the outside edge of the strip as the huge plane turned right onto the runway. I could feel the engines roar, and then she was off—moving slowly at first because she was so heavy with full fuel tanks, a heavy bomb load, and a precious cargo of men. The runway was long, over 2mi. As an aid to the pilots, a huge magenta-colored light was pointed skyward at the far end so they could judge how much runway they had left. The planes had to be airborne by the time they crossed the colored beam or they'd never make it off the ground. It was scary and I prayed hard until I saw the last plane—like a silver-grey dragonfly, its wings headed with tiny lights—lift into the night sky and disappear.

"Then I would turn as the next big bomber lumbered into place, flick on my flashlight, and repeat my ritual for its crew. I didn't know all their names; there were so many that we called them by their rank. Sergeant, mostly, because there seemed to be very few privates or corporals in such a specialized operation. I knew them by the names of the planes they flew in. We'd say, he's from *Miss Shorty*, or *Lassie*, or the *Mary K*, or the *Raiden Maiden*. I admired them and loved them because they were men like my brother, Tom, who was flying a Navy Liberator in the Pacific."

Action in the Pacific

As the 58th BW geared up for the first B-29 strike against the Japanese homeland, things were beginning to happen in the Pacific that would have great bearings on the B-29 program as a whole. At about 4:30pm on June 15, 1944, General Saunders, flying with 468th BG commander, Col. Howard Engler, took off from their forward base in China, heading for Kyushu, Japan. It was a night strike against what was billed as "the Pittsburgh of Japan," the Imperial Iron and Steel Works at Yawata, located on the southern-most home island of Kyushu.

Sixty-eight B-29s were airborne for the mission, but aborts stopped all but forty-seven from making it to the target area. The results of the raid were not too impressive, but the strike against Yawata had psychological impact. Not since the Jimmy Doolittle raid of April 18, 1942, had an enemy airplane darkened the skies above a Japanese home island, and it was the first time B-29s had made such an attack.

The other important development of June 15 was the announcement that a giant Navy task force had landed a Marine invasion force on Saipan. The purpose of this invasion was to secure the island and build a B-29 base from which an all-out assault against the entire main Japanese home islands could begin.

Back in the States, the second B-29 wing, the 73rd BW, had completed its third month of combat training at the same bases in Kansas the 58th

British Admiral Lord Louis Mountbatten, the Southeast Asia theater commander, and Brig. Gen. Roger Ramey prepare to inspect the 40th BG in India. Josh Curtis

BW had vacated when it left for India in April. Like the 58th BW, the 73rd was having to use old B-17s to train with because factories could not supply enough B-29s.

The AN/APQ-13 radar unit in each of the B-29s was so new that very few aircraft commanders, pilots, or even navigators had much faith in it. Each crew had a trained radar operator aboard, but he had a hard time convincing his crew that they should rely on the unit more heavily. Sgt. Francis Boyer, a radar operator in the 462nd BG based at Piardoba, recalls how his crew members became thoroughly convinced of the merits of the radar set: "Once on a mission to Formosa from our India base," he recalls, "we got lost. One engine failed before reaching the target, and then on our way home, a second engine decided to quit. Our pilot told us to start throwing out everything we could pry loose to lighten the plane, so we could try to gain some altitude. I asked him, 'How about the radar set?' He came back with, 'No! Anything but the radar, that's our only hope of reaching base safely!' So it was left up to me as the radar operator to guide us through the mountain passes.

"We were very close to bailing out when we finally located an airfield not very far north of our own base. It was a very dark night and, unfortunately, all the lights on the runways were

turned off because the base was under a Jap air-raid attack. We finally got in touch with the tower and told them about our desperate situation, and they turned the lights on long enough for us to scoot in for a hair-raising landing. But any landing you can walk away from is a good one, so the saying went. Our CFC gunner risked breaking his legs by leaping from the side door before the ladder was lowered, a distance of over 10ft from the ground. He immediately bent down and kissed the ground.

"After that mission, our entire crew's faith in the new-fangled radar unit was strictly enhanced!"

First B-29 Mine-Laying Mission

The Boeing B-29 Superfortress was built specifically for high-altitude precision bombing, with hopes of destroying the Japanese will to continue the war. As hostilities progressed, however, bombing altitudes fluctuated from tree-top level to more than 6mi high. The types of weaponry also varied.

A drastic change from the normal task of the B-29s took place on the night of August 10, 1944, when four-

A 498th BG B-29 rests on its hardstand at Saipan. Speith

teen Superfortresses from the 462nd BG, led by Col. Richard Carmichael, took off to lay mines in the Moesi River at Palembang, Sumatra. This was responsible for a major change in the air war against Japan.

The Palembang mission was part of a three-pronged strike at Japanese targets. Fifty-six B-29s from the 58th BW participated in the mission. Thirty-nine airplanes hit the Pladjoe Oil Refinery complex. One plane was lost. Eight of the mine layers, each plane carrying two mines, made it to their target area, and dropped the mines from altitudes of 100 to 1,000ft. The mission would be the longest made by B-29s in the CBI theater, more than 4,200mi nonstop. Time in the air averaged 19hr. The mission was so long that it was staged from a British base at China Bay near Trincomalee, Ceylon (now known as Sri Lanka).

During this double-barreled attack, a strike force of B-29s struck Nagasaki, one of the home islands of Japan, located in Kyushu. One plane from this force was also lost.

The mine-laying mission illustrates the cooperation established by the Allies working together to defeat Japan. This story of how the B-29s became involved in mine warfare is told, in part, by one of the Navy's experts in the field, R. Adm. K. L. Veth, US Navy (Ret.).

In 1944, Admiral Veth, then a lieutenant commander in the Naval Mine Warfare Section, was assigned to Admiral Lord Louis Mountbatten's Southeast Asia Command. When the decision was made to use B-29s to drop mines, Veth was loaned to the 20th BC to teach B-29 personnel about mine warfare.

In a speech to the 58th BW Association members several years ago, Veth had this to say about the B-29 mining effort: "The post-war analysis revealed an interesting story. The B-29 mining effort against the Japanese homeland consisted of some 1,528 sorties, or 5.7% of the entire B-29 strike force against Japan. Over 12,000 mines were dropped in Japanese waters. These mines, combined with another 13,000 laid by aircraft, submarines, and ships in the so-called outer zone of Malaysia, Indochina, and Pacific islands, had rather phenomenal results.

"In the last six months of the war, these mines sunk and damaged more Japanese shipping than all other forms of attacks put together—that in-

cluded all of the submarines, all the Navy ships' gunfire, and all the Navy and USAAF bombing attacks on shipping during the six months' period. Their combined results were less than the results of the mining attacks, most of which was accomplished by the B-29s.

"The code name 'Operation Starvation' was a most appropriate one. Near the end of the war, a group of Japanese industrialists made a report to the Japanese military that, if the war continued for another year; seven million Japanese would die of starvation. By the summer of 1945, the average calorie intake of each Japanese was less than half that of each American. In fact, it was only about 1,400 calories a day, which is what most doctors consider a weight-losing diet.

"An example to illustrate how desperate the Japanese were for rice. In order to get rice supplies from Korea to Japan with no ships, they were forced to partially fill barrels with rice, dump them in the ocean off Korea, and let them drift by ocean current to the west coast of Japan.

"Monthly shipping through the vital Shimonoseki Straits was reduced from over 500,000 tons in March 1944 to a trickle of only 5,000 tons by August of 1945. Much of the decrease was a direct result of B-29 mining."

In speaking of the overall effect the mine laying effort of the B-29s had on Japan, pertained not only to the later dropping of mines by the 58th BW planes on the dry-docks at Singapore, which was in support of the Philippine Sea war. Other mining missions by the 58th BW were to Saigon, Jahoce Straits, Shanghai and Yangtze. The 313th Bomb Wing's stepped up mining efforts with excellent results.

The second element of the three-pronged strike at Japanese targets was the mine drop on the Moesi River. Ed Perry, Group Navigator for the 462nd Group and sitting in the lead ship with Group Commander Carmichael, had this to say about that historical mission: "The fourteen crews from the 462nd Group were integral, experienced crews. The only substitutions were aboard our aircraft—where Col. Dick Carmichael flew as aircraft commander and mission leader and I replaced the navigator. The normal crew commander [Maj. Conrad Colander] flew co-pilot and Commander Veth flew as observer.

"The plan had called for release of the mines in the river using radar if necessary. However, as we approached the IP, we could see that conditions were very good for visual release. There was a bright, full moon at about 11 o'clock, which reflected off the river surface. Tall trees along the river really highlighted the water surface, with the trees being quite dark and the river surface shimmering from the rays of the moon. Our release points were the furthest down river, therefore, the one closest to the aiming points being attacked by the bombers. Before our release, we could see bombs going off at about 2 o'clock. We could see anti-aircraft fire and searchlights across the area. "Red," our bombardier, and the gunners did some low-level strafing as we went upstream to our release points. Since we were the first low-level aircraft along the river, we had the element of surprise in our favor.

"As we approached the scheduled release for our two mines, we saw a large ship, presumably a tanker, in the channel. Red released our mine before we reached the ship, strafed the ship as we passed overhead, at not more than 350ft altitude, and released the second mine just beyond the ship. The tail gunner reported that both mines entered the channel. At this point, we broke left away from the aiming points for the B-29s dropping the bombs, and started our climb out."

Only eight of the fourteen aircraft loaded with mines reached the target, but all crews made it back to their home base. Thirty-nine of the forty-one aircraft carrying bombs made it to the target, but one plane crew failed to return to home base.

The logistical problem of getting gasoline and bombs to China with which to fly missions out of that forward area to targets in Japan were formidable beyond belief. Washington leaders put the blame, evidently, on the leadership in the field, and General Wolfe, who had shouldered one of the heaviest responsibilities of the B-29 project from its beginning up through the early stages of combat,

would shoulder the blame for the early unsatisfactory results.

Mechanical problems and bad weather teamed up at times, forcing crews flying over the Hump from India to the forward bases in China to bail out over the treacherous Himalayas. Some were more fortunate than others and lived to tell of the experience. Stubbs Roberts, flight engineer on the John Sims crew in the 468th BG, thinks he established a record in B-29 bail-outs: "Twice, I had to hit the silk because of mechanical trouble. Each time with a different crew, my bails took place on both sides of the Hump. Our first two attempts to fly safely over the world's tallest mountains with my regular crew ended in a bail-out when two engines failed just as we entered the crest of the mountains. We turned around to return to our base in India, but when another engine failed, Sims gave the bail-out signal. We all were lucky enough to make it out of the plane and eventually make it back to our base at Kharagpur.

"My second encounter at looking up at a silk canopy of a parachute came on a supply run to Pengshan. Fate had placed me in the flight engineer's seat flying with another crew.

Superfortress being fueled up. These huge bombers carried as much as 8,000gal on long missions. Speith

Jim Patillo's flight engineer reported to sick call the morning of this particular flight, so operations assigned me to fill in for him. This time, the flight went well until we started our descent into A-17, our destination at Pengshan, China. Suddenly, during the descent, propellers on two engines ran away, and the pilot could hardly control the plane. He finally passed the bail-out word, now becoming a familiar word to me. The entire crew made it out of the plane, but we lost the co-pilot and one of the gunners.

"We were eventually picked up by friendly Chinese civilians, and were treated like heroes. After spending a couple of nights in a small village, we were escorted by Chinese soldiers, transporting us by boat and cart to Pengshan. By this time, I was beginning to wonder what kind of card fate was holding for me."

Nineteen forty-four was an eventful year for changes in command. In the spring, General Hansell was put in charge of the 21st BC, relieved as chief

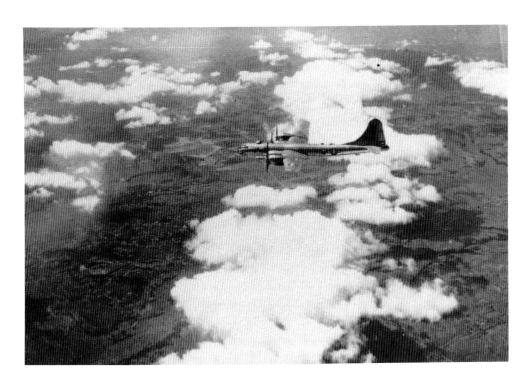

A lone Superfortress over the Indian countryside. Josh Curtis

of staff of the 20th AF by Brig. Gen. Lauris Norstad. And on August 29, 1944, cigar-smoking Maj. Gen. Curtis E. LeMay was named to replace General Wolfe as commander of the 20th BC. As the youngest major general in the US Army at the age of thirty-eight, LeMay had earned quite a reputation as commander of a B-17 Flying Fortress air division in Europe. He was a tough, Patton-type commander, who knew how to get things done.

It didn't take LeMay long to learn that he had stepped up to the plate in an entirely different ball game. The difference between the European air war and the new one he inherited was like going from daylight to nighttime. LeMay came aboard, full of confidence, however, and was equal to the task. He immediately stepped up the frequency of B-29 missions and intensified the training of combat crews. At the same time, he cut back the number of missions out of China in favor of such missions as those to Singapore and other targets flown from base in India where logistical support was manageable.

Some of the crews on the early missions in the CBI theater were for-

tunate enough to find British airstrips in the area on which to make emergency landings. Bill Garland, aircraft commander of *Ready Betty* in the 468th BG, describes such an emergency landing he and his crew made in Burma: "One day, we were returning from Sumatra and were low on fuel. So I decided to attempt a landing on an improvised dirt P-38 strip at Akyab, Burma. The airstrip had been captured by British troops only three days earlier. After landing, we walked over to talk to some British soldiers who were cooking dinner in a large black pot suspended over an open fire on a wooden tripod. The scene reminded us of the comic cartoon of the Katzenjammer Kids.

"Since we needed gas to get back to our base, we did a little bartering with the soldiers. We gave them a few crates of K-rations we had stashed in the back of our B-29, and they responded by giving us many 5gal tins of gasoline, which we poured into our fuel tanks by hand. We thanked them and made a hair-raising takeoff from the short air strip, and returned to our base in China."

B-29s Converted for Photo Reconnaissance

Photo reconnaissance had not reached its zenith during initial 20th

BC operations in the CBI theater. As early as March 1944, the Air Material Command in Washington had directed the Air Technical Service Command, in cooperation with Boeing Co. and Fairchild, to design a photo-reconnaissance version of the B-29. On April 7, 1944, requirement deadlines were set for the modification program, which was designated Project 98115. Initially, twelve airplanes were allocated for the project, all of which were to be completed by August 1; the prototype, to be called F-13, was to be finished by June 1.

It was apparent, because of delays, that the F-13s would not be operational when the 58th BW was ready for the first bombing raid against Bangkok, June 1, so the 21st BC's maintenance division was ordered to convert a B-29 into a photo-reconnaissance aircraft for temporary use in the 58th BW. These aircraft, called FB-29s and nicknamed "Photo Joes," would fill the bill for camera work and some were even equipped with radar countermeasures.

The first converted FB-29 was sent to the 444th BG's forward base at Chengtu, China, on June 15, 1944, which was the day of the first B-29 strike against Japan proper, at Yawata. The crew was scheduled for photo missions that same day, but the airplane crashed on takeoff and the entire crew was lost. The second FB-29, which was assigned to the 468th BG's forward base at Jsinching, China, was also lost after seven photo missions to obtain information for the Army and Navy prior to the Philippine landings in October. One of the most successful FB-29s was a converted B-29 belonging to the 40th BG. It made several post-attack photo missions to Anshan, North China; Palembang, Sumatra; and at Nagasaki and Sasebo, Kyushu. During September 1944, this FB-29 was ordered to cover specific points of interest in Okinawa in conjunction with future carrier strikes by the Navy.

In October 1944, all aircraft assigned to photo work, which included the FB-29s and some regular B-29s that had not been fully converted, were organized into a single unit called the Photo-Reconnaissance Detachment, 20th BC. Maj. Harry B.

Allen was named detachment commander, its headquarters was at the 40th BG forward base of Hsinching, and its airplanes were kept at their home stations of Chengtu, Pengshan, and Hsinching.

The 3rd Photo-Reconnaissance Squadron (PRS), which had trained at Salina, Kansas, was being deployed to Saipan to work with the 21st BC in October. During October, General Hansell ordered some of the F-13s to China for the 20th BC. By the end of the month, four of these planes had reached China and began operations as the 1st PRS.

During World War II, men with special analytical skills served with an organization known as the USAAF Operations Analysis Committee. They served mostly in a civilian capacity, but usually were given a field-grade rank or higher.

As an example of how Operations Analysis worked, consider this request made by the 20th BC. In 1943, after the B-29 combat operations got underway in the CBI theater, the 20th BC

asked the Operations Analysis Committee if they could furnish a gunnery expert to investigate combat losses of the B-29s. Alex E. S. Green, who had considerable experience in conducting air-to-air gunnery, was chosen to go to the combat theater to analyze problems in the B-29 gunnery system and offer suggestions for better performance.

The following is his report on how the B-29 gunnery system was improved: "After several weeks of briefing and study of the B-29's gunnery system and its combat problems at Wright Field, Elgin Field, and the Pentagon, I flew by Air Transport Command (ATC) to the Kharagpur, India, headquarters of the 20th BC. My first trip over the 'Hump' to our advanced base in Chengtu, China, was in a B-29 with General LeMay as the command pilot. My purpose was to gather information from the gunnery officers, intelligence officers, and crews that had witnessed the loss of other planes in their formations. After six weeks involving a second trip to

Dina Might *was a lead plane, as designated by the yellow and black stripes around the tail. Two crew member sit atop the bomb load of twenty-four 500lb bombs.* Teed/Josh Curtis

Chengtu, my analysis showed that we had shot down seventy fighters for each B-29 lost in attacks from the rear, whereas we shot down only three fighters for each B-29 lost in attacks from the front [6]. These results were in direct contradiction to the results of a massive state-side simulated combat study carried out near Alamogordo, New Mexico, which had concluded that the B-29 would be most vulnerable to rear attacks. Nevertheless, the gunnery and intelligence officers endorsed my analysis, and General LeMay modified our formations to bring greater firepower against frontal attacks. I also proposed a simplified way of using the front gunsight to compensate for the short engagement time and this anticipated 'vulnerability' to frontal attacks. By January 1945, the problem was contained."

Airborn *flew with the 444th BG, 58th BW,*
Tinian Island. Ken Rust

Chapter 5

21st Bomber Command Absorbs 73rd Wing

Early organizational plans for the 20th AF called for the 1st BC to have two wings, the 58th and the 73rd, both slated for India with advance bases in China, from which the bombing of Japan would originate. Along with a series of policy changes, only one wing, the 58th, was assigned to the 20th BC.

Original plans called for the 20th AF to have, eventually, three or four bomber commands: the 20th BC in India-China; the 21st BC in the Marianas; the 22nd BC in the Philippines, Formosa, or Okinawa; and perhaps the 23rd BC in Alaska. The total strength of the 20th AF would be 1,000–1,500 operational B-29s and additional escort fighters.

Hampered by the horrible logistical problems of flying bombs and gasoline across the Hump to the forward bases in China, a decision was made in 1943 to step up the invasion of the Marianas, and launch B-29 bombing attacks from at least three islands in that group as early as possible. This decision did not set well with General MacArthur, because he thought the best way to get to Japan was to go through the Philippines.

On November 28, 1943, the 73rd BW, VH, was inaugurated at Salina, Kansas, with Col. Thomas H. Chapman as first wing commander. In December 1943, the Wing did nothing but accumulate personnel, mostly

overages from the 58th BW and the 20th BC. Most of these men were overseas veterans—specialists, pilots, bombardiers, flight engineers, navigators—and were assigned to the 2nd AF, which would be charged with combat operational training of the 73rd BW personnel. They waited up to four months at the collecting point—Clovis, New Mexico, Air Base—for the 58th BW to vacate the four bases at Pratt, Great Bend, Victoria, and Salina.

The sugar mill at Saipan after bombardment by Navy, before the island was invaded. Speith

21st Bomber Command Activated

The 21st BC was activated at Smokey Hill on March 1, 1944. Brig. Gen. Emmett ("Rosey") O'Donnell assumed command of the 73rd BW on March 15, and by March 27, wing

The Twentieth Century Limited *flew with the 881 BS, 500th BG. This aircraft arrived at Saipan in early December 1944. It was commanded by Capt. Tull K. McGuire and flew fifty-one missions, surviving the war. McGuire and crew were lost when they ditched another aircraft, Z-Square-13, after bombing Tokyo.* Hurth Thompkins

headquarters moved to Colorado Springs, Colorado, also home to the 2nd AF. Later, the 21st BC would move to Peterson Field in Colorado Springs, Colorado, to be near the new headquarters of its 73rd BW.

All four of the 73rd BW's groups were activated by General Order No. 176 that activated the wing headquarters. These groups were the 497th BG at Biggs Field in El Paso, Texas; the 498th BG at Clovis Army Air Field in New Mexico; the 499th BG at Davis-Monthan Field in Tucson, Arizona; and the 500th BG at Gowan Field in Boise, Idaho.

Each of the groups originally had four squadrons and a photo lab, but before training got underway, the number of squadrons was reduced to

three for each group. The groups would train with the 58th BW until it left for India.

General Hansell understood the enormous pressure the 21st BC was under to perform. "One major slip," he said, "and the critics would have had their way—the 20th AF would have been dismembered and parceled out to the various theaters."

When the 58th BW moved out of their bases for India in early April 1944, the 497th BG, under the command of Col. Stewart P. Wright, went to Pratt; Col. Wiley D. Ganey, in command of the 498th, went to Great Bend; the 499th BG, under Col. Samuel R. Harris, moved to Salina; and Col. Richard T. King, Jr., in command of the 500th BG, went to Victoria. Combat training began immediately, even though there was an extreme scarcity of B-29s to train with. Like the 58th BW crews before them, the 73rd BW crews were trained primarily on old B-17s.

On June 1, 1944, the 2nd AF Headquarters announced the assignment of four experienced service groups, then stationed at Tinker Field,

Oklahoma, to service the 73rd BW planes at its overseas base. They were the Sixty-fifth, Ninety-first, 303rd, and 330th. The service groups would remain at Tinker Field until time to depart for overseas.

Other support units were being integrated into the 21st BC as extensive combat training got underway. In April 1944, the 3rd Combat Mapping Squadron (CMS) was ordered from its assignment in North Africa to return to the United States for reorganization and training, equipped with the F-13s. The unit arrived at Smokey Hill Army Air Field, to begin training for B-29 support activities.

73rd Wing Combat Training

Combat crew members arriving at their bases in Kansas during April immediately got assignments, met their aircraft commander and other crew members, and happily began flight training as a tight-knit unit.

With a shortage of B-29s to train with, each squadron having only one or two B-29s, old B-17s were used to accomplish some of the training missions. All types of combat-oriented missions were included in the required quota before overseas deployment

Each crew was required to complete a certain number of long-range, mostly over water, missions. With several 100lb bombs aboard, a long-range mission would be scheduled to fly from a Kansas base to the Gulf Coast, south of Houston, Texas, continue at about 3,000ft altitude over water for about 200mi, climb to an altitude of 20,000ft, drop the bombs on a designated little island in the Gulf of Mexico, then proceed to a spot just south of Cuba. Since the United States had the Batista Field USAAF Base in Cuba, the crew was authorized to make an emergency landing there—but only if the airplane was having trouble.

Warren G. Moses, a flight engineer with the 874th BS, 499th BG, 73rd BW, training at Great Bend, Kansas, related an interesting account of the time his crew had to land in Cuba. Kansas was one of two remaining "dry" states, as everyone knew. Moses was the chief monitor of the Superfortress engines, and he was supposed to be the most knowledgeable man aboard to determine the safety factors and performance of the plane. Crew members were always kidding him about not finding something wrong with the airplane, especially on some of the more interesting cross-country training flights—perhaps requiring an emergency landing at a fun-filled town. Even before they took off on the Cuba mission, it was almost a unanimous belief among members of the crew that something would happen to the plane on this trip, causing an emergency landing at Batista Field, with at least an overnight stay and a night on the town of Havana.

"As we flew along," according to Moses, "the intercom was filled with speculative chatter regarding the possibility of landing in Cuba. Like an answer to our prayers, the fuel pressure on our no. 3 engine began to fall off as we began our climb to 20,000ft. I increased the boost, but the pressure continued to drop and the engine began to overheat. It soon became evident that we would have to shut the engine down, so, gleefully, we throttled the engine back, dropped our bombs on the designated target, and headed for Batista Field.

"We didn't make it into Havana that night, but we got our kicks at the Officers' Club on Batista Field. We had a great evening at the Club, enjoying cheap drinks and good tropical food. Then we found out that we could buy liquor by the bottle at the Club at tax-free prices, which came out to about a dollar a bottle. The Club okayed my check, so we proceeded to buy twenty-three cases of scotch, bourbon, and a marvelous Cuban rum, Ron Anejo, which the locals told us was better than scotch. We figured we'd make a lot of long-standing friends when we returned to Kansas with our new-found loot.

"They checked our 'faulty' engine out real good and told me, as if I didn't already know, it was OK and ready to go. Before leaving, however, we got a message from none other than the commanding general of the Caribbean Command, Lt. Gen. George H. Brett, who said he'd sure like to look over the B-29. He had never seen one before, so we took him up for a short hop and he seemed overjoyed.

"After flying the General around the island for about an hour, we land-

Flak Maid—*not bad. This aircraft flew with the 444th BG, 58th BW, Tinian Island.* Ken Rust

ed and soon departed for our home base at Great Bend, Kansas, our contraband well covered and lashed down in the rear of the plane.

"As we neared the Florida coastline, I suddenly felt the all-too-familiar 't-hump' on my throttle handle, the sound of an engine swallowing a valve, and I yelled to Jack Reed, our pilot, to feather the no. 3 engine. This time it was for real. We immediately decided not to try to fly the remaining 1,500mi on three engines, so we landed at Boca Raton, Florida.

"We were, of course, instant celebrities because no B-29 had been seen there before. Since we had arrived from Cuba, the US Customs Inspector was also on hand to greet us. Jack immediately got to the base commanding officer and impressed on him the 'secret' nature of our aircraft. The commanding officer quickly surrounded our plane with MPs, who were instructed to allow no one near it except the crew members. The Customs Inspector was not permitted to go on board, much to our vast relief, because no duty had been paid on the booze."

The B-29 remained on a sort of classified status up through the months the 73rd was in combat operational training. When crews had to make forced landings anywhere in the United States, orders were that they should try to make it to a military air base and before landing request that a military police detachment be available to guard the aircraft to prevent anyone from entering it. On any given cross-country, pilots were given locations of airfields with runways long enough to accommodate the huge B-29.

This author and crew had to make such an emergency landing at Dalhart, Texas, after an over-water trip to Cuba. We were somewhere over west Texas at about 27,000ft altitude when we experienced oil pressure problems in one of the engines. Aircraft commander John Cox looked up the nearest base we could land at, and it happened to be Dalhart. It so happened that the air base had been vacated, with the exception of the permanent base personnel, awaiting the arrival of a B-29 group scheduled to start training there. We called the tower, told them of our need to land there, and asked them to have an MP detachment to guard the plane while were there. We flew around for over a half-hour trying to use up some excess fuel before landing. After landing and taxiing up toward the ramp, we could tell there was a huge crowd lined up by the fence near the parking area. I

Sky Blues *flew from Tinian Island with the 444th BG, 58th BW. Ken Rust*

think every person left on the base was out there to see the Superfortress for the first time. Our chests swelled with pride as we dismounted and looked over toward the people standing there, agog. It was as if we came in on an alien ship from outer space.

At Salina, where I trained with the 878th BS, 499th BG, our group commander, Col. Sam Harris, and his squadron commanders came up with a well-received idea to encourage crews to stay abreast with the training schedules. Each week, squadron Operations would determine which two crews had done well during the week and award them with a B-17 for a cross-country flight anywhere in the United States. This innovative idea gave us something to shoot for. Some of these trips were designated "whiskey runs," and the crew was instructed to negotiate with a liquor wholesaler out there somewhere and bring back a planeload of alcoholic beverages to replenish the supply for the fellows who had put up money with their order.

Saipan Invasion

As B-29 training continued in Kansas at mid-summer, US Marines and Army units began the struggle to capture the island of Saipan, which would become the home of the 73rd BW. Adm. Chester Nimitz's Pacific Fleet put the Marines ashore after one of the heaviest battleship and aerial bombardments of the war.

On June 15, 1944, the Marines led the assault, followed by the Army. More than 30,000 American Marines and soldiers were involved in a battle that lasted until July 4. The cost to capture the island was high, with 47 percent of the invading force killed or wounded in one of the bloodiest battles of World War II.

The 3rd Photo-Reconnaissance Squadron

The 3rd CMS, like the 73rd BW, was attached to the 2nd AF for operational training, and it, too, had to use old B-17s for initial training. The unit was redesignated the 3rd PRS, VH, on May 19, 1944, and later that month, was divided into three flights, each with four aircraft and six crew. Lt. Col. Patrick B. McCarthy was named commander of the 3rd PRS, and Capt. Ralph D. Steakley was named its operations officer. On August 22, 1944, the prototype F-13, a modified B-29 built by Boeing, was delivered to the 3rd PRS in training at Salina.

A modification center was established at Denver to modify B-29s to F-13 configuration. This airplane was a stripped-down version, minus gun turrets, except in the tail section, and test flights indicated that the F-13's range was longer than the B-29's by at least 500mi.

The 3rd PRS's ground echelon left for Saipan to prepare for the acceptance of the aircraft and flying personnel in August. While still awaiting delivery of combat-ready F-13s, it was decided to stage the squadron out of Will Rogers Field in Oklahoma. It would be October 4, 1944, before the unit received its first production F-13. Within two weeks, two planes were ready for deployment to Saipan.

General LeMay's First B-29 Mission

Within a month after Gen. Curtis LeMay assumed command of the 20th BC, in August 1944, he received permission from the 20th AF Headquarters in Washington to go on a B-29 combat mission. The mission he chose to observe was a daylight strike against Anshan, Manchuria, scheduled for September 8.

Lt. Col. James I. Cornett, commander of the 44th BS of the 40th BG, would lead the strike, in which 108 B-29s were participating. Cornett had no inkling that he would be carrying a "special passenger." He explains how he tried to wiggle out of this assignment, to no avail: "Shortly after landing at Chengtu, I was summoned to Col. 'Butch' Blanchard, our group commander. With a straight face, Butch handed me a piece of paper containing a message from the 20th BC which essentially said, 'Lt. Col. James I. Cornett is directed to take General LeMay on the forthcoming mission. He will not abort a takeoff nor the en route flight. He will bomb the primary target and return General LeMay safely to the base of takeoff.'

"My opposition to the idea met on the deaf ears of Colonel Blanchard, however, so we were stuck with the task of getting the head man of the entire Bomber Command to and from a tough target, unscathed.

"We experienced some pretty heavy flak after leaving the target, and two of our crewmen, the radio operator and the CFC gunner, were hit. The next thing I knew after we re-

ceived the report from the rear of the plane, LeMay, minus his parachute, was slithering through the tunnel to go aft and assist in caring for the injured gunner. Luckily, we got him back to Chengtu safely!"

Ira Matthews, now deceased, who was an aircraft commander of the 40th BG, based at Chakulia, India, told a story about the time his 45th BS attacked a Japanese air depot at Mukden, Manchuria, in November 1944: "It was a daylight raid at about 24,000ft altitude and, suddenly, a small speck in the sky progressively grew larger and larger, and low and behold, the speck turned out to be a strange-looking aircraft, a pre-Pearl Harbor, fixed-gear Japanese Nakajima 97.

"At debriefing, almost all of our conversation centered on the Nakajima 97, or 'Nate' as we called them. The intelligence officer took the reports into our group operations section. Soon he returned, with an amused expression on his face. He informed us that a total of seventeen claims had been reported by eight bombardiers, eight upper gunners, and one tail gunner.

"For several days afterwards, we ragged our bombardier and upper gunner on how our crew chief was going to stick 2/17th of a downed enemy fighter decal on our plane's nose."

Heat's On *flew with the 498th BG, 73rd BW, Saipan. This was one of the first B-29s to have its underside painted black when the low-level raids against Japanese cities began. Only a few planes based in Saipan were painted black.* Warren Thompson

Chapter 6

General Hansell Leads 73rd Wing to Saipan

July and August 1944 were crucial months for Hap Arnold's infant 20th AF, especially the newly activated 21st BC. Curtis LeMay's 20th BC personnel in the CBI theater were picking up more experience and a lot more confidence. They were also showing improved results with the Superfortress. A double-barreled assault against Tinian Island just 3mi across the channel from Saipan was carried out by the Marines on July 24, after an assault took place at Guam, 125mi to the south, two days earlier. Tinian Island was declared secure August 2, and Guam, the major island of the Marianas group and a US possession captured early in the war by Japan, was secured later that month.

As fighting continued on each of the islands, engineers and Seabees were being put ashore with equipment to build runways and hardstands for the B-29s.

While the combat crews of the 73rd BW were about halfway through their combat operational training at Kansas bases in August, ground personnel, including the mechanics, the cooks, the clerks, the armorers and medical units were brought to Saipan

Miss Judy takes a whack at Tojo in this creative piece of nose art. This B-29 flew with the 462nd BG, 58th BW, Tinian. Warren Thompson

by transport ships, commonly known as Liberty Ships. They all helped build maintenance facilities, supply dumps, and their own living quarters. At first, tents were set up for living, but later, work began on assembling metal Quonset huts for the flying personnel yet to arrive. Personnel of the 73rd BW Headquarters arrived on the island September 7, ready to set up business.

In the meantime, two more wings, the 313th and the 314th, were in operational training and would occupy the bases at Tinian and Guam. The 313th BW would arrive in December and January at North Field, and would be the third wing to become operational, followed by the 314th BW at Guam.

Trennis Beers, a medic attached to headquarters of the 498th BG, remembers his advance party trip to Saipan: "We rocked and rolled aboard the S.S. *Exchange* across the Pacific Ocean before debarking after a twenty-seven-day trip to Saipan.

"For most of us, it was our first encounter with an ocean-going vessel, and unlike the 'South Seas Cruises' we had always read about, we had heard how boring a troop transport trip always was. To me, the trip wasn't too bad; the one exception was the food. It was terrible. At breakfast one morning, a cook slapped a pile of green spinach on my tray. Now, even if you were not seasick, that stuff was

enough to make your stomach do flip-flops.

"As we were being loaded on trucks, upon arrival, to be taken to our designated area, I asked one of the drivers, 'What the heck is that terrible odor I smell?'

"'Dead Japs!' he said.

"Right then I knew we were in a combat zone, and not on this Pacific Island for recreational purposes."

With the capture of Saipan and Tinian and the recapture of Guam, the Japanese leaders suddenly found themselves in severe shock. Prince Higashi-Kuni, a member of the Supreme War Council and Commander-in-Chief of Home Defense Headquarters in Tokyo, testified after the war that they realized the B-29 was an exceptional airplane after the B-29 Superfortresses began bombing Kyushu from China, knew that they had no means to defend themselves. When Saipan fell, one of the best known Axis villains, Hideki Tojo, the Japanese Premier and former War Minister, resigned. Still in command, the military made plans to attack the airfield on Saipan, which they knew would be built soon.

Airfield Construction

The US Navy played a major part in getting the B-29s of the 20th AF in position to begin the air assault against the Japanese home islands. As the Central Pacific theater comman-

Maj. Jack Catton, pointing, describes the nose compartment of a Superfortress to Admiral King (left), commander of US fleets, as General Hansell, center, looks on. The picture was taken in Hawaii about October 10, 1944, prior to departure to Saipan. Speith

Lt. Col. Robert Morgan, center, standing, and crew of Dauntless Dotty. Morgan and General O'Donnell led the first B-29 mission against Japan on November 24, 1944. Speith

der, Adm. Chester Nimitz was responsible for all logistical and administrative military activities in the area. He and his staff planned the assault on the Marianas, after exhaustive preparations for the amphibious assaults. Nimitz was responsible for formulating plans for constructing airfields large enough to handle the huge Superfortresses. He was also charged with moving the air units from the States, stockpiling fuel and ammunition, and providing logistical and administrative services for the 20th AF wings that would eventually occupy the bases at Saipan, Tinian, and Guam.

To accommodate five wings, each consisting of four groups, it was decided to build a separate base large enough for each wing. Twin 8,500ft runways at each base were constructed. The Army engineers constructed one field at Saipan and two fields on Guam, and the Navy Seabees built two bases on Tinian.

Completion of the bases on Tinian and Guam were delayed at least a month each because of "mop up" activities against the enemy. Further delay in preparing bases on these two islands occurred when Nimitz decided in August 1944, soon after Guam was captured, that he would use that island as a base for the Pacific Fleet. Construction on B-29 bases was drastically curtailed because priority went to the naval base installations and harbor facilities, much to the displeasure of the 20th AF leaders.

Construction of the air base at Saipan was not delayed, however. As soon as the Japanese airfield at the southern end of the island was captured, it was renamed Isley Field in memory of a naval aviator who was killed during one of the first air strikes on the island. The 804th Army Engineer Battalion was the first construction unit to reach Saipan, and they immediately began work on the field by enlarging and lengthening the runway to accommodate the B-29s.

William F. Roos, a construction engineer with the 804th Army Engineer Battalion, relates some of the enormous obstacles that had to be overcome before the runways could be built: "As the enemy was forced back toward the north of Saipan, we knew we had to accomplish three tasks in short order. First, we had to build docks so we could unload our construction equipment and supplies; second, we had to build the roads to get the equipment from the docks to the airfield site; and finally, we had to build the airfield for the B-29s.

"When work began on the B-29 runway at Isley, we found that the topsoil, rather than being about 2ft deep, as forecast, was only a few inches deep. Beneath this thin layer of soil was hard, coral rock that had to be blasted and hacked away a bit at a time. Working on a 24hr basis, engineers were beset by all manner of other difficulties, including enemy air raids at night, during the first few weeks, which caused all work to stop because of the necessary blackouts."

Isley Field was laid out to run, more or less, west to east, and the runway took up almost the entire width of the southern portion of the island. A huge portion of the southernmost mountain was blasted and from it crushed coral rock was used for the base of the runway, and hardstands where the B-29s were to park. An onsite asphalt plant made the asphalt to finish a smooth surfaced runway.

In spite of the overbearing difficulties experienced in blasting and leveling the huge air base, Isley Field was ready to receive the first B-29 on October 12, 1944. The second runway was ready for use on December 15.

North Field, on Tinian, was ready to receive the 313th BW by late December; North Field on Guam was ready for the 314th in January 1945; West Field on Tinian was ready for the transfer of the 58th BW from India-China in April 1945; and by June, the 315th settled in at Northwest Field on Guam. The building of these five air bases, under extreme difficulties, was one of the major accomplishments of World War II.

Gen. "Possum" Hansell, as commander of the 21st BC, was ready to lead his command to Saipan by the first week of October 1944. At this time, the command consisted of the 73rd BW with its four BGs, and he knew the combat crews that would follow to begin the all-out air assault on the Japanese homeland, didn't have enough experience flying in the B-29s.

When time came to move the first units to Saipan, the crews averaged fewer than 100hr of total flying time in the B-29, and the average high-altitude formation flying experience was fewer than 12hr. The engines of the B-29 were still swallowing valves and catching fire. The magnesium crankcases burned with a fury that defied all extinguishing efforts. In addition, gunsight blisters were either blowing out at high altitude or frosting up so badly that it was impossible to see through them. This problem was fixed, however, by extending warm air to them.

In his last meeting with Generals Arnold and Marshall in Washington, in mid-September, Hansell renewed his pledge to attack Japan in November. Leaving the States on October 5, flying a B-29 nicknamed *Joltin' Josie, the Pacific Pioneer*, Hansell headed for Saipan and started the flow which would ultimately become massive. He recalls that flight: "I flew with a crew from the 73rd BW commanded by a bright and capable young major named Jack Catton, who retired in 1979 as a four-star general. Catton and I alternated in the pilot position; I took it from Sacramento to Hawaii; he took it to Kwajalein; and I flew the last lap to Saipan. We took off from

Bird Island, on the northeastern coast of Saipan. Bill Rooney

Mather Field near Sacramento. The original design gross weight of the B-29 was 120,000lb. Wright Field reluctantly permitted an overload weight of 128,000lb. With our spare engine in the bomb bay, and the various kits we carried, we weighed in at about 130,000lb.

"When we arrived at Saipan and circled over the island, we could see the crowd of people gathered at Isley Field. We landed and taxied up to the parking area, and the crowd rushed toward the plane to see the first B-29 to reach the Marianas, and possibly the first B-29 they had seen, period. When I climbed down from the plane, a microphone was handed to me by a reporter. I spoke firmly into the mike expressing my feelings: 'When we've done a little fighting, we'll do a little more talking!' The date was October 12, 1944."

The race for the Marianas really exploded after Hansell's flight. For some, the three-legged flight to Saipan became a hair-raising experience, while others claimed the trip was a "piece of cake." LeRoy Florence, pilot on the Cecil Scarborough crew, 499th BG, tells of their trials and tribulations on the first leg of the flight: "There were quite a number of crews taking off for Hawaii en route to Saipan the day we left Mather Field, and considerable discussion about which crew had the fastest and best B-29. Wagers were laid, with several crews participating, and the crew landing first at John Rogers Field would get the pot. We felt we had the race about won as we made our power

approach toward Diamond Head. Blocking our path as we neared our destination, however, was the Pacific Ocean's ferocious friend, a huge thunderhead. We barreled right into it and 'bam' our radar went out; so did the VHF radio. We had no choice but to pull up right into the middle of the storm. Naturally, the LF radio was not much good in all that lightening.

"While wandering around for what seemed like days, we made several descents with the idea of bailing out or ditching on our minds. We were running very low on fuel.

"We chickened out each time and pulled back up again into the middle of the storm. When the thunderhead began to subside a little, some fighter planes from nearby Hickam Field came up to try to find us. They did, to our great relief, and led us to a hole over the base where we made a Split-S, found the field, and made a smooth landing.

"To the best of my knowledge, all bets were off, and we were left in wonderment thinking if this was going to be a normal Pacific flight in days ahead."

This author had a sort of unusual, and exciting, thing happen to him on his way across the Pacific. I was pilot on the Cox crew (no. 25) in the 878th BS, 499th BG, 73rd BW. Our departure date from Mather Field, California, was November 11, 1944. I had a feeling the departure date itself held

something of a omen. From my earliest childhood memories, I associated November 11 as a day of eternal peace, because on that date I had been taught, the war to end all wars ended, and not just a few people, but everybody, I thought, celebrated that date with some kind of reverence. But here we were about to depart for another World War on this Armistice Day.

We arrived at Mather, our port of debarkation, the day before from our staging base at Herrington, Kansas, where we received our brand-new Boeing B-29 Superfortress, and after several shakedown flights to swing the compass, check the engines, etc., we awoke that morning, long before dawn, ready to go to war.

After takeoff, we immediately entered a light overcast which had turned into a thick soup by the time we reached altitude. The lightning danced across our plexiglass nose and the thunder made its appearance known, even above the roar of our four engines. We hoped, and some of us silently prayed, that our new V-Square-27 B-29 was well bonded. Because if it wasn't, there was a strong chance that a bolt of lightening would do us in. Lucky for us, the only damage from our being struck by lightning once or twice in that thunderstorm was the destruction of our trailing radio antenna.

Excitement was building as we landed at John Rogers Field. Big, beautiful, silver B-29s were departing for the second leg en route to Saipan, while others were arriving from the mainland. It was an exciting time for all of us, and we were getting in the spirit of the times, like the popular

saying making the rounds in those days, "Live it up today, for tomorrow you may die!" I suppose my navigator, J. W. ("Jim") O'Donnel, was the first to bring up the subject, so flight engineer John Huckins and I decided that afternoon to take that saying for granted. We decided to go into Honolulu. We were, of course, restricted to the base; supposedly, the brass didn't want us B-29 flyers getting a little tipsy at some bar downtown and spilling the beans to some sleazy Japanese spy as to where we were going, etc.

After settling down in our assigned quarters in the officers' quarters at John Rogers Field that afternoon, O'Donnell blurted out, "Restricted hell!" he said, "I have heard of Honolulu and Waikiki Beach all my life, and being this close to it, I've just got to see it. Who wants to go to town?" Huckins and I were the two volunteers who were willing to put our USAAF careers on the line by overlooking the restriction rules for B-29 crews passing through. We decided to check out the security system at the main gate. Just outside the gate, buses were leaving for Honolulu every few minutes. We assumed the appearance of "permanent personnel" as best we could, showed our ID cards, and walked casually through the gate. The MP glanced at our cards, snapped a salute, and we were off the base. I suppose the MP thought surely none of the B-29 flyers were dumb enough to take such a risky chance. Our main objective was to check out those grass skirts we thought those Island Queens were wearing.

Our first stop downtown was the cocktail lounge overlooking the famous beach at the Royal American Hotel. I remembered the scene from movies, and subconsciously I kept glancing

around the room expecting to see Humphrey Bogart or some other big movie star. But the place was filled with service people—more sailors than you could shake a stick at—no movie stars—and no girls in grass skirts. We finished our drinks and wandered out the door onto the white sandy beach made famous by song and movies, and there, too, we faced disappointment—more sailors.

We walked out into the street and moseyed along the best we could, dodging soldiers, sailors, and Marines. Down the street we saw a line reaching nearly a block with service guys waiting to get in. At first we thought it must be a good show, or a fine place to eat. We tapped a guy on the shoulder and asked him what the big line was for. "Well," he said, "they're sweating this line here to get into one of the best whorehouses in Honolulu. The girls are all dolls, and the price is only $5." Being fresh from the States, we were not interested in that venture, and since there was a 9 o'clock curfew, we caught a bus back to John Rogers Field. Our fling was a dud, and it would be our last contact with civilization for a long, long time!

War correspondents were thick as flies at John Rogers Field, all trying to catch rides to Saipan. They were certain, they said, the first big raid on Tokyo would be taking place in just a few days. We, of course, didn't believe that, and told them so. "Half of our 499th BG is still back in the States," we'd tell them, "and they can't bomb Tokyo until we get there!"

Clinton Green, war correspondent for the *New York Times*, asked Commander Cox if he could hitch a ride with us. Of course we all said yes. We figured it would be exciting to have a real live correspondent from a big-time newspaper along with us. Now, if we could do something heroic, like shooting down a stray Jap plane en route to Saipan, he might put our names in a news release.

With Green aboard, we took off the next morning and edged our way

Shown here is an innovative way to combat hot weather and high winds, while mechanics work on Fluffy Fuz IV's *engines.* Josh Curtis

A lead aircraft with the 9th BG, 313th BW, Tinian Island. The black and orange stripes on the vertical stabilizer indicate that it is a lead plane. These special markings made rendezvous much easier for squadron airplanes. Josh Curtis

toward the international dateline. Our next stop would be a little flat atoll in the middle of a big ocean called Kwajalein. O'Donnel came on the intercom to announce that we could move our watches ahead 24hr. Instead of November 13, it was then November 14. We spent a "combat zone" night at Kwajalein, with a sudden flash flood and we all thought the island was going to sink into the ocean. The next morning, bright and early, we left Kwajalein, but not for long. One of the engines swallowed a valve, and we had to return to the island. Green threatened to leave us and said he was going to try to catch another plane coming through because he was sure the first raid was about to take place. We talked him out of it, telling him it would be bad luck for him to desert us in the middle of the ocean, so he stayed with us and we spent another night on Kwajalein. Our crew chief, Fred Reid, was with us, and he was able to get us underway the next morning.

We made it on to Saipan without further trouble, and just as soon as we parked the plane, Green rushed off to check in with someone to see if he could go on the Tokyo mission. But before he got out of sight, I yelled to him, "I told you they wouldn't go on that bombing mission to Tokyo without crew no. 25!" Green turned and waved at us and wished us well.

We couldn't wait to get to our living area to see what the heck was going on. We couldn't believe what they were saying up on the line about the mission taking place the next day!

B-29s from the 9th BG head for a target over Japan. Josh Curtis

This photo of the author's crew was taken at Isley Field, Saipan, on June 8, 1945, one day after they had completed a combat tour of thirty missions against Japan. Standing, left to right: John W. Cox, aircraft commander; the author, pilot; John W. Huckins, flight engineer; James R. O'Donnel, navigator; and Herbert Feldman, bombardier. Kneeling, left to right: Robert Slizuski, radar operator; Alvin Torres, radio operator; Kendal Chance, central fire control gunner; George Koepke, right gunner; Arle Lackey, left gunner; and John Sutherland, tail gunner. Our plane was V-Square-27, the V designating that the plane was part of the 499th BG. Japanese flags on the nose mark the ten confirmed victories scored by the gunners. Tail gunner Sutherland was the leading "ace" in the bomber command, with five victories. The winged ball and spear with the name of the aircraft replaced all "girlie" art in the 73rd BW in April 1945. The first B-29 assigned to the crew was destroyed on the ground in December 1944 during a Japanese retaliation raid against Saipan. The crew's second B-29 was shot down over Tokyo on January 27, 1945, while being flown by another crew. Mary Ann was the third B-29 assigned to the crew and had been named by its ground crew chief in honor of his new baby daughter. When the crew went up to the line to look over the new plane, they decided that it would be a bad-luck omen to change the plane's name, so the name stuck for the rest of crew no. 25's tour of duty. Marshall

Chapter 7

B-29s on the High Road to Tokyo

The war correspondents hitching a ride to Saipan were right. The first B-29 raid on Tokyo originally had been set for November 15, one day before our arrival on Saipan.

General Hansell was anxious to fulfill his pledge to bomb Japan from Saipan in November. The November 15 date was set, because the rate of five B-29 crew arrivals per day assured him that by then, more than eighty Superfortresses would be on hand to participate in the first strike.

Initially, the plans for the first B-29 bombing mission from the Marianas called for a combined strike with the Navy, with carrier-based planes helping to divert some of the Japanese fighter planes away from the B-29s. The planned strike was labeled San Antonio I. Six practice missions—four on the island of Truk and two on Iwo Jima—were made by the 497th, 498th, and 500th BGs; the 499th BG didn't participate because it did not arrive on Saipan in time.

But things didn't work out as anticipated. Late in October, the Japanese fleet set out to do the battle in the Philippine Sea. This action disrupted Pacific plans and Adm. Chester Nimitz notified the Chiefs of Staff that the Navy would be unable to launch an attack on the Japanese home island in conjunction with the 21st BC in November. He recommended that the attack on Tokyo be delayed until

the Navy would be in a position to participate. As Hansell saw it, this would have grounded the B-29s indefinitely. He found Nimitz's proposition intolerable. "If the 21st BC could operate only when the Navy was prepared to cooperate," he said, "we might as well disband the 20th AF and put the 21st BC under Admiral Nimitz."

3rd Photo Squadron Arrives on Saipan

Fate dealt a kinder hand to 21st BC at Saipan during October. The 3rd PRS finally got its first modified F-13, specially equipped for high-tech photographic work, on October 4, and the second plane arrived shortly thereafter. By this time, the squadron had been assigned to the 21st BC's 73rd BW on Saipan. On October 27, the squadron was ordered to Saipan.

On November 1, 1944, after flying 33hr to Saipan and with only 5hr of rest, operations officer Captain Steakley and his crew headed off for Tokyo in his plane, nicknamed *Tokyo Rose*. They would fly over the city and other selected targets and photograph the area in order to pinpoint target areas. It would be the first American airplane over Tokyo since the Doolittle raid of April 18, 1942.

General Hansell called the mission results phenomenal: "Captain Steakley insisted upon an immediate mission even though they had just arrived

from the United States. I advised a rest, but the captain and his crew were insistent. Thank God they were. They found clear skies over Japan—a phenomenon. Called *Tokyo Rose*, his aircraft flew above the Japanese capital at an altitude of 32,000ft, photographing a complex of aircraft and engines plants just west of Tokyo and another on the outskirts of Nagoya. They shot over 7,000 excellent photographs in seventeen sorties before the first strike on Tokyo on November 24. Many of the missions were hampered by bad weather, but enough information on the location of aircraft factories was obtained for the first bombing missions. Copies of the photographs were sent to General Arnold for the JCS and to Admirals Nimitz and William Halsey.

"Mosaics were made, strips laid out, initial points and target approaches selected. Every combat crew was required to trace its photo map, mark landmarks and target runs, and then redraw them from memory—over and over."

With this fantastic bit of luck and expert photographic work, General Hansell was indeed confident that his command was ready to launch the B-29 Superfortress attack on Tokyo and the major targets in the Japanese home islands, even if it meant going it alone.

The crew of the Tokyo Rose, *the first B-29 to go over Tokyo on November 1, 1944. Commanded by Capt. Ralph Steakley, the 3rd PRS crew took pictures in Tokyo and other areas to help establish targets for future B-29 strikes. Left to right: Starks, Arnett, Clark, Marvin, Johnson, Hutchins, McCommon, Hart, Burke, Stamaught, and Steakley.* USAAF Photo/Josh Curtis

Japanese Retaliation Raids on Saipan

On November 3, two days after *Tokyo Rose* roamed for more than an hour over Tokyo, nine twin-engine Betty bombers struck back at the Superfortress base on Saipan. The alert came at 1:30am, and even though very little damage was done to Isley Field or the B-29s, the attack did serve notice that Saipan was not out of range of Japanese bombers. Only five fragmentation bombs were dropped on the runway at Isley Field. One of the planes was shot down near Tinian by antiaircraft guns, and another was downed by a P-61 Black Widow night fighter. That downed plane crashed in the engineers' bivouac area, killing four and seriously wounding six other Americans.

The next retaliation strike against Saipan came on November 7, in two separate attacks. The first came at 1:30am when a low-flying aircraft strafed the runway, causing very little damage. The other came at 4:30am, flying over the field and evidently taking photos. Both aircraft escaped without drawing fire.

On the Road to Tokyo

As the B-29s continued to arrive at Saipan, this author and his colleagues sat poised for the initial strike on the Land of the Rising Sun. Soon, we thought, as anxiety climbed like a thermometer's reading on a high-fevered patient, we would be on the road to Tokyo. From this spot of land in the middle of the Pacific Ocean, we were 1,500mi to the south. There was no road, only a red ribbon on a briefing map pointing out the route we would take to the target in the western suburbs of one of the largest cities in the world. There would be no road, just water and a few jutting rock piles sticking up out of the water, some with nothing but volcanic ash and rock showing and some with a bit of vegetation. All had strange names, such as Pagan Island and Iwo Jima. Above Iwo, the string of islands were in the Bonin Group, and all had a name ending with Jima, like Ha Ha Jima, Chi Chi Jima, and so on. Our thorn in the ¬ide, as far as enemy aircraft harassment, would come from Pagan Island just north of Saipan and Iwo Jima. The retaliation raids on Saipan came from Iwo Jima, with Pagan Island used as emergency landings.

Seven Days of Agonized Waiting

Never before in the history of aerial combat had so many men stood by in total frustration as they waited in a "Will we, or will we not?" frame of mind as they contemplated what could or would happen to them or their aircraft on the long, over-water mission.

The raid on Tokyo, with just over 100 B-29s participating, was scheduled for November 17, not two days earlier as Hansell had hoped. As commander of the 21st BC, now poised for its first strike against the heart of Japan, Hansell was experiencing stress he had not been subjected to commanding an air division in Europe. Bad blood was rearing its head between the USAAF and the Navy, all of which could have a bearing on the future of the USAAF's hope for a separate but equal branch of service.

Some of General Arnold's staff expressed grave doubts about launching the initial mission to Tokyo without naval protection. Arnold forwarded the concerns to Hansell and stated his own skepticism, but left the decision up to him. The record would show that Hansell had been warned. In other words, Hansell's USAAF career would be riding on this mission. Even his 73rd BW Commander, General O'Donnell, wrote a letter to him, stating that he, too, had doubts that the mission could be successful without the Navy's help. Instead, he suggested a night raid against a seaport city, which brought this statement from Hansell: "If you are not willing to lead your wing on the planned daylight mission,

Results of the Japanese raids on Isley Field, Saipan, in November and December 1944 and January 1945. Speith

General, I will turn the wing over to Roger Ramey, my deputy, who is anxious to lead it." Given this ultimatum, O'Donnell chose to lead the 73rd BW to Tokyo, riding with Maj. Robert Morgan, who had been among the first B-17 pilots to complete a twenty-five-mission tour and bring his entire original crew back to the States to begin a nationwide bond-selling campaign. Hansell had received orders not to go on the mission because, if captured and tortured, he might reveal that the Japanese secret code, known as Ultra had been broken.

Briefing for the mission would be somber and to the point. At least two major weather fronts would be blocking the 3,000mi over-water flight to and from target no. 357, the Nakajima Aircraft Co.'s Musashino Engine Factory located in the northwestern suburbs of Tokyo. One B-29 crew from the 497th BG flew over Tokyo alone on November 10, not to take pictures, but to "test" Japan's fighter strength and to see how aggressive they were. Results of the flight were not too helpful, but it was estimated that at least 3,000 Japanese fighters were in the Tokyo area, and they were expected to be highly aggressive in trying to protect their capital city. Bombing altitude would be 30,000ft, with each

plane carrying 25 tons of bombs. Takeoff was set for 6am, November 17, 1944. The crews would be awakened 2hr before takeoff so that they could eat breakfast and then go to the line and perform pre-flight inspections on their aircraft.

Crews were told there would be air-sea rescue units along the flight path between Saipan and Japan. Five submarines would be deployed north of Iwo Jima, up to just off the coast of Japan, and two destroyers would roam along the path between Saipan and Iwo Jima.

Clinton Green, the *New York Times* war correspondent who had ridden with us from Hawaii and had assured us that the first raid was about ready to go, even back in Hawaii, would be among the twenty-four war correspondents at Saipan who would break the news to the world.

The Navy's air-sea rescue project was good news to the combat crews as they listened with deadly serious attention as instructions of how the rescue of a downed crew would be attempted. Edwin L. Hotchkiss, of wing

Mechanics had a tough job, constantly having to change those big R-3350 engines when the engines developed troubles. Josh Curtis

headquarters and assigned to communications and air-sea rescue, illustrates how the operation was supposed to work: "Air-sea rescue was begun by the Navy, particularly the submarines. Lifeguard subs would take up station at established coordinates off well-known points near the Empire. If not harassed by enemy air or surface craft, the sub would remain on surface, homing battle-damaged B-29s to them so that if ditching or bailing out were necessary, they would be there to pick up the crews.

"The call signs of these lifeguard submarines were always made up of words containing as many of the letters 'L' as possible—such as 'Sally's Belly' or 'Nellie's Nipple.' Such call signs had two major advantages: Most Japs pronounced the letter 'L' as if it were an 'R,' thus reducing attempts at voice radio deception because the Nips would come out with something that sounded like 'Sarry's Berry' or Nerrie's Nipper.' The second advantage was that such names recalled to our boys some of the better things of life, things

from which they had been too long separated!

"By war's end, the air-sea rescue units had saved 212 downed B-29 crewmen!"

At the briefing, crews from the 499th BG were told that if they had enough fuel when they returned to Saipan, they were to fly to Guam and land on the landing strip near the harbor (later named Harmon Field). This was a question of logistics: Nobody knew what would happen when 100 B-29s or so, all low on gas trying desperately to reach Isley Field, would converge on the field almost simultaneously.

At Saipan, the early-morning hours of November 17, 1944, brought a message of great disappointment to the combat crews anxiously listening for the wake-up call that would send them on their first mission north to Tokyo. The terse announcement over the squadron PA system blared out over the 73rd BW area: "Attention all personnel participating in today's mission. The missions have been postponed 24hr. I repeat, the mission has been postponed!"

What a let down! How could this be? Every man participating in the mission—the cooks preparing the meals, the armorers who had loaded

the bombs on the B-29s, the ground crews, and, of course, the flight crews—were psyched to a point of extreme anxiety to get this initial mission underway. But this would not be the day. This delay was caused by extreme bad weather in the area, but it was only the beginning; the delay message was repeated for a solid week. Three of those mornings, crews actually boarded their aircraft, only to be told, again, that the mission had been delayed. During the agonizing delays, some crew members even thought something or somebody was trying to tell our leaders that bad things would happen if they undertook this mission alone.

November 24 was different from the six previous days. As dawn came to the island that morning, you could feel the excitement which seemed to scream out "This is it!"

One crew member remembers how this day began for his crew: "Before the engine start-up, it is the tail gunner, Sutherland's, duty to start the gasoline auxiliary unit which we call the putt-putt, located in the non-pressurized compartment in the rear of the fuselage. Power from this unit must be switched on to the main electrical circuit line before starting the engines or closing the bomb bay doors, to prevent running the batteries down.

"Sutherland enjoys his lone 'take-off' duty and reports the accomplished fact over the intercom each time in a musical fashion, 'Putt-putt started and on the line, sir,' after which Bombardier Feldman flips a switch and announces, 'Bomb bay doors closed and we are ready to taxi.' The procedure is automatic for crew no. 25. We have practiced it so many times there is no way a foul-up could occur in this phase of our first trip to the Land of the Rising Sun.

"Or is there?

"6:00am—The word is go! No postponement today. It is time to get this show on the road. We are still fidgeting around the plane, talking to the ground crew. There will be at least 20min before we start up. Two groups will proceed us in takeoff.

"Spectators by the hundreds—sailors, Marines, ground personnel from the 73rd BW—people from all over the island have swarmed to Isley

Field and taken up advantageous spots from where they can watch the massive takeoff of the heavily loaded B-29 Superfortresses for this historic mission.

"Across the way, the roar from the engines in the 498th BG has begun and General O'Donnell and Major Morgan, in the lead plane, quickly taxi out to the west end of the runway where the takeoff runs start. There are spotters to direct each plane to the runway at the appropriate time. A flagman and timer will flag each plane off at 60sec intervals.

"The excitement and anxiety is everywhere. You can see it even in the eyes of our ground crewmen. We stand by our plane V-Square-27, in our hardstand near the eastern end of the runway and watch as General O'Donnell lifts off the runway, dips down toward the water of Magicienne Bay to gain airspeed faster, and heads out past Kagman Point before turning north toward Tokyo.

"Cox and I look at each other as we prepare to climb aboard our plane. I think each of us is detecting the feeling of apprehension that we are experiencing.

"Before boarding the plane, I turn to our ground crewmen, and paraphrasing MacArthur's famous remark, exclaim, 'We shall return!'

"Standing by their B-29 ready to board, or already in their positions in their plane, are 111 crews, representing a strike force of 1,221 men from four groups: the 497th, 498th, 499th, and 500th. They are members of the 73rd BW, 21st BC of the 20th AF. They are about to write a new chapter in the history books, by blazing a bombing trail over Tokyo. This is certain to bring a message to the people in the streets of that capitol of the Japanese Empire that the handwriting is on the wall for the warlords of Japan."

The first B-29 raid on Tokyo, in fact the first land-based bombers ever to strike the city, was carried out—not exactly as billed, but like the message sent out after the China-based 58th BW's first mission against a Japanese target a few months before—it was a beginning.

As forecast by the weathermen at the briefing, two massive weather fronts had to be penetrated on the way to Japan, but if there were 3,000 fighters stationed in the Tokyo area, they were either trying to save face or fuel or just plain couldn't estimate the speed of the Superforts at such great heights of 27,000 to 32,000ft.

Ninety-eight B-29s made it to Japan and thirteen of the number that took off for the mission had to abort and return to Saipan. Two aircraft were lost. Gunners from the attacking B-29s claimed seven victories by shooting down that many Japanese fighters, including one victory for my tail gunner, John Sutherland.

The ice had been broken, from here on out, the giant B-29 Superfortresses would earn their keep, and Japan would feel the wrath!

Chapter 8

B-29 Assault on Japan Picks up Steam

With one major mission against Tokyo under their belts, combat crews on Saipan gained more confidence in their Superfortresses. They had listened to the constant roar of those powerful engines for almost 15hr, flown into and escaped two major weather fronts, climbed to a bombing altitude of about 30,000ft, glanced down into the volcanic crater of Mount Fuji, and survived the 45min or so of flak and fighter attacks over Japan itself. Most importantly, the B-29 now left little doubt that the 3,000mi trip, mostly over water, was within its capability.

O'Donnell also left little doubt that there would be no lengthy rest stop between missions for the 73rd crews. The 58th BW, with Gen. Curtis LeMay as its commander, was picking up steam in the CBI area, but that was in a different part of the world. Other B-29 wings would come to the Marianas, but until then the 73rd BW would carry the battle to the heart of Japan alone.

Another mission to Tokyo was scheduled for November 27, just three days after the initial strike. This time, eighty-one Superforts participated. They went back to the same target, no. 357, located in the northwestern sub-

A B-29 from the 498th BG is shown taking off at Isley Field, Saipan. Dick Field

urbs of Tokyo, with instructions to try and improve on the results on the other end of the line. One B-29 was lost on this mission, but before the returning planes reached Saipan, seventeen Japanese Zekes launched from Iwo Jima and paid Isley Field a visit. They approached Saipan lower than 50ft, undetected by the island's radar, and played havoc with the remaining B-29s. They thoroughly strafed the field in the 499th BG area, and extensively damaged the planes parked there. One man was killed during the attack and several in the 500th BG's bivouac area were injured. One of the planes was shot down by antiaircraft gunners, and it hit and exploded near one of the shelters.

Not a single Zeke made it back to Iwo Jima. Antiaircraft guns from Saipan and Tinian shot down thirteen of the planes. One was shot down by a P-47 near Pagan Island, another was destroyed by a P-47 as it attempted to land on a makeshift landing strip on Pagan Island, and one ditched because of battle damage.

Most of us that day who didn't go on the Tokyo raid were about convinced that it was safer in the air over Japan than it was on the ground at Saipan.

Under the command of Gen. James H. Davies, the first aircraft of the 313th BW arrived at North Field on December 21, 1944. The four

groups—the 6th, 9th, 504th, and 505th—completed three practice missions to Truk and Iwo Jima before joining with the 73rd BW in a 110-plane daylight raid on Koebe on February 4.

Retaliation Raids
During December 1944, the Japanese continued their retaliation raids on Saipan and Tinian. Even the propagandist, Tokyo Rose continuously beamed her "report" to Saipan daily, including popular Stateside music in an effort to demoralize the troops. The orderly room people would sometimes put her messages on the PA system.

Five retaliation raids took place in December, with sometimes as many as twenty-five planes participating. The one that left an eternal impression on this author was the December 7 raid. I happened to be the officer of the guard that night. We expected a raid because it was the third anniversary of the Pearl Harbor attack, and we thought they might try to hit us in strength. They did. Gunners on our crew were pulling guard duty that night since policy had been set up to use flight crews to help guard the B-29s up on the line.

My duty was to keep a close check in the area where the B-29s were parked in their hardstands, and to remain alert. The general consensus was that there was a strong possibility

A formation of B-29s from the 498th BG, Saipan, passes near Mount Fuji on its way *to a target in Tokyo.* 73rd BW Photo/ Harold Dreeze

This Superfortress from the 500th BG failed by a few miles making it back to *Saipan. The crew were all saved as ditching took place just offshore.* Speith

that the estimated 8,000 Japanese soldiers holed-up in the jungle-like mountainous area of Saipan would attempt to coordinate an attack on the parked B-29s at Isley Field during or after a Japanese air raid.

My last trip up to the line to check the guards and to carry them coffee took place about midnight. I chatted with each of the guards in our 878th BS before going back down the hill to our living area, which was about 2mi from the flight line. The moon was shining in all its glory that night, and the silver Superfortresses, loaded with bombs all ready for an early-morning strike on Iwo Jima, glistened in the moonlight., offering a big enticement for an attack. As I drove down the hill toward our squadron orderly room; I couldn't help but believe there would be an attack that night. The moon was full, the time was right, and if the Japanese military leaders really meant it when they said they would destroy all the B-29s, this would be the night for a big-time raid.

A light was still shining in the orderly room, and I stopped in to see what the boisterous noise was all about. A poker game was in full blossom, and most of the players, including our operation officer, had been nipping the whiskey ration. I walked in with my shoulder-holstered .45 pistol in full view, and with as much authority as a second lieutenant could muster in front of a few majors and captains, I exclaimed, "You bastards better douse the lights, cut the chatter, and find a hiding place. The Japs are coming tonight!" With that fair warning to my fellow officers, I went to my Quonset hut to get a little nap before going back up to the line to relieve the guards.

I dropped off to sleep almost immediately, and the next thing I heard was the booming of antiaircraft guns. It must have been 2:30 or 3:00am when they struck Isley Field. As always, they came in just above the water and, as almost always, were not detected before dropping bombs on the B-29s. This time they were using some incendiary bombs that scattered on the hardstands and under the planes, before the burning started. Never before had I witnessed such a chaotic experience. The antiaircraft batteries

The A-2 (intelligence) section of the 73rd
BW pose for a group picture on Saipan.
Harold Dreeze

were not only shooting their 50cal machine guns at the low-flying planes, but their searchlights lit up the whole island, it seemed. They scanned the sky and swept across our living area down by the seashore. When the fires caused by the little foot-long incendiary bombs that resembled a large stick of dynamite would reach one of the B-29s, the heavily loaded plane would catch fire. Within minutes, those bombs would explode and the 6,000gal of fuel on fire would envelop the plane and area. Saipan rocked and rolled that night and somebody exclaimed, "They're going to sink the island!"

At the sound of the all-clear signal, I rushed up to the line, expecting to see our gunners' bodies scattered everywhere. Instead, we saw parts of

bodies belonging to the crew of a Japanese "Betty" bomber, shot down near where our plane was supposed to be located, scattered across the taxi strip and area. Where our plane had been was nothing but a hole large enough for a small house.

Three B-29s were totally destroyed, three badly damaged and twenty somewhat damaged from flying shrapnel. Our gunners were not injured, but they were badly shaken up. One guard on the line was killed and two were wounded. The antiaircraft guns on Saipan shot down six planes, including one downed by a mine sweeper off shore, and one by an antiaircraft battery on Tinian.

It was a sobering night, especially for the poker players I had warned.

Tokyo Rose Sends Message

It was really a scary time on Saipan. One night, this author went to see the movie *To Have or Have Not*. The movie was very good, and just as Lauren Bacall walked to the door of Humphrey Bogart's room, opened it and looked around, and said, "If you need me, just whistle. You know how to whistle, don't you?", the lights went out. You've never heard such loud groans of protest. A colonel with his gas mask slung across his shoulder said, "Let me have everyone's attention. The island is now on blue alert

The Pom-Pom Girl *flew with the 315th BW on Guam.* Josh Curtis

This B-29, V-Square-60, remained afloat 17hr after ditching by the Sy Silvester crew *of the 878th BS, 499th BG, Saipan, on December 13, 1944.* Sy Silvester

[like a weather watch; red alert meant the enemy had been sighted en route to the island]. Tokyo Rose said in her latest broadcast that the Japanese Navy was en route to Saipan and that an invasion of Saipan is likely. She says they will destroy all the B-29s and kill all the personnel either by gas or bullets." The colonel gave us orders that every person must have his gas mask with him at all times. Those were sobering words! We'd have to see the movie later to hear Bacall tell Bogart how to whistle.

Having to ditch a B-29 on the way back from a mission, either because it was out of gas or because of damage over the target, was a very real possibility and caused much worry. Of course, there were other reasons for ditching. The navigator had to remain alert at all times so that he would know where the aircraft was. Deviations from course could cause excessive use of fuel, which could cause an engine to run rough or force the pilot to shut the engine down entirely.

Darrell W. Landau, a squadron engineering officer with the 19th BG at Guam, tells how he found the underlying cause of swallowed valves: "When I joined the 19th BG at Guam, the assignment caused me to want to really know why the valves were failing. Having been up all night helping crews change engines, I felt motivated to find out why. Attention was being given to early detection of failures, but not the cause. It soon became obvious that if the oil cooked to carbon, the valve stem would soon wear out and the valve would not seat well and would become hotter and hotter. In time, the head would burn off. But why was the oil cooking? Many must have thought the valves' failure was the cause of the oil cooking. I had the feeling the oil cooked first and then the valve failed.

"Looking up at the engines as I pondered the cause, I became aware of the size and location of the large distributors and prop governor; my gosh, they could block air flow! But the no. 1 cylinder directly behind this obstruction, the only cylinder with a thermal-couple temperature sensor, was not running hot! It was supposed to be the hottest, the worst-case indicator, but that cylinder rarely went out.

"A while later, watching an engine being started, I observed how the air swirled counter-clockwise over the engine. That was it! The hot cylinders were counter-clockwise when observed from the front. Those big mechanical globs on the top front of the engine were designed to block off air flow, especially when the air passage was reduced by the nacelle air duct, which came down sharply so it could house the front exhaust collector ring. The nacelle's cooling air annulus, intended to reduce drag, aggravated the blocking effect.

"When it was necessary to change cylinders, it had always been these hot ones. Once recognized, the cause seemed so obvious. Engine manufacturers had been making radial engines with these parts in this location for years. But the combination of collecting exhaust gas, supercharging for takeoff, large piston sizes relative to frontal area, and extra-high takeoff power setting all added up to exceeding the limits of the design.

"I made a study of how we could hollow certain bolts to get oil into the rocker arms without impairing their function as mounting brackets. I made arrangements to prove this point, but the next day, the war ended. Abruptly the world changed, and all thoughts changed from improving engines to going home.

"Wright Field's solution to cool valve stems had been to convert to fuel injection. To me, this seemed to be a complete unnecessary waste.

"If someone had only found and implemented the above simple solution earlier, there would have been no need for the costly conversion to fuel injection, the tremendous turnover in engines, and the lost operational effectiveness. If this one malfunction and its simple solution had been implemented early, it could perhaps have shortened the war by many weeks. The Japanese were already trying to surrender before the atomic bomb; their surrender might well have been achieved and the A-Bomb might never have been dropped."

Buddy System

Gerald Robinson, aircraft commander and later commander of the 875th BS, 498th BG, Saipan, remem-

A 3rd PRS crew prepares to take off for Japan to take pictures of damage done by a major strike there. John Mitchell

bers an incident in which he and his crew were saved by the buddy system: "We all remember the 'buddy system' that combat crews practiced on the long haul to and from Japan. If you were in trouble and had to leave the formation, someone would drop out and fly along with you to help drive off attacking fighters, report ditching positions, etc. One day, we developed a problem, and a young West Point lieutenant pilot from our squadron dropped back to escort us. We were just off the coast of Japan at an altitude of about 10,000ft, very vulnerable all alone, and the lieutenant gave us our navigational bearing for home. We were in radio contact with each other until we were about opposite Pagan Island, just north of Saipan, our home base. Then we lost contact.

"Several years after the war, I read where they found his wrecked B-29 on the side of the volcanic mountain on Pagan Island. He got us home, but he didn't make it himself. The weather was awful, not much visibility, and I have often wondered how close we came to hitting that same mountain."

High-Altitude Missions

All 73rd BW missions to Japan in December 1944 were high-altitude from 27,000–34,400ft. Most of these missions required the installation of a 640gal bomb bay fuel tank, providing enough gasoline to get the planes back home if all went well. The big drawback was that when these tanks were installed, the bomb load had to be reduced, and at these altitudes, it was almost impossible to get good bombing results, mainly because of the excessive wind speeds at above 28,000ft. At first, most missions were set up to go downwind on the bomb run. With wind speeds sometimes reaching up to 200 knots, that meant the aircraft had a ground speed of more than 500mph. This was unheard-of speed for an aircraft in those days and, consequently, the mechanization in the bombsight could not compensate a correct reading—which meant that it was unusual if the bombs hit their targets.

It took excessive amounts of fuel and high engine settings to climb to these very high altitudes. The increased fuel consumption made it more likely that the B-29s would run out of fuel on their return flights, and the high engine settings were more

The 500th BG theater, where movies and traveling shows are eagerly watched. Bill Rooney

likely to cause swallowed valves. Bombing from very high altitude meant more ditchings on the way home, and many of the planes that ditched were forced to ditch at night.

One of the most unusual ditchings happened in this author's squadron on December 13. Lt. Sy Silvester ran out of gas and was forced to set down in an unfriendly Pacific Ocean with waves more than 14ft high. It was dark, and Sy lined up with the swells and made a perfect landing. All the crew made it out, although the impact of the plane against the water tossed the bombsight loose from its pedestal, and it crashed through the nose with the bombardier following close behind.

He got only a few scratches, and came to about 20ft ahead of the plane. The crew got the life rafts out of the plane and crawled aboard. The incredible thing about this ditching was the fact that the plane floated for 17hr, and when the crew was picked up by the Navy destroyer, USS *Cummings*, the destroyer had to fire more than 40 rounds of 20mm shells into the plane to sink it.

There is an interesting footnote to Silvester's ditching. The first crew to ditch after the initial November 24, 1944, B-29 raid on Japan was Capt. Francis Murray and crew of the 498th BG on Saipan while returning from a December 3 mission. He and nine members of his crew miraculously survived for eleven days on rafts before being picked up. His crew was aboard the *Cummings* when the Silvester

crew was found. Murray's co-pilot went down with the aircraft. The flight engineer of the Murray crew happened to be Silvester's classmate from Western High in Washington, DC.

Another tragic mishap took place when two B-29s were returning from the Nagoya mission the night of December 13. Lt. Garland Ledbetter and crew had nursed their damaged B-29 back to Saipan, and asked for a straight-in approach to the field. They were also running low on gas. Because of the heavy traffic pattern at Isley Field, they were unable to maneuver into a safely spaced-out position to land without hitting another plane. Ledbetter had no choice but to abort the attempted landing, go around, and try to enter the traffic pattern again. The attempt was fatal. Witnesses said the aircraft, after crossing over the end of the runway and trying to gain altitude, suddenly nose-dived into the Magicienne Bay.

A Navy picket boat whose job it was to hover in the area just off the end of the runway, alert for just such emergencies, was on the scene of the crash within minutes, but there would be no rescue this time. The B-29, with the entire crew aboard, disappeared beneath the surface of one of the deepest water holes in the Pacific Ocean. Not even a piece of scrap metal from the wreckage was ever found.

S/Sgt. Murray Juvelier, of the 498th BG on Saipan, tells of the night they crash-landed at Isley Field after a mission: "We had to crash-land after returning to Saipan from a Nagoya mission, December 18, 1944. Our B-29 was so shot up by Japanese fighters, it broke into three pieces upon landing impact. Several crew members were injured, including me, during the crash, but our aircraft commander, Capt. Wilford Turcotte, brought us back alive.

"I was pinned under some of the debris and knocked unconscious during the crash. When I came to, I yelled for help as loud as I could. I was still in shock, but I remember a voice yelling, 'Let's get out of here before she blows!' The guy doing the yelling pulled me from the wreckage and saved my life!

"On May 12, 1983, I attended my first reunion of the 73rd BW Association in Denver. Thirty-nine years had passed since the crash-landing on Saipan. I had sort of shoved the awful memory of that experience from my mind. Soon after checking into my hotel room, a fellow came up to me, shook my hand, gave me a big hug, and said, 'I guess you made it after all, Murray. There's one thing for sure, if you were as heavy then as you are now, I never would have gotten you out of that plane wreckage!' I was standing face to face, for the first time, with the 'stranger' who rushed to our wrecked plane that night and saved my life. The stranger's name was Robert Evans from another group, whose plane landed at Isley Field just ahead of ours that night. He and other members of his crew were the first to reach our debacle and were responsible for saving our crew."

As the 21st BC, under the leadership of General Hansell, continued its high-altitude strategic bombing of targets in Japan, with not much improvements shown in bombing results, General LeMay, commander of the 20th BC in India, was telling journalists that the B-29 was now out of the experimental stage. He had made some changes in operations, scheduling more targets in such places as Rangoon, Singapore, and Formosa and less targets where it was necessary to launch from the forward bases in China.

LeMay was showing improvements, partially because of this decision, because of the adverse logistical problems of having to fly so many supply and fuel trips over the Hump. By avoiding missions from the China bases, LeMay saved wasted time and effort necessary in flying the Hump several times to stockpile enough bombs and fuel in China to launch a mission to Japan or other nearby Japanese targets.

On a December 18, 1944, test mission, General LeMay sent ninety-four B-29s, loaded with 511 tons of M69 incendiary bombs, to Hankow. This raid was extremely successful, and it along with the successful aerial mining missions of the 20th BC would be a determining factor in the Superfortresses' role in knocking Japan out of World War II.

The 20th AF Headquarters in Washington thought the Hankow incendiary mission was so successful that the chief of staff, General Norstad, directed General Hansell to launch a full-scale incendiary attack on Nagoya with at least 100 B-29s. Hansell was reluctant to change tactics from his high-altitude strategic bombing, and he let General Arnold know his feelings. Lt. Gen. Millard F. Harman, commander of Army Forces in the Pacific Ocean area, also was against changing to incendiary bombing against Japanese home islands. He insisted that the main targets should continue to be war industries, not flimsy houses, declaring that "Burning houses will not beat the Japs."

Incendiary bombs were used against Nagoya on the December 22 raid, but not in compliance with Norstad's request. The target, again, was overcast, and very little damage was inflicted.

As 1944 came to an end, those in Washington were coming to a decision that would change the direction of the war. Some of the high-ranking USAAF officers were very unhappy about the end results of the B-29 efforts in the Pacific.

Chapter 9

World War II Countdown Begins

As 1944 sizzled to an end in the Marianas amid Japanese retaliation raids, high-speed winds at high altitude over Japan were causing frustrations at the highest level of command, as well as for the combat crews who were missing targets considerably more often than they were hitting them. After one mission when a whole group of about forty-five planes, having to revert to dropping their cargo by radar, mistook a large lake just north of Tokyo for the target, rumor had it that there were enough dead fish to feed all the hungry people in the city of Tokyo.

As the new year began, there were other winds afloat, other than the puzzling winds over the Japanese Empire. Nobody knew the answer to high speed, but in due time the world would know the high-flying B-29s had discovered what was to be known as the Jet Stream. Also, the new year brought with it a change in the entire 20th AF structure and in the leader of the bomber command.

By year's end, President Roosevelt was demanding to know why the B-29s had not been more productive. Much money and manpower had been

The author's airplane Mary Ann, *V-Square-27, 878th BS, 499th BG, 73rd BW, gets an engine run-up by crew chief Fred Reed at Saipan. The name* Mary Ann *was later painted onto the 73rd BW's winged-ball-and-spear insignia.* Marshall

used to build the B-29s, and many lives were lost to capture the Marianas and to build new bases for them. General Arnold knew something had to be done, and as the new year burst upon the scene, he had made his decision. He would replace his friend, Gen. Haywood Hansell, with cigar-smoking, tough, combat-proven Maj. Gen. Curtis LeMay.

General Norstad, chief of staff of the 20th AF, was dispatched to the Marianas to deliver the bad news to Hansell. Norstad arrived at the 21st BC Headquarters, now at Guam, on January 6. General Arnold had a dispatch sent to LeMay in India that day.

When the dispatch ordering LeMay to proceed to Guam arrived at 20th BC at Kharagpur, a young captain by the name of William A. Rooney, who was an S-2 officer on charge-of-quarters duty that night, took the top-secret message and, according to policy, hand-delivered it to LeMay. Rooney shares this exclusive account of his brush with history in handling one of the most important change-of-command orders involving top-ranking commanders during World War II: "In the bomber command headquarters in Kharagpur, the adjutant's office was manned 24hr a day. Night change-of-quarters duty fell to those rear-rank Ruddys of company grade, as myself. They had to have the additional qualification of be-

ing cleared for handling top-secret material. I casually signed for it, and then began to read it as was my privilege. My hands began to shake just a little when I saw at the top of the message that it wasn't from just an old headquarters, but from the War Department.

"Furthermore, the message was stamped top-secret and 4Z, which meant the highest level of security and the highest level of speed of transmission. Just a little shaky, I proceeded to read the message. It was from Gen. George C. Marshall, Army chief of staff, to LeMay, instructing him to move to the Marianas, where he was to take command of the 21st BC for the purpose of prosecuting the war against Japan. The message was of some length, but reading this far prompted me to go no further, but to get this message to the general as fast as I could.

"LeMay was having dinner in the general's mess in a building connected to headquarters by a breezeway. I had never entered these digs, and, as a lowly captain, I was scared to do so now except that I had to get the general's signature acknowledging receipt of the message. I quietly eased up to LeMay's aide who was sitting beside the general. With great politeness, the aide accepted the message, saying something about having received an alerting message earlier in the day.

Bombs are appropriately decorated before loading for another mission. USAAF Photo

This parade took place on Saipan in May 1945 when the 73rd BW turned out in full to show off for visiting dignitaries and to present medals. The covered nose art on the nearby plane has not been replaced by the wing's symbol, and some high ranking officials in wing headquarters decided that it would be better if the visitors, and especially the newsreels, were not exposed to that particular piece of art. Dick Field

Relieved of my burden, I exited as silently as one of the barefoot Indian houseboys who were serving the meal.

"That message ordering a change of command of the B-29s in the Pacific was a harbinger of a deadly war to come. Arriving on Saipan, LeMay determined early on that the way the war was being waged with the B-29s wasn't going to get the job done. On his own authority, without seeking approval from any higher command, LeMay began low-level, firebomb raids on Tokyo and the other major cities of Japan, thus bringing to the enemy the devastating destruction that was within the plane's capability. The war with Japan turned on that change of command, and my brush with history came about when that message passed through my hands."

LeMay arrived at Guam on January 7 for the meeting that ended with the change of command of the 21st BC. The meeting of the three young generals had to be an uncomfortable situation. All three knew each other well. LeMay had served as a group commander under Hansell in the European war. It was evident that Hansell's reluctance to change his doctrine of high-altitude bombing was the major cause for the change in command.

The change of command would not take place until January 20, 1945, and Hansell would stick with his high-altitude bombing until the end of his tenure. He had fulfilled Norstad's order to conduct a full-blown incendiary raid on Nagoya back in December, but it was launched with ninety-seven B-29s airborne with only sixty planes bombing the primary target. This raid was flown at altitudes of 28,000–31,500ft and didn't receive the hoped-for results. Five B-29s were lost. Tokyo and Nagoya were the next Hansell-ordered missions, both from high altitude, but the results were no better. The mission to Tokyo, January 9 claimed six B-29s, and the Nagoya mission on January 14 claimed five more.

Before the general's final mission on January 19, he had ordered a major reduction in the weight of the aircraft. Steel plates that protected the pilots and one of the bomb bay fuel tanks were removed, reducing the overall

weight of the plane about 6,000lb. Whether this weight reduction was the cause for much better bombing results is a matter of conjecture, but the January 19 mission against the Kawasaki Aircraft Plant at Akashi, near Kobe, turned out to be the best mission to Japan so far. Hansell could return to the States with a bit of consolation about his high-altitude strategic bombing, even over Japan. The planes bombed from altitudes of 25,000–27,000ft. The weather was good, and all sixty-two of the B-29s that participated returned to Saipan. The 3rd PRS planes confirmed that it was a good strike, but the knowledge of just how good it was came after the war, when it was learned that 90 percent of the factory was destroyed on that mission.

The 313th BW on Tinian Island continued their shakedown missions during January as replacement crews started arriving in Saipan to fill the gaps left by downed crews. William G.

Schmidt, navigator on a replacement crew in the 878th BS, 499th BG, recalls disappointments that faced most replacement crews: "As a replacement crew, we got a rude awakening just a few hours after we set our brand-new B-29 Superfortress down on Isley Field, Saipan, and checked in at squadron headquarters.

"We never set foot again in what we thought was 'our airplane.' Our morale took a nose-dive when we were informed that the B-29 we brought over would be assigned to an older crew—one who had been here longer without an assigned airplane. We wondered what 'good news' we'd get next, especially after we found out the quarters we were assigned had been occupied by men who had gone down over Japan a few days earlier. Now that was a sobering thought—not exactly soothing to our nerves.

"It took a while for replacement crews to get used to filling the shoes of downed buddies, in the eyes of veteran

Bombs loaded and awaiting signal for start-up. Gerald Robinson/Josh Curtis

crews. We did our best to fill those shoes, however, and even though we looked pretty forlorn for a while, we finally jelled and then we were looked upon as 'one of them.'"

All the 73rd BW crews flying their B-29s to Saipan made a fueling stop at Kwajalein, a small atoll with just enough room to land and takeoff a heavily loaded B-29. Jack McGregor, an aircraft commander with the 869th BS, 497th BG, had this to say about his stop at the God-forsaken spot of coral rock in the middle of the Pacific Ocean: "About 20mi out of Kwajalein, our refueling stop halfway from Hawaii to Saipan, our future home, we called the control tower for landing instructions. They told us to hold 5mi east of the island at 2,000ft since they had an emergency landing in progress. We circled to watch the unfolding dra-

A downed flyer is pulled aboard a Navy submarine. Lifeguard subs stayed on station near the B-29 routes. These subs stayed on the surface as much as possible, homing battle-damaged B-29s to them so the sub could rescue the crews. Sy Silvester

ma and noticed a large group of people on the apron just off the single runway. One of my crew members sighted an F4U Corsair doing a 360deg overhead turn and landing. We soon received an 'OK 467, Come on in and land!'

"On our approach to the landing strip, we saw the group of people milling around the Corsair. Finally, a jeep roared off toward the building area. After landing, I asked the 'Kwaj' operation folks if the Corsair pilot had been badly hurt. They laughed and said that this was just the regular afternoon 'Freezing the Ice Cream Flight.' Our entire crew laughed over the incident as we enjoyed ice cream for dinner that night!"

Two B-29 crews return to Saipan after being rescued by the Navy. Sy Silvester

The first mission under LeMay's command of the 21st BC was flown by the 313th BW from Tinian Island. It was also that wing's practice mission in the Pacific. The big change had not occurred yet. The 313th's practice strike on Truk Island, a former Japanese stronghold, was from the usual 25,000–26,000ft altitude. After LeMay took over, there were many practice missions. Most of the nearby bypassed islands, with a few Japanese soldiers hiding in the brush, would feel the wrath of the B-29 bombers on practice missions.

The high-altitude raids would continue through February, with the exception of three air-sea rescue missions by the 313th BW at 3,000ft.

On January 27, 1945, LeMay sent seventy-four B-29s, loaded with all-purpose bombs, to the Nakajima plant in Tokyo, again at the familiar high altitude, and results were not much better than before. One thing was different this time, however. Swarms of Japanese fighters came up to challenge the Superfortresses, and they knocked down nine of the attacking force, the largest number of B-29s lost

in a raid to date. Over 900 enemy attacks were hurled at the B-29s, including some trial runs of ramming tactics. No B-29s were rammed during this mission, but six B-29s were shot down, two ditched from fighter damage, and one crashed on landing back at Saipan.

While the Tokyo debacle was taking place, Brig. Gen. Roger M. Ramey, now commander of the 20th BC in the CBI theater, launched a double-whammy mining mission. Twenty-six B-29s laid mines at Saigon, and fifty Superfortresses dropped their mines on the Port of Singapore. These were the first of the mining missions performed by B-29s of the 20th AF, since the initial mining mission at Palembang, Sumatra, by the 462nd BG, 58th BW.

Incendiary Strike on Kobe
February 1945 was the month big new decisions were made and long-held anxieties were beginning to fade.

Sensing that the crews' morale had taken a nose-dive after the tough Tokyo raid of January 27, LeMay requested from Washington that missions should be shifted from heavily defended targets in Tokyo and Nagoya. He suggested that the next mission be an incendiary maximum effort against Kobe. Not only would this relieve some of the tension, he hoped, it would help planners determine the effects of large-scale incendiary raids, since they were unable to get sufficient information from the January 14 incendiary raid on Nagoya.

February 4 was to be one of the most important missions, as far as planners were concerned, in determining whether incendiary bombs should be used on large-scale bombing missions against major cities in Japan.

The mission would include 110 B-29s from the now-ready 313th BW with the 73rd BW bombers. Again, it would be a high-altitude mission at 24,000–27,000ft. It would be a daylight raid, carrying a total of 140 tons of incendiary clusters and 13 tons of fragmentation bombs. Aggressive Japanese fighters shot down one bomber and damaged thirty-five more. Another damaged B-29 crashed and burned upon landing at Isley Field.

The results were a big improvement over the Nagoya incendiary trial mission. Pictures taken by the 3rd PRS revealed that more than 2,500,000sq-ft of Kobe's built-up area was destroyed or damaged.

More encouraging news would soon be announced. Already, rumor had it that an invasion of Iwo Jima would soon take place. There was not much doubt that something was about to take place on Iwo Jima. Seventh USAAF B-24s based on Saipan had, for some time, made daily raids on the airstrip on Iwo Jima, as had B-29s from the 73rd BW and now the 313th Wing.

B-29 Gunners Sink Two Japanese Ships

Arthur Clay, an aircraft commander with the 39th BS, 6th BG on Tinian Island, recalls a run-in with two Japanese surface ships during a Navy assist in a air-sea rescue mission north of Iwo Jima: "With no mission scheduled for my crew that morning of February 14, 1945, I was stripped down to my underwear and getting in a little sack time, when the PA horn blared out, 'Gus Clay, report to operations immediately.' I jumped up, slipped on my clothes and shoes, and, wondering what the heck was up, took off up the street to find out.

"'Get your crew together,' I was told. 'You are to go on an individual plane search mission north of Iwo Jima, complements of the Navy.' A Navy lieutenant was to go with us. Iwo Jima was still in the Japs' hands, and though the mission could be risky for a single B-29 in that area, we accepted the assignment with enthusiasm.

"The Navy had requested assistance for the radar search mission since the area they wanted covered was out of range of the Navy B-24s. The Iwo Jima invasion was coming up soon—thus, the surveillance north of Iwo.

"We made our turn-around at the designated spot, and headed for our base at Tinian Island. The weather, by this time, was getting pretty bad, so I dropped down to about 1,000ft above the water to get under the heavy clouds, when all of a sudden we faced two Jap surface ships dead ahead. They evidently were en route to Iwo Jima. Our Navy observer identified one of the ships as a 7,000-ton freighter, and the other as a 2,500-ton freighter. We contacted one of our submarines we knew to be in the area, who assisted in the rescue of B-29 flyers forced to ditch, to or from bombing missions over Japan.

"Since we had no bombs aboard, I had not even considered trying to 'attack' the ships, and was about to take evasive action to get out of their way, when the ships started firing at us. Turn about was fair play, I thought, so I immediately notified the gunners we were to strafe them. After climbing to about 2,000ft, I turned and made a diving sweep on the larger ship, with our forward guns blazing and the tail

B-29s on their way to their target.

gunner taking over after we passed over the ship. Bingo! As we made our turn for another run, we could see explosions on the ship and, encouraged by the first pass, we turned on the small freighter. It, too, became embroiled in flames. We circled and watched as the larger ship began to sink, as did the second ship. After circling the two stricken ships to make sure they were sinking, we relayed the message to the submarine, explaining to the sub commander that their services were not needed. If I had thought to be more romantic, I'd probably have sent this message: 'Sighted two ships, sank same!'"

314th Wing Arrives at Guam

February brought more good news. Brig. Gen. Thomas S. Power's 314th BW began arriving at North Field, which had recently been carved out of a dense jungle on the north end of Guam. On February 25, the 314th would join the 313th and 73rd BWs in a 229-plane raid, the largest so far against Japan, in Tokyo's urban area. Only three B-29s were lost.

The four BGs in the 314th BW included the 19th, 29th, 39th, and 330th. The 19th BG was almost wiped out when the Japanese struck Clark Field in the Philippines, on December 8, 1941. It was ironic that this group, which had been reactivated to join the 20th AF, would deliver some of the final blows that would force the Japanese to capitulate.

The countdown had begun!

Moonshine Raiders *flew with the 331st BG,*
315th BW on Guam. Gillum/Josh Curtis

Chapter 10

More Help Comes to the Pacific

Early on the morning of February 10, 1945, 118 B-29s from the 73rd and 313th BWs left their bases at Saipan and Tinian Island and headed north toward Japan to bomb a very important target at Ota. It would be a high-altitude mission against the plant producing the new twin-engine airplane called Frank. Intelligence had learned that the new aircraft would be capable of attacking the B-29 at very high altitudes, so it was very important that this plant be destroyed.

This author's crew was one of the strike forces heading north for Ota, located about 60mi inland from the coastline and about 100mi north of Tokyo. It would be an upwind bomb run, because mission planners were still leery of Iwo Jima and dog-legged our route around that island. Rumors of an Iwo Jima invasion were being accepted as a fact. Why else would a steady stream of Navy ships keep passing through the channel separating Saipan and Tinian Island and dropping anchor offshore?

The parade of battleships, carriers—some of which were dubbed "baby flat-tops"—destroyers, landing craft, transport ships, and other vessels was second only to the rendezvous of 100 or more B-29s, circling at high altitude until each plane settled into its designated spot in the formation, then heading across the coastline of Japan toward the target for the day. We

knew it wouldn't be long before the extra mileage around Iwo Jima would be eliminated to and from targets in Japan.

The dog-leg around Iwo Jima for the Ota mission wasn't completely out of sight of the pork chop-shaped, 7mi-long volcanic island. Members of the crew chatted for a while as we passed the island, expressing thanks that soon we'd have a place to land, other than water, if damaged during a raid on Japan.

Passing Iwo Jima, we had not yet started our climb to bombing altitude where we would rendezvous just off the coast of Japan, then go in by groups in train. The B-29s always flew in a very loose formation until nearing the coast to avoid having to jockey the throttles, thus saving gas. Keeping a sharp eye out for surrounding B-29s, we happened to notice what looked like a flight of aircraft directly ahead of us and on our level. At first, they resembled small specks, but this was not the case. The specks got larger and larger. I looked at Cox and said: "Do you see what I see?" Then Herb Feldman, our bombardier, yelled, "Those are Jap planes coming this way!" Not too anxious to play Russian roulette with them at this point, we veered slightly to the right and held our course. It was a very curious sight. A Japanese twin-engine bomber we called a Betty was leading a flight of

six fighter planes we recognized as Zekes or Tojos. They passed within 100yd or so to the left of us, the big red balls on their wings and fuselages shining brightly in our eyes. To this point, it had been the closest we'd been face to face with the enemy. A second close encounter was near at hand.

We crossed the coastline, going slightly north to a certain point we called our Initial Point, and being in the no. 3 position (left wing) of the lead element, our flight leader began a gradual turn to the left, heading directly into a bright and blinding sun.

Every B-29 combat crew member knew it was policy to wear an oxygen mask while in the target or danger area. This precaution was necessary to prevent the crew members from loosing consciousness if the pressurized cabin were to receive flak or shell holes large enough to cause the cabin to depressurize.

The oxygen mask was uncomfortable and I always left it dangling on the side of my face, hooked only to one side on my helmet, until I could see it was time to hook-up. This could have been a fatal habit on this day.

I was in the left seat flying the mission, and my radio was tuned to the interplane channel, not the intercom. All of a sudden, a swarm of fighters found us. They came in droves and out of the sun and we could not see

Two-thousand pounders ready to be loaded for another mission to Japan. Each B-29 could carry a maximum of six of these massive bombs. Chuck Spieth

them until they came barreling through our formation. Three Tojos slammed in on our nose, flying in close formation. I thought about pulling up to try avoiding their attempt to ram us, but there wasn't time for that. They had already zoomed past us. Next came two planes diving out of the sun, and they just barely missed clipping our wing. I fought the controls of the plane, desperately trying to maintain our position in the formation. The next attacker was a twin-engine Tony. The pilot concentrated his firepower on our flight leader, Cecil Scarborough, successfully knocking out one of his engines, making it shudder and almost go out of control before Scarborough and LeRoy Florence could straighten it up. They lost altitude and slid under the formation. To prevent collision with Scarborough, those of us around him had to maneuver away, which resulted in a scattered formation. Just as we were about to close up the formation, the fighters came again. This time, they hit K. B. Smith's plane, which was flying on the

left wing of the element at this time. He dived out of formation and slid under us. By now, we were sitting ducks out on the left of the whole formation. I worked up a sweat trying to hustle back to close the formation. I would not make it before a three-ship attack came in from 9 o'clock and really plastered us. I knew we were hit, but I didn't realize the extent of the damage we had sustained since I still maintained full control of the airplane. My main objective was to close up the positions in the formation vacated by Scarborough and Smith as fast as I could because we all knew the Japs always concentrated their attacks on stragglers, or ships separated from the formation.

As aircraft commander, Cox was generous in sharing flying time with me, even at the controls over the target. To this day, I kid him about how he could foresee the harder missions because I was always at the controls during them. He was on the intercom calling out oncoming fighters to the gunners, and I was monitoring the interplane command radio channel. I could hear flight engineer John Huckins yelling something, but I was too busy in my struggle to maintain control of the aircraft and close up with the formation to understand what he

was trying to tell me. Finally, he unfastened his safety belt and came over and punched my shoulder, gesturing for me to fasten my oxygen mask. He pointed to the cabin pressure altimeter, which normally had a reading of 8,000ft altitude. It was going wild. I was immediately aware that either the pressurization pump had been damaged or destroyed, or we had large holes in the fuselage. The atmospheric condition within the plane was rapidly equalizing with that outside the plane. I immediately snapped on my mask as we gradually closed the formation and crept toward the target, bucking a strong headwind.

Miraculously, as if a hand from Heaven had reached into our plane to prevent further cabin pressure loss, the indicator stopped its spin at a reading of 12,500ft. We all breathed a little easier since we knew if the pump could maintain that level of cabin pressure, we could survive, even without oxygen. At this time, we were totally unaware of what had happened to the oxygen bottles stored in the rear unpressurized compartment.

Within 12min of successfully bombing the target, we made a 180deg turn and were back over the ocean, aided by an unusually strong tailwind. Navigator Jim O'Donnel did some fast calculations and announced that we had been doing a ground speed of 520mph. I was all wrung out, with not a dry stitch of clothing on my body, even down to my socks—even though the outside thermometer read about 35deg below zero. I looked at Cox and said, "Take it, Cox, I'm pooped."

The drama began to unfurl further as we set our course toward home and out of danger of further fighter attacks. Radar operator Robert Slewsuski discovered that an unexploded 20mm shell had ripped through the fuselage and tore into the invertor, making the radar system inoperable. During the bomb run and fighter attacks, he had been sitting on the floorboard hatch. The shell had lodged only 4in below his rear end!

We depressurized the plane as soon as we thought it safe to do so, so that the tail gunner, John Sutherland, could open hatches to his pressurized compartment and come forward, as he always did after leaving a target. To

get to the forward pressurized compartments, Sutherland had to pass through the rear unpressurized section of the B-29 where, among other things, oxygen tanks were stored. After crawling through the tunnel that connected the central fire control gunners' compartment and the forward section, he announced, "Guess what, some shells exploded in the rear compartment and destroyed all the oxygen bottles. They are all busted up and scattered all over the place!"

Opposition in the skies over Japan was picking up. A new record for the number of B-29s lost on a mission was set on this up-wind Ota mission when twelve Superfortresses were lost. More B-29s would not have made it back from that mission had it not been for several extraordinary accomplish-

ments from some of the flight crews whose planes were heavily damaged.

One of the most incredible feats ever accomplished by a B-29 combat crew took place in Cecil Scarborough's plane after it was heavily damaged during the initial fighter attack as the 499th BG made the turn to the bomb run to Ota. During the attack, the throttle cables that controlled power on the no. 3 and 4 engines were severed, causing them to run at dangerously high levels. The pilots had no way to control them. Lt. Howard Guiot, flight engineer, accomplished what seemed to be an impossibility, enabling the crew to make it back to Saipan and to save the Superfortress for another day. He crawled into the bomb bays to survey the situation and finally found the severed cables. With-

Ernie Pyle's Milkwagon *flew with the 6th BG on Tinian Island.* Josh Curtis

out proper tools or equipment, he could not splice them together. Guiot decided to place another crewman at the open hatch leading into the bomb bays to relay messages between the pilot and himself. There was no way to speak directly by intercom from the bomb bays to the pilot, so the message relay system had to work. It did! He relayed the message to Scarborough that he would attempt to lash the broken cables to a spar, after deciding on a constant power setting for the engines. After a period of trial and error, the task was accomplished.

The big sweat was what was going to happen when attempting to land

Bomb bay tanks, each holding 640gal of fuel, ready for installation. The bomb bay tanks were used for high-altitude missions only. At 25,000–30,000ft altitude and above, two of the tanks were used, filling one of the bomb bays and cutting the bomb load in half. The tanks were not dropped during flight; they were reused on later missions. Chuck Spieth

back at Isley Field. The pilot and engineer, after a conference, decided on a plan and hoped it would work. As they neared Saipan, Guiot crawled back into the bomb bays, unleashed the cables, and on final approach to the runway, manipulated them on signals from Scarborough. The landing was not picture-perfect, but it was most incredible.

Date Set for Iwo Jima Invasion

The performance of the B-29 continued to improve in February in both the Pacific and in the CBI theater. During the month, two 100-plus–plane missions were flown to Singapore. Others were made to Saigon, Bangkok, Mingaladon, and Kuala Lumpur.

Big changes were about to take place in the Pacific, as General LeMay had promised. Adm. Chester Nimitz's office had already set the date for the Iwo Jima invasion: February 19. Excitement on Saipan and Tinian Island

grew as the ships that had recently come there left port and headed out to sea. B-29 crews were overjoyed because this Navy and Marine operation was being done, among other reasons, to directly benefit the B-29s with a place to land if running low of fuel or damaged.

Seventh AF B-24s and B-29s had dropped so many bombs on Iwo Jima since the Japanese retaliation raids on Isley Field in November that the general consensus was that the Marines should be able to capture the island in a week or two. They were mistaken. They didn't realize how a Japanese soldier would react when his back was to the wall and his country and Emperor were at stake.

Before the invasion, the plan was to pulverize the island with the heaviest bombardment the battleships could lay down for three days, before the first landing craft headed for shore.

On the morning of February 19, the 73rd and 313th BWs sent 150 B-29s to target no. 357 in Tokyo. My crew was one of the strike force, and again we passed near enough to see what was going on at Iwo Jima. We could see the flashes from the big guns that were filling the air with the largest shells the Navy had. It was, indeed, a strange feeling to know that within a very short time the Marines would be going ashore. My heart went

out for them, but what a relief it would be once that little piece of coral rock and volcanic ash was secured.

The 313th BW's four groups were coming of age quickly. With several practice and air-sea rescue missions under their belt, this was their fourth major mission. Six B-29s were lost.

Another raid on Tokyo, this one on February 25, would be the 21st BC's first three-wing mission. Gen. Thomas S. Power, commander of the 314th BW, was now settled in at North Field on Guam and ready to join the 73rd and 313th BWs in a 229-plane attack. This was one of the last high-altitude, regular missions against Japan. Three planes were lost.

Victor H. King, commanding officer of Consolidated Air Service Groups on Tinian Island, remembers an incident during takeoff for an aerial mining mission from North Field: "Early one spring morning in 1945, a B-29 rolled down the runway at North Field on Tinian Island, loaded with aerial mines to be dropped in the Shimonoseki Straits.

"Prior to liftoff, the pilot encountered a 'no-go' situation. However, he was beyond the point where he could safely abort. He tried desperately to bring the heavily loaded airplane to a halt, but to no avail. Brakes smoking, it ran off the end of the runway, across the overrun, and down a deep slope, and exploded.

"All aboard were blown to bits, except the tail gunner. Sensing that the plane was going to crash, he jettisoned his emergency hatch and dropped onto the runway overrun. Miraculously, he was not injured by the fall. But, as he ran for safety, the explosion blew pieces of a propeller blade in his direction. One of these sliced off a big chunk of his buttocks. He was rushed to the emergency medical unit on the field, where he encountered one of his buddies.

"As he lay with his rear end propped up on the treatment table, his pal exclaimed, 'Boy! That prop sure did a job on you!'

"'That was no prop,' the tail gunner replied. 'That was the Grim Reaper's scythe!'"

The month of March would be the turning point in the war for the B-29s, as three wings were now in operation, one each on Saipan, Tinian Island, and Guam. But a decision had been made to shut down the CBI Super-fortress operation and transfer the entire 20th BC to West Field on Tinian Island. Also, the 20th BC would merge with the 21st BC, headquartered at Guam. The 58th BW, which was the total strength of the 20th BC, would be the fourth wing now under command of General LeMay's 21st BC. The March 29–30 mission to Singapore, with a twenty-nine B-29 strike force, would be the last mission flown from bases in India, as well as the last mission flown by the 20th BC.

From June 5, 1944, to March 30, 1945, the 58th BW, 20th BC, flew forty-nine combat missions from the CBI theater. The missions involved 3,058 sorties in which 11,477 tons of explosives were dropped in Japan proper, Sumatra, North China, and Formosa. They had given support to British Admiral Lord Louis Mountbatten, General MacArthur, and the US Navy during the Battle of the Philippine Sea. They had experimented successfully with incendiary bombs, which was a factor in later decisions by the USAAF Operations Analysis Committee, and later the Joint Target Group, to firebomb major cities in Japan. In addition, the crews of the 58th BW had spear-headed the usage of mines with some very successful aerial mining missions, which were the forerunners of Operation Starvation, the mine-laying in home ports of Japan that eventually developed into a total blockade into and out of Japanese ports.

On March 30, 1945, the entire 20th BC and 58th BW were deployed from bases in India and China to Tinian Island, to join in the big push against the Japanese home islands and merge with the 21st BC.

General LeMay had other surprising changes to spring. After the March 4 192-plane raid, he shut down combat missions for five full days. Rumor had

it that the reason for no scheduled missions during this period was to give mechanics time to try to get all B-29s flying and in tip-top shape for something special. The something special was enough to roll the rumors out in high gear. Most of the crews had been individually practicing dropping 500lb incendiary clusters, one at a time, on one of the nearby islands. This gave food for a lot of thought. At the top of the rumor list was the idea that LeMay was going to send all the planes up to Japan, loaded with aerial mines, and from very low altitude, plant the mines in Tokyo Bay and other shipping ports. This idea was completely demoralizing, conjuring up visions of flying into steel cables, being held up by balloons, and having wings clipped.

During that five-day stand-down, combat crews had plenty time to churn up other demoralizing developments. There had been no such thing as promotions, and, according to the grapevine, our European counterparts were sparkling with higher rank. One of the most frustrating things was the lack of information about length of combat tours. All were anxious to know how many missions would determine our combat stay overseas.

Ground crew personnel had their own brand of problems and mishaps, as they performed around-the-clock maintenance on the Superfortresses. They worried about the length of their tours of duty. No news was forthcoming for the flight crews. Most of them went about their work with the attitude that they were there for the duration, hoping they wouldn't have an unavoidable mishap, such as the one Sgt. Arthur Geminder, with the 504th BG, of the 313th Wing on Tinian Island, almost had: "I was put in charge of the wash rack, washing down dirty B-29s. For help, they were sending me guys who were given extra duties, or guys who had screwed up. The second lieutenant, who was my boss, told me to

Patches *flew with the 875th BS, 497th BG, and was damaged during one of Japan's early retaliation raids on Isley Field in 1944.* Marshall

be very careful with the system of cleaning, which was no more than an air compressor and a drum of kerosene.

"The mixture was sprayed on the planes with long nozzles. There was a gauge on the drum which was not to exceed 150lb. And, yes, you guessed it—I don't know which one of us was responsible, the extra-duty guys, the screw ups, or who—all of a sudden, a loud boom that sounded as if a bomb had gone off shook the area. I glanced around to see the drum flying sky high. The drum, still loaded with lots of kerosene, went up to at least 200ft before reversing its assent and began falling. It landed within a few feet of the B-29 we were washing. I have often wondered what would have happened if that half-filled drum had hit that plane, causing an explosion, which would have destroyed that big B-29. I would be paying for that plane for the rest of my life, I'm sure.

"The name of the aircraft was the *F.D.R.*"

Big Time Operator *was assigned to the Lt.*
W. M. Bloomfield crew, 9th BG, Tinian Is-
land. Larry Smith

Chapter 11

First Fire Raid on Tokyo

By March 8, 1945, rumors about the upcoming B-29 maximum-effort mission were revealed as facts. Those who attended the briefing for that first all-out incendiary raid on Tokyo will never forget the almost shock-effect it had on the crews who would participate. General LeMay was calling for an unbelievable change of policy in the method B-29s would attack Japan. He was advocating such a radical change that most of his own staff thought the loss rate of B-29s and crews would reach astronomical numbers of up to 75 percent. The rumor that came out of that staff meeting was LeMay's so-called reply: "Well, if those figures happen to be correct, then we'll have to send for more B-29 combat crews, won't we?"

The first shocker at the mission briefing was: "The altitude over the target will be 5,000–8,000ft."

The next shocker caused even deeper groans: "All gunners, except one, will stand down for the Tokyo mission. That gunner will ride in the tail gunner position and act as scanner-observer only. No ammunition will be carried because the gun barrels will be removed, saving at least 3,000 extra pounds and thus increasing the bomb payload by that much."

The final shocker was the worst: "This will be an all-night flight; take off at about 6:00pm, hit the target soon after midnight, and return to base after sunup the next day. Crews will fly individually to and from and over the target, and drop their bombs in a selected urban area marked by twelve B-29 pathfinders. These planes will take off an hour ahead of the main strike forces and start fires around the area to be saturated by succeeding planes dropping inside the 'ring of fire'."

All three wings, now in the Marianas—the 73rd, the 313th, and the 314th—would participate in the mission. It would be the largest concentration of B-29s to strike Japan so far, with 325 B-29s scheduled to participate. All planes would drop their load of napalm incendiary bombs in the same general area of urban Tokyo.

Every crew had to adhere to the planned route and cruise control. This was absolutely necessary for the mission to succeed with a minimum of losses due to planes running into each other as they converged upon the target area before arriving in an area that would be illuminated by searchlights and fires. Each squadron in every group participating was assigned certain altitudes. All planes would have enough fuel to make the round trip, but no deviations could be made to or from the target. The navigator and flight engineer would be responsible for spotting any changes in the flight plan. The radar operator would assist the navigator in picking up known landmarks, such as the small islands along the flight path. He was also responsible for monitoring his set and letting the pilots know if blips other than known objects showed up on his screen, indicating that the plane might be on a collision course with another plane in the area.

The decision to use firebombs on Tokyo was made in Washington, but the low-level altitude, over the targets, was LeMay's own decision. According to some of the better known "history-watchers," that decision was one of seven of the most important decisions made by field commanders in World War II that changed the course of the war and had a great effect on bringing it to an end.

Some of the US military leaders, including Chester Nimitz, were against using incendiary bombs on urban areas. Some considered it morally wrong to kill civilians, especially women and children. Others thought that burning down wooden shacks would not win the war, that industries had to be destroyed before any war could be won.

When LeMay first revealed his plans for the fire raids on all major cities of Japan, his staff couldn't believe he was serious. His experts argued their points against his proposals, and each time, the general had a convincing answer for why his plan would work. Why would he take such

Bulldozer operators, building North Field at Tinian Island, wave at a flight of B-29s from Saipan as they pass in salute. Josh Curtis

an unnecessary risk, he was asked, in removing all the guns on this mission? LeMay's answer: According to intelligence reports, there were only two night fighter groups in all four of the main Japanese home islands, so the risk that they could effectively attack a steady stream of B-29s flying over the city would be minimal.

With the B-29s flying at such a low altitude, some thought, the automatic antiaircraft guns would have a field day shooting them down. LeMay's answer: According to Intelligence reports, only two B-29s had been lost to antiaircraft guns. Unlike the German antiaircraft weapons, which were manipulated by radar, the Japanese guns were fired in conjunc-

tion with searchlights and were not controlled automatically by radar, thus allowing a wide range of inaccuracy in hitting fast-moving B-29 targets. Therefore, the general said, the risk of losing large numbers of our planes to Japanese antiaircraft guns would be unlikely.

Also of some concern was the matter of spacing the planes. The B-29s would take off from the three different islands, and planners hoped to get the planes over the target in the shortest time possible. Since the newly arrived 314th BW was located about 125mi south of Saipan and Tinian Island, they would be the first to leave the ground. Calculators determined they should begin their takeoff about 45–50min ahead of the attacking forces on Saipan and Tinian Island.

A takeoff policy had long since been determined for the B-29s participating in bombing missions. It would take a heavily loaded airplane about 1min, after applying power, to begin

the takeoff roll to reach the "point of no return," or near the end of the 8,800ft runways, where there would be no chance of safely aborting the takeoff. A flagman would signal the next plane to begin rolling. During a mission, at either of the bases in the Marianas, a B-29 on each runway would leave the ground at 1min intervals. Each of the bases had two parallel runways, and takeoff rolls were staggered at 30sec intervals, which meant that two planes were leaving the ground each minute.

LeMay didn't see the bombing of urban areas in the Japanese cities as unethical or immoral. It was a known fact, he said, that much of the Japanese industries' war effort took place in the homes of the Japanese people. Therefore, if the goal was to completely destroy Japan's industrial ability to continue the war, this aspect of their production would have to be destroyed also. The American people were also, by now, familiar with the fate of our

Destiny's Tot *was assigned to Capt.*
William Wienert's crew of the 9th BG, Tin-
ian Island. Larry Smith

prisoners of war in Japanese POW
camps, and sought retribution.

The maximum payload of forty M-
69 incendiary bombs was cased in
clusters weighing 500lb each. Each B-
29, loaded with bombs and fuel, would
register a gross weight of up to
140,000lb. On the Tokyo raid, each
plane would average only about 6 tons
of bombs, or almost 12,000lb of incendiaries.

Metal straps contained the incendiary bomb clusters, and the straps
were fused to break at a pre-determined height above the ground, causing the small, individual bombs to
scatter over a large area. One maximum load of clusters would cover an
area up to 0.5mi wide and about 1.5mi
long. The jellied substance in the
bombs would ignite upon impact, and
the fire was very difficult to extin-
guish. Water would spread the fire
rather than douse it.

LeMay designated Gen. Thomas S.
Power his spotter over Tokyo that
night. After leading his 314th BW on
the mission, he would drop his bombs
and then climb to 10,000ft or above,
and send reports back to Guam on
how the raid was progressing.

Sea of Flames Erupts in Tokyo

March 9, 1945, finally arrived.
This would be the day of reckoning for
LeMay's low-level advocates of firebombing urban areas in Tokyo. Late in
the afternoon, crews at Saipan and
Tinian Island were ready to climb
aboard their B-29s. LeMay stood by at
North Field, Guam, to watch General
Power lead the 314th BW crews on the
most daring B-29 mission ever under-
taken, to Japan. He would be carrying
M-47 incendiaries, as would a few of
the other leaders, but the main strike
force would unload the napalm M-69
incendiaries.

It was a few minutes after 6:00pm
when this author and crewmates
cranked up our Superfortress, newly
named *Mary Ann* in honor of our

One of the nights Toyama burned. Chuck
Spieth

A close-up of the incendiary 500lb cluster, before the tail fin is attached. Straps around the cluster could be fused to break at varied altitudes above ground, which scattered the 37lb napalm incendiary bombs. Hurth Thompkins

ground crew chief's daughter born since her dad left the States for Saipan, and prepared to taxi out to takeoff position. Since our hardstand was located near the eastern end of the runway and there was a prevailing easterly wind on Saipan, we had to use up lots of gas to get to the western end of the takeoff strip. There was nothing we could do about the long taxi ride to takeoff position, but on this particular afternoon the thought did cross my mind, *What if we should need this gas we're having to waste to get back to Isley Field tomorrow morning?*

We waved at the line of chaplains lined up near the point where we turned onto the runway, and they were waving at each plane and wishing us well on the mission. The takeoff was normal. Crossing the overrun above the Magicienne Bay, we leveled out just above the water and held our northeasterly course about 5min, and then when we passed Kagman Point, we began turning in a northerly direction toward Tokyo. The trip up was uneventful. Intercom conversation was

subdued, and about all conversation that took place, other than normal business from the navigator telling us to make corrections, was the excitement generated by the beautiful setting sun on our left. There were only a few clouds and they seemed to dance around the beautiful reddish glow of the sun.

Our flight route to Tokyo this night carried us very close to Iwo Jima, and the fighting taking place down below telegraphed a message to us that the struggle for the island was not yet over, and people were still dying down there.

With each mission to Japan, the same ugly feeling seemed to rear its head after passing Iwo Jima: Would our luck hold one more time? Maybe when the Marines finally capture the island, I thought, it will pass away, but on this mission, the feeling was still there. To me, the feeling moved to another level, and precautions became more important, because now we were approaching closer and closer to the front door of the enemy.

An hour or so after passing Iwo Jima, we entered the now-familiar weather front that seemed to linger somewhere along the line between Iwo Jima and Japan. We were flying at about 2,000ft altitude, but decided to get down a little lower to prevent the possibility of colliding with another B-

29 on the way to Tokyo. Our powerful R-3350 engines continued their monotonous roar that let us know that all was well so far.

Finally, our navigator, Jim O'Donnel, asked for a small correction and said it was time to start our climb to our bombing altitude. This was a crucial part of the trip up to the target. We were ordered to fly with our navigational lights off when north of Iwo Jima because of the possibility of there being Japanese ships below to take shots at us. You'd have to be very close to another ship in the soup, anyway, before you could see it, so we were climbing through zero-visibility weather and having to rely on the radar operator to warn us if we were on a collision course with another B-29. Finally, at about 5,000ft, we broke out of the clouds and looked upon one of the most horrifying scenes we had ever witnessed. We were still 50mi or so from landfall, and we could see the fires in Tokyo. Scanning searchlights filled the sky, trying to pick up approaching B-29s. We saw our first B-29 as we came closer to the searchlights. It was a strange feeling to see a few of our planes caught in the lights; you could tell they were being fired on because of the tracer bullets going up to them. We knew that several hundred B-29s should be all around us. Since we were in about the middle of the bomber stream, those nearest us were merging into the same route as our drop zone. How had we missed hitting a plane while climbing in that weather front? Now as we neared what seemed a fiery holocaust, we didn't have time to dwell on what might happen. It was time now to exert all our energy in trying to survive. We donned our dark glasses to try to avoid being blinded if caught in the searchlights. We noticed two B-29s were caught in the lights. When one light would get locked on, other lights would scan over to also lock on, and then they sent up barrages of flak. A B-29 caught in four or five searchlights is a beautiful but horrifying sight. You knew that its crew could be shot out of the sky any minute, but the beautiful silver B-29 gleamed a ghostly white, and you prayed that the people inside would make it through another minute or two.

For awhile, we flew parallel between the two B-29s caught in the searchlights, and lucky for us, all lights in the area were concentrating on those two to give gunners on the ground more time to shoot them down. Finally, we were caught in a fast-moving beam which, after scanning past us, switched back and caught us. It was brighter than daylight. We finally escaped the lights, but a much tougher chore lay ahead. By this time, we were passing over some of the area where the fire was beginning to meet and become a conflagration. Looking down into the streets of Tokyo, you could see flames coming from house windows, and the smell of burning debris was bad, but as we moved on further and opened our bomb bays, we were sickened by the sweet smell of burning human flesh. It was nauseating; I missed

at least two meals before I could eat anything again.

As we dropped our bombs and started to turn to get out of the smoke and flames reaching up to more than 10,000ft by this time, we hit a wind shear. We were lucky. We flew directly into a strong updraft heat thermal that had a G-force stronger than anything I had witnessed in my flying career. We were sucked up like a feather at a tremendous speed. Commander Cox and I both were completely demobilized. We were pinned to our seats, and it was impossible to lift an arm to control the airplane. Within seconds, it turned us loose, and we had gained more than 5,000ft almost instantly. If we had not hit the thermal head-on, we would have experienced what some other crews did in this and other incendiary raids. Several crews who sur-

T. N. Teeny II was assigned to the Capt. Wendell Hutchison crew of the 1st BS, 9th BG, Tinian Island. Larry Smith

vived the experience simply were flipped over on their back, but were lucky enough to get their plane under control before diving into the ground, one of the wings catching in the updraft and flipped the plane over.

For more than 2hr, the B-29s dropped bombs on one of the world's largest cities, and the results of that raid were so successful that there was never another word said about the B-29s not living up to their potential in the Pacific.

General Norstad had come to the Marianas to see how things were going at LeMay's 21st BC headquarters at Guam. After he was briefed on the up-

Daylight raid on Osaka, June 1, 1945. Note that the fires are beginning to spread. Chuck Spieth

A ten-plane flight of Superfortresses from the 29th BG, Guam, heads north. Andy Doty

coming fire raid on Tokyo, scheduled to take place March 9–10, he sent word back to Washington to stand by for word from an outstanding show. When the news about the most successful mission yet performed by the B-29s was released, nobody in Washington had a broader smile than General Arnold. His deep-rooted faith in the plane was now vindicated.

The fires started by the B-29s that night in Tokyo, aided by a 75mph wind, destroyed more than 16sq-mi of the city. Totally demolished were almost 25 percent of all buildings in Tokyo, or more than 267,171 structures. To the B-29 crews that witnessed the events unfolding below them, it was as described as "a nightmare out of Dante's inferno." Tokyo officials estimated that 83,783 people were killed outright, more than would die in the Hiroshima and Nagasaki atomic blasts later. At least 50,000 more were injured in the holocaust and the homes of more than 1,000,000 Tokyo residents were destroyed.

LeMay remained at his headquarters until he received the coded messages from General Powers, who was observing the massive inferno as it developed. The messages were transmitted over 2–3hr as a continuous stream of Superfortresses added their bomb loads on the city. Powers described the raid and its obvious results to LeMay while circling over the area until the last plane departed for its home base.

Raymond ("Hap") Halloran, navigator on the Snuffy Smith crew, had been a prisoner of war since his plane was shot down over Tokyo on January 27, 1945, when the B-29 Superfortresses swooped in over the city at low altitude and dropped their payloads. Halloran, along with some other POWs, was in solitary confinement, in what he called a horse stall, about 5ft wide and 8ft long. Located at the military police compound called Kempai Tai, he was about two or three blocks from the Imperial Palace. Hap recalls some of his thoughts that night: "An antiaircraft gun emplacement was located nearby, and when it was fired, the ground shook. I had often wondered if the guns were shooting down some of my friends, or if the B-29s were really doing much damage when they came over. No bombs had, so far,

fallen near our compound, and of course I had no way of judging.

"Sometime after midnight, I guessed, I was awakened by loud shouts and screaming coming, evidently, from people in the streets outside the compound. As I lay there in my darkened cell, I finally realized an air raid was in progress. I then began hearing the roar of airplanes that seemed to be directly over us at very low altitude. I couldn't imagine what the hell was happening. At first I thought the planes were Japanese, but soon I could recognize the roar that sounded mighty familiar—that of a B-29. It seemed they were coming over, sporadically, every minute or two. Near the ceiling of my cell was a small

opening, the only one in the room, and when I stood up I could see a huge orange glow from fires nearby.

"The frightening shouts and crying continued till late in the morning before dawn as more planes continued to come over. The fires spread rapidly, I was told, aided by a hurricane-force wind, and the resulting inferno looked as if the whole universe was on fire.

"I was suddenly seized with the terrifying thought that I might be burned to death. As the night wore on, and the loud commotion outside the compound continued, I had a fear that the frightened civilians might storm the compound and kill all of us POWs. But beneath the fears for my personal safety, I had a comforting feeling that

Nip Clipper *assigned to the Capt. M. I. Ashland crew, 9th BG, Tinian Island. This aircraft was shot down August 8, 1945, during a daylight raid on Yawata, Japan. The* Clipper *was being flown by the Carl Holden crew that day, and ten of the eleven men on board were taken prisoner by the Japanese. The eleventh crew member was never recovered from sea.* Larry Smith

our B-29 boys were getting the job done, and if they could keep this up, the war would soon be over.

"A guard told me the next morning that there was talk that the prisoners may be shot because of the many civilian deaths caused by the B-29s' attacks on the city. That, of course, was not a comforting thought."

73ʳᵈ WING PHOTOGRAPH

Chapter 12

Preparing for the Knockout Blow

Bolstered by the outstanding success of the March 10 incendiary raid on Tokyo, General LeMay's 21st BC in the Mariana Islands served notice to the military leaders, but also to the Japanese people in the streets of their cities.

In rapid-fire succession, the three wings of Superfortresses from Saipan, Tinian Island, and Guam carried out incendiary raids on Nagoya, Osaka, and Kobe, all important industrial cities and considered major contributors to the Japanese war effort. During the fourteen-day maximum-effort attacks, the six missions, including the Tokyo raid of March 10, 1,729 B-29s took part. They dropped a combined total of 10,858 tons—23,887,600lb—of incendiary clusters on urban areas of the cities. The missions, each carried out at night and flying individually en route to and over the targets, were flown at altitudes ranging from a low of 4,000ft to a maximum of 9,800ft. Twenty-six Superfortresses were lost during the six missions, fourteen of them in the March 9–10 Tokyo raid.

A flight of B-29s from the 498th BG at Saipan practices formation flying near the coast of Saipan. The gun barrels were often removed for low-level fire raids, but guns and gunners were carried on most regular bombing missions. 73rd BW Photo/Harold Dreeze

During this blitz, Tokyo, Osaka, and Kobe were hit only once, while three strikes were made on Nagoya, one of the most heavily saturated industrial cities. Adding up the results of the six strikes, LeMay was assured that the gamble he had taken paid off. The B-29s had fewer mechanical mishaps during the low-altitude attacks, and they had completely destroyed 32sq-mi in four of Japan's greatest cities.

After the six incendiary raids, LeMay received a message from General Arnold, requesting that he relay a message to all three wing commanders. He also instructed that the message be read to all combat crews. The message: "The series of five major strikes which you have performed in fewer than ten days constitute an impressive achievement, reflecting the spirit of your crews, but equally the determinations and the devotion to duty of your ground personnel. Every member of your command is to be commended for his vital share in this superior accomplishment. This is a significant sample of what the Jap can expect in the future. Good luck and good bombing." Arnold's message related to the five incendiary raids preceding the March 9–10 Tokyo fire raid.

That message was a real morale booster, but some of us thought that the many people working in the factories back in the States, building and testing the B-29, should also receive some of the accolades. The Superfortress had now developed into a real workhorse, manned by more confident crews that were getting results.

Nowhere was this more clear than on Iwo Jima. Two weeks after that island was invaded, the first B-29 landed for fuel and repairs, before taking off amidst fanatic fighting to return to its base in the Marianas. Lieutenant Malo and crew of the 9th BG, at Tinian Island, had trouble with fuel transfer over Japan, and because of this and other damage sustained, were faced with the choice of either trying to land on a small fighter strip near the southern tip of the island adjacent to Mount Suribachi or ditch in the ocean. Malo decided to try landing on the volcanic-ash 4,000ft runway. Like all Superfort pilots, he was used to landing on 8,000ft or longer runways, and he thought the outcome might be somewhat doubtful.

The control tower told Malo about the obstructions and fighting going on around the runway. He landed safely, made a few repairs, added enough fuel to get back to Tinian Island, and took off—becoming the first B-29 to land at Iwo Jima. This crew's luck ran out before the end of the war, however. On another mission to Japan, they were shot down and killed.

After Malo's successful stop at Iwo Jima, all crews in the Marianas were warned not to attempt a landing there

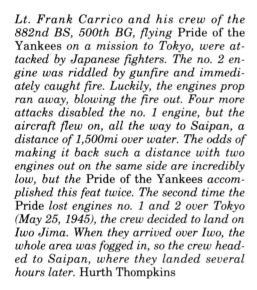

Lt. Frank Carrico and his crew of the 882nd BS, 500th BG, flying Pride of the Yankees *on a mission to Tokyo, were attacked by Japanese fighters. The no. 2 engine was riddled by gunfire and immediately caught fire. Luckily, the engines prop ran away, blowing the fire out. Four more attacks disabled the no. 1 engine, but the aircraft flew on, all the way to Saipan, a distance of 1,500mi over water. The odds of making it back such a distance with two engines out on the same side are incredibly low, but the* Pride of the Yankees *accomplished this feat twice. The second time the* Pride *lost engines no. 1 and 2 over Tokyo (May 25, 1945), the crew decided to land on Iwo Jima. When they arrived over Iwo, the whole area was fogged in, so the crew headed to Saipan, where they landed several hours later.* Hurth Thompkins

Capt. Louis J. Whitten and crew, flying Twentieth Century Sweetheart, *dropped supplies on a POW camp in Shanghai on September 7, 1945.* Josh Curtis

unless theirs was an extreme emergency. For the next two weeks before the island was secured, a small number did land there, including this author and his crew.

Weather forecasting continued to give mission planners major problems. Neither the Russians nor Chinese would help LeMay collect weather data from that part of the world to make reliable forecasts for upcoming weather over the Japanese home islands. Consequently, there was no way to determine weather over a given target 24hr before a scheduled mission.

Finally, a small weather-observer unit composed of eight trained observers and forecasters, called "The Fightin' 55th," was sent to the Marianas to work with the 21st BC. These men, including Jack C. Grantham and

"Ham" Howard, came up with the idea of sending combat crew-manned B-29s, with one of the weathermen aboard with his instruments and equipment, to Japan to send a report back before or while a mission was being planned. Other unit members included Ed Everts, Al Louchard, Bob Moore, Juke Nielson, and Dick Worthen. This worked out very well.

Targets were selected according to good weather advantages. Finally, "weather ships" became a major part of scheduled missions, with up to three weather plane trips to and from the selected target area to forecast weather for the upcoming strike. These planes usually flew across the main island of Honshu, if the mission was to take place anywhere in that vicinity, and from one end to the other, and even west of the island sometimes to check weather in the Sea of Japan. These weather missions culminated at command headquarters at Guam, where the weather observer made his report.

My first "weather strike" and a brush with history on Iwo Jima came during the maximum-effort fire raids in March. We were scheduled to take off before dawn on March 16, fly to Japan, cross Honshu, and generally check the weather conditions all over the island. A weather observer was with us. Altitude was to be 30,000ft over Japan, but as we neared the coastline of Honshu, we experienced a few backfires on one of the engines. Flight engineer John Huckins checked the oil and recommended we not climb any further since oil pressure was not

what it should be. The skies over Japan looked peaceful and almost clear, so rather than continue to climb above the 26,000ft we had already reached, we remained at that level. We felt it was more or less imperative to make a stab at crossing Honshu and send back weather conditions for the scheduled incendiary strike that night on Kobe, so we proceeded across the mountains just north of Mount Fuji. As we made our turn to set a heading to return home, Huckins announced that the oil pressure in the ailing engine had dropped to near zero, so Commander John Cox told him to feather the engine. Crossing over a peaceful-looking bay near the coastline on our return route, we began getting fire from a large destroyer which we had not seen down below. As this was happening, Huckins made another startling announcement: The oil pressure in another engine was beginning to falter. We'd soon be flying with only two engines.

We were flying on a wing and a prayer, and with two engines out, it was difficult to maintain altitude all the way from Japan. We had made a decision, and had set our heading for Iwo Jima. Hopefully, we could make an emergency landing there, and avoid having to ditch our plane in the ferocious Pacific Ocean. Our base at Saipan was still hundreds of miles away. The date: March 16, 1945.

As we neared the gourd-shaped 7mi-long piece of volcanic no-man's land, we could see the fighting taking place with smoke and flashes from artillery guns covering a big part of the northern sector. We called Hotrocks tower for a straight-in approach to the short fighter strip near the base of Mount Suribachi on the southern tip of the island. There was no way to land on a runway under construction on the plateau just north of the fighter strip. The scene throughout the island was one of desolation, and on our descent, the closer we got to the landing strip, the sulfuric stench, mixed with a sweet smell of death, seemed to seep into our cockpit. We landed safely after skidding all the way down the soft volcanic-ash runway. A crowd of Marines, looking as if they were fresh out of the trenches or fox holes, came over to look at our giant Superfortress and chat with us. They tried to make us feel like heroes, but we responded with, "Not us. You fellows are the heroes!" We had to stay over for engine repairs, and that is how I got a real brush with history. On Saipan, the climate is tropical, never cold, but at Iwo Jima it was a different story the night of March 16, 1945. I was not quite sure if I shivered because I was cold or if it was fright.

The Star shells kept the whole island lit up throughout the night, and when dawn finally came, we were told the Island commander had declared Iwo Jima secure. "Secure, hell!" we said, "Those bullets are still flying and people are still dying." But the morning of March 17 went down in history as the date our Marines captured Iwo Jima. Now for almost half a century since that date, like more than 20,000 other B-29 flyers who made emergency landings on Iwo Jima, I still pause periodically and utter an almost-silent prayer: "Thank God for the Marines and Iwo Jima!"

The massive six-mission firebomb blitz depleted the M-69 incendiary bomb supply, but there would be no let-up in attacks against Japan. Now that Iwo Jima had been captured, it was rapidly being turned into a major air base capable of handling large numbers of B-29s low on fuel returning from regular strategic bombing missions. Also, the P-51s were being moved up to Iwo Jima and would shortly begin escorting the Super-

The 500th BG's Big Z Superfortress shower incendiary clusters on a target below. 73rd BW Photo/Harold Dreeze

Lt. Chuck Spieth and crew pose in front of their B-29 while ground crew men inspect the no. 2 engine. Chuck Spieth

Bugger of the 331st BG, 315th BW, has varied mission markers. The parachuting symbol indicates that the crew flew a POW supply drop after the war. The loaded donkey symbol probably indicated that the crew made a forced landing and had to use every method available to get back to base. George Harrington/Josh Curtis

fortresses over Japan and making further attacks on airfields, shipyards, and other targets before joining up with a B-29 "mother ship" to escort them on the 700mi flight back to Iwo Jima. There would be no let up while awaiting for the incendiary bomb supply to be replenished.

The second phase of the attack on the Japanese homeland began as March wound down. The promised aerial mining of harbors and ports around the home islands was about to begin. As far back as January 1945, Admiral Nimitz tried to persuade General LeMay to start the aerial mining and keep it going continuously, but LeMay insisted and General Arnold

agreed that the 20th AF had to get on with its primary responsibility of destroying selected industrial targets. LeMay said that when more B-29s joined the attack, he would begin the mining project, but not until the last of March or April.

The Navy assigned a detachment of mining warfare experts, headed by Cdr. Ellis A. Johnston, to the 21st BC, with orders to instruct the B-29 crews in aerial mining. The 313th BW was assigned the task of delivering the mines to the many harbors and straits in and around all of Japan's main islands, plus some harbors in Korea. This phase was to be known as Operation Starvation. The 58th BW had carried out some very successful mining missions at Singapore, Saigon, Johore Straits, and other targets, before winding down its CBI operation at the end of March. The 58th BWs' last mining mission was a thirty-three–plane strike against the Port of Singapore on March 28–29.

On March 27, the 313th BW sent 102 B-29s on their initial mining drop

on Shimonoseki Straits. Flying at altitudes of 5,000–8,000ft, they dropped 571 tons of aerial mines, some with fuses delayed, to explode when ships passed over. On March 30–31, the 313th went back to the same target. Included this time were ninety-four B-29s carrying 513 tons of mines. The 314th BW sent one of its groups, the 19th, back to Nagoya with all-purpose bombs.

As the aerial mining project was getting underway, Nimitz made another urgent request to LeMay for more help from the B-29s. The Navy had experienced a few suicidal attacks by Japanese fighters during the Philippine operation. The invasion of Okinawa was scheduled to begin April 1, and Nimitz asked LeMay to attack the airfields on Kyushu Island, where he thought the suicide missions would be launched from ships and invasion forces just a little over 300mi south of those fields.

LeMay was again reluctant to change courses in his planned attacks, especially since he thought the Japanese were reeling from the effects of his latest major attacks. He did agree to send his Superfortresses to attack the airfields on Kyushu. On March 31, he sent the 73rd and 314th BWs to bomb airfields while the 313th BW dropped mines in Shimonoseki Straits.

The invasion of Okinawa took place on Easter morning, and the B-29 attack on Kyushu seemed to have been effective. For the next four or five days, the Japanese kamikaze planes stayed away. Then things changed drastically. On April 6, they came in force. Japanese bombers attacked the invaders on land and more than 300 kamikaze pilots began diving into the ships off shore. Admiral Nimitz called for more help with the airfields, and on April 8, General LeMay's B-29s struck six Kyushu airfields. For a short time again, the kamikazes didn't come, but for three weeks, LeMay had to divert his attacks from scheduled targets to the airfields on Kyushu.

On April 7, the 73rd BW went back to Tokyo. This time it would be different. For the first time since the beginning of the B-29 assault on Japan, we would have escort service from the now operative 7th Fighter Command's P-51s off Iwo Jima. This would be a daylight mission going in at the unusually low altitude of 11,000–15,650ft. All four groups would rendezvous just off the coast of Japan, at bombing altitudes. We had orders to circle until all planes assembled by groups, and by then, if the P-51s had not arrived to form a protective umbrella over us, we were to make three more big circles before going in without them. Shortly after starting our second circle, we saw the specks approaching, and as they came to us and positioned themselves in battle formation, I thought that was the most beautiful sight I had ever witnessed: 121 B-29s heading toward their target with about fifty P-51s hovering above them.

As we neared the coastline, I glanced down and saw a twin-engine Japanese fighter climbing up to attack us. The P-51 pilots directly above our plane saw him also, and two P-51s dove straight down across our nose and shot the plane down. Two parachutes appeared before we got out of sight. Capts. Robert T. Down and Richard H. Hintermeier, the two P-51 pilots who attacked the Japanese plane, were credited with shooting down the first Japanese plane, flying land-based American fighter planes, over the Japanese home islands.

Iwo Jima became a beehive of activity after the P-51s moved in; they and the P-61 Black Widows left temporary quarters at Saipan to help locate lost B-29s. The new occupants were trying to make the place livable, even though the many caves that had been bull-dozed shut contained dead bodies.

Soon after Iwo Jima was captured and the tally had been totaled up, word got back to Saipan that some of the statisticians in Washington wondered if the price paid for capturing such a small piece of rock was worth it. The numbers were indeed impressive: When the fighting ended in March 1945, more than 6,800 American Marines had paid the supreme sacrifice, and more than 19,000 were wounded. Only 1,000 of the estimated 21,000 Japanese soldiers defending the island were taken prisoner. The rest died.

Everyone who set foot on Iwo Jima called the volcanic ash-covered piece of no-man's land a "hell on earth."

Maj. Harry C. Crim, commander of one of the P-51 squadrons sent to escort B-29s over the targets in Japan, describes the locale best: "Iwo Jima was perhaps one of the most hostile ground environments a person could find himself in. Dante, in his visions of Hell, could have used Iwo for a model. Nature provided an active volcano, and men provided the war."

As soon as Iwo Jima was made ready to accept B-29s in trouble on a regular basis, a detachment of aircraft mechanics was sent to service the planes that needed fuel or repair. The only trouble was that most of the men sent had received no training on B-29s. As the number of landings increased, the B-29s stacked up to the extent that parking space became a premium. Somebody finally came up with a solution: One experienced me-chanic from each squadron operating from the Marianas, twenty in all, were sent to Iwo Jima to straighten out this tangled mess and to organize an efficient operation. Each mechanic was a specialist in a given field—hydraulics, electrical systems, instruments, and engines. At first, they thought their tour of duty on Iwo Jima would be a short one, but they were sadly mistaken. They all were there when the war ended six months later.

One of these specialists was Allen Hassell, an engine mechanic. He recalls how shocked he and others were when they landed on what he called a "hell on earth": "I am in total agreement with Major Crim's assessment of Iwo Jima being the most hostile ground environment a person could find himself in. The first thing we saw after debarking from the plane that brought us to such a godforsaken place was the steam escaping from the ground all around us. My first thoughts were, *Gosh! The ground is on fire!* The stench from the escaping sulfur fumes made the place smell like a rotten-egg dump. When the truck came to pick us up and carry us to our living area, I got another rude awakening about our new abode. I jumped into the cab with the driver, thinking maybe I could get some 'inside poop' from him. Our conversation went something like this:

"'Do they have any showers around here?'

"'Showers?' he replied, 'I wake up every morning with my eyelids stuck together!'

"'How's the food?'

"'Ha! Ha! Rotten!'

"That conversation served notice that we were in for many more surprises before we settled down to a workable routine. Living conditions, however, never did improve much! When I returned to Saipan, after the Japs threw in the towel, most of my old friends had long since rotated back to the States. But I had lived a part of the war that I could truthfully tell people who listened and who may express some doubts that I had truly 'served in hell on earth and came back!'"

Chapter 13

Build-up for Countdown

The fighting in and around Okinawa by the second week in April 1945 was not progressing very well. The kamikaze planes were still giving the Navy ships a bad time and the Japanese soldiers were putting up a strong defense against the US Army units. As expected, rumor had the B-29s scheduled for a major strike at Okinawa, in support of the fighting there.

There must have been something to the latest rumors, because this author's crew was selected to fly a weather strike to Okinawa, with a weather observer aboard to check the weather for an upcoming major strike there. This would be our second "easy" mission. Some of the crews called weather missions "milk runs," even though they were exposed to the full force of the enemy alone over his territory. We believed scuttlebutt about weather strikes being easy until we had our brush with history at Iwo Jima on March 16–17. This mission, however, would be routine, we were almost certain. We knew the Navy's 58th Task Force was off the coast of Okinawa, and what better protection could we have with all that power on our side?

The flight to our turn-around point, just off the coast of Okinawa,

Twentieth Century Fox *flew with the 501st BG, 315th BW, Guam.* Josh Curtis

was very boring. At 30,000ft, we felt secure against enemy fighter attacks, so we let our guard down. If there ever was a relaxed crew on a combat mission in enemy territory, it was our entire crew that day. On homeward-bound flights, John Sutherland, our tail gunner, would crawl through the tunnel and, after giving the front-end troops the news of what was going in the rear of the plane, would lay between commander John Cox and me and watch the auto-pilot for us. He was pretty good at keeping the indicator lights on the instrument out, which means the plane is flying straight and level when no light is bleeping.

I'm sure we need not worry about a court-martial at this late date, so now it can be told. I can swear to it that every man aboard our plane went to sleep, including the weather observer and our tail gunner, who was the only man supposedly watching the controls of the aircraft at that time.

No one knew how long we remained asleep, but we all suddenly had a rude awakening. Kendal Chance, our central fire control gunner, was the first to shout the alarm that we were being attacked by bogies. But his warnings were ineffective, since four bogies dived down across our nose, and we suddenly had a sinking feeling that we were about to get our ticket punched.

All I could say was, "What the hell!"

Cox came alive and yelled, "Check the back-end and see if the gunners have the gun sights on."

It's too bad if you go into battle with your gun sights off, because it takes a few minutes for them to warm up before becoming operative to fire the guns. No! The guns had not been turned on, so there we were like a ship dead in the water.

Our "secure" position at 30,000ft above a solid overcast didn't seem "secure" anymore. By this time, the bogies were coming in for another attack. But, by this time, also, the whole crew was alert, and the sleepiness had been wiped from our eyes—and some sharp aircraft identification expert on the crew yelled over the intercom, "Oh, heck! They're US Marine planes."

One of the pilots pulled right up under our wing and made an attempt at hand-signaling to us. I signaled to him that I was turning our radio to the frequency he was supposed to be on, and so we made contact. The first thing I heard him say was, "Texas base, we have found the 'bogie' and have identified it as a 'friendly monster'."

He went on to tell me that our IFF (Identification Friend or Foe) was inoperative, and that we were showing up on "Texas Base," his aircraft carrier below, as a bogie. "You better get out

The City of Memphis *screeched in amid a stream of smoke. Handwerker and crew flew with the 19th BG, 314th BW, at Guam.* Jim Handwerker

Aircraft commander Jim Handwerker, center, standing, and crew brought the City of Memphis *all the way from Tokyo to Guam the night of April 1, 1945, after two engines on the same side were lost over the target. Handwerker was awarded the Silver Star.* Jim Handwerker

of the area as fast as you can. We have the whole 58th Task Force around here."

"For God's sake, be sure and emphasize that we are extremely friendly. How about you fellows staying with us awhile to keep them from shooting us down?"

We had a very friendly visit with the Marine pilots, and they stayed with us about 30min to "protect" us from our own Navy ships below.

Bombing strategy took on a new look in April. Multi-wing mass raids to a single target gave way to fewer planes involved in some of the raids. The 73rd BW usually sent out all four of its groups on a strike, but the 313th and 314th scheduled their attacks in squadron and group flights to a single target. Almost daily, B-29s roamed the skies over Japan, especially after beginning the attack on airfields on Kyushu.

Two three-wing attacks took place during April 13–14 when 348 B-29s dropped 2,124 tons of incendiary bomb clusters on Tokyo arsenal from altitudes of 6,000–11,000ft. Seven Superfortresses were lost that night. The night of April 15, the 313th and the 314th BWs dropped 1,110 tons of incendiaries on the urban area of Kawasaki, a city just south of Tokyo. Twelve B-29s were lost that night.

While joining in the attacks on the airfields on Kyushu, at times the 313th continued mine-laying flights. Twice during the month, they mined the port at Hiroshima, and twice they dropped mines in Shimonoseki Straits.

On April 12, General O'Donnell's 73rd BW was scheduled to try once again to knock out the illusive target no. 357, the Musashino Engine Factory at Tokyo; 114 B-29s were scheduled to participate. Again, the P-51s off Iwo Jima would escort the B-29s on this mission. Both the 313th BW, with eighty-two planes scheduled, and the 314th BW, with eighty-five B-29s, were scheduled to hit a chemical plant at Koriyama, about 125mi north of Tokyo.

Action during the daylight raid on Koriyama would result in the first and

only Medal of Honor to a B-29 combat crew member of the 20th AF in World War II. The recipient of the award Sgt. Henry E. ("Red") Erwin, the radio operator on Capt. George A. Simeral's crew of the 52nd BS, 29th BG, 314th BW.

Captain Simeral was a flight leader, and on this particular mission, his flight would be leading the squadron, with the squadron commander, Lt. Col. Eugene Strouse, in the right seat. Simeral remembers the incident vividly: "We arrived over Aoga Shima, our rendezvous area, and began to fly the prescribed pattern to pick up the formation. I motioned for Erwin to fire some flares and then a smoke bomb to attract the attention of our other aircraft in the area and to identify us as the lead plane.

"The flares dropped through the tube without incident, but when Erwin pulled the pin on the phosphorous flare, it malfunctioned and exploded, blowing particles of phosphorous into his eyes and burning off most of his right ear, part of his nose, and most of the skin from his right arm. Patches of skin were seared from his face. Red said afterwards that he felt no pain at the time, but knew he had to get the flare out of the plane.

"The forward section of the plane filled with dense white smoke and became so thick that I could not see my instrument panel. We were at 1,000ft

An unusual shot of Mount Fuji in Japan, looking out over the left wing and engines of a B-29 en route to its target in Tokyo. Kelcie Teague

and fortunately on auto-pilot, except for the elevators. My biggest concern was to avoid placing too much pressure on the control column and causing us to stall, which would have been fatal at that low an altitude.

"In the meantime, Red had packed up the burning phosphorous bomb and crawled with it toward the cockpit. He went past the navigator, who was in the tunnel observing through his blister, unlatched the navigator's table from the gun turret, and lurched toward the co-pilot, shouting for him to open the window.

"With superhuman effort, he raised himself up in front of Colonel Strouse and threw the burning bomb out the window."

On April 19, 1945, at the hospital at Guam, Maj. Gen. Willis H. Hale, commanding general of the Army Air Forces, Pacific Ocean Area, presented Sergeant Erwin, with the Medal of Honor. Standing in the room by his bed were Maj. Gen. Curtis E. LeMay, and Brig. Gen. Thomas Power, Erwin's wing commander. Also present were squadron commanders of the 29th BG and the crew of his B-29. Erwin's gallantry and heroism, above and beyond the call of duty, saved the lives of his comrades.

Balls of Fire

In his foreword to the 9th BG's *War Journal*, commanding officer Col.

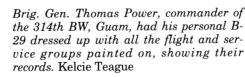

Brig. Gen. Thomas Power, commander of the 314th BW, Guam, had his personal B-29 dressed up with all the flight and service groups painted on, showing their records. Kelcie Teague

Henry C. Huglin said of the 2,500 men in his group: "...[They] were forged in the crucible of war into a brilliantly smooth-working team whose accomplishments will forever be indelibly inscribed in the war annals of the United States as a glowing tribute to themselves and to their country."

As one of the four groups that made up the 313th BW, the 9th BG took part in the aerial mining of the home ports of Japan, as well as many of the incendiary fire raids. The *War Journal* had this recorded account about the group's incendiary attacks: "April 13–14, 1945—With today's effort, we resumed our incendiary attacks against Japan's major cities. Our target was the Tokyo Arsenal area. We had another perfect score, with twenty-eight aircraft scheduled, twenty-eight airborne, twenty-eight striking the primary, and twenty-eight returning safely to base. Sixteen fighter attacks were made and antiaircraft fire was moderate to intense. This mission was one of our most successful and resulted in destruction of approximately 11sq-mi of the city. April 15–16, 1945—Swiftly we followed up our sec-

ond big raid on Tokyo with a blow the next night, at the adjoining city of Kawasaki. This was our toughest, as well as our costliest, mission. Over fifty enemy aircraft were encountered. Approximately a dozen 'Balls of Fire' were sighted by our crews. With over 300 aircraft going over the target, the danger of mid-air collision was ever-present. The antiaircraft fire was both accurate and intense. We were in it longer, too. Heat thermals, one of the serious perils on these raids, were unusually severe. There were thirteen aircraft lost in the Bomber Command. Four of them were ours."

The fire raids on Japanese cities in 1945 instilled memories that will last forever. Anyone who was there witnessing the most destructive fires in the history of the world, as they developed into conflagrations, can close his eyes, even after half a century, and still "see" the devastating holocaust.

At first, combat crews who had to carry out those unbelievable orders vented their fury on General LeMay, the architect of such an unorthodox way of using the high-altitude bomber. Van R. Parker, an aircraft commander in the 28th BS, 19th BG, had a lot of misgivings about LeMay when he heard about the upcoming fire raids. He relates: "Down through the years, I have been amused with published ac-

And the rains came. This was the scene soon after the 314th BW arrived at North Field, Guam—not a pleasant welcome. Kelcie Teague

Fires begin to spread as Superfortresses drop incendiaries on Tarumiza, Kyushu.

counts of thoughts of the combat crew personnel regarding General LeMay's decision to go to low-level firebombing raids on the Japanese cities. My reaction at the time was one of outrage. I felt violated and condemned to a quick demise before I had hardly gotten started in combat. The most good I could say about LeMay was that he had taken full leave of his senses.

"After World War II, I decided to make the USAAF my career, and I got to know General LeMay pretty well, and one day I asked him what was the toughest decision he had ever made. He responded without hesitation, 'My decision to send B-29s in at low level over Japan.'

"The low-level fire raids also caused me to make a personal, unorthodox decision. Following the first Tokyo fire raid, having witnessed the inferno from a very low altitude, I vowed that I would never again wear a parachute over the Japanese homeland. I didn't."

The stress from making these low-level fire raids was not only on the crews, but also on the B-29s themselves, especially when they had to withstand heat thermals after the fires had built into a giant conflagration. Wells Johnson, a flight engineer with the 680th BS, 504th BG, on Tinian Island, describes the experiences one of his friends had after hitting a strong heat thermal: "My friend told me about his experience while his crew and mine were taking a four-day rest leave. He said the updrafts that grabbed their B-29 were so intense that their own bombs, just released, reversed direction and came back into the bomb bays, knocking off a bomb bay door and damaging the vertical stabilizer. He said water flasks and loose equipment seemed to float in mid-air. The over-the-target updrafts were so forceful, and likely very hot, that the B-29 was flipped over, and they found themselves heading back. Maj. Robert Langdale, the aircraft commander, was equal to the task, righting the big bird, making a 180deg turn, and heading back toward the exit route. After the scary maneuvers, the drag of the missing bomb bay door, and other damage, they made it all the way back to Tinian Island without a

Capt. Paul E. Jones lines his crew up in front of the Bataan Avenger, *before takeoff. The* Bataan Avenger *was flipped over on her back during a heat thermal updraft over Osaka on March 13, 1945. No one was seriously injured.* Thomas

Smoke from fires at a target city reach up past bombing altitude. Chuck Spieth

stop at Iwo. None of the crew was injured, except emotionally."

At Saipan, this author often wondered if Admiral Nimitz or any of his staff knew just how much the Navy bolstered the morale of some of the people in the 73rd BW. Some of the groups organized an "Island Whiskey Pool" and charged a membership fee of fifty dollars. The "whiskey ship" always came in about once a month, and members had the privilege of buying their quota, usually two-fifths of whiskey and one-fifth of rum or gin. Elmer Huhta, an intelligence officer in the 872nd BS, 500th Group, 73rd BW, Saipan, tells how he was invited to join the club: "Shortly after I got to Saipan, a young lieutenant from the 21st BC headquarters, then temporarily located at Saipan, came to me and demanded fifty dollars for membership in the Island Liquor Pool. I asked him if it was mandatory that I join the pool, and he replied, 'Hell, yes. All offi-

cers in the 73rd BW have to get in!' After he had explained the rules, including the provision that my money would be refunded when I departed the island, and most of all, the privilege of purchasing incoming whiskey, rum, and gin about once a month for $1.25 a bottle, I quickly handed him my money. As he turned to leave, with a smirk on his face, I could swear he muttered, 'To hell with the ammo, pass the booze!'

"It was almost as if the Marines up in the hills and the Seabees could smell the ships that arrived with our booze, because they all turned up in the 73rd BW area as soon as the ships began unloading. They would happily pay up to $100 a fifth to those of us who were willing to part with some of our spirits. The Marines were no dummies. For a captured Jap sword, the going rate was $150."

As April droned on, all wings continued their support of the Navy and Army at Okinawa by continually bombing airfields on Kyushu. The missions averaged twenty-five or thirty planes on any given target, but they were continuously going back to the airfield to keep them inoperable. There were two exceptions during the latter part of the month. On April 24,

General LeMay sent three wings to bomb an aircraft engine factory at Tachikawa. One-hundred thirty-one B-29s participated, carrying 474 tons of high-explosive bombs. Bombing altitude was 10,000–14,500ft. Five B-29s failed to return. One-hundred six planes loaded with 378 tons of bombs went back to Tachikawa to bomb the air depot from an altitude of 1,700–2,150ft. No B-29s were lost in this raid. A total of forty-seven planes were lost and 120 B-29s made emergency landings at Iwo Jima en route to home bases after missions to Japan during April.

Iwo Jima was fast becoming a way station for B-29s or a mid-way point to stop and get needed repairs or fuel en route to their home bases after bombing raids on Japan. The weather was always causing problems in that part of the Pacific Ocean, and sometimes prevented badly damaged B-29s from landing; those crews were forced to bail out over the island and let their planes continue flying on auto-pilot with hopes that the aircraft would fly out of the area before running out of gas and plunging into the ocean. An abandoned B-29 flying itself near a busy landing strip in the middle of the ocean could present a dangerous situation with other aircraft in the area. To prevent such a tragic mishap from happening, the P-61 squadron at Iwo

B-29 mechanics in the Marianas were never done. Another engine change is underway. Chuck Spieth

Jima was given the assignment of shooting down abandoned B-29s.

Robert D. Thum, a Black Widow pilot in the 549th Night Fighter Squadron, says he shot down two B-29s during his stay at Iwo Jima: "It was kind of a strange feeling to attack one of those beautiful Superfortresses. There was a bit of danger in pulling up to an airplane flying on its own, because you would never know when it would 'turn on you'. I would fly in very close to get a clear view to see if anyone was still in the cockpit. After making the decision that it was clear of personnel, it became a fighter pilot's most exciting challenge in shooting down the B-29."

During a twenty-five–day period beginning April 17 and lasting through May 11, when the airfield bombings ceased, 2,104 sorties were flown by the B-29s from the 73rd, 313th, and 314th BWs. All these missions were daylight strikes on seventeen airfields, and there was seldom a

day that B-29s were not over Japan's two southernmost islands. The pattern for scheduled attacks during the last half of the attacks would send planes from each wing to several different airfields the same day. For instance, on May 3, the 314th BW attacked six airfields with eleven planes. The 313th Wing's policy was essentially the same.

The 313th did, however, revert from the airfield attacks back to mining missions. On May 5–6, all four groups sent ninety-seven B-29s carrying 577 tons of mines back to Shimonoseki Straits.

58th Wing Moves to Tinian Island

During April, the 58th BW completed its move to the newly constructed West Field, located south of the four-runway North Field on Tinian Island, and General Ramey was ready to launch his first attack on the Japanese homeland by May 5. On that date, the 58th BW joined the 73rd BW in a 170-plane attack on Hiro, Japan. Two B-29s were lost on this mission, and sixty-eight planes had to use Iwo Jima's hospitality for repairs and refueling.

Also at this time, the 20th BC was merged into the 21st BC, with General LeMay remaining in command. With the full strength of the 20th AF's B-29s now concentrated in the Mariana Islands, General LeMay, as well as General Arnold in Washington, was anxious to get back to the task of completing what the B-29s were supposed to do: knock Japan out of the war.

With the obligation to assist the Navy at Okinawa now behind him, and with a new supply of the highly successful napalm M-69 incendiary bombs on hand, LeMay was ready. While the 313th Wing was winding down the airfield attacks, on May 10, the 314th Wing sent 132 B-29s to Otake to drop 549 tons of explosives on industrial and oil refinery facilities. One plane was lost during this strike, and twelve planes landed at Iwo Jima.

On May 10, the 58th BW, making their second strike against Japan from the Marianas, sent eighty-eight B-29s carrying 383 tons of explosives to hit industrial and oil storage facilities at O'Shima. On that same date, the 73rd BW sent a 260-plus–plane strike to Tokuyama, one to hit a fuel station facility and the other to hit a coal facility.

On May 14, General LeMay was able to schedule, for the first time, a 500-plus–plane mission. Using all four wings for the first maximum-effort incendiary raid since the April 13–14 fire raid on the Tokyo Arsenal, he launched 524 B-29s carrying 2,515 tons of M-69s on a daylight, 16,000–20,000ft altitude attack on Nagoya. A second fire raid, on May 16–17, with 516 planes participating, hit Nagoya's urban area again. This time, they went in at a lower altitude of 600–1,858ft, carrying a heavier load of 3,609 tons of M-69 clusters. Eleven planes were lost on the first raid, and three were lost on the second. Sixteen planes were forced to land at Iwo Jima on the second raid flown after the island was captured. Tachikawa was attacked next by 309 B-29s attacking from 13,000–26,600ft. And one group from the 313th BW was keeping up their constant attack, dropping mines mostly in Shimonoseki Straits.

On May 23–24, a record-breaking 558 planes hit the Tokyo urban area with firebombs again. This was the largest single-mission attack to date

for the B-29s, the planes carried a record 3,646 tons of bombs and dropped them from 7,000–15,100ft. Seventeen Superfortresses were lost on this mission, and forty-nine had to land at Iwo Jima. The Japanese anti-aircraft gunners were improving, as were attacks from a few night fighters and what some observed as pilotless Baka Bombs.

On May 25–26, the B-29s saturated the Tokyo urban area with fire-bombs once again, using 498 bombers. But again, the Japanese defenders were ready and waiting. A record twenty-six B-29s were shot down or were unable to make it back that night. This turned out to be the biggest loss of B-29s over Japan on a single mission during the war. These two Tokyo raids destroyed an addi-

tional 18sq-mi in the heart of the city near the Imperial Palace.

Every B-29 combat crew had been warned not to drop bombs on the Imperial Palace compound, but during this second mission, parts of the Palace grounds buildings and the Palace itself received fire damage from flying debris. It was learned after the war the Emperor and Empress were in their air raid shelter during the raid and were not injured.

Time and time again, the B-29 Superfortress proved its metal in bringing its crew back after being heavily damaged. There are numerous cases where the pilots brought their planes back after losing two engines or fuselage or suffering tremendous wing damage.

Aircraft commander Claude E.

Goin' Jessie, *the "goingest" B-29 in the 20th AF. Larry Smith*

Hensinger, of the 679th BS, 444th BG, 58th BW, made it back to Iwo Jima from the May 23 incendiary raid on Tokyo in *Jo* after being rammed by another B-29 over the target area. The fantastic story of this plane's combat exploits probably would not have been known Stateside had it not been for the sheet metal workers at the Martin Superfortress plant in Omaha, Nebraska. After working on the plane during its production, they left a note hidden in the cockpit, asking the crew that would be assigned to *Jo* to please keep them informed about their combat experiences. Viva P. Turnbull, one

The flight crew of Goin' Jessie. *The crew included John Fleming, aircraft commander; Charles Chauncey, pilot; Jack Cremer, navigator; Julius Chilipka, bombardier. Kneeling: Prushko, Rice, Scribner, Coldman, Waldron and Roncace.* Charles Chauncey

of the workers, was named correspondent with the yet-to-be-assigned combat crew members. Hensinger kept the metal workers informed of his crew's experiences on Tinian Island and of their combat missions, including the May 23 mission to Tokyo.

The following is a play-by-play account of *Jo's* last hours, as related by Hensinger: "We took off from Tinian Island on the night of May 23 to firebomb Tokyo. Everything went fine until after 'bombs-away,' when the Superfort flew into a large smoke cloud. In the next instant, there was a terrific jar and crash of metal. Whether we had suffered a direct flak hit or had collided with another B-29 was not of any importance at the time, for things began to happen to *Jo*. The pilot's control column went limp and the no. 1 engine quit. The co-pilot and pilot rudder controls went out, all instruments were knocked out on no. 1 and 2 engines, and we soon found ourselves

headed back over Tokyo as a result of the blow.

"The only thing working in the cockpit, it seemed, was the auto-pilot, and that was what got us back to Iwo Jima. We were able to manipulate the ailerons and rudder with the auto-pilot controls, and were able to keep the plane on a straight and level flight. I decided on a wheels-down landing attempt at Iwo, but with no brakes, I knew that would present a real problem. We decided to tie parachutes in the tail gun position and open them just before touchdown to help stop the plane. After a hectic ride down the runway and off the end overrun, a stretch of very rough ground, *Jo* came to a final stop. *Jo* was so beat-up she was never to fly again! But the whole crew debarked from the plane uninjured."

After the two all-out efforts against Tokyo in May, the damage caused to date was over 50 percent total destruction in the entire city. In his assessment of the damage done, General LeMay said he thought the heavy loss of B-29s over Tokyo in May was worth it. Forty-three Superforts were lost in those two missions.

To wind up missions in May, LeMay sent 510 B-29s carrying 2,570

tons of firebombs dropped their loads in the urban area of Yokohama. Seven B-29s were lost on this mission and thirty-nine had to make emergency stop-overs at Iwo Jima. This was a daylight mission with the Mustangs off Iwo Jima escorting the B-29s.

With the success of the May fire raids and the 21st BC's increased strength—with the addition of the veteran 58th BW and new 315th BW—General LeMay was convinced more than ever that the B-29s could knock Japan out of the war without a land invasion. He had already informed General Norstad that his command was now capable of launching 500 or more planes on any given target in Japan, and proposed that his more powerful force be used to further intensify the strikes against Japan. The USAAF had an opportunity to prove the "power of the strategic air arm," destroying Japan's ability and will to wage war "if its maximum capacity is exerted unstintingly during the next six months." Those were strong words, shared by many USAAF people in high places, even as the policy makers were putting in place the works for a ground invasion of Japan to be executed no later than November 1, 1945.

With the Superfortress build-up in the Marianas, it was almost a miracle that there were very few major accidents during takeoffs and landings. One of the worst accidents, with several fatalities, occurred during May 1945. It happened during the mass launching of 313th BW B-29s at North Field on Tinian Island during the early evening of May 23, and the resulting conflagration that suddenly burst into the sky above North Field could be seen from Saipan.

Larry Smith, central fire control gunner on Captain Hutchison's crew, 1st BS, 9th BG, remembers seeing the disaster that destroyed four B-29s and killed ten of the eleven-man crew of *Thunderin' Loretta*, plus two ground crewmen. All planes in the 9th BG were loaded with six 2,000lb mines scheduled to be dropped in Shimonoseki Straits that night: Smith's plane was next in line for takeoff after Lt. William Caldwell, aircraft commander of *Thunderin' Loretta*, released his brakes and added full power for takeoff. Sixty seconds after Caldwell began his roll, Captain Hutchison began his takeoff roll. "About a quarter of the distance down the runway, during our takeoff run, I heard our radio operator, Frank Cappozzo, yell out, 'We're getting the red light from the tower, Captain!' Frank's sentence was hardly finished before the engines had been cut and the brakes applied hard, as Hutch and Pounteny, the aircraft commander and pilot, observed the tragedy unfolding in front of them.

"Before I could scramble back into my top gunner's position, from my takeoff position, to see what was happening, we heard a loud explosion. Caldwell's plane had veered off the runway to the right and collided head-on with a parked B-29. Fifty-caliber ammunition was going off in all directions. The six mines in Caldwell's plane exploded individually. With every explosion, the wings of our plane lifted a little from the concussion, even though it must have been three-quarters of a mile away.

"The runway ahead of us was littered with debris. I could see the entire tail section of Caldwell's aircraft lying some distance behind the conflagration, apparently having been blown off when the first mine exploded.

"We were directed to make a 180deg turn and taxi to another runway to take off for the mission. We continued on to Japan that night in half shock, not knowing the results of the tragedy we had witnessed, until our return.

"The entire Caldwell crew, with the exception of the tail gunner, who jumped from the plane before the explosion, died instantly. And it was a miracle that only two ground crewmen near the parked B-29s were killed."

While the tragedy was unfolding across the channel on North Field, Tinian Island, the 73rd BW on Saipan was taking off for another incendiary raid on Tokyo. This author was among those witnessing the explosion on Tinian Island. We wondered how many people were losing their lives at that moment. It was the worst accident that happened to the B-29 crews in the Marianas.

And it was about as tragic as the accident that took place in the 44th BS, 40th BG, 58th BW while stationed in India. In this accident, nine people

were killed outright and twenty-one were wounded, some seriously. All were crew chiefs and ground crewmen attempting to download one of the planes carrying fragmentation clusters, to be replaced with demolition bombs. One of the clusters accidentally fell and exploded, setting off a fire that spread rapidly, engulfing the B-29. Fragments spread to another plane nearby, which caught fire and was destroyed. Six other B-29s were heavily damaged.

As the strength of the 21st BC increased, so did the popularity of the B-29 Superfortress in the Marianas. A mass launching of a full wing of B-29s was spectacular, and people not associated with the plane would come to the bases to watch the takeoffs. On Saipan, a field hospital on the bluffs to the north and overlooking Magicienne Bay afforded an outstanding view of the 73rd BW takeoffs. We were told that patients would ask to be wheeled out on the porch to watch. Nurses were glad to oblige because then they could watch also. Rumor had it that doctors even pushed operation schedules up so that they, too, could watch the spectacle.

This record-setting maintenance ground crew includes M/Sgt. "Curley" Klabo, crew chief. Klabo was awarded a Legion of Merit award for setting a fifty-mission record on Goin' Jessie *without a single abort, by General Spaatz.* Charles Chauncey

The Marines, Seabees, and Navy personnel were always trying to hitch a ride on a B-29 during an "engineering hop." After an engine change, the plane had to be "slow timed" and the compass had to be aligned. This chore usually fell to the crew that the B-29 was assigned to. During my stay on Saipan, we had to make several hops, which lasted an hour or two. Each time we went to the line to take our plane up, there was always a small group from the Navy asking if they could go with us. On our first hop, we took four chief petty officers from a Seabee battalion stationed on the northern end of the island. We stayed out about 2hr that day, buzzing all the non-captured islands in the area, such as Pagan Island and Rota. The chiefs thought the ride was great, and we told them they'd have to come back and do it again sometime. We were trying to set them up for a return favor.

Before they left us after the ride, we asked them if they could direct us to somebody who could give us some plywood. Since each Quonset hut in the officer's quarters had men from two crews, we needed a back porch so that the crew returning from a mission could sleep while the other men could play cards without disturbing them. We needed enough plywood to build a covered patio-type addition to our hut and, if possible, individual clothes closets and shelves beside each bed.

The next day, a huge 6x6 truck stopped in front of our hut and some men unloaded the whole truckload. From then on, we acted as a kind of travel agent for those chiefs. We'd call them up when we had friends who were going to take their plane up for an engineering hop and make arrangements for the chiefs to be included on the flight.

B-29 crews became staunch friends of the Navy permanent-duty personnel located down near the harbor—including officers who could get you in The World's Longest Bar. The bar was several big Butler huts joined together, and the overall length was separated into three sections, one for junior-grade officers, one for field-grade, and one for senior-grade officers. They served double-size bourbon with Coke, including ice, all for twenty-five cents a drink.

The crews also tried to develop friendships with the Navy cooks. We made friends with a group of them one day when we carried them up on one of our test hops. They invited us down to their enlisted mess hall for a midnight snack. They said not to come until after midnight because by that time most of the officers in charge would have gone to bed, and they could cook us up what we wanted. Now that sounded like the best deal on the island, especially compared to the K-rations: the powdered eggs, the Spam if we were lucky or something that resembled steak, which we called "Argentina horse flesh."

Our first trip to the Navy mess hall revealed that we weren't the only B-29 guys who had made deals with the cooks. We sweated out a line while the cooks kept frying real eggs and ham or ham-and-egg omelets. No question about it, anytime those cooks wanted a ride in a B-29, we saw they got it. And we told them that the next war we fought, we were going Navy!

There was much ado about "nowhere to go, and nothing to do, and no women, even to look at" at the B-29 bases in the Marianas. You had to make your own entertainment, whether it was playing cards or borrowing a jeep or weapons carrier to look over the island. Some, however, got three-day passes to visit some of the other islands.

Clyde A. Emswiler, crew chief on B-29 T-Square-29, the *Tanaka Termite*, with the 874th BS, 498th BG, 73rd BW on Saipan, found a way to get a pass and visit a friend on Tinian Island. He is still amused at what happened to him after his return from that visit: "Wartime duty on a god-forsaken Pacific island was a far cry from being stationed near cities like London in the European theater of war, or in other civilized areas where there were girls.

"When we left the States for overseas destinations, we knew it was farewell to sex life until we got back to civilization. Granted, on Saipan, there were a few nurses at the hospitals and later a few Red Cross girls who passed out doughnuts and coffee to the flight crews. But these girls I saw were all rank-conscious. Even my master-sergeant stripes were not enough rank to get their attention.

"One day I asked for, and was granted, a three-day pass to go over to Tinian Island, which was just 3mi across the channel from Saipan. I got word from home that one of my hometown buddies was stationed on Tinian Island. I asked my buddy at Saipan to get a pass and go over to Tinian Island with me. We knew in advance that the woman situation at Tinian Island was the same as on Saipan, so we had no thought of womanizing during the visit. We had no problem catching a hop over to Tinian Island, found my old friend, had a good visit, and when our three days were up, we caught a plane back over to Saipan. So much for our visit to Tinian Island, and you'd think this would be the end of the trip.

"Lo and behold, on checking the bulletin board in our Orderly Room, we found a notice ordering the two of us, because of our visit to Tinian Island, to report to the dispensary for a 'short-arm inspection!'"

The Fighter Escort Fiasco

Continuing the four-wing missions, with a renewed supply of M-69 napalm clusters on hand, General LeMay sent a strike force of 509 B-29s on a daylight mission to drop on the urban area of Osaka. Bombing altitude ranged from 18,000–28,000ft, and scheduled to escort the Superfortresses over the target area were P-51s from three fighter groups from Iwo Jima. Three modified B-29s, called Navigation B-29s, would lead the fighters, one for each group, to the Japanese coastline. The navigation planes would then circle in the same area until the P-51s completed the escort duty over the target and return to their designated spot to be led back to Iwo Jima. B-29 weather aircraft were also on hand to try to forecast weather before any flights the P-51s made from Iwo Jima.

On June 1, 1945, the stage was set for the big raid on Osaka, but the P-51s, because of foul weather, suffered the worst disaster since the December 7, 1941, Japanese attacks on Wheeler and Bellows Fields on Oahu. The 15th, 21st, and newly arrived 506th Fighter Groups participated in the mission.

Maj. Robert W. Moore, commander of the 45th Fighter Squadron (FS), 15th Fighter Group (FG), who was leading the escort mission, explains how the tragedy happened: "I had an elevated ringside seat and saw the whole thing as it happened. I was leading the 45th FS of the 15th FG, and Col. John Mitchell was the leader of Blue Flight in my squadron. Earlier in the war, Mitchell had led the P-38 strike from Guadalcanal that intercepted and shot down Japanese Admiral Yamamoto over Kihili Airfield on Bouganville.

"About 250mi north of Iwo Jima, we began to encounter varied cloud layers. A weather B-29 ahead of us had radioed back that he had penetrated a small frontal area without any problem, and thought we would be able to do the same. Instead of getting better, the weather got worse, and the three navigator B-29s flew into a solid cloud front. The 506th FG tried to keep them in sight and dove down through the 21st FG in the process. Some pilots—flying close formation one second and totally blind the next—suffered disorientation and subsequently fatal vertigo, while others were victims of mid-air collisions. Many of the pilots radioed their distressed situations, and a bedlam of 'Mayday! Mayday! I'm bailing out!' ensued. This cacophony of distress calls made me aware that a major tragedy was in the making.

"Because of the weather, our entire command had to abort the mission and, luckily, we made it back to Iwo. Final tabulation revealed we lost twenty-seven planes that day and twenty-four pilots. Two pilots from the 506th FG were picked up very soon after the fiasco. The third, 2nd Lt. Arthur A. Burry, a member of my 45th FS, was flying with the 47th FS that day, and he was picked up on June 7 by a submarine.

"What really hurt was that we had lost so many close comrades—not to the enemy, but to the weather. And without a shot having been fired!"

Many things seemed to have gone wrong on the June 1 mission. Eighty-one B-29s in the strike force had to make emergency landings at Iwo Jima, and ten were lost over the target or en route home that day.

Capt. Arthur Behrens of the 458th BS, 330th BG, 314th Wing, had not reached the drop zone and still had his bomb load aboard when he received a direct hit from an antiaircraft gun. The plane suffered serious damage to the control cables on Behrens' side of the cockpit. Co-pilot Lt. Robert M. Woliver was trying to help Behrens when another shell exploded in the cockpit, killing Behrens and seriously wounding Woliver. They were flying as the high group that day at 20,000ft, and when they were hit the second time, the plane went out of control. Woliver finally got the plane under control, but was down to about 200ft above the water at that time. Years later, he wrote his friend, Cleve R. Anno, an aircraft commander in the 29th BG, that, "If the hand of God wasn't involved that

Coming home, on the downwind leg in a landing pattern at Isley Field, Saipan. Chuck Spieth

day, I'll eat my hat! In getting the plane under control from our fast descent, we wandered around so much, the navigator couldn't get any kind of fix on our location. The IFF switches up front were destroyed by the explosion, but our radar operator, Wallace Mussallm, had an emergency switch in his compartment and, luckily, it worked. He turned it on and prayed that someone would hear it.

"About this time, another 'miracle' happened. Art Shepherd and his radar operator were flying along, not too far away, in their P-61 Black Widow. They were about to return to their Iwo Jima base because their primary radar set had malfunctioned. However, they did have an operational IFF scope, which, through a stroke of luck, picked up the IFF signal from our plane, permitting them to find the B-29, way off course."

The story doesn't end here. Even though Shepherd was able to guide Woliver's plane to Iwo Jima, with so many B-29s milling around, all trying to land on the one runway, it was another matter to get the crew safely on

the ground. Woliver began circling the island and the crew members started bailing out of the plane, hoping to come down on the island. After several circles, all the crew got out of the airplane and landed safely. Unable to leave the plane on his own, Woliver would have gone down with Captain Behren's body, which was still strapped in its seat. But Lt. John Logerot, the bombardier, noticed his friend's predicament and threw him from the doomed plane before jumping himself, thus saving Woliver's life.

After everyone was out of the B-29, Shepherd shot down the Superfortress, the *City of Osceola*. Captain Behren's body went down with the plane.

June 1 was indeed a rough day for the 21st BC. It had lost seven B-29s and twenty-seven P-51s of its 567th Fighter Command.

Who notices the name on this 3rd PRS Superfortress? John Mitchell

Chapter 14

Last Two Months before the A-Bomb

When General Ramey brought his veteran 58th BW out of India and China to join with the three B-29 wings then operating from the Mariana Islands against the Japanese homeland, little did he, or anyone else for that matter, know what happened to at least three of his B-29s that made emergency landings on Russian soil.

The fate of the interned B-29 crews was not known until January 1945, when they, with Soviet approval, "escaped" over the Iranian border to freedom. It was much later before the general public knew what happened to the three B-29s.

The urban area of Kobe was next to receive another maximum-effort fire raid. This time, 530 B-29s dropped 3,079 tons of M-69 napalm clusters from 13,000–18,000ft. It was a daylight mission and Kobe was covered with a solid overcast. The bombs were dropped by radar.

The days of missing targets by a wide margin were behind the B-29 crews. Most of the navigators and radar operators with better training were fairly accurate. This is why General LeMay told General Arnold during his visit to the Marianas in June that the days of loading the planes for a mission, then having to postpone the mission because of weather over the target, were long gone. "The crews," he told his commander, "now have more confidence in their radar units, so we are now hitting the targets regardless of bad weather over the targets."

The June 5 Kobe strike was the last mission where B-29 losses were numbered in double digits. Eleven Superfortresses were lost on that mission, and forty-three had to make emergency landings at Iwo Jima.

For the rest of June, with a few exceptions, the strategy was to bomb multiple targets each day. As many as seven cities were hit in any given day. In addition to continuing the mining of Shimonoseki Straits and other ports at such places as Fukuoka, the 313th BW also joined the 58th, 73rd, and 314th BWs in another daylight incendiary raid on the urban area of Osaka on June 15. Five hundred eleven B-29s took part in the mission, and all planes returned to their bases. On June 20, the 73rd and 313th BWs sent 237 B-29s to drop 1,525 tons of incendiaries on Fukuoka; two B-29s were lost.

The 315th Wing Arrives

The new 315th BW settled in at the not-yet-completed Northwest Field on Guam, amid rains and flooded living areas.

But before the 315th Wing could get a single combat mission tucked away, they had to stand by for a top brass dedication ceremony concerning one of their own B-29s. It so happened that General Arnold was making his first visit to the B-29 outfits in the Marianas in June. Somebody had the idea of naming one of the Superfortresses in honor of Admiral Nimitz, who had done such a good job of seeing that the B-29s got what was needed, so a brand-new Superfortress from the 501st BG was selected, and the name *Fleet Admiral Nimitz* with a five-star flag was printed on the nose of the airplane. A painting of the plane now hangs in the Admiral Nimitz Center. Colonel Boyd, 501st BG commander, took part in the ceremony before a crowd of 315th BW spectators and the crew of the *Fleet Admiral Nimitz*, standing at attention. Speeches were given by General Arnold, Admiral Nimitz, and 315th BW commander Gen. Frank Armstrong.

Col. George E. Harrington, the 315th BW's supply chief, said the 315th was supposed to have been located at West Field on Tinian Island and was packed for overseas shipment when orders were received from 21st BC on Guam that plans had been changed.

The uniqueness of the 315th is recalled by Stephen M. Bandorsky, radar navigator, 502nd BG: "All four groups of the 315th BW—the 16th, 331st, 501st, and the 502nd—trained [with a focus on night missions] in aircraft built by the Bell Aircraft Corp. at its Marietta, Georgia, plant, between January and September 1945. These planes were the only true variant of the B-29 ever manufactured. It was called the B-29B, and was a stripped-down version of the standard B-29. The General Electric remote-controlled aiming system was not installed since the only armament on the plane was its tail guns, twin .50cal machine guns, and a 20mm cannon. A variety of other components were also omitted in order to save overall weight and thereby increase the aircraft's bomb-carrying capacity. The resulting reduced, unladened weight of the plane of 69,000lb lessened the strain on the engines and airframe and permitted the bomb load to be increased from 6 tons to 9 tons."

They came ready to show off their new Eagle radar units, capable of identifying a single building in a selected target area by using a wing-shaped radar vane beneath the fuselage. The Eagle radar system was developed by MIT's Radiation Lab, and was designed specifically for bombardment. It was so secret that no B-29 equipped with this system was ever permitted to be photographed, even for official purposes.

"All missions were planned and briefing materials provided that were specifically oriented to radar bombing," Bandorsky remembered. "Pre-mission briefings were so thorough, that the RDOBs had to spend hours

---

Russian Superfortresses

Several years ago, Mauno A. Salo, then a member of the board of directors of the American Aviation Historical Society, sent me an article pertaining to the "lost" B-29s in Russia, with a note that it contained a part of the B-29 history that is not well known. The article, which Salo said was written by an unknown British author, is a documentation of a detailed account of what happened to the crew of the three B-29s confiscated after landing at Vladivostok, Russia, and another crew that had to bail out of their damaged B-29 over Russian soil.

The three B-29s "captured" by the Russians were Superfortresses nicknamed *Ramp Tramp*, serial number (s/n) 42-6256, flown by Capt. Howard R. Jarrell from the 770th BS, 462nd BG; *Ding How*, s/n 42-6358, flown by Lt. William Micklish of the 79th BS, 468th BG; and the *General H. H. Arnold Special*, s/n 42-6365, flown by Capt. Weston H. Price from the 794th BS, 468th BG. The fourth B-29 retained by Russian authorities was s/n 42-93829, from the 395th BS, 40th BG. It crashed in Russia.

The B-29 crews that landed at Vladivostok were treated as an enemy—fired upon by antiaircraft guns and escorted to a landing field by fighters. The crewmen were stunned at their receptions, since the Soviet Union was supposed to be an ally of the United States in World War II.

At the urgency of the American consul, O. Edmund Chubb, the crewmen were allowed to "escape," but the Soviets would not release the aircraft. They used the Soviet-Japanese Alliance as a cover to impound the airplanes and to intern the crews.

With the three flyable B-29s in their hands, Soviet authorities began a project to build their own Super-fortress. They quickly put into action a program of the highest priority: to manufacture exact copies of the American B-29 bomber. Overall responsibility was given to Soviet bomber designer A. N. Tupolev, with A. B. Shvetsoz supervising the production of a direct copy of the R-3350 engine. A wide section of Soviet manufacturing industry and research expertise was brought into the program. Two of the B-29s were stripped down into components and sub-assemblies for technical evaluation. The third B-29 was kept in flying condition for flight-test evaluation.

Many industrial, scientific, and technological problems had to be overcome. A factory on the Volga River was given the task of producing twenty pre-production aircraft for testing various systems. Two factories behind the Ural Mountains were given instructions to tool up for serious production in the summer of 1946. The last of the twenty pre-production aircraft, designated as the Tu-4, were delivered to the flight-test center during the late autumn of 1947. As with the B-29, the Tu-4 was beset by numerous technical and mechanical problems, such as failures in the propeller-feathering mechanisms and the electrically operated landing gear systems, engine fires, and air-locks in the fuel and oil pressure systems of the Shvetsov ASh-73TK engines.

The Soviets must have encountered more problems with the brakes and tires than they bargained for because third parties, acting for the Soviet government, tried to purchase tires, wheels, and brake assemblies in America in 1946. This was brought out during testimony of Gen. Carl Spaatz, USAF chief of staff, before President Truman's Air Policy Committee.

The Soviet copy of the B-29 made its first public appearance at the Soviet Aviation Day Parade on August 3, 1947, when three of the twenty pre-production Tu-4s flew across Tushino Aerodrome in Moscow. They were accompanied by a transport version that used the same wings, engines, and tail assembly on a redesigned fuselage, designated as the Tu-70.

More than 1,400 exact duplications of the B-29 Superfortress were built by the Soviet Union and were the principal component of their long-range aviation arm until the early 1950s. With one stroke, the Soviets had revolutionized their thinking on manned bomber design and tactical deployment.

Rudy L. Thompson, a flight engineer in the 770th BS, 462nd BG, adds a bit of flavor to the story of the Soviets copying the *Ramp Tramp*: "There were many real heroes in the 20th AF who carried out the air assault against the Japanese homeland, and in the end dropped the bombs that forced Japan to capitulate. There were those who say they weren't even 'assistant heroes.' But some of us experienced a part of history being made and deserve a bit of the glory. My claim to fame is that I was the flight engineer on the first B-29 the Russians 'captured' and later copied.

"Our plane was named the *Ramp Tramp* because she was a real dog. That name fit her perfectly—always on the ramp undergoing repairs. The reason our crew was not flying the *Tramp* the day the Russians took control of her was that the 771st BS was short of B-29s and they borrowed our plane for Captain Jarrell and crew to fly to An-shan, Manchuria, to attack the Showa Steel Works. We eventually got a new B-29, which we immediately named *Ramp Tramp II*. We took her to Tinian Island, where we later lost her during takeoff on a mission to Tokyo."

studying radar-targeting materials and were required to draw the details from memory."

General LeMay decided that the 315th would be charged with destroying the oil refineries all over Japan. Even though several missions had already been sent to bomb such targets as the Army Fuel Depot at Iwakuni, he knew that some of the fuel and oil refineries were still operating.

For the 315th's first mission over Japan, thirty-five B-29Bs were sent to bomb the oil refinery and industrial section of Yokkaichi on June 26–27. They dropped 143 tons of bombs from 14,000–17,400ft. Thirty-six Superfortresses went to Kadamatsu on June 29–30 and with 209 tons of bombs hit the oil refinery there. Both missions produced excellent results, and the 315th got off to a good start.

With Fame Came Celebrities and Journalists

During the spring and summer of 1945, several Hollywood celebrities came to the Marianas to entertain the troops that flew and serviced the B-29s. One night, this author and three or four buddies were at the bar of the 499th BG's Officers' Club on Saipan, when somebody opened the front door and let out one of the loudest yells we'd ever heard. In walked the very popular movie comedian, Joe E. Brown. That was one of his trademarks: opening his big mouth and yelling as loudly as he could. Well, he came in and shot the bull with us for a while. He told us that he got word a month or so before, from the War Department, that his son, a B-17 pilot in Europe, had been killed when his plane was shot down.

Not long before Okinawa was captured, Ernie Pyle, America's most popular war correspondent, came to Saipan. He had a nephew on the island and he wanted to check up on the B-29. He stayed for a few days in the Quonset hut of Gerald Robinson, commander of the 875th BS, 498th BG.

Robinson remembers Pyle's excitement in getting to ride in a B-29: "I was privileged to take Ernie up on his only flight of a B-29. Less than two weeks later, while riding in the front seat of a jeep in Ie Shima Island, near Okinawa, a Japanese sniper shot him through

A picture taken by author on June 1, 1945, just prior to entering boiling smoke clouds over Osaka, Japan. Note the B-29 below left wing. Flak from Japanese navy ships hit the nose of Captain Wilkerson's plane and it spun down. All perished. Marshall

the head, killing him instantly.

"These are some of the things he wrote about his B-29 ride with us: 'I sat on a box between the pilots, both on takeoff and landing, and as much as I've flown, that was still a thrill. These islands are all relatively small, and you're no sooner off the ground, than you're out over water, and that feels funny. If the air is a little rough, it gives you a very odd sensation sitting way up there in the nose. For the B-29 is so big that instead of bumping or dropping, the nose has a willowy motion, sort of like sitting out on the end of a green limb when it's swaying around.'"

Ralph Marr, tail gunner with the 15th BS, 16th BG, is proud of the fact that his was the only B-29 crew that lived in the pages of a major magazine. The *Saturday Evening Post* assigned one of its top war correspondents, Richard Tregaskis, to "live and fly with us on the Road to Tokyo, and to report the action first-hand in a weekly series of stories." Capt. Bob ("Pappy") Hain, who flew fifty missions over Europe, was the crew's aircraft commander.

The *Lucky Irish* and *Bataan Avenger*

One of the greatest "sweat jobs" a B-29 combat crew had to endure while

flying a bombing mission to and from the Japanese homeland from the Marianas was the countdown to rotation home. Thirty missions had been set for a combat tour, but the closer a crew came to that magic number, the tougher it became to sweat out the next trip to Japan.

By June 1945, opposition, especially fighter attacks, had diminished to the point that sometimes there was not a single enemy fighter in the air. But they were still able to put up flak barrages that could knock a Superfortress down, there were those terrible weather fronts to fly through on the 3,000mi round trip to and from the target, and there was always that fickle finger of fate, always lingering around the corner—as recorded about the crew of the *Lucky Irish*: As the bombing raids increased with the strong build-up of B-29s coming from the islands, the magic number thirty rolled around for some of the crews. My number thirty came up after the June 7 maximum-effort fire raid on Kobe. My crew and I were dished a

A B-29 Superfortress at Dalhart, Texas, Air Base, shows the Eagle radar antenna beneath fuselage. This is a rare picture of this secret weapon used by 315th BW. The Eagle system, known officially as the AN/APQ-7 radar set, was a great improvement over the older AN/APQ-13 radar units in the B-29As. The Eagle was capable of identifying a single building in a selected target area, allowing the radar operator and bombardier to coordinate their efforts to aim the bombs more accurately. W. H. Keathley

double lucky deal. We had not only survived the thirty-mission tour, but also survived the thirty-mission cut off, by one day. The day after completing our tour of combat duty, we were placed on a holding list, awaiting transportation back to the States for reassignment.

Lt. William A. Kelley, aircraft commander of *Lucky Irish*, remarked after the thirtieth and final mission, "The unusual thing about our crew is that nothing unusual has ever happened to us."

The combat tour of the crew had been unbelievably routine. Assigned to the 870th BS, 497th BG, on Saipan, they began their combat tour on the first B-29 raid on Tokyo, November 24, 1944. None of the men had received the slightest injury, the aircraft had hardly been scratched, and they had flown every mission as scheduled and never aborted. The central fire control gunner, Glenn W. Jomes, complained, "Our good luck seems to charm away the opposition and keeps me from getting any gunnery practice."

Actually, this was the third *Lucky Irish* flown by Kelley's crew. The first was destroyed on the runway at

Saipan by Japanese aircraft from Iwo Jima. The second *Lucky Irish* was lost somewhere north of Iwo Jima on a mission to Japan, having been assigned to another crew for this mission. Yet, flight after flight, the original crew of A-Square-28 wallowed in Irish luck.

The *Irish* were an extremely close crew. They had trained together for more than a year and flown in combat over the vastness of the western Pacific and the Japanese homeland for another six months. Now they were going home: the first Superfortress crew to complete its combat tour of duty, thirty missions. The plane they were to fly back to the United States was the *Dauntless Dotty*, the lead plane for the first B-29 raid on Tokyo on November 24, 1944.

As Kelley and crew boarded the plane for home, he didn't know that his first child, a daughter, had been born a few hours earlier. Compared to the 3,000mi nonstop flights to and from Japan, the return flight would be simple: Saipan to Kwajalein in the Marshalls, Hawaii, and then to California. With an outstanding record of fifty-three missions over Japan and 176,000 combat miles, *Dotty* had just been overhauled. They departed Saipan in the twilight hours of June 6, 1945, and reached Kwajalein just before midnight. They had a snack in the mess hall, and the crew voted on whether to remain overnight and get a little sleep or refuel and proceed to Hawaii. To a man, they decided to push on. At 3am, they were airborne, and 40sec later, the *Dauntless Dotty* plunged into the Pacific Ocean, never to be seen again. Ten of the thirteen men on board perished instantly.

Lt. John F. Neveille, the co-pilot, was thrown through the nose of the aircraft and survived, as did Glenn Gregory, the tail gunner, and Charles McMurry, the left gunner.

News of that crew's disaster wasn't known for some time later, but had this author and his crew known, our mode of transportation back to the States may have been changed. The *Lucky Irish* crew left Saipan on their fatal flight one day before we completed our tour and were eligible for rotation back to the States. We were asked how we wanted to return home: by a Navy transport ship, by Air Transport Command, or wait for a war-weary B-29 to become available and fly it back to the States. We settled on waiting for a "war weary." We had a boring three-week wait before our B-29 was brought from the 6th BG on Tinian Island. We were to return the plane to the States for a complete overhaul, including repair of structural damage suffered during an incendiary raid on Osaka. The name of the aircraft was the *Bataan Avenger*. A newspaper clipping pasted on the pilots' instrument panel told part of the story of the *Avenger*: Before building the plane, workers at the Boeing Aircraft Co. plant in Wichita, Kansas, raised the money to purchase it, and they prophesied that some day the airplane would return to Kansas, victoriously. The flight back to the States was uneventful, if you can overlook the anxiousness that accompanies a person returning from a combat tour of duty. We had to leave the plane in California, after authorities turned deaf ears to our pleas to let us fly the *Avenger* on to Wichita, Kansas. What a gala event that would have been!

B-29s Roam Japanese Skies

By June 1945, the B-29s, now with five wings roaming the skies over Japan, had greatly weakened the opposition. B-29 losses were decreasing at a rapid rate. This meant that the Superfortresses had, at last, overcome the deficiencies that had caused so much early trouble.

As the war continued, strategies changed to suit the situations. With the 313th and 315th BWs tightening their stranglehold on the Japanese population, it was becoming increasingly difficult to get food or oil and gas from outside sources. They tried dropping barrels of much-needed food into the Inland Sea from Asian shores, hoping the easterly currents would deposit it on Japanese western shores. The Japanese air force was curtailed due to the depletion of their oil and fuel supplies, destroyed by B-29s of the 315th BW. Japanese planes didn't have enough fuel to attack Superfortresses now roaming their skies.

The 58th, 73rd, and 314th BWs attacked sixty-six cities in Japan, sometimes with assistance from the 313th BW. The 315th never participated in a combined mission with other units, but instead, with their Eagle radar system, put their full effort into destroying the oil and fuel industry and storage facilities.

Regular attacks were made on cities with as few people as 40,004 (Isezaki) to the larger cities with populations of 6,778,804 or more (Tokyo). LeMay finally had printed notices dropped from B-29s over a city, warning the population to vacate the premises or suffer the consequences, prior to a mission.

William C. Leiby, bombardier with the 28th BS, 19th BG, relates a June 26, 1945, mission his crew, flying the *City of Austin*, made: "Our mission was to the Kawasaki Aircraft Factory at Kagamigahara, Japan. As we were rendezvousing just off the coast of Osaka, Japanese fighters rose to attack our formation. They shot down one of our B-29s and our squadron leader ordered us to leave the formation and drop down to see if we could assist the ditching plane's crew.

"We circled the downed flyers, dropping food, water, emergency radio equipment, and life rafts. Our radio

The ground crew of the 3rd PRS's Double Exposure *know how to clean their airplane.*
John Mitchell

An unusual shot of the V-Square-25, which flew with the 878th BS, 499th BG, Saipan.
Ray Brashear

Two officers chat beside a Superfortress that honors the 4th Marines. Dick Field

operator finally contacted a nearby submarine, who came to the rescue of the downed flyers immediately. After our submarine surfaced near the crew in the water, we headed for a couple of two-masted Japanese schooners that had set out from shore toward the downed crewmen. We tried dropping two bombs on the boats, but missed. Our aircraft commander, Lt. Ed Gammel, then made a higher pass at the boats, bringing the nose down as we got in range so that we could fire all six of our .50cal guns at the same time. As we passed over, the tail gunner got in some good shots. The first boat immediately caught fire and began burning, and we noticed that the second boat was badly damaged. The submarine picked up the downed crewmen and we set our course to our return route to Guam."

Balls of Fire Myth Resolved

As the B-29s increased their missions over Japan into the summer of 1945, so did the crew reports of seeing "balls of fire" following them during their return to base. Some of the gunners fired on the elusive bright light that followed them for miles, and some of the pilots even used sharp, often violent, evasive maneuvers in an effort to shake off what they considered an enemy aircraft with powerful lights to direct Japanese fighter planes to them. But, the pilots said, it was useless, for the lights would stay with them, regardless of the action taken.

In all reports, there was one consistent point: The balls of fire, the airborne-searchlights, or whatever they appeared to be, would always appear off the right wing when going into the Japanese homeland and off the left wing as they returned to their Mariana bases.

By early July, the fireball myth was resolved. All B-29 bomber crews were summarily briefed as follows: "Fly all over the sky, fire all you want, you're not going to shoot this one down. Those 'balls of fire' you've seen out there is the planet Venus, which is extremely brilliant in this region of the world at this time of the year."

Fresh from a record-setting performance in June of amassing a total of more than 6,200 combat hours, Lt. Col. Charles M. Eisenhart's 505th BG was assigned the task of flying all the mining missions. With an average of thirty B-29s on each flight, the 505th scheduled missions every other night to lay mines in areas covering most of the harbors, especially the Shimonoseki Straits, to tighten the stranglehold around Japan's home islands. The group's action was instrumental in virtually halting the 1.5 million tons of merchant shipping Japan needed for her survival. The 505th's effort was the continuation of Operation Starvation, which had been assigned to the 313th BW by General LeMay.

First Capitulation Feelers Appear

Following the B-29s' most destructive raids on Japan's major cities, some Japanese civilian leaders read the handwriting on the wall and argued for discussions to begin in an effort to find ways to end the war. By this time, Tokyo, Nagoya, Kobe, Osaka, Yokohama, and Kawasaki lay in ruin. The combined total urban area of these cities had a total of 257.2sq-mi, of which the B-29s had totally destroyed 105.6sq-mi of the built-up areas. Many of the factories had been burned or put out of operation. Millions of Japanese families had lost their homes during the massive fire raids, and the blockade of all Japanese ports had rendered shipping impossible. It was time now to try and stop the war.

A new Premier, Adm. Kantaro Suzuki, had taken over the Japanese cabinet in April, and the civilian leadership thought Suzuki could be persuaded to at least disauss ways to end the war. Suzuki, who had taken over the top job from Hideki Tojo in April, finally realized that his country was in desperate straits and something had to be done.

Suzuki agreed to seek Moscow's intercession at the right time, but it was not until July that he persuaded his foreign minister, Shigenori Togo, to formally direct the Japanese ambassador in Moscow, Naotake Sato, to seek help from the Soviet leaders. He hoped that their influence with the Allies could help in trying to stop the war.

The Japanese government, still influenced by military leaders as late as July 1945, looked upon themselves as the ones to establish and maintain a lasting peace.

Togo's instructions to Sato seemed to counteract any proposal for stopping the war. Knowing that the United States and England weren't about to lay down any weapons and would

Ray Brashear checks engines during start-up. Note the sixteen missions emblems and three victories over Japanese fighters displayed on his plane. Ray Brashear

Superfortresses from the 878 BS, 499th BG, Saipan, on the way to a target. Ray Brashear

press the attack unless the Japanese would agree to an unconditional surrender, Togo nevertheless instructed Sato to inform the Soviets that this condition would not be accepted by Japan and that if the United States and England persisted in this demand, Japan had no alternative but to see the war through in an all-out effort, for the sake of survival and honor of the homeland.

In Sato's opinion, the Soviets would not go along with any Japanese proposals, and he thought Tokyo's view of the world situation was unrealistic. He told the Foreign Minister this and that, in his opinion, England and America were planning to "take the right of maintaining peace away from Japan." He voiced doubts that Japan was in a position or had the reserve strength to resist the war further, and questioned whether it was necessary to further sacrifice the lives of hundreds of thousands of soldiers and millions of other innocent residents of cities and metropolitan areas.

This would certainly be the outcome if the Imperial General Headquarters continued to gird for such a war of resistance, he predicted.

The fact that the B-29s were able to bomb cities and towns across Japan almost unchallenged was somewhat of a mystery among General LeMay and other Allied leaders. The reasons were not fully known until after the war: Expecting an invasion of their homeland, Japanese military leaders had hoarded at least 8,000 aircraft and hid them in undetected areas, built one-way runways scattered throughout the country, and waited. Most of the airplanes would be flown by kamikaze pilots. The Japanese thought that by delaying an invasion, they could hold out indefinitely and thus demand better surrender terms.

With little or no air opposition, General LeMay continued the leaflet propaganda drops on cities that would be hit the next day. The civilian desire to continue the war correspondingly declined.

The Manhattan Project and the 509th Composite Group

In the best-kept secret the US Government ever involved itself with, a mysterious special project code-named the Manhattan Engineer District, with Brig. Gen. Leslie Groves directing, began work on producing the atomic bomb in 1942. By 1943, it was time to think about how the B-29 would have to be modified to deliver the bomb to a target. General Arnold

instructed his chief assistant for air material, now Maj. Gen. Oliver P. Echols, to have a B-29 modified to meet specifications for carrying the bomb. Echols selected his assistant, Col. Roscoe Wilson, as the special project officer to get the job done. Wilson called on now Col. Donald Putt at Wright Field, who happened to have been the first USAAF officer to fly a B-29, to help carry out the highly secret project.

A B-29 was borrowed from the 58th BW, and its bomb bay was modified to accommodate two bombs of different sizes: one, nicknamed Little Boy, which would be 28in in diameter and 120in long and weigh 9,000lb; and another, nicknamed Fat Man, which would be 60in in diameter and 128in long and weigh about 10,000lb. The bombs would be used separately, not loaded at the same time.

After modifications were done and tested with simulated bombs of the size and weight of the two atomic bombs, a contract was awarded to a firm in Omaha, Nebraska, to modify at least fourteen B-29Bs immediately. The A-bomb modification order eventually was increased to fifty-four, but only forty-six B-29s were modified before war's end.

General Arnold selected Lt. Col. Paul W. Tibbets, Jr., to command a

As the missions against Japan accelerated, so did the scrap pile on Tinian of wrecked Superfortresses and other aircraft. Bill Rooney

new, self-sustaining combat unit, called the 509th Composite Group (CG), in the summer of 1944. Tibbets had been flight-testing the B-29s since shortly after production of the Superfortress began. Before joining the B-29 testing program, Tibbets had completed twenty-five combat missions in B-17s over Europe and North Africa, and he was considered an outstanding pilot.

When Tibbets assumed command of the new combat unit, he alone was informed of the nature of his mission. His initial duties were to find an isolated spot in the United States where the unusual training program could be carried out with the least chances for leaks of what the ultra-secret unit was training for. He was also responsible for selecting personnel for the unit. Wendover, Utah, was selected as the training site. For the nucleus of his combat unit, he chose the 393rd BS, which was then in training with the 6th BG, a unit of the 313th BW, in Nebraska. Maj. Charles W. Sweeney, commander of the 393rd BS, moved his unit to Wendover in September 1944. The 320th Troop Carrier Squadron with its C-54s was attached to the group to move the group's personnel anywhere in the world. The 320th would be called the Green Hornet Airline. The 509th CG also was provided with its own engineer squadron, an air material squadron, and a military police company. By the time the 509th deployed to Tinian Island in 1945, its total strength came to 225 officers and 1,542 enlisted men.

By July, the entire 509th CG was in place on Tinian Island, and located in a special section near North Field, the entire operation was somewhat of a mystery to personnel from the nearby 313th BW.

To emphasize how secretive the 509th CG was, even General LeMay, commander of the 21st BC, was not aware of the atomic bomb program until March 1945. It was then that Col. Elmer E. Kirkpatrick, an engineering officer associated with the project, came to the Marianas to supervise the special construction at Tinian Island in preparation for the arrival of the 509th CG and to inform LeMay of its true nature and how it would fit in with the 21st BC. Soon after, General Arnold informed LeMay about the 509th's mission also, and told him that although the 509th CG would be un-der the 21st BC's control, since the unit would be operating under an experimental nature, it would be controlled initially from his Washington headquarters. General LeMay had nothing to do but go along with his boss. Admiral Nimitz was informed of the secret operation also in February by Cdr. Frederick L. Ashworth, who had been assigned to the 509th and made a special trip to Guam to inform the admiral.

Goin' Jessie

The Superfortresses continued to saturate cities across Japan during July and early August. The efficiency of these airplanes and their ground crews was reaching new heights.

Charles G. Chauncey, pilot on the John D. Fleming crew of the 5th BS, 9th BG, on Tinian Island, tells how proud his crew was about the accomplishments of their *Goin' Jessie*: "When we picked up our brand-new Boeing-Wichita–built B-29, s/n 42-24856, at the Herrington, Kansas, staging base and headed west for our combat destination home on Tinian Island, little did we realize that *Goin' Jessie* would be such a prophetic name.

"In combat, *Goin' Jessie* racked up all kinds of records. On July 10, 1945, at 0118 o'clock over Wakayama, Japan, *Jessie* was credited with dropping the 2,000,000th ton of bombs dropped by the USAAF on the Axis since World War II began. Colonel Luschen, squadron commander, who was riding with us that day, verified the bomb drop and claimed the record for the aircraft. But that accomplishment was minor compared to record-setters that followed.

"We were certain we had a good flight crew, thought we had a good airplane, and we had what we considered an excellent ground crew headed by M/Sgt. Einar S. ('Curley') Klabo. Our thoughts were all justified indeed. We never had to abort a combat mission. *Goin Jessie* lived up to our expectation all the way.

"When we left for the States, after completing our thirty-five–mission combat tour, Lt. William Reynolds and crew took over *Goin Jessie*, and kept the no-abort record intact, up to and including the final large-scale bombing raid on Japan on August 14, 1945. It was *Goin' Jessie*'s fiftieth mission without a single abort. That record means that not once did a crew have to return to base without completing the assigned mission because of mechanical troubles, an outstanding accomplishment indeed.

"When the war ended, *Jessie* had flown 808 combat hours, or 135,000mi, or five-and-one-half times around the world, and had dropped 645,000lb of explosives on targets in Japan.

"Accomplishing this amazing combat record, Jessie had used twelve engines, three sets of tires, 295,000gal of gas, and more than 5,000gal of oil.

"For such an outstanding performance of keeping *Goin' Jessie* going, Sergeant Klabo, who had remained crew chief for the entire record-setting performance of *Goin' Jessie*, was awarded the Legion of Merit medal."

Colonel Huglin, commander of the 9th BG, remembers the circumstances surrounding the awarding of the medal to Sergeant Klabo the day Gen. Carl Spaatz, newly named commander of the US Strategic Air Forces in the Pacific, came to Tinian Island: "General Davis, the 313th BW commander, sent word to us group commanders of the Wing to come to his headquarters to be present at the briefing for General Spaatz and to have lunch with him.

"While driving my jeep to Wing Headquarters, I was speculating on what I would tell the General if he should say to me, 'Well, Colonel, what problems do you have that I can help with?'

"Well, wonder of wonders, I was placed next to General Spaatz at lunch, and he said just that to me! I told him that most everything was going very well in our operations and maintenance, but I was having trouble getting awards for our deserving men in a reasonable length of time. I cited, in particular, Master Sergeant Klabo, the crew chief of a B-29 nicknamed *Goin' Jessie*, which had completed almost fifty combat missions with a perfect maintenance record. I thought Sergeant Klabo deserved a prompt award of the Legion of Merit. General Spaatz said, 'I agree. And furthermore, I will present it to him this afternoon.' And he did. Now, that is command action!"

A bit of flak harassed a flight of B-29s over Tokyo. 73rd BW Photo/Chuck Spieth

The harbor at Guam. Bill Rooney

Chapter 15

Final Blow of World War II

The final days of World War II were ticking down to the final onslaught by the middle of July 1945. Colonel Tibbets, with his 509th CG's full complement of men and machines in place at their Tinian Island home base—even before the first test explosion of the nuclear bomb—was anxiously awaiting the word "Go." Confidence displayed by the scientists and engineers of the Manhattan Engineer District project over-shadowed uncertainty. The ultimate climax was near.

Early on the morning of July 16, two B-29 Superfortresses at Kirkland Field in Albuquerque, New Mexico, took off after a short delay because of weather conditions over their target. The Superfortresses were equipped with a variety of instruments, electronic devices, cameras, and other equipment to record the fireball's intensity and other phenomena that was expected to occur during the explosion of an atomic bomb. The "bomb" was attached to a 100ft-tall steel tower located at a site called Trinity, in the white-sands desert west of Alamogordo, New Mexico. The two B-29s were still several miles from the test sight when a tremendous explosion occurred. The time was a few seconds past 5:20am, and the pilots gasped in amazement at the brightness of the explosion, described by Gen. Leslie Groves as equal to several suns at midday. The explosion, rattled windows in houses over 100mi away in Albuquerque, New Mexico.

At exactly the same time of the explosion, Jim Teague, a B-29 flight engineer in transition training at the Alamogordo Air Base, was pre-flighting his B-29 in preparation for a training flight, when all of a sudden it seemed, he said, "the entire universe lit up and we could see as plain as day." He had just asked his helper to bring the crew chief lights around so he could see to inspect an engine. His helper said, "You don't need a light, the sun is coming up." Teague's reply was, "The sun, hell! That light is coming from the west—a plane must have exploded. At about that time, a major sped down the flight line in his jeep, waving to the crews about ready to crank their planes and take off. 'All planes, cut your engines. We've got orders to delay your takeoff.' It was not until after August 6, 1945, the day Hiroshima was bombed, that we found out why all our planes were grounded for a short time that morning on July 16."

Word of a successful atomic bomb test was flashed to President Truman, who was attending an Allied conference at Potsdam. The president informed Winston Churchill and Chiang Kai-shek about the successful test, and a declaration was issued, calling upon the Japanese government to surrender immediately. The declaration warned that the alternative would be Japan's prompt and complete destruction. Japan's Premier Suzuki dismissed the declaration with a strong determination to fight on to a successful conclusion.

The stage was set. President Truman had approved the dropping of the A-bomb on Japan, so the time set to drop the first atomic bomb was as soon as weather would permit after August 3. Gen. George Marshall and Secretary of State Henry Stimson approved the mission sent to them at Potsdam by acting chief of staff, Gen. Thomas T. Handy, on July 24, and the clock began to tick. The mission directive was dispatched to Gen. Carl Spaatz, who was directed to send a copy of the document to Admiral Nimitz and General MacArthur.

The target for the first drop would be one of a list of four cities: Hiroshima, Kokura, Niigata, or Nagasaki.

As Tibbets' 509th CG stood by awaiting favorable weather, the 21st BC went about sending Superfortresses loaded with mines and firebombs across Japan. B-29s from all five wings were on the prowl over Japan during the night of August 1–2. A

Pilots, man your planes! P-51s of the 21st FG on Iwo Jima ready for takeoff, as seen beneath the three-story tail of a Superfortress "Mother Ship." Josh Curtis

P-51s of the 567th Fighter Command arrived at Iwo Jima soon after the island was captured on March 16, 1945: The Mustangs *were a beautiful sight on the ground but were much prettier when escorting B-29s over Japan.* Marshall

Adm. Chester Nimitz addresses an assembly during the ceremony dedicating a B-29 named in his honor, while the crew of the *plane and Colonel Hubbard and General Armstrong look on.* John Mitchell

record-breaking 836 Superfortresses took part in the mission.

As if waiting for the weather to dictate the exact time when Colonel Tibbets would load up and head for the as-yet-unknown target in Japan with his "secret weapon," General LeMay waited until the night of August 5 to send another force of 635 Superforts to Japan, loaded with fire-bombs, mines, and explosives. The B-29s were back at their bases before an early-morning departure of another B-29, this one with the name *Enola Gay* freshly painted on its nose. Piloted by Tibbets, that B-29 took off from North Field on Tinian Island on a mission that would send shock waves around the world. It was 2:45am, the morning of August 6, 1945.

Hiroshima's Fate Sealed

Three B-29s loaded with weather-observing instruments, proceeded Tibbets' departure by about 1hr. Their mission was to fly to the area of the selected targets in Japan and check and report weather conditions back to the *Enola Gay* as the flight to Japan developed. The city of Hiroshima, with a population of 245,000 residents, had already been selected as the primary target, if the weather was favorable for a visual drop. If not, one of the other three cities would have been the target.

Maj. Claude Eatherly, flying *Straight Flush*, led the weather planes off the runway at North Field, followed by *Jabbitt III* and *Full House*. The latter two planes were to check weather conditions at Kokura and Nagasaki, respectively. At Iwo Jima, Lt. Charles McKnight and his crew stood by in another Superfortress, to take the place of *Enola Gay* if mechanical trouble developed before they reached Iwo Jima. Their stand-by services were not needed.

Two B-29s following the *Enola Gay* off the runway at North Field would play a vital role in the mission. The second plane off was the camera plane, flown by Maj. George Marquardt, followed by Maj. Charles W. Sweeney's plane, loaded with blast gauges and other instruments.

Straight Flush reached Hiroshima shortly after 7am. After crossing over the city twice, Major Eatherly flashed

the word to Tinian Island and to the en route *Enola Gay* that Hiroshima was clear for a visual bomb drop. Hiroshima would be the target.

After passing Iwo Jima, Tibbets and the accompanying planes began their climb to a bombing altitude of 31,500ft. Navy Capt. William ("Deke") Parson, the weaponeer, armed the bomb as the three planes headed for Hiroshima. At 9:15am, the bombardier pushed the button that released the bomb, and 2min later, the explosion took place, timed to go off 2,000ft above the ground. The blast killed more than 78,000 people in Hiroshima and injured another 51,000. More than 48,000 buildings in the city were completely destroyed and an additional 22,178 were badly damaged. More than 176,000 people were made homeless.

During the training for the atomic bombing missions, Colonel Tibbets never clarified the special weapon they were training to drop. He always called it "the Gimmick," never mentioning the term "atomic bomb."

The day before the strike, Colonel Tibbets ordered the name *Enola Gay* be painted on the nose of the plane. The Superfortress actually was assigned to Capt. Robert Lewis, one of Tibbets' hand-picked pilots. Lewis first saw the new name just prior to take-off. According to some who were there, he asked, "Who the hell did that?" He was told that the name *Enola Gay* was painted there by order of Tibbets, and that it was Tibbets' mother's name.

There was no let-up with the dropping of the atomic bomb on Hiroshima. The Superfortresses from the 58th, 73rd, and 313th BWs struck the Toyokawa Arsenal in a 151-plane daylight raid, dropping 124 tons of explosives from 19,000–23,600ft. Again on the night of August 7, the 505th BG of

Diamond Y-3 flew with the 501st BG, 315th BW, Guam. The 315th came to Guam a few months before the Japanese surrendered. Most of their planes were painted black underneath and up the sides to hide them from the Japanese searchlights. Bill Rooney

the 313th BW sent thirty-two B-29s loaded with 189 tons of mines to drop on seven different targets.

The Japanese government, determined to continue the war at all costs, attempted to downplay the atomic attack on Hiroshima. This brought out a 245 B-29 force, on August 8, from the 58th, 73rd, and 313th BWs, again to drop incendiary bombs on the urban area of Yawata in the southern island of Kyushu. At the same time, the 314th BW struck an industrial area of Tokyo with a sixty-plane force. The Japanese fighters and antiaircraft still

The Enola Gay *is parked in its hardstand after dropping the first atomic bomb. Lt. Col. Paul Tibbets, commander of the 509th CG was at the controls of this aircraft when the world was introduced to the power of atomic energy as the bomb demolished the city of Hiroshima, Japan.* Warren Thompson

had a little fight, knocking down four B-29s during the Yawata raid and three at Tokyo.

Second Atomic Bomb

The Japanese showed no indications of being ready to end the war under Allied terms, so a second atomic mission was scheduled for August 9.

After the destruction of Hiroshima, Foreign Minister Togo, along with other Japanese leaders, realized that if their government didn't surrender immediately, their cities were in jeopardy of being totally destroyed and their people killed. On August 8, while the second atomic mission was being readied, Togo met with Emperor Hirohito and advised him to accept the Potsdam Declaration quickly. The Emperor agreed, and said it was time to try to prevent another tragedy like Hiroshima. Togo dispatched the Emperor's message to Premier Suzuki, who, regrettably, was unable to convene the foot-dragging Supreme War Council until the next day.

The plutonium bomb called Fat Man, weighing about 12,000lb, was already loaded on the B-29 called *Bock's Car*, and was ready to leave for the second atomic strike against Japan. Major Sweeney was the aircraft commander, and Fred Olivi was co-pilot that day. The strike plane on the second mission was supposed to have been the *Great Artiste*, but since it had been used as one of the two observation planes on the Hiroshima strike, the wired instruments had not been removed in time to load the bomb for the second mission. Capt. Fred Bock flew one of the observation planes on the second strike.

As in the first mission, alternate targets were selected for the second atomic strike. Kokura was selected as the primary target, with Nagasaki named as alternate. If weather prevented a visual drop at the primary target, they were to proceed to the alternate target immediately.

Jake Beser, the radar countermeasure operator for both missions, said the "Hollywood premier" atmosphere was non-existent for the second mission. It was almost as if they were about to leave on a routine B-29 mission to Japan, similar to the mass raids in the past. Beser was the only person to fly on both strike aircraft, and was considered the most experi-

enced man available to monitor the sensitive equipment. He recalls that the second mission got off to a bad start from the very beginning and got worse as time passed: "I was beginning to feel the effects of the lack of sleep when we got to *Bock's Car* and sat down on the Colonel's jeep until it was time to go. The appointed time came and went, and we still were sitting there. Something was causing a delay in our departure.

"Major Sweeney came over to Colonel Tibbets' jeep several times, and they removed themselves from our presence and had several animated discussions. At one point, Fred Asworth, the assigned weaponeer for this mission, was made privy to the discussions, but obviously neither Bill Laurence, the *New York Times* correspondent who was assigned to cover the mission, nor I could contribute to it, so we weren't told what the trouble was. I learned from one of my enlisted men that there were two concerns: one, the weather over Japan was not clearing as expected; and two, there was some kind of problem with the bomb bay fuel transfer."

The anxious moments before take-off were only a prelude of what was to come. Major Sweeney proceeded to Kokuro to find the entire area covered with a thick layer of smoke, caused by the mass incendiary raid on Yawata the night before. Yawata and Kokuro were located near each other, and the dense smoke still covered both cities. There was nothing to do but to proceed to Nagasaki, the alternate target. There was a nine-tenths cloud coverage over that city also. Sweeney made the decision to fly a second and possibly a third run over the city while Capt. Kermit Beahan searched for a hole in the overcast. By this time, the flight engineer told Sweeney that something would have to be done soon, or they would run out of fuel and not make it back to Iwo Jima. Sweeney tried one more fly-over and this time, Captain Beahan yelled that he could see a slight opening in the clouds. He immediately lowered the bomb bays and prepared to drop the bomb. He flipped the switch, and Fat Man was on its way. A few seconds later, Nagasaki disappeared under the familiar fireball and mushroom clouds that raced toward the sky. An estimated 35,000 people died.

Troubles for the crew were a long way from over. The troublesome fuel transfer pump, discussed back at Tinian Island before takeoff, refused to transfer fuel from one of the storage tanks. A quick check indicated that there was not enough fuel left to make it back to Iwo Jima, so Major Sweeney decided to try the shorter distance to Okinawa, which was not given as an alternate landing site, even though preparations were being made to accommodate General Doolittle's 8th Air Force.

The crew of *Bock's Car* finally found a field, but it was a fighter strip. Sweeney decided to try to land there anyway, because it was doubtful that they could make it any farther. The last foul-up came when the men in the tower refused to believe that *Bock's Car* had been over Japan and dropped the atomic bomb. Finally, Sweeney turned and started the final approach for the short fighter strip, ignoring the tower personnel trying to wave him off. He just barely made it, borrowed some gas, took off, and returned to Tinian Island.

The atomic bomb dropped on Nagasaki was the last one dropped in anger. It served its purpose despite the anxiety it caused that day among the *Bock's Car* crew. Fred Olivi, co-pilot on the plane had this observation of the part he played in the last atomic bomb dropped: "As a participant in the bombing of Nagasaki, I hope that it marked the final chapter in the history of atomic warfare. I will never forget the sight of that ugly mushroom cloud arising from the ruins of Nagasaki.

"The night following the bombing, we huddled around our radios on Tinian Island and heard Japan sue for peace. For the first time, I began to realize the significance of our mission and the importance of our group. Two B-29s altered the course of history."

It would be five days before the Japanese government finally threw in the towel. During this time, hundreds of Japanese citizens became victims of the B-29 onslaught. It was not before the Emperor himself met with the War Cabinet, and in an unprecedented address to the military leaders, which

Sleepy Time Gal *was assigned to the 498th BG, 73rd BW, Saipan.* Dickson

was broadcast to the citizens of Japan, he insisted that Japan should surrender. Capitulation was expected momentarily.

On the night of August 14, no effort had been made by the Japanese government to make contact or formally seek an end of hostilities with the Allies. Hundreds of Superfortresses were scheduled for another strike at targets throughout Japan, and the crews were all told to carefully listen to their radios on the way up to their targets. They were instructed to abort their mission, drop their bombs in the ocean, and return to their bases, if word that the war had ended was received. The message never came that

night, and the Superfortresses completed their last combat mission of World War II.

It would be during the morning of August 15, 1945, that word of Japan's surrender finally came.

Air-Sea Rescue

By the end of World War II, it was appropriate to note and give thanks that the air-sea rescue operation had come of age. With an outstanding record, statistics prove it was highly successful in saving many men who

A copy of one of several leaflets dropped over Japanese cities. During the last few months of the war, many tons of propaganda leaflets were dropped on populated areas of Japan in an attempt to bring the truth of the war's progress. Japanese citizens had not been told that Japan was losing the war. The leaflets were designed to inform the civilians of Japan's military losses and reverses and to warn them of the impending bombing and burning of their cities. Andy Doty

were forced to ditch during the air assault against Japan.

At the peak of the air-sea rescue operation in the Pacific, there were fourteen submarines, twenty-one Navy seaplanes, nine B-29 Super Dumbos, and five surface vessels patrolling the waters between Japan and the Mariana Islands. A total of 2,400 men were assigned to air-sea rescue duty. Of the 1,310 B-29 crew members known to have gone down or ditched at sea, 654, or about 50 percent, were rescued.

Missions of Mercy

When the shooting stopped, the 20th AF set up a project called "Missions of Mercy," to search out and drop medical supplies, food, and clothing to Allied prisoners of war held by the Japanese.

Prisoner of war camps were eventually found in Japan, China, Manchuria, and Korea. The last supply drop by the Superfortresses was on September 20, 1945. By that time, 1,066 B-29s had participated in 900 effective missions to 154 camps. An estimated 63,500 Allied prisoners were provided 4,470 tons of supplies.

During the 'Missions of Mercy," eight B-29s were lost with seventy-seven crew members aboard.

When the prisoners of war were finally liberated, many stories of outrageous atrocities were told. Many prisoners died during captivity. Some had endured the hardships and abuse

Major Track, 411 BS, 502nd BG, 315th BW, flying The Uninvited, *claims the distinction of being the last crew to bomb Japan in World War II. They were the last plane over target at Akita the night of August 14, 1945.* George Harrington

since the fall of the Philippines during the early days of the war, as was the plight of Earl Barton, a crew chief with the 30th BS, 19th BG, stationed at Clark Field in the Philippines when their base was overrun. He eventually ended up at a prisoner of war camp called Shinagawa, located in the Tokyo area. Barton will never forget the inhumane treatment he and others received: "I wound up in a camp near Tokyo, where I witnessed the B-29 bombings and fire raids on Tokyo. What a spectacular show! It was tremendous! After three-and-one-half years of imprisonment, I felt the Japanese deserved every bomb showered on them.

"The B-29 raids literally blew and burned us out of Tokyo. Personally, I never got enough. I wanted the whole island destroyed! The Japanese treated us like caged animals. We were spat on, kicked, forced to eat crap, jeered at, stabbed, poked, slapped, beaten, humiliated, and tortured both physically and mentally. What a relief it was to see and hear the American planes coming over and knowing that the war would have to end soon.

"When people ask me what the fire raids on Tokyo were like, I sum it by quoting an old Army saying, 'The wind blew, the shit flew, and visibility was obscured for days.'"

The Show of Force Mission

The surrender date was set for September 2, 1945. All the main characters who were instrumental in bringing Japan to the surrender table were there on the main deck of the battleship *Missouri*, docked in Tokyo Bay and surrounded by hundreds of US Navy ships. At the head table sat General of the Army Douglas MacArthur presiding over the historic event. Directly behind him stood General LeMay, Admiral Nimitz, and others most responsible for the day's event. Also standing tall was Lt. Gen. Jonathan Wainwright. He looked frail, skinny, and clearly visible in his eyes were the years of abuse he had endured since it came his lot, back on May 5, 1941, to surrender the last stronghold of the American army at Corregidor to the conquering Japanese army.

While the ceremony was taking place aboard the *Missouri*, the big stars of the show roared in from the south, displaying what was billed as "The Show of Force." In battle formation, more than 500 B-29 Superfortresses, representing every unit of the 20th AF, roared across Tokyo Bay, in what was a spine-tingling display of power. Certainly nobody attending the surrender ceremony, including the Japanese official who signed the docu-

ments in the name of the Emperor, would doubt that had it not been for the Superfortresses, the ceremony would not be taking place on that date.

Tallying the Score

The 20th AF operated for fifteen months, had suffered 3,015 casualties—dead, wounded, and missing, and had lost 414 bombers. Only 147 of the bombers lost were attributed to flak or fighter attacks. They had dropped almost 170,000 tons of bombs on enemy targets, and had flown 34,790 sorties during the war.

A couple of significant quotes came to light sometime later. Prince Konoye of the Japanese Royal Family said, "Fundamentally, the thing that brought about the determination to make peace was the prolonged bombing by the B-29s."

Premier Suzuki, who evidently had trouble convincing the War Plans Committee that the war was lost, said, "I, myself, on the basis of the B-29 raids, felt that the cause was hopeless."

A lot of water had gone under the bridges, and the oceans' tides had risen and fallen many times since President Roosevelt pronounced December 7, 1941, the "Day of Infamy."

Chapter 16

Between the Wars

With the war ended, all thoughts turned to going home. For some, beginning the long trip eastward wasn't long coming. A point system was used to determine who went home first.

To get some people home fast, the Superfortresses were turned into transports and loaded with human cargo, rather than supplies or bombs. They called it Operation Sunset.

Since there was no more use for so many Superfortresses in the Marianas bases, a rotation system was set up for men and planes. Operation Sunset originated at Saipan, since the 73rd BW crewmen had been in the Pacific longer than those in other wings, with the exception of the 58th BW, which had transferred from the CBI theater. If a full combat crew were eligible for rotation, they would bring a B-29 back to the States, including additional men. Personal effects were loaded on the aircraft. The Air Transport Command, plus Navy cargo or transport

And then there was one! Long gone are the thousands of B-29 Superfortresses that played a major role in winning World War II, with the exception of fewer than twenty-five on static display in the United States and some foreign countries. Only one is still flying: Fifi, reclaimed and owned by the Confederate Air Force of Texas, participates around the country in Air Shows, much to the delight of those of us who flew them in combat. Glenn Chaney

B-29s line up at Isley Field, Saipan, awaiting orders to load supplies in planes to be dropped at POW camps. Josh Curtis

ships, also brought some of the Sunsetters home.

Some of the last wings to arrive in the Marianas, such as the 315th, and the 314th at Guam, were ordered to remain on station to maintain a stable force until other decisions were made.

B-29 Boneyards

Arrangements were made to deliver the returning B-29s to what some called "boneyards" or open storage areas. Many of the Superfortresses were stored in western states, where the dry humidity would not deteriorate or rust the aircraft as much as if they were stored in more humid areas. Many of the B-29s were mothballed, with exposed parts enclosed in a cocoon to prevent deterioration. These aircraft could be recalled in a very

A prisoner of war camp where Americans were held in Japan. Note the initials "P.O.W." painted on the tops of buildings to aid supply aircraft to find them. John D. Kremer

short time and put back in service if needed. Large numbers of B-29s were stored at Davis-Monthan Air Force Base (AFB) at Tucson, and at China Lake, California, Pyote, Texas, and Tinker Field, Oklahoma.

Many of the Superfortresses fell prey to the chopping block. Consumers were starved for aluminum pots and pans, and since the B-29 was now living out its usefulness as a bomber, entrepreneurs decided they could produce a lot of cookware with all that aluminum.

Norman Lent, who served as a flight engineer in the 3rd PRS during the war and was then working for Lockheed, watched salvage people at Pyote, Texas, convert Superfortresses to aluminum ingots: "The Texas Railroad Co. set up shop at Pyote to scrap out B-29s by the hundreds. They had blast furnaces going day and night to melt down the big bombers. For me, it was a heart-breaking, gruesome sight.

"The salvagers would tow the planes to an area where they removed the engines and some of the internal needs. After this, they would flip the plane over on its back and chop holes in the leading edges of the wings so that they could remove the fuel valves. After the landing gear and wheels were removed, a large knife, which was dropped from a high boom, would cut the fuselage and wings into pieces. A crane would then pick up the pieces and drop them into a furnace, where the once-proud warbirds were converted into almost-pure aluminum ingots. All of the B-29s that remained at Pyote after we had selected the ones to de-moth were scrapped out in this manner."

B-29s Fulfill Post-War Tasks

Not all B-29s were destined for scrapping after the war, however. They remained the Strategic Air

Food and medical supplies were dropped over the POW camps. 73rd BW Photo/ Hurth Thompkins

Force's top bomber until 1948, when they were replaced with the revised Superfortress version, then called the B-50. Soon after that, a brand-new bomber, the B-36, appeared. The B-29s were then designated medium bombers. It was something of a demotion for the most advanced bomber of World War II.

Bikini Atomic Tests

One of the major undertakings after World War II was a project involving further testing with atomic bomb explosions. Operation Crossroads would involve 242 ships, including aircraft carriers, battleships, and cruisers from US, Japanese, and German fleets; 10,000 instruments; and more than 42,000 people. The exercise took place at Bikini Atoll, located 200mi west of Kwajalein.

Two atomic bombs were exploded in separate events, one dropped from a B-29 Superfortress and one at an underwater position near the center of the dispersed ships. The 509th CG was, again, selected to drop the bomb. Col. Paul Tibbets was assigned the duty of dropping the Fat Man-type bomb, and he would again be flying the *Enola Gay*.

The USAAF's element, known as Task Force 1.5, consisted of about 2,000 personnel, drawn mostly from the Strategic Air Forces and under the command of Gen. Roger Ramey. Five B-29s code-named Silverplates and modified to drop an atomic bomb, took part in the exercise. Also participating were one standard B-29 and eight F-13As from the 3rd PRS, responsible for taking pictures after the drop. The Air Weather Service sent three RB-29s to check weather over the test site before the drop.

July 1, 1946, was designated the drop date, which was code-named Able Day. Because of mechanical troubles on drop day, the *Enola Gay* was grounded and *Dave's Dream* was substituted, with another pilot flying it.

Five ships were sunk by the atomic explosion and nine were heavily damaged.

The Superfortresses were also involved in the second phase of "Operation Crossroads." The underwater explosion took place several weeks after Able Day, and the B-29s were used for support functions, such as photographic and data collection.

The Tanker's Role

With the advent of jet fighters, the Air Force had to activate an entirely new type of a support unit for the short-range aircraft. The new designa-

Barrels of supplies were dropped in this photograph. Note POWs outside the buildings anxiously awaiting the landing of the containers. Hurth Thompkins

tion for the unit was air refueling squadrons, and the B-29s were ideal for this task of in-flight refueling.

The Air Force borrowed a British-developed system of trailing hoses and grapnel hooks. Another modification had to convert B-29s to tankers with the aircraft coming from the Strategic Air Forces. In 1948, the Boeing plant at Wichita was re-opened for the express purpose of modifying the B-29s as tankers. These aircraft were designated KB-29Ms. Seventy four B-29s were converted to tankers at the Wichita plant.

The Air Weather Service

World War II experiences with the weather, especially in the Pacific, convinced the USAAF of the need for better weather observation and monitoring, and led to the development of a tracking system to locate and report bad weather, such as typhoons and hurricanes.

The Air Weather Service was organized in 1946 and, using RB-29s, soon became global weather watchers. The first flight over the top of a hurricane was made by an Air Weather Service B-29 on October 7, 1946, and on March 17, 1947, the first RB-29 flight over the North Pole was made.

In 1950, after a complete overhaul, the RB-29s were redesignated again, this time to WB-29.

Col. Ray Brashear was operations officer for the 514th Weather Reconnaissance Squadron, later changed to the 54th Strategic Reconnaissance Squadron at North Guam Air Base, and then again to Anderson AFB. He relates some of the tactics used to

track weather in that part of the world: "The area south and west of Guam is where most typhoons developed. The path of individual typhoons is very erratic, but generally makes a sweeping curve northwest, then north, and finally northeast if they do not dissipate sooner. Some developed and died without ever touching land. Others, at different times, roared across the Philippines, Formosa, Okinawa, the China coast, and even Japan. Needless to say, everyone in that part of the world was vitally interested in the location, strength, and general movement of the storm. Ships at sea had a most urgent need to know where the typhoon was and its general direction and speed of movement.

"When a tropical storm or typhoon developed, the 514th made a morning and afternoon fix on its location. This required flying into the eye to determine the intensity of each quadrant. Depending on its proximity to a suitable refueling base, one airplane might make the morning fix and then linger in the storm area for the late afternoon fix before heading for Iwo Jima, Clark USAAF Base in the Philippines, Okinawa, or back to Guam."

Jim O'Donnell remained in service a while after the war because, he said, "the USAAF suddenly found themselves short of good experienced overwater navigators." He was assigned to a weather squadron in Guam and he recalls one of the flights he made to the Philippines checking on a typhoon; it was the most violent storm he had ever encountered: "Our B-29 was thrown around like a straw, about like [by] the heat thermals over Japan during fire raids. When we landed at Clark AFB, we noticed that the rivets were torn from the fuselage in places. We had to leave the plane at Clark Field, and we learned later it was scrapped."

B-29s Loaned to RAF

Eighty B-29s were "loaned" to the British RAF in 1950. The RAF gave the ex-Superfortresses a new name, Washington, and used them for long-

range observations and to experiment with some very heavy bombs.

All of the B-29s were eventually returned to the USAF.

The B-50

As World War II was heading for the last round-up, Boeing Aircraft Co. was still determined to eliminate the remaining deficiencies in its B-29 Superfortress. Designers came up with a much-improved version of the Superfortress at about the time that the Japanese threw in the towel. The new version was called the B-29D. It had many changes but still resembled the original B-29. The most notable difference was the tail, which was 5ft taller than that of the B-29, bringing the overall height over 33ft.

The 2,200hp Wright R-3350 engines were replaced by 3,500hp Pratt & Whitney R-4350 engines. The B-29D's 141ft wingspan was about the same as that of the original B-29s, as was its 99ft length. Gross weight was increased to 173,000lb, and top speed was 380mph at 25,000ft altitude. Service ceiling was rated at 36,000ft, load was 20,000lb maximum, and range was 4,900mi.

Robert Robbins, left, holds the distinction of having served as experimental test pilot at Boeing, and accumulated more than 470hr on the no. 1 XB-29. During the last few years, he has flown Fifi, becoming the only living person known to have flown the first and the last B-29. Robbins poses at an air show in Florida with Glenn Chaney. Glenn Chaney

In December 1945, the B-29D was redesignated the B-50. It served as an interim bomber, along with some not-yet-retired B-29s, until the jet-powered B-47 came on line.

Boeing built 370 B-50s during the period of 1945 to 1953. There were three bomber conversions—the RB-50 for reconnaissance, the WB-50 for weather, and the KB-50 for tanker service—as well as a version for training (the TB-50) and for testing (the DB-50). Some of the KB-50Js were fitted with two General Electric J-47 turbojet engines of 5,000lb thrust to increase speed for refueling jet aircraft.

The B-50s did not see combat in Korea, but did serve as tankers during the Vietnam War. They were retired from service in 1965.

Chapter 17

B-29s in Korea

They called it the Korean Conflict, the Limited War, or a Political War, but whatever the nomenclature, it was a plain war to the foot soldiers and the air crewmen who risked their lives in the air above the 38th parallel in Korea. The shrapnel from flak barrages and bullets from Soviet-built MiG fighters were just as deadly as the hits that snuffed out the lives of young airmen over Europe and Japan in World War II.

Historians kept dispatching their fading-glory stories about the swan song of the B-29 Superfortress, but on June 25, 1950, just a few months short of her seventh birthday, the gallant old B-29 was called on, once again, to go to war. For two-and-one-half years, she again showed her mettle, despite limitations and restrictions dictated by politicians.

It was on that date, again a Sunday morning, that a horde of Communist North Koreans crossed the 38th parallel and attacked the Republic of Korea to the south. For the southern Korean soldiers guarding the border, it was no contest. The invading North Koreans swept through their ranks and headed south, bent on capturing South Korea.

Beat Up Bastard *bombed the North Koreans from Kadena Air Base on Okinawa.* R. Mann

The nearest US Air Force (USAF) outfit to the trouble spot was the veteran 19th BG, the only combat unit now assigned to the once-proud and potent 20th AF. The 19th BG was located at Anderson AFB on Guam, known during World War II as North Field, where it served with distinction as one of the four B-29 BGs of the 314th BW.

General MacArthur, serving as United Nations Supreme Commander, headquartered in Tokyo, was instructed to support the South Koreans. He immediately ordered the 19th BG, with its twenty-two B-29 strike force, to answer the call and move to Kadena Air Base on Okinawa, from where it would launch an attack on North Korea.

It took the 19th BG only 19hr after receiving MacArthur's orders to strike their opening blow in the Korean War. An element of four B-29s flew to the Munsan area to search out and drop their bombs on targets of opportunity. The planes all returned safely to their base.

As the war heated up, the USAF sent two more of its B-29 groups to make up the Far East Air Force (FEAF), commanded by Maj. Gen. "Rosey" O'Donnell. Joining the FEAF to begin attacks on Korea were the 22nd and 92nd BGs. Col. Jim Edmundson, who served as commander of the 468th BG, 58th BW in India,

China, and Tinian Island in World War II, commanded the 22nd BG. O'Donnell's FEAF was headquartered in Yokota, Japan. In July, two more B-29 groups, the 98th and the 307th, were sent to Japan to join the FEAF.

President Truman let it be known that he was against indiscriminate bombing of North Korea, and bombers were not to fly beyond the borders of North Korea.

By mid-September, General O'Donnell was satisfied that all major strategic targets in North Korea had been neutralized, and he ordered the 22nd and 92nd BGs to return to the United States. With the air war well in hand, he told the other two groups they probably could spend Christmas back in the United States.

But by November, things began to take on a different hew along the Yalu River. The Chinese began a build-up of soldiers and equipment just across the river, poised to join the fray and engulf the American and South Korean troops. General O'Donnell sent his bombers to the bridges across the Yalu, but the river had begun freezing over, making it possible for the Chinese to cross on the ice. By July, the North Koreans had acquired enough MiG fighters that they could mount major air strikes. General MacArthur ordered General O'Donnell to send B-29s to the airfield in North Korea to attempt to neutralize them, but they

Tail gunner Albert E. Conder and crew of 92nd BG, 325th BS, shown taking off from RAF Station Southorp, England, prior to Korean War. Albert Conder

had to pull back to try and stop the invaders from the north. It was touch and go, but B-29s from the 19th BG had some success dropping "Raisin" bombs, which were directed to the target by radio beams. These bombs were the forerunners of the "smart" bombs used against Iraq in Operation Desert Storm.

Negotiations for a peace settlement had been started in 1950, but progress was almost nonexistent.

B-29 of the 580th Air Resupply Squadron on a search and rescue mission assigned at Burtonwood, England, 1953. Robert Tharratt

Albert Conder remembers the cold weather during the winter of 1953 at Lowrey Field, Colorado, where he received gunnery training. Albert Conder

Albert E. Conder, a central fire control gunner with the 92nd BG, tells of how fate stepped in and saved his life as he watched his good friends being shot down near Sinanju in North Korea: "In December 1948, I was assigned to a crew in the 92nd BG, 325th BS, commanded by 1st Lt. James T. Patrick. This crew had a permanently assigned aircraft, a B-29, no. 2084.

"No. 2084, held a very special place in my heart. It was the first B-29

Typhoon Goon II, *a fully modified WB-29 of the 54th Strategic Reconnaissance Squadron (Weather), formerly the 514th Weather Reconnaissance Squadron. The Unit was located at Guam, 1949–1951.* Ray Brashear

B-29 pilots practice formation flying near their base at Lowrey Field, Colorado, before shipping out to join the FEAF command. Albert Conder

that I ever flew on. It was assigned to our crew for more than eighteen months and during that time, we had flown it to Bermuda, England, Africa, Germany, the Azores, Alaska, and all over the United States.

"I saw it come to an untimely end on September 10, 1950, along with

Band leader Phil Harris had a popular novelty song he called "The Thing." Every time he described "the thing" or its contents, a loud drum beat drowned out his words. No one ever found out what "the thing" was. However, crew chief Sergeant Leighty knew The Thing was his WB-29. The plane flew with the 514th Weather Reconnaissance Squadron, later the 54th Squadron during the Korean War. Ray Brashear

some of my very good friends and former crewmates.

"My crew was flying on no. 7326, the lead ship of a three-aircraft formation. The target was far into North Korea, near Sinanju. No. 2084 was flying the right-wing position. As we headed for the target, three shots were fired by antiaircraft guns at our formation. The first was just behind us, the second came between us and no. 2084, actually between the left wing and the horizontal stabilizer of the tail section. The next shot hit engine no. 2 of 2084. I was monitoring the command radio and heard Maj. Zane M. Hoit call a 'Mayday'.

"Major Hoit stated also, that he was going to attempt to make it to the Yellow Sea for a possible ditching. Luck was not with him or his crew, for just few minutes later, the left wing folded and no. 2084 began its death dive.

"I was able to observe everything very clearly from my position as the CFC, top gunner. I counted five 'chutes as the crew exited the falling plane, watching in horror as one of the five landed in the burning wreckage on the ground. Patrick, followed by our left wingman, took our ship down to a very low altitude, in an attempt to help our stranded crewmates. We dropped our survival kits, along with guns and ammo we had on board. We also made several strafing runs, in an attempt to give air-sea rescue time to arrive. As we circled the crash site, we could see what appeared to be thousands of either soldiers or people heading for no. 2084. It looked like an army of ants.

"It was apparent very soon that the air-sea rescue would be of no help, and it was with sad hearts and lumps in our throats that we finally had to leave those brave men to their fate and return to our home base, Yokota AFB, Japan.

"Shortly before we had been ordered to the Far East to participate in the Korean War, Lieutenant Patrick and the flight engineer, T/Sgt. Joseph C. Goslin had been transferred from our crew to another crew. Patrick became the commander of the crew flying no. 7326. I was extremely upset with this turn of events, because I wanted to continue on as the CFC

A nice inflight of a brand new, sleek WB-29. It arrived in Guam in early 1951 ready for assignment with 514th Weather Reconnaissance Squadron based at North Guam AFB, later named Andersen AFB. The weather squadron tracked weather in support of the Korean War from Guam over Japan to a point near Russia. Ray Brashear

A close view of a WB-29. Symbols on the nose indicate nine typhoon penetrations. The crackerbox on the aft fuselage contained weather monitoring equipment and seen below the no. 2 is weather monitoring radar. This plane also flew with the 514th Weather Squadron. Ray Brashear

First Lieutenant Carlyle G. Townswick commanded B-29 number 066 during the Korean War. The aircraft known as Townswick Terrors. *The crew flew missions against North Korea from Yokota AFB in Japan with the 325th BS, 92nd BG.* Conders

The Lt. James T. Patrick crew pose in front of United Notions *at their base at Yokota AFB, Japan. Ten days after this picture was taken,* United Notions *was shot down over North Korea, with another crew flying the plane. Standing left to right: 1st Lt. James T. Patrick, 1st Lt. James S. Murphy, 1st Lt. John B. Wood, Jr. Capt. James R. Cole, and Maj. Homer E. Chatfield. Kneeling, left to right , M/Sgt. Edward D. Hodsdon, S/Sgt. William T. Ayres, and S/Sgt. Paul A. Lenart.* Condor

gunner on his crew. He felt the same way, and with some persuasion, he was successful in effecting my transfer also. I honestly feel that Lieutenant Patrick saved my life, because without his help and the grace of God, I would have been on board no. 2084 that fateful September day in 1950.

"After the armistice, and prisoners were returned, we were told that four of the survivors from no. 2084 had been seen in POW camps in Manchuria. None ever returned."

The 580th Air Resupply and Communications Wing was a little-known unit that saw distinguished service in the Korean War. Robert C. Tharratt

tells about the unit's assignments during the Korean War: "The 580th Air Resupply and Communications Wing was the first of three special B-29 units that flew during the Korean War. Two squadrons [580th and 581st], equipped with modified B-29s with only the tail turret for armament, were reactivated from storage at Warner-Robins Field, Georgia, and began training at Mountain Home AFB, Idaho, early in 1951. The lower-aft turret hole was padded and used to parachute Army Special Forces at night during escape and invasion exercises in the German Alps. Bomb bays were modified to handle cargo, fuel tanks, parachute containers, or leaflet delivery equipment."

The first wing commander was Col. John Kane, a Congressional Medal of Honor recipient in World War II. Colonel Kane participated in the ill-fated first low-level B-24 raid on the Ploesti oil fields in 1943.

The 580th was deployed to Wheelus AFB in Tripoli, Libya, in October 1952 and the 581st went to Clark AFB in the Philippines shortly thereafter. Coincidentally, it was from a North African airbase that Colonel

Kane flew his B-24 on the Ploesti raid just nine years earlier. The final air resupply and communications squadron, the 582nd, trained at Mountain Home and deployed to Molesworth, England, in 1953.

Dubbed "psychological warfare" units, these squadrons were ideally suited for a variety of assignments. Many B-29 flights were long-range night missions to deliver leaflets and supplies, equipment, and personnel to "friendly, isolated forces" in remote areas. The Alps of Southern Europe, North African and Asian deserts in the distant Arabian Gulf, and the battlefield of North Korea, adjacent to Iron Curtain countries, served as an ideal training ground to develop the skill and precision necessary to carry out successful clandestine operations.

Many of the missions were hazardous low-level night flights to avoid radar detection. During one moonless-night transition mission in 1953, B-29 no. 44-61681 literally flew into the ground in the desert near Wheelus Field. Miraculously, six of the ten crew members survived. This aircraft, nicknamed *The Incendiary Blonde*, had flown sixteen missions with the 20th

Circle-W-084 of the 325 BS, 92nd BG is shown dropping demolition bombs on targets in North Korea. The plane was based at Yokota AFB, Japan, and was part of the FEAF, commanded by Maj. Gen. Emmett O'Donnell, who commanded the 73rd BW at Saipan during World War II. Conder

South Sea Sinner was assigned to the 19th BG and bombed targets in North Korea from Kadena Air Base in Okinawa. The 19th BG was the last group of the old 20th Air Force of World War II fame. When

North Korea crossed the 38th parallel to start the Korean War, the 19th BG B-29s were the first to drop bombs on the North Korean invaders. R. Mann

AF during World War II. Three other aircraft from the 580th were lost during the six years of operations. The 581st and 582nd suffered similar operational losses.

The B-29s of the 581st were assigned to duty on Okinawa and flew on leaflet missions over North Korea in 1952–1953. In January 1953, a 581st B-29 was shot down over Manchuria, and the USAF crew reportedly were imprisoned as spies until 1955. The 580th remained in Libya after the Korean War to carry out special assignments during the Cold War build-up. The 580th returned to the United States in 1957 for deactivation, and the 581st and 582nd in 1958, closing another interesting but little-known chapter in the history of the B-29 Superfortress.

America's F-86 Sabre Jets were sent to Korea to try and protect the B-29s from the superior MiG Jets, but the early-model Sabres were no match for the Soviet-built MiG-15, so the B-29s tried night raids and were more successful, until the MiGs learned

Never Hoppen also flew with the 19th BG from their base on Okinawa. R. Mann

Nose artists never missed a stroke between wars as the 19th BG B-29s prove with sophisticated works like this on Top of the Mark. *The black belly indicated the plane did a lot of low-altitude, night flying. R. Mann*

some night fighter tricks and were successful in shooting down several B-29s.

FEAF planners were successful with their strategic campaign of sustained attacks on North Korea's hydro-electricity facilities. They selected four complexes for destruction: Sui-Ho, Chosin, Fusen, and Kyosen. The Navy contributed with carrier-born aircraft from Task Force 77 off the coast of Korea. The raids began on June 24 with the B-29s going in for the first time that night against Chosin. By June 27, it was estimated that nine-tenths of North Korea's electrical-generating capacity had been destroyed.

On July 27, 1953, negotiations for a cease fire were agreed to by all parties, and the Korea Conflict had ended after three years, one month, and two days. It was obvious the B-29 Superfortress had fought its last battle.

The old, tired B-29s had done a respectable job. They had dropped a total of 167,000 tons of bombs on the enemy, and in so doing, lost sixteen B-29s to enemy fighters, four to antiaircraft guns, and fourteen to other causes.

A job well done!

Bug's Buster *bombed North Korea as one of the 19th BG's fleet of B-29s flying missions from Kadena. R. Mann*

Appendices

B-29 Production Summary

Type	No. Built	Plant
XB-29-BO	3	Boeing-Seattle
YB-29-BW	14	Boeing-Wichita
B-29-BW	1,630	Boeing-Wichita
B-29-BA	357	Bell-Atlanta
B-29-MO	531	Martin-Omaha
B-29A-BN	1,119	Boeing-Renton
B-29B-BA	311	Bell-Atlanta
	3965 Total	

Performance Characteristics and Technical Data

Manufacturer/ Type	No. Built (All Models)	Span	Length	Height	Empty Wt. (Pounds)	Gross Wt. (Pounds)	Service Ceiling	Cruise/Top Speed (MPH)	Engines	H.P.	Range	Bomb Load
Boeing B-29	3,654 *	141'3"	99'	27'9"	70,140	110,000	31,850'	220/365	Wright R-3350-23	2,200	5,830	20,000
Boeing/Bell B-29B	311	141'3"	99'	27'8"	68,821	135,744	38,100'	344/354	Wright R-3350-57 R-3350-57A	2,200	6,023	10,000

* Includes B-29s other than B-29Bs.

Dimensions

DIMENSION	AIRCRAFT				
	XB-29	**YB-29**	**B-29**	**B-29A**	**B-29B**
Wing Span (ft. in.)	141' 2.76"	141' 2.76"	141' 2.76"	141' 2.76"	141' 2.76"
Wing Root Chord (ft. in.)	17' 0.00"	17' 0.00"	17' 0.00"	17' 0.00"	17' 0.00"
Wing Tip Chord (ft. in.)	7' 5.00"	7' 5.00"	7' 5.00"	7' 5.00"	7' 5.00"
Wing Area (sq. ft.)	1,736.0	1,736.0	1,736.0	1,739.0	1,736.0
Aileron Span (ft. in.)	25' 10.00"	25' 10.00"	25' 10.00"	25' 10.00"	25' 10.00"
Flap Span (ft. in.)	37' 8.43"	37' 8.43"	37' 8.43"	37' 8.43"	37' 8.43"
Length (ft. in.)	98' 1.92"	99' 0.00"	99' 0.00"	99' 0.00"	99' 0.00"
Height (ft. in.)	27' 9.00"	27' 9.00"	27' 9.00"	27' 9.00"	27' 9.00"
Rudder Height (ft. in.)	14' 7.25"	12' 0.18"	12' 0.18"	12' 0.18"	12' 0.18"
Horizontal Stabilizer Span (ft. in.)	43' 0.00"	43' 0.00"	43' 0.00"	43' 0.00"	43' 0.00"
Horizontal Stabilizer Root Chord (ft. in.)	11' 2.40"	11' 2.40"	11' 2.40"	11' 2.40"	11' 2.40"
Vertical Fin Area (sq. ft.)	237.8	237.8	237.8	238.8	237.8
Horizontal Tail Area (sq. ft.)	330.0	330.0	330.0	330.0	330.0
MLG Track (ft. in.)	28' 5.60"	28' 5.60"	28' 5.60"	28' 5.60"	28' 5.60"
MLG Tire Diameter (in.)	56.00"	56.00"	56.00"	56.00"	56.00"
NLG Tire Diameter (in.)	36.00"	36.00"	36.00"	36.00"	36.00"
Propeller Diameter (ft. in.)	17' 0.00"	17' 0.00"	16' 7.00"	16' 7.00"	16' 7.00"

Bibliography

Books

Anderton, David A. *B-29 Superfortress at War*. New York: Charles Scribner's Sons. 1978.

Berger, Carl. *B-29, The Superfortress*. New York: Ballantine Books, Inc. 1973.

Beser, Jacob. *Hiroshima & Nagasaki Revisited*. Memphis: Global Press. 1988.

Birdsall, Steve. *Saga of the Superfortress*. New York: Doubleday & Co., Inc. 1980.

Birdsall, Steve. *B-29 Superfortress in Action*. Carrollton, Texas: Squadron/Signal Publications, Inc. 1977.

Birdsall, Steve. *Superfortress*. Carrollton, Texas: Squadron/Signal Publications, Inc. 1980.

Gurney, Gene. *B-29 Story*. Greenwich, Connecticut: Fawcett Books. 1961.

Coffey, Thomas M. *Iron Eagle, the Turbulent Life of General Curtis LeMay*. New York: Crown Publishers. 1986.

Hudson, Lionel. *The Rats of Rangoon*. London: Leo Cooper. 1987.

Marshall, Chester. *Sky Giants over Japan*. Winona, Minnesota: Appolo Books. 1984.

Marshall, Chester. *The Global Twentieth, An Anthology, Volume 1*. Winona, Minnesota: Appolo Books. 1985.

Marshall, Chester. *The Global Twentieth, An Anthology, Volume 2*. Memphis, Tennessee: Global Press. 1987.

Marshall, Chester. *The Global Twentieth, An Anthology, Volume 3*. Memphis, Tennessee: Global Press. 1988.

Marshall, Chester. *The Global Twentieth, An Anthology, Volume 4*. Memphis, Tennessee: Global Press. 1992.

Morrison, Wilbur H. *Point of No Return*. New York: Time Books. 1979.

Pimlott, John. *B-29 Superfortress*. Secautus, New Jersey: Chartwell Books, Inc. 1980.

Prange, Gordon W. *At Dawn We Slept*. New York: McGraw-Hill Book Co. 1981.

Sargent, Mary Thomas. *Runway Towards Orion*. Grand Rapids, Michigan: Trimph Press, Inc. 1984.

Thomas, Gordon and Morgan Witts. *Enola Gay*. New York: Pocket Books. 1977.

Albums, Histories, Documents

"The 20th AF Album," by Dick Keenan. Published by 20th AF Association. 1982.

"Strategic Air War Against Japan," by Maj. Gen. Haywood S. Hansell, Jr. Published in 1980, under the auspices of the Airpower Research Institute, Air War College, Maxwell AFB, Alabama.

"Impact, Volume 8," sponsored by the Army Air Forces' Historical Society. Published by *Historical Times*

"The Story of the 73rd BW, the Unofficial History of the 73rd BW at Saipan." First printing 1946 by 73rd Wing headquarters. Reprinted by the Battery Press, Inc., Nashville, Tennessee. 1980.

"The Air Intelligence Report of the 21st BC." Published by 21st Bomber Command, April 1945.

"Saipan, Then and Now" (1972); "Tinian Island, Then and Now" (1977); and "Guam, Then and Now" (1979) by Glenn McClure. Published by Emerson's, Universal City, Texas.

"The Pirate's Log, a Historical Record of the Sixth BG." Published by Engineer Reproductions, Philippines. 1946.

"Story of the 505th BG, 313th BW, Tinian Island." Published by Betty Macintyre, Ogden, Utah. 1946.

"War Journal—Story of the 9th BG, Tinian Island." Published by the 9th Bomb Group. 1946.

"The Unofficial History of the 499th BG, Saipan." Published by Historical Aviation, Temple City, California. 1981

"The Story of the 315th Wing, Guam." Published by the 315th Wing Association, Cocoa Beach, Florida. 1981.

"The B-29 Bibliography," by Denny Pidhayny. Published by the 58th BW Association Recording and Historical Secretary. Updated April 1992.

Index